HYMNS AND HISTORY

AN ANNOTATED SURVEY OF SOURCES

Forrest M. McCann

A·C·U
PRESS

Hymns and History: An Annotated Survey of Sources

ACU Station, Box 29138
Abilene, TX   79699

Type Specifications: Chapter Heading set in Helvetica Black Italics, 30 point. Headline set in Times, 18 point. Subhead set in Helvetica, 80% width, 12 point. Body copy set in Times, 11 point. Endnote set in Times, 10 point.

Typesetting by Stephen B. Carman, LadyBug Communications

To Clara

FOREWORD

A mong the Churches of Christ, whose polity affirms the independence of each congregation under the lordship of Christ, there can never be an "authorized" hymnal. While there have been and continue to be many fine collections from which our congregations may choose, throughout most of the twentieth century *Great Songs of the Church* has, in the judgment of many, come nearer than any other to being "standard" and setting a pattern of excellence for our hymnody.

For many years the author has desired to publish a handbook to this noble hymnal and to this end has collected materials for such a work. Humble thanks are due to God for bringing into the author's life so many encouragers and lovers of Christian song. This handbook is now offered to the public in the hope that it may bless all who sing the praises of our God and of his Christ.

The work consists of five sections: Part I, a history of the hymnals and hymnody of the Stone-Campbell movement; Part II, a history of *Great Songs of the Church*; Part III, a discussion of texts and tunes with the texts given in alphabetical order; Part IV, a series of brief biographies of authors and composers collated in alphabetical order; and Part V, an appendix containing a complete listing of all texts and tunes found in all editions of *Great Songs* since its beginning in 1921.

The author expresses sincere thanks to the administration of Abilene Christian University, to the ACU Press, to the compilers of many standard hymnal handbooks whose works have been indispensable, to colleagues and friends who have been a part of his lifelong education in Christian song, and to that God who is the author and object of all song and whose mercy endures forever.

Forrest M. McCann
Abilene, Texas
February, 1997

Contents

PART I:

The Hymnody of the Restoration Movement

In the 1790s, following the American Revolution, occurred that religious event known as the Second Awakening. This revival began in the East through the efforts of such men as Timothy Dwight of Yale and soon spread generally along the seaboard to the South and over the mountains to the West. Everywhere there was a desire to return to a more fervent expression of faith.[1]

Profiting from this revival of religion and the general desire to serve God, widely separated efforts arose to return to primitive Christianity. In the South James O'Kelly appeared; in the Northeast Abner Jones and Elias Smith; in the West Barton W. Stone and his coadjutors; and, some ten years afterwards, from Ireland, came the Campbells. These early leaders apparently saw the value of song in propagating the ancient gospel, for many had a part in publishing hymnals.

The Christian Connection: The South

James O'Kelly (ca. 1739-1826) united with the Methodist Church and served in it as a presiding elder. After the Revolution, when American Methodism separated itself from its English connections under the leadership of Thomas Coke and Francis Asbury, O'Kelly broke with the Methodists in 1792-93. He and his group denominated themselves "Republican Methodists" in their desire to oppose what they thought to be tyranny, but ultimately they took the name "Christian" and called their assemblies Christian Churches. They represented the southern branch of the so-called Christian Connection. Remnants of this movement still remain in Virginia and North Carolina. [2]

O'Kelly edited *Hymns and Spiritual Songs for the Use of Christians* (1816). The volume contained 350 hymns and was published by Thomas W. Scott at the Minerva Press in Raleigh, North Carolina.[3]

One of the most noted preachers in the South was Joseph Thomas (1791-1835). He joined O'Kelly's group about 1806-07 and worked as an itinerant evangelist. Thomas wore a long white robe on his preaching missions and was known as the "White Pilgrim." He edited *The Pilgrim's Hymn Book* (1815) with subtitle "Offered as a Companion to All Zion Travelers." A second edition containing 216 pages was published in 1817 at Winchester, Virginia, where Thomas was living at the time.

These appear to be the only early hymnals published by the southern branch of the Christian Connection. This group never joined forces with the Campbells and, indeed, opposed many of their views. Around 1840, one of their preachers, Miles Barrett, edited a hymnal, the title of which is unknown.

The Christian Connection: The Northeast

The northern or eastern branch of the Christian Connection centers in the labors of Abner Jones, a physician and member of the Baptist Church, and Elias Smith, a Baptist minister. Smith (1769-1846), from Connecticut, united with the Baptists in Vermont. He withdrew from them in 1804, established independent churches, and founded the first religious newspaper in America, *The Herald of Gospel Liberty*.[4] In 1805 Elias Smith edited his first hymnal, *A Collection of Hymns for the Use of Christians*, which contained 36 pages of hymns of the camp-meeting type. Undoubtedly its title and contents influenced O'Kelly's publication of 1816, as well as others to be mentioned later.

New Englander Abner Jones (1772-1841) became dissatisfied with Baptist doctrines and established a Christian Church at Lyndon, Vermont, in September 1801. In June 1803, he and Smith became co-workers in the cause of religious restoration. Together they edited *Hymns, Original and Selected for the Use of Christians*, probably a revision of Smith's 1805 book. A third edition was published at Exeter, New Hampshire, in 1809. A seventh edition of the "Smith and Jones Hymn Book" was advertised in Smith's autobiography in 1816. It was said to be a "small neat pocket volume" and sold for 62.5 cents per copy. [5]

Robert Foster edited *Hymns, Original and Selected for the Use of Christians* (1826), published by Elias Smith in Portsmouth, New Hampshire. The outer cover bore the title *Christian Hymns*. More than likely this was a further revision of the Smith and Jones hymnal. Nothing is known of Robert Foster, unless he is the person who went west to Kentucky with Barton Stone in May 1796. He was a licensed Presbyterian preacher, but at the time had resolved to quit the ministry.

The Christian Connection: The West

Barton Warren Stone (1772-1844), having been converted by the preaching of James McGready, received a license from the Presbyterians in 1796 and moved west to Kentucky. There he married in 1801 and participated in the great Cane Ridge Revival with McGready. Stone's withdrawal from the Presbyterians was marked by the well-known *Last Will and Testament of the Springfield Presbytery* in 1804. It was twenty-five years later, however, that Stone edited his first hymn book. Assisted by Thomas Adams, Stone published *The Christian Hymn-Book, Compiled and Published at the Request of the Miami Christian Conference* (1829). This volume contained 340 hymns on 370 pages, plus a 14-page index of topics and first lines. The poems were divided into 22 topical sections, with the first hymn being "Come, Ye Sinners, Poor and Needy."

On the final page of the book this note appeared: "We have not secured a copyright for this book; but it is our intention to continue to publish, until our brethren shall advise us to stop."[6]

Thomas Adams (1798-1831) was born near Dayton, Ohio. He joined the Christian Church in 1814 and after many struggles was ordained by the elders at Clarksville, Pennsylvania, in 1819. Although an earnest student of the Bible and a master of ancient and modern languages, Adam's life was filled with tragedy. He fell prey to tuberculosis in 1821; his bride of less than a year died in 1822. Adams died May 8, 1831, in Lexington, Kentucky.

The year after Adams's death, Stone joined with John Telemachus Johnson, his co-editor of the *Christian Messenger*, for a new edition of the *Christian Hymn Book*. This "second edition" sold for 37.5 cents per copy by the dozen or 43.75 cents singly. The book was extremely popular among the Christians in the West and had sold 3,000 copies before it was combined with Campbell's hymnal in 1834.[7]

David Purviance (1766-1847), born in Iredell County, North Carolina, was reared a strict Presbyterian. He moved with his young bride to near Nashville, Tennessee, in 1790, and a year later to Bourbon County, Kentucky, south of Cane Ridge. He was a member of the Cane Ridge Church and served as its ruling elder. Purviance, a popular figure in the community, served several terms in the Kentucky legislature. He, along with Stone, broke with the Presbyterians in 1804. While others went back, he never wavered and was the first of the Kentucky Christians to repudiate infant sprinkling. In 1806 Purviance moved to Ohio, where he preached and served 15 terms in the Ohio legislature. He was also active in the temperance movement.[8]

David Purviance helped to edit one hymnal which John Thompson, one of the signers of the *Last Will and Testament*, published as *The Christian*

Hymn Book (1815). Thompson was the principal editor, and the title page read "John Thompson and others." The "others" were David Purviance, Samuel Websterfield, William Snodgrass, and William McClure. This was a second edition of an earlier book issued in 1810, for by 1815 Thompson had already returned to the Presbyterians.[9] A third edition (date unknown) was printed by Looker and Wallace Publishers, in Cincinnati, Ohio.

Rice Haggard (1769-1819) was a descendant of an English lord who settled in Virginia, apparently because the entire family seemed to love freedom and liberty. Haggard joined the Methodist Church and was ordained by Francis Asbury in 1791. At the General Conference of 1792-93, he sided with O'Kelly against what he considered oppressive ecclesiastical authority. It was Rice Haggard who proposed to O'Kelly "that henceforth and forever the followers of Christ be known as Christians simply."[10] Haggard moved to Kentucky in 1803 and was present at the signing of the *Last Will and Testament*. With full sympathy he cast his lot with Stone and his group and again proposed that men call themselves simply Christians. The name was adopted, and thus began the Christian Church in the West.

Haggard later purchased land in Champaign County, Ohio, and died there in 1819. Many years later, in the obituary of his wife Nancy, the following brief statement appeared: "About the year 1818 he published the first collection of select psalms, hymns, and spiritual songs, on reforming principles, ever to be published in Kentucky."[11] This hymnal had a topical arrangement and contained 365 hymns, 52 of which were in an appendix. The title page read "*A Selection of Christian Hymns* by Rice Haggard. 'Let every thing that hath breath praise the Lord. Praise ye the Lord.' Psalm cl. 6. Lexington, K. John Norvell, Printer. 1818."

The Union of Christians and Reformers

The congregations of the old "Christian Church" or "Christian Connection" had existed for fifteen years before any of the Campbells arrived in America, but within fifteen years more the movement set on foot by the Campbells was the most powerful and appealing of all. After their initial meeting in 1824, Stone and Campbell realized that their efforts stood on the same foundation. In 1831-32 a union of forces was effected in Kentucky, of which Stone afterwards wrote: "This union, irrespective of reproach, I view as the noblest act of my life."[12] After the merger, the Christians in the East and South pursued their own course and either ignored or actively opposed Stone and Campbell.

The Campbell Hymnal

In giving Campbell's motives for publishing a hymnal, Alger Fitch wrote:

> Religious poetry and music impress the memory and sway the heart as prose never can. Aware of this force, Campbell was driven to harness it for service in the coming reformation. Magazines would be read and then set aside. Not so easily could the hymns be forgotten.[13]

Furthermore, while all the denominational hymnals of the day were designed to propound their peculiar creedal sentiments, Campbell designed to publish a hymn book "from which unscriptural sentiments were to be excluded."[14] Hence, in May 1828, he brought out his *Psalms, Hymns, and Spiritual Songs Adapted to the Christian Religion.*

The original 1828 book contained a poem entitled "Elegant Extract," 125 hymns, a preface on "Psalmody," and an appendix on "Prayer." The hymns had a metrical abbreviation at the head of each poem and sold from Bethany at 37.5 cents per copy or $3.75 a dozen.

From 1828 onward the Campbell book grew in size and increased in circulation. A second edition appeared in 1829 and a third in 1832. The number of poems kept increasing slowly, but the essay on "Prayer" was omitted in 1832.[15] The sources for the various poems were not given, a common practice at the time.

With the union between Christians and Reformers in 1831-32, the use of two different hymnals posed a problem. Campbell made overtures to Stone and Johnson that one hymnal be made of the two. It was agreed that A. Campbell and Walter Scott, and Stone and Johnson would meet to do this work, but the meeting never took place. No satisfactory reason was ever given, but while Stone and Johnson were waiting for further details of when and where to meet, Campbell and Scott did the revising themselves and sent Stone the galley sheets for proofreading.[16]

A problem developed when Campbell and Scott made the title page read *The Disciples' Hymn-Book*. Stone objected to the title, for he desired to magnify the name "Christian," over which he and Campbell had already had a dispute. He urged that Campbell remove the prefaces as well and insert certain hymns from Stone's former book. Campbell agreed only to change the title, and thus the book went forth. Doubtless B. W. Stone and John T. Johnson were magnanimous men, or else they would have broken with Campbell over such treatment. Obviously Christian union was more important to them than their hymnal, and they too desired to see a single book in use among lovers of reform.

The title page, as changed after the objections of Stone and Johnson, read: *Psalms, Hymns, and Spiritual Songs, Original and Selected—*

Compiled by A. Campbell, W. Scott, B. W. Stone, and J. T. Johnson—Bethany, Va. 1834. This book contained 240 hymns and sold for 37.5 cents per copy. In 1835, Campbell bought the rights of the other compilers and became the sole owner of the book.

From 1834 to 1843, five editions were produced, and the number of songs continued to increase. The book was stereotyped during this period, and the 1838 printing sold at the reduced price of 25 cents. The hymnal could also be purchased bound together with Campbell's *Pocket Testament* for 50 cents.[17]

In 1843 a new edition appeared with a "Part II," which contained 217 new hymns and a first-line index. The book now had 475 pieces, and the price went back to 37.5 cents per copy. This increase and Campbell's reluctance to enlarge the volume substantially seems to have caused the appearance of competitive hymnals and to have defeated Campbell's desire for one hymnal for the brotherhood. It was also about this time that Campbell acceded to a proposal that proceeds from the sale of the hymnal be used to educate young men for the Christian ministry. (Campbell had founded Bethany College in 1840.) The 1848 edition sold 100,000 copies and brought in $2,000 for this purpose. Campbell continued to use the proceeds from the hymnal for the education of young men at Bethany College as long as he controlled the book.

From 1851 to 1865, at least seven editions were published. The divisions into Parts I and II were eliminated, and the numbering was made consecutive throughout. The tune names formerly printed at the heads of the songs were omitted. Advertisements in the *Millennial Harbinger* for this period indicated that the book was being sold in every state in the Union and also in Canada. The hymnal had grown to 511 pages; and, while the cover bore the title *Christian Hymn-Book*, the title page was slightly emended. It read: "Psalms, Hymns, and Spiritual Songs, Original and Selected. Compiled by A. Campbell, W. Scott, B. W. Stone, and J. T. Johnson, Elders of the Christian Church; With Numerous and Various Additions and Emendations Adapted to Personal, Family, and Church Worship by Alexander Campbell."

By the 1850s and early 1860s, there was in some quarters a growing dissatisfaction with the Campbell book. Several resented the fact that only one book was available. Deeply hurt, Campbell stated that he would do whatever the brotherhood desired if they would make their wishes known. (*Millennial Harbinger*, 1852, pp. 54ff; 1864, p. 524) The American Christian Missionary Society, with Campbell as president, had been founded in 1849. Campbell felt that it represented the churches in America. In 1863 the ACMS appointed a committee, headed by Isaac Errett, to approach Campbell on the idea of a complete revision of the hymnal. In 1864 Errett wrote in the *Millennial Harbinger*:

> It is well known that for several years past there has been a growing
> desire among our brethren for a revision and enlargement of our
> Hymn Book. This desire is now well nigh universal. In view of
> this, and in order to prepare the way for a book which should be
> emphatically *the book of the brotherhood,* an informal meeting of
> brethren from several states was held, in Cincinnati, in October,
> 1863, at which a Committee was appointed to open a
> correspondence with Bro. A. Campbell. (p. 520)

This was done, and in 1864 Campbell transferred his rights to the hymnbook
to the ACMS, which would revise it and publish it. The proceeds from the
sale of the book would be given to the Society for the support of missions.
Campbell printed his last edition of his hymnal in 1865.

That same year the Society's book appeared. Its editors, overseeing
various aspects of publication, consisted of the leading brethren supporting
the Society: R. M. Bishop, C. H. Gould, W. H. Lape, O. A. Burgess, J. B.
Bowman, Isaac Errett, W. K. Pendleton, W. T. Moore, T. M. Allen, A. S.
Hayden, and William Baxter. The new book contained 1324 hymns on 840
pages. All of Campbell's own compositions were omitted. The book sold
for 90 cents per copy and received plaudits from noted Christian leaders
such as Robert Milligan and J. W. McGarvey. Even competitive publishers
hailed it. J. S. Lamar wrote a few years later:

> It should be stated that as the result of the solicitous care and pains
> of the committee, and of their exceptional competency for the task,
> the work produced was perhaps the best and most complete
> hymnbook in the world.[18]

The Society editions from 1865 to 1871 continued the basic
approaches begun by Alexander Campbell and the other compilers
mentioned above. With Campbell's death in 1866, the editors felt free to
make further changes and to take new approaches. All of his life Campbell
had opposed the excesses of the singing schools, the use of choirs, and the
use of instrumental music. Furthermore, he objected to the use of musical
notes in hymnals, believing that they detracted from the content of the
songs. So long as he lived, no notes were printed in his own hymnals nor
those of the ACMS.[19]

In 1870 A. S. Hayden produced a tune book for use with the
Campbell Society book of 1865. The next year (1871), the Society, even
though they would continue to print and sell the 1865 book until 1878,
published an alternative volume with music, which omitted A. Campbell's
name from the title page and which bore the title *The Christian Hymnal.*
The story of the Campbell Society hymnal comes to a close with the two
final editions of 1875 and 1882. The 1875 book was entitled *The Christian*

Hymnal: A Choice Collection of Hymns and Tunes for Congregational and Social Worship. The final edition of 1882, which had been authorized by the ACMS at the 1880 convention, was the *Christian Hymnal: Revised.* The revision committee consisted of A. I. Hobbs, C. L. Loos, J. S. Lamar, A. R. Benton, and Joseph Franklin to oversee the text, with J. H. Fillmore, L. H. Jameson, and T. P. Haley in charge of the music. This, too, was an expensive book and sold in cloth and boards for 90 cents per copy. The competition had become too great. Besides, a controversy was rising which would rend the brotherhood and would find a focus in the dispute between David Lipscomb of the *Gospel Advocate* and Isaac Errett of the *Christian Standard* over the Society and its publications.

Campbell's Nineteenth-Century Competition

The desire of Alexander Campbell for one hymnbook for the entire brotherhood was never fully realized. In one sense Campbell was simply not abreast, or not willing to be abreast, of the times. He had opposed the singing school movement for the most part and had excluded from his hymnals those songs which had come out of that movement. The more stately hymnody preferred by Americans such as Lowell Mason appealed to him. Others in the brotherhood did not share this view; thus, competitive books were bound to come even from Campbell's closest associates.

Amos Sutton Hayden (1813-1880) had begun to publish music as early as 1834. Hayden was a fine singer and a great worker on what was then called the Western Reserve (primarily Ohio). Campbell always seemed to appreciate him. In the *Harbinger* (1835, p. 336) Campbell placed this note:

> Brother Hayden's New Music Book, adapted to our selection of Psalms, Hymns and Spiritual Songs is received here. Orders for it will be filled in conjunction with orders for our works, addressed to M'Vay and Ewing. I learn from those who are much better judges than I am, that this is one of the very best selections of sacred music suited to social worship.

Hayden also published *The Sacred Melodeon* (1849); *The Hymnist* (1863); and *The Christian Hymn and Tune Book* (1870).

Walter Scott (1796-1861), one of Campbell's closest associates, was a fine musician. In 1839 he published *Christian Psalms and Hymns*, which he considered an improved edition of the hymnal which Campbell had published. He and Campbell had a dispute about this. In 1844 he brought out *The Christian Hymn Book, Being a Collection of Psalms, Hymns, and Spiritual Songs, Compiled by the Executive Committee of the Ohio Christian Book Association*. Scott, who also encouraged the use of musical notes and of singing schools, had adapted his revision of the hymnal (1839) to T. B. Mason's *Sacred Harp*. An advocate of the singing schools who seemed especially to have irritated Campbell was Silas White Leonard (1814-1870), a friend of Walter Scott and A. D. Fillmore. With Fillmore he edited the *Christian Psalmist* (1847), which ran to at least eighteen editions. Leonard also published rudiments books, including *The Numeral Singer* (1850) and *The Vocalist* (1850). His last book was entitled *The New Christian Psalmist* (1871).

B. F. Hall (1803-1873), called by Robert Richardson "the evangelist of Kentucky,"[19] was an early associate of Campbell and a coworker of John T. Johnson. In 1852 he published *Christian Songs: Adapted to Individual, Family, and Congregational Worship*. This book contained 386 hymns.

Augustus Damon Fillmore (1823-1870) was one of the great names connected with Christian praise in the 19th century. After his death his sons formed the Fillmore Brothers Music Company in Cincinnati, Ohio, and continued his work. Fillmore published many rudiments books, Sunday School hymnals, and other songbooks. By the age of thirty he had established a permanent reputation. He also invented a mathematical system of notation which had brief popularity in mid-century. An example follows from the Fillmore's *New Harp of Zion* [1872], p.220.

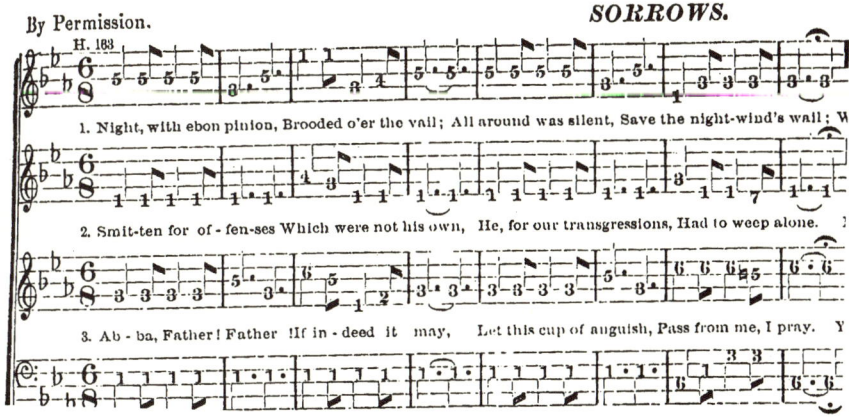

The following advertisement appeared in the *Gospel Advocate* (1855, p. 127) offering a new Fillmore book:

> The Nightingale, or Normal School-singer; designed for Schools, Home Circle, and Private Practice, on a *Mathematically constructed Plan of Notation* . . . Brother Fillmore is admitted to be a beautiful musical composer, and is possessed of fine discrimination in

selecting. Whilst we are not entirely satisfied as to the system of notation, we regard the work as very plain, and worthy of extensive patronage.

Other works by Fillmore include *The Temperance Musician* (1853), *The Polyphonic or Juvenile Choralist* (1863), and *Fillmore's Christian Choralist* (1864). Stanford Chambers (1876-1969) stated in a letter to me on September 22, 1954:

> The first hymn book of my recollection (in the 1880's) used by Shiloh congregation, Sullivan Co., Indiana, and others around, was *Harp of Zion*. The first edition sold well and the second (*New Harp of Zion*, 1872) was expected to sell even better.

Fillmore also edited with Robert Skene *The Concordia* (2d ed.; 1865) and *The Christian Psaltery* (1867).

The evangelist Knowles Shaws (1834-1878) was also a fine musician who published a good deal of Sunday School music. He was prominent among the churches in the 1860s and 1870s until his tragic death in a train wreck near McKinney, Texas. His publications included *Shining Pearls* (1868), *Golden Gate, Sparkling Jewels* (1871), *The Gospel Trumpet* (1875), and *The Morning Star* (1878). These books contained music mostly by Shaw. *The Gospel Trumpet* was designed "for Revivals, Protracted and Tent Meetings."

Christopher Columbus Cline (b. 1848) was a preacher, college professor, and singing teacher. In 1878 he compiled his *Popular Hymns*, which sold two million copies. *Popular Hymns, No. 2* was published in 1901. He also compiled *The Standard Church Hymnal* for the Standard Publishing Company (1888).

From all the foregoing it may be seen that there had been songbook competition to some degree for nearly all the years that Campbell had been publishing his hymnals. After his death matters intensified, and by 1880 the proliferation of songbooks began, which has been the bane and the blessing of congregations ever since.

Major Modern Hymnals

When the *Christian Hymnal: Revised*, the last lineal successor to the Campbell Society books, appeared in 1882, competition had already doomed it to failure. That same year James Henry Fillmore (1849-1936), the leading light in the Fillmore Brothers Music Company, edited *The New Christian Hymn and Tune Book*. It sold for about half the price of the Society book and had practically the same material. The original book contained Parts I and II, and a Part III was added in 1887. This book dominated among the churches into the first decade of the twentieth century.

A veritable stream of Sunday School compilations and popular male quartet arrangements came from the Fillmores at the turn of the century.

Other hymnals also followed. J. H. Fillmore and Gilbert Ellis edited *The Praise Hymnal* (1896); *The New Praise Hymnal* (1906); and *The New Praise Hymnal, Revised* (1927).

The Gospel Advocate Company began publication of its hymnals in 1889. The early Advocate policy was to have one of its editors or a leading preacher oversee the words and to employ a musician, of whatever religious affiliation, to edit the music. The original Advocate hymnal was *Christian Hymns: A Collection of Hymns and Tunes for All Occasions of Work and Worship*, edited by Elisha G. Sewell and R. M. McIntosh, assisted by Leonard Daugherty. This volume was followed by the Sunday School collection *Words of Truth* (1892) by Sewell and McIntosh, assisted by H. R. Christie. In 1895 appeared *Voice of Praise: New Songs for Gospel Meetings and Sunday Schools*, edited by Leonard Daugherty. This book could also be purchased bound in a single volume with *Christian Hymns*. In 1900 A. J. Showalter and Sewell edited *Gospel Praise*, followed by *Seventy-Seven Sweet Songs* (1906) and *The New Christian Hymn Book* (1907), both by T. B. Larimore and W. J. Kirkpatrick. A. B. Lipscomb and Kirkpatrick edited *Praise Him* (1914).

In 1923 the Advocate began to use only members of the Church of Christ (non-instrumental) in editing its hymnals. C. M. Pullias edited several books. In 1923 came *Choice Gospel Hymns* by T. B. Mosley and Pullias with S. P. Pittman. Next were *Sweeter Than All Songs* (1927) and *Greater Christian Hymns* (1931), edited by Pullias alone. In 1933 Lloyd Otis Sanderson was employed by the Gospel Advocate Company as music editor. He edited, in conjunction with Pullias, N. B. Hardeman, E. H. Ijams, and James F. Cox, *Christian Hymns* (No. 1) in 1935. Sanderson was the sole editor of *Christian Hymns, No. 2* (1948) and *Christian Hymns, No. 3* (1966).[20]

One of the most ambitious ventures in hymnal publishing was *Gloria in Excelsis* (1905) by William E. M. Hackleman. Hackleman was a well-trained musician who had begun his own music company in 1896. He was editor-in-chief for the Twentieth Century Hymnal Committee. The book was a large volume of 624 pages and was an attempt to build a hymnal in the historic tradition. It contained "Sentences for Opening Service," "Invocations," "Responsive Sentences," an order for communion and baptism, Psalm selections, and responsive readings. There were 814 songs with music, divided topically and followed by 15 pages of doxologies, benedictions, and ancient chants and canticles. The book closed with a tune and first line index. It was expensive and for most churches just too liturgical. The *Christian-Evangelist*, however, in 1932 (pp. 146-7) called it "the standard hymn book of Disciples of Christ" and "one of the great hymnals of all time." An abridged edition of 503 numbers (omitting most of the quasi-liturgical material) was also offered. The book was published jointly by the Christian Board of Publication in St. Louis, Missouri, and the Hackleman Music Company in Indianapolis. In 1911 Hackleman, assisted by E. O. Excell and with A. B. Philputt and D. R. Dungan as editors of the responsive readings, published *Hymni Ecclesiae or Hymns of the Church*. Part One of the volume was basically the older book (*Gloria in Excelsis*) while Part Two included about 175 "gospel songs."

The Standard Publishing Company also edited a series of hymnals beginning with the Cline *Standard Church Hymnal* (1888). A partial list of their publications includes J. H. Rosecrans and Leonard Daugherty's *Crown of Beauty* (1902); R. M. Hopkins' *Standard Revival Songs* (1903); H. R. Christie's *Christian Church Hymnal* (1906) and *Worship and Service* (1916); W. Stillman Martin, T. B. Mosley, and J. E. Sturgis's *Christian Hymnal* (1924); *Favorite Hymns* by Sturgis alone (1933); and *Favorite Hymns, Revised* (1953). The Standard Publishing Company also published, for some twenty years, the standard note edition of *Great Songs of the Church, Number Two*.

As the churches that supported the missionary society and generally used mechanical accompaniment in singing developed in the 20th century, a serious rift occurred about 1919. At that time the various organized works of the churches were combined under the United Christian Missionary Society. As the years went by, nearly all the leadership positions were occupied by theological liberals, and the old plea of unity by conformity to Scripture standards was abandoned. The "United" leaders began to publish hymnals about this time. J. H. Garrison's *Christian-Evangelist* advertised E. O. Excell and A. C. Smither's

Hymns of the Faith (St. Louis: Christian Board of Publication, c. 1918). Charles Clayton Morrison, editor of the liberal *Christian Century*, edited *Hymns of the United Church* (1924). In 1941 the "Disciples" church, now well-organized with their International Convention, published a hymnal jointly with the Northern Baptist Convention. This was *Christian Worship: A Hymnal*, under the chairmanship of William S. Abernethy (Baptist) and Raphael H. Miller (Disciple). Fred B. Wise was the editor of the work. The most recent hymnal of the Disciples is *Hymnbook for Christian Worship* (1970). Charles Huddleston Heaton was editor, and John Paul Pack (Disciple) and Edward Hughes (American Baptist) were chairmen of the committee.[21]

The Firm Foundation Publishing House of Austin, Texas, has published hymnals since early in the twentieth century. These include Austin

Taylor (1881-1973) and G. H. P. Showalter, *Gospel Songs; Gospel Songs, Number Two* (1919) *Gospel Songs, Number Three* (1924); Taylor, Showalter, James Acuff, and W. D. Everidge, *The New Ideal Hymn Book* (1930); and in 1938, *Wonderful Songs* (title changed shortly after to *New Wonderful Songs*, probably to avoid confusion with a Gospel Advocate revival collection). This work continued for several years as the principal Firm Foundation collection. Thomas S. Cobb and G. H.

P. Showalter edited *Our Leader* (1941). Showalter and Taylor edited the *Majestic Hymnal* (1953). Reuel Lemmons was the editor of *Majestic Hymnal, Number Two* (1959) and *Hymns of Praise* (1978).

Various individual Christians have published hymnals used more or less regionally in the United States and by segments of the Stone-Campbell Movement. Among these, without any effort to be definitive, are the following: S. H. and Flavil Hall, *The Gospel Message in Song* (1910); *Redemption's Way in Song* (1911); and the *Cross and Resurrection* (1920; 1927). The songs included were chiefly by the editors and their friends, and many are intensely sentimental. F. L. Rowe, editor of the *Christian Leader*, published these hymnals. He also published *The Wonderful Story in Song*, edited by Fred A. Fillmore (1917). Will W. Slater was a well-known singer and publisher in the Southwest, and his son, J. Nelson Slater, edited the *Christian Hymnal* (1963), a very fine collection of standard hymns and gospel songs. Tillit S. Teddlie, who died in 1987 at age 102, published many hymnals. Marion Davis of Alabama edited the *Complete Christian Hymnal* (1940), which had a fairly extensive use in the Southeast. J. W. Treat, former professor of foreign languages at Abilene Christian University, edited *Cantos Espirituales* (1947), a hymnal for Spanish-speaking churches. In recent years missionaries have prepared hymnals in other languages: Frank Worgan edited for Dutch churches *Liederen ten dienste van Gementen van Christus* (1959), and a hymnal is in preparation for French-speaking churches. Ellis Crum edited *Sacred Selections for the Church* (1956); Alton Howard, *Songs of the Church* (1971); V. E. Howard, *Gospel Songs and Hymns* (1978); and R. J. Stevens and Dane K. Shephard, *Hymns for Worship* (1987); John Wiegand, *Praise for the Lord* (1992); and Albert E. Winstanley and Graham A. Fisher, *Favourite Hymns of the Church* (1995).

Great Songs of the Church

The first major hymnal by someone in the Restoration Movement who did not use instruments in worship appeared in 1921. Elmer Leon Jorgenson (1886-1968), a native of Nebraska and a fine musician, had had wide experience in leading singing for meetings, had headed the vocal music department at Western Bible and Literary College, Odessa, Missouri, and later was president of the Louisville Choir, Louisville, Kentucky. Jorgenson took an idea originally suggested by J. W. McGarvey (*Millennial Harbinger*, 1864, pp. 260ff.) and turned it into the most enduring hymnal in the history of the Stone-Campbell Movement—*Great Songs of the Church*. McGarvey had said:

> To the uninitiated it appears strange that the last man who publishes a tune book does not reproduce all the popular pieces in all previous publications, and thus combine in one the excellencies of all.

Jorgenson did just that and gave the churches "the best from all the books." The Number One book went through three editions (1921, 1922, 1925) and sixteen printings. In 1937 Jorgenson published *Great Songs of the Church, Number Two*, for which he was elected to the Eugene Field Society and listed in *Who's Who in America*.

Abilene Christian University has owned the shaped-note edition of *GS* since 1957. In 1971 the school's president, John C. Stevens, appointed a committee to add a supplement to the book. The members, who completed their work in 1975, were Bill Davis and Jack Boyd of the ACU Music department and Forrest M. McCann of the English faculty. Sixty new songs and four former end-sheet songs were added, updating the hymnal for current and continuing use. *Great Songs of the Church, Number Two, with Supplement* is still in print, the 60th edition of the *Number Two* and the 9th with *Supplement*, having come from the press in 1994.

The remainder of this book continues the story of *Great Songs of the Church* as we conclude the final decade of the twentieth century.

---

[1] Oliver P. Chitwood and Frank L. Owsley, *A Short History of the American People* (New York: D. Van Nostrand Co. Inc., 1945) I, 548ff.

[2] Nathan Bangs, *A History of the Methodist Episcopal Church* (New York: T. Mason and G. Lane, 1838) I, 351ff.

[3] W. E. MacCleny, *The Life of Rev. James O'Kelly and the Early History of the Christian Church in the South* (reprint Hollywood, CA: Old Paths Book Club, 1950), 127.

[4] James DeForest Murch, *Christians Only, A History of the Restoration Movement* (Cincinnati: Standard Publishing, 1962), 33.

[5] There is a microfilm copy of the autobiography in the Abilene Christian University library.

[6] A microfilm copy is in the ACU library.

[7] Alger Fitch, "Alexander Campbell and the Hymnbook," *Christian Standard* 28 Aug. 1965, p. 7. (Fitch published eighteen articles in the *Standard*, 26 June through 30 October 1965. These are an invaluable source of information.)

[8] Levi Purviance, *The Biography of Elder David Purviance, with Appendix* (Dayton, Ohio: B. F. & G. W. Ells, 1848), 53.

[9] W. P. Strickland, *Autobiography of Rev. James B. Finley; or, Pioneer Life in the West* (Cincinnati: Methodist Book Concern, 1854) 370ff.

[10] *Millennial Harbinger*, Feb. 1863.

[11] Colby D. Hall, *Rice Haggard, the American Frontier Evangelist Who Revived the Name Christian* (Fort Worth: University Christian Church, 1957), 30.

[12] B. W. Stone, *The Life of Barton W. Stone, Written by Himself, with Additions by John Rogers* (1847), 79.

[13] Fitch, 10 June 1965, 5.

[14] Robert Richardson, *Memoirs of Alexander Campbell* (Cincinnati: Standard Publishing Co., 1897) II, 180.

[15] See *Millennial Harbinger*, 1831, 497ff.

[16] William Garrett West, *Barton Warren Stone, Early American Advocate of Christian Unity* (Nashville: Disciples of Christ Historical Society,1954), 191-92.

[17] *Millennial Harbinger*, 1838, 430.

[18] J. S. Lamar, *Memoirs of Isaac Errett with Selections from His Writings* (Cincinnati: Standard Publishing Co., 1893) I, 291.

[19] Richardson, II, 396.

[20] L. O. Sanderson, "One Hundred Years in Song," *Gospel Advocate*, 14 July 1955, 598.

[21] John T. Brown, *Churches of Christ, A Pictorial History* (Louisville: John P. Morton and Co., 1904), 660.

PART II

A History of *Great Songs of the Church*

O n May 16, 1996, *Great Songs of the Church* celebrated its seventy-fifth anniversary. It is the longest-lived hymnal of the Stone-Campbell Movement, is used in every state of the United States, in every province of Canada, and has gone into most of the nations of the English-speaking world. In these seventy years, over two million copies of the hymnal have been sold to churches in and out of the Movement. Its popularity and longevity are unparalleled; its excellence is unquestioned.

How may we account for this unusual hymnal? Its roots lie with its original compiler, who shared an idea that was almost obsessive during most of the nineteenth century among the leaders of the Restoration Movement.

I.

Elmer Leon Jorgenson (1886-1968) was the youngest son of a family of Danish immigrants. His father, Christopher Jorgenson, had been a soldier in the personal guard of the King of Denmark and his mother was a seamstress to the Queen. Since his father died while ELJ was young, he worked to help support the family. His musical talent gave him opportunity to lead singing among the churches at and near his birthplace in Albion, Nebraska, and also in the neighboring state of Missouri. By 1908 he was the head of the Music department of Western Bible and Literary College in Odessa, Missouri. Here he met and married Irene Doty. In 1910 they moved to Louisville, Kentucky, where he ministered to the Highland Church and where he first conceived the idea for *Great Songs of the Church*.

This hymnal was born out of Jorgenson's agreement with the passion for unity that marked the work of Barton W. Stone and Alexander Campbell. Campbell had issued his first hymnal in 1828 and Stone his first in 1829. When they joined forces in the winter of 1831-32, they saw an immediate need for a single hymnal to promote and to preserve that union. Accordingly, in 1834, with the assistance of Walter Scott and John T. Johnson, they issued a combined hymnal for the use of the churches. Campbell expressed his own passion for excellence in hymnody:

> The subject matter of the Christian psalter, psalm or hymn-book, is therefore of the first importance; as, next to the Bible, no book in the world has such influence on the heart. No volume, indeed, ought to be studied with more care, and composed with more special regard to the sacred style, than this book of Christian worship.[1]

In 1835 Campbell purchased the copyrights of the other compilers and published the hymnal in increasingly larger editions until he presented the book to the American Christian Missionary Society, that there might continue to be one hymnal for the churches.[2]

Few competitors to the Stone-Campbell hymnal existed before the 1880s. The united churches used one hymnal, north, south, east, and west. That passion for excellence, however, had not been completely satisfied. Some were seeing the need to incorporate the increasing number of good materials into one book. In 1864 J. W. McGarvey yearned for a hymnal, both for church meetings and for Sunday Schools, that would contain only the best. He said:

> To the uninitiated it appears strange that the last man who publishes a tune book does not reproduce the popular pieces in all previous publications, and thus combine in one the excellencies of all.[3]

McGarvey, however, thought this impossible because of copyright obstacles. Challenged by this "impossibility," Jorgenson, in 1910, began to collect materials for just such a book.

The twenty-four-year-old Jorgenson naively believed that his work would be relatively simple and could be accomplished quickly, but a decade would pass before *Great Songs* (hereafter referred to as *GS*) could appear. Shortly before the hymnal was published, ELJ wrote in the *Word and Work*:[4]

> Heretofore, a peculiar kind of competition has made it impossible to secure certain songs *by anyone*, at any price. All that is altered now. For the first time in about twenty years, the greatest copyrights of *both* Mr. Excell and Mr. Alexander will appear side by side, in the same book.[5]

Then Jorgenson added:

> I am profoundly thankful to the Lord, that, in His over-ruling providence, this remarkable advantage has been sent *our way*. It removes the last obstacle in issuing the greatest Hymnal ever put out, an obstacle that for ten years discouraged my efforts.[6]

Jorgenson had not been idle in pursuing his dream during those ten years. He wrote again:

> For more than ten years, the work of collecting songs, from various lands and languages has been in progress. I find from old letters that negotiations for permissions began in 1911. In the meantime, a four-year course in musical theory, history, harmony and composition was undertaken and completed at the University of Louisville—as a further preparation for this very labor. Also, the counsel of the ablest song leaders and compilers known to me has been freely sought and obtained.[7]

Jorgenson's principles, which were consonant with those of Campbell, were plainly made known to the brethren. He said:

> Next to the Bible, the song book is the most important book in the church, or in the world. Therefore the hardest and most serious labor of my life is going into it. The effort is intended as a *lasting service* to the church of God, for the praise of His name, rather than any money-making venture, or commercial project.[8]

The hymnal was to contain the "really great standard hymns" and "at least an equal number" of gospel songs. But, Jorgenson added, "All its songs are *'spiritual songs,'* no rag-time, no 'jazz,' nor jazzy syncopation. . . . The utmost care is exercised, to make every song ring as true to scripture as if it were an oracle of God." He believed that he was building a useful, working tool for Christian worship and teaching. "Themes that are emphasized in Scripture, as for instance, Missions, the doctrine of the Cross, will be prominent in the hymnal." The heart of all his principles he stated thus:

> The book is being built on this unusual principle: No song can enter there unless it is *indispensable*, or at least *so very excellent*, so scriptural, so beautiful, so useful in saving sinners, or in edifying saints, so true and tried. . . that if we knew the song, we simply would not want to do without it.[9]

On May 16, 1921, *GS* was published. The event was celebrated in Louisville by a great union sing that lasted over five days, and that alternated between the Highland and Portland church buildings. Jorgenson himself led the singing, and disciples came from far and near to participate. Thus began the hymnal which has exercised the greatest influence on the hymnody of the Churches of Christ in the twentieth century.

The first printing of the world's only alphabetical hymnal (an idea that came to ELJ shortly before publication) sold out in slightly over a year. The second printing with a fifty-song *Supplement* appeared on August 19, 1922. Jorgenson wrote the following month:

A few plates were recast for "sharpness," some tunes were worked in where only word-songs appeared before...and fifty noble hymns were added. . . .We have added them chiefly to meet the need of the British brethren among whom the hymnal has won favor—though it is our earnest hope that their use will spread throughout the United States.[10]

The *Supplement* contained such abiding favorites as "All Things Praise Thee," "Dear Lord and Father of Mankind," "Jesus, Thou Joy of Loving Hearts," "Peace, Perfect Peace," "The Lord's My Shepherd," "Thou Art the Way," and "Unto the Hills." "Another Week" and "Lord of Our Highest Love," two communion hymns by the British disciple Gilbert Young Tickle, were also added. *GS* was published in this format until 1925.

The book received high praise from leading singers in the Movement including Austin Taylor and L. O. Sanderson. W. Stillman Martin, composer of the tune "God Will Take Care of You," wrote: "I unhesitatingly say it is the best song book I have seen since the days of the old 'Gospel Hymns' of Moody and Sankey, and it is equal to their combined collection."[11]

A primary reason for the success and quality of the hymnal was its inclusions. J. F. Lilly of Los Angeles, who had been one of Jorgenson's greatest encouragers in the publication of the hymnal, wrote to him in August, 1923, that the book contained every one of the hymns on the list of the world's thirty greatest hymns, which had just been published by *Etude*, except "Come, Thou Almighty King," and that the book had the traditional tune for that poem—"Italian Hymn"—set to other words.[12]

The original hymnal and the edition with *Supplement* were printed only in round notes, but by 1922 Jorgenson noted that the request for a shaped-note edition was heavy. In 1925 he acceded to this demand, which came principally from across the South, and a new edition of *GS* was published. The new shaped-note book appeared in September and the new round-note book in November 1925. Several deletions and additions were made, and the songs from the *Supplement* of 1922 were included in one alphabetical arrangement, still making four hundred fifty numbers in all. Some of the hymns included for the first time in 1925 were "Again the Lord of Light and Life," "Behold a Stranger at the Door," "Have You Been to Jesus," "I Know That My Redeemer Lives" (with the "Bradford" tune), "May the Grace of Christ Our Savior," "O Come, All Ye Faithful," "O Jesus, I Have Promised," "On a Hill Far Away," and "Safe in the Arms of Jesus."

The "revised" *GS* was an immediate bestseller. Between September 1925, and May 1926, three printings were called for, some 10,000 books in all. By the end of 1929, 80,000 copies had been printed. In June 1930, the sales had neared the 100,000 mark. The book had been priced at 65 cents per copy, but during the harsh depression years, beginning in 1932, Jorgenson reduced the price to 50 cents per copy. In 1933 the children's songs section was also published in a separate pamphlet for use in Sunday Schools, and, in 1934, Jorgenson added, on one of the end-sheets, his musical setting of the "Blessing" of Numbers 6: 24-26, "The Lord Bless Thee and Keep Thee." The book was in use in at least one thousand churches across the United States and Canada and on almost every continent. The 1935 sales exceeded those of any previous year, and the book was being marketed not only through the *Word and Work* in Louisville, but also through the *Apostolic Review* of Indianapolis, the Upper Canada Tract Society of Toronto, and by the Union Gospel Press of Cleveland. In April 1936, ELJ wrote:

> From the Canadian Northland to the Gulf, from Maine to California, at least a quarter million disciples in a thousand churches, sing from its pages every Lord's day. It is the first book in our generation to transcend sectional prejudices, and become 'standard' among churches of Christ. It has won the unsolicited, unqualified approval, as the best extant, of hundreds of prominent singers and preachers, and from every continent, and practically every state and province in the U. S. and Canada.[13]

II.

For fifteen years *GS* won its way into the hearts of the Churches of Christ and gained a reputation among denominational and independent publishers and users of church hymnals. By early 1937, ELJ had determined to bring out a complete revision of the hymnal. In July 1937, he published the "Foreword to the New Hymnal" in the *Word and Work*. He said:

> Fifteen years of more mature experience have suggested many improvements. They have been years of unusual opportunities to learn firsthand the needs and capacities of the churches in every section of America—North, South, East, and West; of much contact with the song leaders, and of earnest research in the whole field of sacred music. As the fruit of these, and as the supreme labor of his life, the compiler sends forth this larger, better, 'Great Songs of the Church'—the new 'No. 2.'[14]

Jorgenson was thirty-five years old when he issued the original *GS*; he was now fifty-one. These added years of maturity and dedication had borne fruit. The new book contained 600 numbers, divided into "gospel songs" and "hymns." It retained 350 numbers from the older books and added 250 new ones. The music plates were prepared by Anderson Brothers of Chicago, one of the premier music typographers in America at that time.

He made an effort to include compositions by those he called "disciple brethren," which included names such as J. H. Fillmore, Flavil Hall, L. K. Harding, Richard Maxwell, James Deforest Murch, Austin Taylor, L. O. Sanderson, Tillit S. Teddlie, Lula Klingman Zahn, and himself. Issued in both round and shaped notes, the book was an immediate success upon its publication in September 1937. Jorgenson reported that "Total sales of 'Great Songs of the Church' for September were the largest for any month since publication of the first edition in 1921."[15]

This success story would continue for almost the next fifty years. In the December 1937 *Word and Work*, Jorgenson printed three full pages of commendations which had poured in from church leaders all over America. The commenders included many of the most influential figures in the fellowship: R. S. King, Marion Davis, H. H. Adamson, S. S. Lappin, Flavil Hall, G. C. Brewer, James Lovell, James F. Cox, Batsell Baxter, N. B. Hardeman, A. R. Holton, R. H. Boll, Leonard Burford, W. H. Free, George Klingman, James Deforest Murch, Andy T. Richie, Jr., and Burton Coffman. The edition for 1938 ran to 30,000 copies, and that year he added on the back end sheets the Kurfees-Hopkins unity song "How Blest and How Joyous." By then, rival publishers were praising the new book. Commendations were received from Fleming H. Revell Company, Fillmore Music House, Union Gospel Press, Hope Publishing Company, Frank C. Huston, the *Christian Standard*,[16] and the *Firm Foundation*. As a result of his work, ELJ was listed in *Who's Who in America* and was elected to the Eugene Field Society.

The older book, now called the "No. 1," was kept in print for a time. This hymnal ran through 16 editions, the last printing in 1940, and was finally sold out and allowed to go out of print in 1944. By June 1941, nearly 250,000 copies of the No. 1 and No. 2 books had been sold.

Beginning in 1932, Jorgenson spent a month or two each year on a "song tour" to encourage good singing. Although not for the purpose of selling his hymnal, and always held only in churches already using the book, doubtless this contact with the churches all over the U. S. and Canada greatly enhanced sales. In 1943, 55,000 copies of the hymnal were sold, and 60,000 in 1945. These sales were all the more remarkable since they occurred during the years of the World War II, when paper shortages were constant. Eighty thousand copies of the hymnal were sold in 1946, and because of rising paper costs the price of the hymnal was raised to 75 cents. (It had been at 65 cents since 1937.) By 1947 the price rose to $1.00 per copy.

Sales for 1948 reached 75,000 copies, and that year three styles of the book were offered: the "Louisville" edition in round or shaped notes with the compiler's name on the title page, the "Cincinnati" edition in round notes with a responsive readings supplement by James Deforest Murch;[16] and the "Nashville" edition with Barney Morehead's *World Vision* imprint but without ELJ's name on the title page.[17] In 1949, the hymnal began to be published by the Rand McNally Company of Chicago. In 1950 "Beyond the Sunset" and a male quartet arrangement of "Still, Still with Thee" were added to the end sheets, and by 1952 over one million copies of *GS* had been sold. That year the mailing address for the hymnal was moved from Louisville to Chicago under the now familiar title of Great Songs Press. In 1953, ELJ reported that 5,000 churches were using *GS* and that sales were exceeding all previous years.

In 1954, Jorgenson sold the printing rights for the round-note book to the Standard Publishing Company of Cincinnati, Ohio, and the set of shaped-note plates to the *Christian Chronicle* of Abilene, Texas. By early 1956, the *Chronicle* went into bankruptcy, and in the bankruptcy sale, the shaped-note book was obtained by Frank Riggs, then of Odessa, Texas. He controlled the shaped-note plates until October 1, 1957. On that date E. L. Jorgenson went to Abilene to participate in the sale of the shaped-note book to Abilene Christian College (now University), which has owned and published the hymnal ever since.

On August 25, 1958, Jorgenson suffered a severe heart attack, from which he never fully recovered. During the last decade of his life, however, he never lost interest in his hymnal. In January 1960, he reported that 3,000,000 souls in some 10,000 churches were singing from the book. In 1965 he renewed the copyright to *GS* and said that the latest printing (the 44th) was mechanically as sharp and clear as the earlier ones, for he had used sheets for duplication which had been run off and stored years before the original plates had begun to show any wear. He also added: "...how many millions have been sold we do not any longer know." [18] In 1967 Jorgenson joined financially with Abilene Christian and the Standard Publishing Company to secure permission from Manna Music Company to include "How Great Thou Art" in the hymnal. Negotiations had begun for the hymn in 1965, and this popular composition was included on the end sheets in the 1967 printing.

Elmer Leon Jorgenson died at his home in Louisville, Kentucky, on December 14, 1968. This remarkable man had done more to fix and to elevate the hymnody of the Churches of Christ, and many of the Christian Churches, than any other person. In every hymnal extant among the Churches of Christ today, his work is evident. The hymnody used among the non instrumental churches before 1921 and after 1921, and especially after 1937, is radically different. The difference lies in the employment of the great historic treasury of standard hymns after these dates. E. L. Jorgenson and *GS* were responsible for this change.

III.

The history of *GS* since E. L. Jorgenson's death is one of continuing development.[19] When officials at Abilene Christian University were approached with the idea of updating *GS* (about 1970), they were enthusiastic about the project. Dr. John C. Stevens, then president of the university gave his approval and appointed a committee to add a *Supplement* (1971).[20] After four years of labor seventy selections were added, including two of the former end sheet songs, "We Gather Together" and "Beyond the Sunset." The hymnal with *Supplement* was published in 1975, and since then there have been nine printings of the No. 2.

The experience of publishing the *Supplement* encouraged the committee to continue the work of revising the hymnal. Dr. William J. Teague, president of ACU, appointed the Executive Revision Committee to prepare a hymnal which would retain the best of the older book and maintain in the selection of new materials the high standards of excellence established by E. L. Jorgenson. The committee began its work in April, 1982, and the hymnal was completed and presented both to the university and to the churches at the ACU Lectures on February 12, 1986. The principles which guided the present editors may be found in the "Foreword" to *Great Songs of the Church, Revised* and in a booklet

containing the "Editor's Introduction." This booklet is available without cost from the ACU Press in Abilene.[21] Our sentiments, on being blessed of God to complete the work, are expressed at the end of the *Foreword*:

> We give thanks to the Lord whose mercy endures forever and who inhabits the praises of His people, asking that He may be pleased to accept our work in the name of Jesus, the Lord.[22]

---

[1] *Millennial Harbinger*, May 1842, p. 231.

[2] Ibid., 1852, p. 55.

[3] Ibid., June 1864, 261-2.

[4] *Word and Work*, April 1920. (In 1916 ELJ became associate editor and publisher of the *Word and Work* magazine, ed. by R. H. Boll. He used the cover pages of this publication to boost his hymnal. Unless otherwise indicated, all quotations from *Word and Work* are taken from the covers.)

[5] Charles M. Alexander, singer for evangelists R. A. Torrey and J. Wilbur Chapman, owned hundreds of copyrights to religious hymns and tunes. Edwin O. Excell, singer for evangelists Sam Jones and Gypsy Smith, owned about as many. These men were rivals and would not allow their copyrighted materials to be included together in any hymnal. But shortly before their deaths, they relented, and Jorgenson was the first hymnal compiler to reap the blessings of their change of heart.

⁶ *Word and Work*, April 1920.

⁷ Ibid.

⁸ Ibid.

⁹ Ibid.

¹⁰ *Word and Work*, Sept. 1922.

¹¹ *Word and Work*, 1923, p. 38.

¹² The *Etude* list, in descending order, included the following hymns:

Abide with Me	Sweet Hour of Prayer
Nearer, My God to Thee	When I Survey the Wondrous Cross
Lead, Kindly Light	He Leadeth Me
Rock of Ages	In the Cross of Christ I Glory
Jesus, Lover of My Soul	Onward, Christian Soldiers
Jesus Calls Us	Guide Me, O Thou Great Jehovah
Holy, Holy, Holy	O Mother Dear, Jerusalem
Just as I Am	My Faith Looks Up to Thee
Jesus, Savior, Pilot Me	Come, Thou Almighty King
Will There Be Any Stars	O Love that Wilt Not Let Me Go
All Hail the Power	O Worship the King
Softly Now the Light of Day	Now the Day Is Over
How Firm a Foundation	Come, Ye Disconsolate
In the Hour of Trial	One Sweetly Solemn Thought
What a Friend We Have in Jesus	
I Need Thee Every Hour	

¹³ *Word and Work*, April 1936.

¹⁴ *Word and Work*, July 1937.

¹⁵ *Word and Work*, Sept. 1937, p. 193.

¹⁶ Jorgenson had become good friends with several associated with the *Standard* through the Witty-Murch "unity meetings" held between representatives of Christian Churches and Churches of Christ in the late 1930s and early 1940s. The *Standard* issued a round-note edition of *GS* until well into the 1970s.

¹⁷ Some leaders among Churches of Christ opposed Jorgenson because of his belief in the premillennial return of Christ. By simply leaving his name off the title page, the publishers obviated the objection for many.

¹⁸ *Word and Work*, 1965.

¹⁹ By the grace of God, Dr. and Mrs. Forrest M. McCann obtained from Mrs. E. L. Jorgenson, in 1969, her husband's collection, consisting of some 300 hymnals, from which Jorgenson had compiled the previous editions of *GS*. Mrs. Jorgenson was kind and gracious in this transaction, as she was in every contact with Abilene Christian University. She passed away in Louisville on Jan. 12, 1981.

²⁰ The members of the committee were Bill W. Davis and Jack Boyd of the ACU Music department and Forrest M. McCann of the ACU English faculty. James Fulbright, then director of the ACU Bookstore, obtained copyright permissions and guided the committee in our contacts with music compositors and book manufacturers.

[21] The original members of the Executive Revision Committee were Forrest M. McCann, Chairman; Jack Boyd, Rollie Blondeau, Milton Pullen, Gary Mabry, and Larry McCommas. McCommas, an Abilene businessman and a well-trained musician, was soon relegated to the Advisory Committee because of his business obligations. Mabry went on a leave of absence and later decided not to return to the university. The major work in Abilene was done by the remaining members of the committee and, during the last year before publication, by McCann and Boyd, since by then both Blondeau and Pullen had left the University. A Liaison Committee, which was later included in the Advisory Committee, was also formed in Abilene: James Fulbright was in charge of securing copyright permissions and Ronald Hadfield oversaw book design and production. Rubén Santiago, an Abilene artist, designed the cover and title page of the hymnal. Don Ellingson of Musictype in Omaha, Arkansas, was employed to typeset the hymnal.

[22] More than fifty men and women from across the United States, Canada, Great Britain, and Australia, formed an Advisory Committee and provided invaluable insights and suggestions. They were the following:

Bill W. Davis, Honorary Chairman

Kenneth L. Adams, Jr.	L. D. (Bill) Hilton
Fred Alexander	Wayne Hinds
Tony AshJames	L. Jackson
Joe B. Baisden	Dale A. Jorgenson
Irma Lee Batey	William T. King
Larry M. Bills	Thomas A. Langford
Marca Lee Bircher	Ernest E. Lyon
Terry M. Blake	Gary Mabry
Nick Boone	Bruce Mayhall
Carl Brecheen	Larry McCommas
Marvin A. Brooker, Jr.	Patricia Burke McNicol
George E. Butterfield	Timothy M. Meixner
Gerald Casey	Erle T. Moore
Ralph A. Casey	Anthony Mukitus
H. Decker Clark, Jr.	R. Stafford North
Paul A. Clark	Thomas H. Olbricht
John Clovis	Paul R. Piersall
Bevan Collingwood	Richard David Ramsey
Charles E. Cox	Robert M. Randolph
Max E. Craddock	H. Putnam Reeves, Jr.
Robert M. Cronin	Andy T. Richie III
Dan G. Danner	Jerry Rushford
Kenneth Davis, Jr.	Leon B. Sanderson
Lloyd A. Deal	Arthur L. Shearin
Enos E. Dowling	Tommy Spain
William E. Fowler	Russel N. Squire
James Fulbright	William J. Teague
Neil Fry	Darryl Tippens
Clifton L. Ganus III	Bill B. Totty

Andrew Gardiner   Peggy Spoonts West
Ronald B. Hadfield   Bill Waugh
Jim Hawkins   James Willett
Ken Helterbrand   John F. Wilson

PART III

Texts and Tunes

A Charge to Keep I Have   600

Charles Wesley, 1707-1788

This text, inspired by the words of Leviticus, "Keep the charge of the Lord, that ye die not" (8:35), was first published in Wesley's *Short Hymns on Select Passages of Holy Scripture* (1762, Vol. I, No. 188). This two-volume work contained 2,030 hymns based on biblical texts from Genesis to Revelation, including 16 from Leviticus. Wesley seems to have followed Matthew Henry's commentary on Leviticus 8:35 nearly word for word. The text was the first song in the original edition of *Great Songs* (1921), (hereafter referred to as *GS*), but was omitted in the *Number Two* book (1937). It was returned in the *Supplement* (1975, No. 601).

Boylston

Lowell Mason, 1792-1872

This tune was first published in *The Choir* (1832), set to "Our days are as the grass." Boylston is the name of a city in Massachusetts and also of a street in Boston. Armin Haeussler says that the tune is based on a Gregorian formula, and William Reynolds has pointed out the similarity of the melody to HOBART in I. B. Woodbury's *New Lute of Zion* (1853, p. 149).

A Mighty Fortress Is Our God   104

Martin Luther, 1483-1546

The exact date and the circumstances of composition of this hymn are uncertain. Traditionally it is said to have been written in 1529 following the Diet of Speyer, where the German princes "protested" the revocation of their liberties, and whence arose the term "Protestant." John Julian says it was first published in Joseph Klug's *Geistliche Lieder* (Wittenberg, 1529). No copy of this hymnal exists. The hymn was also included in Michael Blum's *Enchiridion geistlicher Gesänge und Psalmen für die Laien* (1530). The poem is based upon Psalm 46 and has been the marching song of Protestantism through the centuries. The first three stanzas correspond exactly to the natural divisions of Psalm 46, and have been included in *GS* since 1937. The fourth stanza is included for the first time in *Great Songs of the Church, Revised,* (hereafter referred to as *GSR*).

Luther's great poem "Ein' feste Burg ist unser Gott" has been translated many times. The two most famous translations are those by Thomas Carlyle, beginning "A safe stronghold our God is still," and by Frederick H. Hedge (1805-1890). The Hedge translation has always been chosen for *GS*. It was first published in Hedge and F. D. Huntingdon's *Hymns for the Church of Christ* (1853).

Ein' feste Burg

Martin Luther, 1483-1546

The tune was probably included in Klug's *Geistliche Lieder* (1529) and was in A. Raushcer's *Geistliche Lieder* (Erfurt, 1531), and in *Kirchengesange, mit viel schöner Psalmen und Melodien* (Nuremberg, 1531). The present arrangement is by Jack Boyd, music editor of *GSR*.

A Wonderful Savior 467

Fanny J. Crosby, 1820-1915

This text was written by Crosby for Kirkpatrick's tune. It was first published in George D. Elderkin, C. C. McCabe, John R. Sweney, and Kirkpatrick's

The Finest of the Wheat, No. 1 (Chicago, 1890, No. 49). For years this hymn was the opening theme song for *The Herald of Truth*, a nationwide broadcast sponsored by the Churches of Christ. It has been in *GS* since 1921.

Kirkpatrick

William J. Kirkpatrick, 1838-1921

This tune was written in 1890 and prompted Fanny Crosby to write the text above. No other circumstances of the writing are known. It was first published in the hymnal mentioned above, and has been in *GS* since 1921.

Abide with Me 33

Henry F. Lyte, 1793-1847

As Henry Lyte neared the end of his life, he continued to preach as he had since 1815. His daughter said that he often spoke playfully, saying that "It is better to wear out than to rust out." From 1823 until his death, he ministered at Lower Brixham in Devonshire, England. His health declining, he decided to take a trip to the south of Europe. On Sept. 4, 1847, he preached his last sermon and that evening gave a copy of this now famous poem to a near and dear relative. Leaving England soon afterwards, he died at Nice, France, Nov. 20, 1847. The poem is not strictly an evening hymn, but a hymn for the close of life. It is, however, included among evening hymns in most collections. The poem was first published in a leaflet with a tune by Lyte in 1847, and then in the *Remains of Henry Francis Lyte* (1850). The hymn has been a great comfort to believers in times of distress and sorrow and loneliness.

The original poem contained eight stanzas. The 1921 edition of *GS* had stanzas 1, 2, 6, and 8. Stanza 7 entered *GS* in 1937. The three omitted stanzas are as follows:

3
Not a brief glance I beg, a passing word;
 But, as Thou dwell'dst with Thy disciples, Lord,
Familiar, condescending, patient, free,
 Come, not to sojourn, but abide with me!

4
Come not in terrors, as the King of kings,
 But kind and good, with healing in Thy wings,
Tears for all woes, a heart for every plea;
 Come, Friend of sinners, and abide with me.

5
Thou on my head in early youth didst smile;
 And, though rebellious and perverse meanwhile,

Thou hast not left me, oft as I left Thee:
On to the close, O Lord, abide with me.

Eventide

William H. Monk, 1823-1889

This tune was composed for the foregoing hymn and published in
the first edition of *Hymns Ancient and Modern* (1861, No. 14). Two versions
of the circumstance of its composition exist. Monk's widow is said to have
reported that this tune was written in her presence as she and her husband,
during a time of sorrow, were watching the glory of the setting sun. A
second version, which is probably the more reliable, says it was written in
ten minutes at the close of a meeting of the committee compiling *Hymns
Ancient and Modern*. It has been in *GS* with the text since 1921.

Again the Lord of Light and Life   28

Anna L. Barbauld, 1743-1825

This text was written to celebrate the resurrection of Christ and
was first published in Dr. William Enfield's *Hymns for Public Worship*
(Warrington, England, 1772, No. 60). It appeared under the heading "For
Easter Sunday" and was originally in eleven stanzas. Mrs. Barbauld (then
Miss Aiken) published the text with revisions in her *Poems* (London, 1773,
pp. 118-20). Dr. William Bangs Collyer divided the poem into two parts in
his *Hymns* (1812), the first part embracing stanzas 1-4, which is our present
text. Collyer's part one entered *GS* in 1925.

Arlington

Thomas A. Arne, 1710-1778

Arne was England's most famous native-born composer of the
eighteenth century. His opera *Artaxerxes* was performed in London in 1762.
The present arrangement is by the amateur musician, Ralph Harrison (1848-
1810), and is taken from the minuet in the Overture to Arne's opera. It was
first published in Harrison's *Sacred Harmony*, Vol. I (1784). This tune
entered *GS* in 1921, set to Anne Steele's poem "Jesus, In Thy Transporting
Name."

Ah, Holy Jesus   222

Johann Heerman, 1586-1647

The roots of this hymn go back to the Middle Ages. The original is
the seventh of a group of *Meditationes* by several Latin writers. These

were formerly attributed to Augustine of Hippo. The seventh is now known to be the composition of Jean de Fecamp (d. 1078). Heerman's beautiful hymn beginning "Herzliebster Jesu, was hast du verbrochen" was published in 15 stanzas in his *Devote Musica Cordis, Hauss-und-Herts-Musica* (Breslau, 1630).

The English translation is by Robert Bridges (1844-1930), the English poet and literary executor of Gerard Manly Hopkins. The translation is based on both the Latin and German works and was first published in Bridges's *Yattendon Hymnal* (1895-1899). This is the first appearance of the hymn in *GSR*.

Herzliebster Jesu

Johann Crüger, 1598-1662

This tune with harmony was published in Crüger's *Newes vollkomliches Gesangbuch Augsburgishcher Confession* (Berlin, 1640). It is not completely original with Crüger. Its predecessors seem to have been GELIEBEN FREUND in Johann Hermann Schein's *Cantionale* (1627) and a setting for Psalm 23, "Mon Dieu me paist," by Louis Bourgeois in the *Genevan Psalter* (c. 1543). This is the first appearance of this tune in *GS*.

Alas! and Did My Savior Bleed? 215

Isaac Watts, 1674-1748

This text, which has had a great appeal to sinner and saint alike, was first published in Watts's *Hymns and Spiritual Songs* (1707) and entitled "Godly Sorrow arising from the Sufferings of Christ." It was originally in six stanzas, but Watts himself bracketed stanza two in later editions of his work to indicate that it might be omitted. The omitted stanza reads:

> Thy body slain, sweet Jesus, thine—
>> And bathed in its own blood,
> While all exposed to wrath divine,
>> The glorious sufferer stood.

Various emendations have been made in Watts's text over the years. 2:1 originally read "crimes that I had done"; 1:4, "for such a worm as I"; 3:3, "When, God, the mighty Maker." The text, but without the present alterations in 1:4 and 2:1, has been in *GS* since 1921. *GSR* includes all the alterations.

Hudson

Ralph E. Hudson, 1843-1901

It is probable that Hudson either wrote or adapted the words of the refrain to go with Watts's poem. This tune was first published in Hudson's *Songs of Peace, Love, and Joy* (Alliance, Ohio, 1885). The refrain, without being attributed to Hudson, was included with other texts in various nineteenth century hymnals. It has been in *GS* since 1921.

All Creatures of Our God and King   66

Francis of Assisi, 1182-1226
Tr. William H. Draper, 1855-1933

Francis's original poem seems to have been written in the year of his death, during a period of great physical and emotional suffering. It is called "The Canticle of the Sun" (*Canticum solis*), and it is the first great hymn poem in the Italian language. Draper's translation, composed some time between 1899 and 1919, is a metrical rendition of Francis's seven stanza Italian poem. The opening Italian lines:

> Laudato sia Deo mio Signore,
> > con tutte le creature
> > specialmente messer lo Frater Sole

are represented by *GSR* stanza one. *GSR* uses stanzas 1, 3, 5 and 7 of Draper's translation. The text entered *GS* in the *Supplement* (1975).

Lasst uns erfreuen

Geistliche Kirchengesang, 1623

This melody first appeared in the German hymnal *Geistliche Kirchenge-sänge* (Cologne, 1623). Eric Routley has suggested that it may belong to a family of tunes based on the major triad. See MIT FREUDEN ZART (Nos. 109, 288 in *GSR*). The tune name derives from the German text to which it was originally set in the Cologne hymnal: "Lasst uns erfreuen herrlich sehr." The present arrangement is by Jack Boyd, music editor of *GSR*, and was written in 1974 for the *Supplement* (1975).

All Glory, Laud, and Honor   167

Theodulph of Orleans, c. 760-821
Trans. John M. Neale, 1818-1866

This text was composed by Theodulph during his imprisonment at Angers, c. 820. The original poem consisted of 78 lines. A legend says that as King Louis the Pious was celebrating Palm Sunday, AD 821, he passed the prison where he had confined Theodulph and heard this beautiful hymn sung from within the prison. Having learned who the singer was, he freed him, pardoned him, and ordered that this hymn be thereafter sung on each Palm Sunday. The original Latin text begins

> Gloria, laus, et honor tibi sit,
>> Rex Christe redemptor,
> Cui puerile decus prompsit Hosannas pium.

Neale's translation was first published in the *Hymnal Noted*, Pt. II (1853), and the present text with slight revisions was published in the trial edition (1859) and subsequent editions of *Hymns Ancient and Modern* (1859). This is the first inclusion of the hymn in *GS*.

St. Theodulph

Melchior Teschner, 1584-1635

This tune was originally the second voice setting which Teschner made for the German hymn "Valet will ich dir geben" and was published in a twelve page tract entitled *Ein Andachtiges Gebet* (Leipzig, 1615). It was first joined with Theodulph's text (Neale's translation) in *Hymns Ancient and Modern* (London, 1861). The tune is sometimes called VALET WILL ICH DIR GEBEN. This is its first inclusion in *GS*.

All Hail the Power of Jesus' Name

250, 251

Edward Perronet, 1726-1792
Alt. John Rippon, 1751-1836

The first stanza of this hymn appeared in the *Gospel Magazine* (November 1779). The complete eight stanza text was printed in the same journal for April 1780. The original stanza had been set to the tune MILES LANE (originally called SHRUBSOLE) by William Shrubsole (1760-1806), who was organist for the Independent Chapel in London. MILES LANE was included in all previous editions of *GS*, but was dropped from *GSR*. Perronet's poem was emended by various hymnal editors during the eighteenth and nineteenth centuries, but was put in its modern form by John Rippon in his *Selection of Hymns from the Best Authors* (1787). The original complete text may be seen in Julian (p. 41). This hymn is one of the most powerful and widely-used hymns in the English language. It has been used as the opening hymn for the ACU school year since 1906. It has been in *GS* since 1921.

Coronation

Oliver Holden, 1765-1844

Holden composed this tune to accompany "All Hail the Power" in 1792 and published it in his *Union Harmony* (1793). It is one of the earliest American contributions to the great body of hymn tunes. It has been in *GS* since 1921.

Diadem

James Ellor, 1819-1899

This tune was written by Ellor when he was nineteen years old. First sung in the hat factory where he worked, it was received enthusiastically. Afterwards it was copied and sung at the Sunday School anniversary of the Wesleyan chapel at Droylsden, near Manchester, England, and thence passed into popular use. This is its first inclusion in *GS*.

All People That on Earth Do Dwell   74

William Kethe, d. 1594

This famous hymn poem was first published in John Daye's *Psalter* (London, 1561) and in his *Anglo-Genevan Psalter* the same year. Since 1564 it has been printed in all English and Scottish psalters and in most hymnals. *GSR* gives the text as originally written, allowing for modernization of the spelling and the retention of "flock" (2:3), instead of Kethe's "folck" (i.e., folk). Although the authorship has been questioned, as Julian says, "The evidence is certainly in favor of W. Kethe."

Old Hundredth

Genevan Psalter, 1551

Louis Bourgeois either composed or adapted this tune for Psalm 34 in the 1551 edition of the *Genevan Psalter*. It was used as the setting for William Kethe's version of Psalm 100 ("All people that on earth do dwell") in *Four-score and Seven Psalms of David* (Geneva, 1561) and in Daye's *Psalms of David in English Metre* (London, 1561). The tune name derives from its being used in the old metrical psalter of Sternhold and Hopkins (London, 1562) as the setting for Psalm 100.

All Praise to Our Redeeming Lord 391
Charles Wesley, 1707-1788

Entitled "At Meeting of Friends," this text was first published in Wesley's *Hymns for Those That Seek, and Those That Have Redemption in the Blood of Jesus Christ* (1747). It was originally in three eight line stanzas, but since the 1820s has usually been printed in four line stanzas. *GSR* text employs stanzas 1, 2, 3, 5, and 6, with stanzas 2 and 3 reversed. The complete text may be found in *The Methodist Hymn Book* (London, 1933). This is the first inclusion of this text in *GS*.

Armenia
Sylvanus D. Pond, 1792-1871

This tune was originally published in *Musical Magazine*, edited by Thomas Hastings, and collected in *The Musical Miscellany* (1836). It was first set to "Let the sweet hope that Thou art mine" and included in Pond's *United States Psalmody* (1841) and in Hastings's *The Manhattan Collection* (1841). This is its first inclusion in *GS*.

All Praise to Thee, My God, This Night 30
Thomas Ken, 1637-1711

John Julian says: "Bishop Ken is known to Hymnody as the author of the *Morning, Evening,* and *Midnight Hymns,* the first and second of which have found a place in almost every English collection for the last 150 years." (*Dictionary*, 617) This, his evening hymn, exists in texts dated 1693, 1696, and 1709. Our version is that of 1709. Originally in twelve stanzas, the *GSR* text represents stanzas 1, 2, 4, and 12. It has been in *GS* since 1937.

Tallis Canon
Thomas Tallis, c. 1505-1588

TALLIS CANON was composed for inclusion in Matthew Parker's *The Whole Psalter* (London, 1561-67). The original tune was in eight phrases, each phrase being repeated twice. The present 4-phrase form appeared in Ravenscroft's *The Whole Book of Psalms* (London, 1621). This tune was first put with Ken's text in the *Harmonious Companion* (17132) and has rarely been separated from it since. *GS* (1937) used the tune TALLIS' EVENING HYMN, which is but a variant of TALLIS' CANON.

All the Way My Savior Leads Me   651
Fanny J. Crosby, 1820-1915

Fanny Crosby penned this now widely used hymn after she had been especially blessed. Clint Bonner says:

> One day in 1874 Fanny Crosby prayed for more material things. She was short of money and needed five dollars. There was no time to draw on her publishers. So she simply prayed for the money. Rising from her knees, she was walking the room trying to "get in the mood" for another hymn when the doorbell rang. She greeted the strange admirer with "Bless your dear soul," and the two chatted briefly. According to Fanny Crosby's statement, in the parting handshake the strange caller left something in her hand. It was five dollars. (*A Hymn Is Born*, 112)

Out of this experience, she wrote the beautiful lines beginning "All the Way My Savior Leads Me." This text has been in *GS* since 1937.

All the Way
Robert Lowry, 1826-1899

After penning the words above, Fanny Crosby sent them to her friend Robert Lowry, who then composed the tune. The song was first published in W. H. Doane and Lowry's *Brightest and Best* (1875), with the Scripture motto "The Lord alone did lead him" (Deut. 32:12). The tune first entered *GS* in 1937.

All Things Praise Thee   64
George W. Conder, 1821-1871

This hymn was first published in 1874 in Conder's appendix to the *Leeds Hymn Book* (ed. 1853). It was originally in six 6-line stanzas. Nothing further is known of the circumstances under which the poem was written. Our text reduces the hymn to three stanzas. It entered *GS* in 1925.

Dix
Conrad Kocher, 1786-1872
Adpt. William H. Monk, 1823-1889

This tune first appeared in a collection of German hymns entitled *Stimmen aus dem Reiche Gottes* (Stuttgart, 1838). Monk shortened the melody from seven to six lines and used it as the setting for William Chatterton Dix's "As with gladness men of old," hence the tune name. It was first published in *Hymns Ancient and Modern* (1861). The tune entered *GS* in 1925.

All to Jesus I Surrender 604
Judson W. Van de Venter, 1855-1939

This text, according to Van de Venter's own account, was written "in memory of the time when, after a long struggle, I had surrendered and dedicated my life to active Christian service. The song was written while I was conducting a meeting at East Palestine, Ohio, and in the home of George Sebring, who later founded the city of Sebring, Florida. The Sebring camp meeting at Sebring, Ohio, was also founded by him." The text entered *GS* in 1937. It was my privilege to meet the author's second wife in 1946, while I was a student at Florida Christian College (now Florida College) in Temple Terrace (near Tampa), Florida. Her lovely home and citrus grove adjoined the campus on the banks of the beautiful Hillsborough River. She told me that her husband believed "All to Jesus I Surrender" to be his greatest hymn. Our text contains stanzas 1, 2, and 4 of the complete five-stanza poem. The omitted stanzas 3 and 5 read:

> All to Jesus I surrender,
>> Make me, Savior, wholly Thine;
> Let me feel the Holy Spirit—
>> Truly know that Thou art mine.

> All to Jesus I surrender,
>> Now I feel the sacred flame;
> O the joy of full salvation!
>> Glory, glory to His name!

Surrender
Winfield S. Weeden, 1847-1908

Weeden, who was Van de Venter's singer in evangelistic meetings, composed the tune for the foregoing text. It was published in *Gospel Songs of Grace and Glory*, compiled by Weeden, Van de Venter, and Leonard Weaver (1896).

Alleluia! Alleluia! Hearts to Heaven 244
Christopher Wordsworth, 1807-1885

This text was first published in Wordsworth's *The Holy Year* (1862). The hymn was written while Wordsworth was serving as a minister in a country parish in Berkshire, England. All of his hymns have a distinct doctrinal cast, for he believed it "the first duty of a hymn writer to teach sound doctrine, and thus to save souls." The hymn was originally in five stanzas, and the *GSR* text contains stanzas 1, 3, and 4. In 1:5 the original reading "victim" has been altered to "ransom." The omitted stanzas 2 and 5 read:

> Now the iron bars are broken,
>> Christ from death to life is born,
> Glorious life, and life immortal,
>> On this holy Easter morn.

> Christ has triumph'd,
>> And we conquer by His mighty enterprise,
> We with Him to Life eternal
>> By His resurrection rise.

And the final chorus:

> Alleluia! Alleluia! Glory be to God on high;
> Alleluia to the Savior, Who has gained the victory;
> Alleluia to the Spirit, Fount of love and sanctity;
> Alleluia! Alleluia! to the Triune Majesty.

This is the first inclusion of this hymn in *GS*.

Antilutron

Andächtige und auserlesene Gesänge (Würzburg, 1705)

This tune, which is usually called WURZBURG from its place of publication, is in *GSR* called ANTILUTRON because of the alteration made in 1:5 above. The general editor is responsible for this name change. "Antilutron" means "ransom" in Greek. The tune first appeared in the collection mentioned above. No further information is available. This is its first inclusion in *GS*.

Alleluia! Sing to Jesus   253
William Chatterton Dix, 1837-1898

This text grew out of a need felt by the author for more communion hymns for use in the Church of England. It was written in 1866 and first published in his *Altar Songs, Verses on the Holy Eucharist, No. 7* (1867) in five 8-line stanzas. The text is based on Revelation 5:9 and was originally entitled "Redemption in the Precious Blood." *GSR* text omits stanzas 4 and 5. Stanza 5 is a repetition of stanza one. Stanza 4 reads:

Alleluia! King Eternal
   Thee the Lord of lords we own;
Alleluia! born of Mary,
   Earth Thy Footstool, Heav'n Thy Throne:
Thou within the veil hast enter'd,
   Robed in flesh, our great High Priest;
Thou on earth both Priest and Victim
   In the Eucharistic Feast.

This hymn was first included in *GS* in the *Supplement* (1975).

Hyfrydol

Rowland H. Prichard, 1811-1887

This tune was written around 1830, when the Welsh composer was about 20 years old. HYFRYDOL means "good cheer" in Welsh. It was published in his *Cyfaill y Cantorion* (i.e., "The Singer's Friend") in 1844. The range of the tune is only five notes with one exception. It was first included in *GS* in the *Supplement* (1975).

Am I a Soldier of the Cross 546

Isaac Watts, 1674-1748

This text was appended to Watts's *Sermons* (3 vols., 1721-24) as the end of the third volume. The date and circumstances of the writing are unknown. It was originally entitled "Holy Fortitude, or Remedies Against Fear," and is based on 1 Cor. 16:13. *GSR* text contains all six stanzas of the original poem, the only alteration being in 5:4. In place of Watts's "And seize it with their eye," we have adopted a reading found as early as 1831: "By faith they bring it nigh." Previous editions of *GS* have read 5:4 "By faith's discerning eye." This text has been in *GS* since 1921.

Arlington

Thomas A. Arne, 1710-1778

This tune is taken from the minuet in the Overture to Arne's opera *Artaxerxes* (London, 1762). It was arranged by Ralph Harrison and was published in volume one of his *Sacred Harmony—A Collection of Psalm-Tunes, Ancient and Modern*, (2 vols., London, 1794, 1791). The original edition of *GS* (1921) printed only the words of Watts's poem, with an indication to use either ARLINGTON or McANALLY. The 1925 edition printed the words with the tune ST. PETER and noted that it might be sung with ARLINGTON or ST. PETER.

Great Songs, No. 2 (1937) included Watts's poem in both the "Gospel Songs" and the "Hymns" sections, in the former set to McANALLY, with note to use ARLINGTON as an alternate, and in the latter set to PISGAH. *GSR* sets the poem to ARLINGTON, the tune to which the words are usually sung. See also the notes under "Again the Lord of Light and Life."

Amazing Grace   121,122
John Newton, 1725-1807

This text was first published in Newton and William Cowper's *Olney Hymns* (1779). It is based on 1 Chron. 17:16, 17. The poem was originally in six stanzas, but Newton's original stanza six is no longer used. It read:

> The earth shall soon dissolve like snow,
> > The sun forbear to shine;
> But God, who call'd me here below,
> > Will be forever mine.

In place of this stanza, the present stanza six is taken from an anonymous American hymn "Jerusalem, My Happy Home," which appeared in Richard and Andrew Broaddus's *A Collection of Sacred Ballads* (1790). The stanza may be much earlier than this collection. E. O. Excell seems to have been the first editor to join the stanza to Newton's hymn in his *Coronation Hymns* (Chicago, 1910). This text has been in *GS* since 1921. The 1921 edition contained only stanzas 1, 2, 4, and 5. The 1937 hymnal printed the entire six stanzas as they stand in *GSR*.

Amazing Grace

From *Virginia Harmony,* 1831

The first known appearance of this anonymous American hymn tune was in James P. Carrell and David L. Clayton's *Virginia Harmony* (Lebanon, Virginia, 1831). It has been called NEW BRITAIN, HARMONY GROVE, SYMPHONY, SOLON, and REDEMPTION, as well as AMAZING GRACE. *GSR* has two harmonizations of this tune. No.121 is by the music editor, Jack Boyd, and was arranged specially for this edition of *GS*. No. 122 is the traditional arrangement of the tune and is attributed to E. O. Excell in his collection *Make His Praise Glorious* (Chicago, 1900). The harmonization found in *The Southern Harmony* (1854 ed., p. 8) is given below.

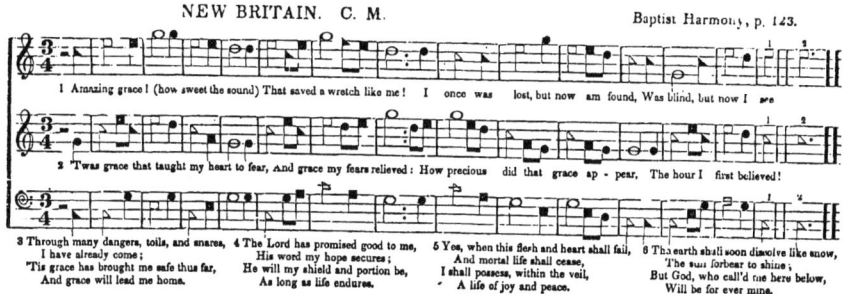

Ancient of Days   56
William C. Doane, 1832-1915

This text was written in 1886 to celebrate the bicentennial of the city of Albany, New York, the first chartered city in the United States. Doane was Protestant Episcopal bishop of Albany. The hymn was first sung in the Episcopal cathedral in Albany that year and, with alterations, was included in the Episcopal *Church Hymnal* (1892). The poem entered *GS* in 1921.

Ancient of Days

J. Albert Jeffrey, 1855-1929

This tune was written at Doane's request to accompany the foregoing poem. Jeffrey was organist at All Saints Cathedral in Albany. It was originally printed in the 1894 music edition of the *Church Hymnal* (1892) and given the tune name ANCIENT OF DAYS. In the music edition of *Hymnal with Tunes Old and New* by J. Ireland Tucker and W. W. Rousseau, the tune is called ALBANY. *The Hymnal* (1940) continued to use this name. This tune entered *GS* in the editions of 1921 and 1922, attributed, apparently by misprint, to T. A. Jeffrey. The poem and tune were omitted in 1925, restored in 1937, and have continued to the present.

Angels from the Realms of Glory   194
James Montgomery, 1771-1854

Montgomery wrote this text for the Christmas Eve edition of the newspaper he edited, *The Sheffield Iris* (1816). It was printed originally in five 6-line stanzas. He republished the poem with alterations in his *Christian Psalmist* (1825). *GSR* prints the first four stanzas as revised by Montgomery. The omitted fifth stanza reads:

Sinners, wrung with true repentance,

Doomed for guilt to endless pains,
Justice now revokes the sentence,
 Mercy calls you, break your chains:
Come and worship,
 Worship Christ, the newborn King.

Regent Square

Henry Smart, 1813-1879

This tune was originally composed as the setting for Horatius Bonar's "Glory Be the God and Father" and was first published in James Hamilton's *Psalms and Hymns for Divine Worship* (London, 1867) The tune name REGENT SQUARE is in honor of the Regent Square Presbyterian Church in London, of which Hamilton was minister.

Angels Holy, High and Lowly   95

John Stuart Blackie, 1809-1895

In 1850 Blackie had been appointed professor of Greek at Edinburgh University. In 1857 he published his *Lays and Legends of Ancient Greece, with Other Poems*, which included this text. It had been first published twelve years earlier in Horatius Bonar's *Bible Hymn Book* (1845). The original version in twelve 6-line stanzas was based on the *Benedicite, Omnia Opera*, or "The Song of the Three Holy Children" from the apocryphal additions to Daniel 3. The 1857 edition of the poem was in seven 4-line stanzas. Blackie said that he composed the text to be set to "the very beautiful Burschen melody, *Alles Schweige,* which will be found in the collection of *Burschen Melodies* that Blackie had published in *Tait's Magazine* in 1840. The *GSR* text includes stanzas 1, 4, 5, and 6 of the seven-stanza version. This is the first inclusion of this hymn in *GS*.

Llanherne

George T. Thalben-Ball, b. 1896

This tune was written while the composer was organist at the Temple Church, London, in 1926. No other information is currently available.

Angels We Have Heard on High   201

Traditional French Carol
Trans. James Chadwick, 1813-1882

The original French text is believed to date from the eighteenth century. It was first published in *Nouveau recueil de cantiques* (1855). The French poem begins "Les anges dans nos campagnes." The English translation is attributed to Bishop James Chadwick, Roman Catholic Bishop of Newcastle (1866), who was previously professor and then president of Upshaw College, Durham, England. The translation was first published in *The Holy Family Hymns* (1860) and then in its present altered form in Henri Frederick Hemy's *Crown of Jesus Music,* Part. II (London, 1862). This is its first inclusion in *GS*.

Gloria

Traditional French Carol
In *Nouveau recueil de cantiques,* 1855

Nothing is known of the origin of this traditional melody. The present harmonization is by Edward Shippen Barnes and was first published in *The New Church Hymnal* (New York, 1937). The tune first appeared as a setting for an English text (Grantham's translation of the French carol "When the Crimson Sun Was Set") in R. R. Chope's *Carols for Use in Church* (1875). This tune, with a different harmony, has been in *GS* since 1937.

Another Week   370

Gilbert Young Tickle, 1819-1888

This British disciple was a widely-known church leader and poet among the British Churches of Christ. He met Alexander Campbell at the dock in Liverpool when Campbell visited England in 1847. It is not known when this text was composed, but it was probably first published in David King's *Hymns for Churches of Christ* (1868). The text has been in *GS* since the first *Supplement* (1922).

Toulon

Genevan Psalter, 1551
Harm. Claude Goudimel, 1510-1572

The original of this tune, either composed or adapted by Louis Bourgeois for the *Genevan Psalter* (1551), is called OLD 124TH. The original name derives from its being set to Psalm 124 in the psalter. Claude Goudimel harmonized the melody for the *Genevan Psalter* (1565). The present arrangement of the tune is merely a shortening of the original melody by omission of the original third line of music. It is called TOULON from the French city of that name. The present shortened version of the tune appeared as early as 1848 in Lowell Mason and George Webb's *The National Psalmist*. This melody first entered *GS* in the *Supplement* (1922).

Anywhere with Jesus   530
Jessie Brown Pounds, 1861-1921
Helen C. Alexander Dixon, 1877-1969

The original text by Jessie H. Brown (later Mrs. John Pounds) was published in the Fleming H. Revell Company's *Hymns Old and New, No. 1* (1887). It was first published in hymnals from the Stone-Campbell Movement in Gilbert J. Ellis and J. H. Fillmore's *The New Praise Hymnal* (Cincinnati, 1906). Sometime between 1910 and 1920, Helen Cadbury Alexander (later Mrs. Amsji C. Dixon) added two more stanzas, giving the hymn a more missionary flavor. She was the wife of the famous singer-evangelist, Charles M. Alexander. *GSR* stanza three is one of her stanzas. The three-stanza poem by Pound entered *GS* in 1921, and the stanza by Mrs. Alexander in 1925.

Security

Daniel B. Towner, 1850-1919

This tune was written for the Pounds's text above and was published with it in Towner's *Hymns Old and New, No. 1* (Fleming H. Revell, 1887) It has been in *GS* since 1921.

Are Ye Able, Said the Master   602
Earl Marlatt, 1892-1976

This text was written for a consecration service at the Boston University School of Religious Education in 1925. It was inspired by Christ's words in Matthew 20:22, which Marlatt had used in a sermon the previous Sunday. The poem was first printed as a leaflet under the title "Challenge." Although originally printed in six stanzas, stanzas 2 and 3 are usually omitted, and the *GSR* text contains stanzas 1, 4, 5, and 6. The hymn was first published in a collection in H. Augustine Smith's *American Student Hymnal* (1928). This is its first inclusion in *GS*.

Beacon Hill

Harry S. Mason, 1881-1964

This tune was composed in April 1924 by Mason to accompany a text by Harry Wright for a song contest at a school. Marlatt overheard the students collaborating in this work and greatly admired the tune. He was disappointed when it took no prize in the contest. Being asked to write a hymn for the consecration of the officers of the Student Association in the spring of 1925, he remembered Mason's tune and discovered that the words of Jesus—"Are ye able"—exactly fit. Marlatt said that the music "miraculously seemed to suggest the words until the whole hymn was finished in a single evening." Beacon Hill, a famous section of Boston, was the former location of the Boston University School of Theology, hence the tune name.

Arise, My Soul, Arise   342
                                           Charles Wesley, 1707-1788

This text was first published in Wesley's *Hymns and Sacred Poems* (1742), under the title "Behold the Man." Originally in five stanzas of six lines each, *GSR* omits stanzas 3 and 4 and alters the text to some degree. 1:4 originally read, "In my behalf appears"; and 5:1 read, "My God is reconciled." This latter was altered to make it scriptural, since we are reconciled to God, not God to us. The omitted stanzas read:

3
Five bleeding wounds he bears,
    Received on Calvary;
They pour effectual prayers,
    They strongly plead for me:
"Forgive him, O forgive," they cry,
    "Nor let that ransomed sinner die!"

4
The Father hears him pray,
    His dear anointed One;
He cannot turn away
    The presence of his Son:
His Spirit answers to the blood,
    And tells me I am born of God.

Towner

                                           Traditional American Melody
                                           Arr. Daniel B. Towner, 1850-1919

The origin of this melody is unknown. Towner's arrangement was prepared for the words above and published in his *The Ideal Song and Hymn Book* (Revell, 1909). It has been in *GS* since 1921.

Art Thou Weary?   332
Attributed to Stephen the Sabaite, d. 794
Trans. John Mason Neale, 1818-1866

Neale published this poem in his *Hymns of the Eastern Church* (1862), and he first claimed it was a translation or paraphrase of Stephen's text, Κόπον τε καì κάματον, which he said he had found in an undated book from Constantinople. In later editions of his work, he disclaimed such a source and said that the English poem contained so little of the original Greek that it should not be considered a translation. It is, perhaps, but not certainly, an original hymn by Neale, which was suggested by ideas he had absorbed in his wide reading in the Greek hymnists. Neale's text originally appeared in seven stanzas. *GSR* contains stanzas 1, 6, 5, and 7. Stanza 7 is much altered. The omitted stanzas and the original stanza 7 read:

2

Hath He marks to lead me to Him,
    If He be my Guide?
"In His feet and hands are wound-prints,
    And His side."

3

Is there diadem, as Monarch,
    That His brow adorns?
"Yea, a crown, in very surety,
    But of thorns."

4

If I find Him, if I follow,
    What His guerdon here?
"Many a sorrow, many a labour,
    Many a tear."

7

Finding, following, keeping, struggling,
    Is He sure to bless?
"Angels, Martyrs, Prophets, Virgins,
    Answer, Yes!"

Stanza 7 was revised to its present form by E. H. Bickersteth in *The Hymnal Companion to the Book of Common Prayer* (1870). The hymn has been in *GS* since 1921.

Stephanos

Henry W. Baker, 1824-1877

This tune was written by Baker for the *Appendix* to the first edition of *Hymns Ancient and Modern* (1868). It was harmonized by W. H. Monk and has been in *GS* since 1921.

Ask Ye What Great Thing I Know   304

John C. Schwedler, 1672-1730
Trans. Benjamin H. Kennedy, 1804-1889

The original of this text, beginning "Wollt ihr wissen, was mein Preis?," is based on 1 Cor. 2:2 and Gal. 6:14, and was first published in the *Hirschberger Gesangbuch* (1741) The original hymn was in six stanzas with the refrain "Jesus, der Gekreuzigte." Kennedy published his translation in *Hymnologia Christiana* (1863). The *GSR* text contains stanzas 1, 4, 5, and 6. This is its first inclusion in *GS*.

Hendon

H. A. Cesar Malan, 1787-1864
Arr. Lowell Mason, 1792-1872

HENDON seems to have been first published in 1827. Malan compiled several collections of hymns and tunes beginning in 1823. Lowell Mason brought the tune to the United States and published it in his *Carmina Sacra* (1841) The name "Hendon" (probably from Old English *hean-dun*, i.e., "high hill") is derived from a village in Middlesex, England, located a few miles northeast of London.

Asleep in Jesus   671
Margaret Mackay, 1892-1887

This hymn poem was printed in *The Amethyst* (1832), an annual published in Edinburgh, Scotland. Its theme was suggested by the author's visit to a rural cemetery at Pennycross Chapel, Devonshire, England. There she found a tombstone with the inscription "Sleeping in Jesus." Of her poem she said:

> This simple inscription is carved on a tombstone in the retired rural burying-ground of Pennycross Chapel, in Devonshire. Distant only a few miles from a bustling and crowded seaport town, reached through a succession of those lovely green lanes for which Devonshire is so remarkable, the quiet aspect of Pennycross comes soothingly over the mind. "Sleep in Jesus" seems in keeping with all around.

The poem was originally in six stanzas. Our text contains stanzas 1-4. The two omitted stanzas read:

> Asleep in Jesus! time nor space
>> Debars this precious "hiding Place";
> On Indian plains or Lapland snows
>> Believers find the same repose.

> Asleep in Jesus! far from thee
>> Thy kindred and their graves may be;
> But thine is still a blessed sleep,
>> From which none ever wakes to weep.

Rest

William B. Bradbury, 1816-1868

This tune was published in 1843 and was written specifically for Mrs. Mackay's words. These words and tune, according to Robert Guy McCutchen, have "perhaps been the best-known and loved 'rest' hymn in the English language." It has been in *GS* since 1921.

At Even, When the Sun Was Set   36

Henry Twells, 1823-1900

This poem was written at the request of Sir Henry Baker for the 1868 edition of *Hymns Ancient and Modern*. Twells, who was at the time headmaster of Godolphin School, Hammersmith, England, wrote the poem one afternoon while his students were writing an exercise. The text originally contained eight stanzas, but we have omitted stanzas 4 and 5. They read:

> 4
> And some are pressed with worldly care,
>> And some are tried with sinful doubt;
> And some such grievous passions tear,
>> That only Thou canst cast them out.

> 5
> And some have found the world is vain,
>> Yet from the world they break not free;
> And some have friends who give them pain,
>> Yet have not sought a Friend in Thee.

Abends

Herbert S. Oakeley, 1830-1903

ABENDS, the German word for evening, was written because Oakeley disliked the tune HURSLEY as a setting for Keble's text "Sun of My Soul." He published it with Keble's poem in the *Irish Church Hymnal* (Belfast, 1874). Later he altered the harmony and republished the tune in *The Church Hymnary* (Edinburgh, 1898). Twells's original reading in the poem above at 1:1, "At even *ere* the sun was set," was altered with his approval about 1882.

Awake, and Sing the Song 153

William Hammond, 1719-1783

This text was first published in Hammond's *Psalms, Hymns, and Spiritual Songs* (London, 1745) under the heading "Before Singing of Hymns, by Way of Introduction." The *GSR* text is a cento from two selections made from the original: the first by George Whitefield in his *Collection of Hymns for Social Worship* (1753)—our stanzas 1 and 2; and the second from Martin Madan's *Collection of Psalms & Hymns* (1760)—our stanzas 3 and 4. The original poem contained fourteen stanzas. This hymn entered *GS* in 1937.

St.. Thomas

Aaron Williams, 1731-1776

ST. THOMAS is a portion of a sixteen-line quadruple short meter tune called HOLBORN, which was first published in Williams's *The Universal Psalmist* (1763). This lengthy tune was a setting for four stanzas of Charles Wesley's "Soldiers of Christ Arise." ST. THOMAS is taken from the setting for the second stanza of Wesley's poem. This shortened version, named for the apostle Thomas, appeared in *The Universal Psalmist*, 5th ed. (1770), and in Isaac Smith's *A Collection of Psalm Tunes* (1770). This tune entered *GS* in 1925.

Awake, My Soul, Stretch Every Nerve 543

Philip Doddridge, 1702-1751

This hymn by Job Orton was published posthumously in Doddridge's *Hymns Founded on Various Texts in the Holy Scriptures* (1755). It was entitled "Pressing on in the Christian Race," with the text Phil. 3:12-14. The hymn originally contained five stanzas. *GSR* omits stanza four:

That prize, with peerle'ss glories bright,
Which shall new luster boast,
When victors' wreaths and monarchs' gems
Shall blend in common dust.

This hymn entered *GS* in 1921.

Christmas

George F. Handel, 1685-1759
Adpt. David Weyman's *Melodia Sacra*, 1815

The source of this tune is the soprano aria "Non vi piacque ingiusti Dei" from Handel's opera *Siroe*, Act II (1728). Weyman adapted it as a setting for Psalm 132 in the hymnal mentioned above. The editors of the *Companion to the (Methodist) Hymnal* (1966) say it was previously adapted in James Hewitt's *Harmonia Sacra* (1812). The tune name derives from the tune's close association with Nahum Tate's "While Shepherds Watched Their Flocks by Night." It is also called LUNENBURG and SANDFORD, and, in *The (Episcopal) Hymnal* (1982), SIROE.

Awake, My tongue, Thy Tribute Bring   67

John Needham, 1710-1787

This text was written while Needham was minister of a Baptist church in Callowhill Street, Bristol, England. It was published in his *Hymns Devotional and Moral on Various Subjects, collected chiefly from the Holy Scriptures* (1768). He is known to have written 263 hymns, but this is the only one to survive in use today. The text entered *GS* in 1921.

Duke Street

John Hatton, d. 1793

This tune was published anonymously in Henry Boyd's *Select Collection of Psalm and Hymn Tunes* (Glasgow, 1793). William Hatton gave John Hatton as the composer in his *Euphonia* (Liverpool, 1805). The tune name derives from the street in St. Helen's, England, where John Hatton lived. This tune and text have been included in hymnals of the Stone-Campbell Movement from the earliest days and have been included in *GS* since 1921.

Away in a Manger 204
Anonymous

Although this hymn has long been attributed to Martin Luther, the evidence is conclusive that he had nothing to do with either the text or tune. For a summation of research on this hymn, see Richard S. Hill, "Not So Far Away in a Manger," *Music Library Association Notes* (December, 1945). Stanzas 1 and 2 were published in the *Little Children's Book for Schools and Families* (Philadelphia, 1885), a publication for the Evangelical Lutheran Church in North America. The third stanza, also anonymous, but sometimes attributed to John Thomas McFarland, was first published in Charles H. Gabriel's *Vinyard Songs* (1892). The text entered *GS* in 1937.

Away in a Manger
James R. Murray, 1841-1905

Murray published this tune in his *Dainty Songs for Little Lads and Lasses* (Cincinnati, 1887). There he said: "Luther's Cradle Hymn. Composed by Martin Luther for his children, and still sung by German mothers to their little ones." Apparently, however, Murray himself is the composer of the tune. It appeared again in John Murray's *Royal Praise for the Sunday School* (John Church Company, Cincinnati, 1888), with the heading "Music by J. R. M." The tune entered *GS* in 1937.

Be Not Dismayed 127
Civilla D. Martin, 1869-1948

This text was first published in John A. Davis's *Songs of Redemption and Praise* (1905). Mrs. Martin said of the composition of the text and tune in 1904:

> I was confined to sick bed in a Bible School in Lestershire, New York. My husband was spending several weeks at the school, making a songbook for the president of the school. "God Will Take Care of You" was written one Sunday afternoon while my husband went to a preaching appointment. When he returned I gave the words to him. He immediately sat down to his little Bilhorn organ and wrote the music. That evening he and two of the teachers sang the completed song. It was then printed in the songbook he was compiling for the school.

This poem entered *GS* in 1921.

God Will Take Care of You

W. Stillman Martin, 1862-1935

For the circumstances of the composition of this tune, see the notes on the text above. It was first published in John A. Davis's *Songs of Redemption and Praise* (1905). It entered *GS* in 1921.

Be Still, My Soul   547

Katharina von Schlegel, b. 1697

Trans. Jane Borthwick, 1813-1897

Little is known of this author and nothing of the circumstances of the writing. The hymn was first published in *Neue Sammlung geistlicher Lieder* (1752). The original German text begins "Stille, mein Wille, dein Jesus hilft siegen" and was in six stanzas. Miss Borthwick omitted stanza three from her translation in *Hymns from the Land of Luther* (1855). The *GSR* text contains Miss Borthwick's stanzas 1, 2, and 4. It entered *GS* in the *Supplement* (1975).

Finlandia

Jean Sibelius, 1865-1957

This tune is an arrangement from Sibelius's symphonic poem *Finlandia* (1899). It was arranged in 1932 by the editors of *The Hymnal* (1933) of the Presbyterian Church, USA. It entered *GS* in the *Supplement* (1975).

Be Thou My Vision   578

Irish poem, 8th century

Trans. Mary E. Byrne, 1880-1931

Versed Eleanor H. Hull, 1860-1935

This anonymous Irish poem dates from the eighth century. Miss Byrne translated it into English prose, and it was first published in *Erin* (Vol. II, 1905). The original sixteen couplets in prose were reduced to twelve rhymed ones in Miss Hull's translation. The poem was first published in Hull's *Poem Book of the Gael* (1912). The text entered *GS* in the *Supplement* (1975).

Slane

Traditional Irish Melody
Arr. Jack A. Boyd, b. 1932

This old melody may be found in Patrick W. Joyce, *Old Irish Folk Music and Songs* (1909), set to the secular song "With My Love on the Road." It was included with a harmony by David Evans in the revision of the *Church Hymnary* (1927), and has become popular since. The tune name SLANE comes from a hill in County Meath near Tara where Patrick is reputed to have lighted the Easter fire in defiance of the Druid priests. The present harmony was made in 1974 for publication in *Great Songs No. 2, with Supplement* (1975).

Be with Me, Lord

579
Thomas O. Chisholm, 1866-1960

This text was written in 1934 and first published in *Christian Hymns* (Nashville, 1935). Leon Sanderson, the son of the writer and a minister in the Church of Christ, wrote in *20th Century Christian* (April, 1986) about the origin of this text and tune:

> He wrote music for a dozen of Thomas O. Chisholm's songs...Chisholm lived in Vineland, New Jersey, about 1000 miles from Springfield, Missouri, where Sanderson served as minister for the South National church. Travel was not easy in 1934, so the two men never met, yet they collaborated in song writing by correspondence. Late one evening Sanderson was working on a hymnal. The tune for "Be With Me, Lord" kept coming to his mind. He stopped and wrote it down to be able to continue his work. Shortly the harmony seemed to clear and he completed it the same night. He searched for words to fit but found none, as the music had an unusual meter of 11/10/11/10. Eight days later he received a letter from Chisholm telling of an incident on this same night. He had gone to bed, yet some words were on his mind. He got up and wrote them down and was sending them to see what Sanderson thought. They were an exact match! Whether coincidental or providential, this particular composition has been sung more widely than any other of Sanderson's songs and has been translated for use in Italian, German, African, and other languages.

Sanderson

Lloyd O. Sanderson, b. 1901

This tune was written in 1934, as given above, and first published in the Gospel Advocate's *Christian Hymns*, edited by Sanderson, C. M. Pullias, and associate editors N. B. Hardeman, E. H. Ijam, and James F. Cox (1935). The tune name was given by the present general editor of *GSR*.

Before Jehovah's Awful Throne　　　　　　　　　110
Isaac Watts, 1674-1748

The predecessors of this text appeared first in Watts's *Horae Lyricae* (1706) and in his *Hymns and Spiritual Songs* (1707). The original poem began "Sing to the Lord with Joyful Voice" and was in five stanzas, under the title "Praise to the Lord from All Nations." Here is the original version:

Sing to the Lord with joyful voice;
　Let every land his name adore;
The British isles shall send the noise
Across the ocean to the shore.

With gladness bow before his throne,
　And let his presence raise your joys;
Know that the Lord is God alone,
　And formed our souls, and framed our voice.

Infinite power without our aid
Figured our clay to human mould;
And when our wandering feet had strayed,
　He brought us to his sacred fold.

Enter his gates with thankful songs,
　Through his wide courts your voices raise;
Almighty God, our joyful tongues
　Shall fill thine house with sounding praise.

Wide as the world, is thy command;
　Vast as eternity thy love;
Firm as a rock thy truth must stand,
　When rolling years shall cease to move.

Watts republished the hymn in 1719 in *The Psalms of David Imitated in the Language of the New Testament*, making certain revisions and adding what is now the *GSR* stanza 3. The present form of the hymn is the work of John Wesley in his *Collection of Psalms and Hymns* (Charleston, 1737). Tillit and Nutter, in their *Hymns and Hymn Writers of the Church* (Nashville,

1911), make the following excellent comment:

> If anyone desires to prove by example as well as by argument the wisdom of allowing judicious editors to alter and improve the original words of the authors when this is called for, hereby rendering a real service to the authors themselves, let him make use of this hymn, which would never have found a place, and least of all, a place of high esteem, in the great hymnals of the Church but for the fact that the original was abridged and otherwise altered by John Wesley.

This hymn entered *GS* in 1921.

Winchester, New

Musikalisches Handbuch, 1690

This tune was first published in the above-mentioned collection in Hamburg in 1690. It was subsequently altered by Freylinghausen in his *Geistreiches Gesangbuch* (Halle, 1704) and by Thomas More in *Psalm-Singer's Delightful Pocket-Companion* (Glasgow, 1762). The present arrangement was made by William H. Havergal in *Old Church Psalmody* (London, 1847) The tune name derives from an ancient city in Hampshire, England. In all previous editions of *GS,* the tune, either indicated or printed, has been OLD HUNDREDTH. This is the first appearance of WINCHESTER, NEW in *GS*.

Behold a Stranger at the Door 340

Joseph Grigg, 1720-1768

This text is based on Rev. 3:20, "Behold, I stand at the door and knock." The original poem was in eleven stanzas. The *GSR* text is comprised of stanzas 1, 3, 2, and 10. A few of the other stanzas read:

4
Rise, touched with gratitude divine;
    Turn out his enemy and thine,
That soul-destroying monster, sin,
    And let the heavenly Stranger in.

5
Yet know, nor of the terms complain,
When Jesus comes, he comes to reign;
To reign, and with no partial sway;
Thoughts must be slain that disobey.

11
Sovereign of souls! thou Prince of Peace!
O may thy gentle Reign increase!
Throw wide the Door, each willing Mind,
And be his Empire all mankind.

This text entered *GS* in the first *Supplement* (1922).

Holley

George Hews, 1806-1872

This tune was written by Hews in 1835. It was named from a village in Orleans County, New York, which took its name from Byron Holley, one of the first canal commissioners of the State of New York. It entered *GS* in the first *Supplement* (1922).

Beneath the Cross of Jesus   229

Elizabeth C. Clephane, 1839-1869

This daughter of a Scottish sheriff, although she died quite young, devoted her life to the service of Jesus who died on the cross. We have no information as to the circumstances that called forth this beautiful poem. It was published posthumously in the *Family Treasury* (1872), a religious magazine, under the general heading of "Breathings on the Border." This text entered *GS* in 1921.

St. Christopher

Fredrick C. Maker, 1844-1927

This tune was composed for Miss Clephane's poem and was first published in the *Supplement* to the *Bristol Tune Book* (Bristol, England, 1881), edited by Alfred Stone. The tune name ST. CHRISTOPHER seems not to bear any special relation to the poem. "Christopher" was the so-called patron saint of travelers. This tune entered *GS* with the preceding text in 1921.

Beneath the Forms of Outward Rite   338

James A. Blaisdell, 1867-1957

The date and circumstances of writing of this text by this Congregational minister are unknown. The text was probably first included in H. Augustine Smith's *American Student Hymnal* (1928). This is its first inclusion in *GS*.

Belmont

From William Gardiner's *Sacred Melodies*, 1812

There is some doubt as to the origin of this tune. It was the setting for the text "Come hither all ye weary souls" in the Gardiner collection. *The Historical Companion to Hymns Ancient and Modern* gives two other possibilities, but Gardiner seems to be the earliest source. This tune has been in *GS* since 1925.

Beyond the Sunset   662

Virgil P. Brock, 1887-1978

This text and the tune following were written one evening in 1936 while the Brocks were guests at Rainbow Point, Winona Lake, Indiana—the home of Homer Rodeheaver. At this date Brock was serving as district evangelist for the Christian Churches in Marion County, Indiana. On that day in 1936, there was a beautiful sunset over the lake, and the Brocks were overcome by its beauty. The question arose in their minds: "What lies beyond the sunset?" In response to this question, they wrote the hymn. It first appeared in Brock, Ralph W. Pollock, Frank C. Huston, and Blanche Kerr Brock's *Songs for the New Day*, published by the Rodeheaver Company. This little collection bears copyright 1935 on the front cover, but the hymn itself gives copyright of 1936. It is Brock's best known hymn. The text entered *GS* in 1950.

Brock

Blanche Kerr Brock, 1888-1958

This tune was written for the preceding text (q.v.) and published in Brock's *Songs for the New Day* (1935). Originally published as a duet, the song appeared in *GS* with E. L. Jorgenson's four part arrangement, in 1950, inside the back cover. It became part of the main collection in the *Supplement* (1975) and in the present edition (1986).

Blessed Assurance   345

Fanny J. Crosby, 1820-1915

Many of Fanny Crosby's texts seem to have come to her almost spontaneously upon hearing a melody. This text was written in 1873, when her friend Phoebe Palmer Knapp played for her a melody she had composed and asked her what it said. Crosby replied with the first stanza of this hymn. It was first published in John R. Sweney's *Gems of Praise* (Philadelphia, 1873). The text was also included in Sankey's *Sacred Songs and Solos* and in his *Gospel Hymns* series and so became popular around the world. The text entered *GS* in 1921.

Assurance

Phoebe P. Knapp, 1839-1908

This tune was composed in 1873 and joined with Crosby's text as detailed above. It was published in Sweney's *Gems of Praise* (1873) and entered *GS* in 1921.

Blessed Jesus, at Thy Word   25

Tobias Clausnitzer, 1619-1684
Trans. Catherine Winkworth, 1827-1878

Clausnitzer's text "Liebster Jesu, wir sind hier" was a poem written to be sung on Sundays before the sermon for the day. It was first published in three 6-line stanzas in the *Altdorffisches Gesang-Büchlein* (1663). Originally published anonymously, it was first attributed to Clausnitzer in 1671. Miss Winkworth's translation appeared first in her *Lyra Germanica*, 2nd Series (1858), and in her *Chorale Book for England* (1863). This is the first inclusion of the hymn in *GS*.

Liebster Jesu

Johann Ahle, 1625-1673

LIEBSTER JESU was written for Franz Joachim Bormeister's advent hymn "Ja er ist's, das Heil der Welt," in 1664, and published in *Neue geistliche auf die Sontage* (Mulhausen, Germany, 1664). The tune has been joined with Clausnitzer's poem since its publication in *Altdorffisches Gesang-Büchlein* (1671). This is its first inclusion in *GS*.

Blessed Savior, We Adore Thee   154

B. B. McKinney, 1886-1952

McKinney was a leader in church music among the Baptists. In 1941 he became head of the Church Music Department of the Sunday School Board. This text was written in 1942 and published that year in *Teacher,* a Sunday School magazine. It was first included in the hymnal *Look and Live Songs* (1945). This is its first inclusion in *GS*.

Glorious Name

B. B. McKinney, 1886-1952

The tune was written for the foregoing text and was published as the preceding paragraph indicates. The tune name was first given by the hymnal committee of the *Baptist Hymnal* (1956).

Blessing and Honor and Glory and Power 174

Horatius Bonar, 1808-1889

This text is part of an ascension hymn beginning "Into the heav'n of heav'ns hath He gone," published in Bonar's *Hymns of Faith and Hope*, third series (1866). It was originally in eight 4-line stanzas. Bonar had just become minister of a large church in Edinburgh, Scotland, the year he wrote this hymn. The original hymn is no longer published, but the cento, which is included in this edition of *GS* for the first time, has been popular. It first appeared in the hymnal *Laudes Domini* (New York, 1884), and consists of stanzas 8, 4, 5, and 7.

O Quanta Qualia

Paris Antiphoner, 1681
Adpt. in *La Feillée's Methode de Plain Chant*, 1808

Nothing is known of the composer or the circumstances of composition of this tune. Austin Lovelace says that La Feillée's work is an important landmark of the changes from modal to tonal harmony and from free to isometric rhythm. See *Companion to the Methodist Hymnal* (1970, p. 592).

Blest Be the Tie 394

John Fawcett, 1740-181

The story of the origin of this text, which is probably true, is that the hymn was written in 1772, when Fawcett, preparing to leave his congregation at Wainsgate, England, could not do it. He had preached his farewell sermon and loaded his wagons for the journey to another church, but the love and tears of his old congregation were too much. He gave up the possibilities of an attractive pulpit in London to remain with them. The hymn was first published in Fawcett's *Hymns Adapted to the Circumstances of Public Worship and Private Devotion* (Leeds, 1782). It was there entitled "Brotherly Love."

The text appeared originally in *GS* (1921) in five stanzas. In the 1925 edition, a sixth stanza was added, giving the complete text of Fawcett's hymn. It has been so printed ever since.

Dennis

Johann Georg Nägeli, 1773-1836
Arr. Lowell Mason, 1792-1872

According to Leonard Ellinwood, the original melody for this arrangement may be Nageli's "O Selig, selig, wer vor dir," which first appeared in *Christliches Gesangbuch* (1828). Mason's arrangement was published in his and George J. Webb's *The Psaltery* (1845) as the setting for the text "How Gentle God's Commands." It has been in *GS* since 1921.

Bread of the World   373

Reginald Heber, 1783-1826

This beautiful communion hymn was first published in the posthumous collection of Heber's poetry, *Hymns Written and Adapted to the Weekly Service of the Church Year* (1827). It is known to have been written some time after 1807, while Heber was Anglican vicar of Hodnet in England. Nothing further is known. The text with the accompanying tune below has been in *GS* since 1921.

Eucharistic Hymn

John S. B. Hodges, 1830-1915

This tune was composed in 1868 and published in the *Book of Common Praise* (1869). Hodges was rector of Grace Episcopal Church, Newark, New Jersey, at the time. The tune name is derived from the Greek word εὐχαριστία meaning "gratitude, or thanksgiving." Jesus "gave thanks" for the loaf in the Passover feast when he ordained the Lord's Supper; hence, the term applied to the communion, the eucharist.

Break Forth, O Beauteous Heavenly Light   200

Johann Rist, 1607-1667
Trans. John Troutbeck, 1833-1889

This text, beginning "Ermuntre dich, mein schwacher Geist," was first published in twelve 8-line stanzas in Rist's *Himmlische Lieder* (1641). It was entitled "A hymn of praise on the joyful Birth and Incarnation of our Lord and Savior Jesus Christ." The text is based on Isaiah 9:2-7. Johann Sebastian Bach used stanza nine (the original of the present text) in his *Christmas Oratorio*. John Troutbeck made this English translation for the Novello Company edition of Bach's work sometime in the 1800s. This is its first appearance in *GS*.

Ermuntre dich

Johann Schop, c. 1590-1664
Harm. J. S. Bach, 1685-1750

This melody first appeared in *Himmlische Lieder* (1641). Schop was the musical editor of this work. Bach made the present arrangement for his *Christmas Oratorio*. This is the first appearance of the tune in *GSR*.

Break Thou the Bread of Life   312

Mary Artemisia Lathbury, 1841-1913

This text was written at the request of John H. Vincent, founder and manager of the Chautauqua Institution in New York, for the use of groups devoting themselves to Bible study. The *GSR* text in two stanzas was written in 1877. It is based on the gospel story of Jesus' feeding of the multitudes and has become a traditional vesper (evening) hymn. Some hymnals add one or two stanzas, but these are not by Miss Lathbury. These additions by Alexander Groves were published in the *Wesleyan Magazine* (London, 1913):

Thou art the Bread of life,
    O Lord to me;
Thy holy Word the truth
    That saveth me;
Give me to eat and live
    With Thee above;
Teach me to love Thy truth,
    For Thou art love.

O send Thy Spirit, Lord,
    Now unto me,
That He may touch mine eyes,
    And make me see;
Show me the truth concealed
    Within Thy word,
And in Thy Book revealed
    I see Thee, Lord.

Bread of Life

William F. Sherwin, 1826-1888

This tune was written for Miss Lathbury's text above and was first published in Charles S. Robinson and Robert S. MacArthur's *The Calvary Selection of Spiritual Songs* (New York, 1878). Both text and tune have been in *GS* since 1921.

Breathe on Me, Breath of God   295
Edwin Hatch, 1835-1889

Hatch wrote this text while serving as vice-principal of St. Mary's Hall, Oxford University. It was first published in a pamphlet entitled "Between Doubt and Prayer" (1878). Eight years later it entered Henry Allon's collection *The Congregational Psalmist* (1886). Allon altered Hatch's original line in 3:2, which had read "Blend all my soul with thine." Allon's revision is now the standard reading. This text was first included in *GS* in the *Supplement* (1975).

Trentham

Robert Jackson, 1842-1914

This tune was written as a setting for Henry W. Baker's "O perfect life of love" and was first published in *Fifty Sacred Leaflets* (1888). Trentham is a village in County Stafford, England. The tune was first included in *GS* in the *Supplement* (1975).

Brethren, We Have Met to Worship   419
Attributed to George Atkins

Many nineteenth century collections attribute this text to Atkins. Nothing is known of this author. The hymn entered *GS* in the *Supplement* (1975).

Holy Manna

William Moore

This tune was composed by Moore (sometimes spelled More) and was published first in his *Columbian Harmony* (1825). This compilation was registered for copyright purposes in the District of West Tennessee and printed in Cincinnati by Morgan, Lodge, and Fisher. It entered *GS* with the preceding text in the *Supplement* (1975).

Brief Life Is Here Our Portion   673
Bernard of Cluny, 12th Century
Trans. John M. Neale, 1818-1866

This text is a free translation of a portion of Bernard's great satire on the vices of the medieval church and the world. John Julian tells of Bernard's composing this "wondrous satire against the vices and follies of his age, which has supplied—and it is the only satire that ever did so—

some of the widely known and admired hymns to the Church today."
(*Dictionary*, 137) The poem, containing nearly 3,000 lines, was entitled
De Contemptu Mundi (On the Contemptibleness of the World) and was
written in a difficult dactylic hexameter containing both end and interior
rhyme. The familiar opening lines of the original show what Bernard
accomplished:

> Hora noviss*ima*, tempora pess*ima* sunt, vigil*emus*.
> Ecce minac*iter*, imminet arb*iter* ille sup*remus*;
> Imminet, imm*inet*, ut mala term*inet*, aequa cor*onet*;
> Recta remun*eret*, anxia lib*eret*, aethera d*onet*;
> Auferet asp*era* duraque pond*era* mentis on*ustae*;
> Sobria m*uniat*, improba p*uniat*, utraque i*uste*.

It was Bernard's view that God's divine power had assisted him to write
the poem. He said, "I am not haughty, but wholly humble, and therefore I
say boldly, that unless the Spirit of wisdom and understanding had been
with me and flowed over me, so difficult a meter and so long a work, I
could not have composed." "Brief Life Is Here Our Portion" is translated
from the stanza beginning

> Hic breve vivitur, hic breve plangitur, hic breve fletur;
> Non breve vivere, non breve plaudere, retribuetur.

The poem was dedicated to Peter the Venerable, Abbot of Cluny (1122-
1156) in Burgundy, in France. The date usually assigned to the poem is
about 1140. "Brief Life" was first included in *GS* in 1937, and it stands a
blessed affirmation of hope in a world that needs hope so desperately.

St. Alphege

Henry S. Gaunlett, 1805-1876

This tune, in its original form with a closing "Alleluia," was
published in W. J. Blew and Gauntlett's *Church Hymn and Tune Book*.
Gauntlett often assigned saints's names to his tunes. Nothing further is
known of the circumstances of its composition. It entered *GS* with the
words above in 1937.

Brightest and Best   211

Reginald Heber, 1783-1826

This text was originally published in the *Christian Observer*
(November, 1811) as one of a series of poems for the Sundays and holy
days of the Anglican church year. It was for the Epiphany (January 6th)
celebration. The hymn was originally in five stanzas, the fifth being a

repetition of the first. The *GSR* text omits Heber's third stanza, which reads:

> Say, shall we yield Him, in costly devotion,
>> Odors of Edom, and off'rings divine?
> Gems of the mountain, and pearls of the ocean,
>> Myrrh from the forest, and gold from the mine?

This hymn first entered *GS* in 1921 with Heber's complete text, but was omitted from the *Number Two* hymnal in 1937. It is now restored in *GSR*.

Morning Star

James P. Harding, 1850-1911

GS originally set the preceding text to a tune by Ira D. Sankey, written in 1891. *GSR* employs the more traditional tune MORNING STAR. This tune comes from an anthem composed by Harding in June 1892, which was to be sung in a mission in the slum district of London. It was first included in *The Church Hymnal* of the Protestant Episcopal Church (1894).

Brightly Beams Our Father's Mercy   420

Philip P. Bliss, 1838-1876

This text was inspired by a sermon illustration from Dwight L. Moody. Moody told of a ship on the Great Lakes trying to get to Cleveland in a raging storm. When the captain asked the pilot if he was sure they were headed to Cleveland, the pilot assured him that they were. Only the light from the great lighthouse could be seen. The captain asked: "Where are the lower lights?" "Gone out, sir," the pilot replied. "Can you make the harbor?" "We must or perish, sir," the pilot said. But in the darkness the channel was missed, and the ship with its many passengers perished in the rocks. Moody concluded: "Brethren, the Master will take care of the great lighthouse; let us keep the lower lights burning!" This text has been in *GS* since 1921.

Lower Lights

Philip P. Bliss, 1838-1876

The tune was written for the preceding text and was published in *The Charm, a Collection of Sunday School Music* (Cincinnati, 1871). It entered *GS* with the text in 1921.

Bring Christ Your Broken Life   326

Thomas O. Chisholm, 1866-1960

This text was first published in *Christian Hymns for Every Purpose in Worship* (Nashville: Gospel Advocate Company, 1935, No. 85) Leon Sanderson, the son of the composer of the tune, in a letter of March 21, 1988, comments on the origin of the text and tune:

> As to *Bring Christ Your Broken Life*, the music was written first and then my dad asked Mr. Chisholm to write the words for it. No subject was given in this particular case and he chose to write the text that now appears as *Bring Christ Your Broken Life*. The tune had just come to my dad's mind, so he put it down and also harmonized it.

Broken Life
Lloyd O. Sanderson, b. 1901

For the origin of this tune, see the text above. The tune was written in 1935 and was first published that year in *Christian Hymns*. The tune name, BROKEN LIFE, was assigned by the general editor of *GSR* (1986).

Built on a Rock
Nikolai F. S. Gruntvig, 1783-1872
Trans. Carl Doving, 1867-1937
Rev. Fred C. M. Hansen, 1888-1965

This powerful hymn, based on Jesus' words in Matthew 16:18, first entered *GS* in the *Supplement* (1975). The original Danish poem, beginning "Kirken den er et gammelt Hus," was in seven stanzas and was first published in *Sang-Vark til den Danske Kirke* (1837). Carl Doving translated the hymn into English in 1909, and it was published in the *Lutheran Hymnary* (1913). Doving's translation in six stanzas may also be seen in *Hymnal for Church and Home* (1927), published by the Danish Evangelical Lutheran Synods in America. The present text is a revision of Doving's translation by Fred C. M. Hansen, prepared for and published in the Lutheran *Service Book and Hymnal* (1958).

Kirken
Ludwig M. Lindeman, 1812-1877

This tune was written for the preceding text and published in Wilhelm Wexel's *Christelige Psalmer* (1840). It was Lindeman's first hymn tune. It entered *GS* in the *Supplement* (1975).

Buried with Christ 355

Thomas O. Chisholm, 1866-1960

This text was first published in L. O. Sanderson and C. M. Pullias's *Christian Hymns for Every Purpose in Worship* (Nashville: Gospel Advocate Company, 1935). The hymn is widely used among Churches of Christ as a baptismal song. In a letter from Leon Sanderson, son of the composer of the tune following, he gives the account of the origin of the text and tune:

> As to *Buried with Christ*, my dad asked Mr. Chisholm to write some words on Romans 6:3-5. He did write these words and sent them back. With that text then my dad wrote the music and harmonized the piece. An interesting side-note about this is that my dad was really concerned about how much truth Mr. Chisholm knew. They never actually met, just corresponded, but he felt that he understood a great deal about what God's word had to say, and this particular assignment was his way of checking into his understanding of baptism.

This text entered *GS* in the *Supplement* (1975).

Buried with Christ

Lloyd O. Sanderson, b. 1901

This tune was written for the preceding text and published with it in Sanderson and C. M. Pullias's *Christian Hymns* (Nashville, 1935). See notes on the text above for fuller information. The tune entered *GS* in the *Supplement* (1975).

By Christ Redeemed, In Christ Restored   374

George Rawson, 1807-1889

Of George Rawson's hymns, John Julian said: "His hymns are distinguished by refinement of thought, and delicacy and propriety of language; and if they do not attain the first rank among the songs of the Christian Church, many are of great excellence." (*Dictionary*, 952) He includes the present text in this evaluation. It was written in 1857 and first published in *Psalms and Hymns for the Baptist Denomination* (1858). It was first included in *GS* in the *Supplement* (1922).

Troyte's Chant, No. 1

Arthur H. D. Troyte, 1811-1857

Nothing is known of the circumstances which produced this melody. Most of Troyte's chants and hymn tunes were written for the *Salisbury Hymn Book* (1857). This tune is known to have been written in 1848, and it was published posthumously in his *Forty-eight Hymn Tunes* (1860). It first entered *GS* in the *Supplement* (1922).

Can You Count the Stars 126

Johann Hey, 1789-1854

Most of Johann Hey's poems were written for children, and this is an especially beautiful text. The German poem begins "Weisst du wie viel Sternlein stehen." It was originally published in his *Fabeln für Kinder*, 2d series (1837). Elmer Leon Jorgenson made this translation for the first edition of *GS* (1921).

Weisst du wie viel Sternlein stehen

German Folk Tune, 16th Century

In my copy of the *Liederbuch für Sontagsschulen* (St. Louis, 1882), this tune is simply denominated "Volksweise" (folk melody). Nothing further is known of its origin. It entered *GS* in 1921.

Cast Thy Burden on the Lord 637

From Rowland Hill's *A Collection of Psalms and Hymns*, 1783

The complete authorship of this poem is difficult to determine. The original authorship is unknown and is assigned by different authorities, by guess, to John Cennick or William Hammond. The first stanza, exchanging "shalt" for "wilt" is exactly as it stands in Hill's *Psalms and Hymns*. It is based on Psalm 55:22. The second stanza is similar to a rewritten version of the Hill poem by George Rawson in the *Leeds Hymn Book* (1853). Rawson's stanza reads:

> Fear not, then, in every storm
> There shall come the Master's form;
> Cheering voice and present aid—
> "It is I, be not afraid."

Nothing like this stanza appears in the poem in Hill's *Collection.* The third stanza is by another and unknown hand. This beautiful and comforting poem in its present form joins the tender mercy of God in the Psalms with that of Christ Jesus in the Gospels—"It is I. Be not afraid" (Matthew 14: 27). This text, included for the first time in *GSR* is a great source of encouragement in times of weakness.

Mercy

Louis M. Gottschalk, 1829-1869

This tune is taken from Gottschalk's piano composition "The Last Hope" (1854). It was first arranged as a hymn tune by Hubert P. Main (1865). The present harmony is by Edwin P. Parker, which was first published in Charles S. Robinson's *In Excelsis* (1896).

Cast Thy Burden Upon the Lord   638
Paraphrase

The text of this hymn is a paraphrase from a portion of a number of the Psalms: Psalm 55:22; 57:10; 110:5; and 25:3, as given in the Authorized Version. It is a part of the libretto for Mendelssohn's oratorio *Elijah*. This is the first inclusion of this text in *GS*.

Elijah

Felix Mendelssohn, 1809-1847

This chorus from Mendelssohn's oratorio *Elijah,* with the preceding libretto, enters *GS* for the first time. *The New Groves Dictionary of Music and Musicians* says: "After a stay in Leipzig he went on his journey to England on 18 August 1846 to rehearse the oratorio *Elijah,* which he had composed in a single creative outburst in the spring and summer of 1846 for the first performance at the Birmingham Music Festival (26 August 1846)." (Vol. 12, p. 142) Indeed, he had completed the oratorio one week before the performance on 11 August 1846. The next fall he revised the musical score for publication, and the work was published the following year in Bonn, Germany. In *The Mennonite Hymnal* (1969), the original text of the cento (the libretto) is attributed to Julius Schubring (b. 1806), with translation by William Bartholomew (1846).

Children of the Heavenly Father   644
Caroline V. Sandell-Berg, 1832-1903
Trans. Ernst William Olsen, 1870-1958

This text was written while the author was still in her teens and is a testimony to the spiritual upbringing she had received in her home. Her father was a minister. The poem was first published in her *Andeliga daggdroppar* (1855). Ernst William Olsen translated the text into English, and it entered *The Hymnal* (1925), published by the Lutheran Augustana Synod. This hymn text now enters *GSR* for the first time.

Tryggare Kan Ingan Vara
Swedish Folk Melody

This tune was first used with Sandell's poem in Frederik Engelke's *Lofsanger och andeliga wisor* (1873). The authorities differ as to the origin of the tune, but it is probably a Swedish folk melody. Mary Kay Stulken gives the different opinions as to its origin in the *Hymnal Companion to the Lutheran Book of Worship* (1981, pp. 474-5). The tune enters *GS* for the first time in our current edition (1986).

Children of the Heavenly King 468
John Cennick, 1718-1755

The short life of John Cennick was especially productive in Christian service. This hymn was published without a title in his *Sacred Hymns for the Children of God, in the Days of Their Pilgrimage* (1742). It originally contained twelve stanzas. Our text includes stanzas 1, 3, 6, 7, and 8. It was first included in 1937.

Pleyel's Hymn
Ignace J. Pleyel, 1757-1831

This tune is an adaptation from Pleyel's *Quartet* No. 4, Op. 7 (c. 1782). It first appeared as a hymn tune in long meter form in *Arnold and Calcott's Psalms* (London, 1791), as a setting for Joseph Addison's "The spacious firmament on high." Benjamin Carr brought the tune to its present form in his *Masses, Vespers, Litanies, and Hymns* (Baltimore, 1805). It has been in *GS* since 1937.

Christ for the World We Sing 400
Samuel Wolcott, 1813-1886

Wolcott wrote this text on Feb. 7, 1869, after attending a YMCA meeting in Cleveland, Ohio, at which he had seen the banner "Christ for the world, and the world for Christ." It was first published in W. H. Doane's *Songs of Devotion for Christian Associations* (1870). This is the first inclusion of this text in *GS*.

Italian Hymn

Felice de Giardini, 1716-1796

This tune was composed for the text of the hymn "Come, Thou Almighty King" and was first published in *A Collection of Psalm and Hymn Tunes Sung at the Chapel of the Lock Hospital* (London, 1769). Martin Madan was the editor of this collection. The tune name derives from the nationality of the composer. It is sometimes called MOSCOW, the city in Russia where the composer died. The tune has been in *GS* since 1921.

Christ in His Word Draws Near   525

Thomas T. Lynch, 1818-1871

This hymn was published in *The Rivulet* (1855), having been written the previous year, according to Lynch's own account: "I will quote the hymn with which I commenced my work of song. It was made on the Monday morning before Christmas day, whilst I was meditating on yesterday's worship." This is its first inclusion in *GS*. It is a hymn which expresses the sentiment of so many scriptures: "Draw nigh to God, and He will draw nigh to you."

Serug

Samuel S. Wesley, 1810-1876

Wesley was the son of Charles Wesley and a well-known musician and professor of organ at the Royal Academy of Music in London. He published some 131 hymn tunes, including SERUG, which is found in his *European Psalmist* (1872). This its first inclusion in *GS*.

Christ Is Made the Sure Foundation   364

From *Urbs beata Jerusalem*, c. 700
Trans. John Mason Neale, 1818-1866

This text originated probably about the end of the eighth century, but maybe even earlier. Richard Chenevix Trench called it a "rugged but fine old hymn." Found in the *Anglo-Saxon Hymnarium* (c. 1100), it has been part of English hymnody for many centuries. In the *Hymnarium* it was entitled "Hymnus in Anniversario Dedicationis Ecclesie" and has been widely used for such dedications. The translation by Neale first appeared in his *Medieval Hymns* (1851). Originally the Latin hymn was in nine stanzas, stanza one beginning "Urbs beata Jerusalem / dicta pacis visio." Our text includes stanzas 5, 7, 8, and 9. Stanza five begins "Angularis fundamentum / lapis Christus missus est." The *GSR* text has been slightly revised for scripturalness, and this is the first appearance of this hymn in *GS*.

Regent Square
Henry Smart, 1813-1879

For information on this tune, see "Angels, from the realms of glory" (*GSR*, No. 194).

Christ Is the World's True Light   402
George Wallace Briggs, 1875-1959

This text was first published in *Songs of Praise* (1931), ed. Percy Dearmer. It was there entitled "The Light of the World." No other information is available. This is its first appearance in *GS*.

St. Joan
Percy E. B Coller, b. 1895

This tune was written in 1941 and was first published in *The Hymnal of the Protestant Episcopal Church in the United States of America, 1940* (1943). ST. JOAN is named for the composer's wife. This is its first inclusion in *GS*.

Christ Jesus Lay in Death's Strong Bands   237
Martin Luther, 1483-1546
Tr. Richard Massie, 1800-1887

This text, beginning "Christ lag in Todesbanden," was first published in seven 7-line stanzas in the *Enchiridion* (Erfurt, 1524), and in *Geistliches Gesangbüchlein* (Wittenberg, 1524). The complete text may be seen in *Kirchen-Gesang-Buch für Evangelisch-Lutherische Gemeinden* (St. Louis, 1849). Massie's translation first appeared in his *Martin Luther's Spiritual Songs* (1854). The translator's opening line read: "Christ lay awhile in Death's strong bands," but was altered to its present form in *Church Hymns* (1871). The *GSR* text includes stanzas 1, 4, 6, and 7 of Luther's original hymn in Massie's translation. This is its first inclusion in *GS*.

Christ lag in Todesbanden
Johann Walther's *Geistliches Gesangbüchlein*, 1524

Walther (1496-1570) was the editor of the hymnal mentioned above. This tune is based on the ancient plainsong melody CHRIST IST

ERSTANDEN (see "Christ the Lord is risen again," *GSR,* No. 247), and is perhaps by Walther himself. This is its first inclusion *GS.*

Christ the Lord Is Risen Today   235
Charles Wesley, 1707-1788

This text has been one of the most popular modern poems on the resurrection of Christ. It was published in eleven 4-line stanzas in Wesley's *Hymns and Sacred Poems* (1739). In 1760 Martin Madan altered several phrases of the text. To Madan we owe the readings in *GSR* 4:3 and 4:4: "Once He died our souls to save" (rather than "Dying once He all doth save") and "Where's thy vict'ry, boasting grave?" (rather than "Where thy victory, O grave"). With these changes the *GSR* text contains stanzas 1-4 of Wesley's poem. It was first included in *GS* in 1921.

Easter Hymn

From *Lyra Davidica*, 1708

This tune was published anonymously in *Lyra Davidica* (1708). In its present form it was first published in John Arnold's *The Complete Psalmist* (London, 1741). John Wesley published it in the *Foundery Collection* (London, 1742) and called it SALISBURY TUNE. It has been known by various other names because of the different texts with which it has been joined. In previous editions of *GS* it was called WORGAN because it was once believed that Dr. J. Worgan had written it. It was first included in *GS* in 1921.

Christ the Lord Is Risen Again   247
Michael Weisse, c. 1488-1534
Trans. Catherine Winkworth, 182701878

Weisse's text beginning "Christus ist erstanden / Von des Todes Banden was published in the first hymnal of the Bohemian Brethren, *Ein Neu Gesengbuchlen* (1531), in seven 4-line stanzas with Alleluia. Winkworth's translation is from her *Lyra Germanica* (1858). The *GSR* text includes stanzas 1, 3, and 5. Duffield suggests that both Weisse and Luther (Christ lag in Todesbanden; see *GSR* No. 237) may be indebted to the Latin sequence *Victimae Paschali laudes*, particularly the stanza beginning "Mors et vita duello / conflixere mirando; / dux vitae mortuus regnat vivus." This sequence, which is attributed to Wipo of Burgundy (d. 1050), was one of the five sequences, out of hundreds, which were retained in the official liturgy of the Roman Catholic Church after the Council of Trent in the sixteenth century. It also contributed to the rise of liturgical drama which would later issue in the Mystery plays, and beyond that to drama in the West. The *Victimae Paschali laudes* was used at the annual Easter season and became part of a little drama during the Matins (morning) service on Easter Day. Various participants in the public service would take the parts of the angels and the women at the tomb of Jesus on the resurrection morning, based on Matthew 28. At the point at which the angel says, "He is not here," those playing the women would face the choir and sing, "Alleluia, the Lord is risen." Then the presiding bishop or senior official would question those playing the women, and he would be answered by stanzas from the *Victimae Paschali* laudes. This is the first inclusion of this text in *GS*.

Christ ist erstanden

Plainsong Melody, 12th century

This tune is based on a Plainsong melody which has been long associated with the *Victimae Paschali laudes* (see above on text). The *GSR* inclusion is based on an arrangement of the tune found in Joseph Klug's *Geistliche Lieder* (1533). This is its first inclusion in *GS*.

Christ, We Do All Adore Thee   155

Theodore Baker, 1851-1934

Baker served as literary editor for G. Schirmer, Inc., from 1892 until 1926. This text was published in 1927, shortly after he retired, as part of the libretto for the *Seven Last Words of Christ*. No other information is available. It was first included in *GS* in 1937.

Adoremus te Christe

Theodore Dubois, 1837-1924

Dubois was *maitre de chapelle* at Sainte-Clotilde in Paris, beginning in 1866. He produced his work "Les Sept Paroles du Christ" on Good Friday 1867. This tune is taken from that work. It was first included in *GS* in 1937.

Christ Will Me His Aid Afford   650

Johnson Oatman, Jr., 1856-1927

This text written by Oatman was first published in E. O. Excell's *Make His Praise Glorious* (Chicago, 1900, No. 10). In Excell's book he indicates that Entwisle copyrighted the song and that it is used by permission. He does not indicate that apparently John J. Hood owned the song in 1900.

Sweeter Than All

J. Howard Entwisle, 1863-1901

This tune was written for and published with the preceding text in 1900. Entwisle originally owned the copyright, but it was later controlled by John J. Hood. It has been in *GS*, with the text, since 1921.

Closer to Thee   573

Austin Taylor, 1881-1973

One day Austin Taylor was sitting in his study trying to write a new song. He had made several efforts but had cast them into a wastebasket because he felt that they did not say what he wanted. During this effort, a preacher friend came by to visit and during their conversation retrieved this text from the wastebasket. He read it and pronounced it worthwhile. Taylor, then, decided to publish it. It has had an extensive use among the Churches of Christ. The text, with the tune that follows, was published in Taylor's *New Songs of Victory* (Austin, Texas: Firm Foundation, 1911). It entered the *Supplement* to *Great Songs, No. 2* in 1975.

Taylor

Austin Taylor, 1881-1973

This tune was written for the preceding text and was published with it in *New Songs of Victory* (1911). It entered *GS* in the *Supplement* (1975).

Come, Christians, Join to Sing   151

Christian Henry Bateman, 1813-1889

This hymn, intended originally for children, was first published in Bateman's *Sacred Melodies for Children* (1843). Although the poem appeared first in five stanzas, with the reading in 1:1 "Come, children, join to sing," Bateman himself reduced it to the three stanzas of our present text in his *Sacred Melodies for Sabbath Schools and Families* (1854). This is the first inclusion of this text in *GS*.

Madrid

Anonymous
Arr. Benjamin Carr, 1769-1831

This tune is current in two versions, which are known by separate names. The present version is for an 8-line stanza with six syllables per line (6.6.6.6, D). (The other version is found in *GSR* No. 652.) Carr made an arrangement of this melody in 1825 and published it as *Spanish Hymn arranged and composed for the Concerts of the Musical Fund Society of Philadelphia by Benjamin Carr, The Air from an Ancient Spanish Melody* (1826). This is the first inclusion of this version in *GS*.

Come, Come, Ye Saints 128
William Clayton, 1814-1879
Alt. Joseph F. Green, b. 1924

The text by William Clayton was prompted by his learning that his wife had given birth to a son in Nauvoo, Illinois. He was making his way to Utah with Brigham Young as a member of the early band of Mormons. The letter from his wife ended with the words "All is well." He probably remembered a text which had appeared in *The Sacred Harp* (184) by J. T. White. That poem in five stanzas began:

What's this that steals, that steals upon my frame!
Is it death, is it death?
That soon will quench, will quench this mortal flame.
Is it death? Is it death?
If this be death, I soon shall be
From ev'ry pain and sorrow free,
I shall the King of glory see.
All is well! All is well!

The present text is an alteration by Green. He deleted from Clayton's poem all the specific Mormon references. His adaptation, made in 1960, was first published in *Christian Praise* (Nashville, 1964). This is its first inclusion in *GS*.

Come Down, Lord 522
Miriam Therese Winter, b. 1938

In a letter to me dated March 8, 1990, Professor Winter gives the following account of the composition of this text and tune:

I wrote the song "Come Down, Lord" in 1965, shortly after the liturgical language and musical repertory of my tradition changed from Latin to the vernacular and we were left without a song to sing. Like all those early songs, they were written as heart response and liturgical response to the biblical reading in the lectionary, specifically in this case, the incident of the centurion's son. I wanted to link that narrative theme with my own heart's experience and with the reality of the wider world, a pattern integral to my understanding of biblical/liturgical spirituality. The text and melody emerged as a unit, with the intent of achieving a natural fit between them as had been my experience with the Gregorian chant. I sang verse 1 in response to the traumatic changes of the 60's, and verse 3 in response to the Vietnam war and other national and global violence.

The song is recorded on my first album, *Joy Is Like the Rain*. An inclusive language version appears in *An Anthology of Scripture Songs*. This is the first inclusion of this beautiful text in *GS*.

Come Down, Lord

Miriam Therese Winter, b. 1938

This tune was written for the text preceding and at the same time. See the account above. This is its first inclusion in *GS*.

Come, Every Soul   327

John H. Stockton, 1813-1877

This text was first published in Stockton's *Salvation Melodies No. 1* (Philadelphia, 1874). *GSR* text includes three of the original five stanzas. Omitted are the following:

Yes, Jesus is the truth, the way,
That leads you into rest;
Believe in Him without delay
And you are fully blest.

O Jesus, blessed Jesus, dear,
I'm coming now to Thee:
Since Thou hast made the way so clear
And full salvation free.

The latter stanza is always omitted from modern hymnals. The original chorus read:

Come to Jesus, come to Jesus,
Come to Jesus now;
He will save you, He will save you,
He will save you now.

Ira D. Sankey altered this chorus to its present form in 1873 and published the song in his *Sacred Songs and Solos* (1875). The hymn entered *GS* in 1937.

Stockton

John H. Stockton, 1813-1877

Stockton wrote this tune for the preceding text and published it in his *Salvation Melodies No. 1* (Philadelphia, 1874). The tune name was first given in *Baptist Hymnal* (1956).

Come, Give Now to Christ All Honor 184

Paul Gerhardt, 1607-1676

Trans. Anonymous

This text by Gerhardt, "Kommt, und lasst uns Christum ehren," was published in eight 4-line stanzas in J. G. Ebeling's *Geistliche Andachten* (1667). The translation in *GSR* is copyrighted by Plough Publishing House, Hutterian Society of Brothers (Rifton, New York). The translator is unknown. No further information is available.

Dignitas

From the *Hohenfurth Manuscript,* 1410

No information is available on the *Hohenfurth Manuscript*. The tune name is derived from the general character of the hymn and was given in this edition of *GS* by the general editor.

Come, Holy Spirit, God and Lord 292

Martin Luther, 1483-1546

Tr. Catherine Winkworth, 1817-1878

This text is based on the eleventh century Latin antiphon *Veni Sancte Spiritus: repletuorum corda fidelium.* During the fifteenth century there existed a single stanza in German from this hymn, beginning "Komm Heiliger Geist, Herre Gott." The authorship is unknown. Martin Luther admired the stanza and added two more. The entire poem was published in the *Enchiridia* (Erfurt, 1524) and in Johann Walther's *Geystliche gesangk Buchleyn* (1524). Miss Winkworth's translation was published in her *Lyra Germanica,* 1st Series (1855), and in her *Chorale Book for England* (1863). This is its first inclusion in *GS*. It is a poem celebrating the events of the first Pentecost as recorded in Acts 2.

Das neuegeborne Kindelein

Melchior Vulpius, c. 1560-1616

Harm. J. S. Bach, 1685-1750

This tune was first published in Vulpius's *Ein schön geistlich Gesangbuch* (Jena, 1609), set to Cyriacus Schneegass's text "Das neugeborne Kindelein." This is its first inclusion in *GS*.

Come, Holy Spirit, Guest Divine   359

Adoniram Judson, 1788-1850

About 1829 Judson wrote a hymn in seven stanzas which was said to have been sung at the baptism of several soldiers at Moulmein, where Judson served as a missionary to Burma. The original first three stanzas were formerly often printed in Baptist and Disciple hymnals, including those of Alexander Campbell. They read:

Our Saviour bowed beneath the wave,
    And meekly sought a watery grave:
Come see the sacred path he trod—
    A path well pleasing to our God.

His voice we wear, his footsteps trace,
    And hither come to seek his face,
To do his will, to feel his love,
    And join our songs with songs above.

Hosanna to the Lamb divine!
    Let endless glories round him shine;
High o'er the heavens for ever reign,
    O Lamb of God, for sinners slain.

The remaining stanzas form the present text. Hymnals of the Stone-Campbell Movement have always changed Judson's "Dove divine" (1:1) to "Guest divine." The general editor has altered "The sealing unction" (4:3) to "Our God's anointing." The Judson text was first printed in Winchell's *Collection* (1832). This text, with the accompanying tune DUKE STREET, first entered *GS* in the *Supplement* (1975).

Duke Street

John Hatton, d. 1793

For information on this tune, see "Awake, My Tongue, Thy Tribute Bring," *GSR,* No. 67.

Come, Let Us Join Our Cheerful Songs 5

Isaac Watts, 1674-1748

This poem, originally in five stanzas, is Watts's paraphrase of Revelation 5:11-13. It was first published in his *Hymns and Spiritual Songs* (1707) and entitled "Christ Jesus, the Lamb of God, worshipped by all the Creation." *GSR* text omits the original fourth stanza:

Let all who dwell above the sky,
    And air, and earth, and seas,
Conspire to lift thy glories high,
    And speak thine endless praise.

This text entered *GS* in 1937.

Gräfenburg

From Johann Crüger's *Praxis Pietatis Melica*, 1647

Arr. Jack Boyd, b. 1932

This tune, also called NUN DANKET ALL, is usually attributed to Johann Crüger, at least in its present form. It was first published in his *Praxis,* 2nd ed. (1647), where it was set to Paul Gerhardt's "Nun danket all und bringet ehr." This is the first inclusion of this tune in *GS.*

Come Now, O Lord of Victory 170

Cynewulf, 8th century

Trans. Forrest M. McCann, b. 1931

Cynewulf flourished in the latter part of the eighth century and was the greatest of the Old English poets. This text is taken from his poem *Christ* (or *The Ascension*), lines 243b-74. Here is the Old English text:

Cum, nu sigores Weard,
Meotod moncynnes,
arfæst ywe!
ðæt we ðin medrencynn
rhytgeryno,
ðæt fædrencynn
ðu ðisne middangeard
ðurh ðinne hercyme,
ond ða gyldnan geatu
heofona heahfrea,
ond usic ðonne gesece
eaðmod to earðan.
Hafað se awyrgda

ond ðine miltse her
Us in eallum neod
motan cunnan,
nu we areccan ne mægon
fier owihte,
milde geblissa
hælende Crist,
ðe in geardagum
hat ontynan,
ðurh ðin sylfes gong
Us in ðinra arna ðearf!
wulf tostenced,

deor dædscua,   Dryhten, ðin eowde,
wide towrecene.   ðæt ðu, Waldend, ær
blode gebohtes,   ðæt se bealofulla
hyne heardlice,   ond him on hæft nimeð
ofer usse nioda lust.   For on we, Nergend, ðe
bidda geornlice   breastgehygdum
ðæt ðu hrædlice   help gefremme
wergum wreccan,   ðæt se wites bona
in helle grund   hean gedreose,
ond ðin hondgeweorc,   hæleða Scyppend,
mote arisan   ond on ryht cuman
to ðam upcundan   æðelan rice,
ðonan us ær ðurh synlust   se swearta gast
forteah and fortylde,   ðæt we, tires wone,
a butan ende   sculon ermðu dreogan,
butan ðu usic   ðon ofostlicor, ece Dryhten,
æt ðam leodsceaðan,   lifgende God,
Helm alwihta,   hreddan wille.

This poem praises Jesus as "sigores Weard" (Lord of victory), who has
come down to earth, identified with mankind, and by his death has
accomplished for all humanity the victory of the kingdom of God. The
translation is by the general editor of *GSR*, and was made during the process
of the present revision expressly for this work.

Sigor

M. L. Daniels, b. 1934

The tune name SIGOR, the Old English word for "victory," was
given by the general editor. The tune was composed expressly for the
preceding text for inclusion in *GSR* by Melvin Lee Daniels, professor of
music emeritus at Abilene Christian University.

Come, Risen Lord   378

George W. Briggs, 1875-1959

Briggs contributed sixteen hymn texts to *Songs of Praise* (London,
1931), of which this is one. It is based on Luke 24:28-31 and is a highly
useful text for communion. This is its first inclusion in *GS*.

Sursum Corda

Alfred M. Smith, 1879-1971

This tune was composed in 1941 for Henry M. Butler's text "Lift Up Your Hearts!" and was submitted anonymously to the committee editing the Episcopal Church's *The Hymnal, 1940.* This is its first inclusion in *GS.*

Come, Sound His Praise Abroad 111

Isaac Watts, 1674-1748

This text was first published in Watts's *The Psalms of David, Imitated in the Language of the New Testament* (1719). It was originally in six stanzas, but stanzas 5 and 6 are never included for obvious reasons in twentieth century hymnals. They read:

But if your ears refuse
    The language of his grace
And hearts grow hard like stubborn Jews,
    That unbelieving race;

The Lord, in vengeance dressed,
    Will lift his hand and swear,
"You that despised my promised rest,
    Shall have no portion there."

Cambridge

Ralph Harrison, 1748-1810
Arr. Samuel S. Wesley, 1810-1876

This tune first appeared in Harrison's *Sacred Harmony—A Collection of Psalm-tunes, Ancient and Modern* (2 vols; London, 1784, 1791). Wesley inserted it in his *European Psalmist* (London, 1782). CAMBRIDGE is named for the site of the ancient English university and is also called WAUGH or CAMBERWELL. This is its first inclusion in *GS.*

Come, Thou Almighty King 88

Anonymous, c. 1757

This hymn has been attributed to Charles Wesley, but there is little real evidence that he is the author. It appeared together with Wesley's hymn "Jesus, Let Thy Pitying Eye," bound in a four-page tract in copies of George Whitefield's *Collection of Hymns for Social Worship* (1757). Wesley never printed the hymn in his collections, never claimed authorship, and as far as is known, never wrote in this meter. The authorship is simply unknown. It appears to be an imitation, for spiritual purposes, of the poem which became England's national anthem, "God Save the King" (1743), and was sung to the common tune for that poem, known in the United States as AMERICA. The poem was originally in five stanzas, but *GSR* text omits 2 and 4:

> 2
> Jesus, our Lord, arise,
>> Scatter our enemies,
> And make them fall!
>> Let thine almighty aid
> Our sure defence be made:
>> Our souls on thee be stayed,
>> Lord, hear our call.

> 4
> Come, Holy Comforter,
>> Thy sacred witness bear,
> In this glad hour!
>> Thou, who almighty art;
> Now rule in every heart,
>> And ne'er from us depart,
>> Spirit of power.

The original 5:1 (*GSR* 3:1) has been altered by hymnal compilers of the Stone-Campbell movement to avoid the direct emphasis on Trinitarian formula and in favor of more biblical language. This text was first included in *GS* in 1937.

Italian Hymn

Felice de Giardini, 1716-1796

For information on this tune, see "Christ for the World We Sing," *GSR*, No. 400.

Come, Thou Fount of Every Blessing   595

Robert Robinson, 1735-1790

This text was written in 1758 and first published in *A Collection of Hymns Used by the Church of Christ in Angel Alley Bishopgate* (1759). The poem was originally in four 8-line stanzas. The fourth stanza, beginning "O, that day when free from sinning," was omitted by Martin Madan in his *Psalms and Hymns* (1760). All succeeding compilers have followed Madan.

The text has had various alterations over the years, usually depending on the theological orientation of the editors of the various collections. The present text is that usually found in hymnals of the Stone-Campbell Movement of the nineteenth century. We have returned, however, to the original reading in 1:1, "Come, Thou Fount."

Nettleton

Traditional American Melody
John Wyeth's *Repository of Sacred Music*, 1813

The origin of this tune is obscure. In Wyeth's collection the tune name was HALLELUJAH. It has been attributed to both Wyeth and Nettleton and was included in Nettleton's *Village Hymns for Social Worship* (1824). Perhaps some third person composed it and named it in honor of Nettleton. Asahel Nettleton was a well-known evangelist of the early nineteenth century. The text above entered *GS* in 1921, and the tune was first printed in our hymnal in 1925.

Come, Thou Long-Expected Jesus   188

Charles Wesley, 1707-1788

This text was first published in *Hymns for the Nativity of Our Lord* (1744). The *GSR* text is exactly as Wesley published it except for 1:3, which changes "relieve" to "release." This change had occurred during Wesley's lifetime. The hymn first entered *GS* in the *Supplement* (1975).

Hyfrydol

Rowland H. Prichard, 1811-1887

Prichard composed this tune when he was about twenty years of age. It was first published in his *Cyfaill y Cantorion* (The Singer's Friend) in 1844. HYFRYDOL means "good cheer" in Welsh. The tune entered *GS* with the preceding text in the *Supplement* (1975).

Come to the Savior   336

George F. Root, 1820-1895

This text was first published in Root's *The Prize* (Chicago: Root & Cady, 1870). It also appeared in Bliss and Sankey's *Gospel Hymns and Sacred Songs* (1875, No. 62). This is its first appearance in *GS*.

Joyful

George F. Root, 1820-1895

This tune was written for the text preceding and appeared with it in Root's *The Prize* (Chicago, 1870). It is now included in *GS* for the first time.

Come to the Savior Now   334

John M. Wigner, 1844-1911

This text was written in 1871 and first published in the *Supplement to Psalms and Hymns* (1880), an English Baptist collection. This hymnal was compiled by Thomas John Wigner, the father of the poet. The *GSR* text is somewhat altered from the original. (See Sankey's *Sacred Songs and Solos,* No. 399.) This is the first inclusion of this text in *GS.*

Invitation

Frederick C. Maker, 1844-1927

This tune was composed for the foregoing text and was first published in *The Bristol Tune Book* (1881, No. 742). This is its first appearance in *GS.*

Come, Ye Disconsolate   338

Thomas Moore, 1779-1852, Stanzas 1, 2
Thomas Hastings, 1784-1872, Stanza 3

This text was first published in Moore's *Sacred Songs* (1816). The original 1:1 read "Come, at God's altar fervently kneel." Moore changed this to the smoother "Come, at the throne of God" in the 1824 edition. Thomas Hastings dropped Moore's original third stanza, which read:

Go, ask the infidel what boon he brings us,
    What charm for aching hearts he can reveal.
Sweet as the heavenly promise hope sings us:
    "Earth has no sorrow that God cannot heal."

He then added a stanza of his own and is responsible for most of the changes which have brought the text to its modern form. Curiously, however, in Hastings's *Presbyterian Psalmodist, a Collection of Tunes Adapted to the Psalms and Hymns of the Presbyterian Church in the United States of America* (Philadelphia, 1855, p. 305), stanza three reads:

Here see the bread of life; see waters flowing
    Forth from the throne of God, boundless in love;

Come to the feast prepared; come, ever knowing
Earth has no sorrows but heav'n can remove.

Hastings published the stanzas as a hymn first in his *Spiritual Songs for Social Worship* (1832). This text has been included in *GS* since 1921.

Consolator

From *A Collection of Motets and Antiphons*, 1792
Arr. from Samuel Webbe, Sr., 1740-1816

This tune appeared in Webbe's *Collection of Motets and Anthems* (1792), arranged as a solo. It was there set to the Latin hymn "Alma redemptoris mater." Thomas Hastings and Lowell Mason arranged it for solo and duet in *Spiritual Songs for Social Worship* (1831). The tune entered *GS* in the first edition (1921).

Come, Ye Sinners, Poor and Needy 329

Joseph Hart, 1712-1768

The original version of this text was first published in Hart's *Hymns Composed on Various Subjects* (1759), in seven 6-line stanzas. There it was entitled "Come, and Welcome, to Jesus Christ." The refrain was not a part of Hart's hymn, but derives from an anonymous nineteenth-century American folk hymn "Far, far away from my loving Father." The refrain originally read:

I will arise and go to Jesus
He will embrace me in His arms;
In the arms of my dear Savior,
O there are ten thousand charms.

Hart's last two lines of his stanza one read: "He is able, / He is willing: doubt no more." The present text employs the first four lines of Hart's stanzas 1, 2, and 3, and the American folk refrain as stanza 4. The omitted stanzas read:

4
Come, ye weary, heavy-laden,
Lost and ruined by the fall;
If you tarry till you're better,
You may never come at all.
Not the righteous,—
Sinners Jesus came to call.

5

Agonizing in the garden,
    Your Redeemer prostrate lies;
On the bloody tree behold Him!
    Hear Him cry, before he dies,
"It is finished!"
    Sinners, will not this suffice.

6

Lo! the incarnate God, ascending,
    Pleads the merit of his blood:
Venture on him, venture freely;
    Let no other trust intrude:
None but Jesus
    Can do helpless sinners good.

7

Saints and angels, joined in concert,
    Sing the praises of the Lamb;
While the blissful seats of heaven
    Sweetly echo with His name:
Hallelulah!
    Sinners here may do the same.

Hart's text originally appeared in *GS* in 1937, with slightly altered versions of his stanzas 2 and 3, and the original refrain of stanza 1 as the chorus. The present text entered *GS* in the *Supplement* (1975), but with the American folk hymn refrain as stanza one.

Arise

Traditional American Melody
Arr. Jack A. Boyd, b. 1932

The tune originally used in *GS* with the foregoing text was called GREENVILLE in American collections and ROUSSEAU'S DREAM in British books. It was taken from Jean Jacques Rousseau's composition "Le Devin du Village" (1752). The present tune, of unknown origin, was published in William Walker's *Southern Harmony* (1835) and called RESTORATION. It was first included in *GS* in the *Supplement* (1975).

Come, Ye Thankful People, Come 590
Henry Alford, 1810-1871

Alford first published this text in his *Psalms and Hymns* (1844). He revised it slightly in *The Poetical Works of Henry Alford* (ed. 1865). The poem was revised again in his *Year of Praise* (1867). Our text is that of 1865. This is a beautiful harvest hymn based on Mark 4:26-29 and Matthew 13:36-43. It first entered *GS* in 1937.

St. George's Windsor 590
George J. Elvey, 1816-1893

This tune was written as a setting for James Montgomery's "Hark, the song of Jubilee," and it was first published in E. H. Thorne's *A Selection of Psalm and Hymn Tunes* (1858). The editors of *Hymns Ancient and Modern* (1861) put the tune with the present text. The tune name derives from St. George's Chapel, Windsor, where Elvey was organist for forty-seven years. It entered *GS* in 1937.

Come, Ye That Love the Lord 68
Isaac Watts, 1674-1748

Watts's text of ten 4-line stanzas was first published in his *Hymns and Spiritual Songs* (1707). The words to some of the stanzas were altered by John Wesley and others. For example, 1:1, 2 originally read "Come, we" and "let our," and 2:3 (originally stanza 3) read "favorites." An unknown author later emended this to "children," the common reading of all modern hymnals. *GSR* text includes Watts's stanzas 1, 3, 9, and 10. The refrain is by Robert Lowry and was added in 1867. The complete original text of Watts's poem may be seen in Samuel Worcester's *Watts and Select* (1850). This text entered *GS* in 1921 with the "Come, we" reading.

Marching to Zion
Robert Lowry, 1826-1899

This tune was composed for this text in 1867 and was first published in Lowry's Sunday School hymnal *Silver Spray* (1868). The tune was first printed in *GS* in 1937. At that time the text reading was altered to "Come, ye that love the Lord."

Comfort, Comfort Now My People   183

John Olearius, 1611-1684
Trans. Catherine Winkworth, 1827-1878

This hymn by Olearius, beginning "Trostet, trostet meine Lieben," was written in 1671 in four 8-line stanzas. It is based on Isaiah 40:1-5 and was written for the holy day commemorating John the Baptist in the ecclesiastical calendar of the Lutheran Church (June 24). It was published in *Geistliche Singe-Kunst* (Leipzig, 1671), one of the most important German hymnals of the eighteenth century. The *GSR* text contains stanzas 1, 3, and 4 of the Winkworth translation as altered in the *Lutheran Book of Worship* (1978). Miss Winkworth's original translation may be found in the *Mennonite Hymnal* (1969) and in various other modern hymnals.

Freu dich sehr

Trente quatre Pseaumes de David, 1551

This tune was originally a French folksong tune for the text "Ne l'oseray je dire" (1505). It was adapted by Louis Bourgeois in *Trente quatre Pseaumes de David,* (Geneva, 1551). The tune was used as a setting for the German funeral hymn "Freu dich sehr, o meine Seele" in J. Rhamba's *Harmoniae sacrae* (Gorlitz, 1613), whence the tune name. This is the first appearance of this tune and the preceding text in *GS*.

Creator of the Stars of Night   160

Anonymous Latin Hymn, 9th Century
Adpt. from John Mason Neale in *The Hymnal*, 1940

Although this hymn has been ascribed to Ambrose, it was rejected as one of his authenticated compositions by the Benedictine editors of his works. Its first known appearance is in a ninth-century manuscript at Bern, Switzerland. The *GSR* text contains stanzas 1, 4, and 5 of the 1940 translation. The complete text marks the poem as an advent hymn. Our text makes it a song of praise to Christ. This is its first appearance in *GS*.

Conditor Alme

Sarum Plainsong, Mode IV

This is the first time that an ancient modal tune has been included in *GS*. This music represents, as nearly as we can duplicate it, the musical forms prevalent in the ancient church. Since the so-called Use of Sarum (that is, Salisbury) was established by Osmund about A.D. 1085 following the Norman conquest of England, this tune dates from at least the eleventh century, as far as its use in England goes. In modal music the meaning of the words always prevails over the appeal of the tune, the tune being merely a chanting vehicle to assist in expressing the thought.

Crown Him with Many Crowns 255
Matthew Bridges, 1800-1894 (Stanzas 1,3,4)
Godfrey Thring, 1823-1903 (Stanza 2)

This text is a composite. Bridges's hymn in six stanzas first appeared in his *Hymns of the Heart* (1848) to illustrate the text from Revelation 19:12, "And on his head were many crowns." The *GSR* text stanzas 1, 3, and 4 come from Bridges's original hymn. Stanza 2 was written by Godfrey Thring in 1874 because he was dissatisfied with Bridges's hymn. Thring's lyric originally began "Crown him with crowns of gold, / All nations great and small." This text has been in *GS* since 1921.

Diademata

George J. Elvey, 1816-1893

This tune was written for the preceding text and was first published in the *Appendix* to *Hymns Ancient and Modern* (1868). The tune name DIADEMATA (διαδήματα) is the Greek term found in the text from Revelation on which the hymn is based. It has been in *GS* since 1921.

Day by Day 134
Caroline V. Sandell-Berg, 1832-1903
Trans. A. L. Skoog, 1856-1934

Caroline V. Sandell-Berg wrote this text in 1865, between the time of the death of her mother and her marriage to C. O. Berg. The original Swedish text began "Blott en dag, ett eoonblick i sander." It was first published in her *Korsblomman* (1866). The English translation by A. L. Skoog appeared in *Mission Hymns* (1921).

Blott en dag

Oscar Ahnfelt, 1813-1882

The tune name BLOTT EN DAG derives from the opening lines of the original Swedish poem. It was first published in Ahnfelt's *Andeliga Sanger* (1872). This is the first inclusion of Sandell's text and this tune in *GS*.

Day Is Dying in the West   37
Mary Artemisia Lathbury, 1841-1913

The first two stanzas of this hymn were written in 1877 at the request of Dr. John H. Vincent, founder of the Chautauqua Institution, as a hymn for vespers, or the evening service. It was sung that year at Chautauqua Lake in New York. As a two-stanza poem, it first appeared in Charles S. Robinson and Robert S. MacArthur's *The Calvary Selection of Sacred Songs* (New York, 1878). Stanzas 3 and 4 were added by Miss Lathbury in 1890.

Chautauqua

William Fisk Sherwin, 1826-1888

CHAUTAUQUA was composed in 1877 for the preceding text while Sherwin was music director at the Chautauqua assembly. It appeared with the text in *The Calvary Selection* (1878). The text and tune have been in *GS* since 1921.

Dear Lord and Father of Mankind   569
John Greenleaf Whittier, 1807-1892

This text is taken from Whittier's "The Brewing of Soma," a 17-stanza poem published in the *Atlantic Monthly* (April, 1872). The poet had read in a Hindu scripture of how the priests of Indra drank a mixture which produced a frenzy in them which they believed brought new joy and life. In the light of this, he thought of the noisy and frenzied camp meetings of his day which offended him. His poem concludes with six stanzas of prayer, which give his view of true worship. Our text contains stanzas 12, 13, 14, and 16 of the original poem. The hymn entered *GS* in the first *Supplement* (1922).

Elton

Frederick C. Maker, 1844-1927

This tune was composed for the foregoing text. It was first published in G. S. Barrett's *Congregational Church Hymnal* (1887). The tune is called REST in some modern hymnals. *GSR* includes the more prevalent tune name, ELTON, which is a common English place name, coming from the Old English "eald tun" (old town).

Dear Master, in Whose Life I See   571
John Hunter, 1848-1917

This text was first published in the *Monthly Calendar* of the Trinity Congregational Church, Glasgow, Scotland. Hunter was minister there from 1887 to 1901. It was first included in a hymnal in Hunter's *Hymns of Faith and Life* (1889). This is its first inclusion in *GS*.

Hursley

Katholisches Gesangbuch, 1774

This tune first appeared in the undated *Katholisches Gesangbuch* (Vienna) set to the text "Grosser Gott, wir loben dich." (See *GSR*, No. 48.) The probable date is 1774. Later the tune was published in J. G. Schicht's *Allgemeines Choral-Buch* (1819). This was a Protestant collection published in Leipzig. The tune name HURSLEY derives from the English parish where John Keble was vicar. He had chosen this tune for his hymn "Sun of My Soul." HURSLEY is an adaptation of the tune GROSSER GOTT, WIR LOBEN DICH. The tune entered *GS* in 1925.

Does Jesus Care   642
Frank E. Graeff, 1860-1919

Although known as a spiritual optimist, Graeff in 1901 was undergoing a time of physical and spiritual despondency. In turning to Jesus for comfort, he found special strength in the promise "He careth for you" (1 Pet. 5:7). This poem came out of his spiritual struggles. It first entered *GS* in 1937.

My Savior Cares

J. Lincoln Hall, 1866-1930

The tune was written for Graeff's text. Hall felt it was his "most inspired piece of music." Although the song was copyrighted in 1901, its first date of publication is unknown. It is included in Herbert J. Lacey, C. Austin Miles, and Maurice A. Clifton's *New Songs of the Gospel, No. 2* (1905). It entered *GS* with the text above in 1937.

Dying with Jesus   528
Daniel W. Whittle, 1840-1901

When Whittle was at the World's Columbian Exposition in Chicago in 1893, the English preacher Henry Varley remarked to him that he did not like the song "I Need Thee Every Hour" because he felt that he needed Him every moment. After reflecting on this remark, Whittle penned these words. The text was first published as a leaflet, but was subsequently published in Ira D. Sankey, James McGranahan, and George C. Stebbins's *Sacred Songs No. 1* (1896).

Whittle

May Whittle Moody, 1870-1963

The tune was composed for the text above by Whittle's daughter, who later married the son of Dwight L. Moody. It was published with the text in the hymnal mentioned above. Both the text and tune have been in *GS* since 1921.

Encamped Along the Hills of Light 498

John H. Yates, 1837-1900

Sankey reported that he first published this text in *The Christian Endeavor Hymnbook* (c. 1891) and in *Gospel Hymns No. 6* (1891). Yates had sent the poem to Sankey. The song also appears in *Young People's Songs of Praise with Christian Endeavor Supplement* (1902). It was first included in *GS* in 1921.

Sankey

Ira D. Sankey, 1840-1908

Sankey wrote the tune for the words above and published them with the text in *The Christian Endeavor Hymnbook* (c. 1891). This tune entered *GS* with the text in 1921.

Eternal Father, Strong to Save 137

William Whiting, 1825-1878

The original version of this text was written in 1860 and published with alterations in the first edition of *Hymns Ancient and Modern* (1861). Whiting's original stanza one read:

> O Thou who bidd'st the ocean deep
>> Its own appointed limits keep,
> Thou who didst bind the restless wave,
>> Eternal Father, strong to save:
> O hear us when we cry to thee
>> For all in peril on the sea.

Whiting accepted most of the alterations of the *HA&M* editors when he made his own revision of the poem in 1869. The *GSR* text agrees with a revision made by Whiting and *HA&M* editors in 1875. Stanza 3 is omitted, according to the custom of our original editor (E. L. Jorgenson) of not including addresses to the Holy Spirit. The omitted stanza reads:

> O Holy Spirit, who didst brood
> > Upon the waters dark and rude,
> And bid their angry tumult cease,
> > And give for wild confusion peace:"
> O hear us when we cry to thee
> > For those in peril on the sea.

This hymn entered *GS* in 1937.

Melita

John B. Dykes, 1823-1876

This tune was written for the preceding text and included in the first edition of *Hymns Ancient and Modern* (1861). MELITA derives from the ancient name of the island of Malta, where the apostle Paul was shipwrecked (Acts 28:1).

Eternal God, Whose Power Upholds 396
Henry Hallam Tweedy, 1868-1953

This hymn text won the first prize in the Hymn Society of America's competition (1928-29). It was written in 1929 and first sung at the Presbyterian Church in Riverdale, New York, May 30, 1930. It was included in the *Methodist Hymnal* (1935). This is its first inclusion in *GS*.

Forest Green

English Folk Melody
Arr. Ralph Vaughan Williams, 1872-1958

This folk song, with its text entitled "The Ploughboy's Dream," was discovered by Vaughan Williams at Forest Green, Surrey, England, in 1903. He harmonized it for inclusion in *The English Hymnal* (Oxford, 1906). This is its first inclusion in *GS*.

Face to Face 660
Carrie E. Breck, 1855-1934

Mrs. Breck sent this poem to Grant Colfax Tullar in 1898, asking that he provide a musical setting. He had just written a tune and text beginning "All for me my Savior suffered" while working in a religious meeting in Rutherford, New Jersey. Mrs. Breck's poem exactly fit his tune, so he discarded his poem and used hers. This text entered *GS* in 1921.

Face to Face

Grant Colfax Tullar, 1869-1950

This tune, written as explained above, was first published in Tullar's *Sermons in Song, No. 2* (1889). It entered *GS* in the first edition (1921).

Fairest Lord Jesus   156
Anonymous in *Münster Gesangbuch,* 1677

Although written as early as 1662, the original of this text appeared first in the *Münster Gesangbuch* (1677). It passed into popular use when A. H. Hoffman von Fallersleben set it to the tune now known as SCHÖNSTER HERR JESU and published it in von Fallersleben and E. F. Richter's *Schlesische Volkslieder* (Leipzig, 1842). The anonymous English translation first appeared as arranged by Richard Storrs Willis in his *Church Chorals and Choir Studies* (New York, 1850). The first three stanzas have been in *GS* since 1921. *GSR* has added for the first time stanza four from Joseph A. Seiss's translation in *The Sunday School Book* (Philadelphia, 1873). The German text of stanza one marks this poem as a hymn originally for Roman Catholics:

> Schönster Herr Jesu
> Herrscher aller Erden
> Gottes und Marien Sohn;
> Dich will ich lieben,
> Dich will ich ehren,
> Du meiner Seele Freud und Kron.

Schönster Herr Jesu
Silesian Folk Melody

Von Fallersleben seems to have discovered this tune being sung by haymakers in the Glaz district of Silesia in 1839. He set it to the preceding text under the caption "Jesu über alles" in his and Richter's *Schlesische Volkslieder* (Leipzig, 1842). The tune is also called ASCALON (in England) and ST. ELIZABETH (because of the use of it in Franz Liszt's oratorio *Legend of St. Elizabeth*, 1862). Willis erroneously called it CRUSADER'S HYMN in his 1850 collection. It has no connection with the crusades. Both text and tune entered *GS* in 1921.

Faith of Our Fathers 494

Frederick W. Faber, 1814-1863

The text appeared in four stanzas in Faber's *Jesus and Mary—Catholic Hymns for Singing and Reading* (1849). It was also printed in his *Hymns* (1862). The *GSR* text contains stanzas 1, 2, and 4. The omitted third stanza originally read:

> Faith of our Fathers! Mary's prayers
> Shall win our country back to thee;
> And through the truth that comes from God
> England shall then indeed be free.

This stanza has been altered in some modern Protestant hymnals to remove the Roman Catholic emphasis on Mary.

St. Catherine

Henri F. Hemy, 1818-1888
Adpt. James G. Walton, 1821-1905

This tune was written for the text "Sweet Saint Catherine, Maid Most Pure," which first appeared in *Crown of Jesus Music* (1864). Hemy was the editor of this work. Walton took the first sixteen measures of Hemy's inclusion, added eight of his own, and published the tune in *Plain Song Music for Holy Communion Office* (1874). Catherine was a fourth-century Christian martyr from Alexandria in Egypt. Both text and tune entered *GS* in the first *Supplement* (1922).

Far and Near 399

John O. Thompson

Little information is available on this gospel song. It is quite a popular missionary hymn among Churches of Christ. It seems to have been written by Thompson about 1885 and was published that year in John H. Vincent's *The Epworth Hymnal containing Standard Hymns* (New York: Phillips and Hunt). It was later owned by Eaton and Main. The text, with the accompanying tune by Clemm, was included in C. C. Cline's *Standard Church Hymns* (1888). It has been in *GS* since the first edition (1921).

Clemm

J. B. O. Clemm

No information is available on this composer. The hymn tune name CLEMM was given by the present general editor of *GSR*. It was first published in Vincent's *The Epworth Hymnal* (1885), as mentioned above.

Father Almighty, Bless Us   568
From the *Berwick Hymnal*, 1886

Nothing is know of this text other than it was published in the hymnal mentioned above. A. W. Oxford edited the *Berwick Hymnal*. He was vicar of St. Luke's Church on Berwick Street, London, England.

Flemming
Friedrich F. Flemming, 1778-1813

The tune was written in 1811 as a setting for Horace's ode "Integer vitae" (Bk. I, 22)—"the unblemished life." It was originally composed for male voices. This is the first inclusion of this text and tune in *GS*.

Father and Friend, Thy Light, Thy Love   115
John H. Bowring, 1792-1872

This text was published the year before Bowring became editor of the *Westminster Review*. It is a poem dealing with the omnipresence of God and appeared in his *Matins and Vespers* (2nd ed., 1824). It entered *GS* in the first *Supplement* (1922).

Hesperus
Henry Baker, 1835-1910

This tune was written while Baker was a student in engineering at Winchester, in 1854. It was published without Baker's knowledge in John Grey's *A Hymnal for Use in the English Church* (1866). Baker claimed it as his in 1871. It entered *GS* in the first *Supplement* (1922).

Father, Hear the Prayer We Offer   564
Love M. Willis, 1823-1908

This text was published anonymously in *Tiffany's Monthly* (1856). The original first line read "Father, hear the prayer I offer." It was also published in J. S. Adam's *Psalms of Life* (1857) in five stanzas of four lines each. The present text was included first in Samuel Longfellow and Samuel Johnson's *Hymns of the Spirit* (1864). It entered *GS* in 1921.

St. Sylvester

John B. Dykes, 1823-1876

This tune was first published in Chope's *Congregational Hymn Book* (1862). It is not to be confused with a tune by the same name written by Joseph Barnby (1867). This tune entered *GS* in 1921.

Father, Hear Thy Children's Call 582

Thomas B. Pollock, 1836-1896

Pollock's reputation rests upon his metrical litanies. The text is part of a three-part litany published in his *Metrical Litanies for Special Services and General Use* (1870). The entire text may be found in the Society for the Propagation of Christian Knowledge's *Church Hymns* (1906, No. 648). *GSR* text contains stanzas 1, 2, 6, and 7 of Part I, and stanza 7 of part II. This text first entered *GS* in 1921.

Gower's Litany

John H. Gower, 1855-1922

Although born and educated in England, Gower had mining interests in the United States. He came to this country in 1887, settled in Denver, Colorado, and served as organist for churches there. This tune was published in his *Original Tunes* (1890). It has been in *GS* with the preceding text since 1921.

Father, Lead Me Day by Day 132

John Page Hopps, 1834-1912

This text was first published in Hopps's *Hymns, Chants, and Anthems for Public Worship* (1877). It was there called a "Child's Prayer for Divine Guidance." This is its first inclusion in *GS*.

Orientibus Partibus

From the Office of Pierre de Corbeil
Harm. Richard Redhead, 1820-1901

This melody was sung in medieval times at the Feast of the Ass (Jan. 14), a festival commemorating the flight of Joseph and Mary with the child Jesus into Egypt (Matthew 22). It is usually dated about 1210, by which date it is found in the *Sens Breviary* as "A Conductus from the Office of the Circumcision." Pierre de Corbeil, who died in 1222, was Archbishop of Sens. Redhead published his modern setting in *Church*

Hymn Tunes, Ancient and Modern (London, 1853). The tune name ORIENTIBUS PARTIBUS derives from the Latin text of de Corbeil's Office: *Orientibus partibus advenivit asinus* ("from the eastern parts came the ass").

Father of Mercies, Day by Day   125
Frederick W. Faber, 1814-1863 (St. 1)
Alice Flowerdew, 1759-1830 (Stanzas 2,3)

This text is a happy blending of two poems. Stanza 1 is an altered version of Faber's hymn "Mother of mercies," first published in his *Jesus and Mary* (1849). The word "Mother" was changed to "Father" by Elmer Leon Jorgenson, and the hymn, with Flowerdew's stanzas, was introduced into *Great Songs of the Church, Number Two* (1937). Stanzas 2 and 3 are by Alice Flowerdew, from a hymn originally beginning "Fountain of mercies, God of love," and published in her *Poems on Moral and Religious Subjects* (3d ed., 1811). "Fountain" was altered to "Father" in Murray's *Hymnal* (1852).

Eleos

Traditional English Melody

Little information is available on this tune. In Hemy's *Crown of Jesus Music* (1864), it is called "an old English air." The tune name ELEOS ("mercy") was given by the present general editor of *GSR*.

Father of Mercy

Anonymous (St. 1)
George William Walton, b. 1941 (Stanzas 2-4)

The source of the text of stanza one is unknown. It first entered *GS* in 1937. Stanzas 2 through 4 were written especially for the present edition of *GS* by G. W. Walton, chairman of the English faculty at Abilene Christian University. These additional stanzas have greatly enlarged the usefulness of the hymn by calling forth the blessings of Father, Son, and Holy Spirit.

Semele

Arr. from George F. Handel, 1685-1759

This tune is arranged from Handel's *Semele*, which was first performed at Covent Garden, London (Feb. 10, 1744). Handel took his libretto from revisions of William Congreve and Alexander Pope. The work

GS since 1937.

Father, We Praise Thee   26

Gregory the Great, 540-604

Trans. Percy Dearmer, 1867-1936

This text is Dearmer's translation of the medieval Latin office hymn *Nocte surgente vigilemus omnes*. The complete Latin text with Old English gloss may be found in the Surtees Society's *The Latin Hymns of the Anglo-Saxon Church* (Durham, 1851, No. 7). Although the hymn has long been ascribed to Gregory (and is so ascribed in *GSR*), no real evidence of his authorship exists. A. S. Walpole in his *Early Latin Hymns* (1922) suggests that Alcuin of York (A.D. 730-804) may be the author. Dearmer's translation was first published in the *English Hymnal* (Oxford, 1906). This is its first inclusion in *GS*.

Christe Sanctorum

Paris Antiphoner, 1681

Arr. from Françoise de La Feillee's

Nouvelle Methode de plain-chant, 1782

CHRISTE SANCTORUM is an ancient plainsong melody adapted for congregational use. It was originally published in the *Paris Antiphoner* (1681). The present arrangement is from La Feillee's *Nouvelle Methode de plain-chant* (5th ed., Paris, 1782) as printed in *The English Hymnal* (1906). This is its first inclusion in *GS*.

Father, We Thank Thee   387

From *The Didache*, c. A.D. 110

Trans. F. Bland Tucker, 1895-1988

The ancient document entitled Διδαχὴ τῶν Δώδεκα Ἀποστόλων, or "The Teaching of the Twelve Apostles," is the earliest book of church order which has come to us outside of the New Testament itself. It is no later than the first half of the second century. Sections IX and X of this document contain an order for the taking of the Lord's Supper. The translation is that of J. Fitzgerald (New York, 1884):

> IX. And concerning the eucharist, thus give thanks First as to the cup: We give thee thanks, our Father, for the holy vine of David thy servant, which thou has made known to us through Jesus thy servant; to thee be glory forever. As to the broken bread: We give thee thanks, our Father, for the life and the knowledge which thou

thee thanks, our Father, for the life and the knowledge which thou hast made known to us through Jesus thy servant; to thee be glory forever. As this broken bread was scattered over the hills, and having been gathered became one, so may thy congregation be gathered from the ends of the earth into thy kingdom; for thine is glory and power forever through Jesus Christ. And let none eat or drink of your eucharist, save those baptized in the name of the Lord, for of this the Lord said, Give not what is holy to dogs.

X. And when you are filled give thanks thus: We give thee thanks, holy Father, for thy holy name which thou hast caused to dwell in our hearts, and for the knowledge, and faith and immortality which thou hast made known to us through Jesus thy servant; to thee be glory forever. Thou Almighty Master, didst make all things for thy name's sake; both food and drink thou hast given to men for enjoyment, that they might give thanks to thee; and on us thou hast bestowed spiritual food and drink and life everlasting, through thy servant. Above all we thank thee that thou art powerful; to thee be glory forever. Remember, Lord, thy congregation to deliver it from all evil and to make it perfect in thy love, and gather it from the four winds, sanctified, into thy kingdom which thou hast prepared for it; for thine is power and glory forever. May grace come and this world pass away. Hosanna to the son of David. If one is holy, let him come; if not, let him repent. Maranatha, Amen.

Tucker's translation is a selection from the sections given above. It was made in 1939 and first published in *The Hymnal, 1940*. This is its first inclusion in *GS*.

Eucharistic Hymn

John S. B. Hodges, 1830-1915

For information on this hymn tune, see "Bread of the World," *GSR* No. 373.

Father, Whate'er of Earthly Bliss   591

Anne Steele, 1716-1778

This poem was published in ten 4-line stanzas in Miss Steele's *Poems on Subjects Chiefly Devotional* (Vol. I, 1760). Stanza one began "When I survey life's varied scene / Amid the darkest hours." Our text consists of stanzas 8, 9, and 10, with a few alterations; 1:1 originally read "And oh, whate'er of earthly bliss / Thy sov'reign hand denies;" 3:2 read

"My path of life attend"; and 3:4, "And bless its happy end." This text entered *GS* in 1937.

Naomi

Hans G. Nägeli, 1768-1836
Arr. Lowell Mason, 1792-1872

This was one of the tunes which Mason brought back from Europe after his visit there in the early 1830s. He had gained a personal acquaintance with Nägeli while in Europe. The tune was first published with the preceding text in his *Occasional Psalm and Hymn Tunes* (1836). NAOMI derives from the Old Testament story of Ruth: she was wife of Elimelech and mother-in-law to Ruth. The tune entered *GS* in 1937.

Fight the Good Fight   442

John S. B. Monsell, 1811-1875

This text was first printed in Monsell's *Hymns of Love and Praise for the Church Year* (1863). It was written for the "Nineteenth Sunday after Trinity" in the Anglican *Book of Common Prayer,* with the motto "Fight the good fight of faith, lay hold of eternal life" (1 Tim. 6:12). In *GSR* Monsell's text is basically unchanged except that the current editors have modernized the pronouns and employed the reading in 4:4, "That Christ is all eternally," so that the phrase might be unified with 1:4. The text with the accompanying tune has been in *GS* since 1921.

Pentecost

William Boyd, 1847-1928

This tune was composed in 1864 at the request of Sabine Baring-Gould. It was first sung at a meeting of Yorkshire colliers on Whitsunday (i.e., Pentecost) 1864 and published in *Thirty-two Hymn Tunes* (Oxford, 1868). Originally it was the setting for the hymn "Come, Holy Ghost, our souls inspire." A few years later Arthur Sullivan, who was editing *Church Hymns* (1874), asked Boyd if he could use the tune. He was given permission, but later Boyd was chagrined to find that Sullivan had set it to "Fight the Good Fight." Boyd remarked later, however, that "judging from the favor with which the tune has been received, I feel that Sullivan was right in so mating the words and music."

Flee as a Bird   275
                                              Mary S. B. Dana, 1810-1883

This text, which is based in part on the language of Psalm 11:1, grew out of Mrs. Dana's many afflictions which commenced in early 1837. Having moved from South Carolina to New York following her marriage, she entered upon what should have been a happy life. That year her favorite sister died at her home in New York. In 1839, her brother died in Alabama. The summer of that year, having moved with her husband to Bloomington, Iowa, on the Mississippi River in an attempt to escape the congestive fevers which were ravaging the country, both her two-year-old son and her husband, Charles E. Dana, sickened and died. Following these calamities, she ultimately managed to return to her childhood home in Charleston, South Carolina. John S. Hart, in *Female Prose Writers of America* (1857), says of this time:

> To give herself mental occupation, she now began to indulge in literary pursuits. She had always been very fond of music, and finding very little piano music that was suitable for Sunday playing, she had for several years been in the habit of adapting sacred words to any song which particularly pleased her. To wean her from her sorrows, her parents encouraged her to continue the practice, and this was the origin of the first work she published, "The Southern Harp."

The hymn text was published in *The Southern Harp* (New York, 1842). It has been in *GS* since 1925.

In Domino Confido

                                                              Anonymous

In the 1925 edition of *GS* and in all following editions, this tune was simply marked "Spanish Air." No further information is available. The tune name IN DOMINO CONFIDO was given by the current general editor of *GSR*.

For All the Saints   450
                                              William W. How, 1823-1897

This text was first published in Earl Nelson's *Hymns for Saints' Days, and Other Hymns, by a Layman* (1864). It is one of the finest hymns on the triumph of faith ever written. The original text was in eleven 3-line stanzas with Alleluia. The *GSR* text includes stanzas 1, 2, 6, 8, 9, and 10. This text entered *GS* in 1925 in five stanzas (1, 2, 6, 9, and 10). In the

Supplement (1975) stanzas 1, 2, 6, 8, and 11 were included. The original opening line of stanza one read "For all thy saints."

Sine Nomine

Ralph Vaughan Williams, 1872-1958

This tune was written for the preceding text and was first published in *The English Hymnal* (Oxford, 1906). It first entered *GS* in the *Supplement* (1975). Previous editions of *GS* had set the text to TROYTE'S CHANT, No. 2. SINE NOMINE means "without a name."

For the Beauty of the Earth   94

Folliot S. Pierpoint, 1835-1917

This hymn, originally in eight stanzas, was published in Orby Shipley's *Lyra Eucharistica* (2nd ed., 1864). The text was written for use as a communion hymn, but it has been widely used as a song of thanksgiving and as a song for children. The *GSR* text, which has been in *GS* since 1937, contains stanzas 1, 3, 4, and 5. The original chorus read: "Christ, our God, to Thee we raise / This our sacrifice of praise." The omitted stanzas show Pierpoint's original intent in his poem as a communion hymn.

3
For the joy of ear and eye;
    For the heart and mind's delight;
For the mystic harmony
    Linking sense to sound and sight:
Christ our God, to thee we raise
    This our sacrifice of praise.

6
For thyself, best Gift divine!
    To our race so freely given;
For that great, great love of thine,
    Peace on earth, and joy in heaven:
Christ our God, to thee we raise
    This our sacrifice of praise.

7
For each perfect gift of thine
    To our race so freely given,
Graces and human and divine,
    Flowers of earth and buds of heaven:
Gracious God, to thee we raise
    This our sacrifice of praise.

8
For thy virgins' robes of snow,
  For thy maiden mother mild,
For thyself, our hearts aglow,
  Jesu, Victim undefiled:
Offer we at thine own shrine
  Thyself, sweet Sacrament Divine.

Dix

Conrad Kocher, 1786-1872

For information on this tune, see "All Things Praise Thee," *GSR*, No. 64.

Forth in Thy Name   501
Charles Wesley, 1707-1788

This text was first published in Wesley's *Hymns and Sacred Poems* (1749) in six stanzas. The original stanza three was omitted from John Wesley's *Collection of Hymns for the Use of the People Called Methodists* (1780). Our text contains stanzas 1, 2, 4, and 6. The omitted stanzas three and five read:

Preserve me from my calling's snare,
  And hide my simple heart above,
Above the thorns of choking care,
  The gilded taints of worldly love.

Give me to bear thy easy yoke,
  And every moment watch and pray;
And still to things eternal look,
  And hasten to thy glorious day.

This is the first inclusion of this hymn in *GS*.

Song   34
Orlando Gibbons, 1583-1625

Gibbon's tune first appeared in George Wither's *Hymnes and Songs of the Church* (1623). The present arrangement was made by the music editor of *GSR* (1986).

Free from the Law 313

Philip P. Bliss, 1838-1876

This fine gospel song contains as good a statement of the freedom from the Law and freedom under Grace as has ever been written outside of the New Testament. Bliss found the inspiration for this text in a bound volume of the English periodical *Things Old and New*, which his wife had given him as a Christmas present. It is based on the general teaching found in Romans 8 and Hebrews 10. The text was published originally in Bliss's *Sunshine for Sunday Schools* (Cincinnati, 1873) and in his *Gospel Songs* (Cincinnati, 1874). This is the first appearance of this text in *GS*.

Once for All

Philip P. Bliss, 1838-1876

This tune was written for and published with the preceding text in the composer's *Sunshine for Sunday Schools* (Cincinnati, 1873). This is its first inclusion in *GS*.

From All that Dwell Below the Skies 78

Isaac Watts, 1674-1748

This text is the second of three paraphrases of Psalm 117 in Watts's *Psalms of David, Imitated in the Language of the New Testament* (1719). This paraphrase is in long meter and the other two in common and short meter, respectively. *GSR* includes this poem for the first time in Watts's two original stanzas.

Lasst uns erfreuen

Geistliche Kirchengesang, 1623

For information on this tune, see "All Creatures of Our God and King," *GSR*, No. 66.

From All the Dark Places 424

Mary B. C. Slade, 1826-1882

Other than the fact that Mrs. Slade, the wife of a Methodist minister in Massachusetts, wrote the text, nothing is known of this poem. *GSR* text has changed the original chorus reading "The kingdom is coming" to "The kingdom is spreading," a standard alteration.

The Kingdom Is Coming

Rigdon M. McIntosh, 1836-1899

This tune with the preceding text was first published in McIntosh's *The School Festival* (1873). It may also be found in Atticus G. Haygood and McIntosh's *Prayer and Praise* (Macon, Georgia, 1883). This is the first inclusion of the text and tune in *GS*.

From Every Stormy Wind That Blows 561

Hugh Stowell, 1799-1865

This text in six stanzas was first published in the *Winter's Wreath, a Collection of Original Compositions in Prose and Verse*, an annual published in London (1828-32). The poem was rewritten in 1831 and published in Stowell's *Selection of Psalms and Hymns Suited to the Services of the Church of England* (1832). Various emendations have been made in the text over the years. The only change adopted in *GSR* from our previous editions is at 4:1—"Ah! there" is read in the place of "There, there"; a change first made in *The Methodist Hymnal* (1935). *GSR* text includes stanzas 1, 2, 3, and 5. The two omitted stanzas read:

4
Ah! whither could we flee for aid,
    When tempted, desolate, dismayed;
Or how the hosts of hell defeat,
    Had suffering saints no mercy seat?

6
Oh! may my hand forget her skill,
    My tongue be silent, stiff, and still;
My bounding heart forget to beat,
    If I forget the mercy seat.

From Heaven Above 199

Martin Luther, 1483-1546
Trans. *Lutheran Book of Worship*, 1978

This beautiful carol derives in part from an old garland song (a song for a singing game involving a riddle in which a young lady had to give her garland to a young man if she could not solve his riddle) popular in Germany in Luther's day. Marilyn Kay Stulken prints both the original German garland song with English translation and Luther's first German stanza in her *Hymnal Companion to the Lutheran Book of Worship* (1981,

p. 153). Luther wrote his text for his family's Christmas Eve celebration. It was published in Joseph Klug's *Geistliche Lieder* (Wittenberg, 1535) in fifteen stanzas and set to the tune "Ich komm aus fremden Landen her." The recent *Lutheran Book of Worship* prints a translation of fourteen of the original fifteen stanzas. My copy of *Kirchen-gesangbuch für Evangelisch Lutherische Gemeinden* (St. Louis, 1849) gives all fifteen stanzas. This is the first inclusion of this hymn in *GS*.

Vom Himmel hoch
From Valentin Schumann's *Geistliche Lieder*, 1539

In Klug's hymnal mentioned above, the poem was set to "Aus fremden Landen," but in 1539 in Schumann's hymnal it was set to the tune to which it has been sung ever since. Most scholars believe that Luther himself wrote the tune VOM HIMMEL HOCH. This is the first inclusion of the tune in *GSR*.

Gentle Mary Laid Her Child
196
Joseph S. Cook, 1859-1933

This text was written for a carol competition sponsored by the *Christian Guardian* (1919) and was published that year in its Christmas issue in Toronto, Canada. This is its first inclusion in *GS*.

Tempus adest floridum
From *Thodoricus Petrus, Piae Cantiones*, 1582
Harm. Ernest McMillan, 1893-1973

This tune is taken from Petrus's *Piae Cantiones,* a notable collection made in Nyland, Finland, in 1582. John Mason Neale used it for his legend of "Good King Wenceslas" (1853). McMillan's harmony was first published in *The Hymnary of the United Church of Canada* (1930, No. 57). In this hymnal the tune is said to be "A Spring Carol, c. 14th century." This is the first inclusion of this tune in *GS*.

Give Me the Bible
299
Priscilla J. Owens, 1829-1907

This text was first published in E. S. Lorenz's *Happy Voices for the Sunday School* (Dayton, Ohio: W. J. Shuey, 1883). It first entered *GS* in 1921. No other information is available.

Grammata

Edmund S. Lorenz, 1854-1942

This tune was first published in Lorenz's *Happy Voices for the Sunday School* (1883). The tune has been in *GS* since 1921. The tune name GRAMMATA ("writings") was given by the present general editor of *GSR*.

Give to the Winds Thy Fears   548

Paul Gerhardt, 1607-1676

Trans. John Wesley, 1703-1791

Gerhardt's poem, beginning "Befiehl du deine Wege," is one of the most consoling hymns ever written. It was first published in Crüger's *Praxis Pietatis Melica* (1653) as an acrostic on Luther's version of Psalm 37:5, "Befiehl dem Herrn deine Wege und hoffe auf ihn, er wird's wohl machen." Each stanza of Gerhardt's poem began with a succeeding word from Luther's text with the exception of stanza two, which used the two words "dem Herrn." The original twelve stanzas were translated by Wesley into sixteen 4-line stanzas in his *Hymns and Sacred Poems* (1739). Wesley omitted Gerhardt's stanzas 5, 9, 10, and 11. The present selection of Wesley's stanzas was first made in *The Methodist Hymnal* (1964) and represents stanzas 9, 10, 13, and 16. The pronouns have been modernized in *GSR*. The complete German text may be seen in *Kirken Gesang-buch für Evangelisch Lutherische Gemeinden* (St. Louis, 1849) and the complete Wesley translation, omitting stanza 8, in *The Methodist Hymn-Book* (London, 1933). This is the first inclusion of the of the text in *GS*.

St. Bride

Samuel Howard, c. 1710-1782

This tune first appeared in William Riley's *Parochial Psalmody* (1762) as a setting for Tate and Brady's *New Version* rendering of Psalm 130. It was there called ST. BRIDGET'S TUNE. The present tune name is for St. Bride Church (a contraction of Bridget) in Fleet Street, London. Howard was organist there. The church building was destroyed in an air raid December 29, 1940. This is its first inclusion in *GS*.

Glorious Things of Thee Are Spoken   447

John Newton, 1725-1807

This text is based on Psalm 87:3, "Glorious things are spoken of thee, O city of God." It was first published in the *Olney Hymns* (Bk. I,

1779) in five 8-line stanzas. The *GSR* text contains stanzas 1, 2, and 5. The two omitted stanzas read:

3
Round each habitation hovering,
See the cloud and fire appear!
For a glory and a covering,
Showing that the Lord is near:
Thus deriving from their banner
Light by night, and shade by day;
Safe they feed upon the manna,
Which he gives them when they pray.

4
Blest inhabitants of Zion,
Wash'd in the Redeemer's blood!
Jesus, whom their souls rely on,
Makes them kings and priests to God:
'Tis his love his people raises
Over self to reign as kings,
And as priests, his solemn praises
Each for a thank-off'ring brings.

This text, with the tune which follows, has been in *GS* since 1925.

Austrian Hymn

Franz Joseph Haydn, 1732-1809

After his visit to England in 1794, Haydn, who had heard Britain's national anthem, desired to write one for Austria. The emperor's birthday on February 12, 1797, gave him occasion to do so. He used Lorenz Hauschka's national anthem "Gott erhalte Franz den Kaiser" as the setting and apparently based his tune on a Croatian folk song, "Vjatvo rano se ja vstanem." The tune was first used for a hymn in England in Edward Miller's *Sacred Music* (London, 1802).

Glory Be to the Father 76

Anonymous, 4th century

This poem, given as used in the ancient English church, is based on the Latin text of the *Lesser Doxology*: "Gloria Patri et Filio et Spiritus Sancto." The *Gloria Patri* is from an ancient Greek text which goes as far back as Clement of Rome, who lived in the late first and early second centuries. The earliest Greek form seems to have been Δόξα πάτρι ἐν υἱῶ καὶ διὰ πνεύματος, i.e., "Glory to the Father in the Son and through the Holy Spirit." After the Arian controversy during the third and fourth centuries, the prepositions were omitted and the text became Δόξα Πάτρι καὶ Υἱῶ καὶ ἁγίω Πνεύματος καὶ νῦν καὶ εἰς τοὺς αἰώνας των αἰώνων; and this is still the reading in the Greek Church. Upon this Greek text the Latin Gloria Patri is based: *Gloria Patri et Filio et Spiritui Sancto":* *Sicut erat in principio, et nunc, et semper, et in saecula saeculorum. Amen.* The present English text is a translation, but not a literal one, of the Latin. This text entered *GS* in 1937.

Gloria Patri (Meineke)
Charles Christoph Meineke, 1782-1850

The music is from the "Evening Prayer" in his *Music for the Church ...Composed for St. Paul's Church, Baltimore* (1844). Meineke was organist there, serving until his death in 1850. This is the first appearance of this tune in *GS*.

Go to Dark Gethsemane   218
James Montgomery, 1771-1854

Montgomery published two versions of this text. The first, entitled "The Last sufferings of Christ," was published in Thomas Cotterill's *A Selection of Psalms and Hymns for Public and Private Use* (9th ed., London, 1820). The second, entitled "Christ our example in suffering," appeared in Montgomery's *Christian Psalmist* (1825). *GSR* employs the 1825 text except in 3:5, where "Hear their" (1825) is discarded in place of "Hear Him" (1820). The original texts contained a fourth stanza:

> Early hasten to the tomb,
> > Where they laid his breathless clay;
> All is solitude and gloom,
> > —Who hath taken him away?
> Christ is risen:—He meets our eyes;
> > Savior, teach us so to rise.

This stanza is omitted by nearly all modern hymnals. The text is included in *GSR* for the first time.

Arfon
Traditional Welsh Melody

This tune is either of Welsh or of French origin. Most editors call it a Welsh tune. It was published in G. Legeay's *Noels Anciens* (1875) and in John Roberts's *Caniadau y Cyssegr* (1878). This is the first inclusion of the tune in *GS*.

God Be with You Till We Meet Again   14
Jeremiah E. Rankin, 1828-1904

Rankin said that this text was written as a Christian good-by and was sung first in a Sunday evening gospel meeting at the First Congregational Church, Washington, D.C. After writing the poem, Rankin sent it to two friends for possible tunes. He chose the tune by Tomer, a teacher in the New Jersey public schools, and the music was revised by Rankin's organist, Dr. J. W. Bischoff. The hymn was first published in Bischoff, Otis F. Presbrey, and Rankin's *Gospel Bells* (1880). This text entered *GS* in 1921 with words only. The version with music and refrain entered *GS* in 1937. *GSR* omits the familiar but rather difficult refrain, thus returning to our earlier tradition.

God Be with You

William G. Tomer, 1833-1896

See the text above for the circumstances of the writing of this tune. The music was first published in *Gospel Bells* (1880). It entered *GS* in 1937.

God Calling Yet! Shall I Not Hear   316
Gerhardt Tersteegen, 1697-1769
Trans. Sarah Borthwick Findlater, 1823-1907

The original German text, beginning "Gott rufet noch; sollt ich nicht endlich hören," was published in Tersteegen's *Geistliches Blumengärtlein inniger Seeler* (2d ed., 1735). It was originally in eight 4-line stanzas. The translation was apparently made by Sarah Borthwick Findlater and published in *Hymns from the Land of Luther* (Second series, 1855), to which volume both she and her sister Jane Borthwick contributed. Jane told John Julian, the hymnologist, that Sarah translated this poem. The present arrangement of the text was made by Edward A. Park in *The Sabbath Hymn Book* (Andover, 1858). He shortened the text to five stanzas and placed it in Long Meter. This is the first inclusion of this poem in *GS*.

Federal Street

Henry K. Oliver, 1800-1885

Oliver, affected emotionally by his reading of Theodore Hook's novel *Passion and Principle*, recalled the line from Anne Steele's poem on a child's death which said, "So fades the lovely blooming flower," and was prompted to write this tune. It was written in 1831 and published in Lowell Mason's *Boston Academy Collection of Church Music* (1836). This is the first inclusion of the tune in *GS*.

God Himself Is with Us   7

Gerhardt Tersteegen, 1697-1769

Trans. Composite

The original German poem beginning "Gott ist gegenwärtig" was published under the title "Remembrance of the glorious and delightful presence of God" in Tersteegen's *Geistliches Blumengärtlein* (1729). The translation of stanza one is by Frederick W. Foster and John Miller, as prepared for the *Moravian Hymn Book* (1789) and altered in William Mercer's *The Church Psalter and Hymn Book* (1855). *GSR* stanza two is taken with slight alterations from *The Lutheran Hymnal* (1941). The two stanzas represent translations of Tersteegen's original first and third stanzas. The hymn first entered *GS* in the *Supplement* (1975).

Arnsberg

Joachim Neander, 1650-1680

This tune is also called WUNDERBARER KÖNIG, from the hymn by Neander to which it was first set. It was published in his *Alpha und Omega. Joachimi Neandri Glaub-und Liebesübung* (1680). This tune first entered *GS* in the *Supplement* (1975).

God Is Calling the Prodigal   322

Charles H. Gabriel, 1856-1932

Arr. Jack A. Boyd, b. 1932

The original text of this gospel song was published by Gabriel in 1889. It entered *GS* in 1921. The words were arranged and set to the tune which follows by the music editor of *GSR* especially for this edition (1986).

Orr

Jack A. Boyd, b. 1932

This tune was written for the preceding arranged text and first published in *GSR* (1986). The tune name ORR is from the maiden name of the composer's wife Joanne.

God Is Love; His Mercy Brightens 119
John Bowring, 1792-1872

One of the most popular of Bowring's poems, this text was published in his *Hymns* (1825) in five stanzas, stanza five being stanza one repeated. The *GSR* text is Bowring's original poem, except that in 3:2 "gloom" is substituted for the original "mist," a change first made by Godfrey Thring in his *Collection* (1880). This text entered *GS* in 1937.

Stuttgart
From *Psalmodia Sacra*, 1715

The original of this tune was printed in A. C. Ludwig and C. F. Witt's *Psalmodia Sacra* (1715). It was set to the poem by Christoph Titius, "Sollt es gleich bisweilen scheinen." Witt is thought to have been the composer. Henry J. Gauntlett adapted the tune for the first edition of *Hymns Ancient and Modern* (1861). The tune entered *GS* in 1937.

God Is the Fountain Whence 129
Benjamin Beddome, 1717-1795

This text, originally beginning "Love is the fountain whence," was published posthumously in *Hymns adapted to Public Worship or Family Devotion, now first published from the Manuscripts of the late Rev. B. Beddome, M.A.* This work contained 830 poems and was edited with an introduction by Robert Hall (1817). The poem entered *GS* in 1921.

Gerar
Lowell Mason, 1792-1872

In the sources available to me, this tune is always attributed to Lowell Mason and is dated 1839. Mason often gave the tunes he composed or adapted Old Testament names. "Gerar" is mentioned in Genesis 10:19. The tune entered *GS* in 1921.

God Moves in a Mysterious Way   139
William Cowper, 1731-1800

Cowper first published this hymn text in *Twenty-six Letters on Religious Subjects, to which are added Hymns, by Omicron* (1774). "Omicron" was Cowper's friend John Newton. It was reprinted in July 1774 in the *Gospel Magazine* and in the *Olney Hymns* (1779). The hymn originally bore the title "Light shining out of darkness." It entered *GS* for the first time in 1925.

Dundee

Scottish Psalter, 1615

This tune was first published in Andro Hart's *One Hundred Fifty Psalms of David* (Edinburgh, 1615). It was there called "French Tune" and was one of twelve "common" tunes, that is, tunes that could be used with many texts which were included in the hymnal. Thomas Ravenscroft first called the tune DUNDEE (or DUNDY) in his *Whole Book of Psalms* (London, 1621). This tune entered *GS* in 1921, set to the Quaker poet Bernard Barton's "Lamp of Our Feet" (No. 172). It was there attributed to "Guillaume Franc."

God of Grace and God of Glory   581
Harry Emerson Fosdick, 1878-1969

This text was written in the summer of 1930 at the author's summer home in Boothbay Harbor, Maine. He wrote it for the opening of the Riverside Church in New York City, October 5, 1930, and desired that it be sung to one of his favorite tunes, REGENT SQUARE. It was also sung at the dedication of the church on February 8, 1931. Set to REGENT SQUARE, it was first published in the hymnal *Praise and Service* (1932), edited by H. Augustine Smith. This hymn entered *GS* in the *Supplement* (1975).

Cwm Rhondda

John Hughes, 1873-1932

This tune was written in 1907 for the annual Baptist Cymanfau Ganu (singing festival) at Capel Rhondda, Pontypridd, Wales. It was written on Sunday morning at a Welsh country church (Salem Chapel). The tune was arranged by E. Edwin Young in *The Voice of Thanksgiving, No. 4* (1927), but the circumstances surrounding this copyright are unknown. In England, the tune first appeared in *Fellowship Hymn-Book* (1933) and in

The Methodist Hymn-Book (1933). The copyright is now controlled by Mrs. Dilys S. Webb of Glamorganshire, England. The first joining of this tune with the preceding text was in *The Methodist Hymnal* (1935), edited by Robert G. McCutchan. Fosdick always objected to this, preferring REGENT SQUARE, as in the beginning. The tune first entered *GS* in the *Supplement* (1975).

God of Our Fathers   566
Daniel C. Roberts, 1841-1907

This text was originally written for a Fourth of July celebration in Brandon, Vermont, in 1876. The hymn was later published in various papers and was selected as the official hymn for the centennial celebration of the adoption of the Constitution. Its first inclusion in a hymnal was in the *Hymnal*_(1892) of the Protestant Episcopal Church, set to the tune RUSSIAN HYMN. (See *GSR*, No. 586.) It entered *GS* in 1937.

National Hymn

George W. Warren, 1828-1902

This tune was composed for the preceding text and was used at the Columbia celebration of St. Thomas's Church in Brandon, Vermont, October 8, 1892. The text and tune appeared together in J. I. Tucker and W. W. Rousseau's music edition of the Protestant Episcopal *Hymnal* (1894). The tune entered *Great Songs, No. 2* in 1937.

God of Our Life, Through All the Circling Years   114
Hugh T. Kerr, 1872-1950

This text was written for the fiftieth anniversary of the Shadyside Presbyterian Church, Pittsburgh, Pennsylvania, in 1916. Kerr was the minister for this congregation at the time. *GSR* includes this hymn for the first time.

Sandon

Charles H. Purday, 1799-1885

This tune was first published in Purday's *Church and Home Metrical Psalter and Hymnal* (1860). It was set to the words of Newman's hymn "Lead, Kindly Light." The tune was originally called LANDON, and the present name may have come about as a typographical error.

God of the Earth, the Sky, the Sea   97
Samuel Longfellow, 1819-1892

This hymn was first published in Samuel Longfellow and Samuel Johnson's *Hymns of the Spirit* (1864), in five stanzas. *GSR* text includes stanzas 1, 3, 4, and 5. This is its first inclusion in *GS*.

Herr Jesu Christ, Mein's Lebens Licht
From *As Hymnodus Sacer*, 1625

This tune was originally a folksong melody for the German text beginning "Ich fahr dahin" in the *Lochamer Liederbuch*, a manuscript collection dating from between 1455 and 1460. It was also published in 1602 in a manuscript in Königsburg, Prussia. The tune name derives from its being published in *As Hymnodus Sacer* (Leipzig, 1625) with Martin Behm's text "Herr Jesu Christ, mein's Lebens Licht." This is its first inclusion in *GS*.

God Sent His Son   653
Gloria Gaither, b. 1942
William J. Gaither, b. 1936

The Gaithers wrote this text against the background of the prolific and intensifyingly sinful world of the twentieth century. It was written just after the birth of their third child. The assurance of the risen Jesus which provided a refreshing contrast to the general world situation gave the inspiration for this hymn as they held their infant son in their arms. It was written and published in 1971. This is its first inclusion in *GS*.

Resurrection
William J. Gaither, b. 1936

This tune was written for the preceding text in 1971. It was first called RESURRECTION in the *Baptist Hymnal* (1975), edited by William J. Reynolds. This is its first inclusion in *GS*.

God the Almighty One   586
Henry F. Chorley, 1808-1872
John Ellerton, 1826-1893

The text of this hymn is composite. Chorley's original hymn was written for Lvov's tune and was published in four stanzas in John Hullah's *Part Music* (1844). This text may be seen in the current edition of *Hymns*

Ancient and Modern (No. 491, 1950). During the Franco-Prussian War, Ellerton wrote a hymn in imitation of Chorley's poem beginning "God the almighty, in wisdom ordaining" (1870). A combined version of the poems appeared in *Church Hymns* (1871), and since that time the various hymnals have given combined versions with textual alterations. In the *GSR* text, stanzas 1 and 2 basically belong to Chorley and stanza 3 to Ellerton. It was first included in *GS* in the *Supplement* (1975).

Russian Hymn

Alexis F. Lvov, 1799-1870

This tune was composed in 1833 when Czar Nicholas I commanded a new Russian national anthem to replace the one in former use, which was "God Save the King" with Russian words set to the tune AMERICA. It first appeared with the preceding text in John Hullah's *Part Music* (1844). This tune entered *GS* in the *Supplement* (1975).

Good Christian Men, Rejoice   206
Medieval Latin Carol, 14th Century
Trans. John Mason Neale, 1818-1866

This macaronic carol (i.e., a poem having alternating Latin and vernacular, in this case German, lines) was first mentioned in the fourteenth century by a writer who attributes the text to the mystic Heinrich Suso (d. 1366), who supposedly heard it sung to him by angels. The earliest existing manuscript of the hymn is dated 1400. It was published in Joseph Klug's *Geistliche Lieder* (2nd ed., 1533). The original poem began thus:

> In dulce jubilo
> Singet und sit vro.
> Aller unser wonne
> Layt in presepio
> Sy leuchtet vor dy sonne
> Matris in gremio
> Qui alpha est et O.
> *Qui alpha est et O.*

Neale's translation was first published in his *Carols for Christmastide* (1853). This is the first inclusion of this text in *GS*.

In dulci jubilo

Traditional German Carol, 14th Century

This tune with the text above is first found in the *Leipzig MS* dated

1400. It was printed in the Klug hymnal, *Geistliche Lieder* (2nd ed., 1533). This is its first inclusion in *GS*.

Gracious Spirit, Dwell with Me   297
Thomas Toke Lynch, 1818-1871

This text was published in Lynch's *The Rivulet: Hymns for Heart and Voice* (1855). Because of the personal nature of many of his poems, this volume caused a furor among the Congregationalists among whom he ministered. This is its first inclusion in *GS*.

Redhead, No.   76
Richard Redhead, 1820-1901

This tune was first published in Redhead's *Ancient Hymn Melodies and Other Church Tunes* (1853), where it was called LXXVI. It is now named for its composer. The tune has also been called PETRA. This is its first inclusion in *GS*.

Great God, We Sing That Mighty Hand   141
Philip Doddridge, 1702-1751

This text first appeared in Job Orton's edition of Doddridge's hymns, published posthumously as *Hymns Founded on Various Texts in the Holy Scriptures* (1755). It is based on Acts 26:22 and was first sung, just after it was written, by Doddridge's congregation. This is its first inclusion in *GS*.

Wareham

William Knapp, 1698-1768

This tune was first published in Knapp's *Sett of New Psalm Tunes and Anthems* (London, 1738). It was named by the composer for his birthplace in Dorsetshire, England. Also called ALL SAINTS and BLANDFORD TUNE, the melody, with but one exception, moves in steps up and down the scale. WAREHAM first entered *GS* in the *Supplement* (1922).

Great Is Thy Faithfulness   147
Thomas O. Chisholm, 1866-1960

This text was written in 1923 and was one of a number of poems which Chisholm sent to William M. Runyan. It has become a very popular gospel song and was first published in Runyan's *Songs of Salvation* (Chicago, 1923). This is its first inclusion in *GS*.

Faithfulness
Willam M. Runyan, 1870-1957

This tune was written for the preceding text in Baldwin, Kansas, in 1923. Runyan, devoted coworker of T. O. Chisholm's, said that he prayed that his tune would be worthy to carry the message of the poem. Runyan first named the tune for inclusion in the *Baptist Hymnal* (1956). This is its first inclusion in *GS*.

Guide Me, O Thou Great Jehovah   587
William Williams, 1717-1791
Trans. Peter Williams, 1722-1796 (St. 1)
Trans. William Williams (?) (Stanzas 2,3)

This hymn was written in Welsh, beginning "Arglwydd arwain trwy'r anialwch," and was entitled "Nerth i fyned trwy'r Anialwch" (Strength to pass through the Wilderness). Originally in five 6-line stanzas, it was published in Williams's *Alleluia* (1745). The entire original poem and all succeeding translations may be found in Julian (p. 77, 78). William Williams's brother Peter translated the original stanzas 1, 3, and 5 into English in his *Hymns on Various Subjects* (1771). This translation contained our now familiar first stanza. In 1772, either William or his son John made a translation of stanzas 3 and 4 into English, retained Peter's translation of stanza 1, and then added another stanza to the make the present poem. This version was first printed in a leaflet and then included in the Countess of Huntingdon's collection of hymns (c. 1772). The added fourth stanza is now usually omitted from modern hymnals:

> Musing on my habitation,
>> Musing on my heavenly home,
> Fills my soul with holy longings:
>> Come, my Jesus, quickly come;
> Vanity is all I see;
>> Lord, I long to be with Thee!

The only further revision, made by an unknown hand in the late eighteenth century, is found in 3:3, where "Bear me through the swelling current" replaces the original "Death of deaths, and hell's destruction." This text has been in *GS* since 1921.

Cwm Rhondda

John Hughes, 1873-1932

All previous editions of *GS* have used the tune ZION as the setting for Williams's poem. The editorial committee for *GSR* decided that CWM RHONDDA was a much stronger tune for congregational use. For information on this tune, see "God of Grace and God of Glory," *GSR*, No. 581. The tune first entered *GS* in the *Supplement* (1975).

Hail, Gladdening Light   32

Greek Evening Hymn, 3d Century

This anonymous text, beginning φῶς ἱλαρὸν ἁγίας δόξης, is at least as old as the third century. It was quoted by Basil, bishop of Caesarea (c. 330-379). The Greek text was first printed in Archbishop Ussher's *De Symbolis* (1647) and may be found in Daniel, in Julian, and in J. H. Newman's *Lyra Apostolica*. The translation by Keble first appeared in the *British Magazine* (1834) and in *Lyra Apostolica* (1836). It was first included in *GS* in the *Supplement* (1975).

Sarum

Joseph Barnby, 1838-1896

SARUM was written in 1869 and included in *The Sarum Hymnal* (London, 1869), whence its name. "Sarum" is the old name for Salisbury in southern England, once one of the most important religious centers of that nation. The tune entered *GS* in the *Supplement* (1975).

Hail Morning Known Among the Blest   21

Ralph Wardlaw, 1779-1853

This text was first published in Wardlaw's *Selection of Hymns* (1803) as a hymn for "Sunday morning." Although the poem is somewhat prosaic, it has had a popularity, especially among British brethren. It first entered *GS* in the *Supplement* (1922).

Canonbury

Robert Schumann, 1810-1856
Arr. J. Ireland Tucker, 1819-1895

This tune is an adaptation of Schumann's "Nachtstücke" (i.e., night pieces), Op. 23, No. 4 (1839). It was first published as a hymn tune in J. Ireland Tucker's *Hymnal with Tunes, Old and New* (1872, No. 522). In

Tucker's collection it was used with the text "My hope, my all, my Savior Thou!" This is its first appearance in *GSR*.

Hail the Day That Sees Him Rise 236
Charles Wesley, 1707-1788

This text was first published in Wesley's *Hymns and Sacred Poems* (1739), in ten 4-line stanzas. It was entitled "Hymn for Ascension Day." This has been one of Charles Wesley's most popular texts, but it has undergone modifications over the years, mostly for the better. The *GSR* text is principally that which appeared in Cotterill's *Selection* (9th ed., 1820). The reader will find the most important emendations in Julian (p. 478). The complete text appears in the *Supplement* to the *Collection of Hymns for the Use of the People Called Methodists* (1830, No. 630). *GSR* text, which includes this hymn for the first time, contains stanzas 1, 2, 5, and a sort of merging of stanzas 8, and 10.

Llanfair
Robert Williams, c. 1781-1821
Harm. John Roberts, 1822-1877

This tune was taken from Williams's manuscript notebook and bears the date of July 14, 1817. It was there called BETHEL. Harmonized by Roberts, it was first published in Joseph Parry's *Peroriaeth Hyfryd* (1837). The tune name LLANFAIR is an abbreviated form of Llanfiarynghornwy, the area from which Williams came in Anglesey, Wales. This is its first inclusion in *GS*.

Hail to the Brightness 425
Thomas Hastings, 1784-1872

Hastings wrote this text in 1830, and it was first published in his and Lowell Mason's *Spiritual Songs for Social Worship* (1832). It has been in *GS* since 1921.

Wesley
Lowell Mason, 1792-1872

This tune was written, apparently for the preceding text, in 1830, according to Henry L. Mason, and appeared in Hastings and Mason's *Spiritual Songs for Social Worship* (1832). It first entered *GS* in 1921.

Hallelujah, Praise Jehovah   50

From Sabbath School Psalmist, 1866

The words of this hymn are based on Psalm 148, but the author is unknown. It appeared in the *Sabbath School Psalmist, Prepared expressly for use in the Families, Sabbath-Schools and Congregations of the United Presbyterian Church* (Philadelphia: James M. Ferguson, 1866). The text was also published in *The Psalter* of the United Presbyterian Church (1887), set to Lowell Mason's tune HARWELL (1840) in eight 4-line stanzas. *GSR* employs stanzas 1-6 and uses stanza 7 as the refrain. The omitted eighth stanza reads:

> He his people's pow'r exalteth
>> All his saints to praise accord;
> Jacob's seed, a people near him:
>> Hallelujah. Praise the Lord.

The text has been in *GS* since 1921.

Ainos

William J. Kirkpatrick, 1831-1921

This tune was written and published by Kirkpatrick about 1893. The tune name AINOS ("praise" in Greek) was assigned by the present general editor of *GSR*. The tune was called KIRKPATRICK in the *Psalter Hymnal of the Christian Reformed Church* (1934, No. 321). It entered *GS* in 1921.

Happy the Home When God Is There   438

Henry Ware, Jr., 1794-1843
Alt. Bryan Jeffery Leech. b. 1931

The original text of this poem was first published in Mrs. Herbert Mayo's Selection of Hymns and Poetry for the Use of Infant and Juvenile Schools and *Families* (3rd ed., 1846). Ware's text may be seen in *The Methodist Hymnal* (1964, No. 516). The *GSR* text is the revision by Leech, which was published in Fred Bock's *Hymns for the Family of God* (Nashville, 1976). This is its first inclusion in *GS*.

St. Agnes

John B. Dykes, 1823-1876

This tune was published to be used with the text "Jesus, the Very Thought of Thee" (*GSR*, No. 265), in John Grey's *A Hymnal for Use in the*

English Church (London, 1866). Agnes, for whom the tune was named, was a Christian girl who was martyred on January 21, 304, at the age of 13, for refusing to marry a young pagan nobleman. The tune has been in *GS* since 1921.

Hark! The Gentle Voice 320
Mary B. C. Slade, 1826-1882

The text was first published in R. M. McIntosh's *Good News* (Boston: Oliver Ditson and Co., 1876). Under the title "Come Unto Me," the text also appeared in Atticus G. Haybood and McIntosh's *Prayer and Praise* (Macon, Georgia: 1883, No. 222). It was first published in hymnals of the Stone-Campbell movement in E. G. Sewell and McIntosh's *Christian Hymns* (Nashville, 1889, No.18), by permission R. M. McIntosh" who owned the copyright. This text has been in *GS* since 1921.

Everett
Asa Brooks Everett, 1828-1875

No information is available on this tune.

Hark! The Herald Angels Sing 203
Charles Wesley, 1707-1788

This text in ten 4-line stanzas was published in Wesley's *Hymns and Sacred Poems* (1739). The first stanza originally began:
> Hark how all the welkin rings,
> Glory to the King of kings.

This was altered to its present form in George Whitefield's *Collection of Hymns for Social Worship* (1753). Later alterations were made by Martin Madan in *A Collection of Psalms and Hymns* (1760). In Tate and Brady's *New Version of the Psalms of David* (ed. 1782), the text was printed with all of Whitefield and Madan's alterations. The stanzas were doubled and the opening lines of stanza one were used as a refrain. This is the text now included in *GSR*. This hymn has been in *GS* since 1921.

Mendelssohn
Felix Mendelssohn, 1809-1847
Arr. William H. Cummings, 1831-1915

This tune is adapted from the second movement of Mendelssohn's *Feste-gesang*, Op. 68, No. 7, a section written in celebration of the art of printing and in praise of Gutenberg. Cummings made his arrangement in 1855, and it was published in R. R. Chope's *Congregational Hymn and Tune Book* (1857). This tune has been in *GS* since 1921.

Hark! The Voice of Jesus Calling   416
Daniel March, 1816-1909

This popular missionary hymn text was written on an impulse to follow a sermon which March was to preach to the Philadelphia Christian Association in the Clinton Street Church of that city. His text was Isaiah 6:8, "Here am I, send me." This event occurred on October 18, 1868. The text was originally in four 8-line stanzas. *GSR* includes 1:1-4; 4:1-4, with lines 3 and 4 first; 3:1-4; 4:5-8, with some alterations. The omitted portions of the poem read as follows:

1:5-8
Loud and long the Master calleth
    Rich reward he offers free;
Who will answer, gladly saying,
    "Here am I, send me, send me"?

2:1-8
If you cannot cross the ocean,
    And the heathen lands explore,
You can find the heathen nearer,
    You can help them at your door:
If you cannot give your thousands,
    You can give the widow's mite;
And the least you give for Jesus
    Will be precious in his sight.

3:5-8
If you cannot rouse the wicked
    With the judgment's dread alarms,
You can lead the little children
    To the Saviour's waiting arms.

This text has been in *GS* since 1921.

Unser leben gleicht der Reise
Swiss Melody, 1812

The tune used for the preceding text in all previous editions of *GS*, beginning in 1921, was entitled MARTHA and was written by Elmer Leon

Jorgenson. It was named for his little daughter, Martha Jane, who died in 1926. Since it had fallen into disuse generally among our churches, it was felt best to use a different tune. The editorial committee chose the UNSER LEBEN tune as best. No information is available on this tune other than that given in the heading.

Have Faith in God, My Heart 499
Bryn Austin Rees, b. 1911

This poem was submitted in manuscript form to the editors of *Congregational Praise* (1951) and was published in that hymnal. This is its first inclusion in *GS*.

Franconia
From Johann B. König's *Harmonischer Liederschatz*, 1738
Arr. William Havergal, 1793-1870

This tune first appeared in König's collection, but the composer is unknown. Havergal adapted the original tune with several alterations in his *Old Church Psalmody* (1847). It was then published in *Hymns Ancient and Modern* (1861). It entered *GS* in the *Supplement* (1922).

Have Thine Own Way 597
Adelaide A. Pollard, 1862-1934

This hymn poem was written in 1902, during a time of great personal distress which grew out of her unsuccessful effort to raise funds for a missionary trip to Africa. It was at a prayer meeting that she found peace and completely submitted herself to God's will, after which she penned this hymn. The text was first published in George C. Stebbin's *Northfield Hymnal with Alexander's Supplement* (1907). This text entered *GS* in 1921.

Adelaide
George C. Stebbins, 1846-1945

This tune was written for Pollard's text and published in the hymnal mentioned above. It has been in *GS* since 1921.

Have You Been to Jesus 330
Elisha A. Hoffman, 1839-1929

Hoffman published this text in his and J. H. Tenney's *Spiritual*

Songs for Gospel Meetings and the Sunday School (Cleveland, 1878). In 1881 it was published in Sankey's *Sacred Songs and Solos*. The poem has become one of the most popular gospel song texts ever written and is universally known. Vachel Lindsey, the American poet, used a variant of part of the text in his "General William Booth Enters Heaven." It has been in *GS* since 1925.

Washed in the Blood

Elisha A. Hoffman, 1839-1929

This tune was written for the preceding text and published in Hoffman and Tenney's *Spiritual Songs for Gospel Meetings and the Sunday School* (Cleveland, 1878). It has been in *GS* since 1925.

He Leadeth Me   133

Joseph H. Gilmore, 1834-1918

This hymn was written on March 26, 1862, during the Civil War and shortly after Gilmore's graduation from Brown University. At the time, he was a visiting preacher for the First Baptist Church in Philadelphia. The day he wrote the text, he had preached on Psalm 23, and the words "He leadeth me" took special hold on him. While in conversation with Deacon Wattson of the church, he penciled the text just as we have it on the back of his sermon notes. A few months later his wife sent his poem to the Baptist *Watchman and Reflector*, where it was first printed. It entered *GS* in 1921.

He Leadeth Me

William B. Bradbury, 1816-1868

Bradbury saw the poem as printed in the *Watchman and Reflector* and set it to music in 1864. It was printed that year in his *Golden Censor* (New York, 1864). The text as published by Bradbury was identical with Gilmore's, except that Bradbury altered and slightly added to the chorus, including the phrase "His faithful follower I would be." Gilmore did not know the poem had been set to music until the following year. This tune has been in *GS* since 1921.

Hear the Sweet Voice of Jesus Say   319

Charles H. Gabriel, 1856-1932

This text was written by Gabriel in 1890. It was first published in J. H. Kurzenknabe and W. W. Bentley's *Fair as the Morning, Hymns and Tunes for Praise in the Sunday School* (Harrisburg, Pa.: J. H. Kurzenknabe and Sons, 1891). It has been in *GS* since 1921.

Only a Step

Charles H. Gabriel, 1856-1932

This tune was written for the foregoing text in 1890 and published in the hymnal mentioned above in 1891. It first entered *GS* in 1921.

Heavenly Father, God Over All Things 593

Ukranian Folk Hymn
Tr. Stephen Bilak, b. 1926
Versed Jack A. Boyd, b. 1932

The origin of the Ukranian poem is unknown. The translation and versing were done in 1973. This is the first publication of this text and tune in *GS*.

Bilak

Ukranian Folk Tune
Arr. Jack A. Boyd, b. 1932

Nothing is known of the origin of this tune. The arrangement was made for *GSR* in 1986. The *GSR* hymnal committee named it for the translator.

Here at Thy Table, Lord 376

May P. Hoyt

Little information is available on this hymn text. It may be found in Edward A. Bedell's *The Church Hymnary* (New York, 1891). This is its first inclusion in *GS*. May Pierpont Hoyt's identity is unknown.

Bread of Life

William F. Sherwin, 1826-1888

For information on this tune, see "Break Thou the Bread of Life" (*GSR*, No. 312).

Here Before Thee, Savior 377

Frank C. Huston, 1871-1959

This hymn text was written in 1896 while Huston was living in Indianapolis, Indiana, and preaching for the Christian Church there. It was later owned by the Standard Publishing Company. The text and tune have been in *GS* since 1937.

Huston

Frank C. Huston, 1871-1959

This tune was written for the preceding text. The tune name HUSTON was given by the present general editor of *GSR*. It has been in *GS* since 1937.

Here, O My Lord, I See Thee   381

Horatius Bonar, 1808-1889

The poet's brother, John J. Bonar, asked him to supply a hymn to be used after the communion service, and which would be printed in leaflet form for distribution among the members of the congregation of St. Andrews Free Church, Greenock, Scotland. This was done on the first Sunday in October 1855. The hymn was first published in slightly revised form in Bonar's *Hymns of Faith and Hope* (1857). The text was originally in ten stanzas. *GSR* includes stanzas 1, 2, and 10. Some of the omitted stanzas read:

> This is the hour of banquet and of song;
>> This is the heavenly table spread for me;
> Here let me feast, and feasting, still prolong
>> The brief, bright hour of fellowship with Thee.

> Too soon we rise: the symbols disappear;
>> The feast, though not the love, is past and gone;
> The bread and wine remove: but Thou art here,
>> Nearer than ever,—still my shield and sun.

> I have no help but Thine; nor do I need
>> Another arm save Thine to lean upon;
> It is enough, my Lord, enough indeed;
>> My strength is in Thy might, Thy might alone.

> I have no wisdom save in Him who is
>> My wisdom and my teacher both in one;
> No wisdom can I lack while Thou art wise,
>> No teaching do I crave save Thine alone.

> Mine is the sin, but Thine the righteousness;
>> Mine is the guilt, but Thine the cleansing blood;

Here is my robe, my refuge, and my peace—
Thy blood, Thy righteousness, O Lord, my God.

Reynolds
Arr. from Felix Mendelssohn, 1809-1847

This tune derives from Mendelssohn's "Adagio non troppo," from his *Songs Without Words* (Op. 30, No. 3, Bk. II). Various revisers and adapters have had a hand in bringing the arrangement to its present form. A setting of part of the melody appeared in W. Mercer's *The Church Psalter and Hymn Book* (1864) with harmony by John Goss. Adolphus Levy seems to have brought the arrangement to its present form in Charles S. Robinson's *Spiritual Songs* (1875). The arrangement is credited to Levy in *The Church Hymnal* (1894), edited by Charles L. Hutchins. In previous editions of *GS* the tune name is spelled RAYNOLDS. It has also been called CONSOLATION and BERLIN. It has been in *GS* since 1921.

Here We Are But Straying Pilgrims 555
I. N. Carman, 19th Century

Nothing definite is known of the circumstances surrounding the writing of this poem. It was first published in A. D. Fillmore and C. L. Fillmore's *The Polyphonic* (Cincinnati: R. W. Carroll and Co., 1863). It was also included in the *Christian Hymn Book* (1865), edited by the committee appointed by the American Christian Missionary Society, and continued to be printed in succeeding editions down to the last ACMS book, *The Christian Hymnal, Revised* (1882). Moses Lard called the piece "a silly Jim-Crow lay," but it has been fairly popular among Churches of Christ since being reintroduced in *Great Songs, No. 2* (1937). The original poem was in four stanzas with chorus. The omitted stanza read:

Here, our shadowed homes are transient,
    And we meet the stranger's frown;
But we'll sing with joy while going
    E'en to death's dark billow down.

Perkins
W. O. Perkins, 1831-1902

No information is available on the origin of this tune. It was called HERE AND YONDER in *The Christian Hymnal, Revised* (1882). The tune entered *GS* in 1937.

Hold Thou My Hand   **520**
Fanny J. Crosby, 1820-1915

This text was published under one of Fanny Crosby's pen names, Grace J. Frances, in Robert Lowry and W. H. Doane's *Good as Gold: A New Collection of Sunday School Songs* (1881, No. 142). The fact of the author's blindness makes the message of this hymn especially powerful. The text entered *GS* in 1925.

Main

Hubert P. Main, 1839-1925

This tune was written for the words above in 1880 and published in Lowry and Doane's *Good as Gold* (1881). It has been in *GS* since 1925.

Holy God, We Praise Thy Name   **48**
From the *Te Deum*, 4th Century
Attributed to Ignaz Franz, 1719-1790

The *Te Deum laudamus* is the most famous non-biblical hymn of the Western world. Its origin is obscure, but it is fairly confidently attributed to Nicetas of Remesiana in Dacia (now Romania). The German paraphrase is, with uncertainty, attributed to Ignaz Franz about 1774. The hymn appeared that year in Maria Theresia's *Katholisches Gesangbuch* (Vienna). Clarence Walworth's translation appeared in *Catholic Psalmist* (Dublin, 1858), but it is dated 1853 in Hall and Lasar's *Evangelical Hymnal* (Barnes & Co., New York, 1880). It entered *GS* in the *Supplement* (1975). The original German paraphrase began "Grosser Gott, wir loben dich." Vincent Higginson says that Walworth "wrote the translation for a Redemptorist mission manual, c. 1850."

Grosser Gott

Katholisches Gesangbuch, Vienna, c. 1774

The present form of the melody appeared in J. C. Schicht, *Allegemeiner Choralbuch* (Leipzig, 1819). The tune with the German text had been published in *Katholisches Gesangbuch* in 1774. Many variants of the tune are extant. One of these, HURSLEY, is included in *GSR*, Nos. 42 and 571.

Holy, Holy, Holy   69

Reginald Heber, 1793-1826

Heber wrote this text for use in the Anglican celebration of Trinity Sunday. It was to be used between the reading of the Nicene Creed and the sermon. He composed the poem at Hodnet, Shropshire, England, sometime between 1807 and 1823, as a paraphrase of Revelation 4:8-11. It appeared posthumously in *A Selection of Psalms and Hymns for the Parish Church of Banbury* (3d ed., 1826) and in the following year in *Hymns Written and Adapted to the Weekly Service of the Church Year* (1827). Hymnals of the Stone-Campbell Movement have long used the non-Trinitarian reading in 1:4, "God over all and blest eternally." This text entered *GS* in 1921.

Nicaea

John B. Dykes, 1823-1876

Dykes's tune appeared first in *Hymns Ancient and Modern* (1861). He named it after the Council of Nice (A.D. 325), which had especially defined the doctrine of the Trinity. It entered *GS* in 1921.

Holy Spirit, Light Divine   293

Adapt. from Andrew Reed, 17871862

This text was first published in Reed's *Supplement to Watts' Psalms and Hymns* (1817), and in his *Hymn Book* (1841). The opening words of each stanza originally read "Holy Ghost with..." This is the first inclusion of this poem in *GS*.

Mercy

Louis M. Gottschalk, 1829-1869
Arr. Edwin P. Parker, 1836-1925

This tune is adapted from Gottschalk's piano composition "The Last Hope" (1854). It was arranged by Parker about 1867 and later published in one of the hymnals of Charles S. Robinson. The tune, sometimes called LAST HOPE, has been in *GS* since 1921, and, until this edition, was set to William Cowper's "'Tis My Happiness Below."

Hosanna, Loud Hosanna   164

Jeannette Threlfall, 1821-1880

The hymns of Miss Threlfall, according to her own testimony, were written at "idle moments." This poem was first published in her *Woodsorrel, or Leaves from a Retired Home* (1856). It was reprinted in her *Sunshine and Shadow* (1873). This is its first appearance in *GS*.

Ellacombe

Gesangbuch der h. w. k. Hofkapelle, 1784

This tune originally appeared in *Gesangbuch der herzoglichen württem-bergischen katholischen Hofkapelle* (1784). Its origin, if any beyond this source, is unknown. There are several variations of the tune published in Catholic hymnals. Xavier Ludwig Hartwig published it in England in 1833 and dated the tune 1700. "Ellacombe" is a town in Devonshire, England. This is its first appearance in *GS*.

How Brightly Beams the Morning Star   186

Philipp Nicolai, 1556-1608
Tr. from The Lutheran Service Book and Hymnal, 1955

This hymn text, which has been called the "Queen of Chorales," was first published in Nicolai's *FrewdenSpiegel dess ewigen Lebens* (1599). The translation is anonymous and is credited to the editors of *The Lutheran Service Book and Hymnal*, who were associated in the Commission on the Liturgy and Hymnal. This is its first appearance in *GS*.

Wie schön leuchtet

Philipp Nicolai, 1556-1608

This tune, usually credited to Nicolai, seems to be his reconstruction of the setting for Psalm 100, "Jauchzet dem Herren, alle Lande," in Wolff Kophel's *Psalter* (1538). This is its first appearance in *GS*.

How Firm a Foundation   493

From John Rippon's Selection of Hymns, 1787

This text appeared ascribed to "K" in Rippon's *Selection*. The identity of the author is really unknown. He is sometimes identified as Richard Keen, song leader in the London Baptist church where Rippon was minister. Others have identified "K" as George Keith. All of this is just guessing until further evidence is available. The poem was originally in seven stanzas, but *GS* has always omitted stanza two:

> In every condition—in sickness, in health;
>   In poverty's vale, or abounding in wealth;
> At home and abroad; on the land, on the sea—
>   "As thy days may demand, shall thy strength ever be."

Foundation

From Joseph Funk's *Genuine Church Music*, 1832

This tune is an anonymous folk tune which appeared in Funk's collection in 1832. It was also printed in William Caldwell's *Union Harmony* (1837), in B. F. White's *Sacred Harp* (1844), and in William Walker's *Southern Harmony* (3rd ed., 1854). Funk called the tune PROTECTION; White called it BELLEVUE; and Walker called it THE CHRISTIAN'S FAREWELL, probably because he set it to the poem beginning "Farewell, dear brethren, the time is at hand." Most modern harmonizations of this tune are traceable to R. M. McIntosh's *Tabor: or, the Richmond Collection of Sacred Music* (1866). This tune first entered *GS* with the preceding text in 1925. In the editions from 1921 to 1924, the text was set to PORTUGUESE HYMN. (See *GSR*, No. 210. PORTUGUESE HYMN is another name for ADESTE FIDELIS.) President Andrew Jackson said in 1843 that this was his favorite hymn.

How I Praise Thee, Precious Savior 596
Mary E. Maxwell, 1837-1915

The circumstances of the writing of this hymn poem are not certainly known at this time. Even the identity of the author is questionable, but the general editor of *GSR* has concluded that she is more than likely Mary Elizabeth Braddon Maxwell, who wrote many hymns and was associated with the Keswick Convention in northern England. This song is included under "Special Solos" in J. H. Allan's *Redemption Songs, A Choice Collection of 1000 Hymns and Choruses for Evangelistic Meetings, Solo Singers, Choirs, and the Home* (Glasgow: The Scottish Bible and Book Society, c. 1909, No. 781). This is its first inclusion in *GS*.

Channels

Ada Rose Gibbs, 1865-1905

This tune was published with Maxwell's poem in *Twenty-Four Gems of Sacred Song* (1900). This is its first inclusion in *GS*.

How Shall the Young Secure Their Hearts 302
Isaac Watts, 1674-1748

This text was first published in Watts's *Psalms of David* (1719). It is based on selected verses from Psalm 119 and entitled "Instructions from Scripture." The original poem contained eight stanzas, representing the following verses: (1) 9; (2) 130; (3) 105; (4) 99, 100; (5) 104, 113; (6, 7) 89, 105, 90, 91; (8) 160, 140, 9, 116. The *GSR* text contains stanzas 1, 3, and 8. This hymn entered *GS* in 1921.

Neaniskoi

Attributed to Ludwig van Beethoven

This tune, which has been in *GS* with the preceding text since 1921, is attributed to Beethoven. I have been unable to find the source of this tune. The tune name NEANISKOI was given by the present general editor of *GSR* and means "youths" in Greek.

How Sweet, How Heavenly Is the Sight   390

Joseph Swain, 1761-1796

This beautiful and touching hymn on the Communion of Saints, entitled originally "The Grace of Christian Love," was first published in Swain's *Walworth Hymns* (1792). A few minor alterations have been made in Swain's original text over the years, but the hymn is substantially as he wrote it. This text has been in *GS* since 1921.

Brown

William B. Bradbury, 1816-1868

This tune first appeared in Bradbury's *The Psalmodist* (1844). It was there the setting for the text "I love to steal awhile away." It has been in *GS* since 1921. The origin of the tune name BROWN is unknown.

How Sweet the Name of Jesus Sounds   279

John Newton, 1725-1807

This text was originally published in the *Olney Hymns* (1779) in seven stanzas under the title "The Name of Jesus." The *GSR* text contains the original stanzas 1, 2, 6, and 7. The omitted stanzas read as follows:

3
Dear name! the rock on which I build
    My shield and hiding-place,
My never-failing treasury filled
    With boundless stores of grace.

4
By Thee my prayers acceptance gain,
    Although with sin defiled;
Satan accuses me in vain,
    And I am owned a child.

5
Jesus, my Shepherd, Husband, Friend,
  My Prophet, Priest, and King,
My Lord, my Life, my Way, my End,
  Accept the praise I bring.

Stanza four is never printed in modern hymnals, and 5:1 is usually altered to "Jesus, my Shepherd, Brother, Friend." Both text and tune have been in *GS* since 1921, though not together.

St. Peter

Alexander Reinagle, 1799-1877

This tune was first published in Reinagle's *Psalm Tunes for the Voice and Pianoforte* (Oxford, 1836). It was there set to a paraphrase of Psalm 118, "Far better 'tis to trust in God." He named it ST. PETER in his collection of *Psalm and Hymn Tunes* (1840) after the church St. Peter's-in-the-East, Oxford, where he was organist. In previous editions of *GS*, Newton's words have been set to Thomas Hasting's ORTONVILLE. ST. PETER'S, set to other words, has been in our hymnal since 1921.

I Am Resolved   361

Palmer Hartsough, 1844-1932

The original version of this text was written as a delegation song for Ohio delegates to the World Christian Endeavor Convention in San Francisco in 1896. The popularity of the song prompted Hartsough to write words appropriate for a hymn text. It was first published in Gilbert J. Ellis and J. H. Fillmore's *The Praise Hymnal* (Cincinnati: Fillmore Bros., 1896). It entered *GS* in the *Supplement* (1975).

Resolution

James H. Fillmore, 1849-1936

This tune was written for the preceding text and was first published in Ellis and Fillmore's *The Praise Hymnal* (Cincinnati, 1896). It entered *GS* in the *Supplement* (1975).

I Am the Vine   262

Knowles Shaw, 1834-1878

This text was published in Knowles Shaw's *The Morning Star* (Cincinnati: Central Book Concern, 1877). Outside Shaw's hymnals it appeared as early as 1883 in J. H. Garrison, J. H. Hardin, and George D. Smitherwood's *The Christian Sunday School Hymnal* (St. Louis, 1883, No. 136). It was printed in C. C. Cline's *Popular Hymns No. 3* (St. Louis, 1910) and then entered *GS* in 1921. The text is based on John 15:1-8, and has been widely used among the Churches of Christ since it appeared in *GS*.

Ampelos

Knowles Shaw, 1834-1878

This tune was written for and published with the preceding text. The arrangement is by Elmer Leon Jorgenson from the first edition of *GS* (1921). AMPELOS is the Greek word for "vine" and was given by the general editor of *GSR*.

I Am Thine, O Lord   599

Fanny J. Crosby, 1820-1915

This text resulted from a conversation between Crosby and W. H. Doane on the nearness of God. The evening of the day of their conversation she wrote the words. Some time later Doane composed the tune, and the song was published in Doane and Robert Lowry's *Brightest and Best* (1875). The words are based upon the scripture "Let us draw near with a true heart" (Hebrews 10:22). The text entered *GS* in 1921.

I Am Thine

William H. Doane, 1832-1915

This tune was written in accordance with the information given above and was first published in Doane and Lowry's *Brightest and Best* (1875). It entered *GS* in 1921.

I Bring My Sins to Thee   347

Frances R. Havergal, 1836-1879

This hymn text, written in June, 1870, was entitled "Resting in Jesus." It was printed in the *Sunday Magazine* (1870) and subsequently in *Home Words* (1872), *Under the Surface* (1874), and in the posthumous collection *Life Chords* (1880). This text and the accompanying tune have been in *GS* since 1921.

My Sins

Philip P. Bliss, 1838-1876

This tune was written for the preceding text and published in Bliss and Sankey's *Gospel Hymns No. 2* (1876). It entered *GS* in 1921.

I Come to the Garden Alone 588

C. Austin Miles, 1868-1946

This text was written one day in March 1912 while the author was sitting in his darkroom where he had both his photographic equipment and his organ. He was reading in the Bible from John 20, the story of Jesus and Mary Magdalene. He said in his own account of the event that he suddenly felt a part of the scene. In succession Mary, John, and Peter visited the biblical tomb, and after the apostles left, Mary returned. The weeping Mary turned, saw Jesus, and cried out, "Rabboni!" Miles said he suddenly awakened as from a vision and quickly wrote down the words of the poem. Later that evening he wrote the music.

Garden

C. Austin Miles, 1868-1946

See the account above for the writing of this tune. With the text it was first published in *The Gospel Message No. 2* (Philadelphia: Hall-Mack Pub. Co., 1912). Both text and tune have been in *GS* since 1921.

I Gave My Life for Thee 315

Frances R. Havergal, 1836-1879

While on a visit to Germany, Miss Havergal had seen underneath a painting which she observed in the study of a German preacher the motto: "I did this for thee; what hast thou done for Me?" She copied down these lines on January 10, 1858, and was inspired to write this beautiful hymn. Her sister said: "Reading them over she thought them so poor that she tossed them on the fire, but they fell out untouched. Showing them some months after to her father, he encouraged her to preserve them." They entered *GS* in 1921 in an altered form, beginning: "Thy Life was given for me! / Thy Blood, O Lord, was shed," a version of the text first published in the SPCK *Church Hymns* (1871). The original was restored in *Great Songs No. 2* (1937) and has continued ever since.

Kenosis

Philip P. Bliss, 1838-1876

This tune was composed for the text above and dedicated to the "Railroad Chapel Sunday School, Chicago." It was first published in *Sunshine for Sunday Schools* (Cincinnati, 1873). The tune name KENOSIS is the Greek word "emptying" and is found in Philippians 2:7, where Christ is said to have "emptied himself, taking the form of a servant." The tune has been in *GS* since 1921.

I Have a Savior   328

Samuel O'Malley Clough, 1837-1910

This text was written in 1860 and printed in leaflet form. Sankey seems not to have known the author, but he found the poem in the leaflet and wrote the tune for it. It was published with his tune in *Sacred Songs and Solos* (1873) just as used in the Moody-Sankey meetings in the British Isles that year. In America it was first published in Bliss and Sankey's *Gospel Hymns and Sacred Songs* (1875). The text first appeared in *GS* in 1921.

Intercession

Ira D. Sankey, 1940-1908

This was the second tune that Sankey wrote. (The first was a melody for Horatius Bonar's "Yet there is Room.") See Bliss and Sankey's *Gospel Hymns and Sacred Songs* (1876, No. 81). It was published in England in *Sacred Songs and Solos* (1875). *GS* first included the tune in 1937, all previous editions containing only the words of the text.

I Heard an Old, Old Story   517

E. M. Bartlett, 1885-1941

This text was written in 1939 under the title "Victory in Jesus." It was first published in James D. Vaughn's *Gospel Choruses* (1939). The copyright was later sold to the Stamps-Baxter Music Company, and when the copyright was renewed in 1967, the song was assigned to Albert Brumley, Powell, Missouri. This is its first inclusion in *GS*.

Hartford

E. M. Bartlett, 1885-1941

The tune was written for the text above and was published in

Vaughn's *Gospel Choruses* (1939). The tune name derives from Bartlett's home town of Hartford, Arkansas, and from the Hartford Music Company, which he founded. It was named by his son, Gene Bartlett. This is its first inclusion in *GRS*.

I Heard the Voice of Jesus Say 343
Horatius Bonar, 1808-1889

This text was written in Kelso, Scotland, while the author was minister there. It was first published in his *Hymns Original and Selected* (1846) and entitled "The Voice from Galilee." This poem and the accompanying tune have been in *GS* since 1921.

Spohr

Ludwig Spohr, 1784-1859

This tune is adapted from a solo in Spohr's oratorio *Des Heilands letzte Stunden* (1834). William Reynolds says that the text and tune were joined as early as Edwin P. Parker's *Song Flowers for the Sunday School* (Hartford, Connecticut, 12th ed., 1874). This tune entered *GS* in 1921.

I Know Not Why God's Wondrous Grace 537
Daniel W. Whittle, 1840-1901

According to William J. Reynolds, this text was first published in *Gospel Hymns, No. 4* (1883). My copy of *No. 4* is dated 1881, so there must have been a revised issue in 1883. The text does not appear in *Gospel Hymns No. 4* (1881) nor in *Gospel Hymns Consolidated* (1883), which contained *Nos. 1-4*. It is found as No. 272 in *Gospel Hymns Nos. 1-6 Complete* (1894). In the margin of this hymnal appear the words "Copyright, 1883 & 1887, by James McGranahan." The words were credited to El Nathan, which was Whittle's pen name. El Nathan means "the God of Nathan."

El Nathan

James McGranahan, 1840-1907

This tune was written for the foregoing text and apparently appeared with it in a revised printing of *Gospel Hymns No. 4* (1883). Both the text and tune entered *GS* in 1921.

I Know That My Redeemer Lives   552
Samuel Medley, 1738-1799

This text appeared anonymously in George Whitefield's *Psalms and Hymns* 21st ed., 1775). Medley published it over his name in his *Hymns: The Public* Worship and Private Devotions of True Christians, Assisted in Some Thoughts *in Verse: Principally Drawn from Select Passages of the Word of God* (1800). The hymn was originally in nine stanzas and began:

I know that my Redeemer lives.
What comfort this sweet passage gives!

The *GSR* text contains stanzas 1, 3, 8, and 9. In all previous editions of *GS*, beginning in 1925, 1:2 has read, "What comfort this sweet sentence gives." The present editors have adopted the reading which first appeared in *The Methodist Hymnal* (1849).

Truro

Anonymous in Thomas Williams's *Psalmodia Evangelica*, 1789

This tune was first published in *Psalmodia Evangelica: A Collection of Psalms and Hymns in Three Parts for Public Worship*. It was originally the setting for the hymn poem "Now to the Lord a noble song." The hymn and tune form a great affirmation of Jesus as "the Living One." Both text and tune entered *GS* in 1921.

I Know That My Redeemer Lives   507
Arr. Fred A. Fillmore, 1856-1925

This hymn seems to be a free arrangement by Fillmore of Charles Wesley's hymn of twenty-three stanzas "Rejoicing in Hope," which was published in his *Hymns and Sacred Poems* (1742). It was first published in Fillmore's *The Wonderful Story in Song* (Cincinnati: F. L. Rowe, 1917, No. 153). The copyright is owned today by the Gospel Advocate Company of Nashville, Tennessee. It has been a most popular hymn among the Churches of Christ. It first entered *GS* in the *Supplement* (1975).

Confidence

Fred A. Fillmore, 1856-1925

This tune was written for the preceding text and was first published in Fillmore's *The Wonderful Story in Song* (Cincinnati, 1917). The present general editor of *GSR* assigned the tune name CONFIDENCE.

I Know That My Redeemer Lives 557
Charles Wesley, 1707-1788

This text, which is considered to be one of Wesley's best hymns, is taken from a poem originally in twenty-three stanzas which was published in Wesley's *Hymns and Sacred Poems* (1742) under the title "Rejoicing in Hope. —Rom. 12:12." It entered *GS* in 1925.

Bradford
George F. Handel, 1685-1759

This tune is taken from Handel's great oratorio *Messiah*, which was first performed in Dublin, Ireland, in 1741. The origin of the tune name is unknown. In former editions of *GS* it was called MESSIAH, but the editorial committee of this revised edition has used the more common BRADFORD, since there is another popular tune by Louis F. J. Hérold called MESSIAH. (See "Take My Life and Let It Be," *GSR*, No. 608).

I Love Thy Kingdom, Lord 408, 410
Timothy Dwight, 1752-1817

This hymn text is probably the longest-lived American hymn in common use. It was written in 1800 and published in *The Psalms of David...by I. Watts, D.D. A New Edition in which the Psalms Omitted by Dr. Watts are Versified, Local Passages Are Altered, By Timothy Dwight, D.D. President of Yale College. At the Request of the General Association of Connecticut* (Hartford, 1801). The original poem was in eight stanzas, and *GSR* text contains stanzas 1, 2, 5, 6, and 8. Stanza 7 may be seen at *GSR,* No. 410. The two stanzas not included in our text read as follows:

3
If e'er to bless her sons
    My voice or hands deny,
These hands let useful skill forsake,
    This voice in silence die.

4
If e'er my heart forget
    Her welfare, or her woe,
Let every joy this heart forsake,
    And every grief o'erflow.

This text has been in *GS* since 1921.

St. Thomas

Aaron Williams, 1731-1776

ST. THOMAS is a portion of a sixteen-line quadruple short meter tune called HOLBORN, which was published in Williams's *The Universal Psalmist* (1763). This shorter version, called ST. THOMAS, probably after the Apostle Thomas, appeared in *The Universal Psalmist* (5th ed., 1770) and in Isaac Smith's *A Collection of Psalm Tunes* (1770). This tune first entered *GS* in 1937.

Bealoth

From T. B. Mason's *Sacred Harp*, 1843

This tune bears the name of the Old Testament city which was located in the south of Judah. The Masons were fond of naming their hymn tunes after Old Testament places. Among older hymnals of the Stone-Campbell Movement, this tune was sometimes called PHILPUTT. The reason for this is unknown. The tune was first published in Mason's *Sacred Harp* (1843). It has been in *GS* with the preceding text since 1921.

I Love to Tell the Story   309

Catherine Hankey, 1834-1911

These stanzas are from a long poem in two parts by Miss Hankey, probably written about 1866. Part I was entitled "The Story Wanted" and Part II "The Story Told." W. H. Doane had taken some stanzas from Part I and published them as "Tell Me the Old, Old Story" in 1867. This text is from Part II and was published in *Heart to Heart* (1870). The refrain seems to have been added by the composer of the tune to which this text is always sung. They were added about 1869. This text has been in *GS* since 1921.

Hankey

William G. Fishcher, 1835-1912

This tune was first published with the preceding text in *Joyful Songs Nos. 1-3 Combined* (Philadelphia, 1869). It also appeared in Philip Bliss's *Gospel Songs* (Cincinnati, 1874) and in Ira Sankey's *Gospel Hymns and Sacred Songs* (1875). The tune was not printed in *GS* until 1937.

I Need Thee Every Hour   574

Annie S. Hawks, 1835-1918

This text was written during a time when the author was filled with a strong sense of the nearness of Jesus. It appeared first in a small collection compiled for the use of the National Baptist Sunday School Convention, held at Cincinnati in November 1872. The next year it was published in Robert Lowry and W. H. Doane's *Royal Diadem for the Sunday School* (1873). Originally in five stanza, *GSR* text contains stanzas 1, 2, 3, and 5. Stanza four reads:

> I need Thee every hour;
> Teach me Thy will;
> And Thy rich promises
> In me fulfill.

The hymn was first used evangelistically in the Moody-Sankey meetings held in London's East End in 1874. The text entered *GS* in 1921.

Need

Robert Lowry, 1826-1899

Lowry, who was minister of Mrs. Hawks's congregation, wrote this tune for her words. He also wrote the words for the refrain and then published them as indicated above. The tune entered *GS* in 1921.

I Sing the Mighty Power of God 92

Isaac Watts, 1674-1748

Originally in eight 4-line stanzas, this poem first appeared in Watts's *Divine Songs for Children* (1715), entitled "Praise for Creation and Providence." This collection became the seminal volume for all succeeding children's hymnals. The poem is rarely printed today except in the *GSR* three-stanza form. Although the original opening line read "I sing th'almighty power of God," the *GSR* reading (a standard alteration) was adopted as better fitting the tune ELLACOMBE.

Ellacombe

Gesangbuch der...Hofkapelle, 1784

For information on this tune, see "Hosanna, Loud Hosanna" (*GSR*, No. 164).

I Stand Amazed 230

Charles H. Gabriel, 1856-1932

This text first appeared in E. O. Excell's little hymnal *Praises* (Chicago, 1905, No. 3). Nothing is known of the circumstances of the writing. It has been in *GS* since 1921.

My Savior's Love

Charles H. Gabriel, 1856-1932

The tune was written for the preceding text and published in E. O. Excell's *Praises* (Chicago, 1905). It has been in *GS* since 1921.

I Will Sing of My Redeemer   404, 407

Philip P. Bliss, 1938-1876

Shortly after Christmas in 1876, Bliss and his wife perished in a tragic train wreck. The text of this hymn was found in his trunk following the wreck. Nothing further is known of the origin of the hymn poem. It first entered *GS* in 1925.

Hyfrydol

Rowland H. Prichard, 1811-1887

For information on this tune, see the notes on "Alleluia! Sing to Jesus" (*GSR*, No. 253) and "Come, Thou Long-Expected Jesus" (*GSR*, No. 188).

My Redeemer
James McGranahan, 1840-1907

Shortly after the death of Philip Bliss, McGranahan was invited to join the Moody-Sankey team. He wrote this tune while on a visit to Chicago to discuss this matter. The song was afterwards sung to Bliss's text by a male quartet to a great audience assembled in the tabernacle in Chicago. This tune and the preceding text were also sung and recorded by George C. Stebbins, making this one of the earliest songs to be recorded by Thomas Edison. It was first published in Robert Lowry, W. H., Doane, and Ira D. Sankey's *Welcome Tidings, A New Collection for the Sunday School* (1877). The tune with the preceding text has been in *GS* since 1925.

I Will Sing the Wondrous Story   165

Francis H. Rowley, 1854-1952

This text was written during a revival meeting at the First Baptist Church of North Adams, Massachusetts, in 1886. Peter Bilhorn had suggested to Rowley that he write a text for which Bilhorn would supply the music. Rowley did so. Ira D. Sankey, who held the copyright on the song and who published it in 1887, made changes in the text without the author's knowledge. The original stanzas 2, 3, and 4 read:

2

I was lost: but Jesus found me,
Found the sheep that went astray,
Raised me up and gently led me
Back into the narrow way.

3

Faint was I, and fears possessed me,
Bruised was I from many a fall;
Hope was gone, and shame distressed me:
But his love has pardoned all.

4

Days of darkness still may meet me,
Sorrow's path I oft may tread;
But his presence still is with me,
By his guiding hand I'm led.

Certainly Sankey's emendations have improved the poem. The text was first published in Sankey's *Gospel Hymns, No. 5* (1887). It entered *GS* in 1937.

Wondrous Story

Peter P. Bilhorn, 1861-1923

Bilhorn wrote this tune for the preceding text as described above. Haldor Lillenas harmonized the tune and introduced both it and Bilhorn to Ira D. Sankey. After Bilhorn showed Sankey the song, Sankey included it in his *Gospel Hymns, No. 5* (1887) and in the edition of *Sacred Songs and Solos* which was published that year. It entered *GS* in 1937.

I Would Be True

427

Howard A. Walter, 1883-1918

This poem, entitled "My Creed," was written January 1, 1907. The author sent the verses to his mother, and she sent them to *Harper's Bazaar*, where they were published in May 1907. The original poem was in three stanzas, but Walter added a fourth in 1928, which he sent to his cousin, Theodore Ainsworth Greene, a minister in New Britain, Connecticut. The two stanzas omitted from *GS* are:

3

I would be learning day by day the lessons
    My heav'nly Father gives me in His Word;
I would be quick to hear His lightest whisper,
    And prompt and glad to do the things I've heard.

4

I would be prayerful through each busy moment,
    I would be constantly in touch with God;
I would be tuned to hear His slightest whisper,
    I would have faith to keep the path Christ trod.

This is the first inclusion of this text in *GS*.

Peek

Joseph Y. Peek, 1843-1911

Peek met Walter in the summer of 1909 and received a copy of the three original stanzas of the poem. After the melody occurred to him, he whistled it to Grant Colfax Tullar, the well-known singer and music publisher, who wrote down the tune and harmonized it for Peek. The tune is included in *GSR* for the first time.

If You Are Tired of the Load of Your Sin 317

Leila N. Morris, 1862-1929

Mrs. Morris was attending a revival meeting at Mountain Lake Park, Maryland, and many people, after the manner of Methodism in that day, had come to the "altar." Attempting to help one woman in her prayers, she said to her, "Just now your doubtings give o'er." H. L. Gilmour, the singer for the meeting added, "Just now reject Him no more." The preacher for the meeting, L. H. Baker, pleaded with the words, "Just now throw open the door." And Mrs. Morris concluded: "Let Jesus come into your heart." She remembered these pleading words and wrote the song, both text and tune, before the meeting closed. It was first published in William J. Kirkpatrick and Gilmour's *Pentecostal Praises* (Philadelphia, 1898). The chorus has been in *GS* since 1937. The complete text is included in *GSR* for the first time.

McConnelsville

Leila N. Morris, 1862-1929

The tune was written for the preceding text under the circumstances mentioned above and was published in Kirkpatrick and Gilmour's *Pentecostal Praises* (Philadelphia, 1898). It was named for McConnelsville, Ohio, Mrs. Morris's home, and was first so named in the *Baptist Hymnal* (1956). The music for the chorus was first printed in *GS* in 1937 and the complete score in *GSR* (1986).

I'm Not Ashamed to Own My Lord 504
Isaac Watts, 1674-1748

This widely-used hymn text first appeared in Watts's *Hymns and Spiritual Songs* (1707). The poem was originally in four stanzas, but *GSR* text omits stanza two:

> Jesus, my God, I know his name—
> His name is all my trust;
> Nor will he put my soul to shame,
> Nor let my hope be lost.

The original reading in 3:4 was "Appoint my soul a place." This text entered *GS* in 1921.

Azmon
Carl Gläser, 1784-1829
Arr. Lowell Mason, 1792-1872

AZMON appeared anonymously in Lowell Mason's *Modern Psalmist* (1839). Mason said he obtained the tune on his European tour, which preceded this publication. In 1859, in his *The Sabbath Hymn and Tune Book*, he called the tune DENFIELD and credited it to "C. G." (i.e., Carl Gläser). "Azmon" is a Hebrew word meaning "fortress" and is an Old Testament place name. This tune entered *GS* in 1921, joined to the text above.

I'm Pressing On 630
Johnson Oatman Jr., 1856-1922

Oatman wrote this text in 1898. It has had a wide use as a gospel song and was a favorite in camp meetings of days gone by. The poem was published with Gabriel's tune in John R. Sweney, Frank M. Davis, and J. Howard Entwisle's *Songs of Love and Praise, No. 5* (1898). The text entered *GS* in 1921.

Higher Ground

Charles H. Gabriel, 1856-1932

Gabriel said that he wrote this tune in 1892. He sold it for five dollars. The tune was purchased by J. Howard Entwisle of Philadelphia, who published it in the hymnal mentioned above. It has been in *GS* since 1921.

I've a Home Prepared   670

James W. Acuff, 1864-1937

No specific information is available concerning the circumstances of the writing of this text. It was published in Emmett S. Dean, Acuff, and William D. Everidge's *Glad Hosannas* (Waco, Texas: The Trio Music Co., 1906, No. 105). The song must have been written about that time.

Dean

Emmett Sidney Dean, b. 1876

This tune was written for the preceding text about 1906 and was copyrighted that year and published in *Glad Hosannas* (Waco, Texas, No. 105). It was considered one of Dean's most popular songs. Both text and tune are included in *GS* for the first time.

I've Wandered Far Away from God   351

William J. Kirkpatrick, 1838-1921

This text was first published in *Winning Songs,* edited by John R. Sweney, H. L. Gilmour, and Kirkpatrick (Philadelphia, 1892). It entered *GS* in 1937.

Coming Home

William J. Kirkpatrick, 1838-1921

This tune was written for and published with the preceding text in Sweney, Gilmour, and Kirkpatrick's *Winning Songs* (Philadelphia, 1892). It entered *GS* in 1937.

Immortal Love, Forever Full   444

John Greenleaf Whittier, 1807-1892

This text comes from Whittier's poem "Our Master" (1866). The complete poem contains thirty-eight stanzas and was published in his *Tent on the Beach and Other Poems* (1867). This text entered *GS* in the *Supplement* (1922) and contains stanzas 1, 5, 13, 14, and 15 of Whittier's poem.

Serenity

William V. Wallace, 1814-1865
Arr. Uzziah C. Burnap, 1834-1900

This arrangement is taken from a love song written by Wallace, entitled "Waft Ye Winds," and beginning "Ye winds that waft my sighs to thee," written in 1856. Burnap published his arrangement in Robinson and MacArthur's *The Calvary Selection of Spiritual Songs* (1878) and in *The Hymnal of the Methodist Episcopal Church with Tunes* (1878). In the latter work it was the setting for "See Israel's gentle Shepherd stands." This is the first time for this tune to be included in *GS*. Previously *GS* had used a tune by Elmer Leon Jorgenson, which he had written for the preceding text in 1922.

Immortal, Invisible, God Only Wise 75

Walter Chalmers Smith, 1824-1908

Based on 1 Timothy 1:17, this text first appeared in Smith's *Hymns of Christ and the Christian Life* (1867). He made several revisions of the poem at the suggestion of Garrett Horder for the latter's *Congregational Hymns* (1884). The present text was printed in Horder's *Worship Song* (London, 1905), except that in *GSR*, and in most modern hymnals, the fourth stanza is made up of the first two lines of stanzas four and five of the original. It enters *GS* for the first time in *GSR*.

St. Denio

From John Roberts's *Canaidau y Cyssegr*, 1839

This tune is derived from the Welsh folk song "Can Mlynedd i 'nawr'" (A Hundred Years from Now). It was first used as a hymn tune in Roberts's *Canaidau y Cyssegr* (1839). The tune appeared with Smith's text in *The English Hymnal* (1905). This is its first inclusion in *GS*.

In Christ There Is No East or West 392

John Oxenham, 1852-1941

Oxenham, whose real name was William Arthur Dunkerly, wrote by invitation of the London Missionary Society the libretto for *The Pageant of Darkness and Light* (London, 1908). This text was part of that libretto.

It first appeared in Oxenham's *Bees in Amber* (1913) and then in his *Selected Poems* (1924). It was included in H. Augustine Smith's *Hymns for the Living Age* (1923, No. 383). This text entered *GS* in the *Supplement* (1975).

St. Peter

Arthur Reinagle, 1799-1877

For information on this tune, see "How Sweet the Name of Jesus Sounds" (*GSR*, No. 279).

In Heavenly Love Abiding   649

Anna L. Waring, 1823-1910

This text was first published in Miss Waring's *Hymns and Meditations by A. L. W.* (1850). It appeared under the text "I will fear no evil, for thou art with me" (Psalm 23:4). Of this hymn Tillett and Nutter have said: "A faith like that embodied in this beautiful hymn makes a heaven of this life and turns earth into a paradise" (p. 237). The hymn entered *GS* in1921.

Seasons

Felix Mendelssohn, 1809-1847

In the hymnals of the Stone-Campbell Movement, this tune has been called WARING or SEASONS. There are, however, other well-known tunes which are called by those names. In previous editions of *GS* the name WARING has been used. The melody is taken from Mendelssohn's *Opus 59*. It has been in *GS* since 1921.

In Loving-Kindness Jesus Came   264

Charles H. Gabriel, 1856-1932

This text was first published under Gabriel's pseudonym, Charlotte G. Homer, in D. B. Towner and Charles M. Alexander's *Revival Hymns* (Chicago, 1905). The text has been in *GS* since 1921.

In Memory of the Savior's Love   375

Thomas Cotterill, 1779-1823

The original version of this text appeared in six stanzas in Jonathan Stubb's *A Selection of Psalms and Hymns for Public and Private Use* (1805). Cotterill had assisted in this compilation. The full text begins "Bless'd with the presence of their God." The *GSR* text contains stanzas 3, 5, and 6 with several alterations: 3:1 originally read "In memory of his dying love"; 5:1, 2 read "Symbolic of his broken flesh, / We take the broken bread"; 6:1 began "Under his banner"; and 6:3 read "so" instead of "here." The text entered *GS* in two stanzas in 1925, and in the present *GSR* in three stanzas (including stanza two) in 1937.

Winchester, Old

Thomas Est's *Whole Book of Psalms*, 1592

George Kirbye (c. 1560-1634) is credited with the hymn arrangement of this tune. It appears to be based on Christopher Tye's setting for the eighth chapter of *The Acts of the Apostles* (1553). The present form of the tune originated in *Hymns Ancient and Modern* (1861). It entered *GS* in 1921.

In the Cross of Christ I Glory   480

John Bowring, 1792-1872

This text was first published in Bowring's *Hymns* (1825) in five stanzas, the fifth stanza being merely a repetition of the first. A traditional story has Bowring writing this hymn after viewing the ruins of a cathedral in Macao, China, whose cross still stood. If such a scene inspired Bowring, the inspiration must have been second-hand, because he did not go to China until 1849, many years after he wrote this hymn. The text entered *GS* in 1921.

Rathbun

Ithamar Conkey, 1815-1867

This tune was written for the preceding text in 1849 while Conkey was organist for Central Baptist Church in Norwich, Connecticut. It was first published in Greatorex's *Collection of Psalm and Hymn Tunes* (1851). Robert G. McCutchan says it was written on one rainy Sunday afternoon which found Conkey discouraged because so few members of his choir had attended the morning service. The minister of the church, Doctor Hiscox, had been preaching a series of sermons on "The Words of the Cross." As Conkey sat practicing the music for the evening service, the words of Bowring's hymn, suggested by the sermon theme, ran through his mind. He then and there composed the tune. It entered *GS* in 1921.

In the Hour of Trial   538
James Montgomery, 1771-1854

Montgomery's original manuscript of this hymn is dated October 13, 1834. He sent copies to twenty-two friends. The poem was not published, however, until it appeared in his *Original Hymns for Public, Private, and Social Devotion* (1853). The text is based on Luke 22:31-34, and its sequel, Luke 22:54-62, all involving Peter's denial of Jesus. The hymn has undergone considerable alteration over the years. Originally 1:2 read "Jesus, pray for me." Godfrey Thring altered it to our present text in his *A Church of England Hymnal* (1880). 2:1 originally read "With its witching pleasures," but was altered to the present text by Frances A. Hutton in H. W. Hutton's *Supplement and Litanies* (n.d.). The poem was originally published in four stanzas, the last two drastically altered by Mrs. Hutton. Our text contains stanzas 1, 2, and 3. Montgomery's original last two stanzas read:

> If with sore affliction
>   Thou in love chastise,
> Pour thy benediction
>   On the sacrifice.
> Then upon thine altar
>   Freely offered up,
> Though the flesh may falter
>   Faith shall drink the cup.
>
> When in dust and ashes
>   To the grave I sink,
> While heaven's glory flashes
>   O'er the shelving brink;
> On thy truth relying,
>   Through that mortal strife,
> Lord, receive me dying
>   To eternal life.

This hymn entered *GS* in 1921.

Penitence

Spencer Lane, 1843-1903

This tune was written hurriedly one Sunday afternoon. Not liking one of the tunes which had been chosen for the evening service by his minister, Lane wrote this one to replace it. It was sung that same Sunday evening in 1875 in St. James Episcopal Church, Woonsocket, Rhode Island.

The tune was first published in Charles L. Hutchins's *The Church Hymnal* (1879). It entered *GS* in 1921.

In the Hush of Early Morning 274
Mrs. R. N. Turner, 19th Century

No information is available on the original publication of this hymn. Kirkpatrick wrote the tune about 1890 and copyrighted it that year. The copyright later passed to Hope Publishing Company. The earliest hymnal of the Stone-Campbell Movement to contain the text is T. B. Larimore and William J. Kirkpatrick's *The New Christian Hymn Book* (Nashville: McQuiddy Printing Co., 1907, No. 151). It entered *GS* in 1921.

Proios
William J. Kirkpatrick, 1838-1921

No information is available on this tune except as given above. It entered *GS* with the foregoing text in 1921. PROIOS means "early" in Greek. The tune name was assigned by the present general editor of *GSR*.

In the Land of Fadeless Day 661
John R. Clements, 1868-1946

This text was published in Ira D. Sankey and James McGranahan's *Church Hymns and Gospel Songs* (New York: Bigelow and Main, c. 1898). The copyright later passed to Hope Publishing Company. No further information is available on this hymn. It entered *GS* in 1921.

No Night There
Hart P. Danks, 1834-1903

See the data given in connection with the text above. No other information is available. It entered *GS* in 1921.

In Vain in High and Holy Lays 273
Edmund S. Lorenz, 1854-1942

This text was first published under the pseudonym "E. D. Mund" in Lorenz's *Happy Voices for the Sunday School* (Dayton: W. J. Shuey, 1883). It entered the hymnals of the Stone-Campbell Movement in E. G. Sewell and R. M. McIntosh's *Christian Hymns* (Nashville: Gospel Advocate Publishing Co., 1889, No. 242). It has been in *GS* since 1921.

Wonderful Love

Edmund S. Lorenz, 1854-1942

This tune was written for the preceding text and has been in *GS* since 1921. See above for all available information.

Infant Holy, Infant Lowly   209

Traditional Polish Carol

Paraphrase Edith M. G. Reed, 1885-1933

This text and the tune following probably date from the thirteenth century. The English translation of this traditional Polish carol, "W zlobie lezy" ("in a manger lies") first appeared in *Music and Youth*. Edith Reed was editor of this publication from 1923-1926. It was first included in a hymnal in George Thalben-Ball's *School Worship* (1926). This is its first inclusion in *GS*.

W zlobie lezy

Traditional Polish Carol

The origin of this tune is unknown, but perhaps is as early as the thirteenth century. Miss Reed arranged it for publication in *Music and Youth*. The *GSR* arrangement was made by the music editor, Jack Boyd. This is the first inclusion of this melody in *GS*.

Into the Heart of Jesus   618

Oswald J. Smith, b. 1889

This hymn was written by the famous minister and missions encourager of the People's Church, Toronto, Canada. It was written between 1911 and 1914 and published the latter year in five stanzas. The twenty-one year-old Smith was at the time traveling secretary of the Pocket Testament League, founded by Mrs. Charles M. Alexander Dixon. He had come to Woodstock, Ontario, to preach at the Central Methodist Church (Aug. 13, 1911). As he was walking to the church for the service, the melody and the words "Into the heart of Jesus / Deeper and deeper I go" formed in his mind. He wrote down the melody after the service. The stanzas were completed in 1914 while he was minister of First Presbyterian Church, Bellwood, Ontario. The hymn in five stanzas emphasizes the steps of progression toward Jesus: heart, will, cross, joy, and love. The *GSR* text omits stanza five:

Into the love of Jesus
Deeper and deeper I go,
Praising the One who brought me
Out of my sin and woe
And through eternal ages
Gratefully I shall sing:
"Oh how He loved! O how He loved!
Jesus, my Lord and King."

This text first entered *GS* in 1937.

Deeper and Deeper

Oswald J. Smith, b. 1889

This tune was written for the text above and published in 1914. It entered *GS* with the text in 1937.

Is It for Me, Dear Savior? 171

Frances R. Havergal, 1836-1879

The love which Miss Havergal had for Jesus is redolent in every line of her poetry. This text was first published in her work *Under the Surface* (1874) and again in her *Life Mosaic* (1879). The hymn entered *GS* in 1921.

Soter

Tullius C. O'Kane, 1830-1912

The tune name SOTER ("savior" in Greek) was given by the present general editor of *GSR*. This tune entered *GS* with the preceding text in 1921. No further information is available.

It Came Upon the Midnight Clear 195

Edmund H. Sears, 1810-1876

This text was written in Wayland, Massachusetts, and published in the *Christian Register* (December 29, 1849). The *GSR* text includes stanzas 1, 2, 3, and 5 of the original poem. The omitted stanza four reads:

And ye, beneath life's crushing load,
Whose forms are bending low,
Who toil along the climbing way
With painful steps and slow,

Look now! for glad and golden hours
Come swiftly on the wing:
O rest beside the weary road,
And hear the angels sing.

This text entered *GS* in 1921.

Carol

Richard Storrs Willis, 1819-1900

This tune is an arrangement of Study No. 2 in Willis's *Church Chorals and Choir Studies* (New York, 1850). Originally the tune was a setting for "See Israel's Gentle Shepherd Stand." Some years later, according to Willis, he expanded the tune as a setting for "While shepherds watched their flocks by night." This tune entered *GS* with the preceding text in 1921.

It May Be at Morn   281

H. L. Turner, 19th Century

This text was first published in Ira David Sankey's *Gospel Hymns No. 3* (1878), under the scripture reference John 14:3, "I will come again, and receive you unto Myself." It also appeared in J. E. White's *Supplement to Song Anchor, containing all additional music in 2nd edition* (Battle Creek, Michigan: Review and Herald Press, 1880). The poem entered *GS* in 1937.

Christ Returneth

James McGranahan, 1840-1907

This tune was written for Turner's text and first appeared in Sankey's *Gospel Hymns No. 3* (1878). It entered *GS* with the foregoing text in 1937.

It Only Takes a Spark   459

Kurt Kaiser, b. 1934

Kurt Kaiser and Ralph Carmichael collaborated to author the youth musical *Tell It Like It Is* (1969). Kaiser said that the need for an invitation number restating the biblical doctrine "Go ye into all the world and preach the gospel" was the impetus for the text. It first appeared in a major hymnal in Don Hustad's *Hymns for the Living Church* (Carol Stream, Ill.: Hope Publishing Company, 1974). This is its first inclusion in *GS*.

Pass It On

Kurt Kaiser, b. 1934

This tune was written for the preceding hymn text. It was written by the fireplace in the den of Kaiser's home in Waco, Texas. The tune is sometimes called BROOKS DRIVE, the street on which Kaiser lives in Waco. This is its first inclusion in *GS*.

Jesus Calls Us

614, 615
Cecil F. Alexander, 1818-1895

This text was written in celebration of the feast day of the Apostle Andrew, as celebrated in the Anglican Church, and published in SPCK's *Hymns for Public Worship* (1852). The original second stanza is now generally omitted:

> As of old Saint Andrew heard it
>   By the Galilean lake,
> Turned from home and toil and kindred,
>   Leaving all for His dear sake.

GSR contains all the other stanzas as originally written, with the exception of the fourth stanza. Mrs. Alexander herself made several revisions for the poem's inclusion in *Church Hymns* (1881). The 1852 reading of 4:2 was "Savior, may we hear Thy call." This changed in 1881 to "Savior, make us hear Thy call." This text entered *GS* in 1921.

Burford

Leonard Burford, 1905-1961

This tune was written for the preceding text during the 1940s by Burford, who was the long-time head of the Music Department at Abilene Christian University. The tune was first published in a *Supplement* which Burford prepared to accompany the Gospel Advocate Company's *Christian Hymns* (1935). It entered *GS* in the *Supplement* to the *Number Two* book (1975).

Galilee

William H. Jude, 1851-1922

This tune was written for Mrs. Alexander's text and was first published in *Congregational Church Hymnal* (1887), edited by G. S. Barrett and E. J. Hopkins. In previous editions of *GS*, it has borne the tune name JUDE. It entered our hymnal in 1921.

Jesus, I My Cross Have Taken   536
Henry F. Lyte, 1793-1847

This poem appeared first in Lyte's *Sacred Poetry* (1824) with the title "Lo! we have left all and followed Thee" (Mark 10:28) and was signed "G." Lyte claimed authorship in his *Poems, Chiefly Religious* (1833). The text was originally in six 8-line stanzas, and *GSR* contains stanzas 1, 2, 5, and 6. Stanza 5 originally began "Take, my soul, thy full salvation." The omitted stanzas read:

3

Man may trouble and distress me,
    'Twill but drive me to Thy breast;
Life with trials hard may press me,
    Heaven will bring me sweeter rest.
O 'tis not in grief to harm me,
    While Thy love is left to me;
O 'twere not in joy to charm me,
    Were that joy unmixed with Thee.

4

Haste thee on from grace to glory,
    Armed with faith, and winged by prayer;
Heaven's eternal day's before thee,
    God's own hand shall guide thee there.
Soon shall close thy earthly mission,
    Swift shall pass thy pilgrim days,
Hope shall change to glad fruition,
    Faith to sight, and prayer to praise.

The *GSR* stanzas 1, 2, and 5 entered *GS* in 1921 as a complete entry, and stanzas 5 and 4 as a separate entry. The *GSR* text, omitting stanza 4, brings the two parts of the poem together once more.

Ellesdie

Attributed to Wolfgang A. Mozart, 1756-1791
From Joshua Leavitt's *The Christian Lyre*, 1831

This tune appeared in Leavitt's *Christian Lyre,* Vol. II (1831). Hubert P. Main harmonized it in C. C. McCabe and D. T. Macfarlan's *Winnowed Hymns* (1873). In that hymnal it was attributed to Mozart, but no Mozart source has ever been found. The tune name ELLESDIE, according to Robert G. McCutchan, is a "made name" from the initials "L. S. D." The tune entered *GS* in 1921.

Jesus Is All the World to Me   500
Will L. Thompson, 1847-1909

This text was first published in Thompson's *New Century Hymnal* (1904). It first entered *GS* in 1937.

Elizabeth

Will L. Thompson, 1847-1909

This tune was written for and published with this text in the *New Century Hymnal* (1904). The tune name was first devised for the *Baptist Hymnal* (1956) and is for Miss Elizabeth Johnson, who became Thompson's wife in East Liverpool, Ohio, in 1891. The tune entered *GS* in 1937.

Jesus Is Lord   159
Anonymous, Stanza 1
Larry Simpson, b. 1954 (Stanza 2)
Jack Boyd, b. 1932 (Stanza 3)

The first stanza of this text is anonymous. Stanza 2 was written by Dr. Larry Leonard Simpson when he was eighteen years old. He gave the following account of its origin: "I composed the second verse to 'Jesus Is Lord' while mowing my front yard at 8820 SW 124 Street, in Miami, Florida, in the spring or summer of 1972. It was first sung by a group at a youth retreat held by the Central Church of Christ of Miami, Florida, shortly after that. I still hate mowing the lawn and frequently sing (including gospel songs) to pass the time.

The song's second verse was brought to Abilene Christian by a loosely knit, little known and forgotten social club of no official standing known as the 'TFEENSTTHGAMS' (Third Floor Edwards East North Side of the Hall Gang and Mission Society). Dr. Jack Boyd approached me during my junior year and asked to include the stanza in *GS*."

The third stanza was written by Jack Boyd and published in the *Supplement* to *GS* (1975). Stanza 4, containing the Alleluias, was added in this edition of *GS* (1986).

Egerthe

Anonymous

This tune is of unknown origin. The tune name EGERTHE, which means "one arose" in Greek, derives from John 11:29—"ἠγέρθη ταξυ." The name was given by the present general editor of *GS*. It entered our hymnal with the text above in the *Supplement* (1975).

Jesus Is Tenderly Calling Thee Home   321
Fanny J. Crosby, 1829-1915

This text, under the scripture motto "Arise, he calleth thee" (John 11:28), was first published in *Gospel Hymns No. 4* (1883). George Stebbins, in his *Memoirs and Reminiscences*, said that there was no particular incident which prompted the writing of the text or his tune to accompany it. He was surprised at the popularity and success of this fine gospel invitation hymn. It entered *GS* in 1921.

Calling Today

George C. Stebbins, 1846-1945

This tune was written for the Crosby text and first published in Ira D. Sankey, James McGranahan, and Stebbins's *Gospel Hymns No. 4* (1883). It entered *GS* in 1921.

Jesus, Keep Me Near the Cross   627
Fanny J. Crosby, 1820-1915

Doane first wrote the tune and brought it to Fanny Crosby for the words. This was the case with several of their hymnic collaborations. The text and tune were first published in W. B. Bradbury, W. F. Sherwin, and Chester G. Allen's *Bright Jewels* (1869). It first entered *GS* in 1921.

Near the Cross

William H. Doane, 1832-1915

This tune was written and brought to Fanny Crosby that she might supply a text. It was published in accordance with the note above. This tune was first printed in *GS* in 1925.

Jesus Lives and So Shall I   550
Christian F. Gellert, 1715-1769
Tr. J. D. Lang, 19th Century

The original German text, beginning "Jesu lebt, mit ihm auch ich," was published in Gellert's *Geistliche Oden und Lieder* (1757). It was entitled "Easter Hymn" and was in six 6-line stanzas. The hymn is based on John 14:19, "Because I live, ye shall live also." The English translation by Dr. J. D. Lang was first published in his *Aurora Australis* (1826), in Sydney, Australia. It was first published in the United States in the *Plymouth Collection* (1855) This is its first inclusion in *GS*.

Jesu, Meine Zuversicht
Anonymous in Johann Crüger's *Praxis Pietatis Melica*, 1653

The composer of this beautiful hymn tune is unknown. In the 1668 edition of the *Praxis*, it was attributed to Crüger. He may have written it or adapted it from a previously existing melody. Some have attributed it to Luise Henriette, Electress of Brandenburg (1627-1667), but there is scant evidence for this. The tune name means "Jesus, my confidence." It is included in *GSR* for the first time.

Jesus, Lover of My Soul 276, 278
Charles Wesley, 1707-1788

This text was written shortly after Wesley's conversion in 1738. It was published in his *Hymns and Sacred Poems* (1740) and there entitled "In Temptation." Because the language of the opening line was felt to be too sensual, John Wesley omitted the hymn from his *Collection of Hymns for the Use of the People Called Methodists* (1780). The poem finds its basis in Peter's attempted walk on the water in Matthew 14:28-31 and, perhaps, in the Wesley brothers' own experiences in crossing the Atlantic. Modern Methodist editors justify the phrase "Lover of my soul" by pointing out that it occurs in the apocryphal Wisdom of Solomon 11:26. The *GSR* text, in common with a practice springing from the time of Wesley himself, omits the original stanza 3:

> Wilt Thou not regard my call?
>> Wilt Thou not accept my prayer?
> Lo! I sink, I faint, I fall—
>> Lo! on Thee I cast my care:
> Reach me out Thy gracious hand!
>> While I of Thy strength receive,
> Hoping against hope I stand,
>> Dying, and, behold, I live!

GSR includes for the first time Wesley's original stanza 4 as our stanza 3. This hymn entered *GS* in 1921.

Aberystwyth
Joseph Parry, 1841-1903

Parry wrote this tune at Welsh University College in Aberystwyth, Wales, where he was professor of music. It was first published in E. Stephen and Joseph David Jones's *Ail Llyfr Tonau ac Emynau* (1879), set to the Welsh poem "Beth sydd i mi yn y byd." This is its first inclusion in *GS*.

Martyn

Simeon Butler Marsh, 1798-1975

This tune came to Marsh as he rode his horse from Amsterdam to Johnstown, New York, on the way to teach a singing school. It was first published in Thomas Hastings's *Musical Miscellany* (1836), set to John Newton's "Mary, at her Savior's tomb." It was first joined with Wesley's words in Hastings's *Sacred Songs for Family and Social Worship* (1842). This tune with Wesley's words was first printed in *GS* in 1925.

Jesus, Meek and Gentle   572

George R. Prynne, 1818-1903

This text was written in 1856 and published in the author's *Hymnal Suited for the Services of the Church* (1858). It was later republished in the first edition of *Hymns Ancient and Modern* (1861) and thus passed into popular use. Prynne also included the poem in his *The Soldier's Dying Visions and Other Poems* (1881) with this note:

This little hymn has found its way into most English Hymn-books. It is commonly thought to have been written for children, and on this supposition I have been asked to simplify the fourth verse. The hymn was not, however, written specially for children. Where it is used in collections of hymns for children, it might be well to alter the last two lines in the fourth verse thus:

Through earth's passing darkness,
To heaven's endless day.

This text entered *GS* in 1921.

Dowston Castle

Clarence Hudson, 19th Century

Nothing is known at present concerning this tune. It is rarely used in modern hymnals, but it is well adapted to the text above and has been widely used among the Churches of Christ. The tune entered hymnals of the Stone-Campbell Movement in the publications of the Fillmore Music House in the late nineteenth century. Hudson edited a hymnal entitled *Oldham Psalmody* (1890). Nothing further is known.

Jesus My Lord Will Love Me Forever   461

Norman J. Clayton, b. 1903

Clayton wrote these stanzas and the refrain for the tune below in

1943. They were published in his *Word of Life Melodies No. 1* (1943). This is the first inclusion of the text in *GS*.

Ellsworth
Norman J. Clayton, b. 1903

This tune was written about 1942 while Clayton was living on Long Island in Malverne, New York. A year later when he was compiling the hymnal mentioned above, he remembered the tune and wrote the words for it. This is the first inclusion of the tune in *GS*.

Jesus, Priceless Treasure 350
Johann Franck, 1618-1677
Tr. Catherine Winkworth, 1827-1878

This text was published originally in six stanzas in Johann Crüger's *Praxis Pietatis Melica* (5th ed., Berlin, 1653). Franck's original opening lines read: "Jesu, meine Freude, / Meines Herzens Weide, / Jesu, meine Zier." They were patterned after the love song by Heinrich Alberti "Flora, meine Freude, meiner Seele Weide," written in 1641. Miss Winkworth's English translation was published in her *Chorale Book for England* (1855) and in her *Christian Singers of Germany* (1869). The *GSR* text is taken from the latter source and represents stanzas 1, 2, and 6 of Franck's original poem. This text entered *GS* in the *Supplement* (1975).

Jesu, Meine Freude
Traditional German Melody
Adpt. Johann Crüger, 1598-1662

This tune, together with the preceding German text, was included in Crüger's *Praxis Pietatis Melica* (1653). The original tune was probably an old plainsong melody. This tune entered *GS* in the *Supplement* (1975).

Jesus, Rose of Sharon 486
Ida A. Guirey, 20th Century

This text was first published in Homer A. Rodeheaver and Charles H. Gabriel's *Rodeheaver's Gospel Songs* (Chicago, 1922, No. 83). It first entered *GS* in 1937.

Sharon

Charles H. Gabriel, 1856-1932

The tune was written for the preceding text and published with it in *Rodeheaver's Gospel Songs* (Chicago, 1922). It entered *GS* in 1937.

Jesus Saves Forever   657

Edward Boatner, 19th Century
Arr. Baylus B. McKinney, 1886-1952

The original source of this old song is unknown. The chorus seems to be of camp meeting origin. Various texts have been used with the chorus, including one beginning "Anchored in Jehovah, I shall not be moved." The words are attributed to Edward Boatner, on whom no information is available. McKinney arranged Boatner's poem, and his arrangement was published in Robert Coleman' *Majestic Hymns* (1927). This text is dear to me as the first religious song I ever learned as a child. It is included here in *GS* for the first time.

I Shall Not Be Moved

Traditional Melody
Arr. Baylus B. McKinney, 1886-1952

This tune, with its easy harmonies and repetition of musical phrase, is certainly out of the camp meeting tradition. The *GSR* arrangement was first published in Robert Coleman's *Majestic Hymns* (1927). It is included in *GS* for the first time.

Jesus, Savior, Pilot Me   534

Edward Hopper, 1816-1888

This text appeared anonymously in the *Sailor's Magazine* (March 3, 1871) in six stanzas. It was also published in *The Baptist Praise Book* (1871), but there reduced to four stanzas. After the hymn was published in *Spiritual Songs* (1875), Hopper claimed authorship. He had written the hymn for the sailors who attended his Church of the Sea and Land in New York City. Our text contains the original stanzas 1, 5, and 6. This hymn entered *GS* in 1921.

Pilot

John E. Gould, 1822-1875

This tune was composed for the preceding text and was published in *The Baptist Praise Book* (1871). It has been in *GS* since the first edition (1921).

Jesus Shall Reign Where'er the Sun 261
Isaac Watts, 1674-1748

This text, entitled "Christ's Kingdom among the Gentiles," was first published in Watts's *Psalms of David, Imitated in the Language of the New Testament* (1719). It is the second part of his paraphrase of Psalm 72. Part One began "Great God, whose universal sway." The *GSR* text contains stanzas 1, 4, 6, 7, and 8 of Part Two. The omitted stanzas from that part read:

2
Behold the islands, with their kings,
    And Europe her best tribute brings;
From north to south the princes meet,
    To pay their homage at His feet.

3
There Persia, glorious to behold;
    There India shines in eastern gold;
And barbarous nations at His word,
    Submit, and bow, and own their Lord.

5
People and realms, of every tongue,
    Dwell on His love with sweetest song;
And infant voices shall proclaim
    Their early blessings on His name.

This text entered *GS* in the *Supplement* (1922)

Duke Street
John Hatton, d. 1793

The preceding text had been set to the tune MAINZER (see "Thy Supper Lord, Before Us Spread," *GSR* No. 384) until the present edition. The editors felt that DUKE STREET was a more fitting tune. For a discussion of this tune, see "Awake, My Tongue, Thy Tribute Bring (*GSR*, No. 67). DUKE STREET first entered *GS* in 1921.

Jesus, the Very Thought of Thee   265
Attributed to Bernard of Clairvaux, 1091-1153
Trans. Edward Caswall, 1814-1878

The earliest text of this famous poem may be found in a late twelfth-century manuscript and contains forty-two stanzas. By the close of the thirteenth century, it was being attributed to Bernard. Recent scholarship has attributed the poem to an Englishman who lived at the end of the twelfth century. (See F. J. E. Raby in the *Bulletin of the Hymn Society of Great Britain and Ireland,* October, 1945.) The matter must be left undecided with the present information. *GSR* includes stanzas 1, 2, 3, and 40 of the original Latin text. Caswall's translation was published in his *Lyra Catholica* (1849). It entered *GS* in 1921.

St. Agnes

John B. Dyles, 1823-1876

This tune was composed for the preceding text and was first published in John Grey's *A Hymnal for Use in the English Church* (London, 1866). Agnes, for whom the tune was named, was a Christian girl who was martyred on January 21, 304, at the age of thirteen, for refusing to marry a young pagan nobleman. This tune has been the setting for Bernard's text since the first edition of *GS* (1921).

Jesus, Thou Joy of Loving Hearts   263
Attributed Bernard of Clairvaux, 1091-1153
Trans. Ray Palmer, 1808-1887

This text, as the one just preceding, is taken from the Latin "Jubilus rithmicus de amore Jesu," a devotional poem based on the Song of Solomon which continually repeats the name "Jesu." The *GSR* text represents stanzas 4, 3, 20, 28, and 10 of the original Latin poem, beginning "Jesu, dulcedo cordium, / fons vitae, lumen mentium." Palmer's translation was first published in Edward A. Park, Austin Phelps, and Lowell Mason's *The Sabbath Hymn Book* (Andover, 1858). This hymn entered *GS* in the *Supplement* (1922).

Maryton

H. Percy Smith, 1825-1898

This tune was originally written as a setting for John Keble's "Sun of My Soul" and was published in *Church Hymns with Tunes* (London, 1874). The tune name MARYTON derives from an English manor house.

It entered *GS* in the *Supplement* (1922).

Jesus, Thy Boundless Love to Me 621
Paul Gerhardt, 1607-1676
Tr. John Wesley, 1703-1791

One of the most comforting hymns of all time, its German text begins "O Jesu Christ, mein schönster Licht," and was translated by John Wesley from the *Herrnhut Gesangbuch* (1735) while he lived in the colony of Georgia, about 1738. The original translation included all of Gerhardt's sixteen stanzas, but it was reduced to nine in the *Collection of Hymns for the Use of the People called Methodists* (1780). Gerhardt's poem first appeared in Crüger's *Praxis Pietatis Melica* (5th ed., 1653). The *GSR* text contains stanzas 1, 3, and 9 of Wesley's 1780 version. The last two lines of stanza one originally read:

> Thine wholly, thine alone, I am,
>> Be thou alone my constant flame.

This was altered to the present text in *The Methodist Hymnal* (1935). The text is included in *GSR* for the first time.

St. Catherine

Henri F. Hemy, 1818-1888
Adpt. James G. Walton, 1821-1905

For information on this tune, see "Faith of Our Fathers" (GSR, No. 494).

Jesus, Thy Name I Love 656
James G. Deck, 1802-1884

Deck's hymns deal mainly with the second coming of Christ. This text was written in 1853 after Deck had settled in New Zealand. It was apparently published in *Psalms and Hymns for Public and Social Worship* (1855). It has been in *GS* since 1921.

Lyte

Joseph P. Holbrook, 1821-1888

No information in available on this tune. There are other tunes called LYTE. Holbrook was one of the editors of the 1878 *Methodist Hymnal,* but the tune does not occur there or in any other Methodist hymnal available to me. The tune entered *GS* in 1921 with the preceding text.

Jesus, Wonderful Thou Art   562
Forrest M. McCann, b. 1931

This text was written in 1973 while work on the *Supplement* to *Great Songs of the Church No. 2* was in progress. In seeking to maintain the former alphabetical arrangement of the main hymnal in the *Supplement*, Bill Davis and I discovered we needed to fill a half page. He told me he had written a tune some years before and gave me the meter of his tune. I had been reading the book of Colossians in my own private study at the time, and this poem was the overflow of that study and designed to fit the meter of Davis's tune. When we brought his tune and my words together, they seemed to fit well, and it was decided to include the hymn in the *Supplement* (1975).

Davis

Bill W. Davis, b. 1917

This tune was written in the early 1950s, and was first published in *GS* in the *Supplement* (1975). It is named for the composer. See the notes on the preceding text for the occasion of the joining of tune and text.

Joy to the World   256
Isaac Watts, 1674-1748

This text comprises the second part of a two-part paraphrase of Psalm 98, and was entitled "The Messiah's Coming and Kingdom." The poem was first published in *The Psalms of David, Imitated in the Language of the New Testament* (1719). The *GSR* text stands just as Watts wrote it. It has been included in *GS* since 1921.

Antioch

George Frederick Handel, 1685-1759
Arr. Lowell Mason, 1792-1872

This tune was written in 1836 and first published in Mason's *Occasional Psalms* (1836). It was there marked as "Arr. from Handel." The tune took its present form in *The National Psalmist* (1848) and seems to have received its inspiration from Handel's *Messiah:* the music for "Glory to God in the highest" and "Comfort ye my People." The tune name ANTIOCH is apparently from the great Syrian city from whence the joy of God's salvation in Jesus went forth into all the earth. The tune has been in *GS* since 1921.

Joyful, Joyful We Adore Thee   55
Henry Van Dyke, 1852-1933

Van Dyke's son Tertius said that his father wrote this poem while on a preaching visit to Williams College in 1907. He gave the poem to the college president one morning at breakfast, saying: "Here's a hymn for you. Your mountains (the Berkshires) were my inspiration. It must be sung to the music of Beethoven's 'Hymn to Joy.'" The poem was included in the 3d edition of Van Dyke's *Poems* (1911), but it is there dated 1908. The text first entered *GS* in the *Supplement* (1975).

Hymn to Joy
Ludwig von Beethoven, 1770-1827

This tune is taken from the final movement of Beethoven's *Ninth Symphony*, composed 1817-1823 and published in 1826. The tune seems to have been part of Van Dyke's inspiration for the poem. The present arrangement is by Edward Hodges, an organist for Trinity Church, New York, and was published in S. P. Tuckerman's *Trinity Collection of Church Music* (1864). The tune was first published with Van Dyke's text in the *Presbyterian Hymnal* (1911), but with a different arrangement. *GSR* uses the Hodges's arrangement. This tune entered *GS* in the *Supplement* (1975).

Judge Eternal, Throned in Splendor   433
Henry S. Holland, 1847-1918

This text was published in the journal of the Christian Social Union, the *Commonwealth* (1902), of which Holland was editor. It was included in *The English Hymnal* (Oxford, 1906), for which Holland was an associate editor. Originally in four stanzas, this is Holland's only published hymn. Since the poem was originally written with the British Empire in view, in 1:4 "realm" has been changed to "land," and in 3:5 "empire" has been changed to "nation." The users of *GSR* will note that the section of hymns, numbers 427-436, deal with social and national concerns. We have had few such hymns in our collections during our history, but the author observes that Christians ought to be constructively involved with society on every level. This is the first inclusion of this text in *GS*.

Rhuddlan
Traditional Welsh Melody

This arrangement of the traditional tune first appeared in *The English Hymnal* (1906). The traditional words to the tune begin "Dowch i'r Frwydr'" ("Come to the battle") and may be found in Edward Jones's *Musical Relicks of the Welsh Bards* (1794). This is its first inclusion in *GS*.

Just a Few More Days   556
Charles H. Gabriel, 1856-1932

This text first appeared in Homer A. Rodeheaver and Charles H. Gabriel's *Victory Songs* (Chicago, 1920, No. 18). It first entered *GS* in 1925.

Where the Gates Swing Outward Never
Charles H. Gabriel, 1856-1932

This tune was written for and published with the preceding poem in Rodeheaver and Gabriel's *Victory Songs* (Chicago, 1920). It entered *GS* in 1925.

Just as I Am   346
Charlotte Elliott, 1789-1871

This text was first published in a leaflet in 1835, having been written the preceding year. The circumstances of the writing were purportedly as follows: While Elliott's brother was engaged in raising money for a college where the daughters of poor ministers might be educated inexpensively, she felt herself quite useless since she was a complete invalid. Out of this anguish of heart, she wrote this appealing hymn. Originally in six stanzas in the leaflet, in 1836 it was published in seven stanzas in her *Hours of Sorrow, Cheered and Comforted (or Thoughts in Verse)*. The poem was first included in a hymnal in *The Invalid's Hymn Book* (2d rev. ed., 1841). The seventh stanza, which may be found in some British hymnals, reads as follows:

> Just as I am—of that free love,
> "The breadth, length, depth, and height" to prove,
> Here for a season, then above—
> O Lamb of God, I come!

This text entered *GS* in the first edition (1921).

Woodworth
William B. Bradbury, 1816-1868

This tune was first published in the *Third Book of Psalmody* (1849), edited by Thomas Hastings and Bradbury. This work is also called the

Mendelssohn Collection. It was there set to the poem "The God of love will sure indulge." This tune and the preceding text were first joined in Bliss and Sankey's *Gospel Hymns and Sacred Songs* (1875, No. 54). The tune entered *GS* in 1921.

King of My Life 231
Jennie Evelyn Hussie, 1874-1958

This text was first published in *New Songs of Praise and Power, No. 3* (1921). This is its first inclusion in *GS*.

Duncannon
William J. Kirkpatrick, 1828-1921

This tune was first published in *New Songs of Praise and Power, No. 3* (1921), the year Kirkpatrick died. The tune name was first given in the *Baptist Hymnal* (1975). It is named for Kirkpatrick's hometown of Duncannon, Pennsylvania. This is its first inclusion in *GS*.

Lead, Kindly Light 583
John Henry Newman, 1801-1890

Newman has given his own account of the mental and spiritual struggles out of which his hymn poem came in his *Apologia pro Vita Sua* (1864). After writing his work on the Arians (1832), he went with his friend Hurrell Froude to the south of Europe. All the while, his words to the Catholic Cardinal Wiseman kept running through his mind: "We have a work to do in England." He yearned to return home, but because of illness and unavailable passage, he was prevented for some months. At last finding passage on an orange boat bound from Palermo, Sicily, to Marseilles, France, he set out, but the ship was becalmed an entire week in the Straits of Bonifacio between Corsica and Sardinia. Here he wrote most of the poems published in his *Lyra Apostolica* (1836), including "Lead, Kindly Light," which he penned June 16, 1833. The poem was first published in the *British Magazine* (February 1834) and then in the *Lyra*. It has been in *GS* since 1921.

Lux Benigna
John B. Dykes, 1823-1876

This tune was composed on August 29, 1865, while Dykes walked along the Strand in London. It was first published in D. T. Barry's *Psalms and Hymns for the Church School and Home* (1867) and called ST.

OSWALD. The following year the tune was revised and set to Newman's poem in the *Appendix* to *Hymns Ancient and Modern* (1868). It entered *GS* in 1921.

Lead Me to Some Soul Today   421
Will H. Houghton, 1887-1947

This text seems to have appeared in one of Wendell P. Loveless's *Radio Songs and Choruses of the Gospel* (5 vols.). It appears in *Tabernacle Hymns Number Four* (Chicago, 1941, No. 313), where it bears copyright 1936, with the note "Used by permission of Moody Bible Institute." It entered *GS* in 1937, as part of the short chorus material E. L. Jorgenson had selected to fill out pages.

Loveless
Wendell P. Loveless, 1892-1987

See notes on the text above. The tune entered *GS* in 1937.

Lead On, O King Eternal   259
Ernest W. Shurtleff, 1862-1917

Shurtleff wrote this hymn to be sung at the commencement exercises of his graduating class at Andover Theological Seminary in 1887. It was published that year in his *Hymns of the Faith*. The text first entered *GS* in 1937.

Lancashire
Henry Smart, 1813-1879

This tune was composed for a music festival at Blackburn, England, celebrating the three hundredth anniversary of the Reformation. The event occurred on October 4, 1835. The tune first appeared in a hymnal several years later—Smart's *Psalms and Hymns for Divine Worship* (London, 1867). The tune has been in *GS* since 1937.

Lead Us, O Father   540
William H. Burleigh, 1812-1871

This text was written before 1859 and published in *The New Congregational Hymn-Book* (1859). It was also included in the English collection of C. D. Cleveland, *Lyra Sacra Americana* (1868). This is its first inclusion in *GS*.

Langran
James Langran, 1835-1909

This tune appeared in a leaflet printed in 1861 as a setting for "Abide with Me." It was first published in a hymnal in John Foster's *Psalms and Hymns Adapted to the Services of the Church of England*. It is now included in *GS* for the first time.

Let All Mortal Flesh Keep Silence 386
From the Liturgy of St. James, 5th Century
Trans. Gerard Moultrie, 1829-1885

This text comes from the ancient Syrian rite, the so-called Liturgy of St. James of Jerusalem. In that ritual, as the priest brings in the elements for the Communion service, the public readers sing a hymn to God, and the priest chants the Greek prayer "Σιγησάτω πασα σάρξ βροτεία." It is as least as old as the fifth century. The Greek text may be seen in *Historical Companion to Hymns Ancient and Modern* (1962, p. 346). Moultrie's translation was published in Orby Shipley's *Lyra Eucharistica* (2d ed., 1864). This is the first inclusion of this hymn in *GS*.

Pleading Savior
Leavitt's *The Christian Lyre*, 1830

This tune is probably a folk melody, a pentatonic tune, which appeared in Joshua Leavitt's *The Christian Lyre* (1830). The tune name comes from John Leland's hymn "Now the Savior stands a-pleading," for which PLEADING SAVIOR was the setting in Leavitt's collection. This is its first inclusion in *GS*.

Let All the World in Every Corner Sing 81
George Herbert, 1593-1633

This poem is taken from the volume on which Herbert's reputation rests, *The Temple* (1633). In this collection it was entitled "Antiphon" since lines 1 and 2 and 7 and 8 were designed to be a refrain sung by a chorus and lines 3 to 6 by a solo voice, thus creating an antiphonal effect. Herbert gave the manuscript of *The Temple* to his friend Nicholas Ferrar, the English theologian, just three weeks before Herbert died, and Ferrar published the poems that year (1633). Herbert has attained great stature as a religious and philosophical poet in recent years. This is the first inclusion of this text in *GS*.

Let All Together Praise Our God   192

Nicolaus Hermann, c. 1485-1561

Trans. Arthur Tozer Russell, 1806-1874

This text in eight 4-line stanzas, beginning "Lobt Gott ihr Christen all-zugleich," was published in Hermann's *Die Sonntags-Evangelia über des gantze Jahr, in Gesenge verfasset, für die Kinder und christlichen Haussvetter* (Wittenburg, 1560). Russell's translation, which appears in *GS* for the first time, represents stanzas 1, 3, 6, and 8 of the original German text. It was published in his *Psalms and Hymns, Partly Original, Partly Selected, for the Use of the Church of England* (1851).

Lobt Gott, ihr Christen

Nicolaus Hermann, c. 1485-1561

This tune was first published in *Ein christlicher Abendreihen* (Leipzig, 1554), as the musical setting for Hermann's children's hymn "Kommt her, ihr lieben Schwesterlein." It was published in his "Lobt Gott" in *Die Sonntags-Evangelia* (1560). This is its first inclusion in *GS*.

Let Every Heart Rejoice and Sing   49

Henry S. Washburne, 1813-1903

Washburne wrote many of his hymns for special occasions, but this seems to be for general praise. Nothing is known of the circumstances of the composition of this text. It was first published in Baron Stow and S. F. Smith's *The Psalmist, a New Collection of Hymns for the Use of Baptist Churches* (Boston: Kendall and Lincoln, 1843). It entered *GS* in 1921.

Washburne

George J. Webb, 1803-1887

Nothing is known at present of the circumstances of the composition of this tune. It may have been a singing school exercise. It entered *GS* in 1921.

Let the Whole Creation Cry   58

Stopford A. Brooke, 1832-1916

Brooke was for many years a minister in the Church of England, but in 1881, he left the English church and became an independent. That year he published his *Christian Hymns* for the use of his congregation. This text, entitled an "Invitation to Praise God," was No. 47 in his collection.

It is an imitation of Psalm 148 and was originally published in 4-line stanzas. This is its first inclusion in *GS*.

SALZBURG

Jacob Hintze, 1622-1702
Harm. J. S. Bach, 1685-1750

This tune was included in the nineteenth edition of Christoph Runge's *Praxis Pietatis Melica* (Berlin, 1678). In the 1690 edition of this work, the tune was attributed to Hintze. The harmony is a simplified version of Johann S. Bach's setting in his *Choralgesänge*. The tune was originally a setting for J. G. Albinus's "Alle Menschen müssen sterben" and is sometimes called by that name. This is its first inclusion in *GS*.

Let Us With a Gladsome Mind 84

John Milton, 1608-1674

This translation of Psalm 136 was done in 1624 when Milton was fifteen years old and a student at St. Paul's School, London. He was greatly influenced by the psalters of the time, especially by the version of Sternhold and Hopkins (1547). The *GSR* text includes Milton's stanzas 1, 7, 8, and 22, and then repeats stanza 1. This text entered *GS* in 1937.

Monkland

John Antes, 1740-1811
Arr. John Bernard Wilkes, 1785-1869

This tune was composed by John Antes and published in *A Collection of Hymn Tunes chiefly composed for private amusement by John Antes* (c. 1790). This was a manuscript volume. John B. Wilkes found the tune in John Lee's *Hymn Tunes for the United Brethren* (Manchester, 1826), but he did not know the source. He arranged it for *Hymns Ancient and Modern* (1861). The tune name is that of the town in England where Wilkes was organist. This is the first inclusion of MONKLAND in *GS*. The previous editions have set the words to INNOCENTS, a tune published in the *Parish Choir* (November 1850) and sometimes attributed to Handel.

Lift High the Cross 224

George William Kitchin, 1827-1912
Rev., Michael Robert Newbolt, 1874-1956

The original text was written by Kitchin and revised by Newbolt for the 1916 *Supplement* to *Hymns Ancient and Modern*. It was written as a processional hymn in twelve 2-line stanzas. The *GSR* text includes stanzas 1, 2, 3, 8, 11, and 12, with stanza 1 used both as refrain and stanza and as beginning and ending of each stanza. This is the hymn's first inclusion in *GS*.

Crucifer
Sydney H. Nicholson, 1875-1947

Nicholson wrote this tune for the preceding text while he was musical editor of *Hymns Ancient and Modern* under W. H. Frere. It was published in that hymnal in the *Supplement* (1916). This is its first inclusion in *GS*.

Lift Up, Lift Up Your Voices Now   448
From Charles L. Hutchins's *The Church Hymnal*, 1892

This anonymous hymn is a cento from several sources. Stanza one is taken directly from John Mason Neale's "The foe behind, the deep before," published in his *Carols for Eastertide* (1854). This poem may be seen in the Standard Edition of *Hymns Ancient and Modern* (1916, No. 498). Other stanzas are taken from Neale's translation of the Latin hymn "En dies est dominica" and from Mrs. Elizabeth's Charles's translation of the Latin hymn "Aurora licis." This is the first inclusion of this text in *GS*.

Waltham
John Baptiste Calkin, 1827-1905

This tune was composed as a setting for the text "Fling out the banner! let it float." It was first published in *The Hymnary* (London, 1872) and is the traditional setting for "I heard the bells on Christmas day." The tune first entered *GS* in 1925. In all previous editions it has been called CAMDEN, from Camden Road Chapel, where Calkin was organist for five years.

Lift Up Your Heads, Ye Mighty Gates   191
Georg Weissel, 1590-1635
Trans. Catherine Winkworth, 1827-1878

This text was first published in the *Preussische Fest-Lieder* (1642). The opening German line is "Macht hoch die Thur, das Thor macht weit." The original poem was in five 8-line stanzas and may be seen in *Kirchen-Gesang-Buch für Evangelisch-Lutherische Gemeinden* (St. Louis, 1849). Winkworth's translation was first published in her *Lyra Germanica* (1855) and included all five stanzas of Weissel's poem. The *GSR* text, which includes the poem for the first time, has stanza 1, 4, and 5. The omitted stanzas read:

> 2
> The Lord is just, a helper tried,
>   Mercy is ever at His side,
> His kingly crown is holiness,
>   His scepter, pity in distress,
> 'The end of all our woe He brings;
>   Praise, O my God, to Thee!
>   O Saviour, great Thy deeds shall be.

> 3
> O, blest the land, the city blest,
>   Where Christ the ruler is confest!
> O happy hearts and happy homes
>   To whom this King in triumph comes!
> The cloudless sun of joy He is,
>   Who bringeth pure delight and bliss;
> Praise, O my God, to Thee!
>   Comforter, for Thy comfort free!

GSR also omits the refrain, which appeared in both the original and the translation.

Truro

From Thomas Williams's *Psalmodia Evangelica*, 1789

For information on this tune, see the notes on "I Know That My Redeemer Lives," (*GSR*, No. 552).

Like a Shepherd, Tender, True   272
John R. Clements, 1858-1946

This text was first published in Henry Date's *Pentecostal Hymns, No. 2, A Winnowed Collection for Evangelistic Services, Young People's Societies, and Sunday-Schools* (1898). The poem was written in 1893. It was first included in *GS* in 1937.

Jesus Leads

John R. Sweney, 1837-1899

This tune was written for the preceding text in 1893 and was published in Date's *Pentecostal Hymns, No. 2* (1898). It has been in *GS* since 1937.

Lo! He Comes with Clouds Descending   289
John Cennick, 1718-1755
Alt. John Wesley, 1703-1791

The original version of this text was published by Cennick in his *Collection of Sacred Hymns* (5th ed., 1752) in six stanzas. Cennick's complete text may be seen in Julian (p. 681). His first stanza read:

Lo! He cometh, countless trumpets
Blow before His bloody sign!
Midst ten thousand saints and angels,
See the crucified shine.
Allelujah!
Welcome, welcome, bleeding Lamb!

John Wesley heard Cennick's hymn, was moved by it, and decided to write a better version. Wesley's text in four stanzas has become one of the most powerful hymns on the second coming of Christ. The *GSR* text omits Wesley's stanza 3:

The dear tokens of his passion
Still his dazzling body bears;
Cause of endless exultation
To his ransomed worshipers;
With what rapture,
Gaze we on those glorious scars!

The *GSR* text also alters 1:6, where Wesley had "God appears on earth to reign"; and 3:6, where Wesley read "Everlasting God, come down." This text with the tune following has been included in *GS* since 1921. In 1921, 1:6 read "Jesus now shall ever reign." This was altered by E. L. Jorgenson in 1937 to "Jesus Christ shall ever reign" in order to avoid exacerbating the premillennial controversy which had arisen among Churches of Christ.

Regent Square

Henry Smart, 1813-1879

This tune was first published in the Presbyterian collection *Psalms and Hymns for Divine Worship* (London, 1867), edited by James Hamilton. It was there set to Horatius Bonar's "Glory be to God the Father." The tune name derives from Regent Square Presbyterian Church in London, whose minister edited the collection in which the tune first appeared. It entered *GS* in 1921.

Lo, How a Rose E'er Blooming   180
From *Alte Catholische Geistliche Kirchengesang*, 1599
Stanzas 1, 2, trans. Theodore Baker, 1851-1934
Stanza 3, anon. Berlin, 1844; trans. Harriet Spaeth, 1875

Interest in the prophecy of Isaiah 11:1 began quite early in Christian writings. Cosmas the Melodist in the eighth century wrote a hymn beginning "Rod of the Root of Jesse, Thou, Flower of Mary born." The original German text "Es ist ein Ros' entsprungen" probably dates from the fifteenth century. A manuscript version is known to have been written between 1582 and 1588. The earliest printed text is in the *Alte Catholische Geistliche Kirchengesang* (Cologne, 1599). The text was in 23 stanzas and retold the birth of Christ based on Matthew 2 and Luke 1-2. Baker's translation of stanzas 1 and 2 was published in 1894. The original of *GSR* stanza 3 appeared in Berlin (1844) and was translated by Harriet Spaeth in 1875. This is the first inclusion of this hymn in *GS*.

Es ist ein Ros'
From *Alte Catholische Geistliche Kirchengesang*, 1599

This anonymous composition appeared in the aforementioned hymnal in 1599. This is its first inclusion in *GS*.

Look, Ye Saints! The Sight Is Glorious   252
Thomas Kelly, 1769-1855

This hymn text is based on Revelation 11:15, "And he shall reign forever and ever." It was first published in Kelly's *Hymns on Various Passages of Scripture* (3d ed., 1809). It first entered *GS* in the *Supplement* (1922).

Bryn Calfaria
William Owen, 1814-1893

Owen (also known by his Welsh name Prysgol) wrote this tune for the gospel hymn "Gwaed y groes sy'n codi fynny." It was published in Volume II of his collection of anthems and hymn tunes entitled *Y Perl Cerddorol* (The Pearl of Music). The present arrangement was first published in *The English Hymnal* (1906). BRYN CALFARIA means "Mount Calvary." This is its first inclusion in *GS*, all previous editions having used the setting CROWN HIM by George C. Stebbins (1919).

Lord Christ, When First Thou Cam'st to Men   288
Walter Russell Bowie, 1881-1969

The editors of *Songs of Praise, Enlarged Edition* (1931), searching for a text which would be the modern equivalent of the medieval *Dies irae* (Day of Wrath), requested Bowie to write one. The text merges the love and the wrath of God, as it merges ideas of the first and second comings of Jesus Christ. This is its first inclusion in *GS*.

Mit Freuden zart
Bohemian Brethren's Kirchengesange, 1566

This tune was published in *Kirchengeseng darinn die Heubtartickel des Christlichen Glaubens gefasset* (1566), edited by Georg Vetter (1536-1599). It seems to be derived from the tune used with Psalm 138 in *Trente quatre Pseaumes de David* (Geneva, 1551) and bears affinity to other tunes both sacred and secular of that century. This is its first inclusion in *GS*.

Lord, Dismiss Us with Thy Blessing   10
John Fawcett, 1740-1817

The text, originally in three stanzas, circulated anonymously for several years. It appeared in the *Supplement to the Shawbury Hymn Book* (1773). Tillit and Nutter, in their *Hymns and Hymn Writers of the Church* (1911), say the hymn was signed "Fawcett" in John Harris's *Collection of Hymns for Public Worship* (1774). Fred Gealy in *Companion to the (Methodist) Hymnal* (1970), says the attribution to Fawcett did not occur until the seventh edition of Harris's hymnal in 1791, but that it did appear in the *York Selection of Hymns for Social Worship* (1786). John Julian felt that "the author is very probably Dr. Fawcett." The present reading in 1:6, "Traveling through this wilderness," was substituted for the original "In this dry and barren place" by R. Conyers in *A Collection of Psalms and Hymns from Various Authors* (3d ed., 1774). Fawcett's third stanza, now universally omitted, read:

> So whene'er the signal's given
> > Us from earth to call away,
> Borne on angels' wings to heaven,
> > Glad the summons to obey,
> May we ever
> > Reign with Christ in endless day.

This text entered *GS* in 1921.

Sicilian Mariners

W. D. Tattersall, *Improved Psalmody*, 1794

The origin of this tune is unknown. A tradition says that the German Lutheran minister and poet Herder brought the tune from Italy in 1788-89. He published it in *Stimmen der Völker in Liedern* (1807). But the tune had already been published in Ralph Shaw's *The Gentleman's Amusement* (1794) and in Merrick and Tattersall's *Improved Psalmody*. There is no known connection with Sicily. The tune was first joined with "Lord, Dismiss Us" in William Little's *Easy instructor* (1798). Until the *Number Two* edition of *GS,* the preceding text was always set to DIJON, an old German melody attributed to J. G. Bitthauer. SICILIAN MARINERS entered *GS* in 1937 in a shortened 4-line version. The present revised edition (1986) gives the full form of the tune which is in common use.

Lord Jesus Christ, Be Present Now   3

J. Niedling's *Lutherisch Handbüchlein*, 1638

The original source of this hymn is reported variously in recent hymnals. Some trace the text to Wilhelm II, Duxe of Saxe-Weimar, who served with distinction during the Thirty Years War. His authorship is uncertain. The poem's original date of publication may have been as early as 1638 in Niedling's *Lutherisch Handbuchlein*, or in *Pensum Sacrum* (Altenburg, 1648).

Marilyn Kay Stulken, in her *Hymnal Companion to the Lutheran Book of Worship* (1981), says the *Cantionale Sacrum* (1651) is the earliest source. The present text, much altered, is the translation of Catherine Winkworth in her *Chorale Book for England* (1863). It enters *GS* for the first time in the present edition.

Herr Jesu Christ, dich zu uns wend

Cantionale Sacrum, 1651
Harm. J. S. Bach, 1685-1750

One tradition traces this tune back to John Hus. The earliest documented publication, however, is the *Cantionale Germanicum* (1628). The tune was joined to the preceding text in 1651. This is its first inclusion in *GS.*

Lord Jesus, I Long to Be Perfectly Whole   631

James Nicholson, c. 1828-1876

This poem was first published in a pamphlet entitled "Joyful Songs

No. 4" (1872). The poem was first anthologized in Sankey's *Sacred Songs and Solos* (1876). Each stanza originally opened "Dear Jesus." The present version is taken from Sankey, James McGranahan, and George C. Stebbins's *Gospel Hymns, Nos. 1 to 6 Complete* (1894). The text first entered *GS* in 1921.

Fischer

William G. Fischer, 1835-1912

The pamphlet mentioned above was published by the Methodist Episcopal Book Room in Philadelphia and contained twelve songs, seven of which were by Fischer. This tune was one of them. The tune name was first given in the *Baptist Hymnal* (1956). The tune was first printed in *GS* in 1925.

Lord, Jesus, Think on Me   529

Synesius of Cyrene, c. 375430
Trans. Allen William Chatfield, 1808-1896

Synesius published a series of ten hymns in which he set forth Christian doctrine in accordance with the Neo-Platonic views which he had adopted. This is the last of the ten poems. Chatfield first published a five-stanza translation in his *Songs and Hymns of the Earliest Greek Christian Poets* (1876). He added four more stanzas shortly afterwards, and the translation in nine stanzas appeared in his *Collected Psalms and Hymns* (1876). The opening line of the Greek hymn (μνῶ'εο Χριστέ) is a prayer for remembrance by Christ. This is its first appearance in *GS*.

Southwell

William Damon, *The Psalms of David in English Meter*, 1579

This is an early short meter tune which appeared in Damon's collections and in Thomas Ravenscroft's *The Whole Book of Psalms* (1621). Ravenscroft called it a "Northerne Tune," and it was harmonized by Martin Pierson. Lowell Mason published it in America in *The National Psalmist* (1848). This is its first inclusion in *GS*.

Lord of All Being, Throned Afar   113

Oliver Wendell Holmes, 1809-1984

This text and tune have been in *GS* since 1922. Holmes published the poem in the *Atlantic Monthly* (December 1859). It concluded the final essay in his series entitled "The Professor at the Breakfast Table." Hymnals have traditionally given 1848 as the date of composition, and it may have been written that year.

Arizona

Robert H. Earnshaw, 1856-1929

No information is available on this tune as to the date or circumstances of composition. It entered *GS* in the *Supplement* (1922), and I have found it printed in various British and Canadian Hymnals, including *The Book of Praise* (c. 1918), *The Believer's Hymn Book* , (Pickering and Inglis, c. 1925), and *The Hymnary of the United Church of Canada* (Toronto, 1930).

Lord of Our Highest Love 379

Gilbert Young Tickle, 1819-1888

No exact information is available on the writing of this text. See the data at "Another Week" (*GSR*, No. 370). It was probably published originally in *Hymns for Churches of Christ* (Birmingham, England, either the edition for 1868 or 1888). It was first included in *GS* in the *Supplement* (1922).

Franconia

Johann B. König's *Harmonischer Liederschatz*, 1738
Harm, W. H. Havergal, 1793-1870

This tune is probably by König himself and was published in the hymnal mentioned above. The harmony by Havergal was first published in his *Old Church Psalmody* (1847). It has been in *GS* since the *Supplement* (1922).

Lord, Speak to Me 622

Frances R. Havergal, 1836-1879

This text was written on April 28, 1872, at Winderdyne, Bewdley, England, and was first printed in leaflet form. It was later printed in Miss Havergal's *Under the Surface* (1874), under the heading "A Worker's Prayer: None of us liveth unto himself. Romans 14:7." It entered *GS* in 1921.

Holley

George Hews, 1836-1879

Although this tune was first composed to accompany George W. Doane's "Softly Now the Light of Day," it has long been associated with the text above. HOLLEY was first published in the *Boston Academy Collection of Church Music* (3d ed., 1835). The tune name may be derived from a village in Orleans County, New York. It has been in *GS* since 1921.

Lord, We Come Before Thee Now   4

William Hammond, 1719-1783

The original text of this poem contained eight 8-line stanzas and was published in Hammond's *Psalms, Hymns, and Spiritual Songs* (1745). The entire hymn is never printed in modern hymnals but may be found in *Lyra Brittanica* (London, 1867). Martin Madan reduced Hammond's poem to six stanzas of four lines each in 1760, and he changed the wording in our present stanza four. The original couplet read:

Grant that those who seek may find
Thee a God sincere and kind.

The *GSR* text contains Madan's stanzas 1, 2, 3, and 6. The omitted stanzas read:

Send some message from thy word,
That may joy and peace afford;
Let thy Spirit now impart
Full salvation to each heart.

Comfort those who weep and mourn;
Let the time of joy return;
Those who are cast down, lift up,
Make them strong in faith and hope.

This text has been in *GS* since 1921.

Hendon

Henri A. C. Malan, 1787-1864

For information on this tune, see the notes on "Ask Ye What Great Thing I Know" (*GSR*, No. 304). The tune entered *GS* in 1921.

Love Divine, All Loves Excelling 267
Charles Wesley, 1707-1788

This text was first published in *Hymns for Those That Seek, and Those That Have, Redemption in the Blood of Jesus Christ* (1747). A few alterations have been made in the *GS* text: in 2:5, Wesley originally wrote "our power of sinning" and in 2:4, the "second rest." Martin Madan changed the opening line to "Love divine, all love excelling," an alteration which was included in *GS* from 1921 to the present edition. We have restored Wesley's original reading. In 4:2, Wesley wrote "Pure and sinless." The text with the tune following has been in *GS* since 1921. Wesley's text in its opening phrases seems to have been modeled on John Dryden's poem "Fairest isle, all isles excelling."

Beecher

John Zundel, 1815-1882

This tune was composed for the foregoing text and was first published in Zundel's *Christian Heart Songs* (1870). The name BEECHER is for Henry Ward Beecher, for whom Zundel was organist over a period of twenty-eight years. It has been in *GS* since 1921.

Love for All and Can It Be? 353
Samuel Longfellow, 1819-1892

This text first appeared in *Hymns of the Spirit* (1864), which was edited by Longfellow and Samuel Johnson (1822-1882). It was a poem designed for the Lenten season and was entitled "The Prodigal Son." It has been in *GS* since 1921.

Horton

Xavier Schnyder von Wartensee, 1786-1868

Little information is available on this tune. Henry L. Mason, in his *Hymn Tunes of Lowell Mason*, says this is an arrangement from Schnyder. No date is given. The hymn tune name is not explained. The tune entered *GS* in 1921.

Low in the Grave He Lay 245
Robert Lowry, 1826-1899

This popular gospel song of the resurrection was written in 1879. It was published in W. H. Doane and Lowry's *Brightest and Best* (New

York, 1875). It has been in *GS* since 1921.

Christ Arose

Robert Lowry, 1826-1899

The tune was written for the preceding text and was published in Doane and Lowry's *Brightest and Best* (New York, 1875). It entered *GS* in 1921.

Majestic Sweetness Sits Enthroned   260

Samuel Stennett, 1717-1795

This text was first published in John Rippon's *A Selection of Hymns from the Best Authors, Intended to Be an Appendix to Dr. Watts' Psalms and Hymns* (1787). It is based on Song of Solomon 5:10-16 and was entitled "Chief among ten thousand; or the Excellencies of Christ" The hymn has been included in *GS* since 1921 and contains stanzas 3, 4, 5, 7, and 9 of the original hymn. The omitted stanzas read:

1
To Christ, the Lord, let every tongue
    Its noblest tribute bring:
When He's the subject of the song,
    Who can refuse to sing.

2
Survey the beauties of His face,
    And on His glories dwell;
Think of the wonders of His grace,
    And all His triumphs tell.

6
His hand a thousand blessings pours
    Upon my guilty head;
His presence gilds my darkest hours,
    And guards my sleeping head.

8
To heaven, the place of His abode,
    He brings my weary feet;
Shows me the glories of my God,
    And makes my joy complete.

Manoah

Henry Greatorex's Collection, 1851

This tune was printed in Greatorex's *Collection of Psalm and Hymn Tunes* (1851), but no source was assigned. Perhaps he either wrote or adapted it from an unknown source. The tune name MANOAH seems to be derived from Samson's father (Judges 13:2ff). No other particular significance is known. It been in *GS* since 1921.

Make Me a Captive, Lord 617

George Matheson, 1842-1906

This text was written at Row, Dumbartonshire, Scotland, in 1890. It was published that year in Matheson's *Sacred Songs* and entitled "Christian Freedom." It had as a motto the text, "Paul, the prisoner of Jesus Christ" (Ephesians 3:1). This is its first inclusion in *GS*.

Diademata

George J. Elvey, 1816-1893

This tune was written for the text "Crown Him with Many Crowns." See the notes on that text (*GSR*, No. 255).

Marvelous Grace of Our Loving Lord 124

Julia H. Johnston, 1849-1919

This hymn was written in 1910. It was first published in Daniel B. Towner's *Hymns Tried and True* (Chicago, 1911). This is its first inclusion in *GS*.

Moody

Daniel B. Towner, 1850-1919

This tune was written for the preceding text and published with it in Towner's *Hymns Tried and True* (Chicago, 1911). The tune name MOODY was given by the editors of the *Baptist Hymnal* (1956) for the Moody Bible Institute of Chicago, where Towner headed the music department. This is its first inclusion in *GS*.

May the Grace of Christ Our Savior 17

John Newton, 1725-1807

This poem was originally published in one 8-line stanza in the

Olney Hymns (1779). It is based on 2 Corinthians 13:14. The present version appeared in *The Methodist Hymnal* (1878). This is its first inclusion in *GS*.

Stuttgart

Ludwig and Witt's Psalmodia Sacra, 1715
Adapt. Henry J. Gauntlett, 1805-1876

For information on this tune, see the notes on "God Is Love; His Mercy Brightens" (*GSR*, No. 119).

Men and Children Everywhere   93

John J. Moment, 1875-1959

This text first appeared in *The Hymnal* of the Presbyterian Church, USA, edited by Clarence Dickinson in 1933. It is there dated 1930. This is the first inclusion of the hymn in *GS*.

Rock of Ages

Traditional Hebrew Melody

This tune is a Hebrew melody known as MOOZ TSUR, sung in homes at the beginning of the Feast of Lights (Hannukah). The song derives from the English translation of a German poem by Leopold Stein, translated by M. Jastrow and G. Gottheil. The translation begins "Rock of Ages, let our song / Praise Thy saving power." This is its first inclusion in *GS*.

More About Jesus   626

Eliza E. Hewitt, 1851-1920

John R. Sweney encouraged Miss Hewitt in the writing of poetry, and they collaborated on many songs, such as "More About Jesus." This text was first published in Sweney and W. J. Kirkpatrick's *Glad Hallelujahs* (1887). It has been in *GS* since 1921.

Sweney

John R. Sweney, 1837-1899

Sweney wrote this tune for the preceding text. It was published in his and W. J. Kirkpatrick's *Glad Hallelujahs* (1887). It has been in *GS* since 1921.

More Holiness Give Me 488
Philip P. Bliss, 1838-1876

This text was first published in the author's second collection of hymns, *Sunshine for the Sunday Schools* (1873). It entered *GS* in 1921.

My Prayer
Philip P. Bliss, 1838-1876

This tune was written for and published with the preceding text. The author-composer named the tune. It entered *GS* in 1921.

More Love to Thee, O Christ 613
Elizabeth P. Prentiss, 1818-1878

This poem was first printed in a leaflet in 1869, although it may have been written as early as 1856. Her husband reported as follows concerning its composition:

> Like most of her hymns, it is simply a prayer put into the form of verse. She wrote it so hastily that the last stanza was left incomplete, one line having been added in pencil when it was printed. She did not show it, not even to her husband, until many years after it was written; and she wondered not a little that, when published, it met with so much favor.

The *GSR* text contains stanzas 1, 2, and 4 of the original poem. The omitted third stanza reads:

> Let sorrow do its work,
>   Come grief or pain;
> Sweet are thy messengers,
>   Sweet their refrain,
> When they can sing to me,
>   More love, O Christ, to Thee,
> More love to Thee.

This text entered *GS* in 1921.

More Love to Thee
William H. Doane, 1832-1915

This tune was composed for the preceding text and was first published in Doane's *Songs of Devotion* (1870). It entered *GS* in 1921.

Morning Has Broken   470
                                      Eleanor Farjeon, 1881-1965

When the great British hymnal *Songs of Praise* was being revised
and enlarged, the editors (Percy Dearmer, Ralph Vaughan Williams, and
Martin Shaw) wished to include the Gaelic tune BUNESSAN, but they
could find no suitable words. They appealed to Miss Farjeon to write a
poem which would fit the meter and would deal with the theme of daily
thanksgiving. This text was the result. This is its first inclusion in *GS*.

Bunessan

                                      Traditional Gaelic Melody
                                      Arr. Jack A. Boyd, b. 1932

According to James Moffatt, in his *Handbook to the Church
Hymnary* (1927), this tune was written down by Alexander Fraser, who
had heard it sung by a wandering singer in the Highlands of Scotland. It
was first printed in *Songs and Hymns of the Gael* (1888). It was also
published in the *Irish Church Hymnal* (1917) and arranged by David Evans
for the *Church Hymnary* (rev. ed. 1927). The text and tune were first brought
together in *Songs of Praise Revised and Enlarged* (1931). The *GSR*
arrangement was made by Jack Boyd, music editor for *GSR* (1986).

Must Jesus Bear the Cross Alone   629
                            Thomas Shepherd, 1665-1739, and Others

The history and development of this text is complicated. The current
form of the hymn derives from Henry Ward Beecher's *Plymouth Collection*
(1855), the text of which was taken from George N. Allen's *The Oberlin
Social and Sabbath Hymn Book* (1844). Allen's text was apparently an
altered version of a hymn appearing in Thomas Shepherd's *Penitential
Cries* (1693). Shepherd's poem began:

> Must Simon bear the cross alone,
>> And all the world go free?
> No, there's a cross for every one,
>> And there's a cross for me.
> Yes, there's a cross on Calvary,
>> Through which by faith the crown I see;
> To me 'tis pardon bringing;
>> O that's the cross for me.

The modern text entered *GS* in 1921.

Maitland

George N. Allen, 1812-1877

Allen composed this tune for the preceding text and published it in *The Oberlin Social and Sabbath Hymn Book* (1844). The reason for the tune name MAITLAND is unknown. Beecher called the tune a "Western melody" and also named it CROSS AND CROWN.

My Brethren, Let Us Be as One   395

Victor Vadney, b. 1950

This text was written in 1983 by a former student of the general editor at Abilene Christian University. Dr. Vadney is at present a practicing physician in Abilene, Texas. It is a good expression of the desire and the need for Christian unity. Its first appearance in print is its first inclusion in *GS*.

Daniels

Melvin L. Daniels, b. 1931

This tune was written for the preceding text in 1984 in Abilene, Texas. Dr. Daniels, a former member of the Music faculty at Abilene Christian University from 1959 to 1993 and chairman of the department fifteen years of that time, is a well-known composer. This is its first inclusion in *GSR* (1986).

My Faith Looks Up to Thee   584

Ray Palmer, 1808-1887

Palmer graduated from Yale in 1830 and went to New York to teach in a school for young women. He lived with the family of the woman who was in charge of the school and penned this hymn in her home. Palmer said of the hymn:

> It had no external occasion whatever. Having been accustomed from childhood, through an inherited propensity perhaps, to an occasional expression of what his heart felt, in the form of verse, it was in accordance with this habit, and in an hour when Christ, in the riches of his grace and love, was so vividly apprehended as to fill the soul with deep emotion, that the lines were composed. There was not the slightest thought of writing for another eye, least of all writing a hymn for Christian worship.

He further said: "It is well remembered that when writing the last line, 'a ransomed soul,' the thought that the whole work of redemption and salvation was involved in those words, and suggested the theme of eternal redemption, moved the writer to a degree of emotion that brought abundant tears." This text entered *GS* in 1921.

Olivet

Lowell Mason, 1792-1872

About two years after the preceding text had been written, Lowell Mason met Palmer on the street in Boston and requested some hymns for a new collection which he and Thomas Hastings were bringing out. Palmer showed Mason his poem, and Mason copied it. It was published with the tune which Mason wrote in Mason and Hastings's *Spiritual Songs for Social Worship* (1832). Of this hymn Mason said to Ray Palmer: "Mr. Palmer, you may live many years and do many good things, but I think you will be best known to posterity as the author of "My Faith Looks Up to Thee!" This tune, OLIVET, entered *GS* in 1921.

My God, I Love Thee   451

Attributed to Francis Xavier, 1506-1552
Trans. Edward Caswall, 1814-1878

This hymn is usually attributed to Francis Xavier, who may have written it about 1546. It has also been attributed to the Roman Catholic Saint Teresa. The original is thought to have been a Spanish poem, beginning "No me mueve, mi Dios, para quererte." From this came Xavier's Latin text, "O Deus eo amo Te, / Nec amo Te ut salves me." Caswall made his translation from the text found in *Coeleste Psalmetum* (1669), and it first appeared in his *Lyra Catholica* (1849). This is the first inclusion of the hymn in *GS*.

Kingsfold

English Folk Tune

Ralph Vaughan Williams heard a variant of this folk tune in an English village in Surrey called Kingsfold, hence the tune name. The melody is in the Aeolian mode and was included in *The English Hymnal* (Oxford, 1906). This is its first inclusion in *GS*.

My God, My Father, Though I Stray   611

Charlotte Elliott, 1789-1871

This text first appeared in the appendix of *The Invalid's Hymn Book* (1834). The original poem was in eight stanzas and was obviously based on the Lord's Prayer: "Thy will be done on earth as it is in heaven." 1:1 originally read "My God and Father." The *GSR* text includes stanzas 1, 2, 7, and 8. Some of the omitted stanzas are touching also:

3
What though in lonely grief I sigh
    For friends beloved no longer nigh:
Submissive still would I reply,
    "Thy will be done!"

4
If thou shouldst call me to resign
    What most I prize—it ne'er was mine:
I only yield thee that is thine;
    "Thy will be done!"

6
Let but my fainting heart be blest
    With thy sweet Spirit for its guest,
My God, to Thee I leave the rest;
    "Thy will be done!"

This is the first inclusion of this hymn in *GS*.

Hanford
Arthur S. Sullivan, 1842-1900

    This tune was written in 1871 at Hanford, Dorsetshire, England, in the home of Mrs. Gertrude Clay-Ker-Seymer. Sullivan was a guest there at the time. This is its first inclusion in *GS*.

My Hope Is Built on Nothing Less   558
Edward Mote, 1797-1874

    The text of this hymn was written in London in 1834. The author wrote in *The Gospel Herald* magazine that he was contemplating writing a hymn on the "Gracious Experience of a Christian" and that as he walked Holborn Street one day the words of the chorus came into his mind. During that same day he wrote four stanzas of the hymn. He then met a Brother King and with him called on his sick wife. In that home they together sang the poem which Mote had written. The stanzas were first printed in a leaflet for distribution and then anonymously in *Spiritual Magazine*. The hymn was printed in 1836 in a hymnal (title unknown) by "a Brother Rees" and credited to Rees in the 1837 edition. Mote had published it under his own name in his *Hymns of Praise* (1836). Here is the original form of the hymn:

> Nor earth, nor hell, my soul can move,
>   I rest upon unchanging love;
> I dare not trust the sweetest frame,
>   But wholly lean on Jesus' name.
> On Christ, the solid Rock, I stand,
>   All other ground is sinking sand.

> My hope is built on nothing less
>   Than Jesus' blood and righteousness;
> 'Midst all the hell I feel within,
>   On his completed work I lean;
> On Christ, the solid Rock, I stand,
>   All other ground is sinking sand.

> When darkness veils his lovely face,
>   I rest upon unchanging grace;
> In every rough and stormy gale,
>   My anchor holds within the veil;
> On Christ, the solid Rock, I stand,
>   All other ground is sinking sand.

> His oath, his covenant, his blood,
>   Support me in the sinking flood;
> When all around my soul gives way,
>   He then is all my hope and stay.
> On Christ, the solid Rock, I stand,
>   All other ground is sinking sand.

> I trust his righteous character,
>   His council, promise, and his power;
> His honor and his name's at stake
>   To save me from the burning lake;
> On Christ, the solid Rock, I stand,
>   All other ground is sinking sand.

> When I shall launch in worlds unseen,
>   O may I then be found in him,
> Dressed in his righteousness alone,
>   Faultless to stand before the throne.
> On Christ, the solid Rock, I stand,
>   All other ground is sinking sand.

This text has been in *GS* since 1921.

Solid Rock

William Bradbury, 1816-1868

This tune was composed for Mote's text in 1863. It was published in Bradbury's *Devotional Hymn and Tune Book* (1864). It entered *GS* in 1921

My Jesus, As Thou Wilt 533

Benjamin Schmolke, 1672-1737

Trans. Jane L. Borthwick, 1813-1897

This text, beginning "Mein Jesu, wie du willst," was first published in Schmolke's *Heilige Flammen der himmlisch gesinnten Seele* (1704) in eleven stanzas. Miss Borthwick translated the poem for her *Hymns from the Land of Luther* (1854), omitting stanzas 2, 6, 7, and 9. Our text contains stanzas 1, 2, 4, and 7 of Borthwick's translation. The hymn is based on 1 Samuel 3:18 and Mark 14:36. It has been in *GS* since 1921.

Jewett

Carl Maria von Weber, 1786-1826

Arr. Joseph P. Holbrook, 1821-1888

This tune derives from the overture to von Weber's opera *Der Freischutz* (1820). It was arranged as a hymn tune by Holbrook and was first published in Charles S. Robinson's *Songs of the Church, or Hymns and Tunes for Christian Worship* (1862). It entered *GS* in 1921.

My Jesus, I Love Thee 453

William R. Featherstone, 1846-1873

This hymn text was written by sixteen-year-old Featherstone and sent to his aunt, Mrs. E. Featherstone Wilson, in Los Angeles, California. She suggested that it be published, and it subsequently appeared in the *London Hymn Book* (1864). It was also published in D. L. Moody's *Northwestern Hymn Book* (Chicago, 1868). The text entered *GS* in 1921.

Gordon

Adoniram J. Gordon, 1836-1895

Gordon composed this tune for the preceding text, and it was first published in S. L. Caldwell and Gordon's *The Service of Songs for Baptist Churches* (Boston, 1876). The tune has been in *GS* since 1921.

My Lord Has Garments So Wondrous Fine 277

Henry Barraclough, b. 1891

Barraclough wrote this poem based on the sermon notes of J. Wilbur Chapman on Psalm 45:8. He had heard Chapman in an evening service, for which he himself was the pianist, at the Presbyterian conference grounds at Montreat, North Carolina, in 1915. Afterwards he wrote the stanzas and the refrain, and the hymn was sung shortly after at the conference. It was first published in *Alexander's Hymns, No. 3* (London, 1915). The text first entered *GS* in 1925.

Montreat

Henry Barraclough, b. 1891

The tune was written for the preceding text at the time mentioned above. It was first published in *Alexander's Hymns, No. 3* (London, 1915) and has been in *GS* since 1925.

My Lord, My Truth, My Way 575

Charles Wesley, 1707-1788

This text, entitled "For Believers," was published in Wesley's *Hymns and Sacred Poems* (1749) in seven 8-line stanzas. The original opening line ran "Jesus, my Truth, my Way." Our text contains Wesley's stanza one as stanzas one and two and the first half of Wesley's stanza five. This is the first inclusion of this hymn in *GS*.

Ferguson

George Kingsley, 1811-1884

This tune was published in 1843, probably in Ferguson's *The Harp of David* (1844). It seems originally to have been joined to Samuel Francis Smith's 1832 baptismal poem "Down to the Sacred Wave." It was joined to the preceding text in *The Methodist Hymnal* (1927). This is its first inclusion in *GS*.

My Shepherd Will Supply My Need 645

Isaac Watts, 1674-1748

This text, which is a paraphrase of Psalm 23, was first published in Watts's *The Psalms of David Imitated in the Language of the New Testament, and Apply'd to the Christian State and Worship* (1719). This is its first inclusion in *GS*.

Resignation

William Walker's *Southern Harmony*, 1854

This tune appeared anonymously in Walker's *Southern Harmony* (1854, p. 38) in three-part harmony. This four-part arrangement was published in Walker's 1855 edition. It is included in *GS* for the first time.

My Soul, Be on Thy Guard 531

George Heath, 1750-1822

This hymn was published in Heath's *Hymns and Poetic Essays Sacred to the Public and Private Worship of the Deity* (1781). It was entitled "Steadfastness." This text entered *GS* in the *Supplement* (1975).

Laban

Lowell Mason, 1792-1872

This tune, originally called CONFLICT, was published in Mason's *Spiritual Songs for Social Worship* (1832). It entered *GS* in the *Supplement* (1975) and was there called GUARD. The *GSR* editor has returned to the more usual tune name LABAN.

My Stubborn Will at Last Hath Yielded 349

Leila N. Morris, 1862-1929

This text was written in 1900 and published in George D. Elderkin, John R. Sweney, and William J. Kirkpatrick's *Songs of the Century, for Missionary and Revival Meetings, Sabbath Schools.* (Chicago: George D. Elderkin, 1900). It entered *GS* in 1921.

Sweet Will of God

Leila N. Morris, 1862-1929

This tune was written for the foregoing text and first published in the hymnal mentioned above. It has been in *GS* since 1921.

My Times Are in Thy Hands 508

W. F. Lloyd, 1786-1852

This hymn was first published in *The Tract Magazine* (March 1824), under the motto "My times are in thy hand, *Psalm* xxxi. 15." It was signed "Spes," the Latin word for hope. It is not known when it was first published in a hymnal. This is the first inclusion of this text in *GS*.

Aldersgate

G. P. Merrick

The circumstances of the composition of this tune or the reason for the tune name are unknown. "Aldersgate" was the English birthplace of John Wesley. In various hymnals of the late nineteenth century, the date of composition is given as 1887. This is its first inclusion in *GS*.

Nearer, My God, to Thee   636
Sarah F. Adams, 1805-1848

This text is one of thirteen poems which Mrs. Adams submitted for inclusion in William J. Fox's *Hymns and Anthems* (1841). This hymnal was for use in the Unitarian South Place Chapel, Finsbury, England, where Fox ministered. The first inclusion in an American hymnal was in J. F. Clarke's *The Disciples' Hymn Book* (1844). It entered *GS* in 1921.

Bethany

Lowell Mason, 1792-1872

This tune was written expressly for the poem at the request of Edward A. Park and Austin Phelps for their *Sabbath Hymn and Tune Book* (1859). Mason's own account of the origin of the tune comes from a letter to a friend in 1868: "They applied to me for a musical setting for the hymn 'Nearer, My God, to Thee.' The metre was irregular. But one night some time after, lying awake in the dark, eyes wide open, through the stillness of the hours the melody came to me, and the next morning I wrote down the notes of BETHANY." The tune has been in *GS* since 1921.

Nearer, Still Nearer   483
Leila N. Morris, 1862-1929

The text was written by Mrs. Morris and published in *Pentecostal Praises* (1898). This collection was edited by William J. Kirkpatrick and H. L. Gilmour. The text first entered *GS* in 1921.

Morris

Leila N. Morris, 1862-1929

This tune was written for her text and published in Kirkpatrick and Gilmour's *Pentecostal Praises* (1898). It has been in *GS* since 1921.

Night with Ebon Pinion 212
Love H. Jameson, 1811-1892

This hymn text was first published in 1854, but the circumstances of composition are unknown. It was published in *The Christian Hymn-Book* (1865), the ACMS successor to the hymnal published for many years by Alexander Campbell. It was also published in A. D. and J. H. Fillmore's *New Harp of Zion* (Cincinnnati, 1872, pp. 220-21). It entered *GS* in the *Supplement* (1975).

Sorrows

Joseph P. Powell, 19th Century

The date and circumstances of composition of this tune are unknown. It was first published in A. D. and J. H. Fillmore's *New Harp of Zion* (Cincinnati, 1872, pp. 221) and entitled SORROWS. Another tune by Jameson himself, entitled THE AGONY (p. 220) preceded it. This Jameson tune was called "Night with Ebon Pinion" in *The Christian Hymnal, Revised* (Christian Pub. Co.: St. Louis, 1882). The tune appeared with the text that same year in J. H. Fillmore's *New Christian Hymn and Tune Book* (Cincinnati, 1882). It entered *GS* in the *Supplement* (1975).

Now Rest Beneath Night's Shadow 82
Paul Gerhardt, 1607-1676
Stanza 1, alt. trans. Frances Elizabeth Cox, 1812-1897
Stanza 2, alt. trans. Catherine Winkworth, 1827-1878

The original German text beginning "Nun ruhen alle Wälder" was published in Johann Crüger's *Praxis Pietatis Melica* (3d ed., 1648) in nine 6-line stanzas. The hymn was an immediate favorite and often has been used as a children's hymn because of its simple language, beautiful imagery, and expression of childlike trust in God. The hymn has appeared in many English-language hymnals, chiefly in two translations: "The duteous day now closeth" by Robert Bridges in his *Yattendon Hymnal* (1899) and the present text of *GSR*. Our text is taken from the version as altered in *The Common Service Book with Hymnal of the Lutheran Church* (1917). Stanza 1 is the translation of Frances Elizabeth Cox in her *Hymns from the German* (2d ed., 1864), and stanza 2 is an alteration from Catherine Winkworth's translation in her *Lyra Germanica* (1855). The text entered *GS* in 1937.

Nun ruhen alle Wälder
> Attributed to Heinrich Isaac, 1450-1517
> Arr. J. S. Bach, 1685-1750

This tune is also called INNSBRUCK and O WELT, ICH MUSS DICH LASSEN. It is the top part of a musical setting by Isaac in Georg Foster's *Ein Auszug guter alter und neue Teutscher Liedlein* (Nürnberg, 1539), made for the secular song "Innsbruck, ich muss dich lassen." The harmony in *GSR* is that of Johann Sebastian Bach in his *Choral gesange*. The tune entered *GS* in 1937.

Now Thank We All Our God   59
> Martin Rinkart, 1586-1649
> Trans. Catherine Winkworth, 1827-1878

This hymn, beginning "Nun danket alle Gott," was written during the Thirty Years War (1628-1648) in the midst of terrible suffering at Eilenburg in Saxony. It is sometimes called the German *Te Deum*. The text was probably first printed in Rinkart's *Jesu-Hertz-Büchlein* (1636), but no copy survives. It is found in the 1663 edition of this hymnal. It also appeared in Johann Crüger's *Praxis Pietatis Melica* (1647). Miss Winkworth's translation was first published in her *Lyra Germanica, Second Series* (1858) and in her *Chorale Book for England* (1863). It entered *GS* in 1921.

Nun Danket
> Johann Crüger, 1598-1662

This tune was published anonymously in Cruger's *Praxis Pietatis Melica* (4th ed., Berlin, 1647). Felix Mendelssohn altered and arranged the tune for six voices in his *Lobgesang* (1840). The *GSR* version is a four-part emendation from Mendelssohn, which is used in all modern hymnals. In preceding editions of *GS* since 1937, the musical setting for the preceding text was called a "17th-Cent. Melody" harmonized by J. S. Bach. NUN DANKET first entered *GS* in the *Supplement* (1975).

Now the Day Is Over   34
> Sabine Baring-Gould, 1834-1896

This text was written in 1865 and published that year in the *Church Times*. In 1868, it was included in the *Appendix* to *Hymns Ancient and Modern*. It entered *GS* in 1921.

Merrial
Joseph Barnby, 1838-1896

MERRIAL was written by Barnby in 1868 and published in his *Original Tunes to Popular Hymns* (1869). Charles S. Robinson published it in his *Spiritual Songs for Social Worship* (1878) and in *Spiritual Songs for the Sunday School* (New York, 1881, No. 176) under the name EMMELAR, a word derived from his daughter's initials, M. L. R. Later he changed it to MERRIAL to represent her name, Mary L. The tune is also called TWILIGHT and EVENING. In all previous editions of *GS,* the name EVENING was used. The tune entered *GS* in 1921.

Now the Green Blade Rises   243
John M. C. Crum, 1872-1958

This text was written to provide words for an old French tune, the Christmas carol "Noel nouvelet." The words celebrate the resurrection of Christ. It was first published in *The Oxford Book of Carols* (1928). This is its first inclusion in *GS.*

French Carol
Traditional French Carol
Arr. Martin Shaw, 1875-1958

Shaw made this arrangement of the old French carol for Crum's words. It was published in *The Oxford Book of Carols* (1928). This is its first inclusion in *GS.*

O Be Joyful in the Lord   90
Curtis Beach, b. 1914

This text, a paraphrase of Psalm 100, was published in the *Pilgrim Hymnal* (Boston, 1958, No. 26). This is its first inclusion in *GS.*

Rock of Ages
Traditional Hebrew Melody

This tune is known in the Jewish tradition as MOOZ TSUR, a melody sung in homes at the beginning of the Feast of Lights (Hanukkah). The tune name derives from the English translation of a German poem by Leopold Stein, translated by M. Jastrow and G. Gottheil. The translation begins "Rock of Ages, let our song / Praise Thy saving power." This is its first inclusion in *GS.*

O Beautiful for Spacious Skies   435
Katherine Lee Bates, 1859-1929

During the summer of 1893, Miss Bates was lecturing on English religious drama in Colorado Springs, Colorado. At the close of the session she went with a group to the top of Pike's Peak, where she gazed out briefly over the magnificent view. There the opening lines of this poem came to her mind.

Before leaving Colorado Springs, she had written the original four stanzas. They were laid aside and, two years later, sent to and published in the *Congregationalist* (July 4, 1895). In 1904 Miss Bates rewrote the hymn and much improved it. This revised version which is printed in *GSR* was published in the *Evening Transcript* (Boston, Nov. 19, 1904). A few years later she revised the opening lines of stanza three (omitted from *GS*) a second time. They read:

O beautiful for heroes proved
     In liberating strife,
Who more than self their country loved,
     And mercy more than life!
America! America! May God thy gold refine,
     Till all success be nobleness,
And every gain divine.

This patriotic hymn has been in *GS* since 1937.

Materna

Samuel A. Ward, 1847-1903

The circumstances of the composition of this tune are uncertain. One version says that Ward wrote it while crossing New York harbor coming back from Coney Island in 1882, jotting the tune down on the cuff of his shirt sleeve. Ward's son-in-law, however, said it was composed in memory of Ward's oldest daughter, Clara, who had died in 1885. The tune was written as a setting for "O Mother Dear, Jerusalem" and was first published in *The Parish Choir* (VIII, No. 378). It was included in Charles L. Hutchin's *The Church Hymnal (1894),* and joined with Miss Bates's words in 1922. It entered *GS* in 1937.

O Brother Man, Fold to Thy Heart Thy Brother   428
John Greenleaf Whittier, 1807-1892

This text was the Quaker poet's attempt to contrast the excesses and carnalities of pagan worship with what he considered to be the essential duty of man. The motto of his poem was James 1:27, "Pure religion and undefiled before our God and Father is this: to visit the fatherless and widows in their affliction and to keep oneself unspotted from the world." The text was written in 1848 and published in Whittier's *Labor and Other Poems* (1850). The *GSR* text contains stanzas 13, 11, 14, and 15. The original poem is in fifteen stanzas and entitled "Worship." It first entered *GS* in the *Supplement* (1975).

Henderson

O. C. Henderson, 1896-1970
Harm. Rollie Blondeau, b. 1935

This is the first inclusion of this tune in *GS*. It was written some years ago by the father-in-law of Rollie Blondeau, one of the associate editors of *GSR* (1986). The harmony was done about 1960. When the preceding text was published in *Great Songs, Number Two, with Supplement* (1975), a tune called WINDSOR by Joseph Barnby was used. This current tune, HENDERSON, is much better fitted for congregational use.

O Come, All Ye Faithful   210

Anonymous Latin Hymn
Attributed to John Francis Wade, c. 1710-1786
Trans. Frederick Oakeley, 1802-1880

Dom John Stephan, in *The Adeste Fidelis: A Study of Its Origin and Development* (1947), concludes that this text was first published in manuscript in 1743 and was written by John Francis Wade. Wade's poem was in four stanzas of Latin. It was translated in 1841 by Oakeley and used in the Anglican chapel All Saints, Margaret Street, in London. The Oakeley translation has been altered by many hands over the years to give our present text. The Latin was first printed, according to Vincent Higginson, in *The Evening Office of the Church* (1760) and in *An Essay on Church Plain Chant* (1782). Benjamin Carr published the poem in the United States in his *Musical Journal* (II, No. 29, Dec., 29, 1800). The hymn entered *GS* in 1925.

Adeste Fidelis

John Francis Wade, c. 1710-1786

Stephan also concluded that Wade was the composer of the tune. (See on words above.) The 1743 manuscript gives it in plainsong notation, and it was first printed in England in *An Essay on the Church Plain Chant*

(1792) by Samuel Webbe. The tune was there arranged in 4/4 time. It first entered *GS* in 1925.

O Come, O Come, Emmanuel　　　　　　　　　　182

A Metrical Version of the *Magnificat Antiphons*
in Psalteriolum Cantionum Catholicarum, 1710
Stanzas 1,2: trans. John Mason Neale, 1818-1866
Stanzas 3,4: trans. Henry Sloan Coffin, 1877-1954

This text is a versification of five of the Great Antiphons (called the Great O's, since each begins with "O") written in the sixth or seventh centuries. They were chanted in the medieval Church from December 17 to 23, leading up to the Christmas celebration. The Latin text was first found printed in the *Appendix* to *Psalteriolum Cantionum Catholicarum* (7th ed., Cologne, 1710). The *GSR* text contains stanzas 1 and 2 from the translation by J. M. Neale for his *Mediaeval Hymns and Sequences* (1851) as revised in *Hymns Ancient and Modern* (1861). Our stanzas 3 and 4 are from a translation by Henry Sloan Coffin made in 1916 and published in his *Hymns of the Kingdom of God* (1923). This is the first time for the text to be included in *GS.*

Veni Emmanuel

Adpt. from Plainsong, Mode I by Thomas Helmore, 1811-1890

This tune was an arrangement by Helmore for *The Hymnal Noted* (Part II, London,. 1854), of a melody which he said he copied from J. M. Neale, who had taken it from a French missal. Austin Lovelace says: "In the *Musical Times,* September, 1966, Mother Thomas More, a canoness of St. Augustine, wrote that she had found the manuscript in the National Library of Paris, where the tune was set to a 'Libera' trope, a devotional hymn for the dead, with the text 'Bone Jesu dulcis cunctis.'" (See *Companion to the Methodist Hymnal,* p. 305.) This is the first inclusion of the tune in *GS.*

O Day of God, Draw Nigh　　　　　　　　　　440

Robert B. Y. Scott, b. 1899

This text was written in 1937 for the use of the Fellowship for a Christian Social Order. It was published in *Hymns for Worship* (1939). This is its first inclusion in *GS.*

St. Michael

From *Genevan Psalter*, 1551
Adpt. William Crotch, 1775-1847

The original of this tune appeared in the *Geneva Psalter* (1551). There it was set to Clement Marot's paraphrase of Psalm 101. A decade later it was set to the paraphrase of Psalm 134 in the *Anglo-Genevan Psalter*. Crotch shortened the tune, altered the last phrase, and gave it its present name. It was published in his *Psalm Tunes* (London, 1836). This is its first inclusion in *GS*.

O for a Closer Walk with God 576

William Cowper, 1731-1800

Cowper wrote this hymn text on December 9, 1769, during the serious illness of his friend Mrs. Mary Unwin. It was first published in Richard Conyer's *A Collection of Psalms and Hymns from Various Authors* (2d ed., 1772). With a few alterations, Cowper published it in the *Olney Hymns* (1779) under the heading "Walking with God," with a reference to Genesis 5:24. The hymn was originally in six stanzas. The *GSR* text contains stanzas 1, 2, 5, and 6. The omitted stanzas read:

3
What peaceful hours I once enjoyed!
    How sweet their memory still!
But they have left an aching void,
    The world can never fill.

4
Return, O holy Dove, return,
    Sweet messenger of rest;
I hate the sins that made thee mourn,
    And drove thee from my breast.

This hymn first entered *GS* in 1937.

Beatitudo

John Bacchus Dykes, 1823-1876

This tune was written for the hymn "How bright these glorious spirits shine," published in *Hymns Ancient and Modern* (1875). The tune name, a Latin term first coined by Marcus Tullius Cicero (43 B.C.), means "the condition of blessedness." It entered *GS* in 1937.

O for a Faith That Will Not Shrink 505

William H. Bathurst, 1796-1877

This text was first published in Bathurst's *Psalms and Hymns for Public and Private Use* (1839). It was entitled "The Power of Faith" with reference to Luke 17:5. The hymn was originally in six stanzas, and over the years various emendations have been made in the text. *GSR* contains stanzas 1, 2, 3, and 6. The omitted stanzas read:

4
That bears, unmoved, the world's dread frown,
    Nor heeds its scornful smile;
That seas of trouble cannot drown,
    Nor Satan's arts beguile.

5
A faith that keeps the narrow way
    Till life's last hour is fled,
And with a pure and heavenly ray
    Lights up a dying bed.

This text first entered *GS* in 1921.

Azmon

Carl Gläser, 1784-1829
Arr. Lowell Mason, 1792-1872

For information on this tune, see the notes on "I'm Not Ashamed to Own My Lord" (*GSR*, No. 504).

O for a Heart to Praise My God 491

Charles Wesley, 1707-1788

This text was published first in *Hymns and Sacred Poems* (1742) in eight stanzas. Slight alterations in wording were later made by Martin Madan, John Wesley and others. For example, 3:1 originally read "An humble, lowly, contrite heart." Our text contains stanzas 1, 2, 3, and 8. In Wesley's text, the *GSR* 4:1 began "Thy nature, gracious Lord, impart." This hymn entered *GS* in 1921.

Armenia

Sylvanus D. Pond, 1792-1871

This tune was first published in *The Musical Miscellany* (1836).

The publication was issued by Ezra Collier and contained the music published in the *Musical Magazine,* edited by Thomas Hastings. The tune was later published in Pond's *United States Psalmody* (1841) and Hastings's *The Manhattan Collection* (1841). In all previous editions of *GS,* the preceding text was set to BALERMA, a tune by Robert Simpson (1790-1832) adapted from F. H. Barthélèmon (1741-1808). This is ARMENIA's first appearance in *GS.*

O for a Soul (aglow with Love)   457
William J. Kirkpatrick, 1838-1921

Kirkpatrick published this text in 1900. Its first inclusion in a hymnal of the Stone-Campbell Movement seems to have been in T. B. Larimore and W. J. Kirkpatrick's *The New Christian Hymn Book* (Nashville, 1907). This is its first inclusion in *GS.*

Agape
William J. Kirkpatrick, 1838-1921

This tune was written for the preceding text and published in 1900. The tune name AGAPE means "love" in Greek and was given by the current general editor of *GSR.* This is its first inclusion in *GS.*

O for a Thousand Tongues to Sing   2
Charles Wesley, 1707-1788

This poem in eighteen stanzas was written to commemorate the anniversary of Charles Wesley's conversion. The first stanza began "Glory to God and praise and love" and was probably written in May 1739. It was subsequently published in Wesley's *Hymns and Sacred Poems* (1740). Richard Conyers made the first selection from the original poem and published it in *A Collection of Psalms and Hymns from Various Authors* (1767). Conyers made Wesley's seventh stanza his first, and the one that continues to be first in all modern editions. John Wesley published the poem with a few alterations in his *Collection of Hymns for the Use of the People Called Methodists* (1780). The *GSR* text is comprised of Wesley's stanzas 7, 8, 9, and 10. This hymn entered *GS* in 1937.

Azmon

Carl G. Gläser, 1784-1829
Arr. Lowell Mason, 1792-1872

For information on this tune, see the notes on "I'm Not Ashamed to Own My Lord," (*GSR*, No. 504).

O God of Bethel, by Whose Hand   140

Philip Doddridge, 1702-1751
Alt. in Scottish Paraphrases, 1745

This fine hymn was written by Doddridge on January 16, 1737. It is based on Genesis 28:20-22. The text was revised by Doddridge himself and by John Logan to take the form we have in *GSR* and was published in *Scottish Paraphrases (1745)*. Stanza 3 is entirely Logan's. The text entered *GS* in the Supplement (1922).

Dundee

Scottish Psalter, 1615

For information on this tune, see the notes on "God Moves in a Mysterious Way" (*GSR*, No. 139).

O God of Earth and Altar   434

Gilbert K. Chesterton, 1874-1936

This hymn text was written to be set to the tune AURELIA (see "The Church's One Foundation," *GSR*, No. 365). It was first printed in the *Commonwealth*, the journal organ of the Christian Social Union, and included in *The English Hymnal* (Oxford, 1906). In that hymnal it was set to the tune KING'S LYNN. This is its first inclusion in *GS*.

Llangloffan

Traditional Welsh Melody
From David Evans's *Hymnau a Thonau*, 1865

This tune was printed in Evans's *Hymnau a Thonau yr Gwasanaeth yr Eglwys yng Nghymru* (1865). An English folksong variant is entitled "The Painful Plough." This is its first inclusion in *GS*.

O God, Our Help in Ages Past 136
Isaac Watts, 1674-1748

This powerful hymn text was first published in Watts's *Psalms of David, Imitated in the Language of the New Testament* (1719). Watts had there published a sequence of five poems on Psalm 90. The first was a long meter poem beginning "Through every age, eternal God" and was entitled "Man mortal, and God immortal." The second, our present text, paraphrased verses 1-5 and was entitled "Man frail, and God eternal." The third poem began "Lord, if thine eyes survey our faults," covered verses 8, 11, 9, 10, and 12, and was entitled "Mortality, and Preparation for Death." The fourth poem paraphrased verses 13 to the end, and began "Return, O God of love, return." It was entitled "Breathing after heaven." The final poem began "Lord, what a feeble piece," covered verses 5, 10, and 12, and was entitled "The Frailty and Shortness of life." Originally Watts began his second poem "Our God, our help in ages past." John Wesley altered it to its present form and also provided the current text for *GSR* 6:3, where Watts had written "Be thou our guide while troubles last." This text entered *GS* in 1921.

St. Anne

William Croft, 1678-1727

This tune was first published in *A Supplement to the New Version by Dr. Brady and Mr. Tate* (6th ed., London, 1708). It was there set to Tate's "As pants the hart." Philip Hart first attributed the tune to Croft in his *Collection* (London, 1720). The tune is named for St. Anne's Church, Soho, where Croft served as organist. In the original editions of *GS* (1921-1936) HARVEY'S CHANT was the only tune printed. ST. ANNE was printed as a second tune in 1937. Since the former tune was almost never used, thus causing the neglect of this tune, the current editors of *GSR* felt it needful to set forth only the tune which is universally used for the preceding text.

O God, We Praise Thee and Confess 70
Based on the *Te Deum*, 4th Century in
A Supplement to the New Version, 1700

This paraphrase of the *Te Deum* was published in Nahum Tate and Nicholas Brady's *Supplement to the New Version*. The *New Version* was a psalter designed to replace the old Sternhold and Hopkins version. The original text contains 13 stanzas in two parts, which may be seen in *The Book of Common Prayer...Together with The Psalter or Psalms of David*

(Oxford, 1852), in the section of Hymns following the *Psalter.* The *GSR* text contains stanzas 1, 2, 3, and 5. In 3:4, the original "ray" has been altered to "sway." This is the first inclusion of this hymn in *GS.*

Tallis' Ordinal

Thomas Tallis, c. 1505-1588

Matthew Parker published *The Whole Psalter* (London, 1561-1567) with tunes by Tallis. This tune was the ninth in the musical *Appendix* to Parker's work. Eric Routley, in his *Companion to Congregational Praise,* calls this the simplest of all hymn tunes and declares it to be the first common meter tune in history. The tune name is derived from the use of this tune with the Latin hymn *Veni, Creator Spiritus,* which was used at the ordination of priests in the Anglican Church. This is its first inclusion in *GS.*

O Heart Bowed Down with Sorrow   337

Franklin E. Belden, 1858-1945

This text was published by Belden in his *Gospel Song Sheaf* (1895), and the copyright was owned by William J. Kirkpatrick. It entered hymnals of the Stone-Campbell Movement as early as T. B. Larimore and Kirkpatrick's *The New Christian Hymn Book* (Nashville, 1907) and was also published in Belden's *Christ in Song, Revised and Enlarged* (Washington, D. C., 1908). It was entitled "Come Unto Me" and, in Belden's compilation, has the scripture motto "For my yoke is easy and my burden is light"—Matt. 11:30. It first entered *GS* in 1921.

Belden

Franklin E. Belden, 1858-1945

This tune was written for the foregoing text and published in the *Gospel Song Sheaf* (1895). It first appeared in *GS* in 1921, and the tune name BELDEN was assigned by the current general editor of *GSR* (1986).

O Holy City, Seen of John   431

Walter Russell Bowie, 1881-1969

In 1909 Henry Sloan Coffin and A. W. Verson were editing the hymnal *Hymns for the Kingdom of God* (1910). Coffin requested Bowie to write a hymn that would show that the beginnings of God's kingdom or reign over the hearts of men must start here rather than in a far-off future. He did so, producing this hymn which cries out for disciples of Christ to strive for social justice and to avoid the greed for gain. This is its first inclusion in *GS*.

Morning Song

From John Wyeth's *Repository of Sacred Music, Part Second,* 1813

This tune is also called CONSOLATION (see "The King shall come when morning dawns, *GSR*, No. 284); but, with the last two lines repeated, we have chosen to use the other common name, MORNING SONG. The tune may be traced back to Wythe's *Repository* (1813) and to Ananias Davidson's Kentucky *Harmony* (1816). It is a traditional melody resembling old English ballads and carols. This is its first inclusion in *GS*.

O How He Loves You and Me 232

Kurt Kaiser, b. 1934

This text was written in 1975 in a period of ten minutes. Kaiser often jots down ideas for tunes or lyrics as they occur to him. He had run across the phrase "O, how he loves you and me" in his reading and decided to write a melody to fit the words. The melody and the resulting text just seemed to flow from his pen. The text and tune have been very popular. Kaiser attributes this popularity to the fact that the Swedish gospel singer Evie Tornquist Karlson recorded the song soon after he wrote it. I am indebted to Dr. William J. Reynolds for assisting me in securing this information. The text entered *GS* for the first time in the revised edition of 1986.

Kaiser

Kurt Kaiser, b. 1934

This tune was written for the preceding text in accordance with the information given above. It enters *GS* for the first time in the current revised edition (1986).

O How Kindly Hast Thou Led Me 142

Thomas Grinfield, 1788-1870

This text was first published in *A Century of Original Sacred Songs Composed for Favourite Airs* (London, 1836). It was there entitled "Remembrance of the Way." The text has been in *GS* since 1921.

Middletown

Traditional English Melody

No information is currently available on this tune. It first entered *GS* in 1921.

O How Shall I Receive Thee   189

Paul Gerhardt, 1607-1676

Trans. Arthur Tozer Russell, 1806-1874

This is one of Gerhardt's most beautiful Advent hymns, beginning "Wie soll ich dich empfangen." It was first published in Christoph Runge's *D. M.* Luthers und anderer vornehmen geistreichen und gelehrten Manner geistliche *Lieder und Psalmen* (Berlin, 1653). Russell's translation was published in his Psalms and Hymns, Partly Original, Partly Selected, for the Use of the Church *of England* (1851). This is its first appearance in *GS*.

St. Theodulph

Melchior Teschner, 1584-1635

For information on this tune, see "All Glory, Laud, and Honor," (*GSR*. No. 167). The tune is sometimes called VALET WILL ICH DIR GEBEN.

O Jesus, I Have Promised   620

John E. Bode, 1816-1874

This poem was written in 1866 as a hymn to be used at the confirmation service for Bode's two sons and a daughter. It was first published in leaflet form in 1868 and then included in the *Appendix* to SPCK's *Psalms and Hymns for Public Worship* (1869). The text was originally in six 8-line stanzas. It first entered *GS* in 1925.

Angel's Story

Arthur H. Mann, 1850-1929

This tune was composed for Emily H. Miller's "I love to hear the story that angel voices tell" (whence the tune name) and was first published in *The Methodist Sunday School Tune-Book* (1881). It entered *GS* in 1925.

O Jesus, My Savior 446
Anonymous
Arr. *GSR*, 1986

No information is available on the composition of this text. It appeared with the accompanying tune in Jeremiah Ingall's *Christian Harmony, or Songster's Companion* (Exeter, New Hampshire: Henry Ranlet, 1805). The text first entered *GS* in the *Supplement* (1975). The first stanza of the text in the *Supplement* began "I love Thee, I love Thee, / I love Thee, my Lord." This stanza has been omitted in the present edition because of the monotony of the words. The order of the three remaining stanzas is now stanza 3, 4, and 2 of the original poem.

Charity

Anonymous in Jeremiah Ingalls's
Christian Harmony, 1805

This tune was published in the hymnal mentioned above. It first entered *GS* in the *Supplement* (1975).

O Little Town of Bethlehem 193
Phillips Brooks, 1835-1893

Brooks visited Bethlehem in 1865 while on a tour of the Holy Land. He wrote this text in 1868, and it was sung at a Sunday School Christmas service in his church in Philadelphia. Widely distributed in leaflet form, it was first printed in a hymnal in *The Church Porch, A Service Book and Hymnal for Sunday Schools,* ed. William R. Huntington (New York, 1874). Brooks's poem was originally in five stanzas. The omitted stanza 4 reads:

> Where children, pure and happy
> Pray to the Blessed Child;
> Where misery cries out to thee,
> Son of the Mother mild;
> Where charity stands watching,
> And faith holds wide the door,
> The dark night wakes, the glory breaks,
> And Christmas comes once more.

This hymn entered *GS* in 1921.

St. Louis

Lewis H. Redner, 1830-1908

This tune was written for the preceding text at the request of Phillips Brooks. It was sung first on December 27, 1868, in Holy Trinity Church, Philadelphia, and was published with the text in Huntington's *Church Porch* (1874). The reason for the tune name is unknown. It entered *GS* in 1921.

O Lord of Heaven and Earth and Sea   149

Christopher Wordsworth, 1807-1885

This text was published in Wordsworth's *The Holy Year, or Hymns for Sundays and Holydays* (3d ed., 1863). It was entitled "Charitable Collections" and was originally in nine stanzas. It entered *GS* in the *Supplement* (1922) and contained stanzas 1, 2, 3 ,4, 6, and 8. The *GSR* text includes stanzas 1, 2, 4, 5, and 6. The omitted stanzas 7 and 9 read:

> We lose what on ourselves we spend,
> > We have, as treasure without end,
> Whatever, Lord, to thee we lend,
> > Who givest all.

> To thee, from whom we all derive
> > Our life, our gifts, our power to give;
> O may we ever with thee live,
> > Who givest all!

Meyer

J. D. Meyer's *Geistliche Seelenfreud,* 1692

This tune, composed by Meyer, appeared in his *Geistliche Seelenfreud: oder Davidische Hauss-Capell* (1692). It is also called ES IST KEIN TAG, from the German text to which it was first set. This is its first inclusion in *GS,* all previous editions having used John Bacchus Dykes's ALMSGIVING (1865).

O Lord, My God   60

Carl Boberg, 1859-1940

Trans. Stuart K. Hine, b. 1899

Boberg's now popular hymn was originally written in the summer of 1885 after he had been inspired by the beauty of nature and the ringing sound of church bells. It was published in his hometown newspaper, the *Monsteras Tidningan,* on March 12, 1886. A few years later to his surprise he heard the hymn sung to the Swedish folk tune to which it has ever since been joined. He then published the hymn and tune in 1891 in the *Sanningsvittnet,* of which he was editor. The history of the hymn thereafter is obscure until it was made popular during a Billy Graham crusade in Canada in 1955, but it had come a long and interesting journey. The poem was translated into German in Estonia in 1907 by Manfred von Glehn. The German translation began "Wie gross bist Du." In 1922, it was translated into Russian by I. S. Prokhanoff. Hine learned of the Russian text in 1927, but he did not make his English version until the late 1930s while he was residing in Subcarpathian Russia as a missionary. His poem retains only a few phrases literally translated from the Russian text or contained in Boberg's original. It is practically an original poem.

O Store Gud

Swedish Folk Melody
Arr. Stuart K. Hine. b. 1899

The tune name derives from the original Swedish opening lines of Boberg's poem. The origin of the melody is unknown. As aforementioned, it was published in 1891 with Boberg's text, and in 3/4 time. In 1894 the tune appeared in its modern 4/4 time in *Svenska Missionsforbundet Sangbok*. It entered *GS* in 1967.

O Lord, Our Lord

54
Horatio R. Palmer, 1834-1907

This paraphrase of Psalm 8 was published in Palmer's *Song Monarch* (1874). It was reprinted in his elaborate singing school text *The Choral Union* (1884). *The Psalter of the United Presbyterian Church* included it in 1887. Both poem and tune entered *GS* in 1925, reprinted from Palmer's *Choral Union*.

Palmer

Horatio R. Palmer, 1834-1907

The present arrangement is that of Palmer as published in his *Choral Union* (1884) with the exception of the tenor countermelody which was prepared by Jack Boyd, music editor of *GSR* (1986). The tune name PALMER was given by the current general editor of *GSR*.

O Love, How Deep, How Broad, How High   397
Anonymous Latin hymn
O Amor quam ecstaticus, 15th Century

This hymn, sometimes attributed to Thomas à Kempis (1380-1471), is a cento from the original hymn of twenty-three stanzas, which begins "Apparuit benignitas / Dei nec non humanitas / Ex caritate nimia / Ad nos atque gratuita." Benjamin Webb translated eight of the stanzas which were included in *The Hymnal Noted* (Part II, 1854). The *GS* text is an arrangement from Webb's translation and is substantially that which appears in *The Hymnal 1940* and other modern collections. This is its first inclusion in *GS*.

Deus tuorum Militum

From *Grenoble Antiphoner*, 1753

In the sixteenth and seventeenth centuries, there was a transition in French hymnody from the medieval plainsong to the measured modern hymn. This melody comes out of that transition. The current form of the hymn tune was introduced in *The English Hymnal* (Oxford, 1906) and was taken from the *Grenoble Antiphoner* (1753). The tune name means "God of your soldiers." This is its first inclusion in *GS*.

St. Margaret

Albert L. Peace, 1844-1912

This tune was written for the foregoing text and published in *The Scottish Hymnal* (1884). Peace had been requested by the hymnal committee to prepare the tune. He said: "After reading it (i.e., the poem) over carefully, I wrote the music straight off, and may say that the ink of the first note was hardly dry when I finished the tune." The tune entered *GS* in 1921.

O Master, Let Me Walk with Thee   441
Washington Gladen, 1836-1918

This text was first published in Gladden's magazine *Sunday Afternoon* in 1879. It was entitled "Walking with God" and included in "The Still Hour," a column designed for devotional reading. The poem was originally in three 8-line stanzas, but Charles H. Richards turned it into a 4-line hymn poem and published it in his *Songs of Christian Praise* (1880). Richards omitted the second stanza, which was not appropriate for devotional purposes:

O Master, let me walk with thee
>Before the taunting Pharisee;
Help me to bear the sting of spite,
>The hate of men who hide thy light,
The sore distrust of souls sincere
>Who cannot read thy judgments clear,
The dullness of the multitude,
>Who dimly guess that thou art good.

This text first entered *GS* in the *Supplement* (1922).

Maryton

H. Percy Smith, 1825-1898

This tune was composed by Smith for John Keble's hymn "Sun of My Soul," and was first published in *Church Hymns with Tunes* (London, 1874). It entered *GS* as a setting for Gladden's text in the *Supplement* (1922).

O My Soul, Bless God the Father   123
From *The Book of Psalms*, 1871

This metrical paraphrase of Psalm 103 first appeared in *The Book of Psalms* (1871), published by the United Presbyterian Church. The poem was originally comprised of sixteen stanzas, covering all the verses of the psalm. The complete text may also be found in *The Psalter of the United Presbyterian Church* (1887). The *GSR* text is comprised of the original stanzas 1, 2, 8, 11, 12, and 16. Minor alterations have been made in the text over the years, principally the substitution of the word "Father" for "Jehovah" in 1:1. This is the first appearance of this text in *GS*.

Stuttgart

From *Psalmodia Sacra*, 1715
Adapt. Henry J. Gauntlett, 1861

For information on this tune, see the notes on "God Is Love, His Mercy Brightens" (*GSR*, No. 119).

O Praise the Lord   46
Anonymous paraphrase of Psalm 117

The information on this text is uncertain. *The Dictionary of American Hymnology* project (DAH) attributes this paraphrase to C. W. Naylor in George F. Roots's *The Hour of Praise: for Praise Meetings, and*

Congregational and Sunday School Singing (Cincinnnati: John C. Church, 1872). No other information is available.

Hill

Will Hill

No information is available on this composer. The tune name HILL was assigned by the current general editor of *GSR*.

O Sacred Head   221

Attributed to Bernard of Clairvaux, 1091-1153
German trans. Paul Gerhardt, 1607-1676
English trans. James W. Alexander, 1804-1859

GSR continues to attribute this original hymn to Bernard of Clairvaux. The evidence is questionable, however, and some editors suggest that Arnulf of Louvain (1200-1251) may be the author. It has not been found in any manuscript earlier than the fourteenth century, but it is possible that earlier parts of the poem were by Bernard and the latter by Arnulf or some other poet. The original hymn is in seven parts and addresses various parts of the suffering body of Christ: Part I, *"Salve mundi salutare"* to the feet; II, *"Salve Jesu, Rex sanctorum"* to the knees; III, *"Salve Jesu, Pastor bone"* to the hands; IV, *Salve Jesu, summe bonus"* to the sides; V, *"Salve salus mea"* to the breast;" VI, *"Summi regis cor aveto"* to the heart; and VII, *"Salve caput cruentatum"* to the face. The modern poem derives from Part VII, and the Latin text may be seen in *Historical Companion to Hymns Ancient and Modern* (1962, p. 198). Gerhardt's translation was first published in Johann Crüger's *Praxis Pietatis Melica* (Berlin, ed. 1656) in ten stanzas. This translation appears in my copy of *Kirchen Gesangbuch für Evangelisch Lutherische Gemeinden* (St. Louis, 1844). Alexander published his translation in eight stanzas in Joshua Leavitt's *The Christian Lyre* (1830). The *GSR* text contains stanzas 1 and 6 of Alexander's translation. This hymn has been in *GS* since 1921.

Passion Chorale

Hans Leo Hassler, 1564-1612
Harm. J. S. Bach, 1658-1750

This tune was first published in Hassler's *Lustgarten neuer Deutscher Gesang* (Nuremberg, 1601), set to the love song "Mein G'muth ist mir verwirret einer Jungfrau zart." It was first published as a hymn tune in *Harmoniae Sacrae* (3d ed., Gorlitz, 1613), set to "Herzlich thut mich verlangen." Crüger first used it for a setting for Gerhardt's poem in his *Praxis Pietatis Melica* (1656). Bach's harmony comes from his *St. Matthew Passion* (1729), in which he used the tune five times. It has been in *GS* since 1937. The Number One editions of *GS* used words only; the 1921 book suggested using the tune DOLORES by E. L. Jorgenson; the 1922 and 1925 editions suggested AURELIA.

O Savior, Bless Us Ere We Go 13
Hans Leo Hassler, 1564-1612
Harm. J. S. Bach, 1685-1750

This touching and extensively used evening prayer was written for use at the London Roman Catholic Oratory in 1849. The original opening lines were "Sweet Savior, bless us." This text was published in Faber's *Jesus and Mary* (1852) in five stanzas. It first entered *GS* in the *Supplement* (1922) in four stanzas, but was reduced to the present three in 1925. The *GSR* text contains Faber's stanzas 1, 3, and 4. Stanzas 2 and 5 (the latter included as stanza four in the 1922 edition) read as follows:

> 2
> The day is done, its hours have run,
> And Thou hast taken count of all,
> The scanty triumphs grace hath won,
> The broken vow, the frequent fall.
> Through life's long day, etc.

> 5
> For all we love, the poor, the sad,
> The sinful unto Thee we call;
> O let Thy mercy make us glad"
> Thou art our Jesus, and our all.
> Through life's long day, etc.

Stella

Anonymous
Arr. Henri F. Hemy in *Easy Tunes for Catholic Schools*, 1852

STELLA is an old English melody whose composer and date of composition are unknown. The present arrangement was made by Hemy in 1852. Robert McCutchan relates the story told by James Lightwood that Hemy heard school children singing a song to this tune at Stella, a village near Newcastle. Others derive the tune name from the Latin poem *Stella maris* ("Hail, Queen of Heaven, the ocean star"). This tune entered *GS* in the *Supplement* (1922).

O Sons and Daughters, Let Us Sing   246
Jean Tisserand, d. 1494
Trans. John Mason Neale, 1818-1866

This French text, entitled "L'aleluya du jour des Pasques," was probably written by Tisserand. It is first found printed in the early decades of the sixteenth century. The complete Latin text in nine stanzas may be seen in *Historical Companion to Hymns Ancient and Modern* (1962). Neale's translation first appeared in his *Medieval Hymns and Sequences* (1851). The editors of *Hymns Ancient and Modern* (1861) changed Neale's opening line, "Ye sons and daughters of the King," to its present form and made other alterations in the text which we have retained in the *GSR* text. This is the first inclusion of this hymn in *GS*.

O Filii et Filiae

Traditional French Melody, 17th century

The tune may be contemporary with the words, but its first known appearance was in *Airs sur les hymnes sacrez, odes et noëls* (Paris, 1623). This is another example of ancient modal music, and the tune is included in *GS* for the first time.

O Soul, Are You Weary and Troubled   311
Helen Howarth Lemmel, 1864-1961

Mrs. Lemmel saw the following words in a pamphlet by the missionary Lillias Trotter in 1918: "So then, turn your eyes upon HIM. Look full into His face and you will find that the things of earth will acquire a strange, new dimness." These words inspired the text, the chorus immediately and the stanzas within a week. It was first published in a pamphlet entitled "The Heavenly Vision" by C. C. Birchard in London (1918). It was thereafter published in the National Sunday School Union's *Glad Songs* (1922) and in Harry D. Clarke's *Gospel Truth in Song, No. 2* (1924). This is its first appearance in *GS*.

Lemmel

Helen Howarth Lemmel, 1864-1961

This tune was written for the preceding text and published in the Sunday School Union's *Glad Songs* (1922). This is its first inclusion in *GS*.

O Splendor of God's Glory Bright   158
Ambrose of Milan, c. 338-397
Trans. Compilers of *Hymns Ancient and Modern*, 1904

It is almost certain that Ambrose is the author of the Latin hymn text "Splendor paternae gloriae." Fulgentius of Ruspe, who died A.D. 553, attributed it to him, as did the Venerable Bede in the eighth century. Furthermore, internal evidence from the writings known to belong to Ambrose seems conclusive. In his treatise *De Fide,* he calls the Son of God "Splendor paternae gloriae." This is a beautiful morning hymn and a hymn of praise to Christ. It is included in *GS* for the first time.

Solemnis haec festivitas

From *Paris Gradual,* 1689
Arr. Jack Boyd, 1986

This tune is found in the *Paris Gradual* (1698). No other information is available. It was arranged especially for this edition of *GS* by the music editor and is included for the first time.

O Spread the Tidings Round   290
Francis Bottome, 1823-1921

This text was first published in Thomas Harrison's selection entitled *Precious Hymns for Times of Refreshing and Revival* (Philadelphia, 1890). The poem entered *GS* in the *Supplement* (1975). The current edition omits the chorus.

Comforter

William J. Kirkpatrick, 1838-1921

This tune was written for the preceding text and first published in Harrison's hymnal mentioned above in 1890. Kirkpatrick and John R. Sweney collaborated in editing the collection. The tune first entered *GS* in the *Supplement* (1975).

O Thou, in Whose Presence   634
Joseph Swain, 1761-1796

This text derives from a paraphrase of portions of the Song of Solomon entitled "A Description of Christ by His Graces and Power." It was published in Swain's *Experimental Essays on Divine Subjects in Verse* (1791) in nine 8-line stanzas. It is included in *GS* for the first time.

Dulcimer

Attributed to Freeman Lewis in John Wyeth's
Repository of Sacred Music, Part Second, 1812
Harm. Austin C. Lovelace, 1964

This tune has been known by various names and was called WYETH in the first printing of *GSR*. It is also known as DAVIS, MEDITATION, and MY BELOVED. The tune has been credited to one Freeman Lewis, but Ausin Lovelace says that "it is almost certainly an American folk hymn" (*Companion to the Hymnal,* p. 339).

O Thou, to Whose All-Searching Sight   510

Nicolaus von Zinzendorf, 1700-1760
Trans. John Wesley, 1703-1791

The German text, beginning "Seelen-Bräutigam, O du Gottes-Lamm," was first published in the *Sammlung geistlicher und lieblicher Lieder* (1725). Wesley probably saw it in the *Hernnhut Gesangbuch* (1735) as he traveled with the Moravians to America. He translated only a portion of Zinzendorf's original text and added one stanza, which he translated from J. A. Freyling-hausen's "Wer is wohl, wie du." The hymn in six stanzas was first published in *A Collection of Psalms and Hymns* (1738). It subsequently appeared in Wesley's *Collection of Hymns for the Use of the People Called Methodists* (1780). It has had a continuing use among the Methodists and is a fine hymn of trust in God through difficulties. This is its first inclusion in *GS.*

Rockingham (Mason)

Lowell Mason, 1792-1872

This tune was written in 1830 and first published in *The Choir* (1832). It is sometimes called ROCKINGHAM (New) or, in some of the old oblong shape-note books, GRAVITY. This is its first inclusion in *GS.*

O to Be Like Thee   624

Thomas O. Chisholm, 1866-1960

This text originally appeared in W. D. Kirkland, James Atkins, and W. J. Kirkpatrick's *Young People's Hymnal* (1897). This was a collection for youth in the Methodist Church, South. It was also included in succeeding editions of this hymnal and has had a wide use as a gospel song. It has been in *GS* since 1921.

Rondinella

William J. Kirkpatrick, 1838-1921

This tune was written for and published with the text above in *Young People's Hymnal* (1897). The tune name is for Pasquale Rondinella, one of Kirkpatrick's music teachers. The tune entered *GS* in 1921.

O Word of God Incarnate 298

William W. How, 1823-1897

This is one of How's most popular texts. Appearing under the motto from Proverbs 6:23—"For the commandment is a lamp; and the law is light; and reproofs of instruction are the way of life"—the text is based on Psalm 119:105, and was first published in How and T. B. Morell's *Psalms and Hymns* (1854) and again in their *Supplement* (1867). It first entered *GS* in the *Supplement* (1975).

Munich

Neuvermehrtes Gesangbuch, 1693
Harm. Felix Mendelssohn, 1809-1847

This tune was published in the *Neuvermehrtes und zu Übung christl. Gottseligkeit eingerichtetes Meiningisches Gesangbuch* (Meiningen, 1693). Marilyn Kay Stulken, in her *Hymnal Companion to the Lutheran Hymn Book* (p. 309), says that the melody line seems to be made up from certain tunes by Hieronymus Gradenthaler as published in Wok Helhard von Hehenbert's psalter, *Lust und Arztneigarten* (Regensburg, 1675). The tune in its present form is from Mendelssohn's "Cast thy burden upon the Lord," in his *Elijah* (1847). It was first included in *GS* in the *Supplement* (1975).

O Worship the King 87

Robert Grant, 1779-1838

This text was first published in Henry Bickersteth's *Christian Psalmody* (1833). It is based on William Kethe's paraphrase of Psalm 104, which appeared in the *Anglo-Genevan Psalter* (1561). Originally in six stanzas, the *GSR* text contains Grant's stanzas 1, 4, and 5. The omitted stanzas are as follows:

2
O tell of His might, O, sing of His grace
  Whose robe is the light, whose canopy, space.
His chariots of wrath the deep thunder-clouds form,
  And dark is His path on the wings of the storm.

3

The earth, with its store of wonders untold,
    Almighty, Thy power hath founded of old,
Hath 'stablished it fast by a changeless decree
    And round it hath cast, like a mantle, the sea.

5

O measureless Might! ineffable Love!
    While angels delight to hymn Thee above,
The humbler creation, though feeble their lays,
    With true adoration shall lisp to Thy praise.

This text entered *GS* in 1921.

Lyons

Attributed to Johann Michael Haydn, 1737-1806 in
William Gardiner's *Sacred Melodies*, 1815

    This arrangement was first published in Gardiner's *Sacred Melodies from Haydn, Mozart, and Beethoven* (Vol. 12, 1815) as the setting for the text "O praise ye the Lord, prepare a new song." Although he attributed it to Haydn, no exact source has been found for the tune. It first entered *GS* in 1921.

O Zion, Haste, Thy Mission High Fulfilling   414
Mary Ann Thomson, 1834-1923

    The major portion of this hymn was written in 1868 on an evening when she was sitting up with one of her children who was suffering from typhoid fever. She wished to write a missionary hymn that would fit the usual tune (PILGRIMS) of "Hark, hark, my soul"! Angelic songs are swelling." She was unable, however, to complete a suitable refrain. Three years later in 1871, she wrote the refrain. Originally in six stanzas, the text in *GSR* includes stanzas 1, 2, 5, and 6. The omitted stanzas read:

3

'Tis thine to save from peril of perdition
    The souls for whom the Lord his life laid down;
Beware lest, slothful to fulfill thy mission,
    Thou lose one jewel that should deck his crown.

4
Proclaim to every people, tongue, and nation
    That God in whom they live and move is love;
Tell how he stooped to save his lost creation,
    And died on earth that they might live above.

This text was first included in a hymnal in *The Hymnal* (1892) of the Protestant Episcopal Church. It has been in *GS* since 1921.

Tidings

James Walch, 1837-1901

This tune was written as a setting for the text "Hark, hark, my soul! Angelic songs are swelling." It was published in *The Hymnal Companion to the Book of Common Prayer* (London, 1877). It was later published in the United States in Charles L. Hutchins's *The Church Hymnal, containing the Hymns set forth by the General Convention of 1892, and authorized for Use in the Protestant Episcopal Church* (1894). It has been in *GS* since 1921.

On a Hill Far Away 655

George Bennard, 1873-1958

Bennard gave his own account of the writing of the words and tune for this song:

I was praying for a full understanding of the cross, and its plan in Christianity. I read and studied and prayed. I saw Christ and the cross inseparably. The Christ of the cross became more than a symbol. The scene pictured a method, outlined a process, and revealed the consummation of spiritual experience. It was like seeing John 3:16 leave the printed page, take form, and act out the meaning of redemption. While watching this scene with my mind's eye, the theme of the song came to me, and with it the melody; but only the words of the theme, "The Old Rugged Cross," came. An inner voice seemed to say, "Wait"! I was holding evangelistic meetings in Michigan, but could not continue with the poem. After a series of meetings in New York state, the following week, I tried again to compose the poem, but could not. It was only after I had completed the New York meeting, and returned to Michigan for further evangelistic work, that the flood-gates were loosed. Many experiences of the redeeming grace of God through our Lord Jesus Christ during those meetings had broken down all barriers. I was enabled to complete the poem with facility and dispatch. A friend aided in putting it into manuscript form.

(See George W. Sanville, *Forty Hymn Stories*, p. 15) The poem was completed in 1913 and was first published in *Heart and Life Songs, for the Church Sunday School, Home and Campmeeting* (1915). This collection was edited by Joseph H. Smith, Bennard, and Iva Durham Bennard. The text entered *GS* in 1925.

Old Rugged Cross

George Bennard, 1873-1958

See the notes on the text above. This tune was first published in Joseph H. Smith, Bennard, and Iva Durham Bennard's *Heart and Life Songs, for the Church, Sunday School, Home and Campmeeting* (1915). It first entered *GS* in 1925.

On Jordan's Stormy Banks   666

Samuel Stennett, 1727-1795

This text was written by Stennett, an English Baptist, and published in John Rippon's *Selection of Hymns* (1787). It was there entitled "Heaven Anticipated" and consisted of eight 4-line stanzas, according to William J. Reynolds. I have been unable to find the eighth, but three of the omitted stanzas read:

> There generous fruits, that never fail,
> > On trees immortal grow:
> There rocks, and hills, and brooks, and vales,
> > With milk and honey flow.

> O the transporting, rapturous scene,
> > That rises to my sight;
> Sweet fields arrayed in living green,
> > And rivers of delight.

> No chilling winds nor poisonous breath|
> > Can reach that healthful shore;
> Sickness and sorrow, pain and death,
> > Are felt and feared no more.

The original reading of 2:1 began "All o'er" and 4:2 read "Can here" rather than "Would here." Stennett's poem seems to have been modeled on Isaac Watts's "There is a land of pure delight." The text entered *GS* in 1921, containing only the present stanzas 1 through 3. It was enlarged to five stanzas in 1937, including "O the transporting, rapturous scene" as given above. *GSR* omits this stanza.

Promised Land

American Folk Hymn
Arr. Rigdon M. McIntosh, 1836-1899

The original of this tune (see below) was first published in William Walker's *Southern Harmony* (1835). It was there attributed to "Miss M. Durham," of whom nothing is known. Originally written in the key of F sharp minor, it was altered to F major by R. M. McIntosh and published in Harvey R. Christie's *Gospel Light* (1895). Christie was a well-known singing teacher in the Stone-Campbell Movement. This tune first entered *GS* in 1937. (See McIntosh's arrangement below.)

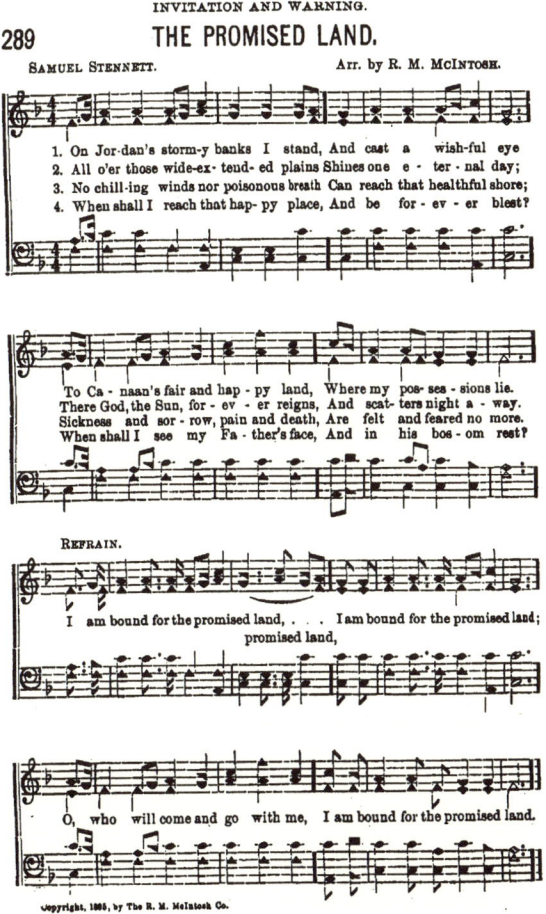

On Zion's Glorious Summit   177
John Kent, 1766-1843

This text first appeared in Kent's Collection of *Original Gospel Hymns* (1803). It has been a very popular hymn among the descendants of the Stone-Campbell Movement. The origin of the text of the Sanctus is unknown. This hymn entered *GS* in 1921.

Skene

Robert Skene, 19th Century

This tune was called ST. LOUIS when it was published in the *New Harp of Zion* (1872), edited by A. D. Fillmore and his son James H. Fillmore. The exact date of composition is unknown. An abbreviated form of the *Sanctus*, with the Skene tune, also appeared in the Fillmore book. An expanded version of this *Sanctus* may be found in R. M. McIntosh's *Hermon: a New Collection of Sacred Music* (New York, 1873). Robert Skene, the composer of the tune, was the son of Benjamin Skene, a longtime advocate of religious reform who died in 1859. Robert resided in Louisville, Kentucky, and was an associate of the Fillmore's. This tune entered *GS* in 1921. The tune name SKENE was assigned by the current general editor of *GSR*.

One Day   283
J. Wilbur Chapman, 1859-1918

Charles H. Marsh, the composer, said that he received the words of this song from Chapman about 1908 or 1909, while they were working together in a Bible conference at Stony Brook, Long Island. Just when Chapman may have written the poem is unknown, but probably about the time that he gave it to Marsh. This text has been in *GS* since 1921.

One Day

Charles H. Marsh, 1886-1956

This tune was written for the preceding text by Marsh at the time of the Bible conference mentioned above, probably in 1909. William J. Reynolds tells of the copyright fight over this hymn in his *Companion to the Baptist Hymnal* (1976). The song was first published in *The Message in Song* (Praise Publishing Company, 1911). This tune entered *GS* in 1921.

One Step at a Time 541

T. J. Shelton, 1849-1929

This text was first published in J. H. Fillmore's *Joy and Gladness* (Cincinnati: Fillmore Bros. Publishers, 1880). It also appeared in the *New Christian Hymn and Tune Book* (Cincinnati, 1887). It entered *GS* in 1925.

Rosecrans

James H. Rosecrans, 1844-1926

No information is available as to the original date or circumstances of composition of this tune. It appeared with the text in the hymnals mentioned above. It has been in *GS* since 1925. The tune name ROSECRANS was assigned by the present general editor of *GSR*.

Only in Thee 477

Thomas O. Chisholm, 1866-1960

This text was first published in Daniel B. Towner and Charles M. Alexander's *Revival Hymns* (Chicago, 1905). No other information is available. It has been in *GS* since 1921.

Monos

Charles H. Gabriel, 1856-1932

This tune was written for the preceding text and published in Towner and Alexander's *Revival Hymns* (Chicago, 1905, No. 127). It entered *GS* in 1921. The tune name MONOS (meaning "only" in Greek) was assigned by the present general editor of *GSR*.

Onward, Christian Soldiers 412

Sabine Baring-Gould, 1834-1896

This powerful and stirring hymn text was written for a children's festival at Horbury Bridge, near Wakefield, England, in 1864. The children were to use it as a processional hymn as they made their way from one village to another. It was first printed in the *Church Times* (October 15, 1864) and in the *Supplement* to *Hymns Ancient and Modern* (1868). The *GSR* text contains stanzas 1, 2, 5, and 6. Stanza 3 reads:

Like a mighty army
Moves the church of God;
Brothers, we are treading
Where the saints have trod;

> We are not divided,
>> All one body we,
> One in hope and doctrine,
>> One in charity.

Stanza 4, omitted here, is no longer used in any hymnal:
> What the saints established,
>> That I hold for true;
> What the saints believed,
>> That believe I too.
> Long as earth endureth
>> Men that faith will hold,
> Kingdoms, nations, empires
>> In destruction rolled.

This hymn first entered *GS* in 1921.

St. Gertrude

Arthur Sullivan, 1842-1900

This tune was written for *The Hymnary* (London, 1872), which was edited by Sullivan, but it was first published in the *Musical Times* (December, 1871). The tune is named for Mrs. Gertrude Clay-Ker-Seymer of Dorsetshire, in whose home the tune was composed. It was published in the United States in John R. Sweney's *Gems of Praise* (Philadelphia, 1873). The tune entered *GS* in 1921.

Open My Eyes, That I May See   607

Clara H. Scott, 1841-1897

The exact date of the writing of this poem is unknown. It was first published in E. A. Hoffman and H. F. Sayles's *Best Hymns No. 2* (1895). This text first entered *GS* in 1921. It was omitted from the *Number Two* (1937) and restored in the *Supplement* (1975).

Open Now Thy Gates of Beauty   83

Benjamin Schmolck, 1672-1737
Trans. Catherine Winkworth, 1827-1878

The German poem beginning "Tut mir auf die schöne Pforte" was first published in Schmolke's *Kirchen-Gefährte* (1732) in seven stanzas.

Catherine Winkworth published her translation in her *Chorale Book for England* (1863). The *GSR* text represents the first two stanzas of her translation. This is its first appearance in *GS*.

Neander
Joachim Neander, 1650-1680

This tune is found in Neander's *Glaub-und Liebesübung* (Bremen, 1680). Lines 5 and 6 of the tune were originally in triple time. The present arrangement dates from E. P. Züchlein's *Geistreiches Gesang-Buch* (Darmstadt, 1698). This tune is also called UNSER HERRSCHER. It first entered *GS* in 1937.

Our Day of Praise Is Done
16
John Ellerton, 1826-1893

The original text of this hymn consisted of four stanzas from W. J. Blew's translation of Charles Coffin's Latin hymn *Grates peracto jam die*. The original was published in Blew's *Church Hymn and Tune Book* (1852). To the four stanzas of Blew's translation, Ellerton added three of his own, and the hymn was used at the Nantwich Festival of Choirs (1868). Our present text consists of three stanzas from a complete revision of the poem by Ellerton in the SPCK *Church Hymns* (1871). The revised poem is really Ellerton's, but the line of thought is from Blew. *GS* includes stanzas 1, 2, and 5 of Ellerton's 6-stanza revision. This text entered GS in the *Supplement* (1922). It was omitted in 1937 and is here restored in *GSR*.

St. Thomas
Aaron Williams, 1731-1776

For information on this tune, see "Awake, and Sing the Song" (*GSR*, No. 153). The preceding text was set to SCHUMANN in the 1922 *Supplement,* but ST. THOMAS became the setting in 1925.

Out of My Bondage
352
William T. Sleeper, 1819-1904

Having previously collaborated with Stebbins on the fine gospel hymn "Ye Must Be Born Again," Sleeper, when he wrote this hymn text about 1886, sent it to Stebbings for the musical setting. It was first published in Ira D. Sankey, James McGranahan, and Stebbins's *Gospel Hymns No. 5* (1887). This text entered *GS* in 1921.

Jesus, I Come

George C. Stebbins, 1846-1945

Stebbins received the preceding text from W. T. Sleeper in 1886 with the request to write a musical setting. He did so, and the hymn and tune were published together in Sankey, McGranahan, and Stebbins's *Gospel Hymns No. 5* (1887). The tune has been in *GS* since 1921.

Out of the Depths I Cry to You   549

Martin Luther, 1483-1549
Trans. Gracia Grindal, b. 1943

This beautiful version of Psalm 130 was a favorite with Luther. The poem was sung at his funeral. It was first published in a broadsheet in Madegburg in 1523 and was printed in the *Etlich Christlich lider* in Wittenburg (1524). The present translation is by Gracia Grindal and was first published in the *Lutheran Book of Worship* (1978). It represents the first four stanzas of Luther's revised hymn. This is its first inclusion in *GS*.

Aus Tiefer Not

Attributed to Martin Luther, 1483-1546
Arr. Jack A. Boyd, b.1932

This melody is usually attributed to Luther himself and was first published in Johann Walther's *Geystliche gesangk Buchleyn* (1524). It is in what the medieval musicians called the Phrygian mode (the ancient Greek Dorian, i.e., formed on the octave e-é) and is well-adapted to Luther's text. The *GSR* arrangement was prepared by the music editor and included for the first time in *GS*.

Peace, Perfect Peace   475

Edward H. Bickersteth, 1825-1906

In the summer of 1875, Bickersteth was on a holiday to Harrogate in the north of England. There on an August Sunday morning, he heard a sermon based on Isaiah 26:3: "Thou wilt keep him in perfect peace whose mind is stayed on thee." The minister remarked that in the Hebrew "perfect peace" was literally "peace, peace." In the afternoon Bickersteth visited an aged and dying relative, Archdeacon Hill of Liverpool, and desiring to express comfort to Hill, took pen and paper, wrote the hymn exactly as it stands, and then read it to Hill. The hymn was originally in seven stanzas, and when the text first entered *GS* in the *Supplement* (1922), all seven were included. Stanza 6 was omitted in 1937. It reads:

Peace, perfect peace, death shadowing us and ours:
Jesus has vanquished death and all its powers.

Bickersteth's original text ended the first line of the first six stanzas with a question mark, making the second line a response. *GS* has always substituted a colon.

Pax Tecum

George T. Caldbeck, 1852-1918

The Latin hymn name means "Peace be with you." The tune was written for the text preceding. It was revised by Dr. Charles Vincent, harmonized by him, and then published in *The Hymnal Companion to the Book of Common Prayer* (2nd ed., 1877). It entered *GS* in 1921.

Praise God 62

William T. Moore, 1832-1926

This doxology first appeared in *The Christian Hymn Book, a Compilation of Psalms, Hymns, and Spiritual Songs, Original and Selected* by A. Campbell and Others (Cincinnati: Bosworth, Chase and Hall, 1865, No. 728). Moore was one of the compilers of this hymnal for the American Christian Missionary Society. Alexander Campbell, of course, had nothing to do with the compilation of the hymnal, but it was the successor to the line of Campbell hymnals which had begun in 1828. This text first entered *GS* in 1937.

Troyte's Chant, No. 1

Arthur H. D. Troyte, 1811-1857

This tune was written in 1848 and first published in Troyte's *Forty-eight Hymn Tunes* (1860). It first entered *GS* in the *Supplement* (1922) as a setting for Godfrey Thring's "The radiant morn hath passed away." It became the setting for Moore's text in 1937.

Praise God from Whom All Blessings Flow 73

Thomas Ken, 1637-1710

This well-known doxology formed the concluding stanza of Ken's "Morning and Evening Hymns." These hymns, including also a "Midnight Hymn," were written in 1674 when Ken published *A Manual of Prayers for the Use of the Scholars of Winchester College*. The Manual makes mention of the three hymns. For additional information see the notes on

"All Praise to Thee, My God, This Night" (*GSR,* No. 30). Ken's original concluding stanza, printed as early as 1693 by Henry Playford, read in line 3, "Praise Him above, the angelick host." This was altered to the present reading in 1709. This text entered *GS* in 1921, set to OLD HUNDREDTH. The music was omitted in 1925. In the 1937 edition of *GS*, the "Doxology" was not included separately, but appeared as part of the "Morning Hymn"— "Awake My Soul, and with the Sun" and the "Evening Hymn"—"All Praise to Thee, My God, This Night." *GSR* returns to the 1921 tradition.

Old Hundredth

Genevan Psalter, 1551
Attributed to Louis Bourgeois, c. 1510 to c. 1561

This tune appeared in the 1551 edition of the *Genevan Psalter,* which Bourgeois edited. He either composed the tune or adapted it, and used it as a setting for Psalm 134. It appeared as a setting for Psalm 100 in William Kethe's *Fourscore and Seven Psalms of David* (Geneva, 1561) and in Day's *Psalms of David in English Meter* (London, 1561). From these psalters came the tune name OLD HUNDREDTH. This tune entered *GS* in 1921 as a setting for the Doxology.

Praise Him! Praise Him!   169

Fanny J. Crosby, 1829-1915

This hymn text, first entitled "Praise, Give Thanks," was published in W. B. Bradbury, W. H. Doane, W. F. Sherwin, and Chester G. Allen's *Bright Jewels* (New York, 1869). It first entered *GS* in 1937.

Joyful Song

Chester G. Allen, 1838-1878

This tune was written for the preceding text and published in *Bright Jewels* (New York, 1869). The tune name was first given in the *Baptist Hymnal* (1956). It entered *GS* in 1937.

Praise, My Soul, the King of Heaven   53

Henry F. Lyte, 1793-1847

In 1834 Lyte published a collection of free paraphrases of the Psalms. This hymn poem is the second of his three versions of Psalm 103. These paraphrases, as his other hymns, were written for his church in the small fishing village of Lower Brixham, Devonshire, where he ministered from 1823 until his death in 1847. The original fifth line of each stanza reads "Praise Him! Praise Him!" Our text, as is usual in modern hymnals, omits Lyte's original stanza 4:

> Frail as summer's flowers we flourish;
>> Blows the wind and it is gone;
> But while mortals rise and perish,
>> God endures unchanging on.
> Praise Him! Praise Him!
>> Praise the high eternal One.

Lyte himself, in the 1834 printing of his poem, suggested that stanza 4 might be omitted without marring the poem. This text (words only) was included in the *Supplement* (1922), but omitted from *GS* until the present edition.

Lauda Anima (Andrews)

Mark Andrews

This tune, with the addition of "Andrews," is to be distinguished from a tune by the same name by Sir John Goss. It was written for the preceding text in 1931 and published that year by G. Schirmer, Inc. It was written as an anthem, dedicated to "Channing Lefebre and the Trinity Alumni Association. This is its first inclusion in *GS*.

Praise the Lord, His Glories Show 72

Henry F. Lyto, 1793-1847

This poem was first published in two stanzas of eight lines in his *Spirit of the Psalms* (1834). It is a paraphrase of Psalm 150. The *GSR* text contains the original first stanza and one-half of stanza 2 (making our stanzas 1-3). The omitted lines read:

> Strings and voices, hands and hearts,
>> In the concert bear your parts;
> All that breathe, your Lord adore;
>> Praise Him, praise Him, evermore.

This stanza was included in the ACMS edition of A. Campbell's *Christian Hymn Book* (1865, No. 58). This is the first inclusion of this hymn in *GS*.

Gwalchmai

Joseph D. Jones, 1827-1870

This tune by the Welsh composer was first published in Stephen's *Llyfr Tonau ac Emynau* (1868). "Gwalchmai" was the name of a Welsh bard who lived in the twelfth century. This is the first inclusion of this tune in *GS*.

Praise the Lord! Ye Heavens, Adore Him   99, 100
The Foundling Hospital Collection, 1796

This text appeared pasted in the aforementioned collection of twenty-two hymns in 1796. The original collection contained sixteen hymns and was published as *Psalms and Hymns and Anthems of the Foundling Hospital* (1774). The authorship and exact date of composition is unknown. In previous editions of *GS,* the text was attributed to J. Kempthorne. I have been unable to identify such a person. The text entered *GS* in 1921.

Austrian Hymn

Franz Joseph Haydn, 1722-1809

For information on this tune, see the notes on "Glorious Things of Thee Are Spoken" (*GSR*, No. 447). This tune entered *GS* in 1925.

Perez

Lowell Mason, 1792-1872

The origin of this tune is unknown. Thomas Hastings, in his *Presbyterian Psalmist* (185), ascribed it as "Arranged from the German by Lowell Mason." It has been in *GS* since 1921.

Praise the Savior, Ye Who Know Him   162
Thomas Kelly, 1769-1855

This text was first published in Kelly's *Psalms and Hymns extracted from Various Authors* (2d ed., 1806). It was there entitled "Praise of Jesus." The hymn was widely used in the Moody-Sankey evangelistic campaigns in Great Britain during 1873-1875. This is its first inclusion in *GS*.

Acclaim

Traditional German Melody

This tune appeared in Sankey's *Sacred Songs and Solos* (enlarged edition, 1903). Donald Hustad says that it has become known as a German melody. Its source is unknown. This is its first inclusion in *GS*.

Praise to God, Immortal Praise   80

Anna L. Barbauld, 1743-1825

This text was first published in W. Enfield's *Hymns for Public Worship* (1772) in nine 4-line stanzas. It was entitled "Praise to God in Prosperity and Adversity." The *GSR* text is a cento, including the author's original stanza 1, the first two lines of stanza 2, and the remainder of the hymn from other sources. It first entered *GS* in 1925.

Song 13

Orlando Gibbons, 1583-1625

Gibbons composed this tune as one of sixteen which he made for George Wither's *The Hymns and Songs of the Church* (London, 1623). It is also called CANTERBURY and SIMPLICITY. It was set to the thirteenth song in Wither's collection (whence the name), which was a paraphrase of a portion of the Song of Solomon beginning "Oh my love, how comely now," a poem in six lines. Gibbons's music for the last two lines is omitted in the *GS* version. This is the first inclusion of this tune in our hymnal.

Praise to the Lord, the Almighty   45

Joachim Neander, 1650-1680

Neander's original text, based on Psalm 103:1-6 and Psalm 150, was published in his *Glaub- und Liebesübung* (1680). Julian calls the hymn "a magnificent hymn of praise to God, perhaps the finest production of its author, and of the first rank in its class" (I, 683). The original opening line is "Lobe den Herren, den mächtigen König der Ehren." Miss Wentworth's translation appeared in her *Chorale Book for England* (1853). This hymn was added to *GS* in the *Supplement* (1975).

Lobe den Herren

Stralsund Gesangbuch, 1665

The original tune was set to the German poem "Hast du denn, Liebster" in *Ander Theil des erneuerten Gesangbuchs* (2d ed., Stralsund, 1665). Neander published it with his poem in his *Glaub- und Liebesübung* (1680). Johannes Zahn believes the melody to be based on an old secular air. Both tune and translation were published in Miss Winkworth's *Chorale Book for England* (1863). This tune entered *GS* in the *Supplement* (1975).

Prince of Peace! Control My Will   478
Mary Ann Serrett Barber, 1801-1864

This poem was first published in the *Church of England Magazine*
(March 3, 1838), entitled "He is our Peace." The poem was erroneously
attributed by Julian to Mary S. B. Dana Shindler. The modern text differs
considerably in some places from the original, which was in four 8-line
stanzas:

Prince of Peace, control my will;
    Bid this struggling heart be still;
Bid my fears and doubtings cease,
    Hush my spirit into peace.
Thou hast bought me with thy blood,
    Opened wide the way to God:
Peace I ask, but peace must be,
    Lord, in being one with thee.

Thou who stilled the raging deep
    Placidly to childlike sleep;
Thou whose voice the maniac heard,
    Knew, and straight confessed his Lord;
Thou, who hushed the mourner's cry
    Mid maternal agony,
Chase these doubtings from my heart;
    Faith and perfect peace impart.

King of Salem! strong to save,
    No ecstatic joy I crave;
Let thy Spirit's soothing calm
    Glide into my soul like balm;
Raise my heart to things above,
    Modulate my soul to love:
May thy will not mine, be done;
    May thy will and mine be one.

Savior! at thy feet I fall;
    Broken is the parting all;
Thou the foe hast reconcil'd;
    Tamed the rebel to the child.
Lord of glory, I am thine;
    Let thy peace around me shine,
And thy happy servant be
    One with God, and one with thee.

Who made the present alterations is not known. This hymn has been in *GS* since 1921.

Hatfield

W. T. Porter

Nothing is known of this composer. The tune, with the present text, appeared in *The Christian Hymnal, Revised: a Collection of Hymns and Tunes for Congregational and Social Worship* (1882, No. 704). This was the last revision of the series of hymnals begun by Alexander Campbell in 1828. It was published by the American Christian Missionary Society through Bosworth, Chase, and Hall in Cincinnati. The tune entered *GS* in 1921.

Purer in Heart, O God 484

Fannie E. Davison, 1851-1887

This text was written by Mrs. Asa Lee Davison (nee Fannie Estelle Church) and published in *Songs of Gratitude* (1877) by J. H. Fillmore in Cincinnati. It has been in *GS* since 1921.

Purer in Heart

James H. Fillmore, 1849-1936

Fillmore wrote this tune for the preceding text. It was published in his *Songs of Gratitude* (Cincinnati, 1877) and entered *GS* in 1921. In the *Book of Common Praise* (Philadelphia, 1943, NO. 503) the tune is called PASTOR.

Purer Yet and Purer

Anonymous in *Iphigenia in Tauris*, 1851

This poem, which has been in *GS* since 1921, is of unknown authorship. It appeared in a translation of J. W. von Goethe's *Iphigenie auf Tauris* (1851). This and several other poems were attached to the translation. The 1921 *GS* attributed the poem to Goethe; the 1925 book added a question mark after the attribution; the 1937 edition simply said "From Goethe." The poem is not by Goethe, but the sentiment is drawn from Goethe's *Iphigenie*. In summing up the purport of his drama, Goethe once said to a friend:

> Alle menschliche Gebrechen
> Sühnet reine Menschlichkeit.

(For each human fault and failure
    Pure humanity atones.)

The poem was first used as a hymn in the American *Sabbath Hymn Book* (1858).

Excelsior

Silas J. Vail, 1818-1884

This tune has been erroneously called LYNDHURST in every edition of *GS* since 1922 (indexes). The musical movement is similar to LYNDHURST, but it is really another tune. LYNDHURST is an anonymous tune, first published in *Church Praise* (1883). The tune EXCELSIOR was written by Vail, but its first place of publication is unknown to me. It has been in *GS* since 1921.

Redeemed, How I Love to Proclaim It   357

Fanny J. Crosby, 1820-1915

This text was first published in John R. Sweney, C. C. McCabe, T. C. O'Kane, and Kirkpatrick's *Songs of Redeeming Love* (Philadelphia, 1882). This is its first inclusion in *GS*.

Redeemed

William J. Kirkpatrick, 1838-1921

This tune was written for and published with the preceding text in Sweney, McCabe, O'Kane, and Kirkpatrick's *Songs of Redeeming Love* (Philadelphia, 1882). It now enters *GS* for the first time.

Rejoice, the Lord Is King   474

Charles Wesley, 1707-1788

Based on Philippians 4:4, this text appeared in Wesley's *Hymns for Our Lord's Resurrection* (1746). The confidence and joy of the believer which grows out of the kingship and reign of Christ is the theme of this hymn. The original poem contained six stanzas. Our text contains stanzas 1, 2, 3, and 6, with some alterations made since 1935. Stanza 2 originally began "Jesus, the Savior, reigns"; stanza 3 read "Are to our Jesus given"; stanza 6, "Jesus the Judge shall come"; and stanza 6 ended with a different refrain:

We soon shall hear the archangel's voice;
    The trump of God shall sound, "Rejoice."

The two omitted stanzas read:
He sits at God's right hand
Till all his foes submit,
And bow to his command,
And fall beneath his feet.
(Refrain)

He all his foes shall quell,
And all our sins destroy;
Let every bosom swell
Witgh pure seraphic joy.
(Refrain)

This is the first inclusion of this text in *GS*.

Darwall's 148th

John Darwall, 1731-1789

This tune was published as a setting for a paraphrase of Psalm 148 (whence the tune name), beginning "Ye boundless realms of joy," in Aaron Wills, *The New Universal Psalmist* (5th ed., 1770). This particular meter, 66.66.88., is labeled H.M. in many early American hymnals ("Hallelujah Meter" because of its joyfulness).

Rejoice, Ye Pure in Hoart   466

Edward H. Plumptre, 1821-1891

This text, based on Psalm 10:4 and Philippians 4:4, was written for a choir festival at Peterborough Cathedral, England, which was held in May 1865. It was published by Novello & Company that year with a musical setting, and also in words only in Plumptre's *Lazarus and Other Poems* (2d ed., 1865). The poem originally contained eleven stanzas of four lines each. It was included in the *Appendix* to *Hymns Ancient and Modern* (1898). The entire poem may be seen in *Hymns Ancient and Modern* (Standard edition, No. 202). The *GSR* text contains stanzas 1, 6, 8, and 9. It has been in *GS* since 1921.

Marion

Arthur H. Messiter, 1834-1916

This tune was written for the preceding hymn in 1883. It was published a decade later in the *Hymnal with Music as Used in Trinity Church*

(New York, 1893). Messiter, the editor of this hymnal, named the tune for his mother. The tune first entered *GS* in 1921.

Renew Thy Church   423
Kenneth L. Cober, b. 1902

This hymn was written as part of the five-year program Baptist Jubilee Advance as Cober traveled across the country working for his denomination. It was designed specifically for the theme of the second year: "The Renewal of the Church: Imperative for Evangelism." It was sung at the American Baptist Convention, May 1960. This is its first inclusion in *GS*.

All Is Well

Traditional English Melody
Adpt. from J. T. White, *The Sacred Harp*, 1844

For information on this tune, see the notes on "Come, Come, Ye Saints (*GSR*. No. 128).

Rescue the Perishing   411
Fanny J. Crosby, 1820-1915

Fanny Crosby described the circumstances of the writing of this hymn thus: W. H. Doane had sent her the subject for the hymn "Rescue the Perishing." A few days later she was speaking to a group of working men. As she spoke, the thought kept recurring to her heart that some mother's boy needed to be rescued from sin that night or not at all. After her appeals, a young man came to her saying that was just his case. She prayed with him that he might find God. That night the circumstances of the evening and of Doane's subject would not leave her mind. She wrote the hymn text before she went to bed and sent it to Doane the next day. This occurred in 1869, and the hymn was published with Doane's tune in his *Songs of Devotion* (New York, 1870). This text has been in *GS* since 1925.

Rescue

William H. Doane, 1832-1915

This tune was written for the preceding text and under the circumstances outlined above. It was published in Doane's *Songs of Devotion,* (New York, 1870) and has been in *GS* since 1925.

Ride On! Ride On in Majesty 216
Henry H. Milman, 1791-1868

Possibly written as early as 1823, this text was published in Bishop Heber's *Hymns Written and Adapted to the Weekly Service of the Church Year* (1827). The text was originally in five stanzas. *GSR* includes stanzas 1, 2, and 3. The omitted stanzas read:

4
Ride on! ride on majesty!
    Thy last and fiercest strife is nigh:
The Father on His sapphire throne
    Expects His own anointed Son.

5
Ride on! ride on in majesty!
    In lowly pomp ride on to die;
Bow thy meek head to mortal pain,
    Then take, O God, thy power, and reign.

This is the first inclusion of this hymn in *GS*.

Winchester, New

George Rebenlein's *Musikalische Handbuch*, 1690
Arr. William H. Havergal, 1793-1870

This tune was first published in the *Musikalische Handbuch* (Hamburg, 1690). The tune has been variously altered in arrangements, but was put into its present form by Havergal in his *Old Church Psalmody* (London, 1847). This is the first inclusion of this tune in *GS*.

Rise Up, O Men of God 405
William P. Merrill, 1867-1954

Nolar R. Best suggested to the author that a hymn on brotherhood was needed for the Presbyterian Brotherhood Movement. About this same time, Merrill read an article by S. Lee entitled "The Church of the Strong Men," which inspired him to write this text. It was written while Merrill was crossing Lake Michigan on a steamer bound for Chicago. The text was first published in the *Continent* (Feb. 16, 1911) and with music in *The Pilgrim Hymnal* (1912). It first entered *GS* in the *Supplement* (1975).

Festal Song

William H. Walter, 1825-1893

This tune was first published in J. Ireland Tucker and W. W. Rousseau's *Hymnal Revised and Enlarged* (1894). There it was the setting for William Hammond's "Awake, and Sing the Song." In the *Pilgrim Hymnal* (1912), it first became the setting for "Rise Up, O Men of God," with which it has been joined ever since. The tune entered *GS* in the *Supplement* (1975)

Rock of Ages   356

Augustus M. Toplady, 1740-1778

In the list of the thirty-two greatest hymns, based on a poll taken by *The Etude* in 1937, this hymn ranked number one. It is still widely used and must, therefore, possess a universal quality that speaks to the hearts of believers everywhere. The original impetus for this hymn text began in the *Gospel Magazine* (October 1775) in an article written by Toplady entitled "Life a Journey," and signed "Minimus." The article said in part: "Yet, if you fall, be humbled; but do not despair. Pray afresh to God who is able to raise you up, and to set you on your feet again. Look to the blood of the covenant, and say to the Lord, from the depth of your heart,

> Rock of Ages, cleft for me,
> Let me hide myself in thee!
> Foul, I to the fountain fly:
> Wash me, Saviour, or I die.

In the same magazine for March 1776, there appeared a curious article on England's national debt, leading on to the tremendous sin debt we all owe. At the end of the article, the complete original text of "Rock of Ages" appeared in four stanzas, entitled "A living and dying Prayer for the Holiest Believer in the World." The title may have represented a sneer at the doctrine of holiness as set forth by the Wesleys. The *GSR* text is an exact representation of Toplady's original poem except for the first word in 3:5. There the term "Vile" is substituted for the original "Foul." The omitted stanza four reads:

> Whilst I draw this fleeting breath—
> When my eye-strings break in death—
> When I soar through tracts unknown—
> See Thee on thy Judgment-Throne—
> Rock of Ages, cleft for me,
> Let me hide myself in Thee!

The text was revised by Toplady himself and by other editors over the years. It has been in *GS* since 1921.

Toplady

Thomas Hastings, 1784-1872

This tune was written in 1830 and harmonized in three parts in the key of D. It was first published in Hastings and Lowell Mason's *Spiritual Songs for Social Worship* (1832). The tune has been in *GS* since 1821.

Safe in the Arms of Jesus   647

Fanny J. Crosby, 1820-1915

W. H. Doane came to Crosby's apartment one summer day in 1868 with a new tune which he had written. He was on his way to a Sunday School convention in Cincinnati and had only a short time before leaving. As Fanny Crosby listened to Doane's tune, she reflected on a scripture text which had been running through her mind that day: "Underneath are the everlasting arms" (Deut. 33:27). She then told Doane that his tune said "Safe in the Arms of Jesus." Within a few minutes she had completed the poem, and Doane went on his way to present the new hymn at the convention. This text entered *GS* in 1925.

Brachioni

William H. Doane, 1832-1915

The tune was written in accordance with the circumstances related above. Doane published the tune in 1869, in *Bright Jewels*. The hymn tune name has been assigned by the present general editor. It is Greek for "in the arms." The tune entered *GS* in 1925.

Savior, Again to Thy Dear Name   11

John Ellerton, 1832-1915

This hymn was written for the Malpas, Middlewich, and Nantwich Choral Association in 1866. Originally in six stanzas, Ellerton abridged the poem to four for the *Appendix* to *Hymns Ancient and Modern* (1868). This text has been in *GS* since 1921 in three stanzas. The omitted stanza three from Ellerton's version reads:

> Grant us thy peace, Lord, through the coming night,
>> Turn Thou for us its darkness into light;
> From harm and danger keep thy children free,
>> For dark and light are both alike to thee.

Ellers

Edward J. Hopkins, 1818-1901

This tune, probably deriving its name from the poet Ellerton, is now used exclusively with "Savior, Again to Thy Dear Name." It was composed for this hymn and published in Robert Brown-Borthwick's *Supplemental Hymn and Tune Book* (1869). There it was a unison tune with varied instrumental accompaniments written for each stanza. At the request of Samuel Smith, a voice harmonization was made by Hopkins for Smith's *Appendix to the Bradford Tune Book* (1872). This latter is basically the harmony used in *GS*. The tune has been in our hymnal since 1921.

Savior, Breathe an Evening Blessing   40

James Edmeston, 1791-1867

This text appeared in Edmeston's *Sacred Lyrics* (1820) in two 8-line stanzas. He used as a motto above the poem a quotation from Salte's *Travels in Abyssinia*: "At night their short evening hymn 'Jesus Mahaxaroo' (Jesus, forgive us) stole through the camp." The text was used soon after as a hymn and first published in Edward Bickersteth's *Christian Psalmody* (1833). This hymn poem has been used among churches of the Stone-Campbell Movement in America since the days of A. Campbell's hymnals. Our text contains the original poem, but it is divided into four 4-line stanzas and contains the alteration of "light" to "bright" in 4:4. The tune entered *GS* in 1921.

Evening Praye

George Coles Stebbins, 1846-1945

This tune was written in 1876 as a response to be sung after prayer during the morning service at the church in Boston where Stebbins was music director. Two years later he put the tune with Edmeston's text, and it was published that year in Sankey, McGranahan, and Stebbins's *Gospel Hymns No. 3* (1878).

Savior, Grant Me Rest and Peace   479

Lucinda Beal Bateman, b. 1843

This is one of a large number of Sunday School hymns written by Mrs. Bateman and published by the Fillmore Brothers Music House of Cincinnati, Ohio. The earliest collection which I have found containing this hymn is J. H. Fillmore's *Hours of Song: Revised, A Book of Rudiments and A Collection of New Music, Sacred and Secular for Singing Classes and Conventions* (1879, No. 75). The original collection had been published in 1875. This text was published under Mrs. Bateman's pen name "Grace Glenn." It entered *GS* in 1921.

Bateman

James H. Fillmore, 1849-1936

BATEMAN is the name which I have given to this tune. It was written for the preceding text and published with it in Fillmore's *Hours of Song* (1879) or, possibly, in the original edition (1875).

Savior, Like a Shepherd Lead Us 606
Hymns for the Young, 1846
Attributed to Dorothy A. Thrupp, 1779-1847

This text was published anonymously in Miss Thrupp's *Hymns for the Young* (4th ed., 1836). In June 1838, it was published in Carus Wilson's *Children's Friend* and signed "Lyte." In the same year, the poem was published in Mrs. Herbert Mayo's *Selection of Hymns and Poetry for the Use of Infant and Juvenile Schools*. Although Miss Thrupp contributed signed poems to this collection, Mrs. Mayo did not give her credit for this one; thus the evidence is against Miss Thrupp's authorship and uncertain with regard to Henry Lyte. This text first entered *GS* in 1937.

Bradbury

William B. Bradbury, 1816-1868

Bradbury composed this tune for the hymn poem above and published it in his *Oriola* (1859), a collection of hymns for the Sunday School. The tune entered *GS* in 1937.

Savior, Teach Me Day by Day 413
Jane E. Leeson, 1807-1882

This text is based on 1 John 4:19, "We love Him, because He first loved us." It was first published in four 8-line stanzas in Leeson's *Hymns and Scenes of Childhood, or a Sponsor's Gift* (1842). It was entitled "Obedience." The hymn entered *GS* in 1921 in three stanzas (*GSR* stanzas 1, 2, and 4) and with the present four stanzas in 1937. The *GSR* text is composed of Leeson's stanzas 1:1-4; 2:1-4; 3:5-8; and 3:1-4.

Seymour

Carl Maria von Weber, 1786-1826

This tune is taken from Weber's last opera, *Oberon*, composed in 1825-1826. This work was performed in London's Covent Garden, April 12, 1826, and the melody, also known as WEBER, comes from the opening chorus. It has been in *GS* sinced 1921.

Savior, Thy Dying Love   609

Sylvanus D. Phelps, 1816-1895

This text was written in 1862 and published in the *Watchman and Examiner* (March 17, 1864). The original version was radically different from our present text:

> Something, my God, for Thee,
>   Something for Thee:
> That each day's setting sun may bring
>   Some penitential offering:
> In Thy dear name some kindness done;
>   In Thy dear love some wanderer won;
> Some trial meekly borne for Thee,
>   Dear Lord, for Thee.
>
> Something, my God, for Thee,
>   Something for Thee:
> That to Thy gracious throne may rise
>   Sweet incense from some sacrifice—
> Uplifted eyes undimmed by tears,
>   Uplifted faith unstained by fears,
> Hailing each joy as light from Thee,
>   Dear Lord, from Thee.
>
> Something, my God, for Thee,
>   Something for Thee:
> For the great love that Thou hast given,
>   For the great hope of Thee and heaven,
> My soul! her first allegiance brings,
>   And upward plumes her heavenward wings,
> Nearer, my God, to Thee,
>   Nearer to Thee.

This hymn poem seems to have been rewritten at the request of Robert Lowry for his and W. H. Doane's collection *Pure Gold for the Sunday*

School (1871). It was published in that hymnal with the motto, "Lord, what wilt Thou have me to do?" (Acts 9: 6). This text entered *GS* in 1921.

Something for Jesus
Robert Lowry, 1826-1899

This tune was written for the preceding text and published in Lowry and Doane's *Pure Gold for the Sunday School* (1871). It has been in *GS* since 1921.

Shall I Crucify My Savior   269

No complete information is available on this text. It was probably written about 1896, the year that G. C. Tullar first copyrighted the music. Mrs. Breck often composed her poems as she did her daily work. The text also appeared in the Tullar-Meridith Company's hymnal *The Dawn Immortal* (1914). It first entered *GS* in 1937.

Tullar
Grant Colfax Tullar, 1869-1950

Tullar published this tune in 1896. No further information is available. The tune entered *GS* in 1937 in a male quartet arrangement. This is the first time this gospel song arrangement, made by the current music editor, has been included in *GS*.

Shall We Gather at the River   551
Robert Lowry, 1826-1899

Robert Lowry has given the following account of the writing of this text:

> One afternoon in July, 1864, when I was pastor at Hanson Place Baptist Church, Brooklyn, the weather was oppressively hot, and I was lying on a lounge in a state of physical exhaustion. I was almost incapable of bodily exertion, and my imagination began to take to itself wings. Visions of the future passed before me with startling vividness. The imagery of the Apocalypse took the form of a tableau. Brightest of all were the throne, the heavenly river, and the gathering of the saints. My soul seemed to take new life from the celestial outlook. I began to wonder why the hymn-writers had said so much about the "river of death" and so little about "the pure water of life, clear as crystal, proceeding out of the throne of God and of the Lamb." As I mused the words began to construct

themselves. They came first as a question of Christian inquiry, "Shall we gather?" Then they broke out in a chorus, as an answer of Christian faith, "Yes, we'll gather." On this question and answer the hymn developed itself. The music came with the tune.

This piece was first published in Lowry and Doane's Sunday School hymnal *Happy Voices* (1865) in five stanzas with refrain. The text entered *GS* (words only) in 1921.

Hanson Place

Robert Lowry, 1826-1899

See the preceding account for the writing of this tune. HANSON PLACE is named for the church where Lowry was preaching in 1864. The tune was printed first in *GS* in 1925.

Shepherd of Souls, Refresh and Bless   146

Collection of Hymns...
of the United Brethren, 1832

Nothing is available at present as to the authorship or the date of writing of this text. It first entered *GS* in the *Supplement* (1975).

Windsor

From William Damon's *Booke of Musicke*, 1591

This tune was first published anonymously in Damon's *Former Booke of Musicke* (1591) and in Thomas Est's *The Whole Booke of Psalms* (1592), in which it was harmonized by George Kirbye. The tune is similar to one used by Christopher Tye for his metrical version of *The Acts of the Apostles* (1553). This is one of the oldest common meter tunes still in use. It was first included in *GS* in the *Supplement* (1975).

Shepherd of Tender Youth   166

Clement of Alexandria, c. 160-210
Trans. Henry M. Dexter. 1821-1890

This text is one of the earliest of writings in use as a Christian hymn outside of the New Testament itself. It was written around A.D. 200. The text is taken from the closing lines of Titus Flavius Clement's work Παιδαγωγός (i.e., Paidagogos, or The Tutor). That work was a guide for Christians in their spiritual lives, and the poem sums up the main themes of the work. It exalts Christ as teacher and guide. Many recent hymnals alter the opening line to read "Shepherd of Eager Youth." The original Greek line reads: Στό'μιον πῶλων αΔαῶν. The hymn has been in *GS* since 1937.

Kirby Bedon
Edward Bunnett, 1834-1923

The original tune name was probably KIRKBY BEDON ("the church near Bedon"), for there is such a place near Norwich, England. The tune was written in 1887 and published that year in *The Congregational Church Hymnal* (London). The tune first entered *GS* in 1937.

Silent Night, Holy Night
202
Joseph Mohr, 1792-1848
Trans. John F. Young, 1820-1885 (stanzas 1-3)
Trans. Anonymous (stanza 4)

The original text, beginning "Stille Nacht, heilige Nacht," was written for a Christmas Eve service at St. Nicholas Church, Oberndorf, near Salzburg, Austria (1818). The earliest known manuscript dates from 1833, and it was first printed in the *Leipziger Gesangbuch* (1838). The translation by Young was first published in John C. Hollister's *The Sunday School Service and Tune Book* (1863). This is the most popular translation of the original text. It enters *GS* here for the first time. Heretofore a text traceable at least as far back as the ACMS *Christian Hymn Book* (Cincinnati, 1865) has been included.

Stille Nacht
Franz Gruber, 1787-1863

Originally composed for two voices with guitar, this tune was first sung by Mohr and Gruber. Karl Mauracher, an organ repairman, copied the song and spread it across the Tyrolian region of Austria, calling it a "Tiroler Volkslied." It was published in the *Leipziger Gesangbuch* (1838). In the United States, the tune was first printed in *The Devotional Harmonist* (1849). It has been in *GS* since 1921.

Simply Trusting Every Day
514
Edgar Page Stites, 1836-1921

Stite's poem first appeared in a newspaper and was seen there by D. L. Moody, who passed it to Ira Sankey for a tune. Sankey agreed to do so if Moody would vouch for the doctrine taught in the poem. Moody said he would do so, and the hymn was published in Sankey's *Gospel Hymns No. 2* (1876). This text entered *GS* in 1937.

Trusting Jesus

Ira David Sankey, 1840-1908

This tune was written for the preceding text at the instigation of Dwight L. Moody and published in Sankey's *Gospel Hymns No. 2* (1876). It entered *GS* in 1937.

Sin Sorrow of Six Thousand Years   382

George Wilmeth Ewing, b. 1923

This text was written for a hymn competition conducted through the Music department of Abilene Christian University in 1982. It won first place that year and was sung by the A Capella Chorus at the annual ACU lectures in February. It is a fine communion hymn and is here offered to the churches for the first time.

The Lamb of God

George Wilmeth Ewing, b. 1923

The tune was written for the preceding text and performed under the circumstances given above. The tune name was provided by the composer/poet, and it is here included in *GS* for the first time.

Sing Hallelujah, Praise the Lord   179

John Swertner, 1746-1813

This text was taken from the hymnal of the Hutterite Society published in Rifton, New York, by the Plough Publishing Company. The poem was first published in 1789. Nothing further is known about the origin of this hymn.

Bechler

John C. Bechler, 1784-1857

No complete information is available on this tune. The GSR text was taken from the Hutterite hymnal mentioned above. It appears in *Offices of Worship and Hymns* 3d ed., revised and enlarged (Bethlehem, Pa.: Moravian Publications Office, 1896), and in the *Hymnal of the Moravian Church* (1969, No. 565). This is the first inclusion of this tune and of the preceding text in *GS*.

Sing On, Ye Joyful Pilgrims   473
Fanny J. Crosby, 1829-1925

I am indebted to Prof. Harold Holland of Pepperdine University for identifying Carrie M. Wilson as Fanny J. Crosby. Crosby wrote under a number of pen names, some of them very confusing. This text was first published in 1886 in one of the many collections of John R. Sweney, *Songs of Joy and Gladness*. It has been in *GS* since 1921.

Sing On

John R. Sweney, 1837-1899

This tune was written for and published with the preceding text in Sweney's *Songs of Joy and Gladness* (c. 1886). It entered *GS* in 1921.

Sing Praise to God Who Reigns Above   109
Johann J. Schutz, 1640-1690
Trans. Frances E. Cox, 1812-1897

This text was first published in Schutz's *Christliches Gedenkbüchlein* (Frankfurt, 1675). Cox's translation was published in *Lyra Eucharistica* (1864) and in her *Hymns from the German* (2d ed., 1864). In 1868, the hymn was printed in the Lutheran *Church Book* in Philadelphia. This is its first inclusion in *GS*.

Mit Freuden Zart

Bohemian Brethren's *Kirchengesänge*, 1566

The present form of this tune may be traced to the hymnal edited by Georg Vetter, *Kirchengeseng darinn die Heubtartickel des Christlichen Glaubens gefasset* (1566). An earlier version can be found in *Trente quatre pseumes de David* (Geneva, 1521), and it is said to bear a resemblance to a French secular song published as early as 1529. The tune may have originated in the late Middle Ages. This is its first inclusion in *GS*.

Sing the Wondrous Love of Jesus   669
Eliza E. Hewitt, 1851-1920

This text first appeared with the tune by Wilson in W. J. Kirkpatrick and Henry L. Gilmour's *Pentecostal Praises* (1898). It apparently grew out of the two ladies' association at the Methodist camp meetings at Ocean Grove, New Jersey.

Heaven

Emily D. Wilson, 1865-1942

See the notes on the text above. The tune name HEAVEN was first given to this melody in the *Baptist Hymnal* (1956). Both text and tune entered *GS* in 1937.

Sing Them Over Again to Me

303

Philip P. Bliss, 1838-1876

This text was first printed in *Words of Life* (1874), a Sunday School paper published by Fleming H. Revell in New York City. It was subsequently published in *Gospel Hymns, No. 3*, which Bliss helped to edit.

Words of Life

Philip P. Bliss, 1838-1876

This tune was written for the preceding text and published with it in the Sunday School paper *Words of Life* (1874). It was later published in Ira Sankey's *Gospel Hymns, No. 3*, of which Bliss was co-editor. Both text and tune entered *GS* in 1921.

Sing to Me of Heaven

672

Ada Powell

No information is available on this gospel song. It was written and published about 1914. This is its first inclusion in *GS*.

Beall

B. B. Beall

Little information is available on this tune. Mr. Beall was living in Douglasville, Georgia, when he wrote this tune about 1914. It appeared in A. J. Showalter's *Waves of Salvation* (Dalton, Georgia, 1922). This is its first inclusion in *GS*.

Sing With All the Sons of Glory

249

William J. Irons, 1812-1883

This text was first published in Irons's *Psalms and Hymns for the Church* (1873) with the text "Now is Christ risen from the dead" (1 Cor. 15:20) as the motto. The original last four lines of stanza one read:

Even now the dawn is breaking,
  Soon the night of time shall cease;
And in God's own likeness waking,
  Man shall know eternal peace.

This is the first inclusion of this text in *GS*.

Hymn to Joy

Ludwig van Beethoven, 1770-1827
Arr. Edward Hodges, 1796-1867

For information on this tune, see the notes on "Joyful, Joyful We Adore Thee," (*GSR*, No. 55). The tune first entered *GS* in the *Supplement* (1975)

Sinners Jesus Will Receive   324

Erdmann Neumeister, 1671-1756
Trans. Emma Frances Bevan, 1827-1909

The original German poem beginning "Jesus nimmt die' Sunder an!" was published in eight 6-line stanzas, and was written as the conclusion to a sermon on Luke 15:2. It appeared in Neumeister's *Evangelischer Nachklang* (1718). Mrs. Bevan's translation was first published in her *Songs of Eternal Life* (1858). This text has been in *GS* since 1921.

Albertson

Phoebe Palmer Knapp, 1839-1908

No information is currently available on the date or the circumstances of composition of ALBERTSON. The preceding text with the tune NEUMEISTER first entered *GS* in 1921 and has continued until the present edition. *GSR* has dropped the older tune and has gone to the present tune ALBERTSON in order to produce a more pleading effect, which the chorus of the older tune did not attain.

Softly and Tenderly Jesus Is Calling   323

Will L. Thompson, 1847-1909

This tenderest of invitation songs seems to have been written by Thompson in 1880 and copyrighted that year. It may have been published that year in J. Calvin Bushey's *Sparkling Gems, Nos. 1 and 2 Combined.* it was certainly published in J. S. Kiskip's *Songs of Triumph* (1882). The text and tune were being published in hymnals of the Stone-Campbell Movement by the late 1880s: J. H. Fillmore's *New Christian Hymn and Tune Book, Part III* (1887), C. C. Cline's *Standard Church Hymnal* (1888), and E. G. Sewell and R. M. McIntosh's *Christian Hymns* (1889). The text has been in *GS* since 1921.

Thompson

Will L. Thompson, 1847-1909

This tune was written for the preceding text and published either in 1880 or 1882, as mentioned above. The tune name THOMPSON was first given in the *Baptist Hymnal* (1956). It has been in *GS* since 1921.

Softly Now the Light of Day   35

George W. Doane, 1799-1859

This hymn in two 8-line stanzas was published in Doane's *Songs by the Way, Chiefly Devotional: with Translations and Imitations* (1824). The poem is based on Psalm 141:2. The *GSR* text contains the first twelve lines of Doane's poem, or what have become stanzas 1, 2, and 3. The fourth stanza (Doane's last four lines) seems inferior to the rest of the poem and is omitted. It reads:

> Thou, who, sinless, yet hast known
> All of man's infirmity;
> Then from Thine eternal throne,
> Jesus look with pitying eye.

In this edition of *GS,* the editors have changed the pronouns from singular to plural to make the poem more appropriate for congregational use as a prayer hymn. This text has been in *GS* since 1921.

Seymour

Carl Maria von Weber, 1786-1826

SEYMOUR, also called WEBER, is an arrangement from von Weber's last opera, *Oberon,* performed at Covent Garden, London, April 12, 1826. The tune was brought to America by Thomas Day Seymour, a professor at Western Reserve College, whose uncle sang in the choir at Center Church, Hartford, Connecticut. Henry W. Greatorex, the organist for Center Church, arranged the tune and named it for Seymour's uncle. This tune was first printed in *GS* in 1925.

Soldiers of Christ, Arise 401

Charles Wesley, 1707-1788

This poem originally appeared either at the end of John Wesley's *Character of a Methodist* (1742) or in an undated broadside about the same time. It was printed in a hymnal in Wesley's *Hymns and Sacred Poems* (1749). The original poem was in sixteen 8-line stanzas. The *GSR* text includes Wesley's stanza 1 (*GSR* 1 and 2), 2a (*GSR* 3), 4a (*GSR* 4), and 2b (*GSR* 5). This text has been in *GS* since 1921.

Kirkwood

William B. Bradbury, 1816-1868

The date and circumstances of composition of this tune are unknown. The earliest appearance which I have found in the hymnals of the Stone-Campbell Movement is in C. C. Cline's *Standard Church Hymnal* (1888). The tune has been in *GS* since 1921.

Something Beautiful 511

Gloria Gaither, b. 1942

In her book *Make Warm Noises* (1971), Gloria Gaither writes:
Suzanne meant to make something beautiful. She had all the right materials: a fine sheet of construction paper, new paints and brushes, scissors and glue. And it started out all right. But right in the middle of the page when she was about half through, she dropped a big glob of paint by mistake. She tried to wipe it up, which only made the glob bigger. Then she tried to paint over it. That didn't work either. Then she tried rubbing it out, but that made a hole in the paper and on it went. It wasn't long before she was in tears. "Mommy, I tried to make you something beautiful, and just look! After that first mistake it just kept getting worse. Now it's just a mess and I can't fix it!" Her words managed to get through her disappointed sobs. I put my arms around her and tried to tell her that I loved her anyway. Then I remembered the extra sheet of paper I had up on the shelf. Now she could start again. Delighted with a new chance she skipped away to begin anew.

Out of this incident, Mrs. Gaither, thinking of how God our Father gives us many chances to begin again, wrote this beautiful text.

Something Beautiful

William J. Gaither, b. 1936

This tune was written for the preceding text and published in 1971. See the notes on the text above for the circumstances out of which it was written.

Son of God, Eternal Savior   161

Somerset Lowry, 1855-1932

This text was written in 1893 and published in *Goodwill* (Feb. 1894). It was first included in a hymnal in the *Christian Social Union Hymn Book* (1895). This is its first inclusion in *GS*.

In Babilone

From *Oude en Nieuwe Hollantse Boerenlities en Contradansen*, c. 1710

Harm. Julius Röntgen, 1912

This tune was one of several hundred mainly folk melodies published as *Oude en Nieuwe Hollantse Boerenlities en Contradansen* (Amsterdam, c. 1710). Julius Röntgen republished many of these tunes in his *Old Dutch Songs and Country Dances Transcribed for the Piano* (London, 1912). The present setting is that of Röntgen, which appeared in the *English Hymnal* (1906). This is its first inclusion in *GS*.

Sowing in the Morning   443

Knowles Shaw, 1834-1878

This gospel song was first published anonymously in Shaw's *The Golden Gate for the Sunday School* (Cincinnati, 1874). It appears with Shaw's name in his collection *The Morning Star, a New Collection of Sunday School Music* (St. Louis: Christian Publishing Co., 1877). The text has been in *GS* since 1921.

Bringing in the Sheaves

George A. Minor, 1845-1904

Shaw had published a tune with his poem, upon which the Minor tune is based. It was, however, much less singable than Minor's melody. The *GSR* tune was composed for the preceding text and published in Minor's *Golden Light No. 1, for Sunday Schools* (Richmond, 1879). This tune has been in *GS* since 1921.

Stand Up, and Bless the Lord 85

James Montgomery, 1771-1854

This text was written for the Sunday school anniversary of Red Hill Wesleyan Sunday School, Sheffield, England, March 15, 1824. Originally line 2 of stanza 1 read "ye children," but Montgomery changed it to "people" when it was published in his *Christian Psalmist* (1825). This is the first inclusion of the text in *GS*.

Festal Song

William H. Walker, 1825-1893

For information on this tune, consult the notes on "Rise Up, O Men of God" (*GSR*, No. 405). The tune first entered *GS* in the *Supplement* (1975).

Stand Up, Stand Up for Jesus 403

George Duffield, 1818-1888

This text was inspired by the last sermon of Dudley A. Tyng during a great revival in 1858. Tyng died in an accident about three days after he preached to five thousand men in the YMCA in Philadelphia on the theme "Stand Up for Jesus." In preaching at his own church in Philadelphia the following Sunday, Duffield spoke from Ephesians 6:14, and concluded with this hymn which he had written for the occasion. It was published in the Presbyterian *Church Psalmist* (1859). The hymn was originally in six stanzas, and *GSR* text includes stanzas 1, 3, 4, and 6. The omitted stanzas read:

2
Stand up!—stand up for Jesus!
    The solemn watchword hear:
If while ye sleep he suffers,
    Away with shame and fear;
Where'er ye meet with evil,
    Within you or without
Charge for the God of Battles,
    And put the foe to rout!

5
Stand up!—stand up for Jesus!
    Each soldier to his post;
Close up the broken columns,
    And shout through all the host!

> Make good the loss so heavy,
> In those that still remain,
> And prove to all around you
> That death itself is gain.

This text has been in *GS* since 1921.

Webb

George J. Webb, 1803-1887

Webb migrated to the United States from his native England in 1830. He wrote this tune while on shipboard coming over the Atlantic. Later he set it to the poem "'Tis dawn, the lark is singing" and published it in *The Odeon* (Boston, 1837). This was a collection of secular melodies. Samuel Duffield in his *English Hymns* (1886) said that William Bradbury was the first to join the text and tune. The tune entered *GS* in 1921.

Standing on the Promises   554

R. Kelso Carter, 1849-1928

This text was published in John R. Sweney and Carter's *Songs of Perfect Love* (1886). It was originally in five stanzas. The *GSR* text omits stanza 3, which reads:

> Standing on the promises I now can see
> Perfect, present cleansing in the blood for me;
> Standing in the liberty where Christ makes free,
> Standing on the promises of God.

The text entered *GS* in 1921.

Promises

R. Kelso Carter, 1849-1928

This tune was written for the preceding text and published in Sweney and Carter's *Songs of Perfect Love* (1886). The tune name PROMISES was first given in the *Baptist Hymnal* (1956). This tune was not printed in *GS* until 1937, all preceding editions containing words only.

Still with Thee, O My God 612

James D. Burns, 1823-1864

This text was published in Burns's *The Evening Hymn* (1857) and in the Baptist *Psalms and Hymns* (1858). John Julian said, "Although mainly included, because of its beautiful simplicity, in children's hymn books, it is yet better adapted for congregational use" (*Dictionary*, 1094). The *GSR* hymnal committee believes it is indeed a fine congregational hymn. It is included for the first time in *GS*.

Prosopon

M. L. Daniels, b. 1931

This tune was composed expressly for the text above and for inclusion in *GSR* by a distinguished member of the music faculty at Abilene Christian University. The tune name PROSOPON, a Greek word meaning "face" or "countenance" (πρόσωπον), was given by the present general editor of *GSR* and derives from the sentiment of the hymn poem.

Still, Still with Thee 641

Harriet Beecher Stowe, 1811-1896

This hymn text was written in the summer of 1853 while Mrs. Stowe was on a visit to the home of a friend. She often arose early to enjoy both the birds and the dawn. Out of such an occasion came this reflection on Psalm 139·18, "When I awake I am still with thee." The poem was first published in the *Plymouth Collection of Hymns* (1855), edited by her brother, Henry Ward Beecher. The text first entered *GS* in 1950 as a male quartet and was printed on the back flyleaf. It was included in the *Supplement* (1975).

Metasou

Ira David Sankey, 1840-1908

This tune was written by Sankey and included in his *Sacred Songs and Solos* (No. 951, ed. 1903). It was printed under the motto "We dwell in Him and He in us."—1 John. 4:13. Before the text was included in the *Supplement* (1975), it was set to a tune by W. H. Gerrish. No information is available on this tune or composer. METASOU was named by the current general editor of *GSR* and is the Greek for "with thee" (μετὰ σοῦ).

Sun of My Soul   42
John Keble, 1792-1866

This text is a selection of stanzas from Keble's poem for Evening Prayer, published in his *The Christian Year* (1827). The poem was written November 25, 1820. *GSR* text contains stanzas 3, 7, 8, and 14 of the original poem. It has been in *GS* since 1921.

Hursley

Arr. from *Katholisches Gesangbuch*, Vienna, c. 1774

For information on this tune, consult the notes on "Dear Master, In Whose Life I See" (*GSR*, No. 571). This tune has been in *GS* since 1921.

Sweet Hour of Prayer   559
Attributed to W. W. Walford, 1771-1850

The authorship of this hymn remains in doubt. For a rather full account of the possibilities and alternatives, see *Companion to the Baptist Hymnal* (1976). Thomas Salmon (1800-1854) attributed the hymn to "the blind preacher" Walford in *The New York Observer* (Sept. 13, 1845). No records have been found which identify a W. W. Walford or that he was blind. The hymnologists over the years have identified this man with William Walford, a Congregational minister of Homerton Academy in England. Joseph F. Green has found several similarities between the language of "Sweet Hour of Prayer" and a work by William Walford entitled *The Manner of Prayer* (1836). We simply do not know who wrote the hymn. This text has been in *GS* since 1921.

Sweet Hour

William B. Bradbury, 1816-1868

This tune was composed for the hymn above and published first in Bradbury's *Golden Chain* (1861). It is possible that it might have been published earlier in one of the editions of Bradbury's *Cottage Melodies*. The music was first printed in *GS* in 1925.

Sweetly, Lord, Have We Heard Thee Calling   426
Mary B. C. Slade, 1826-1882

This hymn text by Mrs. Slade was first published in *The Amaranth* (Nashville, 1871). This was one of several supplementary and Sunday

School collections which were edited by Atticus G. Haygood and R. M. McIntosh. The poem was originally in seven stanzas. *GSR* text incudes stanzas 1, 2, 3, and 6. The omitted stanzas read:

4

Thou, dear Lord, in Thy pathway keeping,
  We follow Thee;
Through the gloom of that place of weeping,
  Gethsemane!

5

If Thy way and its sorrows bearing,
  We go again,
Up the slope of the hill-side, bearing
  Our cross of pain.

7

Then at last, when on high He sees us,
  Our journey done,
We will rest where the steps of Jesus
  End at His throne.

This text has been in *GS* since 1921.

Footsteps

Asa B. Everett, 1828-1875

This tune was composed for the preceding text and published in Haygood and McIntosh's *The Amaranth* (Nashville, 1871). Nothing further is known of the circumstances of composition. The tune has been in *GS* since 1921.

Take My Life, and Let It Be Consecrated   608

Frances R. Havergal, 1836-1879

This text was written on Feb. 4, 1874, after a visit to Areley House, Worcestershire, the preceding December. Miss Havergal said:

I went for a little visit of five days. There were ten persons in the house, some unconverted and long prayed for, some converted but not rejoicing Christians. He gave me the prayer: Lord, give me all in this house. And He just did! Before I left the house everyone had got a blessing. The last night of my visit I was too happy to sleep, and passed most of the night in renewal of my consecration, and these little couplets formed themselves and chimed in my heart one after another, until they finished with "Take myself, and I will be, Ever, only, all for thee."

The poem was published in Charles B. Shepp and Havergal's *Songs of Grace and Glory* (1874). This text has been in *GS* since 1921.

Messiah

Louis J. F. Herold, 1791-1833
Arr. George Kingsley, 1811-1884

This tune was arranged from a melody by Herold which he called MESSIAH. Kingsley retained the name with his arrangement. It was first published in *The Sacred Choir* (1839), set to the well-known poem "Rock of Ages." Two different tunes have been used in previous editions of *GS*: from 1921 to 1924, a tune by M. Lindsay was used; in 1925 MOZART entered the hymnal and so continued until *GSR* was published in 1986.

Take My Life, O Father, Mold It   603
From C. A. Bartol's *Hymns for the Sanctuary*, 1849. Alt.

This hymn text, which is probably of New England Unitarian origin, was published anonymously in Bartol's *Hymns*. It appears to have been originally in four stanzas, but stanza one has been considerably altered and the other stanzas to lesser degrees. The original stanza one read:

Take my heart, O Father, keep it,
    Make and keep it all Thine own;
Let Thy Spirit melt and break it—
    This proud heart of sin and stone.

In *Hymns of the Spirit* (1864), "mold it" appeared in the place of "take it." The source of the other alterations is unknown. Our text contains stanzas 1, 2, and 3. It entered *GS* in 1937.

Teleios

Philip P. Bliss, 1838-1876

This tune was first published in Ira D. Sankey, James McGranahan, and George C. Stebbins's *Gospel Hymns No. 3* (1878). In that hymnal this tune was the setting for the words "Take my life and let it be / Consecrated, Lord, to Thee" by Miss Havergal. Bliss probably added the refrain. This is the first inclusion of this tune in *GS*. The tune name TELEIOS (τέλειος), meaning "perfect" in Greek, was given by the current general editor. In the 1937 edition of *GS,* the preceding text was set to a tune said to be "Arr. from Bortnianski." There seems to be no concrete evidence for this attribution. The "Bortnianski" tune was first published as a glee in John Steven's *A Selection of Popular National Airs* (1818).

Take the Name of Jesus with You 524
Lydia Baxter, 1809-1874

Mrs. Baxter felt that the very utterance of the name of Jesus carried to her a deeper understanding. This text, which was used extensively in the Moody-Sankey gospel campaigns, was written in 1870. It was published in Robert Lowry and W. H. Doane's *Pure Gold for the Sunday School* (1871). This text first entered *GS* in 1921.

Precious Name

William H. Doane, 1832-1915

This tune was written for the preceding text and published with it in Lowry and Doane's *Pure Gold for the Sunday School* (1871). The music was first printed with the text in *GS* (1925).

Take Thou My Hands and Lead Me 527
Julie Hausmann, 1825-1901
Trans. Martha D. Lange

Miss Hausmann was living in Riga, Latvia, where she had gone to care for her aged father in 1859. She continued to live there after his death in 1861 and worked among the poor. Her friend Olga von Karp saw some of her poetry and sent it to Gustav Knak, a minister in Berlin. Knak wished to published the poetry, but Miss Hausmann consented only on the stipulation that it be published anonymously and that the proceeds go to an orphanage in Hong Kong. Her text "So nimm denn meine Hände und führe mich" was published in Knak's *Maiblumen, Lieder einer Stillen im Lande* (1862). I have been unable to identify Martha D. Lange or when she made the *GSR* translation. A translation of Miss Hausmann's text by Elmer Leon Jorgenson was included in *GS* in 1921(No. 301), but it was omitted in the 1925 edition and in all succeeding ones. This translation enters *GSR* for the first time.

So Nimm Denn Meine Hände

Friedrich Silcher, 1789-1860

This tune was first published in Silcher's *Kinderlieder für Schule und Haus*, III (1842). There it was the setting for "Wie könnt ich ruhig schlagen." The tune entered *GS* in 1921, was omitted in 1925, and is now restored in *GSR* (1986).

Take Thou Our Minds, Dear Lord   605

William B. Foulkes, 1877-1961

The text of this hymn was written at the request of the author's friend Calvin W. Laufer after they had met by chance on the railway station platform in Stony Brook, Long Island, New York. Laufer hummed the tune which he had not yet written down and suggested that it would make a good setting for a young people's hymn. Foulkes wrote three of the stanzas on an envelope while riding on the train. He wrote the fourth some time later while he was at a youth conference in Blairstown, New Jersey. This is the first inclusion of this text in *GS*.

Hall

Calvin W. Laufer, 1874-1938

The tune referred to in the notes on the preceding text was first called STONY BROOK. It was renamed by the author and composer to honor their friend William Ralph Hall. The text and tune were first published in *Conference Songs* (1918). This is its first inclusion in *GS*.

Take Time to Be Holy   487

William D. Longstaff, 1822-1894

The circumstances under which this text was written are in dispute. Ira Sankey said that it was written after Longstaff heard a sermon on 1 Peter 1:6 at New Brighton, England. Stebbins, the composer of the tune, said the words derived from a statement by Griffith John, a missionary to China, as quoted at a meeting in Keswick, England. William J. Reynolds says that he is inclined to accept Stebbins's version. Robert McCutchan says that this hymn first appeared in an English publication in 1882 and later in *Hymns of Consecration*, a collection used at Keswick. The text entered *GS* in 1921.

Holiness

George C. Stebbins, 1846-1945

This tune was composed while Stebbins was assisting Dr. George F. Pentecost and Bishop Thoburn in meetings at various places in India. A friend had clipped the poem from a periodical and had given it to Stebbins some months before. When Stebbins found the poem among his materials which he had brought with him, he composed the tune and sent it to Ira Sankey. The text and tune were published in Sankey's *Winnowed Songs for the Sunday School* (1890) and in *Gospel Hymns No. 6* (1891). This tune entered *GS* in 1921.

Take Up Your Cross 503

Charles W. Everest, 1814-1877

This hymn was first published in Everest's *Visions of Death, and Other Poems* (1833). The original text has been somewhat altered, and the alterations seem to have been first made in the *Salisbury Hymn Book* (1857). They thence passed into *Hymns Ancient and Modern* (1861). Our text is from the *Hymns A&M version,* which contains stanzas 1, 2, 3, and 5. It enters *GS* for the first time.

Germany

From William Gardiner's *Sacred Melodies,* 1815

This tune was first published in Gardiner's *Sacred Melodies from Haydn,* Mozart, and Beethoven, adapted to the best English Poets, and appropriated *to the Use of the British Church* (1815). In his *Music and Friends* (1838), Gardiner said that the tune is "somewhere in the works of Beethoven but I cannot point it out." The tune may have been a folk melody, or it may be by Gardiner himself. Leonard Ellinwood has said that there is a similarity between the beginning and ending of this tune and Beethoven's *Allegro ma non troppo* movement in his *Piano Trio*, Op. 170, No. 2. This tune first entered *GS* in 1937 as the setting for the great urban hymn "Where Cross the Crowded Ways of Life."

Tarry With Me, O My Savior 635

Caroline Sprague Smith, 1827-1866

Mrs. Smith's account of the writing of this text is recorded by Julian as follows:

> About the year 1853 (in the summer of 1852), I heard the Rev. Dr. Dexter preach a sermon on "The Adaptedness of Religion to the

Wants of the Aged." I went home and embodied the thought in the hymn "Tarry with me, O my Saviour!" I sent it to Mr. Hallock for *The Messenger.* He returned it as "not adapted for the readers of the paper." Years after I sent it, without any signature, to the little Andover paper.

Julian took the account from Hatfield's *Poets of the Church* (1884). The original poem, given in Hatfield, was in seven 6-line stanzas. In the *Plymouth Collection* (1855), the poem appeared altered to five 4-line stanzas. In Charles S. Robinson's *A Selection of Spiritual Songs for Use in the Church and the Choir* (1878), the poem is in six 4-line stanzas. This text was included in *GS* in 1921, set to J. B. Dykes's tune ST. SYLVESTER (see *GSR,* No. 564, "Father, Hear the Prayer We Offer"), and was given its present setting in the 1937 edition of our hymnal.

Rest

Knowles Shaw, 1834-1878

Shaw's tune was first published in his *Shining Pearls, A Collection of Choice Music for Revivals and Sunday Schools* (1868). Shaw used one of the stanzas of Mrs. Smith's poem as a chorus. This had been the second stanza in *GS* (1921). This tune entered *GS* in 1937.

Teach Me Your Way, O Lord 523

B. Mansell Ramsey, 1849-1923

Certain information on this hymn text is scant. The copyright holder could supply none. The *Anglican Hymn Book* (1965) gives the date of composition as 1919 and states that it appeared in a leaflet published by John T. Park in 1925. The hymn is based on Psalm 27:11. This is its first inclusion in *GS*.

Camacha

B. Mansell Ramsey, 1849-1923

The tune seems to have been written for and published with the text above. The tune name CAMACHA derives from the name of Ramsey's residence in Chichester, Sussex, England. This is its first inclusion in *GS*.

Tell Me the Story of Jesus 305

Fanny J. Crosby, 1820-1915

This text was published with Sweney's tune in William J.

Kirkpatrick and Sweney's *The Quiver of Sacred Song* (Philadelphia, 1880). The tune and the text have been in *GS* since 1925.

That Dreadful Night 372
Joseph Hart, 1712-1768

This text, altered, is taken from the *Supplement* (1762) to Hart's *Hymns Composed on Various Subjects, with the Author's experience* (1759). The original poem was in two 8-line stanzas and entitled "Holy Communion," with the first line beginning "That doleful night." This text entered *GS* in the *Supplement* (1975).

The Solemn Feast
Lloyd O. Sanderson, b. 1901

This tune was composed for the preceding hymn text and was first published in C. M. Pullias and Sanderson's *Christian Hymns* (Nashville, 1935). It is widely used among the Churches of Christ. The tune was first included in *GS* in the *Supplement* (1975).

The Church's One Foundation 365
Samuel J. Stone, 1839-1900

This hymn originated out of the controversy that arose in the Church of England over the views of Bishop John Colenso concerning the interpretation of the biblical text. Colenso had adopted the so called documentary hypothesis with regard to the Pentateuch. His views were ably answered by Bishop Robert Gray, and this led Stone to write the hymn. Stone published twelve hymns on the twelve articles of the Apostles' Creed, and the present text deals with Article Nine: "I believe in the holy Catholic church." The original poem was in seven 8-line stanzas; the *GSR* text contain stanzas 1, 2, 4, and 5. The entire hymn, with Stone's revisions and additions, may be seen in Julian (p. 1146). This text has been in *GS* since 1921.

Aurelia
Samuel S. Wesley, 1810-1876

This tune was written in 1864 for John Keble's hymn "The voice that breathed o'er Eden," but was first published in Charles Kemble's *A Selection of Psalms and Hymns* (London, 1864) as a setting for "Jerusalem the Golden." It was first set to Stone's text in the Appendix to *Hymns Ancient and Modern* (1868). The tune name was suggested by Wesley's wife and derived from the Latin *aureus,* that is, "golden." The tune entered *GS* in 1921.

The Day of Resurrection   242
John of Damascus, 8th century
Trans. John Mason Neale, 1818-1866

John of Damascus was one of the greatest of the Greek poets of the Eastern church. He died about A.D. 780. This beautiful resurrection hymn, Ἀναστάσεως ἡ'μέρα, is the first of eight odes which form what is called "The Golden Canon." Neale's translation first appeared in *The Ecclesiastic and Theologian* (1853). The translation of all eight odes may be seen in his *Hymns of the Eastern Church* (1862). Julian describes the circumstances surrounding the use of this hymn in the Greek Church (p. 62). The poem was included in the first edition of *GS* (1921) and in all printings until the *Number Two* book (1937). We are happy to restore this great text in *GSR.*

Lancashire

Henry Smart, 1813-1879

For information on this tune, see the notes on "Lead On, O King Eternal," (*GSR* No. 259.) It has been in *GS* since 1937.

The Day Thou Gavest, Lord, Is Ended   39
John Ellerton, 1826-1893

This text is an evening hymn written in 1870 and published that year in *A Liturgy for Missionary Meetings*. It was revised for the SPCK *Church Hymns* (1871) in five stanzas. Our text contains stanzas 1, 2, 4, and 5. The omitted stanza 3 reads:

As o'er each continent and island
    The dawn leads on another day,
The voice of prayer is never silent,
    Nor dies the strain of prayer away.

Sheng En

Su Yin-Lan, 1915-1937

SHENG EN was composed in 1934 while Su Yin-Lan was a student at Yenching University in Peking (Beijing), China. Bliss Wiant, her teacher and head of the Music department there, wrote an original harmony. The present harmony was composed for *GSR* by its music editor, Jack Boyd, in

1985. This is the first inclusion of this tune in *GS* and, indeed, the first inclusion of an example of oriental music in any hymnal published among non-instrumental Churches of Christ. All previous editions of our hymnal used ST. CLEMENT by C. C. Scholefield as the setting for Ellerton's text. The text first entered *GS* in the *Supplement* (1922).

The First Noel   208
Traditional English Carol

The origin of this carol is unknown. It was first printed anonymously in Davies Gilbert's *Some Ancient Christmas Carols* (1823) in nine 4-line stanzas. The GSR text contains stanzas 1, 2, and 3. "Noel," a term referring to the birth of Christ, became an expression of joy at the commemoration of Christ's birth. This text and tune have been in *GS* since 1937.

The First Noel

Traditional English Carol
Arr. John Stainer, 1840-1901

This tune first appeared in William Sandys's *Christmas Carols, Ancient and Modern* (1833). Millar Patrick believed that the tune may have been a treble part, sung above the melody, for the tune ST MAGNUS (See *GSR*, No. 257, "The Head that Once was Crowned with Thorns") Patrick's discussion is found in his *Handbook to the Church Hymnary Supplement* (1935). This tune has been in *GS* since 1937.

The God of Abraham Praise   43
Daniel ben Judah Dayyan, 14th century
Trans. Thomas Olivers, 1725-1799

John Julian, in his *Dictionary*, gives a full account of the composition of this poem. Olivers reportedly translated the Hebrew *Yigdal* (or Doxology) in 1770 and said: "I have rendered it from the Hebrew, giving it, as far as I could, a Christian character, and I have called on Leoni, the Jew, who has given me a synagogue melody to suit it; here is the tune, and it is called *Leoni*" (p. 1149).

Julian also includes the original Hebrew text and a literal rendering by Dr. Adler, once a British rabbi. Oliver's text is in thirteen 8-line stanzas. *GSR* includes stanzas 1, 2, and 4, exactly as Olivers translated them. The original text was written by Daniel ben Judah Dayyan about 1400. The poem was a metrical version of the creed drawn up for the Jewish faithful by Moses Maimonides (1130-1205). This text entered *GS* in 1921.

Leoni

Traditional Hebrew Melody

The origin of this tune is unknown. It seems to be an ancient Hebrew synagogue melody. Meyer Lyon (Leoni) probably sang it with the congregation as a unison piece. It first entered *GS* in 1921.

The Great Physician   173

William Hunter, 1811-1877

This hymn text, entitled "Christ the Physician," was published in Hunter's *Songs of Devotion* (1859). It was originally in seven stanzas, and *GSR* text contains 1, 3, 4, and 7. The omitted stanzas read as follows:

2
Your many sins are all forgiv'n,
    Oh! hear the voice of Jesus;
Go on your way in peace to heav'n,
    And wear a crown with Jesus.

5
The children too, both great and small,
    Who love the name of Jesus,
May now accept the gracious call
    To work and live for Jesus.

6
Come, brethren, help me sing his praise,
    Oh, praise the name of Jesus;
Oh, sisters, all your voices raise,
    Oh, bless the name of Jesus.

This text first entered *GS* in 1921.

Great Physician

John H. Stockton, 1813-1877

This tune was written for the preceding text and published at least as early as 1869 in *Joyful Songs, Nos. 1, 2, and 3 Combined* (Philadelphia: Methodist Book Concern). It was later published in Stockton's *Salvation Melodies No. 1, for the Friends of Jesus* (Philadelphia, 1874), and in O'Kane, C. C. McCabe, and J. R. Sweney's *Joy to the World or Sacred Songs for Gospel Meetings* (New York, 1878). The latter hymnal contains words only, indicating the popularity and knowledge of the text and tune. The tune entered *GS* in 1921.

The Greatness of God 190

T. S. N in *Songs of Praise with Music*, 1931

This text is credited to T. S. N. in the aforementioned hymnal without further identification. The text was originally written to celebrate the traditional Epiphany season (January 6), or the revelation of Christ to the Gentiles in the coming of the Magi. In the *Oxford Book of Carols*, this poem is entitled "Infinite Light." This is its first inclusion in *GS*.

Bramley

Traditional English Carol

This tune, also called A VIRGIN UNSPOTTED, is a traditional English carol tune of unknown origin. The tune name BRAMLEY derives from this tune's being set to a poem by H. R. Bramley (1833-1917) in *The English Hymnal* (1933, No. 29). The *GSR* setting is by Martin Shaw (1875-1958), as found in the *Oxford Book of Carols* (1928). This is its first inclusion in *GS*.

The Head That Once Was Crowned with Thorns 257

Thomas Kelly, 1769-1854

This text was published in six stanzas in Kelly's *Hymns on Various Passages of Scripture* (5th ed., 1820). It was entitled "Perfect through sufferings" and was based on Hebrews 2:10. The *GSR* text omits Kelly's stanza five:

> They suffer with their Lord below,
>> They reign with Him above;
> Their everlasting joy to know
>> The mystery of His love.

The poem appears in *GSR* just as Kelly wrote it with the exception of 2:2, which originally read "Is His, is His by right." This text first entered *GS* in the *Supplement* (1922).

St. Magnus

Jeremiah Clark, c. 1670-1707

This tune was attributed to Clark in the volume in which it first appeared, Henry Playford's *The Divine Companion, or David's Harp New Tun'd* (2d ed., London, 1707). The tune name derives from the St. Magnus church which was built by Christopher Wren in London in 1675. The tune name ST. MAGNUS was first given by William Riley in his *Psalms and Hymns* (1762). This tune has been in *GS* since 1921.

The Heavens Declare Thy Glory, Lord   112

Isaac Watts, 1674-1748

This poem was one of several in various meters on Psalm 19, which Watts printed in his *Psalms of David, Imitated in the Language of the New Testament.* Our text includes the first four stanzas of the original six-stanza poem. Watts based his method of handling the Old Testament text on that of the Apostle Paul in Romans 10:18—he applied the language. This may be seen clearly in the omitted stanzas 5 and 6:

5
Great Sun of Righteousness, arise;
    Bless the dark world with heavenly light;
Thy gospel makes the simple wise,
    Thy laws are pure, thy judgments right.

6
Thy noblest wonders here we view,
    In souls renewed, and sins forgiven:
Lord, cleanse my sins, my soul renew,
    And make thy word my guide to heaven

This is the first inclusion of this text in *GS.*

Uxbridge

Lowell Mason, 1792-1872

Little information is available on this tune. Lowell Mason either composed it or adapted it in 1830. It is named for a town in south central Massachusetts near the Rhode Island border. The city in Massachusetts was named for an ancient English town. Other tunes are also known as UXBRIDGE. This is its first inclusion in *GS.*

The King of Love My Shepherd Is   118

Henry W. Baker, 1824-1877

The text was published in the Appendix to the first edition of *Hymns, Ancient and Modern* (1868). It is a paraphrase of Psalm 23, and it is said that the last words of Baker were stanza three in his paraphrase. This is its first inclusion in *GS.*

St. Columba

Traditional Irish Melody

There are several hymns bearing this tune name, but this is the traditional melody. It is named for the famous Irish church leader Columba (A.D. 521-597). He migrated to the Island of Iona about A.D. 563 and established there a center for missionary and educational endeavors which brought the gospel to the Picts of Scotland. He as also known for his musical abilities. This is the first inclusion of this tune in *GS*.

The King Shall Come When Morning Dawns 284
John Brownlie, 1859-1925

This text was first published in Brownlie's *Hymns from the East, Being Centos and Suggestions from the Service Books of the Holy Eastern Church* (1907). He did not give any particular source for this poem, and most editors believe that it is Brownlie's own composition, growing out of his thorough knowledge of the Greek hymns. The *GSR* text contains stanzas 1-4 and 7 of the original seven-stanza poem. This is its first inclusion in *GS*.

Consolation

From John Wyeth's
Repository of Sacred Music, Part Second, 1813

This tune was first published anonymously in Wyeth's *Repository* (Harrisburg, Pa., 1813), set to Isaac Watts's "Once more my soul, the rising day." Its authorship remains uncertain. This is the first inclusion of this tune in *GS*.

The Lone, Wild Bird 589
Henry Richard MacFayden, b. 1877

MacFayden was a Presbyterian minister and a field worker for the Nashville Presbytery. He noticed that a hymn-writing contest was to be conducted in *The Homiletic Review*, wrote the hymn poem in late 1923, and sent it in. He was awarded third prize in the contest, and the poem was published in the *Review* in 1923. The present text is an alteration by David N. Johnson in 1968. The original reading in 1:1 was "The lone, wild fowl," and in 2:2, "The sea's dark deep and no man's land." This is the first inclusion of this hymn in *GS*.

Prospect

Southern Folk Hymn in William Walker's
Southern Harmony, 1854

This tune appeared in the *Southern Harmony* (1854, p. 92), set to Isaac Watts's hymn poem "Why should we start, or fear to die?" from his *Hymns and Spiritual Songs* (1707). The tune is attributed to "Graham." Nothing further is known of this tune. This is its first inclusion in *GS*.

The Lord Bless You and Keep You   632
Paraphrase of Numbers 6:24-26

This text is a paraphrase, with seven-fold amen, of Numbers 6:24-26,

And the Lord spake unto Moses, saying, Speak unto Aaron and unto his sons, saying, On this wise ye shall bless the children of Israel, saying unto them, The Lord bless thee and keep thee:
The Lord make his face to shine upon thee, and be gracious unto thee:
The Lord lift up his countenance upon thee, and give thee peace.
And they shall put my name upon the children of Israel; and I will bless them.

This hymn first entered *GS* in the *Supplement* (1975). In editions of *GS* beginning about 1934, a version of the "Blessing" by E. L. Jorgenson entered *GS*. It has been omitted in *GSR*.

Lutkin

Peter C. Lutkin, 1858-1931

Peter Lutkin was the first dean of the school of music at Northwestern University. He also helped to edit *The Methodist Hymnal* (1905), in which this arrangement of the Old Testament "Blessing" appeared (No. 748). It had been previously copyrighted by C. F. Summy Company, but the date is not available to me. The sevenfold amen was not included in this 1905 hymnal. The tune first entered *GS* in the *Supplement* (1975). With the text preceding, this hymn is used to close each school year at Abilene Christian University. In previous editions of *GS*, a tune for the text without the sevenfold amen by E. L. Jorgenson was included. That tune was named BENEDICTION and is omitted from *GSR*.

Hieron

William J. Kirkpatrick, 1838-1921

This tune was composed by Kirkpatrick and copyrighted by the Hope Publishing Company in 1900. Its first place of publication is unknown to me. The current general editor of *GSR* assigned the tune name HIERON (ιερόν), which means "temple" in Greek. This tune entered *GS* in 1921.

The Lord Jehovah Reigns 105

Isaac Watts, 1674-1748

This text, a paraphrase of Psalm 148, first appeared in Watts's *Hymns and Spiritual Songs* (1707). *GSR* employs the version of the poem used in most modern hymnals because the hymn, especially stanza three, has been variously emended. The original stanzas 3 and 4 read as follows:

3
Through all his ancient works,
    Surprising wisdom shines;
Confounds the powers of hell,
    And breaks their cursed designs:
Strong is his arm—
    And shall fulfill
His great decrees,
    His sovereign will.

4
And can this mighty King
    Of glory condescend—
And will he write his name,
    My Father and my Friend?
I love his name,
    I love his word;
Join, all my powers,
    And praise the Lord.

This is the first inclusion of this text in *GS*.

Millennium

Plymouth Collection, 145

This tune is a popular Southern camp meeting melody. It was first included in Henry Ward Beecher's *Plymouth Collection* (1855). This is its first inclusion in *GS*.

The Lord My Shepherd Is   145

Isaac Watts, 1674-1748

This text first appeared in Watts's *The Psalms of David, Imitated in the Language of the New Testament, and apply'd to the Christian State and Worship* (1719). Originally in six stanzas, the poem in *GSR* includes stanzas 1-3. The remaining stanzas read:

4
While he affords his aid
    I cannot yield to fear!
Though I should walk in death's dark shade,
    My Shepherd's with me there.

5
In spite of all my foes,
    Thou dost my table spread;
My cup with blessings overflows,
    And joy exalts my head.

6
The bounties of thy love
    Shall crown my following days;
Nor from thy house will I remove,
    Nor cease to speak thy praise.

This text has been in *GS* since 1921.

Cambridge

Ralph Harrison, 1748-1810
Arr. Samuel S. Wesley, 1810-1876

Harrison published the original of this melody in his *Sacred Harmony—A Collection of Psalm-tunes, Ancient and Modern* (2 vols., London, 1784, 1791). Wesley printed his arrangement in the *European Psalmist* (London, 1872). This is the first inclusion of this tune in *GS*. In all previous editions of our hymnal, beginning in 1921, an anonymous tune was used, with the notation /s s. m r f m. f s/ in the first phrase.

The Lord Will Come and Not Be Slow   282

John Milton, 1608-1674

This text is a cento drawn from several Psalm paraphrases which

Milton wrote in 1648 during the English Civil War. His head note to these Psalms read: "Nine of the Psalms done into Meter, wherein all but what is in a different Character, are the very words of the Text, translated from the Original." He put the literal translation in roman type and the words of his own composition to make the paraphrase in italic (i.e., "a different Character"). The *GSR* text runs as follows: Stanza 1 from Psalm 85:13. (Milton actually wrote:

> Before him Righteousness shall go
> > His Royal Harbinger,
> Then will he come, and not be slow,
> > His footsteps cannot err.

We do not know who first made the change to the present text.) Stanza 2 from Psalm 85:11; stanza 3 from Psalm 82:8; stanza 4 from Psalm 86:9; and stanza 5 from Psalm 86:10. This is the first inclusion of this text from one of our greatest poets in *GS*.

St. Stephen

William Jones, 1726-1800

This tune first appeared in *Ten Church Pieces for the Organ* (London, 1789), set to the version of Psalm 23 found in the old *Sternhold and Hopkins Psalter*. It is named for the first Christian martyr, a favorite biblical character of the composer. This is its first inclusion in *GS*.

The Lord's My Shepherd 143

From the *Scottish Psalter*, 1650

This text was published in *The Psalms of David in Meter: Newly Translated, and diligently compared with the original Text, and former Translations: More plaine, smooth, and agreeable to the Text, than any heretofore* (1650). This is the most famous of all the Scottish Psalters. The present text is indeed a result of a comparison "with the former Translations"; for it is a mosaic of lines from seven former versions, according to Millar Patrick in his *Four Centuries of Scottish Psalmody* (1949). This text first entered *GS* in the *Supplement* (1922).

Crimond

Jessie Seymour Irvine, 1836-1887

This tune was first published in William Carnie's *Northern Psalter* (Aberdeen, 1872) and was there credited to David Grant. In 1911 Miss Irvine's sister claimed that Grant had merely harmonized the melody but that her sister had written it. A controversy ensued, but after the *Scottish Psalter* (1929) credited it to Miss Irvine, her authorship has been accepted. "Crimond" is the Scottish town in which Miss Irvine's father was a longtime minister. This is the first inclusion of the tune in *GS*. All previous editions, beginning in 1922, have used the tune ORLINGTON by John Douglas Sutherland Campbell, who was son-in-law to Queen Victoria and one-time Governor-General of Canada, and the 9th Duke of Argyle.

The Sands of Time Are Sinking   668
Anne R. Cousin, 1824-1906

This hymn poem is based on phrases found in the letters of the famous Scottish preacher Samuel Rutherford (1600-1661), which Mrs. Cousin had read. Her daughter said she composed the lines as she sewed in her home at Irvine, in which place her husband was minister of the Scottish Free Church. The poem was first published in *The Christian Treasury* (1857). It was sung at the bedside of the dying Spurgeon in 1892 and was a favorite hymn of Dwight L. Moody. This text first entered *GS* in 1921.

Rutherford

Chretien D'Urhan, 1788-1845
Arr. Edward F. Rimbault, 1816-1876

The tune name RUTHERFORD comes obviously from the association with the writings of Rutherford mentioned above. The tune is based on a melody by D'Urhan in *Chants Chretien* (1834). Rimbault's arrangement was published in *Psalms and Hymns for Divine Worship* (1867). This tune has been in *GS* since 1921.

The Spacious Firmament   91
Joseph Addison, 1672-1719

Addison's fame rests in part upon his contributions to an early English periodical, *The Spectator*. In 1712, he wrote an article entitled "The Right Means to Strengthen Faith," in which he said:

> The Supreme Being has made the best arguments for his own existence in the formation of the heavens and the earth...The Psalmist has very beautiful strokes of poetry to this purpose in that exalted strain (Psalm xix). As such a bold and sublime manner of thinking furnished very noble matter for an ode, the reader may see it wrought into the following one.

He then concluded his essay with his now famous poem. This text has been in *GS* since 1925.

Creation
Franz Joseph Haydn, 1732-1809

This tune in an adaptation from Haydn's oratorio *The Creation* (1798). It appeared in George Kingsley's *The Sacred Choir* (New York, 1838), set to "Awake, my soul, and with the sun." Later adaptations were made by William Gardiner in his *Sacred Melodies* (London, 1812) and by Lowell Mason in *The Choir* (1832). The tune and text were first joined in Lowell Mason and George J. Webb's *The National Psalmist* (1848). This tune entered *GS* in 1925.

The Statutes of the Lord   301
From *The Psalms of David in Metre: According to the Version approved by The Church of Scotland*, 1650

This text is an adaptation from the *Scottish Psalter* (1650), probably made by James McGranahan when he wrote the accompanying tune. The words and tune were published in 1897 and owned by Hope Publishing Company. The text from the *Scottish Psalter* on which this text is based reads as follows in the paraphrase of Psalm 19:8-13:

8
The statutes of the Lord are right,
    and do rejoice the heart:
The Lord's command is pure, and doth
    light to the eyes impart.

9
Unspotted is the fear of God,
    and doth endure for ever:
The judgments of the Lord are true
    and righteous altogether.

10
They more than gold, yea, much fine gold
    to be desired are:
Than honey, honey from the comb
    that droppeth sweeter far.

11

Moreover, they thy servant warn
    how he his life should frame:
A great reward provided is
    for them that keep the same.

12

Who can his errors understand?
    O cleanse thou me within
From secret faults. Thy servant keep
    from all presumptuous sin:

13

And do not suffer them to have
    dominion over me:
Then righteous and innocent
    I from much sin shall be.

This paraphrase has been in *GS* since 1921.

O How Love I Thy Law

James McGranahan, 1840-1907

The tune name is the title under which the song was first published. It was written by McGranahan about 1897, copyrighted first by Charles M. Alexander and then later by Hope Publishing Co. Where it was first published I cannot determine. It has been in *GS* since 1921 with the preceding text, the stanzas of which come from Psalm 19 and the refrain from Psalm 119:97.

The Strife Is O'er, the Battle Done   238

Latin Hymn, *Finita jam sunt praelia*, c. 1695
Trans. Francis Pott, 1832-1909

This Latin text first appeared in *Symphonia Sirenum Selectarum* (Cologne, 1695). Its authorship and date of composition are unknown. John Mason Neale printed it in his *Hymni Ecclesiae* (21851). Pott's translation was first published in his *Hymns Fitted to the Order of Common Prayer* (1861). This text was first included in *GS* in the *Supplement* (1922). In 1925, a Hallelujah prelude was added. The hymn was omitted from the *Number Two* book in 1937. We are glad to restore this great hymn of hope to *GS*.

Victory

Giovanni P. da Palestrina, 1525-1594

This tune is an arrangement from Palestrina's *Gloria* in his *Magnificat Tertii Toni* (1591). William H. Monk made an initial arrangement which he published in the *Parish Choir* (1851) and then made this improved composition for the first edition of *Hymns Ancient and Modern* (1861). The arrangement differs vastly from the Palestrina original. This is its first inclusion in *GS* since the 1922-1936 editions. It was omitted in the 1937 edition.

The Sun Declines O'er Land and Sea 38

Robert Walmsley, 1831-1905

This text, written in 1893, was intended as an evening hymn for the celebration of Whitsuntide, or Pentecost. It was first published in Walmsley's *Sacred Songs* (1900). This text first entered *GS* in 1925.

Wentworth

Frederick C. Maker, 1844-1927

This tune was first published in the second series of *The Bristol Tune Book* (1876, No. 522). *GSR* uses the original tune but repeats the last two phrases. Jack Boyd, music editor of *GSR*, made the present arrangement in 1985. Beginning in 1925, and until the publication of *GSR*, a tune by Horatio R. Palmer called VINCENT had been the setting for Walmsley's poem.

There Is a Balm in Gilead 314

Traditional American Spiritual

This anonymous text came out of the folk tradition of American slaves and is based on Jeremiah 8:22. The *GSR* version of the hymn is taken from Frederick J. Work and John W. Work's *Folk Songs of the American Negro, No. 1* (Nashville, 1907, p. 31). It was first included in *GS* in the *Supplement* (1975).

Balm in Gilead

Traditional American Spiritual

This arrangement of the traditional tune was made by Jack A. Boyd, music editor of *GSR* for the *Supplement* to *Great Songs, Number Two* (1975).

There Is a Fountain Filled with Blood   217
William Cowper, 1731-1800

This text was originally in seven stanzas and was first published in R. Conyers's *A Collection of Psalms and Hymns from Various Authors* (2d ed., 1772). It was also included in the *Olney Hymns* (1779) and there entitled "Praise for the fountain opened—Zech. 13:1." This text has been in *GS* since 1921. From 1921 through 1985, all printings contained only Watts's stanzas 1, 3, and 4. *GSR* includes all the stanzas except 6 and 7. The two omitted stanzas read:

6
Lord, I believe thou hast prepared,
    Unworthy though I be,
For me a blood-bought, free reward,
    A golden harp for me.

7
'Tis strung and tuned for endless years,
    And formed by power divine,
To sound in God the Father's ears,
    No other name but thine.

Cleansing Fountain

Traditional American Melody

This anonymous tune is often denominated "Western Melody" in various nineteenth-century tune books. It seems to be a typical camp meeting tune. Some have erroneously ascribed it to Lowell Mason because of the similarity between it and Mason's tune COWPER. The Mason tune probably derives from CLEANSING FOUNTAIN. It has been in *GS* since 1921.

There Is a Green Hill Far Away   226
Cecil Frances Alexander, 1818-1895

This text was written while the poet was sitting beside the bed of a sick child. It was first published in her *Hymns for Little Children* (1848) as one of a series of poems attempting to make the Apostles' Creed meaningful to children. This hymn centered on the phrases "Suffered under Pontius Pilate, was crucified, dead and buried." Originally in five stanzas, the *GSR* text incudes all but Mrs. Alexander's stanza three:

He died that we might be forgiven,
    He died to make us good;

That we might go at last to heaven,
Saved by His precious blood.

This text has been in *GS* since 1921.

Meditation
John H. Gower, 1855-1922

This tune was composed for the familiar old hymn "There is a land of pure delight." First published in Gower's *Original Tunes* (Denver, 1890), this is its first inclusion in *GS*. In previous editions of our hymnal, other tunes have been used. From 1921-1936, a tune by George C. Stebbins was employed, with the final stanza used as a chorus. This tune dates from 1919. When the *Number Two* book was published in 1937, it contained the text with music by E. L. Jorgenson, which was called COMMUNION CHANT.

There Is a Habitation 664
Love H. Jameson, 1811-1892

No specific information is available on this text. L. H. Jameson was an evangelist, writer, and singer of the Stone-Campbell Movement, who lived in Indianapolis, Indiana. A. Campbell spoke of him as the brother "whose praise is in all the churches in Indiana" (*Millennial Harbinger,* 1851, p. 14). The hymn appears in J. H. Fillmore's *New Christian Hymn and Tune Book* (Part II; Cincinnati, 1882, No. 619). The text has been in *GS* since 1921.

Jameson
James Holmes Rosecrans, 1844-1926

No specific information is available on this tune. When it appeared in J. H. Fillmore's *New Christian Hymn and Tune Book* (Part II; Cincinnati, 1882, No. 619), it bore the tune name O SION, SION. This tune by Rosecrans was not printed in *GS* until 1937. The text appeared from 1921 to 1924, was omitted from 1925 to 1936, and restored with tune in 1937.

There Is a Name I Love to Hear 455
Frederick Whitfield, 1829-1904

This text was written in 1855 and circulated first in leaflet form. It was thereafter published in Whitfield's *Sacred Poems and Prose* (1861). The chorus, which is not a part of the original hymn, is found used with many texts in nineteenth-century American Collections. The refrain first entered *GS* in 1937, used with Watt's "Alas! and did my Savior bleed." The stanzas of the hymn enter *GS* for the first time in this edition (1986).

Oh, How I Love Jesus
American Folk Hymn, 19th Century

The origin of this tune is unknown. It appears in many nineteenth century American collections, with such texts as "Alas! and did my Savior bleed" and Newton's "Amazing grace." It entered *GS* in 1937.

There Is a Place of Quiet Rest   482
Cleland B. McAfee, 1866-1944

Katherine McAfee Parker, the daughter of Cleland B. McAfee, has said that this hymn was written in 1901 just after the death of the two little daughters of McAfee's brother Howard from diphtheria. McAfee was accustomed to writing a hymn for each communion service of the Presbyterian church where he ministered in Chicago, Illinois. This hymn came out of the grief and loss he felt at the deaths of his nieces. It was first sung outside his brother's house, which was under quarantine, and also at the services the next day. The text was first published by the Lorenz Publishing Company in its hymnal *The Choir Leader* (1903). This text entered *GS* in the *Supplement* (1975).

McAfee
Cleland B. McAfee, 1866-1944

The tune was written for the preceding text. The name McAFEE was first given to the tune in the *Baptist Hymnal* (1956). It entered *GS* in the *Supplement* (1975).

There Is, Beyond the Azure Blue   107
Aaron W. Dicus, 1888-1978

This text, currently very popular among Churches of Christ, was written by Aaron Wesley Dicus, a physicist, inventor, educator, and gospel preacher. After his retirement as dean of Florida Christian College (now Florida College), in Temple Terrace, Florida, in 1954, he gave himself to hymn writing. This song was published in 1966. This is its first inclusion in *GS*.

Dicus

Aaron W. Dicus, 1888-1978

This tune was written for and published with this text in 1966. It was published shortly thereafter in Ellis Crum's *Sacred Selections for the Church* (Kendalville, Indiana). This is its first inclusion in *GS*.

There Is Sunshine in My Soul 463

Eliza Edmunds Hewitt, 1851-1920

This text was written while the author was recovering from an injury. She had been teaching school in Philadelphia when an unruly student whom she had been attempting to correct struck her across the back with a heavy slate board. She had to spend six months in a cast. When her physician at last permitted her to go for a short walk, her heart overflowed for joy. After her walk, she wrote this fine gospel song. It entered *GS* in 1937.

Sunshine

John R. Sweney, 1837-1899

This tune was written for Miss Hewitt's text and published with it in William J. Kirkpatrick and Sweney's *Glad Hallelujahs* (Philadelphia, 1887). The tune name was given by the hymnal committee of the *Baptist Hymnal* (1956). It entered *GS* in 1937.

There's a Call Comes Ringing 439

Charles H. Gabriel, 1856-1932

Gabriel wrote this text in 1890 after he became a chorister at Grace Methodist Episcopal Church in San Francisco. It was published in his *Scripture Songs* (San Francisco, 1891), with the inscription "Written expressly for the Easter service of the Grace M. E. Sunday School, San Francisco, California." It was also published that same year in *The New Song for the Sunday School* (Chicago: George F. Rosche & Co.). The original refrain contained sixteen measures and began with a bass lead. This original version, owned by George F. Rosche, may be seen in *Wonderful Songs for Work and Worship* (Austin: Firm Foundation Publishing House, 1938), edited by Thomas S. Cobb and G. H. P. Showalter. The text has been in *GS* since 1921.

McCabe

Charles H. Gabriel, 1856-1932

The tune was written for the preceding text in 1890 (See above for the circumstances). The tune name was first given in the *Baptist Hymnal* (1956). It is named for Chaplain C. C. McCabe, who helped to popularize the song. The tune entered *GS* in 1921.

There's a Glad New Song 469

Albert C. Fisher, 1886-1946

Fisher wrote this song in 1940 and entitled it "Redeeming Love." He sold it to Robert H. Coleman that year, and it remained in the files of unpublished materials until the Coleman firm was purchased by the Baptist Sunday School Board in 1945. Walter Hines Sims, the editor of the *Baptist Hymnal* (1956), discovered the song in the unpublished materials and included it in his hymnal. This is its first inclusion in *GS*.

Redeeming Love

Albert C. Fisher, 1886-1946

This tune was written for the preceding text in 1940. Its history is that of the text above. The *Baptist Hymnal* (1956) used the title which Fisher had given his poem as a tune name. This is its first inclusion in *GS*.

There's a Land That Is Fairer Than Day 659

Sanford F. Bennett, 1836-1898

Bennett, a druggist in Elkhorn, Wisconsin, wrote this poem shortly after the close of the Civil War. He gave the following account of its writing:

Mr. Webster, like many musicians, was of an exceedingly nervous and sensitive nature, and subject to periods of depression, in which he looked upon the dark side of all things in life. I had learned his peculiarities so well that on meeting him I could tell at a glance if he was melancholy, and had found that I could rouse him by giving him a new song to work on.

He came into my place of business, walked down to the stove, and turned his back on me without speaking. I was at my desk writing. Turning to him I said, "Webster, what is the matter now?" "It's no matter," he replied, "it will be all right by and by." The idea of the hymn came to me like a flash of sunlight, and I replied, "The Sweet By and By! why would not that make a good hymn?"

"Maybe it would," he said indifferently. Turning to my desk I penned the words of the hymn as fast as I could write. I handed the words to Webster. As he read his eyes kindled, and stepping to the desk he began writing the notes. Taking his violin, he played the melody and then jotted down the notes of the chorus. It was not over thirty minutes from the time I took my pen to write the words before two friends with Webster and myself were singing the hymn.

This text entered *GS* in 1921.

Sweet By and By
Joseph P. Webster, 1819-1875

This tune was written for the preceding text in accordance with the account given above. The song was published in Webster's *The Signet Ring, a New Collection of Music and Hymns, Composed for Sabbath Schools* (1868). Only the text was printed in *GS* in 1921, with indication to use this tune. The music was first printed in our hymnal in 1925.

There's a Wideness in God's Mercy   308
Frederick W. Faber, 1814-1863

This text was first published in Faber's *Oratory Hymns* (1854). It was originally printed in thirteen 4-line stanzas. The *GSR* text includes stanzas 4, 5, 6, and 13. The original first stanza read:

Souls of men! why will ye scatter
   Like a crowd of frightened sheep?
Foolish hearts! why will ye wander
   From a love so true and deep?

This text is included in *GSR* for the first time.

In Babilone
Traditional Dutch Melody
Arr. Julius Röntgen, 1855-1932

For information on this tune, see the notes on "Son of God, Eternal Savior" (*GSR*, No. 151). This tune is included in *GS* for the first time.

There's Within My Heart a Melody   465
Luther B. Bridgers, 1884-1948

Bridgers lost his wife and children in a house fire at her parents' home in Georgia while he was away conducting a meeting at a Methodist church in Kentucky. It is believed that he wrote this text in 1909 following that tragic loss. The text was first published in Charlie D. Tillman's *The Revival No. 6* (1910). In 1917 Robert H. Coleman purchased the hymn and published it in his widely-circulated *Popular Hymnal* (1918). This is the first inclusion of the text in *GS*.

Sweetest Name

Luther B. Bridgers, 1884-1948

This tune was written for the preceding text at the time of the incident described above and was published in Charlie D. Tillman's *The Revival No. 6* (1910). This is its first inclusion in *GS*.

Thine Is the Glory   240
Edmond L. Budry, 1854-1932
Trans. R. Birch Hoyle, 18751939

The original French text, beginning "A toi la gloire," was attributed to Budry in the hymnal of the World Student Christian Federation, *Cantate Domino* (1925). The text was apparently written in 1884. Hoyle's translation appeared in the hymnal mentioned above in 1923. The is the first inclusion of the text in *GS*.

Judas Maccabeus

George Frederick Handel, 1685-1759

This tune is taken from the chorus "See the conquering hero comes" in Handel's oratorio *Judas Maccabeus* (1745). It was not in the original score of the oratorio, but was transferred to it from Handel's *Joshua* in 1751. It was first published as a hymn tune in Thomas Butts's *Harmonia Sacra* (1760), where it was set to Wesleys "Christ the Lord Is Risen Today." This is its first inclusion in *GS*.

This Is My Father's World   103
Maltbie D. Babcock, 1858-1901

Babcock, a minister, would often take morning walks "to see my Father's world." Apparently one of these walks inspired this poem. It was first published posthumously in a little volume of his sermons and poems entitled *Thoughts for Everyday Living* (1901). The poem consisted originally of sixteen 4-line stanzas. The *GSR* text contains stanzas 2, 3, 4, 5, 14, and 16. It was first included in *GS* in the *Supplement* (1975).

Terra Beata

Franklin L. Sheppard, 1852-1930

This tune first appeared in *Alleluia* (1915), a Presbyterian young people's hymnal edited by Sheppard. In that book he ascribes the tune (No. 180) as a "Traditional English Melody, Arranged by S. F. L., 1915." S. F. L. are pseudonymous initials for Sheppard. Modern editors disagree as to the source of the composition, but it does appear to be based upon the traditional English melody called RUSPER, found in the *English Hymnal* (1906, No. 379). It was first included in *GS* in the *Supplement* (1975).

This Is the Day of Light 23

John Ellerton, 1826-1893

Ellerton wrote this hymn in 1867, and it was published that year in Dean Howson's *Hymns for Special Services and Festivals* (Chester, 1867, No. 51). The original poem was in five 4-line stanzas. Our text contains stanzas 1-4. This is its first inclusion in *GS*.

Swabia

Johann Speiss, d. ca. 1772

SWABIA has been attributed to various composers. In earlier hymnals it was simply called a "German" tune. Later it was said to have been adapted from Johann Crüger's *Pietatis Melica* (1698). More recently hymnologists attribute the tune to Johann M. Speiss in his *David's Harpffen Spiel* (1745), where it was set to "Ach wachet, wachet auf." The present arrangement is by W. H. Havergal in *Old Church Psalmody* (1847). This is its first inclusion in *GS*.

This Is the Day the Lord Hath Made 18

Isaac Watts, 1674-1748

This text, first published in Watts's *Psalms of David* (1719), is the fourth part of a paraphrase of Psalm 118. The five original quatrains represent verses 24-26 of the psalm. Watts entitled the poem "Hosanna; the Lord's Day; or Christ's Resurrection, and Our Salvation." The *GSR* text omits the original stanza two:

> Today He rose and left the dead,
> And Satan's empire fell;
> Today the saints His triumphs spread,
> And all His wonders tell.

This is the first inclusion of this text in *GS*.

Twenty-Fourth

Lucius Chapin, 1760-1842

This melody, first published in 1813, is a folk tune and may be found in such oblong hymnals as *Kentucky Harmony* (1815) and the *Sacred Harp* (1844). The composer was probably Lucius Chapin. In 1813 it appeared in John Wyeth's *A Repository of Sacred Music, Part II* and in Robert Patterson's *Church Music,* the same year. Which had it first is unknown. This is its first inclusion in *GS*.

Thou Art Merciful, O Father   106

Elmer Leon Jorgenson, 1886-1968

This paraphrase of Psalm 103:8-22 is by the original compiler-editor of *GS*. It was included in the original edition (1921), but was omitted from the editions of 1925 and 1937. The *Supplement* committee restored it in 1975. It is one of the finest of E. L. Jorgenson's poems.

Jorgenson

Wolfgang Amadeus Mozart, 1756-1791

This tune is an arrangement by Jorgenson, from Mozart's composition K. 331. The *Supplement* committee shortened the last phrase, which required repetition of the final line of each stanza. It first appeared in the 1921 edition of *GS,* was omitted from those of 1925 and 1937, and restored in the *Supplement* (1975).

Thou Art the Way   260

George W. Doane, 1799-1859

This hymn was first published in Doane's *Songs by the Way, Chiefly Devotional with Translations and Imitations* (1824) under the motto "I am the way and the Truth, and the Life" (John 14:6). It is the only hymn by an American writer in the original edition of *Hymns Ancient and Modern* (1861). The text first entered *GS* in the *Supplement* (1922). Doane's text was originally in four stanzas. The *GSR* text contains stanzas 1-3. Stanza four reads as follows:

> Thou art the Way, the Truth, the Life:
> > Grant us that way to know,
> That truth to keep, that life to win,
> > Whose joys eternal flow.

Sawley

James Walch, 1837-1901

According to R. G. McCutchan in his *Hymn Tune Names*, this tune was first published in 1857. The name SAWLEY derives from the name of the town in England near where Walch was born. This tune first entered *GS* in the *Supplement* (1922).

Thou, Whose Almighty Word   101

John Marriott, 1780-1825

This hymn text is said to have been written in 1813. It was quoted by Thomas Mortimer, lecturer of St. Olave's, Southwark, at a meeting of the London Missionary Society, May 12, 1825, and printed in June of that year in the *Evangelical Magazine*. The original poem is in four stanzas and began "Thou Whose Eternal Word." *GSR*, according to E. L. Jorgenson's usual practice, omits the overtly Trinitarian stanza 4, as well as the direct appeal to the Holy Spirit of stanza 3. The omitted stanzas read:

3
Spirit of truth and love,
    Life-giving, Holy Dove,
Speed forth thy flight;
    Move on the water's face,
Bearing the lamp of grace,
    And in earth's darkest place
Let there be light!

4
Holy and blessed Three,
    Glorious Trinity,
Wisdom, Love, Might;
    Boundless as ocean's tide
Rolling in fullest pride,
    Through the world far and wide
Let there be light!

This text first entered *GS* in 1937. Samuel W. Duffield, in his *English Hymns: Their Authors and History*, says Marriott's text was first published in Dr. Raffle's *Collection* (1816).

Braun

Johann Georg Braun, 1675

The general editor of *GSR* originally assigned the tune name BRAINE in *GSR,* but no information was found on the composer W. R. Braine. The name is an error which has been in *GS* since 1937, when the text and tune entered our hymnal. In all succeeding editions of the hymnal the tune name will be given as BRAUN, for J. G. Braun who published the tune in his *Hymnodiae Coelestis* (Ubthal, 1675).

Through All the Changing Scenes   52

Tate and Brady, New Version, 1696

This paraphrase of Psalm 34 appeared in Nahum Tate and Nicholas Brady's *New Version of the Psalms of David* (1696). It was revised somewhat in the second edition (1698). Psalm 34 contains 22 verses, which the New Version paraphrases in 22 4-line stanzas. The *GSR* text includes stanzas 1, 3, 8, 9, and 22. This is first inclusion in *GS.*

Irish

From *A Collection of Hymns and Sacred Poems,* 1749

This tune is probably an Irish folk song. James Hogg, the Scottish poet, associates it with an old poem called "The Cameronian Cat" in his *Jacobite Relics of Scotland.* It has also been attributed to John F. Lampe (1702-1751), an associate of John Wesley in Dublin in 1749. The tune first appeared in *A Collection of Hymns and Sacred Poems* (Dublin, 1749). Caleb Ashworth gave the tune its present name in his *Collection of Tunes* (c. 1760). This is its first inclusion in *GS.*

Through the Love of God Our Savior   117

Mary Bowly Peters, 1813-1856

Mrs. Peters was the wife of an Anglican minister. This text was first published in her *Hymns intended to help the Communion of Saints* (London: Nisbet & Co., 1847). It is a beautiful poem intended to emphasize security in Christ. This is its first inclusion in *GS.*

Ar Hyd Y Nos

Traditional Welsh Melody

This traditional melody was published in Edward Jones's *Musical Relics of the Welsh Bards* (Dublin, 1784). It first entered *GS* in 1937. In all previous printings of our hymnal since that date, it was set to the familiar words by Sir Harold Edwin Boulton, "Sleep, my child, and peace attend thee" (All Through the Night).

Thy Supper, Lord, Before Us Spread 384
Joseph F. Green, b. 1924

William Reynolds says that this text was written at the request of Bill F. Leach as part of a study of the Lord's Supper. It first appeared in an anthem setting in *The Church Musician* (December 1961). The hymnal version was arranged for *The Junior Hymnal* (Nashville, 1964). This is the first inclusion of this text in *GS*.

Mainzer
Joseph Mainzer, 1801-1851
Harm. Austin C. Lovelace, b. 1919

This tune first appeared in the composer's *Choruses* (London, 1841) as a setting for a paraphrase of Psalm 107. It was also used as a setting for Psalm 102 in Mainzer's *Standard Psalmody of Scotland* (1845). In order to give more variety to the tune, Austin Lovelace provided the present harmonization of the melody. MAINZER first entered *GS* in the *Supplement* (1922), as the setting for "Jesus Shall Reign Where'er the Sun."

Till He Come 383
Edward H. Bickersteth, 1825-1906

This beautiful poem presents, as the author said, "one aspect of the Lord's Supper which is passed over in many hymnals, 'Ye do show forth the Lord's death till He come;' and also our communion with those of whom we may say 'We bless Thy holy name for all Thy servants departed this life in Thy faith and fear.'" The text was written in 1861 and was first published in Bickersteth's *The Blessed Dead* (1862). It entered *GS* in the *Supplement* (1922).

Halle
Attributed to Franz Joseph Haydn, 1732-1809

This tune seems to be derived from GROSSER GOTT, WIR LOBEN DICH (See *GSR,* No. 489, "Holy God, We Praise Thy Name"). The hymnals I have examined that include it ascribe it variously. *The Hymnbook* (1955), edited by David H. Jones for the Presbyterian and Reformed Churches in America, attributes the tune to Haydn. *The Psalter*

Hymnal of the Christian Reformed Church (1934) attributed the arrangement to Thomas Hastings. The old *Psalter of the United Presbyterian Church* (Pittsburgh, 1887) gives Peter Ritter as the composer and assigns the date as 1798. This is the first inclusion of this very singable tune in *GS*. All previous editions of the hymnal since 1922 have either indicated or printed the tune WELLS as the setting.

'Tis Midnight and on Olive's Brow   213
William B. Tappan, 1794-1849

This text, entitled "Gethsemane," was published in Tappan's *Poems* (1822). His original words in 2:2, "Immanuel wrestles," and in 2:3, "E'en the disciple that," were altered to the present text in the *Hymnal of the Methodist Episcopal Church* (Cincinnnati, 1878). This hymn has been in *GS* since 1921.

Olive's Brow

William B. Bradbury, 1816-1868

This tune was written for the preceding text and was first published in Bradbury and George F. Root's *The Shawm* (New York 1853). The tune entered *GS* in 1925, all previous editions containing words only with an indication to use OLIVE'S BROW as the tune.

'Tis So Sweet to Trust in Jesus   497
Louisa M. E. Stead, c. 1850-1917

No certain information is available concerning the circumstances under which this hymn text was written. It may have been composed after her husband's death in 1879. It was first published in John R. Sweney and William J. Kirkpatrick's *Songs of Triumph* (1882). It has been in *GS* since 1921.

Trust in Jesus

William J. Kirkpatrick, 1838-1921

This tune was composed for the preceding text and was first published in Sweney and Kirkpatrick's *Songs of Triumph* (1882). It entered *GS* in 1921.

'Tis the Blessed Hour of Prayer   560
Fanny J. Crosby, 1820-1915

This text was first published in Robert Lowry and W. H. Doane's *Good as Gold* (1880). It has been in *GS* since 1921. Nothing is known of the circumstances out of which the poem developed.

Blessed Hour

William H. Doane, 1832-1915

This tune was written for the preceding text and published in Lowry and Doane's *Good as Gold* (1880). It first entered *GS* in 1937. All previous editions of our hymnal had used a tune written in 1892 by E. Maude Cline.

To Canaan's Land I'm on My Way   665
William M. Golden

The date and circumstances surrounding the writing of this text are unknown. According to George Pullen Jackson, Golden was from Mississippi. The text and tune appeared as early as 1922 in R. E. Winsett's *Songs of the Coming King: The Message Due the World* (Ft. Smith, Arkansas).

Golden

William M. Golden

No information is available on this tune. See notes on the text above. The tune name GOLDEN was given by the current general editor of *GSR*.

To God Be the Glory   79
Fanny J. Crosby, 1820-1915

This text was published in W. H. Doane and Robert Lowry's *Brightest and Best* (1875), a Sunday school hymnal. This was a notable collection in that it also included "All the Way My Savior Leads Me" (*GSR*, No. 651); "I Am Thine, O Lord" (*GSR*, No. 599), "Savior, More Than Life to Me," and "Up from the Grave He Arose (*GSR*, No. 245). The poem was not included, however, in Sankey's popular *Gospel Hymns* series and never caught on in America. Among the hymnals of the Stone-Campbell Movement, the only one known to me to have included it was *The Christian Sunday School Hymnal; a Compilation of Choice Hymns and Tunes for Sunday Schools* (St. Louis: Christian Publishing Company, 1883). This collection was edited by J. H. Garrison, J. H. Harder, and George D. Smitherwood. It was not included in *The Christian Hymnal* (1882). The hymn entered *GS* in the *Supplement* (1975).

To God Be the Glory

William H. Doane, 1832-1915

This tune was first published with the preceding text in Doane and Robert Lowry's *Brightest and Best* (1875). It entered *GS* in the *Supplement* (1975).

To Love Someone More Dearly Every Day   460

Maude Louise Ray

F. H. Pickup

This text in two stanzas was written by Ray in 1903. A third stanza was added by Pickup in 1913. The hymn, owned by the Lorenz Publishing Company, appeared in Edmund S. Lorenz's *The Church Hymnal, The Official Hymnal of the Church of the United Brethren in Christ* (Dayton, Ohio, 1935, No. 377). It first entered *GS* in 1937.

My Task

Emma Hindle Ashford, 1850-1930

At age twelve Mrs. Ashford was organist at Kewanee, Illinois, and after her marriage, lived in Nashville, Tennessee, where her husband was superintendent of buildings and grounds at Vanderbilt University. This tune was written one Sunday morning in 1905 after a friend had brought her the lines and had gone on to church services. It may be found in the Lorenz hymnal mentioned above. The tune entered *GS* in 1937.

Trying to Walk in the Steps of the Savior   518

Eliza Edmunds Hewitt, 1851-1920

This text and the tune following were first published in John Wanamaker and John R. Sweney's *Living Hymns for Use in the Sabbath School, Young People's Meetings, the Church and Home* (Philadelphia: J. J. Wood, 1890, No. 23). William J. Kirkpatrick copyrighted the hymn in 1890, and it was later assigned to the Hope Publishing Company. It appeared in Hope's 1898 collection, *Pentecostal Hymns, No. 2*, edited by Henry Date. This is its first inclusion in *GS*.

Ichnos

William J. Kirkpatrick, 1838-1921

This tune was written for the text above in 1890. It was published in Wanamaker and Sweney's *Living Hymns*, that same year. This is its first inclusion in *GS*. The tune name ICHNOS (ἴχνος), which is the Greek term for "step," was given by the current general editor of *GSR*.

'Twas on That Night 367

John Morison in *Scottish Paraphrases*, 1781

This text comes from a revision of the Scottish *Translations and Paraphrases* of 1745, in which Morison assisted, and which was published in 1781. The original poem was in six stanzas. The *GSR* text represents an alteration made by E. L. Jorgenson and containing stanzas 1-4, except that 3:3 has "sacred feast" rather than "sacred rite." The *GSR* stanza five contains Morison's 5:1, 2, and two more lines based on Morison's stanzas five and six. The original stanzas read:

5
"My blood I thus pour forth," He cries,
To cleanse the soul in sin that lies;
In this the covenant is sealed,
And heaven's eternal grace revealed.

6
"With love to man this cup is fraught;
Let all partake the sacred draught;
Through latest ages let it pour,
In memory of my dying hour."

The text entered *GS* in 1925.

Windham

Daniel Read, 1757-1836

The preceding text has been set to the tune ROCKINGHAM, OLD in all former editions of *GS*, beginning in 1925. That tune, however, had fallen into disuse in recent years and the hymn was not being used. The current hymnal committee felt that the text was too good to lose and hence set it to WINDHAM, which is one of the earliest of American hymn tunes. It is found in The *American Singing Book* (1785). This is its first inclusion in *GS*.

Under His Wings   643
William O. Cushing, 1823-1902

These words were written in the 1890s, but the exact year is unknown. We have ventured 1896. The hymn is based on Psalm 17:8, "Hide me under the shadow of thy wings." It was published in Ira D. Sankey's last major collection, *Sacred Songs No. 1* (1896). This text entered *GS* in 1937.

Hingham

Ira David Sankey, 1840-1908

This tune appeared in Sankey's last major song collection, *Sacred Songs No. 1* (1896). The tune name derives from Cushing's birthplace, Hingham Center, Massachusetts. The name was first used in Donald Hustad's *Hymns for the Living Church* (1974). It entered *GS* in 1937.

Unto the Hills   148
John D. S. Campbell, 1845-1914

This text is a metrical version of Psalm 121. It was published in Campbell's *Book of Psalms* (1877), which appeared after he had married the fourth daughter of Queen Victoria and the year before he became Governor-General of Canada. The text has been a special favorite in Canada. It was first included in *GS* in the *Supplement* (1922), which was added "to meet completely the need of those churches throughout the British Empire in which such selections are most often used." It has become a special favorite among the Churches of Christ in the United States as well as in Canada.

Sandon

Charles H. Purday, 1799-1885

This tune, first published in Purday's *Church and Home Metrical Psalter and Hymnal* (London, 1860), was set to the text "Lead, Kindly Light." It was there called LANDON, and the present tune name may have resulted from a typographical error. There is, however, an English residence called "Sandon." This tune entered *GS* in the *Supplement* (1922).

Wake, Awake, for Night Is Flying 286
Philip Nicolai, 1556-1608
Trans. Catherine Winkworth, 1827-1878

This text, often called "the King of Chorales," was first published in Nicolai's *Frewden-Spiegel dess ewigen Lebens* (1599). He desired to set forth in this work a testimony to his faith in the Christian hope that it might comfort others. The original German poem is a reversed acrostic, forming the initials of Nicolai's student, Graf zu Waldeck—W. Z. G.: W(achet), Z(ion), G(loria). The poem is based principally on Matthew 25:1-13 and Revelation 19:6-9 and 21:1, with echoes of the prophecies of Isaiah and Ezekiel. Winkworth's translation appeared in her *Lyra Germanica, Second Series* (1858). This is the first inclusion of this text in *GS*.

Wachet Auf

Philip Nicolai, 1556-1608

This tune was published in Nicolai's *Frewden-Spiegel* (1599). It was probably based on Hans Sachs's "Silberweise" (c. 1513). The melody was harmonized by J. S. Bach. This is its first inclusion in *GS*.

Walk in the Light 625
Bernard Barton, 1784-1849

This text in six 4-line stanzas appeared first in Barton's *Devotional Verses, Founded on Select Texts of Scripture* (1826). It was based on 1 John 1:7. Our text contains the original stanzas 1, 2, 4, and 6. This is its first inclusion in *GS*.

Manoah

Henry W. Greatorex's *Collection of Psalm and Hymn Tunes*, 1861

Although this tune was included in Greatorex's *Collection,* no source was assigned. He either wrote it himself or adapted it from some unknown source. Manoah was the father of Samson, but otherwise the tune name seems to have no particular significance. The tune entered *GS* in 1921 as the setting for "Majestic Sweetness Sits Enthroned" (See *GSR,* No. 260).

Walking Alone at Eve 41
Thomas R. Sweatmon

J. Nelson Slater, the son of the composer of the tune following, has told me that he believes this poem was probably written about 1915 while Sweatmon and his father were students together at the Eureka Normal Music School in Stigler, Oklahoma. Sweatmon's religious affiliation is unknown, but he was a minister and singing teacher and later resided in Georgia and in Louisville, Kentucky. This text enters *GS* for the first time in the present edition (1986).

Slater
William Washington Slater, 1885-1959

Slater acquired the preceding text from Sweatmon and then wrote the tune. It was first published in 1917. No other information is available. This is its first inclusion in *GS*. The tune name SLATER was given by the current general editor of *GSR*.

Walking in Sunlight   462
Henry J. Zelley, 1859-1942

Zelley wrote this text for the tune below by G. H. Cook. Afterwards Zelley and Cook sold the song to H. L. Gilmour, who copyrighted both text and tune and published them in W. J. Kirkpatrick and Gilmour's *Gospel Praises* (Philadelphia, 1899). This hymn entered *GS* in 1937.

Sunlight
George H. Cook

Cook wrote this tune and brought it to Zelley, asking him to provide a text for it. It was then sold to H. L. Gilmour, as mentioned above, and published in Kirkpatrick and Gilmour's *Gospel Praises* (1899). It entered *GS* in 1937.

Watchman, Tell Us of the Night   181
John Bowring, 1792-1872

This plaintive, yet reassuring, text was first published in Bowring's *Hymns* (1825). It is based on Isaiah 21:11,12. It first entered *GS* in 1937.

Aberystwyth
Joseph Parry, 1841-1903

This tune was first published in E. Stephen and Joseph David Jones's *Ail Llyfr Tonau ac Emynau* (1879). It was there set to the Welsh poem "Beth sydd i mi yn y byd." The tune name is derived from the Welsh city where Parry was professor of music at the Welsh University College. This is its first inclusion in *GS*. In all previous printings of our hymnal, the preceding text has been set to the antiphonal hymn tune WATCHMAN by Lowell Mason.

We Are Called to Be God's People   436
Thomas A. Jackson, b. 1931

This text was written in 1973 for the accompanying tune and for use in a service in the McLean Baptist Church, McLean, Virginia, where Jackson served as minister. Its first hymnal inclusion was the *Baptist Hymnal* (1975). This is its first inclusion in *GS*.

Austrian Hymn
Franz Joseph Haydn, 1732-1809

For information on this tune, see the notes to "Praise the Lord, Ye Heavens Adore Him," *GSR*, NO. 99). This tune first entered *GS* in 1925.

We Are One in the Spirit   456
Peter Scholtes

This text was first published in Roger D. Nachtway's *Hymnal for Young Christians* (Chicago: FEL Publications, 1966). No further information is available. This is its first inclusion in *GS*.

St. Brendan's
Peter Scholtes

Repeated efforts to secure information from FEL Publications about this tune or the accompanying text have failed. Other than the facts given above, no other information is available. This tune is included in *GSR* for the first time.

We Bless the Name of Christ the Lord   358
Samuel F. Coffman, 1872-1954

This text was written by Coffman in 1926. It was first published in the *Mennonite Church Hymnal* (Scottdale, Pennsylvania, 1927), edited by J. D. Brunk and S. F. Coffman. This is the first inclusion of the text in *GS*.

Retreat

Thomas Hastings, 1784-1872

This tune was composed in 1840 for the text "From Every Stormy Wind That Blows" (See *GSR*, NO. 561). Since 1921 this tune has been joined with that text in *GS*. RETREAT was first published in Hastings's *Sacred Songs for Family and Social Worship* (1842). The present editors wished to include the preceding text with this tune to remedy a paucity of songs for baptismal services in the churches.

We Gather Together 1

From Adrianus Valerius's *Nederlandtsch Gedeckclanck*, 1626

Trans. Theodore Baker, 1851-1934

This fine opening hymn is from an anonymous Dutch hymn beginning "Wilt heden nu treden voor God den Heere." It was written in the late sixteenth century to celebrate Dutch independence from Spain. The text was originally published in Valerius's *Nederlandtsch Gedenckclanck* (1626). Baker made his translation in 1894, and it was first published in Coenraad v. Bos, *Dutch Folksongs* (1917). The text entered *GS* in 1944.

Kremser

Netherlands Folk Tune

Arr. Edward Kremser, 1838-1914

The poem above and tune KREMSER were discovered by Edward Kremser and published in his *Sechs Antniederlandische Volkslieder* (1877). This text and tune entered *GS* in 1944. E. L. Jorgenson made slight modifications in the text: 2:4 originally read "Thou Lord, wast at our side; the glory be thine"; 3:1 read "Thou leader in battle"; and 3:4, "O Lord, make us free."

We Give Thee But Thine Own 610

William W. How, 1823-1897

This text was written in 1858, and first published in T. B. Morrell and How's *Psalms and Hymns* (1864). The biblical text "He that hath pity upon the poor lendeth unto the Lord" (Proverbs 19:17) served as a motto for the hymn. It was originally published in six stanzas. Our text contains stanzas 1, 2, and 6. The omitted stanzas indicate that the hymn was meant to be a poem of social consciousness and awareness of the needs of the poor:

3
Oh, hearts are bruised and dead,
And homes are bare and cold,
And lambs, for whom the Shepherd bled,
Are straying from the fold.

4
To comfort and to bless,
To find a balm for woe,
To tend the lone and fatherless,
Is Angels' work below.

5
The captive to release,
To God the lost to bring,
To teach the way of life and peace,
It is a Christ-like thing.

This hymn text has been in *GS* since 1921.

Schumann

From Mason and Webb's *Cantica Laudis*, 1850

This tune was printed and arranged in Lowell Mason and George J. Webb's collection *Cantica Laudis* and called WHITE. They claimed that they had arranged the melody from Robert Schumann, but Clara Schumann, the composer's wife, told James Love, the Scottish hymnologist, that she could find no such tune in her husband's works. This tune entered *GS* in 1925. In the previous editions, beginning in 1921, the preceding text had been set to LISBON by Daniel Read, the early American composer.

We Have Heard the Joyful Sound 307

Priscilla J. Owens, 1829-1907

The usual date given for the composition of this text is 1882. It was written for an anniversary meeting of a Sunday school in Baltimore, Maryland, and adapted to the chorus "Vive le Roi," from Meyerbeer's opera *Les Huguenots*. It should be remarked, however, that some editors claim it was published as early as 1868 in *The Revivalist*. I cannot confirm this latter claim. The original first line, "I have heard a joyful sound," was changed to its present reading in Sankey's *Gospel Hymns No. 5* (1887). This text entered *GS* in 1937.

Jesus Saves

William J. Kirkpatrick, 1838-1921

This tune was composed for the foregoing text and was first published in John R. Sweney, C. C. McCabe, T. C. O'Kane, and Kirkpatrick's *Songs of Redeeming Love* (Philadelphia, 1882). It first entered *GS* in 1937.

We Praise Thee, God   63

Attributed to Nicetas of Remesiana, 335-416

The *Te Deum laudamus* is, with the *Gloria in excelsis*, the most famous of Western non-biblical hymns. Once attributed to Augustine and Ambrose, who were supposed to have composed alternate lines and to have sung the hymn antiphonally at Augustine's baptism in A.D. 387, the hymn is now attributed to Nicetas. He was bishop of Remesiana in Dacia (a part of modern Romania) and probably wrote the hymn about A.D. 414. Our translation, which is anonymous, represents only the first two lines of the original poem:

Te Deum laudamus: Te Dominus confitemur
Te aeternum Patrem: omnis terra veneratur.

This translation of the *Te Deum* has been in *GS* since 1937.

Te Deum Laudamus

James Turle, 1802-1882

The date and circumstances of the composition of this chant are unknown. Turle was a practicing musician from 1819 to 1875, the year of his retirement, and the tune was written some time during these years. The present arrangement is by the music editor of *GSR* (1986).

We Praise Thee, O God   61

William P. Mackay, 1839-1885

Mackay wrote this text in 1863 and revised it to its present form in 1867. The *GSR* text contains the full five-stanza original. This hymn is based on Habakkuk 3:2, "O Lord, revive thy work." It first entered *GS* in 1921.

Revive Us Again

John J. Husband, 1760-1825

Husband's tune, as William Reynolds suggests, may have first been used with a different text. Its first use with Mackay's poem seems to have been in Bigelow and Main's *New Praises of Jesus* (c. 1867). It has been in *GS* since 1921.

We Praise Thee, O God, Our Redeemer, Creator 44

Julia Cady Cory, 182-1963

Over a two-week period during a school vacation in 1902, Julia Cady wrote this beautiful hymn. J. Archer Gibson, organist for the Brick Presbyterian Church, New York, asked her to write new words for the tune KREMSER, and the present poem was the result. It was first sung during Thanksgiving in 1902 at Brick Presbyterian and at the Church of the Covenant, New York, that year at Christmas. For that occasion, at which her minister father, J. Cleveland Cady presided, she wrote a Christmas stanza to be added to the hymn:

> Thy love Thou didst show us, Thine only Son sending,
> > Who came as a babe and whose bed was a stall,
> His blest life He gave us and then died to save us;
> > We praise Thee, O Lord, for Thy gift to us all.

This text is now included in *GS* for the first time.

Kremser

Netherlands Folk Song
Arr. Edward Kremser, 1838-1862

For information on this hymn tune, see the notes on "We Gather Together" (*GSR* No. 1). The tune entered *GS* in 1944.

We Saw Thee Not 495

Anne Richter, c. 1857
Recast by John H. Gurney, 1802-1962

Mrs. Richter's original poem was published anonymously in *Songs from the Valley: A Collection of Sacred Poetry* (1834). The poem was in eight 6-line stanzas. It was completely recast by J. H. Gurney in four stanzas in his Lutterworth collection: *Collection of Hymns for Public Worship* (1838). The hymn was further altered by Henry J. Buckoll (1803-1871) in Buckoll and Goulburn's *Psalms and Hymns* (1843). The final revision, after which only minor changes have been made by unknown editors, appeared in J. H. Gurney's *Psalms and Hymns for Public Worship, Selected for some of the Churches in Marylebone* (1851). Each of these texts may be seen in Julian (1242). The hymn has been in *GS* since 1921.

Shaw

Knowles Shaw, 1834-1878

This tune appeared with the preceding text in one of Shaw's Sunday school collections. I have been unable to determine which had it first. It was also published in J. H. Fillmore's *The New Christian Hymn and Tune Book, Part III* (1887). It entered *GS* in 1921.

We Would See Jesus   496

Anna B. Warner, 1820-1915

This poem is based on an episode found in John 12:20ff and was first printed in the novel *Dollars and Cents* (1852), which Miss Warner published under the pseudonym Amy Lathrop. It was also included in her *Hymns of the Church Militant* (1858) and that same year in Thomas Hastings's *Church Melodies*. The original text, in six stanzas, is usually reduced to four. These omitted stanzas 4 and 5 read:

> We would see Jesus: yet the spirit lingers
> Round the dear objects it has loved so long,
> And earth from earth can scarce unclasp its fingers;
> Our love to thee makes not this love less strong.

> We would see Jesus: sense is all too binding,
> And heaven appears too dim, too far away.
> We would see thee, thyself our hearts reminding
> What thou hast suffered, our great debt to pay.

This text entered *GS* in 1921 with Miss Warner's stanzas 1, 2, and 6. Her stanza 3 was added in 1937.

Reynolds

Arr. from Felix Mendelssohn, 1809-1847

This hymn tune is taken from Mendelssohn's *Songs without Words,* Op. 30, No. 32, Bk. II. The tune name is sometimes given as CONSOLATION, but Mendelssohn called it "Adagio non troppo." The arrangement is sometimes credited to Adolphus Levy (1880), but arrangements had already appeared in E. J. Hopkin's *The Temple Church*

Hymn Book (1869) and in Charles S. Robinson's *Spiritual Songs* (1875). In older editions of *GS*, the tune name was spelled RAYNOLDS. In the first edition of our hymnal, it was called CONSOLATION, but this was returned to REYNOLDS in succeeding editions in order to avoid confusion with the tune of No. 284. This tune entered *GS* in 1937. In the editions from 1921 to 1936, a tune by Lowell Mason was employed.

Welcome, Delightful Morn 20
"Hayward" in John Dobell's Selection, 1806

Although sometimes ascribed to Thomas Hayward, the authorship of this hymn is really unknown. It was first published in John Dobell's *A New Selection of Seven Hundred Evangelical Hymns, for Private, Family, and Public Worship* (London, 180-6). It was there signed "Hayward." This text has been included in *GS* since 1921.

Lischer
Friedrich Schneider, 1786-1853

LISCHER is an arrangement of a tune by Friedrich Johann Christian Schneider, who was court conductor at Dessau, Germany, after 1821. Lowell Mason published his arrangement in *Carmina Sacra: or Boston Collection of Church Music* (1841). Mason's arrangement, which has appeared in *GS* since 1921, has been slightly simplified for the present edition.

Were You There? 228
Traditional Negro Spiritual
Adpt. from *Folk Songs of the American Negro*, 1907

This traditional song originates from slavery days in the United States. The first known printed text is found in William Barton's *Old Plantation Hymns* (Boston, 1899). The *GSR* text is taken from *Folk Songs of the American Negro* (Nashville, 1907), edited by John W. Work, Jr. (1901-1967) and Frederick J. Work (1879-1942). It was first included in *GS* in the *Supplement* (1975).

Were You There
American Folk Hymn
Arr. Jack A. Boyd, b. 1932

There were earlier forms of this tune appearing in the Barton collection mentioned above. The *GSR* inclusion is from the Works' *Folk*

Songs of the American Negro (1907). The arrangement is by the music editor of *GSR*. The tune entered *GS* in the *Supplement* (1975).

What a Fellowship 108
Elisha A. Hoffman, 1839-1929

According to Haldor Lillenas in *Modern Gospel Songs Stories*, A. J. Showalter had been involved in expressing his sympathy to two friends whose wives has recently died. He quoted Deuteronomy 33:27 to both of them: "The eternal God is thy dwelling place, / And underneath are the everlasting arms." Believing that these words would make a good basis for a song, he sent the music and the words for the refrain to Hoffman. Hoffman then wrote the stanzas, and the completed text appeared in Showalter, L. M. Evilsizer, and S. J. Perry's *The Glad Evangel for Revival, Camp, and Evangelistic Meetings* (Dalton, Georgia, 1887). This text entered *GS* in 1937.

Showalter
Anthony J. Showalter, 1858-1924

This tune was written as indicated above and published in *The Glad Evangel* (1887). It entered *GS* in 1937.

What a Friend We Have in Jesus 567
Joseph Scriven, 1819-1886

This text was written to comfort his mother in a time of sorrow, with no thought of any wider use. It was written about 1855. During the author's last illness, he said to a friend who saw the manuscript, "The Lord and I wrote it between us." This text was first published anonymously in H. L. Hastings's *Social Hymns, Original and Selected* (1865). It has been in *GS* since 1921.

Erie
Charles C. Converse, 1832-1918

This tune was composed for Scriven's words in 1868. It was first published in *Silver Wings* (1870). Converse edited this hymnal under the pseudonym "Karl Reden." The hymn and tune were also published in Philip Bliss and Ira D. Sankey's *Gospel Hymns and Sacred Songs* (1875), where the words were mistakenly attributed to Horatius Bonar. The hymn was substituted at the last minute for another, and Sankey later said that "the last hymn that went into the book became one of the first in favor." This tune has been in *GS* since 1921.

What a Wonderful Change in My Life 471
Rufus H. McDaniel, 1850-1940

These words were written in 1914 to express the faith of the author following the death of his son. This is its first inclusion in *GS*. It was first published in leaflet form and used in a Billy Sunday campaign in Philadelphia in 1915. Afterwards it was published in Homer Rodeheaver's *Songs for Service* (1915).

McDaniel
Charles H. Gabriel, 1856-1932

This tune was written by Gabriel in 1914 for the preceding text. They were published together for a Billy Sunday campaign in leaflet form (1915) and that same year appeared in Rodeheaver's *Songs for Service*. The tune name was given in the *Baptist Hymnal* (1956). This is its first inclusion in *GS*.

What Can Wash Away My Sin? 344
Robert Lowry, 1826-1899

This text was first published in William H. Doane and Lowry's *Gospel Music* (New York, 1876) with the motto "Without the shedding of blood there is no remission of sin" (Heb. 9:22). The hymn was originally in six stanzas. *GSR* includes stanzas 1-3. The omitted stanzas read:

4
This is all my hope and peace,
    Nothing but the blood of Jesus;
This is all my righteousness,
    Nothing but the blood of Jesus.

5
Now by this I'll overcome—
    Nothing but the blood of Jesus,
Now by this I'll reach my home—
    Nothing but the blood of Jesus.

6
Glory! Glory! this I sing—
    Nothing but the blood of Jesus,
All my praise for this I bring—
    Nothing but the blood of Jesus.

This text entered *GS* in 1921. In the 1921 edition, stanza 4 was included. It was omitted first in 1937, and we have continued the omission.

Nothing but the Blood

Robert Lowry, 1826-1899

This tune was written for the preceding text and was published in Doane and Lowry's *Gospel Music* (New York, 1876). In the *Baptist Hymnal* (1956), the tune is called PLAINFIELD, from Plainfield, New Jersey, where Lowry ministered from 1875 to 1885 and where he made his home until his death. This tune was first printed in *GS* in 1937, all previous editions containing words only.

What Child Is This?   207

William Chatterton Dix, 1837-1898

This text is taken from Dix's poem *The Manger Throne*. It was written in 1865 after Dix had been reading Matthew 2:1-12, which text is read in the Anglican Church on Epiphany (January 6). This is its first inclusion in *GSR*.

Greensleeves

Traditional English Melody, 16th Century

This traditional folk tune is known to have existed by September 1580, at which date one Richard Jones licensed with the Stationer's Company "A New Northern Dittye of the Lady Greene Sleeves." Shortly thereafter it was used as a setting for a religious song. Shakespeare refers to the tune in *The Merry Wives of Windsor* (II, i; c. 1597), and it is known to have been used as a setting for the New Year's carol "The old year now away is fled" in *New Christmas Carols* (1642). This is its first inclusion in *GS*.

What Wondrous Love Is This?   225

American Folk Hymn
Attributed to Alexander Means

This text is attributed to Alexander Means, a Methodist minister from Oxford, Georgia, in William Hauser's *The Hesperian Harp* (1848). It was apparently a revision or recasting of an older text. The hymnals print the stanzas variously. The older text appeared in Stith Mead's *A General Selection of the Most Admired Hymns and Spiritual Songs* (2d ed., Lynchburg, Virginia, 1811), and the same year in Starke Dupuy's *Hymns and Spiritual Songs* (Frankfort, Kentucky). The text and the tune following first entered *GS* in the *Supplement* (1975).

Wondrous Love

American Folk Hymn
Attributed to "Christopher" in
William Walker's *Southern Harmony*, 1843

The origin of this tune is unknown, other than the vague attribution in the *Southern Harmony*. George Pullen Jackson connects it with a ballad text and tune about the pirate Captain Robert Kidd, who was executed in 1701. The old ballad runs:

My name was Robert Kidd, when I sailed, when I sailed,
    My name was Robert Kidd, when I sailed;
My name was Robert Kidd, God's laws I did forbid,
    So wickedly I did when I sailed, when I sailed,
So wickedly I did when I sailed.

This connection has been disputed by Ellen Jane Lorenz Porter in her essay published by the Hymn Society of America (1975): "Two Early American Tunes: Fraternal Twins?" William Walker attributed the tune to "Christopher" in the 1843 appendix to his *Southern Harmony* (1843), but in his *Christian Harmony* (1866), he noted that the tune was "arranged by James Christopher of Spartanburg, S. C." This tune first entered *GS* in the *Supplement* (1975). The arrangement is by the music editor of *GSR*.

When All My Labors and Trials Are O'er 658

Charles H. Gabriel, 1856-1932

This text was inspired by the life and faith of Ed Card, the superintendent of the Sunshine Rescue Mission in St. Louis, Missouri. Because of his exuberant Christian joy, all called him "Old Glory Face," and he nearly always ended his prayers with "And that will be glory for me." Gabriel's poem was first published in his *Make His Praise Glorious* (1900). This text has been in *GS* since 1921.

Glory Song

Charles H. Gabriel, 1856-1932

Because of the general content of the poem, the tune has always been known as the "Glory Song." It was written for and published with the text preceding in Gabriel's *Make His Praise Glorious* (1900). The tune entered *GS* in 1921.

When All Thy Mercies, O My God   131

Joseph Addison, 1672-1719

This hymn, as certain others by Addison, appeared at the end of one of his essays. This text was appended to an essay on "Gratitude" which was published in the *Spectator,* August 9, 1712. The hymn has been in *GS* since 1921 and contains stanzas 1, 5, 10, and 13. The verses omitted are probably as useful as the ones included. They read as follows:"

2

O how can words with equal warmth
    The gratitude declare,
That glows within my ravished heart?
    But thou canst read it there.

3

Thy providence my life sustained,
    And all my wants redressed,
When in the silent womb I lay,
    And hung upon thy breast.

4

To all my weak complaints and cries
    Thy mercy lent an ear;
Ere yet my feeble thoughts had learned
    To form themselves in prayer.

6

When in the slippery paths of youth,
    With heedless steps I ran,
Thine arms, unseen, conveyed me safe,
    And led me up to man.

7

Through hidden dangers, toils, and deaths,
    It gently cleared my way;
And through the pleasing snares of vice,
    More to be feared than they.

8

When worn with sickness, oft hast thou
    With health renewed my face;
And, when in sins and sorrows sunk,
    Revived my soul with grace.

9
Thy bounteous hand with worldly bliss
    Hast made my cup run o'er;
And in a kind and faithful friend
    Hast doubled all my store.

11
Through every period of my life
    Thy goodness I'll pursue;
And after death in distant worlds
    The glorious theme renew.

12
When nature falls, and day and night
    Divide thy works no more,
My ever grateful heart, O Lord,
    Thy mercies shall adore.

Winchester, Old

Thomas Est's *Whole Book of Psalms*, 1592

This tune was published anonymously in Est's psalter, but the tune arrangement there was attributed to George Kirbye, a contemporary of Est. The source of the tune is probably from *The Acts of the Apostles* (London, 1553), a musical setting of Acts 8 by Christopher Tye. The *GSR* setting is taken from *Hymns Ancient and Modern* (1861). It entered *GS* in the *Supplement* (1922) as a setting for G. T. Noel's "If Human Kindness Meets Return" and from 1925 to the present edition has been used as the setting for Thomas Cotterill's "In Memory of the Savior's Love" (see *GSR*, No. 375). In all previous editions of *GS,* the setting for "When All Thy Mercies" has been John Cole's tune GENEVA, published in Joseph Funk's *Harmonia Sacra* (1805).

When Day's Shadows Lengthen

544
Frederick G. Lee, b. 1832

This text was written as a poem on old age and was first published in the *People's Hymnal* (1867). It was first included in *GS* in 1937. No other information is available.

Montani

From W. Becker's *Gebet- und Gesangbüchlein,* 1872
Arr. Nicola A. Montani, 1880-1948

This tune was originally published in Becker's *Gebet- und Gesangbüchlein* (1872). Montani adapted and arranged it in his *The Saint Gregory Hymnal* (1920), where he called it a traditional melody. It entered *GS* in 1937.

When I Survey the Wondrous Cross   233
Isaac Watts, 1674-1748

This text was first published in Watts's *Hymns and Spiritual Songs* (Bk. III, 1707) in five stanzas. The original stanza four has been omitted. It read:

> His dying crimson, like a robe,
> > Spreads o'er his body on the tree;
> Then am I dead to all the globe,
> > And all the globe is dead to me.

Line 1:2 originally read "Where the young Prince of glory died." This hymn has been in *GS* since 1921.

Hamburg

Based on Gregorian Psalm Tone, Mode I
Arr. Lowell Mason, 1792-1872

In commenting on the use which Mason made of the Gregorian Psalm tones, J. Vincent Higginson said that this tune was one of his most popular. Of HAMBURG Higginson says: "The first and fourth phrases follow the chant melody with only a slight variation. The second phrase is a condensation of the whole chant tune" (*The Hymn,* 1967, p. 41f.). This tune was arranged in Savannah, Georgia, and was first sung in the First Presbyterian Church of that city. It was subsequently published in the *Handel and Haydn Society Collection of Church Music* (3d ed., 1825). The tune first entered *GS* in 1921.

When Morning Gilds the Skies   152
Katholisches Gesangbuch, 1828
Trans. Edward Caswall, 1814-1878

This German text, beginning "Beim frühen Morgenlicht," appeared anonymously in *Katholisches Gesangbuch* (Würzburg, 1818) in fourteen

4-line stanzas. It was published in various emended versions thereafter, but its origin is obscure. Caswall's translation seems to have been made from a later version. It was first published in Henry Formby's *Catholic Hymns* (1854) in six stanzas. In Caswall's *Masque of Mary* (1858), all 14 stanzas are translated. This text entered *GS* in 1937.

Laudes Domini
Joseph Barnby, 1838-1896

This tune was written for Caswall's text and was first published in the Appendix to *Hymns Ancient and Modern* (1868). The tune name means "Praise the Lord" and comes from the repetition "May Jesus Christ be praised." The tune entered *GS* in 1937.

When My Love to Christ Grows Weak   219
John R. Wreford, 1800-1881

This text was first published, along with fifty-four others by Wreford, in J. R. Beard's *Collection of Hymns for Public and Private Worship* (1837). Line 1:1 originally read "When my love for God grows weak." This text has been in *GS* since the *Supplement* (1922).

Albertson
Phoebe Palmer Knapp, 1839-1908

No information is available on this tune.

When Peace Like a River   646
Horatio Gates Spafford, 1828-1888

In 1873 Mr. Spafford, upon the advice of his physician, planned a trip to Europe to improve his wife's health. Their four daughters were to accompany them. When business engagements delayed him, he sent the family on ahead, planning himself to follow shortly. On the high seas their vessel, the *S.S. Ville du Havre,* was struck by an English sailing ship the *Lochearn* and went down almost immediately. Mrs. Spafford was saved, but the children were all drowned. Upon hearing the news, Spafford sailed to be with his wife, and while passing near the spot of the sinking, as indicated by the captain, he wrote this hymn of comfort. The text has been in *GS* since 1921.

Ville du Havre

Philip P. Bliss, 1838-1876

This tune was composed for the preceding text and published in Ira D. Sankey and Bliss's *Gospel Songs No. 2* (1876). The tune name derives from the ship on which the four daughters of Horatio Spafford were drowned in the Atlantic. This tune entered *GS* in 1921.

When Storms Around Are Sweeping   542

Anonymous

This text appeared as early as 1872 in George F. Root's *The Hour of Praise: for Praise Meetings and Congregational and Sunday School Singing* (Cincinnati: John Church Co.). It first entered *GS* in 1937 as a male quartet. That arrangement was copyrighted by the Hope Publishing Company (1912). The present arrangement for mixed voices is by the music editor of *GS*. No other information is available.

Remember Me

Attributed to Johanna Kinkel, 1810-1858

This tune, attributed to Johanna Kinkel, arranged from her work, is found in Ira D. Sankey and George C. Stebbins's *Male Chorus, No. 1 for Use in Gospel Meetings, Christian Associations and Other Religious Services* (Chicago: Bigelow & Main Co., 1888; No. 76). No other information is available on the composer or the composition.

When the Trumpet of the Lord Shall Sound   437

James M. Black, 1856-1938

Black wrote this gospel song text in 1893, and it was published in his and Joseph F. Berry's *Songs of the Soul* (1894). It was also published that same year in Henry F. Date's *Pentecostal Hymns* (Chicago). Black, as reported by Ira D. Sankey in *My Life and the Story of the Gospel Songs,* said he wrote this poem while he was serving as a teacher in a Sunday School in which a poor girl had enrolled. One evening as he called the roll, she was absent, and he said to the group assembled, "O God, when my name is called up yonder, may I be there to respond!" Out of this thought came the hymn, which he wrote that same evening. The text has been in *GS* since 1937.

Roll Call

James M. Black, 1856-1938

Having written the words to this gospel song, as discussed in connection with the preceding text, Black went to his piano and played the music. It has never been altered in any way. The tune entered *GS* in 1937.

When This Passing World Is Done 652

Robert M. McCheyne, 1813-1843

This hymn, in nine 6-line stanzas, was written about 1837. It entered *GS* in the *Supplement* (1922) in three stanzas, words only, but with an indication to sing the text to SPANISH HYMN. Our fourth stanza was added in 1925. Other stanzas of this text by McCheyne, which have never been in *GS,* were popular in former years among Calvinists. The following stanzas represent a selection from the larger hymn:

Chosen not for good in me,
    Waked from coming wrath to flee,
Hidden in the Saviour's side,
    By the Spirit sanctified.
Teach me, Lord, on earth to show,
    By my love, how much I owe.

Oft I walk beneath the cloud,
    Dark as midnight's gloomy shroud:
But, when fear is at the height,
    Jesus comes, and all is light;
Blessed Jesus, bid me show
    Doubting saints how much I owe.

Oft the nights of sorrow reign—
    Weeping, sickness, sighing, pain;
But at night Thine anger burns—
    Morning comes and joy returns:
God of comforts! bid me show
    To Thy poor how much I owe.

When in flowery paths I tread,
    Oft by sin I'm captive led;
Oft I fall, but still arise—
    Jesus comes—the tempter flies:
Blessed Jesus! bid me show
    Weary sinners all I owe.

Spanish Hymn

Traditional Spanish Melody
Arr. Benjamin Carr, 1769-1831

In 1825 Carr secured a copyright for variations which he had written for a popular tune of the time. He published it in 1826 under the title *Spanish Hymn Arranged and Composed for the Concerts of the Musical Fund of Philadelphia by Benjamin Carr, the Air from an Ancient Spanish Melody.* The flyleaf of this publication indicates that the music was first performed December 29, 1824. It should be noted that two versions of this hymn are extant. SPANISH HYMN is the name of the tune when used with 6-line stanzas of seven syllables (7.7.7.7.7.7.). When used with an 8-line stanza of six syllables per line, the tune is called MADRID (See "Come, Christians, Join to Sing, *GSR,* No. 151). This music was first printed in *GS* in 1925.

When Upon Life's Billows   545
Johnson Oatman Jr., 1856-1922

This popular gospel song was first published in E. O. Excell's *Songs for Young People* (Chicago, 1897). No other information is available. It has been in *GS* since 1921.

Blessings

Edwin O. Excell, 1851-1921

This tune was written for the preceding text and first published in Excell's *Songs for Young People* (Chicago, 1897). The tune name was first given in the *Baptist Hymnal* (1956). It entered *GS* in 1921.

When We Meet in Sweet Communion   366
Tillett Sidney Teddlie, 1885-1987

In the summer of 1921, Teddlie heard a sermon by Foy E. Wallace Jr. on the subject of "The Duty of Constant Communion." Eighteen souls responded to the invitation at that time, and the sermon inspired Teddlie to write the text. He wrote it during the winter of 1922, and it was published by the Firm Foundation Publishing House of Austin in 1923. The text first entered *GS* in the *Supplement* (1975).

The Lord's Supper

Tillet Sidney Teddlie, 1885-1987

Teddlie wrote this tune for the preceding text under the circumstances given above. It has proved to be one of the most widely used communion hymns among the Churches of Christ. It entered *GS* in the *Supplement* (1975)

When We Walk with the Lord 513
John H. Sammis, 1846-1919

When D. L. Moody was conducting a meeting in Brockton, Massachusetts, Daniel B. Towner was his singer. During one of the meetings, a young man arose and said: "I am not quite sure—but I am going to trust, and I am going to obey." Towner, struck by the words, wrote them down and sent them to Sammis. Sammis the wrote the chorus first and afterwards composed the stanzas. The text was first published in *Hymns Old and New* (1887). It has been in *GS* since 1921.

Trust and Obey
Daniel B. Towner, 1850-1919

The occasion for the writing of the text is given above. After Sammis wrote the text, Towner wrote the tune for the text, and they were published in Fleming H. Revell Company's *Hymns Old and New* (1887). This tune entered *GS* in 1921.

Where Charity and Love Prevail 452
Latin Hymn, *Ubi caritas et amore*, c. 9th century
Trans. Omer Westendorf, b. 1916

This text is a translation of an anonymous Latin antiphon which dates from the time of Charlemagne or even earlier. The English translation is by Omer Westendorf, who, under the pseudonym "J. Clifford Evers," published it in the *People's Mass Book* (Cincinnati, 1961). This is its first inclusion in *GS*.

Twenty-Fourth
From John Wyeth's *Repository of Sacred Music,*
Part Second, 1813
Attributed to Lucius Chapin, 1760-1842

This tune appeared in Wyeth's *Repository* (1813) and that same year, or even a little earlier, in Robert Patterson's *Church Music* (Cincinnati). In the Wyeth collection it was set to Isaac Watts's "Salvation! Oh, the joyful sound," and in his index it was attributed to "Chapin." Modern editors have assigned it to Lucius Chapin. This is the first inclusion of this tune in *GS*.

Where Cross the Crowded Ways of Life   415
Frank Mason North, 1850-1935

Several factors gave us this powerful, graphic "city" hymn. First, North had firsthand experience with the crowds of New York City. Second, he had been urged by Caleb T. Winchester, an editor of the *Methodist Hymnal* (1905), to provide a new missionary hymn for that compilation. Third, shortly before writing this hymn, he had preached on Matthew 22:9, "Go ye therefore into the partings of the highways, and as many as ye shall find, bid to the marriage feast." The text was first printed in the *Christian City* (June, 1903) and was included in the *Methodist Hymnal* (1905). It first entered *GS* in 1937.

Germany

Attributed to Ludwig van Beethoven, 1770-1827
in William Gardiner's *Sacred Melodies*, 1815

For information on this tune, see "Take Up Your Cross, *GSR,* No. 503. This tune entered *GS* in 1927.

Where Restless Crowds Are Thronging   430
Thomas C. Clark, 1877-1953

Clark, who was poetry editor for the *Christian Century,* was a well-known musician and poet. The present text was his last hymn, written in October, 1953. It was selected by the Hymn Society of America for use at the Urban Convention at Columbus, Ohio (February, 1954). Clark did not get to hear it sung there, for he died on December 7, 1953. This its first inclusion in *GS*. The present editors of our hymnal felt a need for more "city" hymns, since our nation and our churches have become so urbanized. This hymn is one of the best of urban texts.

Llangloffan

Traditional Welsh Melody in David Evans's
Hymnus a Thonau, 1865
Rev. in *Revised Church Hymnary,* 1927

This traditional Welsh melody was first published in Evans's *Hymnau a Thonau er Gwasanaeth yr Eglwys ynd Nghymru* (i.e., Hymns and Tunes, etc.) in 1865. The tune was joined with Clark's poem in 1954. This is its first inclusion in *GS*.

While Jesus Whispers to You 331

William E. Witter, b. 1854

This text was written in 1877 while the twenty-three year-old Witter was teaching school in Wyoming Valley, New York, and staying on a farm. He was in anxiety over two of his pupils. One Saturday afternoon, while he was bunching hay on the farm, the words and tune came to him. At the same period of his life, he was touched by the recent death of Philip P. Bliss (d. 1876), and he asked God to help him write hymns to touch hearts. He went to his lodgings from the hay field and wrote down the hymn. It was published in Sankey's *Gospel Hymns No. 5* (1882). This text entered *GS* in 1921.

HAMARTOLOI

Horatio R. Palmer, 1834-1907

Palmer composed this tune in 1879, apparently for the preceding text. In 1921, when the tune entered *GS,* the song was used by permission of Arthur W. Palmer. Nothing further is known of the circumstances of composition. The tune name HAMARTOLOI was given by the current general editor and means "sinners" (ἁμαρτωλοί) in Greek.

While on the Sea 539

Trans. Stephen Bilak, b. 1926

Versed by Jack Boyd, b. 1932

The origin of this text is unknown. It was translated from the Russian by Stephen Bilak, a native Ukrainian, in 1974 and versed by Jack Boyd, music editor for *GSR*, that same year. The text was then published in the 1975 *Supplement* to *GS*. The poem has special poignancy when one realizes that Bilak, once exiled from his native Russia because of Communist domination, for years could not return. Only recently has the situation changed. The poem expresses, beyond physical love of country, the desire for "a better country, that is, a heavenly" (Hebrews 11:16).

Ukraine

Ukrainian Folk Melody

The origin of this tune is unknown. It first entered *GS* in the *Supplement* (1975).

While Shepherds Watched Their Flocks   197
Nahum Tate, 1652-1715

This text was first published in *The Supplement to the New Version of Psalms by Dr. Brady and Mr. Tate* (1700). *The Supplement* contained metrical paraphrases of great biblical hymns (*Benedictus, Magnificat*, and *Nunc dimittis*) and several medieval hymns (*Veni Creator* and *Te Deum*). It also contained hymns for morning, evening, and communion. This text was entitled "Song of the Angels, at the Nativity of our Blessed Saviour, Luke 11:8-15." It has been in *GS* since 1937.

Christmas

From George F. Handel, 1685-1759 in
James Hewitt's *Harmonia Sacra*, 1812

For information on this tune, see the notes to "Awake, My Soul, Stretch Every Nerve" (*GSR*, No. 543). The tune entered *GS* in 1921.

Who at the Door Is Standing?   341
Mary B. C. Slade, 1826-1882

This text, with the first line originally "Who at my door is standing," was written about 1875. It was published in R. M. McIntosh's *Good News* (Boston, 1876). At the time when this text first entered *GS* in 1921, it was used by permission of the Standard Publishing Company, Cincinnati, Ohio.

Thura

Asa Brooks Everett, 1828-1875

This tune was written shortly after the preceding text by Mrs. Slade and expressly for it. It was published in McIntosh's *Good News* (Boston, 1876). The tune name THURA was given by the current general editor and is the Greek word for "door" (θύρα). It is sometimes called EVERETT. The tune entered *GS* in 1921.

Whosoever Heareth   335
Philip P. Bliss, 1838-1876

This text was inspired by a series of sermons by Henry Moorhouse, the English evangelist. Bliss worked with him in a meeting and heard him preach on John 3:16 every night. The hymn text was written during the winter of 1869-70 and first published in George F. Root's *The Prize* (1870). It first entered *GS* in 1925.

Whosoever

Philip P. Bliss, 1838-1876

This tune was written for the preceding text and first published in George F. Root's *The Prize* (1870). It has been in *GS* since 1925.

Why Did My Savior Come to Earth   369

James Gerald Dailey, b. 1854

Little information is available on this hymn, which is widely used among the Churches of Christ. It was written by J. G. Dailey of Philadelphia, Pennsylvania, in 1892. Sometime after this, the copyright was obtained by the Gospel Advocate Company of Nashville, Tennessee, who renewed it in 1920. The hymn appears in C. M. Pullias's *Sweeter Than All Songs* (Nashville, 1927) with the first line as title, but with subcaption "The Love Song." The hymn has been in *GS* since 1921.

Dailey

James Gerald, Dailey, b. 1854

This tune was written for the preceding text. See above for what little information is available. The tune name was given by the current general editor.

Without Him I Could Do Nothing   515

Mylon R. LeFevre, b. 1945

This text was written by LeFevre in 1963 when he was eighteen years old. No other information is available.

Without Him

Mylon R. LeFevre, b. 1945

This tune was written for the text above in 1963. No other information is available.

Work, for the Night Is Coming   418

Annie L. Walker, 1836-1907

At eighteen Miss Walker (later Mrs. Coghill) had come from England to visit her brothers in Canada. She wrote the hymn text during her visit, and it was published in a newspaper in Canada in 1854. Later it was included in her *Leaves from the Backwoods* (Montreal, 1861). In the original poem, the fourth line of each stanza had six syllables and the eighth line read "Night, when man's work is done." The present alterations were made without the author's consent by Lowell Mason. This text has been in *GS* since 1921.

Work Song

Lowell Mason, 1792-1872

This tune was set to the preceding text and published in a school music book which Mason edited—*The Song Garden* (Bk. 2d, 1864). Mason altered Walker's words to fit his tune. It has been in *GS* since 1921.

Worthy of Praise   168
Tillit S. Teddlie, 1885-1987

This text was written at Belton, Texas, February 1929, as the author was preparing a sermon to be based on Revelation 4:10, 11 and 5:12-14. He wrote it on the flyleaf of his copy of B. W. Johnson's *People's New Testament with Notes* and later scribbled the chorus while sitting on the steps of his home in Belton. The hymn was first published in C. M. Pullias's *Greater Christian Hymns* (Nashville, 1921) by the Gospel Advocate Company. It entered *GS* in the *Supplement* (1975). The chorus, revised for publication in 1931, originally read:

Worthy of honor, praise, and thanksgiving,
Worthy of glory, honor and power!
Worthy, thrice worthy, King of salvation,
Worthy art Thou! Worthy art Thou!

The original manuscript of this hymn, as well as many other of Teddlie's compositions, is in the archives of Abilene Christian University.

Worthy Art Thou

Tillit S. Teddlie, 1885-1987

This tune was written for the preceding text at the time and under the circumstances described above. Teddlie's original manuscripts reside in the library of Abilene Christian University, Abilene, Texas. This tune entered *GS* in the *Supplement* (1975).

Would You Be Free   339
Lewis E. Jones, 1865-1936

This text was written while the author was attending a camp

meeting at Mountain Lake Park, Maryland. It was first published in H. L. Gilmour and William J. Kirkpatrick's *Songs of Praise and Victory* (Philadelphia: Pepper Printing Co., 1899) and that same year in Kirkpatrick, Gilmour, and J. Lincoln Hall's *Gospel Praises* (Philadelphia). The text has been in *GS* since 1921.

Power in the Blood
Lewis E. Jones, 1865-1936

This tune was written for the preceding text at Mountain Lake Park, Maryland, and published as detailed above. The tune name was first officially given in the *Baptist Hymnal* (1956). This tune has been in *GS* since 1921.

Would You Live for Jesus? 628
Cyrus S. Nusbaum, 1861-1937

Nusbaum was a Methodist minister who, according to his own account recorded in Haldor Lillenas's *Modern Gospel Song Stories,* had spent his first year as a circuit preacher in "one of the poorest circuits in our district." At the end of 1898, he and his wife attended the annual conference hoping to receive something better:

> Naturally, we had prayed and hoped that at this conference I might be appointed to a better charge, but when the Bishop read the appointments the last night of the conference I was named as pastor of the same old "hard scrabble circuit." It was with heavy hearts that we repaired to our lodging place that night. Mrs. Nusbaum sensibly retired early, but I remained in the little parlor with no one to disturb me. I was very unhappy and a spirit of rebellion seemed to possess me. About midnight I finally knelt in prayer beside my chair. After some struggles a deep peace came stealing into my heart. I told the Lord I would be willing to let Him have his way with me regardless of the cost. With that feeling of surrender to the will of God came the inspiration for the song now so well known throughout Christendom.

Nusbaum sold his manuscript to Dr. H. L. Gilmour, who was then living in Wenonah, New Jersey, and the text and tune were included in William J. Kirkpatrick, J. Lincoln Hall, and Gilmour's *Gospel Praises* (1899). This text has been in *GS* since 1921.

Nusbaum

Cyrus S. Nusbaum, 1861-1937

This tune was written for the text preceding and published in Kirkpatrick, Hall, and Gilmour's *Gospel Praises* (1899). It entered *GS* in 1921. The tune name NUSBAUM was given by the hymnal committee for the *Baptist Hymnal* (1956).

Ye Servants of God   175

Charles Wesley, 1707-1788

This text was first published in six stanzas in Wesley's *Hymns for Times of Trouble and Persecution* (1744). It and three other hymns had the title "Hymns to be sung in a Tumult." The "tumult" seems to refer to the times of trouble suffered by the Methodists during the Jacobite rebellion in England during the 1740s. Our text contains stanzas 1, 4, 5, and 6. The two omitted stanzas, which are never printed in modern hymnals, read:

The waves of the sea have lift up their voice,
    Sore troubled that we in Jesus rejoice;
The floods they are roaring, but Jesus is here;
    While we are adoring, He always is near.

Men, devils engage, the billows arise
    And horribly rage, and threaten the skies;
Their fury shall never our steadfastness shock,
    The weakest believer is built on a rock.

This text now enters *GS* for the first time.

Hanover

William Croft (?) in *Supplement to the New Version*, 1708

This tune, which has been known under various names, was at first thought to have been written by Handel, who was court conductor at Hanover in 1710. It is now believed to have been composed by Croft. It, as well as Croft's famous ST. ANNE tune, appeared in John Playford's edition of *The Supplement to the New Version of the Psalms by Dr. Brady and Mr. Tate* (6th ed., 1708). HANOVER is included in *GS* for the first time.

Years I Spent in Vanity and Pride   268

William R. Newell, 1868-1956

William Reynolds, in his *Companion to the Baptist Hymnal* (1976), recounts the writing of this text as follows:

> This hymn was written by William R. Newell while he was associated with Moody Bible Institute of Chicago. The words had been vaguely in his mind for a few weeks and then, one day, on his way to lecture, they suddenly began crystallizing in his mind. He stepped into an unoccupied classroom and wrote them down quickly on the back of an envelope as they now appear. Proceeding to his class, he met Daniel B. Towner, then director of music at the Institute, handed him the verses and suggested that he compose suitable music for them. When the author returned from his class, Dr. Towner had completed the tune, and they sang it together.

It was first published in *Famous Hymns* (1895) and was first included in *GS* in 1937.

Calvary

Daniel B. Towner, 1850-1919

The tune was written as described above in the comments on the text. It was published in *Famous Hymns* (1895). This tune first entered *GS* in 1937.

Yes, For Me, For Me He Careth 639

Horatius Bonar, 1808-1889

This text was published in Bonar's *Songs for the Wilderness, No. 2* (1844). It has been included in *GS* since 1921. In our original edition the text was set to the tune MABYN by Thomas Hastings. This tune continued in *GS* until the present edition. In 1937 a second tune, with slightly altered text by Lloyd Otis Sanderson, was also included.

Merimna

M. L. Daniels, b. 1931

This tune, written expressly for the preceding text, is published for the first time in *GSR*. Dr. Daniels is a distinguished former member of the Music faculty of Abilene Christian University. The editors of *GSR* hope that this tune will bring into wider and more frequent use the comforting words of Bonar's hymn. The tune name MERIMNA, the Greek word for "cares" (μέριμνα), was given by the current editor of *GSR*.

PART IV
Authors, Composers, and Translators

Acuff, James W.

Acuff, James W. (b. Freestone County, Texas, 1864; d. Georgetown, Texas August 1, 1937) was a well-known and beloved singer and song writer among the Churches of Christ in Texas. He wrote several popular gospel songs, often led the singing for protracted meetings, and assisted in compiling hymnals for the Firm Foundation Company of Austin, Texas. The most popular of these was Austin Taylor, Acuff, J. W. Everidge and G. H. P. Showalter's *The New Ideal Gospel Hymn Book* (Austin, 1930). Before he moved to Georgetown, he lived for several years in Granger, Texas. His career as a singer and song writer spanned nearly fifty years.

I've a Home Prepared (670)

Adams, Sarah Flower

Adams, Sarah Flower (b. Harlow, Essex, England, February 22, 1805; d. London, England, August 14, 1848) was the younger daughter of Benjamin Flower, editor of the *Cambridge Intelligencer* and the *Political Review*. She married William Bridges Adams in 1834. For some years she was an actress, but retired because of ill health and turned to poetry. She was a member of the South Place Unitarian Church, London, and her minister, William Johnson Fox, published her poems in his journal, the *Monthly Repository,* and in his hymn compilation for the use of his congregation, *Hymns and Anthems* (1840-41). Her most famous hymn, "Nearer, My God to Thee," appeared in the latter work. She was also the author of *Vivia Perpetua,* a dramatic poem dealing with the conflict between heathenism and Christianity (1841), and *The Flock at the Fountain,* a collection of her poems (1845). She and her sister Eliza were great friends of the Romantic poet William Wordsworth, and Eliza was the music editor for Fox's *Hymns and Anthems*. Both sisters were always in fragile health, and Sarah died of tuberculosis in 1848.

Nearer, My God, to Thee (636)

Addison, Joseph

Addison, Joseph (b. Milston, Wiltshire, England, May 1, 1672; d. London, England, June 17, 1719) was the son of Lancelot Addison, an Anglican minister and onetime Dean of Lichfield. He was educated at the Charterhouse and at Magdalen College, Oxford. Although destined for a career in the church, he turned to law and politics, rising through various posts to be chief secretary for Ireland. In 1716 he married Charlotte, Countess of Warwick. His fame rests chiefly on his association with Richard Steele and his contributions to *The Spectator*, the journal which he founded in 1711. He also contributed to such journals as *The Tatler*, *The Guardian*, and *The Freeholder*. His poems included in *Great Songs, Revised* (hereafter referred to as *GSR*) were all published in connection with his essays in *The Spectator*. He died at Holland House, Kensington, London, in 1719.

The Spacious Firmament on High (91)
When All Thy Mercies, O My God (131)

Ahle, Johann Rudolf

Ahle, Johann Rudolf (b. Mülhausen, Thüringia, December 24, 1625; d. Mülhausen, July 8, 1673) was educated at Göttingen and Erfurt and served as cantor at St. Andreas Church, Erfurt. Later he was organist at St. Blasius's Church, Mülhausen, and in 1661 was elected Bürgermeister (mayor) of that city. Ahle was interested in the reform of church music and published *Compendium pro tenellis* (1648), a work designed to improve choir music. He edited a number of hymnals and collaborated with Heinrich Albert (1604-1651) in introducing a new style of melody into the church. He and Albert called these pieces "sacred arias" because of their debt to Italian opera. His son succeeded him as organist at Mülhausen, and he was succeeded by Johann Sebastian Bach.

LIEBSTER JESU, WIR SIND HIER (25)

Ahnfelt, Ocar

Ahnfelt, Ocar (b. Gallup, Sweden, May 21, 1813; d. Karlshamm, Sweden, October 22, 1882) was the son of a Swedish minister and grew up in a home filled with music and good literature. He was tutored by his older brothers and entered Lund University (1829), intending to be a minister. His interest in his studies waned, however, and he earned his living as a tutor before going to Stockholm to study music. There he became a disciple of Carl Rosenius, the leader of the conventicle movement, and traveled over Scandinavia playing his guitar. The famous singer Jenny Lind underwrote his first collection of hymns, *Andeliga Sånger* (1850), which contained many hymns by Carolina Sandell (see *GSR*, Nos. 134, 644). In all he published twelve volumes of texts and tunes, the last in 1877.

    BLOTT EN DAG (134)

Alexander, Cecil Frances

    Alexander, Cecil Frances (b. Redcross, County Wicklow, England, 1818; d. Londonderry, Ireland, October 12, 1895) was the daughter of Major John Humphreys. Her mother was Elizabeth Reed. She received the advantages of being born into a wealthy family and could remember Sir Walter Scott, the poet and novelist, visiting her home when she was a child. In 1835 her family moved to County Tyrone, Ireland, and there she published her *Hymns for Little Children* (1848). Her reputation rests chiefly on her children's hymns. In 1850 she married William Alexander, an Anglican minister who became primate of all Ireland in 1893. She seems to have been a tireless coworker with her husband and was especially interested in works of mercy. She also published *Verses from the Holy Scriptures* (1846), *Narrative Hymns for Village Schools* (1853), and *Hymns Descriptive and Devotional* (1858).

    Jesus Calls Us (614,615)
    There Is a Green Hill Far Away (226)

Alexander, James Waddell

    Alexander, James Waddell (b. Hopewell, Virginia, March 13, 1804; d. Sweet Springs, Virginia, July 31, 1859) was the son of Archibald Alexander, a Presbyterian minister. He was educated at the College of New Jersey (now Princeton University) and ordained to the Presbyterian ministry in 1825. He was minister at Trenton, New Jersey (1829-1832), professor of rhetoric at Princeton (1834-1844), minister in New York City (1844-1849), and professor of church history in Princeton University (1849-1851). From that time until his death, he was minister at Fifth Avenue Presbyterian Church in New York City. Waddell always maintained an interest in hymnology, and he published articles in the *New York Observer* and the *Princeton Review*. His translations of Latin and German hymns appeared posthumously in *The Breaking Crucible and Other Translations* (1861).

    O Sacred Head, Now Wounded (91)

Alford, Henry

Alford, Henry (b. London, England, October 7, 1810; d. Canterbury, England, January 12, 1871) was the son of Henry Alford, an Anglican minister. He was educated at Ilminster Grammar School, Somerset, and at Trinity College, Cambridge. He graduated with high honors, was ordained to the ministry in 1833, and became a Fellow of Cambridge in 1834. His ancestors for five generations had been clergymen in the Church of England. Alford is best known for his critical commentary on the Greek New Testament, which consumed twenty years of his life. He was also a member of the New Testament Committee which helped to produce the English Revised Version (1881). His poetical works are many and are listed by Julian in his *Dictionary*. Alford's hymns, both original and translated, were published in *Psalms and Hymns* (1844), *Poetical Works* (1853), and *The Year of Praise* (1867). He became dean of Canterbury (1857).

Come, Ye Thankful People, Come (590)

Allen, Chester G.

Allen, Chester G. (b. 1838; d. 1878). No information is available on this composer other than that he collaborated with William B. Bradbury, W. H. Doane, and William F. Sherwin in the publication of Sunday School hymnals.

JOYFUL SONG (169)

Allen, George Nelson

Allen, George Nelson (b. Mansfield, Mass., Sept. 7, 1812; d. Cincinnati, Ohio, Dec. 9, 1877) graduated from Oberlin College in 1838, and taught music there until 1864. His work with the college Music department contributed to the founding of the Oberlin Conservatory of Music in 1865. He compiled *The Oberlin Social and Sabbath Hymn Book* (1844) and contributed several tunes to this collection.

MAITLAND (629)

Ambrose of Milan

Ambrose of Milan (b. probably at Treves in Gaul (Germany) about 340; d. Milan, Italy, April 3, 397) was the son of a prefect of Gaul and was educated at Rome for a civil career. He studied law at Milan, and there became prefect of Liguria (i.e., northern Italy). Upon the death of Auxentius, bishop of Milan, in 374, he was chosen bishop, although he was but a catechumen and not yet baptized. The Emperor Valentinian urged him to assume this task. The appointment set him in opposition to Justina, the wife of the emperor, who was an Arian, but he waged valiant battle with Arianism all the rest of his life. Ambrose, called "the father of Latin hymnody," initiated the so-called Ambrosian Chant, which became part of the musical reforms carried through by Gregory I, bishop of Rome. He wrote simple hymns for congregational use.

O Splendor of God's Glory Bright (158)

Mark Andrews

Mark Andrews (b. Gainsborough, Lincolnshire, England, March 21, 1875; d. Montclair, New Jersey, December 10, 1939) studied under John Thomas Ruck at Westminster Abbey. He came to the United States in 1902 and served as organist and choir director for churches in Montclair, New Jersey. Andrews was active in the American Guild of Organists and composed in various musical forms, including works for the organ, cantatas, and choral anthems.

LAUDA ANIMA (Andrews) (53)

Antes, John

Antes, John (b. Frederick, Pennsylvania, March 24, 1740; d. Bristol, England, December 17, 1811) was the son of Heinrich Antes, who purchased land in Pennsylvania and North Carolina for Moravian immigrants. His father also established a school for young men, and here John received both his academic and musical training. In 1764 he went to the important Moravian center at Herrnhut, Saxony (Germany), to study for the ministry. He also learned the trade of watchmaking. In 1769, having been ordained to the Moravian ministry, he went to Egypt as the first American missionary to that country, where he remained until 1781. During his stay in Egypt he was beaten and imprisoned by the bey and wrote several important musical pieces while in prison. In 1781 Antes returned to Germany for two years, became acquainted with Joseph Haydn, and then settled in Fulneck, England, where he was treasurer for the Moravian congregation. Antes invented a new method for tuning the violin, as well as an improved violin bow, and improved piano hammers. He retired in 1808 and moved with his wife to Bristol, where he lived until his death in 1811.

MONKLAND (84)

Arne, Thomas Augustine

Arne, Thomas Augustine (b. London, England, March 12, 1710; d. London, March 5, 1778) was the son of an upholsterer. He studied at

Eton and briefly entered the practice of law, but his first love was music. He wrote the music for Joseph Addison's *Rosamund* (1733), for twelve other masques and operas, and for two oratorios. The finale of the opera *Alfred* (1740) contains the famous "Rule, Brittania." Although his music was far less popular than that of Handel, who dominated the then current taste in England, Arne was recognized as the greatest English composer of the eighteenth century. He was among the first musicians to introduce parts for female voices in choral compositions. Although he was a Roman Catholic, Oxford University conferred upon him the honorary Mus.D. degree in 1759.

ARLINGTON (28, 546)

Ashford, Emma Louise Hindle

Ashford, Emma Louise Hindle (b. Newark, Delaware, March 27, 1850; d. Nashville, Tennessee, September 22, 1930) showed musical talent at an early age. Her parents were from England, and her father was a singing teacher. At age twelve she was organist for the Episcopal church in Kewanee, Illinois. In 1864 the family moved to Seymour, Connecticut, where she was organist for St. Peter's Episcopal Church. After her marriage to John Ashford, she moved with him to Nashville, Tennessee, where he served on the music faculty and then as superintendent of buildings and grounds at Vanderbilt University. John Ashford, a native of Bath, England, was also soloist at St. James's church (Nashville) under Dudley Buck. Mr. and Mrs. Ashford served in musical capacities for various churches, and even for a Jewish synagogue. Her hymn tunes EVELYN and SUTHERLAND were published in the *Methodist Hymnal* (1905).

MY TASK (460)

Atkins, George

Atkins, George.
No information is available on this author.
Brethren, We Have Met to Worship (419)

Babcock, Maltbie Davenport

Babcock, Maltbie Davenport (b. Syracuse, New York, August 3, 1858; d. Naples, Italy, May 18, 1901) was a member of a socially prominent family in Syracuse and was educated at Syracuse University and Auburn Theological Seminary. He excelled in athletics, drama, music, and in his academic work at Syracuse. Babcock became a Presbyterian minister and served churches in Lockport, New York, and Baltimore, Maryland. In 1899 he succeeded Henry Van Dyke as minister of the Brick Presbyterian Church in New York City. He died eighteen months later as he traveled to the Holy Land. Selections from his sermons and poems were published after his death under the title *Thoughts for Every-Day Living* (1901).

This Is My Father's World (103)

Bach, Johann Sebastian

Bach, Johann Sebastian (b. Eisenach, Germany, March 21, 1685; d. Leipzig, Germany, July 21, 1750) felt he had a divine call to give to the church the best possible music. His family has been distinguished musically, and he received his musical education at Ohrdruf and Lüneburg. He served briefly as organist at Arnstadt and Muhlhausen, and then began the great creative periods of his life: at Weimar (1708-1717), at Anhalt-Cothen (1718-1723), and at Leipzig (1723-1750). Bach's son Karl Philip Emmanuel became Kapellmeister to King Frederick the Great of Prussia in 1740. He wrote over 300 cantatas and provided scores of harmonizations for Lutheran chorales. The Bach inclusions in modern hymnals came chiefly from his harmonizations. His published works, the *Bach-Gesellschaft* (1851-1900), comprise some 46 volumes. All the Bach inclusions in *GSR* are harmonizations of the following tunes:

SALZBURG (58)
INNSBRUCK (82)
HERR JESU CHRIST, MEIN'S LEBENS LICHT (97)
ERMUNTRE DICH (200)
PASSION CHORALE (221)
WACHET AUF (286)
DAS NEUGEBORNE KINDELEIN (292)
JESU, MEINE FREUDE (350)

Baker, Henry

Baker, Henry (b. Nuneham, Oxfordshire, England, 1835; d. Wimbledon, England, April 15, 1910) was the son of an Anglican minister and studied engineering at Winchester and Cooper's Hill. He spent many years in India constructing railroads. Baker had a keen interest in music. He was encouraged by John Bacchus Dykes and earned a B.Mus. degree from Exeter College, Oxford (1867). His tunes appeared in Garret Horder's *Worship Song* (1905).

HESPERUS (115)

Baker, Henry Williams

Baker, Henry Williams (b. Vauxhall, England, June 21, 1821; d. Monkland, England, February 12, 1877), the eldest son of Admiral Henry Loraine Baker, was educated at Trinity College, Cambridge. He became an Anglican minister in 1844 and vicar of Monkland in 1851, where he remained until his death. He was knighted by Queen Victoria in 1859. Baker was one of the leading lights in the publication of *Hymns Ancient and Modern* (1861), serving as chairman of the committee which compiled it. He was responsible for securing many of the great nineteenth century English musicians who contributed to this famous hymnal. The language of Baker's hymns is always simple, smooth, and earnest. Julian says: "The last audible words which lingered on his dying lips were the third stanza of his exquisite rendering of the 23rd Psalm, "The King of Love, my Shepherd is"—

> Perverse and foolish, oft I strayed,
>> But yet in love He sought me,
> And on His shoulder gently laid,
>> And home, rejoicing, brought me.

STEPHANOS (332)
The King of Love My Shepherd Is (118)

Baker, Theodore

Baker, Theodore (b. New York, New York, June 3, 1851; d. Dresden, Germany, October 13, 1934) was first trained for a business career but turned his interest to music. He began studying in Leipzig (1874), where he received the Ph.D. degree in 1882. His dissertation was a study of the music of the Seneca Indians in North America. Baker was literary editor for G. Schirmer, Inc., from 1892 until 1926. Upon his retirement, he returned to Germany where he spent his remaining years. Baker published a *Dictionary of Musical Terms* (1895), *A Pronouncing Pocket Manual of Musical Terms* (1905), and *Baker's Biographical Dictionary of Musicians* (1st ed., 1900)

> *Christ, We Do All Adore Thee* (155)
> *Lo, How a Rose E'er Blooming* (180)
> *We Gather Together* (1)

Barbauld, Anna Laetitia

Barbauld, Anna Laetitia (b. Kibworth-Harcourt, Leicestershire, England, June 20, 1743; d. Newington Green, England, March 9, 1825) was the daughter of John Aiken, a dissenting minister who was later tutor in the dissenters' academy at Warrington, England. Five of her hymns were published in William Enfield's *Hymns for Public Worship* (1772). In 1774 she married a Unitarian minister of French descent, Rochemony Barbauld, who was minister of a church at Palgrave, Suffolk, where she assisted him in conducting a boarding school until 1785. Mr. Barbauld was subsequently minister at Hampstead and at Newington Green. In this latter place Mrs. Barbauld remained until her death. Her poems appeared in various Unitarian hymn collections during her life, and shortly after her death, her niece, Lucy Aiken, published her works under the title *The Works of Anna Laetitia Barbauld, with Memoir* (1825).

> *Again the Lord of Light and Life* (28)
> *Praise to God, Immortal Praise* (80)

Barber, Mary Ann Serrett

Barber, Mary Ann Serrett (b. 1801; d. Brighton, England, March 9, 1864) was the daughter of Thomas Barber. She published poems in the *Church of England Magazine* and also published several books., Her autobiography was published posthumously as *Bread Winning; or, The Ledger and the Lute, an Autobiography* (1865).

> *Prince of Peace, Control My Will* (478)

Baring-Gould, Sabine

Baring-Gould, Sabine (b. Exeter, England, January 28, 1834; d. Lew-Trenchard, Devon, England, January 2, 1924) was the eldest son of Edward Baring-Gould. He was educated at Clare College, Cambridge and spent much of his early life in Germany and France. Following his ordination to the Anglican minister in 1864, he served at Horbury and cared for the mission at Horbury Bridge. He wrote his best-known hymns for the children at this mission. Baring-Gould also served at Dalton in Yorkshire and at East Mersea in Essex, and following his father's death, he inherited the family estate at Lew-Trenchard and became rector there. His varied interests may be seen in the titles of his published works: *Lives of the Saints* (15 vols., 1872-1877); *The Origin and Development of Religious Belief* (1869-1870); *Curious Myths of the Middle Ages* (1866-1868); *Songs and Ballads of the West* (1889-1891), a collection of folk songs from Devon and Cornwall; and *A Garland of Country Song* (1894). He later collaborated with Cecil J. Sharp, England's foremost authority on folk song, in publishing *English Folk-songs for Schools*.

> *Now the Day is Over* (34)
> *Onward, Christian Soldiers* (412)

Barnby, Joseph

Barnby, Joseph (b. York, England, August 12, 1838; d. London, England, January 28, 1896) was a talented musician from his youth. At age seven he was chorister at York Minster, the organist there at twelve, and choirmaster at age fourteen. He was educated at the Royal Academy of Music under Cipriani Potter (1854) and was organist and choirmaster at St. Andrew's, London (1863-1871), and St. Anne's, Soho (1871-1876). At the latter church be began conducting an annual singing of Bach's passion music (1871). Barnby was also an advisor to Novello and Company, precentor of Eton College, and principal of the Guildhall School of Music. He was knighted by Queen Victoria in 1892. Barnby edited five hymnals: *The Hymnary* (1872); *The Congregational Mission Hymnal* (1890); *The Congregational Sunday School* (1891); *The Home and School Hymnal* (1893); and *The Cathedral Psalter,* with other editors (1873). He composed 246 hymn tunes which were published in a single volume after his death.

> *SARUM* (32)
> *SEYMOUR* (34)
> *LAUDES DOMINI* (152)

Barraclough, Henry

Barraclough, Henry (b. Windhill, York, England, December 14, 1891) was educated at Bradford Grammar School and at age five began training in the organ and piano. He first made his living as a claims adjuster for the Car and General Insurance Company in Bradford and later was secretary to Sir George Scott Robertson, M.P. (1911-1913). In 1914 he joined the evangelistic team of J. Wilbur Chapman and Charles M. Alexander as pianist and came with them to the United States. He served as a soldier in the American army during World War I. From 1919 to 1961, Barraclough was an officer in the General Assembly of the Presbyterian Church, USA. Bloomfield College and Seminary of New Jersey awarded him the honorary LL.D. degree. Following his retirement, he lived in Elkins Park, Pennsylvania.

> *MONTREAT* (277)

Bartlett, Eugene Monroe

Bartlett, Eugene Monroe (b. Waynesville, Missouri, December 24, 1885; d. January 25, 1941) was the son of Hiram Bartlett. He was educated at Hall-Moody Institute in Martin, Tennessee. From 1918 to 1935, he was president of the Hartford Music Company, Hartford, Arkansas. Bartlett published a large number of song books and edited the music magazine

Herald of Song. In later years he was affiliated with the Stamps-Baxter Music Company of Dallas, Texas, and with the James D. Vaughn Music Company of Lawrenceburg, Tennessee.

I Heard an Old, Old Story (517)
HARTFORD (517)

Barton, Bernard

Barton, Bernard (b. London, England, January 31, 1784; d. Woodbridge, England, February 19, 1849), known as the "Quaker Poet," educated at the Quaker school at Ipswich. He was apprenticed for a time to a shopkeeper in Halstead, Essex, England, and later was associated with his brother in the coal and corn business in Woodbridge, Suffolk (1806). Upon the death of his wife, to whom he had been married but one year, he moved to Liverpool and served as a tutor. In 1810 he returned to Woodbridge, where he worked as a bank clerk for the rest of his life, about forty years in all. During these later years at Woodbridge, he was a friend of several of the writers connected with the English Romantic Movement, including Charles Lamb, Lord Byron, Walter Scott, and Robert Southey. He published ten volumes of poetry, beginning in 1812 with *Metrical Effusions* and concluding in 1845 with *Household Verses*. The *GS* inclusion comes from his *Devotional Verses* (1826).

Walk in the Light (625)

Bateman, Christian Henry

Bateman, Christian Henry (b. Wyke, England, August 9, 1813; d. Carlisle, England, July 27, 1889) was the son of John Bateman. In his early years he studied for and became a minister in the Moravian Church. In 1843, he became a Congregational minister, serving in Edinburgh, Scotland, at Hopton in Yorkshire, and at Reading in Berkshire. He then took orders in the Church of England (1869) and served various churches until his retirement in 1884. Bateman edited with James Gall and Robert Inglis *Sacred Melodies for Sabbath Schools and Families* (1843), which sold over six million copies. He also edited *The Children's Hymnal and Christian Year* (1872).

Come, Christians, Join to Sing (151)

Bateman, Lucinda M. Beal

Bateman, Lucinda M. Beal (b. December, 1843). I am indebted to Prof. Harold Holland of Pepperdine University for most of the information on Mrs. Bateman. She lived in Ionia, Michigan, in 1891, where she and her husband, Zadok H. Bateman, operated a secondhand furniture store. She lived in Detroit in 1900, apparently with her daughter, Grace M. Bateman, who was a music teacher. She was associated with J. H. Fillmore and with James Holmes Rosecrans, and her compositions were published by the Fillmore Brothers Music House of Cincinnati, Ohio, in their publication *The Musical Messenger* and in their hymnals. Her poems appeared in *Grateful Praise* (1884), *Gems and Jewels* (1890), and *Christian Work Songs* (1892). She was also associated with the temperance movement, and Fillmore published her work *The Prohibition Speaker, a Collection of Readings, Recitations, Dialogues, Tableaux and Songs for Temperance and Prohibition Entertainments, Original and Written* (1889). She often wrote under the pen name "Grace Glenn."

Savior, Grant Me Rest and Peace (479)

Bates, Katherine Lee

Bates, Katherine Lee (b. Falmouth, Massachussetts., August 12, 1859; d. Wellesley, Massachussetts, March 28, 1929) was the daughter of William Bates and the granddaughter of Joshua Bates, both ministers in the Congregational Church. Joshua was president of Middlebury College (1818-1838). She was educated at Wellesley and Newton high schools and graduated from Wellesley College in 1880. She taught in high school for six years and then taught at Wellesley College and served as head of the English department. Her works as author or editor include *American Literature* (1908); *America, the Beautiful* (1911); *Fairy Gold* (1916); and *The Pilgrim Ship* (1926). She was awarded the honorary Litt.D. degree from Middlebury College (1914) and from Oberlin College (1916). She was granted the LL.D. by Wellesley College in 1925.

O Beautiful for Spacious Skies (435)

Bathurst, William Hiley

Bathurst, William Hiley (b. Clevedale, England, August 28, 1796; d. Lydney Park, Gloucestershire, England, November 25, 1877) was the son of Charles Bragge, member of Parliament for Bristol, but took the name Bathurst upon inheriting his uncle's estate at Lydney Park. He was educated at Winchester and Christ Church, Oxford, and became an Anglican minister. He was rector of the church at Barwick-in-Elmet, Leeds, from 1820 until 1852. At that time Bathurst resigned his ministry and retired to private life because he could no longer reconcile his religious views with certain parts of the *Book of Common Prayer,* relating to baptism and the burial of the dead. His published works include *Psalms and Hymns for Public and Private Use* (1831); *Metrical Musings,* or *Thoughts on Sacred*

Subjects in Verse (1849); *The Georgics of Virgil* (1849); and, posthumously, *The Roman Antiquities of Lydney Park* (1879).

O for a Faith That Will Not Shrink (505)

Baxter, Lydia

Baxter, Lydia (b. Petersburg, New York, September 8, 1809; d. New York, New York, June 22, 1874) was converted, along with her sister, under the preaching of Eben Tucker, a Baptist minister. Thereafter she and her sister helped to form a Baptist church in Petersburg. She married and moved to New York to continue her Christian work. In later years she became an invalid, but her home was always a meeting place for Christian leaders. Mrs. Baxter published one collection of religious verse, *Gems by the Wayside* (1855).

Take the Name of Jesus with You (524)

Beach, Curtis

Beach, Curtis (b. Cambridge, Massachussetts, February 9, 1914) is a descendant of several generations of ministers. He was educated at Harvard and the Boston University School of Theology and holds the Ph.D. degree from the University of Southern California. He served as minister of the Neighborhood Church, Pasadena, California (1943-1959), and since that time has been minister for the Smithfield Congregational Church of Pittsburgh, Pennsylvania. Beach published *The Gospel of Mark: Its Making and Meaning* (1959), and his hymns have been widely used in both Protestant and Roman Catholic hymnals and in the hymnal of the United Church of Japan.

O Be Joyful in the Lord (90)

Beall, Benjamin Burke

No other information is available on this composer, except that he conducted B. B. Beall and Company, which published hymnals during the early decades of the twentieth century.

BEALL (672)

Bechler, Johann Christian

Bechler, Johann Christian (b. Oesel, an island in the Baltic Sea, January 7, 1784; d. Herrnhut, Germany, April 15, 1857) came to the United States in 1806, as one of the first professors of the Moravian Theological Seminary at Nazareth, Pennsylvania. For the next thirty years he served as

professor, principal, and pastor among the Moravians. He ministered to churches in Philadelphia, Staten Island, and Lititz, Pennsylvania. Bechler also composed many hymns, anthems, and ariettas. He became a bishop among the Moravians in 1836 and thereafter served in Russia. About 1813, he published *VIII Hymns Selected from the Common Prayer Book of the Episcopal Church* (New York).
    BECHLER (179)

Beddome, Benjamin

Beddome, Benjamin (b. Henley-in-Arden, Warwickshire, England, January 23, 1717; d. Bourton, Gloucestershire, England, September 3, 1795) was the son of John Beddome, a Baptist minister. He was apprenticed to a surgeon in Bristol, but went to London, joined the Baptist church in Prescott Street, and was called to the ministry. In 1740, he began to preach at Bourton, where he remained for the rest of his life. Beddome was a highly respected minister during his lifetime and received an honorary M.A. degree from Providence College in Rhode Island. Julian says: "It was his practice to prepare a hymn every week to be sung after his Sunday morning sermon." (121) His hymns found their way into the English Baptist hymn collections and thence to a wider use.
    God Is the Fountain Whence (129)

Beethoven, Ludwig van

Beethoven, Ludwig van (b. Bonn, Germany, December 16, 1770; d. Vienna, Austria, March 26, 1827) was a musical genius who was playing publically by age eight and composing at age ten. He studied under Neefe and was introduced to the works of Bach. He visited Vienna at age sixteen and played before Mozart, whom he impressed greatly. Beethoven studied briefly under Haydn and, in the years following produced a vast amount of musical compositions. He began to suffer deafness at age twenty-eight, and was totally deaf at age forty-five. Beethoven never heard some of his most beautiful compositions, including HYMN TO JOY, taken from the finale of his *Ninth Symphony.*
    HYMN TO JOY (55, 249)
    GERMANY (415)
    NEANISKOI (302)

Belden, Franklin Edson

Belden, Franklin Edson (b. Battle Creek, Michigan, March 21, 1858; d. December 2, 1945) was the son of Stephen Belden and Sarah

Harmon Belden. His aunt was Ellen Harmon White, the Adventist prophetess. He moved with his family to California and later settled in Colorado for a time, where he married a musician. He thereafter moved back to Battle Creek and was associated with the Seventh-day Adventist publishing house. He published hymnals, the most important of which was *Christ in Song* (1900; 2d ed., 1908), and served as superintendent of the Review and Herald Publishing Association. His other published works include, with Edwin Barnes, *The Seventh-day Adventist Hymn and Tune Book for Use in Divine Worship* (1886); *Gospel Song Sheaf* (1895); and *Songs for the King's Business* (1910). In 1910 he began writing songs for Billy Sunday's evangelistic efforts.

O Heart Bowed Down with Sorrow (337)

BELDEN (337)

Bennard, George

Bennard, George (b. Youngstown, Ohio, February 4, 1873; d. Reed City, Michigan, October 10, 1958) was the son of a coal miner. In his youth he lived in Albia and Lucas, Iowa. At the age of sixteen he was converted in a Salvation Army meeting. He desired to become a minister, but the death of his father prevented his receiving an education. He studied on his own, however, and after his move to Illinois and his marriage, he and his wife worked in the Salvation Army. In later years he joined the Methodist Church and spent many years evangelizing in the United States and Canada. After his first wife's death, he married Hannah Dallstrom, and for a number of years before his death, they lived in Reed City, Michigan. In recognition of his living contribution to Christian song, "The Old Rugged Cross," wooden crosses were erected at both Reed City, Michigan, and Youngstown, Ohio.

On a Hill Far Away (655)

Bennett, Sanford Fillmore

Bennett, Sanford Fillmore (b. Keden, Erie Co., New York, June 21, 1836; d. Richmond, Indiana, June 12, 1898) at the age of two moved with his family to Plainfield, Illinois. He was educated at Waukegan Academy and the University of Michigan. Although converted in a Methodist meeting, he declared himself a Universalist. Bennett served two years as superintendent of schools in Richmond, Illinois. Later he was associate editor of the *Independent*, a weekly paper published at Elkhorn, Wisconsin. During the Civil War, Bennett was a second lieutenant in the Fortieth Wisconsin Volunteers. He studied medicine after the war and received a medical diploma from Rush Medical College in 1874. He practiced medicine for twenty-two years.

There's a Land That Is Fairer than Day (659)

Bernard of Clairvaux

Bernard of Clairvaux (b. Castle Fountaines, near Dijon, France, c. 1090; d. Clairvaux, France, August 20, 1153) was born into a noble family and became one of the foremost religious leaders of the twelfth century. His mother was a great influence in his life. He was educated at Chatillon, but chose to reject the possibilities of this world for religion. Bernard entered the monastery at Citeaux in 1112, and in 1115 he founded the Cistercian monastery at Clairvaux, of which he was abbot until his death. An exceedingly zealous and able man, he helped to bring unity into the Catholic Church of his day. Bernard is also remembered for preaching in favor of the disastrous Second Crusade in 1147.

Jesus, the Very Thought of Thee (265)
Jesus, Thou Joy of Loving Hearts (263)
O Sacred Head (221)

Bernard of Cluny

Bernard of Cluny (b. probably at Morlaix, Bretagne, early twelfth century) was of English parentage, and was a monk in the abbey of Cluny under Peter the Venerable (1133-1156). In this splendid monastery, Bernard wrote his satire of some 3000 lines against the vices of his age, the *De Contemptu Mundi*. Nothing further is known of Bernard's life.

Brief Life Is Here Our Portion (673)

Bevan, Emma Frances

Bevan, Emma Frances (b. Oxford, England, September 25, 1827; d. Cannes, France, 1909) was the daughter of Philip Nicholas Shuttleworth, who was warden of New College, Oxford, and later bishop of Chichester. In 1856 she married R. C. L. Bevan, a London banker. She published two volumes of verse, which contain her translations of German hymns: *Songs of Eternal Life* (1858) and *Songs of Praise for Christian Pilgrims* (1859).

Sinners Jesus Will Receive (324)

Bickersteth, Edward Henry

Bickersteth, Edward Henry (b. Islington, England, January 25, 1825; d. London, May 16, 1906) was the son of Edward Bickersteth, an

Anglican minister and compiler of the important hymnal *Christian Psalmody* (1833; enlarged 1841). He was educated at Trinity College, Cambridge and became an Anglican priest in 1848. He ministered at Banningham, Norfolk; at Christ Church, Tunbridge Wells; at Hinton-Martell (1852); and at Christ Church, Hempstead (1855). In 1885 Bickersteth was appointed dean of Gloucester and that same year became bishop of Exeter. He published several volumes of poems, and also edited *Psalms and Hymns* (1858); *The Hymnal Companion* (1870); and *The Hymnal Companion, Revised and Enlarged* (1876). All of his religious poems and hymns are directed to the individual and are highly personal.

> *Peace, Perfect Peace* (475)
> *Till He Come* (383)

Bilak, Epi Stephan

Bilak, Epi Stephan (b. Western Ukraine, Russia, May 13, 1926), the son of Dmitri and Anna Bilak, attended high school in the Ukraine. Bilak was taken from his home to a forced labor camp in Germany in 1942. After the war, while in a Displaced Person Camp, a Ukrainian couple gave him a New Testament. He was led to Christ and baptized in 1946. In 1954 he came to the U. S. and studied at David Lipscomb College (now University) in Nashville, Tennessee, where he met and married Reba Denny. After receiving a B.A. degree from Lipscomb, he did graduate work at Wayne State University and at McGill University in Montreal, Canada. After the Communists occupied his country, he chose not to return to the Ukraine, which branded him as a traitor so that he could not return safely. He chose rather to take Christ to his nation and to Eastern Europe by radio. The Bilaks now live in Lausanne, Switzerland. He is the voice of radio broadcast "Slavic World for Christ," sponsored by the Minter Lane Church of Christ in Abilene, Texas, and carried weekly over shortwave stations in Monaco and Malta. This program began in 1959 under oversight of the Rochester Church of Christ, Rochester, Michigan, and, since 1974, of the Abilene Church.

> *Heavenly Father, God Over All Things* (593)
> *While on the Sea* (539)

Bilhorn, Peter Philip

Bilhorn, Peter Philip (b. Mendota, Illinois, July 22, 1865; d. Los Angeles, California, December 13, 1936) was the son of a Bavarian carriage maker. His father, having immigrated to the United States, was killed in the Civil War three months before Peter was born. The original family name was Pulhorn, but was changed to Bilhorn in a court presided over by

Abraham Lincoln at Ottawa, Illinois. He and his brother carried on their father's trade for a time in their business, the Eureka Wagon and Carriage Works. Bilhorn had a fine singing voice and was popular in the German concert halls and beer gardens in Chicago. Converted during a meeting held by George F. Pentecost and George C. Stebbins in 1883, he decided to study music seriously thereafter and did so under Frederick W. Root and George C. Stebbins. Later he was involved in evangelistic work with D. D. O'Dell, George F. Pentecost, and John Currie. He invented a small organ to be used in the evangelistic singing, and this instrument was produced by the Bilhorn Folding Organ Company, Chicago, for several years. He was widely known as a gospel singer, was Billy Sunday's song leader until 1908, and in 1900 conducted a 4,000—voice choir at the World's Christian Endeavor Convention in London. While there, by special invitation of Queen Victoria, he sang his hymns in the chapel of Buckingham Palace. Bilhorn edited several hymnals, including *Crowning Glory No. 1* (1888), *Crowning Glory No. 2*, *Soul Winning Songs*, *Choice Songs*, *Sunshine Songs*, and *Bilhorn's Male Chorus* (Columbian Issue, 1893).

     Wondrous Story (165)

Black, James Milton

     Black, James Milton (b. South Hill, Sullivan Co., New York, August 19, 1856; d. Williamsport, Pennsylvania, December 21, 1938) was educated in singing and organ playing. He became a singing-school teacher and edited over a dozen songbooks which were published by the Methodist Book Concern (New York), the McCabe Publishing Company (Chicago), and the Hall-Mack Company (Philadelphia). His most popular collection was *Songs of the Soul* (1894). He was a member of the joint Commission for the *Methodist Hymnal* (1905), but none of his hymns were included in the collection. Black was a member of the Pine Street Methodist Church in Williamsport, Pennsylvania, from 1904 until his death.

     When the Trumpet of the Lord Shall Sound (437)

Blackie, John Stuart

     Blackie, John Stuart (b. Glasgow, Scotland, 1809; d. Edinburgh, Scotland, 1895) was educated at Marischal College, Aberdeen, and at Edinburgh University. He became an attorney in 1834. In 1841 Blackie was appointed professor of Latin in Marischal College, and in 1850 he became professor of Greek at Edinburgh University. His published works include *Lyrical Poems* (1860) and *Songs of Religion and Life* (1876). Blackie also served as editor of the *Sunday Magazine*.

     Angels Holy, High and Lowly (95)

Blaisdell, James Arnold

Blaisdell, James Arnold (b. Beloit, Wisconsin, December 15, 1867; d. Claremont, California, January 29, 1957) was educated at Beloit College and Hartford Theological Seminary. He was a minister in the Congregational Church and served in Waukesha, Wisconsin and Olivet, Michigan. Blaisdell was professor of Biblical literature in Beloit College (1903-1910) and president of Pomona College, Claremont, California (1910-1928). He was awarded honorary degrees by Hartford Theological Seminary, Occidental College, and the University of California.

Beneath the Forms of Outward Rite (388)

Bliss, Philip Paul

Bliss, Philip Paul (b. Clearfield, Co., Pennsylvania, July 9, 1838; d. near Ashtabula, Ohio, December 19, 1876) was born in a log cabin and in his early years worked on the farm and in the lumber camps. At the age of twelve, he joined the Baptist church near Elk Run, Pennsylvania. He received musical training from J. G. Towner, the father of D. B. Towner, and attended a musical convention conducted by William B. Bradbury. Bliss married Lucy J. Young in 1859 and worked for his father-in-law that year. In 1860 he became a professional music teacher, teaching in the winters and attending singing normals in the summers. He sold his first song to Root and Cady of Chicago in 1864 and was a member of their firm until 1868. Through the encouragement of D. L. Moody and others, he gave up music teaching and became a singing evangelist. In 1874 he joined the gospel campaigns of Major D. W. Whitle as singer. In 1876, following a revival meeting in Peoria, Illinois, he spent Christmas with his family in Rome, Pennsylvania, and then he and his wife left by train for a meeting in Moody's tabernacle in Chicago. While the train was crossing a railway bridge near Ashtabula, Ohio, the bridge gave way, and Bliss's car plunged with several others into a ravine. The cars caught fire, and Bliss, having at first escaped from the wreckage, went back into the car to rescue his wife, where both perished in the flames. Bliss wrote many gospel songs and assisted in the compilation of many significant hymnals, including *The Charm, a Collection of Sunday School Music* (1871); *Gospel Songs* (1874); *Gospel Hymns and Sacred Songs* (1875); and *Gospel Hymns No. 2* (1876).

Free from the Law - ONCE FOR ALL (313)

Sing Them Over Again to Me - WORDS OF LIFE (303)

KENOSIS (315)

MY SINS (347)

Whosoever Heareth - WHOSOEVER (335)

I Will Sing of My Redeemer (404, 407)

Brightly Beams Our Father's Mercy - LOWER LIGHTS (420)
More Holiness Give Me - MY PRAYER (488)
TELEIOS (603)
VILLE DU HAVRE (646)

Blondeau, Rollie Earl

Blondeau, Rollie Earl (b. Brenham, Texas, March 19, 1935) is the son of Earl Elwood and Evelyn Summers Blondeau. He was educated at Trinity University of San Antonio, Texas (Mus.B., 1957), Yale University (M.Mus,1960), and the University of Iowa (D.M.A., 1976). Blondeau taught at Abilene Christian University for several years and rendered invaluable assistance as a member of the Executive Committee for *GSR*. He and his wife Colleen now live in San Antonio, Texas, where he is associated with a real estate firm.

HENDERSON (428)

Boatner, Edward

No information is available on this author.
Jesus Saves Forever, I Shall Not Be Moved (657)

Boberg, Carl Gustaf

Boberg, Carl Gustaf (b. Monsteras, Sweden, August 1616, 1859; d. Kalmar, Sweden, January 7, 1940) was the son of a carpenter who worked at Monsteras on Sweden's southeast coast. He went to sea for a time, then attended a craft school at Nybro, Sweden, and taught crafts at Monsteras. He was converted at age nineteen, attended the Bible school at Kristinehamm, and began preaching in Monsteras. He was editor of the Christian weekly *Sanningsvittnet* (Witness of the Truth) from 1890 to 1916 and served as a member for Monsteras in the Upper House of the Swedish Parliament (1912-1934). Boberg was a popular speaker and published several volumes of poems.

O Lord, My God (60)

Bode, John Ernest

Bode, John Ernest (b. St. Pancras, England, February 23, 1816; d. Castle Camps, Cambridgeshire, England, October 6, 1874), the son of William Bode, was educated at Eton and at Christ Church, Oxford. He became an Anglican priest in 1841 and was rector at Westwell, Oxfordshire (1847), and at Castel Camps, Cambridgeshire (1860). Bode delivered the

Bampton Lectures at Oxford in 1855. He also published *Ballads from Herodotus* (1853), *Short Occasional Poems* (1858), and *Hymns from the Gospel of the Day for each Sunday and Festivals of Our Lord* (1860).

O Jesus, I Have Promised (620)

Bonar, Horatius

Bonar, Horatius (b. Edinburgh, Scotland, December 19, 1808; d. Edinburgh, July 31, 1889) was a descendant of a family, some of whose members had been ministers in the Church of Scotland for two hundred years. He was educated at the University of Edinburgh and ordained a minister of the Church of Scotland (1837). He left the church in 1843 and was instrumental in founding the Free Church of Scotland that year. Bonar was editor of *The Border Watch*, the official organ of the Scottish Free Church, and because of his keen interest in prophecy, was also editor of the *Journal of Prophecy*. In 1866 he became minister of Chalmers Memorial Free Church, Edinburgh, which was named in honor of Thomas Chalmers, the first moderator of the Free Church and a former professor of Bonar at Edinburgh. Bonar himself became Moderator of the General Assembly of the Free Church of Scotland in 1883. His published works include *Songs for the Wilderness* (1843); *The Bible Hymn Book* (1845); *Hymns, Original and Selected* (1846); *Hymns of Faith and Hope* (1857; 1861); *The Song of the New Creation* (1872); and *Hymns of the Nativity* (1879).

Blessing and Honor (174)
I Heard the Voice of Jesus Say (343)
Here, O My Lord, I See Thee (381)
Yes, For Me, For Me He Careth (639)

Borthwick, Jane Laurie

Borthwick, Jane Laurie (b. Edinburgh, Scotland, April 9, 1813; d. Edinburgh, September 7, 1897) was the older daughter of James Borthwick, manager of the North British Insurance Office in Edinburgh. At the urging of her father, she collaborated with her sister Sarah (Mrs. Eric Findlater) in the translation of German hymns. Together they published *Hymns from the Land of Luther* in four series (1854, 1855, 1858, and 1862). Of the 122 hymns included in these series, 69 are by Jane. She signed her poems "H. L. L.," from the title of the series. Jane Borthwick is probably second only to Catherine Winkworth as a translator of German hymns. She was also active in the support of missions and of social agencies.

God Calling Yet! Shall I Not Hear? (316)
My Jesus, As Thou Wilt (553)
Be Still, My Soul (547)

Bottome, Frank

Bottome, Frank (or Francis) (b. Belper, Derby, England, May 26, 1923; d. Travistock, Devon, England, 1894) migrated to the United States and entered the ministry of the Methodist Episcopal Church in 1850. He received an honorary D.D. degree from Dickinson College, Carlisle, Pennsylvania (1872). His published works include *Centenary Singer* (1869) and *Round Lake* (1872), in which a number of his hymns are included.

O Spread the Tidings Round (290)

Bourgeois, Louis

Bourgeois, Louis (b. Paris, France, c. 1510; d. c. 1561) was cantor (1540) and choirmaster (1545) in St. Peter's Church in Geneva, Switzerland. John Calvin appointed him musical editor of the *Genevan Psalter* (1542-1557). He was a popular citizen of Geneva and was admired for his teaching of children. He composed and adapted many tunes for the psalters published in Geneva. He also published *Le droit chemin de musique* (1550). Bourgeois left Geneva in 1557. He published harmonizations for the psalter tunes in 1547 (Geneva) and 1561 (Paris). He disappears after the latter date.

OLD HUNDREDTH (73, 74)

Bowie, Walter Russell

Bowie, Walter Russell (b. Richmond, Virginia, October 8, 1882; d. Alexandria, Virginia, April 23, 1969) was educated at Harvard and at Virginia Theological Seminary. He was ordained a priest in the Episcopal Church in 1909 and served churches in Virginia and New York as rector. During World War I, he was a hospital chaplain in France. Bowie became associated with his alma mater, Virginia Theological Seminary (now Protestant Episcopal Theological Seminary) first as dean of students and then as professor of practical theology and of homiletics. He delivered the Lyman Beecher Lectures (1934) and the Hale Lectures (1939). He was editor of the *Southern Churchman* and a member of the committee which prepared the Revised Standard Version of the Bible. His hymns have been widely used both in the United States and Great Britain.

Lord Christ, When First Thou Cam'st to Men (288)
O Holy City, Seen of John (431)

Bowring, John

Bowring, John (b. Exeter, England, October 17, 1792; d. Exeter, November 23, 1872) was one of the most important men of his day. His parents were Puritans, but he became a Unitarian. He left school at age fourteen to assist his father in the manufacturing business and traveled much on the continent. By age sixteen he spoke fluently German, Dutch, Spanish, Portuguese, and Italian. He was one of the world's great linguists, claiming to speak 100 languages and to read 200. In 1825 he succeeded Jeremy Bentham as editor of the radical *Westminster Review*. He was twice a member of parliament, beginning in 1835, was consul at Canton, China in 1849, minister to China (1854) and governor of Hong Kong. Bowring was knighted by Queen Victoria in 1854. His hymns were first printed in various Unitarian collections, but many of them have come into common use.

> *Father and Friend, Thy Light, Thy Love* (115)
> *God Is Love; His Mercy Brightens* (119)
> *In the Cross of Christ I Glory* (480)
> *Watchman, Tell Us of the Night* (181)

Boyd, Jack Arthur

Boyd, Jack Arthur (b. Indianapolis, Indiana, February 9, 1932) is the son of Arthur Pierce and Stella Cunningham Boyd. He was educated in the public schools of Indianapolis and holds a B.S. degree in music education and vocal music from Abilene Christian University. He received his Masters degree in Music Composition and Theory from North Texas State University (now the University of North Texas), Denton, Texas (1959), and his Ph.D in choral literature at the University of Iowa, Iowa City, Iowa (1971). He is married to the former Joann Ruth Orr, and they have three children. Boyd is the co-editor of *Children, Rejoice!* (R. B. Sweet Company, Austin, Texas) and the author of *Rehearsal Guide for the Choral Director* (1970), *Teaching Choral Sight Reading* (1975), and *Leading the Lord's Singing* (1982). He is also a widely published short story writer, including *One God, One Man* (a series of religious short stories published by ACU Press (1989) and *Life As It's Lived* (Texas Tech University Press). Jack Boyd is the music editor of *GSR* and has been my faithful fellow worker both on the ACU faculty for more than twenty years and in the editing and publication of *GS* since 1970.

> *AMAZING GRACE* (122)
> *BALM IN GILEAD* (314)
> *BILAK* (593)
> *Heavenly Father, God Over All Things* (593)
> *Jesus Is Lord* (159)
> *LASST UNS ERFREUEN* (66)
> *ORR* (322)
> *SLANE* (578)
> *WERE YOU THERE* (228)

While on the Sea (539)
WONDROUS LOVE (225)

Boyd, William

Boyd, William (b. Montego Bay, Jamaica, 1847; d. Paddington, England, February 16, 1928) composed music by age ten. He was educated at Hurstpierpoint, where he studied under Sabine Baring-Gould, and at Worcester College, Oxford. He was ordained an Anglican priest in 1882; was rector of Wigginholt, Sussex (1884-1889); and vicar of All Saints, Norfolk Square, London (1893-1918). Boyd harmonized Baring-Gould's *Folk Music of Iceland* and contributed to *Thirty-Two Hymn Tunes,* composed by fourteen members of Oxford University (1868).

PENTECOST (442)

Bradbury, William Batchelder

Bradbury, William Batchelder (b. York, Maine, October 6, 1816; d. Montclair, New Jersey, January 7, 1868) was a pioneer music teacher. At the age of fourteen, he moved with his family to Boston, where he attended the Boston Academy of Music and sang in the Bowdoin Street Church choir under Lowell Mason. In 1840 he was organist for the First Baptist Church of Brooklyn and in 1841 for the Baptist Tabernacle in New York City. His singing classes, patterned after those of Mason in Boston, resulted in the teaching of music in the New York public schools. From 1847 to 1849, Bradbury moved with his family to Europe and studied in Leipzig under Hauptmann and Moschelles. Upon returning to the United States, he gave himself to the teaching of music and to publication. With his brother he founded the Bradbury Piano Company in 1854. Between 1841 and 1867, he edited some sixty collections of music. These included *The Young Choir* (1841), *The Psalmodist* (1844), *The Mendelssohn Collection* (1849), *The Shawm* (1853), *The Jubilee* (1858), *The Golden Chair* (1861), *Devotional Hymn and Tune Book* (1864), and *The Golden Censer* (1864).

BROWN (390)
BRADBURY (606)
He Leadeth Me (133)
KIRKWOOD (401)
Olive's Brow (213)
REST (671)
Solid Rock (558)
Sweet Hour (559)
WOODWORTH (346)

Brady, Nicolaus

Brady, Nicolaus (b. Bandon, County Cork, Ireland, 1659; d. Richmond, Surrey, England, 1726) was educated at Westminster, at Christ Church, Oxford, and at Trinity College, Dublin. He was ordained an Anglican priest and served as chaplain to King William III. He ministered at Richmond from 1696 until his death in 1726. In the former year he was associated with Nahum Tate in producing the *New Version* of the English psalter. This was a revision of the older version by Sternhold and Hopkins. Many of his sermons are extant. He was the author of a tragedy, *The Rape, or the Innocent Imposters* (1692) and also published a translation of part of Virgil's *Aeneid* (1726).

Through All the Changing Scenes (52)

Braine, W. R.

No information is available on this composer. It seems to be an error of long standing in the attribution in *GS*. See the next entry.

BRAINE (101)

Braun, Johann Georg

He published *Hymnodiae Coelestis* (1675) in Ubthal and was also organist at Eger, Germany. No other information is available.

BRAUN (101)

Breck, Carrie E.

Breck, Carrie E. (b. Walden, Vermont, January 22, 1855; d. Portland, Oregon, May 27, 1934) spent her childhood in Vermont, lived briefly in New Jersey, and then, after her marriage to Frank A. Breck, moved to Portland, Oregon, where she remained for the rest of her life. She had five daughters. A deeply committed believer and a member of the Presbyterian Church, she often composed her poems while going about her household chores. Although she herself could not carry a tune, she loved music and wrote over 2,000 poems.

Face to Face with Christ My Savior (660)

Shall I Crucify My Savior (269)

Bridgers, Luther Burgess

Bridgers, Luther Burgess (b. Margarestville, North Carolina, February 14, 1884; d. Atlanta, Georgia, May 27, 1948) began to preach at age seventeen and was a student at Asbury College in Kentucky. He preached for various Methodist churches, being widely-known for his evangelistic fervor. In 1910 his wife and three sons burned to death at his father-in-law's house in Harrodsburg, Kentucky, where Bridgers was holding a meeting. Beginning in 1914 he became a general evangelist among the Methodists. Following World War I, he was a missionary to Belgium, Czechoslovakia, and Russia. He married Aline Winburn, a music teacher at Shorter College, Rome, Georgia, in 1914 and in later years served churches in Georgia and North Carolina. He lived in retirement in Gainesville, Georgia, his wife's home-town, until his death.

There's Within My Heart a Melody - SWEETEST NAME (465)

Bridges, Matthew

Bridges, Matthew (b. Maldon, Essex, England, July 14, 1800; d. Sidmouth, Devonshire, England, October 6, 1894), the younger son of John Bridges, was educated in the Church of England. In 1828 he published a book against the Roman Catholic Church entitled *The Roman Empire Under Constantine the Great*. In 1848, under the influence of the Oxford Movement and John Henry Newman, he became a Roman Catholic. After his conversion, he spent some years in the Province of Quebec, Canada. He published *Hymns of the Heart* (1847; enlarged 1851) and *The Passion of Jesus* (1852). Some of his hymns were included in Henry Ward Beecher's *Plymouth Collection* (1855). He returned to England and spent his final years at the guest house of the Convent of the Assumption in Sidmouth. He was buried in the convent's private graveyard.

Crown Him with Many Crowns (255)

Bridges, Robert Seymour

Bridges, Robert Seymour (b. Walmer, Kent, England, October 23, 1844; d. Boar's Hill, Abingdon, Berkshire, England, April 21, 1930) was an English physician, musician, scholar, and poet laureate. He was educated at Eton, at Corpus Christi College, Oxford, and at St. Bartholomew's Hospital in London. In 1881 he gave up his medical practice because of ill health and retired to Yattendon in Berkshire to devote himself to literature and hymnody. In 1924 he received the honorary LL.D. degree from the University of Michigan at Ann Arbor, and in 1929 was awarded the Order of Merit for his work *The Testament of Beauty*. He married Mary Monica Waterhouse in 1884 and was appointed poet laureate in 1913. Bridges also received honorary doctorates from Oxford, St. Andrews, and Harvard.

Ah, Holy Jesus (222)

Briggs, George Wallace

Briggs, George Wallace (b. Kirkby, Northamptonshire, England, December 14, 1875; d. Hindhead, Surrey, England, December 30, 1959) was educated at Emmanuel College, Cambridge and ordained in the Church of England. He was a chaplain in the Royal Navy (1902-1090), vicar of St. Andrew's Norwich (1909-1918), rector of Loughborough College, canon of Leicester Cathedral (1927-1934), and canon of Worcester (1934-1956). Briggs was present at the meeting between President Franklin D. Roosevelt and Prime Minister Winston Churchill aboard the H.M.S. *Prince of Wales*, August 10, 1941, at the signing of the Atlantic Charter, and read the following prayer:

> Stablish our heart, O God, and strengthen our resolve, that we fight not in enmity against men, but against the power of darkness enslaving the souls of men; till all enmity and oppression be done away, and the peoples of the world be set free from fear, to serve one another; as children of one Father, who is above all, and through all and in all.

Christ Is the World's True Light (402)
Come, Risen Lord (378)

Brock, Blanche Kerr

Brock, Blanche Kerr (b. Greenfork, Indiana, February 3, 1888; d. Winona Lake, Indiana, January 3, 1958) was the wife of Virgil P. Brock and a member of the Christian Church (Independent). She studied voice at the Indianapolis Conservatory of Music and at the American Conservatory in Chicago. She married Virgil P. Brock on September 24, 1914. From 1914 to 1922, she accompanied her husband as a singer in connection with his work as a general evangelist. From 1923 to 1936, she worked with him in evangelistic work in Marion County, Indiana, They returned to general evangelistic work in 1937, in which work she engaged with her husband until her death.

BROCK (662)

Brock, Virgil Prentiss

Brock, Virgil Prentiss (b. Celina, Ohio, January 6, 1887; d. Youth Haven Ranch, River Junction, near Jackson, Michigan, March 12, 1978) was a Quaker in early life but later became a member of the Christian Church (Independent), and a successful evangelist. He married Blanche Kerr on September 24, 1914. From 1914 to 1922, the Brocks were a respected evangelistic team in general work all over the United States.

After 1922 he served as evangelist for the churches in Marion County, Indiana. He returned to general evangelistic work in 1937. Mrs. Brock died in 1958. He then married Martha Anderson (1959), and she died in 1969.

Beyond the Sunset (662)

Brooke, Stopford Augustus

Brooke, Stopford Augustus (b. Glendoen, Letterkenny, County Donegal, Ireland, November 14, 1832; d. The Four Winds, Surrey, England, March 18, 1916) was educated at Kingstown, Kidderminster and at Trinity College, Dublin, where he received prizes for his English verse. He became an Anglican priest in 1857, served churches in England, and was chaplain to the British embassy in Berlin for two years. In 1867 he leased Bedford Chapel where he continued to preach until his retirement in 1894. Brooke withdrew from the Church of England in 1880 because of his liberal views and became an Independent. He had Unitarian leanings, but never joined any denomination. His published works include the *Life and Letters of the Late F. W. Robertson* (1865), *Theology in the English Poets* (1874), *Primer of English Literature* (1876), *Christian Hymns* (c.1878), *and Poems* (1888).

Let the Whole Creation Cry (58)

Brooks, Phillips

Brooks, Phillips (b. Boston, Massachussetts, December 13, 1835; d. Boston, January 23, 1893) was educated at Boston Latin School, Harvard University, and Virginia Theological Seminary. He was ordained an Episcopal priest in 1859 and served churches in Philadelphia, becoming rector of Trinity Church in Boston in 1868. He served until he was consecrated bishop of Massachusetts in 1891. Brooks was recognized as one of America's greatest preachers and in 1877 delivered the Lyman Beecher Lectures at Yale University. He made a trip to the Holy Land (1866) and preached later before Queen Victoria and at St. Paul's Cathedral and Westminster Abbey. He became good friends with Dean Stanley, dean of Westminster. Oxford University gave him the honorary D.D. degree in 1885.

O Little Town of Bethlehem (193)

Brownlie, John

Brownlie, John (b. Glasgow, Scotland, August 3, 1857; d. Crieff, Perth, Scotland, November 18, 1925) was educated at the University of Glasgow and at Free Church College in Glasgow. He began to serve as a minister in the Free Church of Scotland in 1885. He was also interested in public educational matters and became a member of the school board in Portpatrick, Wigtownshire in 1888. Thereafter he was governor of the Stranrear High School (1897) and chairman of the governors (1901). Brownlie was a fine classical scholar and made many translations from Greek and Latin hymns. His publications and translations include *Hymns of the Early Church* (1896), *Hymns from East and West* (1898) *Hymns and Hymn-Writers of the Church Hymnary* (1899); and *Hymns of the Greek Church* (four series: 1900-1906).

The King Shall Come (284)

Buckoll, Henry James

Buckoll, Henry James (b. Siddington, Gloucester, England, September. 9, 1803; d. Rugby, England, June 6, 1871) was the son of James Buckoll, rector of Siddington near Cirencester. He was educated at Rugby and Queen's College, Oxford. In 1827 he was ordained an Anglican priest but turned his attention to education and was assistant master at Rugby from 1826 until his death. Buckoll made several translations of German hymns into English. He is believed to have edited the Rugby school collection *Psalms and Hymns for the Use of Rugby School Chapel*. He also edited *Collection of Hymns* for the use of Rugby parish church. Buckoll's name does not appear in the text of *GSR* with the hymn below since he, with J. H. Gurney, was the author of an intermediate version between the original and the final poem.

We Saw Thee Not When Thou Didst Come (495)

Budry, Edmond Louis

Budry, Edmond Louis (b. August 30, 1854; d. November 12, 1932) was a student of theology with the "Faculte libre" in Lausanne, Switzerland. In 1881 he was minister at Cully and in 1889 became minister of the Free Church in Vevey, Switzerland, where he remained for thirty-five years. He wrote the texts for more than sixty chorales, several of which have been included in French hymnals. He also translated hymns from German, English, and Latin. Budry retired in 1923, but he continued to write poetry.

Thine is the Glory (240)

Bunnett, Edward

Bunnett, Edward (b. Shipham, Norfolk, England, June 26, 1834; d. Norwich, England, January 5, 1923) was a chorister at Norwich Cathedral at age eight and began the study of the organ at age fifteen. He was assistant to his teacher, Zechariah Buck, from 1855 to 1877. Bunnett was educated at Cambridge and served as conductor for the Norwich Musical Union for over twenty-one years. He gained much attention and favor while serving as organist at St. Peters, Manscroft, beginning 1877.

KIRBY BEDON (166)

Burford, Leonard

Burford, Leonard (b. near Abilene, Texas, September. 30, 1905; d. Abilene, September 2, 1961) was the son of J. L. and Lillian Frances Fisher Burford. He was educated at Abilene Christian College (now University; B.A., 1925), and at Columbia University (M.A., 1937; Ph.D., 1952). He and his brother Jack and sister Mabel all lost their sight at an early age. Leonard learned Braille at age fourteen and went completely blind at age twenty-eight in 1933. Burford was the first head of the Music department at ACU, serving from 1932 to 1961. He directed the A Capella chorus, taught voice, piano, music education, and music history in the department. His best known work is *Come Unto Me*, which has been performed widely in the Southwest. He married Mrs. Mary Telk Titsworth (December 1957).

BURFORD (614)

Burleigh, William Henry

Burleigh, William Henry (b. Woodstock, Connecticut, February 2, 1812; d. Brooklyn, New York, March 18, 1871) was educated in the public schools of Plainfield, Connecticut. He worked as a printer and a journalist. In 1837 he published the *Christian Witness* and the *Temperance Banner* in Pittsburgh and afterwards moved to Hartford, Connecticut, where he edited an anti-slavery paper, *Christian Freedom*. Burleigh was secretary of the New York Temperance Society (1849-1855). He published his *Poems* (1841; enlarged 1871). During his later years, he was Harbor Master for the City of New York, holding this post until 1870. Although he was a Unitarian, his hymns are more usually included in the hymnals of other religious groups.

Lead Us, O Father (540)

Burnap, Uzziah Christopher

Burnap, Uzziah Christopher (b. Brooklyn, New York, June 17, 1834; d. Brooklyn, December 8, 1900) was a successful dry goods merchant in Brooklyn. In his youth he had studied music in Paris, France, and served as organist of the Reformed Church in the Heights, Brooklyn, for thirty-seven years. He was the music editor for the Reformed Church hymnal, *Hymns of the Church: with Tunes* (1869). Burnap also joined with John K. Paine and James Flint, serving as music editor for *Hymns and Songs of Praise* (1874).

SERENITY (1878)

Burns, James Drummond

Burns, James Drummond (b. Edinburgh, Scotland, February 18, 1823; d. Mentone, France, November 27, 1864) was educated at the University of Edinburgh. He was minister of the Free Church in Dunblane at the time of the organization of the Free Church of Scotland. His health failed, and in 1848 he became minister of the Presbyterian Church at Funchal in the Madeira Islands. In 1855 he returned to England and became minister of the Hampstead Presbyterian Church in London. His publications include *The Vision of Prophecy: and Other Poems* (1854; enlarged 1858) and *The Evening Hymn* (1857). Other of his hymns, including translations from the German, appeared in *Memoir and Remains of the Late Rev. James D. Burns* by James Hamilton (1869). Burns wrote the article "Hymn" for the eighth edition of the *Encyclopedia Brittannica*.

Still with Thee, O My God (612)

Byrne, Mary Elizabeth

Byrne, Mary Elizabeth (b. Dublin, Ireland, July 1, 1880; d. Dublin, January 19, 1931) was educated at the Dominican Convent in Dublin and at the University of Ireland. She was expert in the ancient Gaelic language and worked as a researcher for the Board of Intermediate Education of Ireland. She also contributed to the *Old and Middle Irish Dictionary* and to the *Dictionary of the Irish Language* and assisted in compiling the *Catalogue* of the Royal Irish Academy. Byrne also authored *England in the Age of Chaucer.*

Be Thou My Vision (578)

Caldbeck, George Thomas

Caldbeck, George Thomas (b. Waterford, Ireland, 1852; d. Epsom, Surrey, England, January 29, 1918) was educated at the National Model School in Waterford and at Islington Theological College, London, intending to become a missionary. While in college, he wrote his hymn tune PAX TECUM. Because of ill health, he was not accepted for missionary work, so he returned to Ireland to become a schoolmaster and evangelist.

In 1888 he went to London, served as an evangelist, and sold scripture cards from door to door.

PAX TECUM (475)

Calkin, Jean Baptiste

Calkin, Jean Baptiste (b. London, England, March 16, 1827; d. London, April 15, 1905), the son of James Calkin, received his musical training first from his father. At the age of twenty, he became organist at St. Columba College, Rathfarnham, Dublin, Ireland. He returned to London in 1853 and was organist at various chapels until 1884. In 1883 he became a professor in the Guildhall School of Music. Calkin was also a member of the Council of Trinity College, London, and a Fellow of the Royal College of Organists.

WALTHAM (448)

Campbell, John Douglas Sutherland

Campbell, John Douglas Sutherland (b. St. James, Westminster, England, August 6, 1845; d. East Cowes, Isle of Wight, May 2, 1914) was chief of the Campbell clans and the ninth Duke of Argyle. He was educated at Eton, St. Andrews, and Trinity College, Cambridge. He married Princess Louisa Alberta, daughter of Queen Victoria (1871), and served as governor-general of Canada (1878-1883). Campbell was popular with the Canadians and wrote two books about the country. The Canadian province of Alberta is named for his wife. After his return to England, he served in parliament as a member for South Manchester. He was a great friend of the poet laureate Alfred Tennyson.

Unto the Hills (148)

Carman, I. N.

Little information is available on this author. He studied at Bethany College in Bethany, Virginia (now West Virginia), under Alexander Campbell and for a time was a minister of the Christian Church. He left the church in the late 1850s.

Here We Are But Straying Pilgrims (555)

Carr, Benjamin

Carr, Benjamin (b. London, England, September 12, 1769; d. Philadelphia, Pennsylvania, May 24, 1831) was educated in music and sang with the London Ancient Concerts. He came to the United States in

1793. With his father, Joseph, and brother, Thomas, he entered the music publishing business. The Carr family was quite successful, having stores in Philadelphia, New York, and Baltimore. Carr edited the weekly *Musical Journal* and was cofounder of the Musical Fund Society of Philadelphia (1820). He greatly encouraged contemporary musicians both at home and abroad. His publications included *Masses, Vespers, and Litanies* (1805), *A Collection of Chants* (1816), and *The Chorister* (1820). We are indebted to Carr for the publication of much American popular, patriotic music such as "Yankee Doodle" and, in 1814, Francis Scott Key's "Star Spangled Banner." (See "Spanish Chant: An Intruder's Adventures into Hymnology," by R. T. Boehm in *The Hymn* (January 1881) 32:17-24.

MADRID (151)
SPANISH HYMN (652)

Carter, Russell Kelso

Carter, Russell Kelso (b. Baltimore, Maryland, November 18, 1849; d. Catonsville, Baltimore Co., Maryland, August 23, 1926) was a member of the first graduating class of Pennsylvania Military Academy (1867), where he was an outstanding baseball pitcher and gymnast. He taught in his alma mater almost continuously from 1869 to 1887. From 1873 to 1876, he engaged in sheep raising in California. In 1887 he became a minister in the Methodist Church and was active in the Holiness movement in that body. Carter wrote much in the areas of mathematics, science, and religion. With A. B. Simpson, the leader of the Christian and Missionary Alliance, he published *Hymns of the Christian Life* (1891). In later life, he took up the study of medicine and practiced in Baltimore.

Standing on the Promises - PROMISES (554)

Caswall, Edward

Caswall, Edward (b. Yately, Hampshire, England, July 15, 1814; d. Edgbaston, Birmingham, England, January 2, 1878) was the son of R. C. Caswall, vicar of Yately. He was educated at Brasenose College, Oxford, ordained in the Church of England in 1838, and served as curate at Stratford-sub-Castle near Salisbury. Under the influence of the Oxford Movement, he resigned his curacy in 1847. After his wife died in 1849, he joined John Henry Newman as a Catholic priest at the Oratory of St. Philip Neri at Edgbaston. His life thereafter was spent in his priestly duties, with interest in the poor and in little children. He is recognized as second only to John Mason Neale as a translator of Latin hymns.

Jesus, the Very Thought of Thee (265)
When Morning Gilds the Skies (152)

Cennick, John

Cennick, John (b. Reading, Berkshire, England, December 12, 1718; d. London, England, July 4, 1755). Although his parents were Quakers, Cennick was brought up in the Church of England. He worked as a land surveyor, but gave this up to join with John Wesley in teaching religion. His ministry was to the children of coalminers at Kingswood. He left the Wesleys, however, and joined with George Whitefield for a time. Later, in 1745, he joined the Moravian Church, was ordained as a preacher in 1749, and preached in Germany and in Ireland. His publications include *Sacred Hymns for the Children of God in the Days of Their Pilgrimage* (1741), *Sacred Hymns for the Use of Religious Societies* (1743) *A Collection of Sacred Hymns* (1749) and *Hymns to the Honour of Jesus Christ, composed for such Little Children as desire to be saved* (1754).

    Children of the Heavenly King (468)
    Lo! He Comes with Clouds Descending (289)

Chapin, Lucius

Chapin, Lucius (b. Hamilton Co., Ohio, 1760; d. Springfield, Massachusetts, December 24, 1842) was a descendant of Samuel Chapin, who came to America in 1636. His father was a deacon and a song leader in the church at Springfield. Lucius enlisted as a fifer in the Continental army in Boston and served throughout the Revolutionary War, including the terrible winter with Washington at Valley Forge, where he received severe frost- bite, from which he suffered the rest of his life. After the war he became an itinerant singing teacher, traveling over the New England states and later south into Virginia. He married Susan Rousseau of Staten Island, New York, in 1791. They returned to Virginia, but in 1794 removed to Kentucky, where he lived and taught for the next forty years. He not only taught singing schools himself, but sent out his more talented students on their own. He retired in 1835 and moved to Hamilton County, Ohio, where he remained until shortly before his death.

    TWENTY-FOURTH (18)

Chatfield, Allen William

Chatfield, Allen William (b. Chatteris, Cambridgeshire, England, October 2,1808; d. Much Marcle, Hertfordshire, England, January 10, 1896) was the son of an Anglican priest. He was educated at Charterhouse School and at Trinity College, Cambridge. He was ordained to the Anglican ministry in 1832 and served as vicar of Stotfold, Bedfordshire (1833-1847), and Much Marcle from 1847 until his death. He is best known for his translations and his renderings into Greek of the litany, the *Te Deum*, and other parts of the English Church offices. He published his *Songs and Hymns of Earliest Greek Christian Poets, Bishops, and Others, translated into English Verse* (1876)

    Lord Jesus, Think on Me (529)

Chesterton, Gilbert Keith

Chesterton, Gilbert Keith (b. Kensington, London, England, May 29, 1874; d. Beaconsfield, England, June 14, 1936) was educated at St. Paul's School, London, and the Slade School of Art. His art reviews in the *Bookman* and the *Speaker* gained him fame throughout the literary world. He married Frances Blogg in 1901, and she helped him in all practical affairs so that he could be free to write. Through the influence of Hilaire Belloc, he converted to Roman Catholicism in 1922. Chesterton felt the Middle Ages to be the golden age of history and advocated the medieval trade system as the cure for England's economic ills. He wrote a series of detective stories in which a priest, Father Brown, is the hero. Chesterton published his poems in 1927 and wrote biographical studies of Francis of Assisi, Robert Browning, Charles Dickens, and George Bernard Shaw. He was a man of enormous size (weighing between 300 and 400 pounds) and of intemperate habits, which ultimately led to his death.

    O God of Earth and Altar (434)

Chisholm, Thomas Obediah

Chisholm, Thomas Obediah (b. near Franklin, Simpson Co., Kentucky, July 29, 1866; d. Ocean Grove, New Jersey, February 29, 1960) received a meager education, but made good use of his opportunities. He taught school at age sixteen in the country schoolhouse where he had received training. At twenty-one he was associate editor of the weekly *Franklin Favorite*. He was converted in 1893 during a meeting held in Franklin by H. C. Morrison. Afterwards he moved to Louisville, Kentucky, and became office editor and manager of Morrison's *Pentecostal Herald.* Chisholm was ordained to the ministry of the Methodist Church, but because of poor health gave it up, spent five years on a farm near Winona Lake, Indiana, and about 1909, went into the insurance business in Winona Lake. In 1916 he moved with his family to Vineland, New Jersey, where he continued his business and retired in 1953. His final years were spent in the Methodist Home for the Aged in Ocean Grove. Chisholm wrote over 1200 poems, many of which have been used as hymn texts. He has become known among Churches of Christ through his collaboration on some songs with Lloyd Otis Sanderson.

Great Is Thy Faithfulness (147)
Be with Me, Lord (579)
Bring Christ Your Broken Life (326)
Buried with Christ (355)
O to Be Like Thee (624)
Only in Thee (477)

Chorley, Henry Fothergill

Chorley, Henry Fothergill (b. Blackley, Lancashire, England, December 15, 1808; d. London, England, February 16, 1872) was educated at the Royal Institution, Liverpool. Showing literary skill, he gave up his job with a Liverpool merchant to become a musical journalist. He wrote for the *London Athenaeum* (1839-1865) and was its musical editor. He was also music critic for the *Times* (London). His *Autobiography, Memoir and Letters* was published posthumously (1873).

God, the Almighty One (586)

Clark, Jeremiah

Clark, Jeremiah (b. England, c. 1669; d. London, England, December 1, 1707) served in his youth as a chorister in the Chapel Royal. He was organist at Winchester College (1692-1695) and at St. Paul's (1695). He was organist jointly with William Croft at the Chapel Royal in 1705 and also served as music master to Queen Anne. He ended his own life by shooting himself with a pistol because of an unhappy love affair.

ST. MAGNUS (257)

Clark, Thomas Curtis

Clark, Thomas Curtis (b. Vincennes, Indiana, January 8, 1877; d. December 7, 1953) was the son of a minister of the Christian Church. After his father moved to Bloomington, Indiana, to preach for a congregation there, Clark attended the University of Indiana. He taught high school and for a time was a singing evangelist and worked in the piano business. In 1906 he began editorial work for Christian publications. He was poetry editor for the *Christian Century* (1912-1948), editor of the *Twentieth Century Quarterly* beginning in 1919, and on the staff of the *Christian Century Pulpit* beginning 1929. He published several collections of his poetry and also wrote librettos for four oratorios by the composer Bethuel Gross of Chicago. He married Hazel P. Davis in 1910.

Where Restless Crowds Are Thronging (430)

Clausnitzer, Tobias

Clausnitzer, Tobias (b. Thurn, near Annaberg, Saxony, c. February 5, 1619; d. Weiden, Germany, May 7, 1684) studied at several universities and graduated from the University of Leipzig (1643). He was chaplain to the Swedish forces stationed in Leipzig in 1644 and preached the thanksgiving sermon at St. Thomas Church celebrating the accession of Queen Christiana to the throne of Sweden. In 1649 he became minister for the church at Weiden in the Upper Palatine, where he remained until his death.

Blessed Jesus, at Thy Word (25)

Clayton, Norman John

Clayton, Norman John (b. Brooklyn, New York, January 22, 1903) was converted and took a part in the South Brooklyn Gospel Church. He married Martha A. Wistendahl in 1925. Beginning in 1942, he was associated with Jack Wyrtzen's Word of Life ministry and also worked with the Sunday Morning Radio Bible Class and with Bellerose Baptist Church. Clayton went into the music publishing business in 1945 and published about thirty song books between then and 1959, when he sold his business to the Rodeheaver Company and joined Rodeheaver as writer and editor. Since 1960 he has lived in Centerport, New York.

Jesus, My Lord, Will Love Me Forever (461)

Clayton, William

Clayton, William (b. Penwortham, Lancashire, England, July 17, 1814; d. Salt Lake City, Utah, December 4, 1879) came to the United States and in 1837 was converted to Mormonism. He returned to England for three years as a missionary, and then came back to the United States and settled in Nauvoo, Illinois, in 1840. He was city treasurer and clerk of the Temple in Nauvoo and was Joseph Smith's private secretary until Smith's death in 1844. Afterward he traveled to Utah with Brigham Young, reaching the site of Salt Lake City in 1847. He was a member of the Nauvoo Brass Band and played second violin in the Salt Lake Theatre Orchestra.

Come, Come, Ye Saints (128)

Clement of Alexandria

Clement of Alexandria (b. probably Athens, Greece, c. 170; d. c. 220). His full name was Titus Flavius Clemens. Nothing is known of his parentage, but he seems to have had an interest in matters of the mind from his youth. He studied the Greek philosophers and may himself have been a Stoic. Clement was taught the Christian faith by Pantaeus, the master of the Catechetical School in Alexandria, Egypt. Upon the retirement of Pantaeus, he succeeded to the leadership of the school (c. 190-203). Origin was one of his pupils. He was driven from Alexandria by the persecution under the Emperor Severus, and the remainder of his life is uncertain. It may have been he who carried a letter from Alexander, bishop of Cappadocia, and one of his old pupils, to Antioch in Syria around 211.

Shepherd of Tender Youth (166)

Clements, John Ralston

Clements, John Ralston (b. County Armagh, Ireland, November 28, 1868; d. Binghamton, New York, 1946) came to the United States at the age of two. He entered business at age thirteen, and over the years was successful as a retail and wholesale grocer. Clements was converted under the preaching of Dwight L. Moody in 1886. He was an active worker in the Christian Endeavor movement and at one time served as president of the New York State Christian Endeavor Union. He spoke at many of their International Conventions. Clements edited several hymnals; one of the most popular, with I. Allan Sankey, son of Ira D. Sankey, was *Best Endeavor Hymns*. He was friends with such noted hymnists as Fanny Crosby and W. S. Weeden and served as a deacon in the Presbyterian Church of Binghamton, New York.

In the Land of Fadeless Day (661)
Like a Shepherd, Tender, True (272)

Clemm, J. B. O.

No information is available on this composer.
CLEMM (399)

Clephane, Elizabeth Cecilia

Clephane, Elizabeth Cecilia (b. Edinburgh, Scotland, June 18, 1839; d. Melrose, Scotland, February 19, 1869) was the daughter of Andrew Clephane, Sheriff of Fife. After her father's death, she moved with her family to Melrose, near Abbotsford, the home of Sir Walter Scott. She devoted much time to the alleviation of the ills of the poor. Her eight hymns were published posthumously in William Arnot's *The Family Treasury* (1872-1874). Miss Clephane's beautiful and popular hymn text "The Ninety and Nine" was brought to the attention of Ira Sankey while he and Dwight

L. Moody were holding a meeting in Edinburgh in 1873.
        Beneath the Cross of Jesus (229)

Clough, Samuel O'Malley Gore

Clough, Samuel O'Malley Gore (b. Dublin, Ireland, 1837; d. Timahoe, Queen's County, Ireland, 1910). His name is sometimes spelled Cluff. He was educated at Trinity College, Dublin, and was ordained a minister in the Church of Ireland (Anglican). He left the Irish Church in 1874 and united with the Plymouth Brethren, and, perhaps, later with a "holiness" group. Clough published some songs under the title *Timogue Leaflets.*
        I Have a Savior (328)

Cober, Kenneth L.

Cober, Kenneth L. (b. Dayton, Ohio, July 12, 1902) is the son of Baptist missionaries and grew up in Puerto Rico. He was educated at Bucknell University and Colgate Rochester Divinity School and was minister to Baptist churches in Canandaigua, New York, and Buffalo, New York. He held offices in the American Baptist Convention until his retirement in 1970. His publications include *The Church's Teaching Ministry* (1964) and, as a member of the joint committee of the American Baptists and Disciples of Christ (Christian Church), the *Hymnbook for Christian Worship* (1970).
        Renew Thy Church, Her Ministries Restore (423)

Coffin, Henry Sloan

Coffin, Henry Sloan (b. New York, New York, January 5, 1877; d. Lakeville, Connecticut, November 25, 1954) was educated at Yale University, New College in Edinburgh, Scotland, the University of Marburg, Germany, and Union Theological Seminary. A Presbyterian minister, he served churches in New York City, taught theology and hymnology at Union Theological Seminary, and became president of that institution in 1926. He was elected Moderator of the Presbyterian Church, USA in 1943. Coffin was co-editor of *Hymns of the Kingdom* (1910).
        O Come, O Come, Emmanuel (182)

Coffman, Samuel Frederick

Coffman, Samuel Frederick (b. near Dale Enterprise, Rockingham Co., Virginia, June 11, 1872; d. Vineland, Ontario, Canada, June 28, 1954) was educated at Elkhart, Indiana High School and the Moody Bible Institute. He was ordained to the ministry in April 1895 and preached at the Moyer Mennonite Church in Vineland, Ontario. In 1903 he was appointed Bishop of the Mennonite churches in the Niagara district. He organized the Ontario Mennonite Bible School and served as its principal until he retired (1907-1952). From 1911 to 1947, Coffman served in various capacities in regard to the hymnody of the Mennonite Church. He helped publish *Church and Sunday School Hymnnal Supplement* (1911), *Life Songs* (1916), *Songs of Cheer for Children* (1928), and *Life Songs, No. 2* (1938). He was the chief editor for the Mennonite *Church Hymnal* (1927).

We Bless the Name of Christ the Lord (358)

Coller, Percy E. B.

Coller, Percy E. B. (b. Liverpool, England, 1895) was a chorister at Liverpool and Oxford Cathedrals and served as sub-organist at Liverpool at age fifteen. He was educated at Liverpool University, served in World War I, and was for many years organist at St. Peter's Church, Mount Royal, Montreal, Canada. His one inclusion in *GSR* helps to express the modern missionary concept that "In Christ all races meet." It was published anonymously in *Songs of Praise* (1931) and named for his wife.

ST. JOAN (402)

Conder, George William

Conder, George William (b. Hitchin, Herts, England, November 30, 1821; d. Forest Hill, England, November 8, 1874) was the only son of George Conder. He was educated at Highbury College, London, and became co-minister of the High Wycombe Congregational Church in 1845. He later served churches in Leeds, Manchester, and finally in 1870, Queen's Road, Forest Hill, London. He helped compile the *Leeds Hymn Book* (1853), to which he published an Appendix (1874).

All Things Praise Thee (64)

Conkey, Ithamar

Conkey, Ithamar (b. Shutesbury, Massachusetts, May 5, 1815; d. Elizabeth, New Jersey, April 30, 1867). Nothing is known of his early life. He went to New York City around 1848, where he sang in the choir of Trinity Church. Previous to this he served as organist at Central Baptist Church in Norwich, Connecticut. In 1850 he was bass soloist at Calvary Episcopal Church in New York, from 1852 to 1854 participated in musical services at Trinity Church, and in 1861 was a choir leader in the Madison

Avenue Baptist Church in New York. He seems to have been exceedingly popular as a soloist. His single inclusion in our hymnal was named for Mrs. Beriah S. Rathbun, the leading soprano in the choir of Central Baptist Church in Norwich, Connecticut.

RATHBUN (480)

Converse, Charles Crozat

Converse, Charles Crozat (b. Warren, Massachusetts, October 7, 1832; d. Highwood, New Jersey, October 18, 1918) was educated in the academy at Elmira, New York. He went to Germany in 1855, studied music under Plaidy, Richter, and Hauptmann, and was associated with Liszt and Louis Spohr. Upon returning to the United States in 1859, he attended Albany University, where he obtained a law degree in 1861. For many years he practiced law in Erie, Pennsylvania. Converse composed a great deal of music in different genres and was also associated with William Bradbury in editing hymnals. He often wrote under the German form of his name, "Karl Reden." Among the hymnals he edited was *The Standard Hymnal for General Use* (New York: Funk and Wagnalls Company, 1896).

ERIE (567)

Cook, George Harrison

Cook, George Harrison (b. 1864; d. Ocean Grove, New Jersey, 1946). Little is known of this composer. He was converted at age fourteen, and spent his life in the ministry of preaching and singing and in training gospel singers. After his retirement he lived out his life in Ocean Grove, New Jersey.

Heavenly Sunlight (462)

Cook, Joseph Simpson

Cook, Joseph Simpson (b. Durham County, England, December 4, 1859; d. Toronto, Canada, May 27, 1933) grew up as a youth in England, then migrated to Canada, and graduated from Wesley College of McGill University, Montreal. He was at first a Methodist minister, but later joined the United Church of Canada.

Gentle Mary Laid Her Child (196)

Corbeil, Pierre de

Corbeil, Pierre de (d. c. 1222)
Almost nothing is known of this author/composer except that he

was archbishop of Sens, France. The melody for which he seems responsible is found in the Sens Breviary, about 1210.

ORIENTIS PARTIBUS (132)

Cory, Julia Bulkley Cady

Cory, Julia Bulkley Cady (b. New York, New York, November 9, 1882; d. Englewood, New Jersey, May 1, 1963) was the daughter of the well-known architect J. Cleveland Cady. Educated at Brearley and Reynolds Schools in New York, she was a member of the Brick Presbyterian Church in New York. She married Robert Haskell Cory in 1911. In her later years she lived in Englewood, New Jersey.

We Praise Thee, O God, Our Redeemer, Creator (44)

Cotterill, Thomas

Cotterill, Thomas (b. Cannock, Staffordshire, England, December 4, 1779; d. Sheffield, England, December 19, 1823) was the son of a woolstapler. Cotterill was educated at his local grammar school, at the Free School, Birmingham, and St. John's College, Cambridge. He was ordained to the ministry of the Church of England and served as curate of Tutbury, Lane End, Staffordshire, and finally of St. Paul's Sheffield from 1817 until his death. Cotterill is best known for his compilation of a *Selection of Psalms and Hymns* (1st ed., 1810). In those days only the poems in the approved Psalters were used in the Anglican churches, but he attempted to introduce his collection of songs into his church. Opposition arose, and the archbishop of York persuaded Cotterill to withdraw his hymnal. A ninth edition was accepted in 1820—somebody must have been using the intervening eight—and became the first such hymnal accepted for use in the Church of England.

In Memory of the Savior's Love (375)

Cousin, Anne Ross Cundell

Cousin, Anne Ross Cundell (b. Hull, York, England, April 27, 1824; d. Edinburgh, Scotland, December 6, 1906) was the only daughter of David Ross Cundell, a physician of Leith, England. She was reared in the Church of England, but she later became a Presbyterian and was married to William Cousin, a minister in the Scottish Free Church. She contributed poems to several periodicals, and her hymns were included in various Presbyterian hymnals.

The Sands of Time (668)

Cowper, William

Cowper, William (b. Berkhampstead, Herts, England, November 15, 1731; d. East Dereham, Norfolk, England, April 25, 1800) was one of the greatest poets of his age. His father was chaplain to King George II; his mother was a descendant of John Donne, the preacher and poet. She died when Cowper was six years old. He attended Westminister School, studied law, and was admitted to the bar in 1745. He never practiced law, however, and in the next few years fell into a melancholy and a madness. He lived with the family of Morley Unwin, a minister, and Unwin's wife became his friend and his guardian. After Mr. Unwin's death, at the suggestion of John Newton, Mrs. Unwin moved to Olney, and Cowper came to live in her home. He resided there for nineteen years (1767-1796). Here he wrote his great poem *The Task* (1785) and, with Newton, produced the famous *Olney Hymns* (1779). Mrs. Unwin died in 1796, and thereafter Cowper fell into despair and died in 1800. His life is one of the great tragedies of English literature and of Christian poetry.

God Moves in a Mysterious Way (139)
O for a Closer Walk with God (576)
There Is a Fountain Filled with Blood (217)

Cox, Frances Elizabeth

Cox, Frances Elizabeth (b. Oxford, England, May 10, 1813; d. Headington, England, September 23, 1897), the daughter of George V. Cox, was one of the finest translators of German hymns. She was assisted in this enterprise by her friend Baron Bunsen, Prussian Ambassador to England. Her works are found in her *Sacred Hymns from the German* (1841) and *Hymns from the German* (1864).

Now Rest Beneath Night's Shadow (82)
Sing Praise to God Who Reigns Above (109)

Croft, William

Croft, William (b. Nether Eatington, Warwickshire, England, December 30, 1678; d. Bath, England, August 14, 1727) was a chorister at St. James Chapel Royal. He was organist at St. Anne's, Soho, from 1700 to 1711. He was also organist at the Chapel Royal (1707) and at Westminster Abbey (1708). Croft composed secular music in his early life, but in his later years he devoted himself wholly to sacred music, that is, music for sacred texts and services. We are indebted to him for the true development of the English psalm tune.

HANOVER (175)
ST. ANNE (136)

Crosby, Fanny Jane

Crosby, Fanny Jane (b. South East, Putnam Co., New York, March 24, 1820; d. Bridgeport, Connecticut, February 12, 1915) was probably the greatest writer of gospel hymns who ever lived. She became blind at the age of six weeks when a country doctor applied mustard poultices to her inflamed eyes. She was educated in the New York City School for the Blind and taught there for eleven years. Miss Crosby wrote poems for George F. Root, the musician and publisher, and in 1858 she married Alexander Van Alstyne, a teacher in the school for the blind and a musician. In the early 1860s, she turned from secular to sacred song, and her poems represented the epitome of the American gospel song. At one period in her life, she was under contract to the Bigelow and Main Company to produce up to three hymns a week. She was a Methodist and lived most of her life in New York City.

A Wonderful Savior (467)
All the Way My Savior Leads Me (651)
Blessed Assurance (345)
Hold Thou My Hand (520)
I Am Thine, O Lord (599)
Jesus Is Tenderly Calling (321)
Jesus, Keep Me Near the Cross (627)
Praise Him! Praise Him! (169)
Redeemed, How I Love to Proclaim It (357)
Rescue the Perishing (411)
Safe in the Arms of Jesus (647)
Sing On, Ye Joyful Pilgrims (473)
Tell Me the Story of Jesus (305)
'Tis the Blessed Hour of Prayer (560)
To God Be the Glory (79)

Crotch, William

Crotch, William (b. Green's Lane, Norwich, England, July 5, 1775; d. Taunton, England, December 29, 1847) was a musical genius. He gave public recitals at age four, studied with John Randall at Cambridge at eleven, played organ at Trinity and King's Colleges, and began his theological studies at Cambridge at age thirteen. At fifteen he became organist at Christ Church, Cambridge and received his degrees in 1794 and 1799. He was professor of music at Cambridge from 1797 to 1807. Crotch became the first principal of the new Royal Academy of Music (1822-1832). He is chiefly remembered for the seventy-four chants which he wrote to be used in the worship services of the Church of England.

    ST. MICHAEL (440)

Crüger, Johann

Crüger, Johann (b. Gross-Briesen, Prussia, April 9, 1598; d. Berlin, Prussia (now Germany), February 23, 1662) was educated at the Jesuit College of Olmutz and at a "Poet's School" at Regensburg, where he studied under Paul Homberger. He came to Berlin (1615) and finished his studies at the University of Wittenburg. He became cantor of the Lutheran Cathedral of St. Nicholas in Berlin (1622) and held this post until his death. Crüger composed chorale settings for the great Lutheran hymnists of his day: Franck, Herrman, Rinkart, and Rist. His *Praxis Pietatis Melica* (1st ed. 1644) passed through forty-four editions and was the greatest hymn collection of the seventeenth century.

    GRÄFENBURG (5)
    NUN DANKET (59)
    JESU, MEINE FREUDE (350)
    JESUS, MEINE ZUVERSICHT (550)

Crum, John Macleod Campbell

Crum, John Macleod Campbell (b. Mere Old Hall, Cheshire, England, October 12, 1872; d. Farnham, Surrey, England, December 19, 1958) was educated at Eton and at New College, Oxford. He was a minister in the Church of England, ordained deacon in 1897 and priest in 1900. Afterwards he held various posts, including assistant curate at St. John the Evangelist, Darlington (1897-1901), domestic chaplain to the Bishop of Oxford (1901-1910), vicar of Mentmore (1910-1912), rector of Farnham (1913-1928), and canon of Canterbury (1928-1943). He was the author of several theological works: *Road Mending on the Sacred Way* (1924); *What Mean Ye by These Stones?* (1926); and *St. Mark's Gospel, Two Stages of Its Making* (1936). He wrote his hymns for special occasions or for children.

    Now the Green Blade Riseth (243)

Cushing, William Orcutt

Cushing, William Orcutt (b. Hingham Center, Massachusetts, December 31, 1823; d. Lisbon, New York, October 19, 1902) decided at age eighteen that he wished to be a minister and served in the Christian Church (Disciples of Christ) for more than twenty years. He married Rena Proper in 1854, and they worked together until shortly before her death at Searsburg, New York (1870). After her death, he was afflicted with a paralysis which ultimately deprived him of his power of speech. Then he made his home with a minister friend, E. E. Curtis, in Lisbon Center, New York. He wrote some 300 texts for Sunday School songs and gospel songs which were set to music by George F. Root, Robert Lowry, Ira Sankey, and others.

Under His Wings (643)

Cynewulf

Cynewulf (flourished in the 8th century A.D.) was the greatest poet of the Golden Age of Old English poetry. His finest poem is *Christ*.

Come Now, O Lord of Victory (170)

D'Urhan, Chretien

D'Urhan, Chretien (b. Montjoie near Aix-la-Chapelle, France, February 16, 1790; d. Belleville, Paris, France, November 2, 1845) came to the attention of the Empress Josephine and was sent to Paris to develop his musical skill at the age of fifteen. He became a noted violinist and was a member of the orchestra of the Opera Française and concertmaster in 1831. He was also organist at the Church of St. Vincent de Paul in Paris. D'Urhan was an ascetic and deeply religious. Several of his melodies composed for secular pieces have been adapted for hymn tunes.

RUTHERFORD (668)

Dailey, James Gerald

Dailey, James Gerald (b. 1854; d. ?). Little information is available on this author-composer. He was a resident of Philadelphia. In the 1880s he published temperance songs. (See George Ewing, *The Well-Tempered Lyre*, Dallas: SMU Press, p. 162.) Dailey seems to have been a member of the Church of Christ. In 1900 he lived in Fredonia, Chautauaua County, New York.

Why Did My Savior Come to Earth - DAILEY (369)

Damon, William

Damon, William (b. c. 1540; d. c. 1590), musician to Queen Elizabeth I, was one of the earliest composers to provide part settings for the English Psalters. His compositions were included in John Day's *The Psalms of David in English Meter* (1579) and in Thomas Est's *The Former Book of Music of M. William Damon* (1591).

WINDSOR (146)
SOUTHWELL (529)

Dana, Mary Stanley Bunce Palmer

Dana, Mary Stanley Bunce Palmer (b. Beaufort, South Carolina, February 15, 1810; d. Texas, February 8, 1883) was the daughter of Benjamin M. Palmer, a minister of the Independent, or Congregational, Church in Beaufort. At the age of four she moved with her family to Charleston, where her father was minister to the Independent Church there. She grew up with the advantages of the best antebellum Southern society. She was educated in Charleston and in several ladies' seminaries in Hartford, Connecticut; Elizabethtown, New Jersey; and New Haven, Connecticut. In 1835 she married Charles E. Dana, and they moved to New York City. The Dana's first child, a son, was born in 1837, but then a series of calamities began to strike the family. Mrs. Dana's favorite sister died at her home in New York. Her brother died while away from the family in Alabama. In 1838 the Danas moved west. Terrible fevers were sweeping the country in 1839, and in an attempt to escape these, she began a trip up the Mississippi River for St. Louis and Bloomington, Iowa, with her husband and little son. Both son and husband contracted the fevers and died. Mrs. Dana then returned by a long and circuitous route to Charleston and to her parents and thereafter gave herself to literary pursuits. Her works include *The Southern Harp* (1840), *The Parted Family and Other Poems* (1841), and *The Northern Harp* (1843). She also published much temperance verse. In 1848 she married Robert D. Shindler, a minister of the Episcopal Church. They lived first in Upper Marlborough, Maryland, then in Shelbyville, Kentucky, where Mr. Shindler taught at Shelby College, and finally in Texas, where Mrs. Shindler died. The place of her death is unknown.

Flee as a Bird (275)

Daniels, Melvin Lucas, Jr.

Daniels, Melvin Lucas, Jr. (b. Cleburne, Texas, January 11, 1931) is the son of Melvin Lucas Daniels, Sr. and Ruby Mae Bickle Daniels. He was educated at Abilene Christian University (B.A., 1955; M.A., 1956) and the University of North Texas (formerly North Texas State University; Ph.D., 1964). He is married to the former Elaine Stewart. Daniels was a professor in the department of Music of ACU, was honored as a Piper Professor (1982), and has won the National School Orchestra Association's composition contest three times. He has also done staff arranging for several companies, including Warner Brothers, and Music Corporation of America.

DANIELS (395)
MERIMNA (639)
PROSOPON (612)
SIGOR (170)

Danks, Hart P.

Danks, Hart P. (b. New Haven, Connecticut, 1834; d. Philadelphia, Pennsylvania, 1903) moved with his family to Saratoga Springs, New York, as a boy. He was a carpenter by trade, a good bass singer, and a self-taught musician and composer. He later moved to Chicago, Illinois. Danks was the author of the well-known sentimental favorite "Silver Threads among the Gold." He died in poverty. After his death, scribbled on a piece of paper found on his desk were the words: "It's hard to die alone."
No Night There (661)

Darwall, John

Darwall, John (b. Haughton, Staffordshire, England, 1731; d. Walsall, England, December 18, 1789) was educated at Manchester Grammar School and at Brasenose College, Oxford (1756). He took orders in the Church of England and was minister to St. Matthew's Parish Church, Walsall, for the remainder of his life. Darwall was an amateur musician and wrote tunes for all the Psalm texts in Tate and Brady's *New Version*.
DARWALL'S 148 (474)

Davis, Bill W.

Davis, Bill W. (b. Dallas, Texas, April 5, 1917) is the son of Andrew P. and Minnie Ora Balch Davis. He was educated at North Texas State University (now the University of North Texas; B.M., 1941), and at Southern Methodist University (M.M., 1952). He is married to Maureen Lamm Davis. In early life he experienced a close association with hymn singing, both at home and in the church. He served as a song leader in the church for over fifty years, as well as a music teacher in the Dallas school system and other Texas schools as band, orchestra, and choral director for some twenty years. He taught at Abilene Christian University in the fields of band, orchestra, music history and literature, and church music for nineteen years, retiring in 1979. He and his wife now reside in George West, Texas. Their grandson Paul lives in Lake Dallas, Texas, with his wife Linda, and their children, Lisa and Brian.
DAVIS (562)

Davison, Fanny Estelle Church

Davison, Fanny Estelle Church (b. Cuyahoga Falls, Ohio, 1851; d. Chicago, Illinois, March 10, 1887) was the daughter of Philo and Sara Ann Linsted Church. Her father was killed when she was ten years old. Her mother then married Henry Christian Warner, and the family moved to Carthage, Missouri. She married Asa Lee Davison, a court reporter, and they resided first in Chicago and later in Madison, Wisconsin. She was buried at Carthage, Missouri, where her mother still lived at the time. Her hymns were published by the Fillmore Brothers Music House (Cincinnati), and she often collaborated with James Henry Fillmore in the writing of hymns.

Purer in Heart, O God (484)

Dayyan, Daniel ben Judah

Dayyan, Daniel ben Judah (late 14th century) is the reputed arranger of the Hebrew Yigdal (doxology) as it is used in Hebrew congregations and wherever the poem is sung in its various forms. No other information is available.

The God of Abraham Praise (43)

Dean, Emmett Sidney

Dean, Emmett Sidney (b. Conecuh County, Alabama, 1876; d. 1950) was a singing school teacher and for many years president of the Trio Music company, which was organized in 1895 by F. L. Eiland and H. W. Elliott, with Dean as an associate. With Eiland, Dean edited the popular hymnal *The Gospel Gleaner* (1902). After Eiland's death in 1909, Dean became editor of the periodical *The Musical Trio*.

DEAN (670)

Dearmer, Percy

Dearmer, Percy (b. Somerset House, Kilburn, Middlesex, England, February 27, 1867; d. Westminster, England, May 29, 1936) was educated at Westminister School and Christ Church, Oxford. He entered the Anglican ministry as deacon (1891) and priest (1892). He was vicar of St. Mary's, Primrose Hill, London (1901-1915); secretary of the London branch of the Christian Social Union (1891-1912); a chaplain in World War I; and professor of ecclesiastical art at King's College, London. From 1931 until his death, he was canon of Westminster. His publications include *The English Hymnal*, with Ralph Vaughan Williams (1906); *Songs of Praise*, with Martin Shaw and Vaughan Williams (1925); *The Oxford Book of Carols* (1928); *Songs of Praise Enlarged* (1931); and *Songs of Praise Discussed* (1933). He was one of the most influential hymnologists of the first half of the twentieth century.

Father, We Praise Thee (26)

Deck, James George

Deck, James George (b. Bury St. Edmunds, England, 1902; d. New Zealand, 1884) was the son of John Deck. He was educated for the army and served in India. After his retirement, he joined the Plymouth Brethren and ministered at Wellington, Somerset, beginning in 1843. In 1851 he migrated to New Zealand. His hymns, many of which dealt with the second coming of Christ, were published in *Hymns for the Poor of the Flock* (1837-1838), *Psalms and Hymns* (1842), the *Wellington Hymn Book* (1857), and *Hymns and Spiritual Songs* (1860).

Jesus, Thy Name I Love (656)

Dexter, Henry Martyn

Dexter, Henry Martyn (b. Plympton, Massachusetts, August 13, 1821; d. Boston, Massachusetts, November 13, 1890) was educated at Yale and at Andover Theological Seminary. He was ordained a Congregational minister (1844) and ministered at Manchester, New Hampshire. He was editor of *The Congregationalist, The Congregational Quarterly*, and *The Congregationalist and Recorder*. He also served as minister of the Berkeley Street Congregational Church in Boston for eighteen years. In 1880 he published *The Congregationalism of the Last Three Hundred Years, as Seen in Its Literature*. The translation of the poem listed below seems to have his only excursion into verse.

Shepherd of Tender Youth (166)

Dicus, Aaron Wesley

Dicus, Aaron Wesley (b. Festus, Missouri, May 30, 1888; d. Temple Terrace, near Tampa, Florida, September 1978) moved with his family in childhood to Swayzee, Indiana. He married his first wife, Bertha Jane, in 1908 and resolved to become a teacher and minister in the Church of Christ. While preaching for the church in Bloomington, Indiana, he received an assistantship to the University of Indiana (1925). In 1929 he became head of the Physics department at Tennessee Tech University in Cookeville, Tennessee. There he trained graduates in nuclear studies for the work at Oak Ridge, Tennessee. In 1949 he was appointed academic dean of Florida Christian College (now Florida College) in Temple Terrace, Florida, remaining in this post until his retirement in 1954. He married his second wife, Flora, in 1953. Dicus was the inventor of the turn signal now used on all automobiles.

Our God, He Is Alive - DICUS (107)

Dix, William Chatterton

Dix, William Chatterton (b. Bristol, England, June 14, 1837; d. Clifton, England, September 9, 1898) was the son of John Dix, a surgeon who was also the author of a *Life of (Thomas) Chatterton*, for whom he named his son. He was educated at the Bristol Grammar School and entered the mercantile business, rising to become manager of a marine insurance company in Glasgow. Although possessing scanty academic training, he was a proficient student, and some of his hymns are metrical renderings of the English translations from the Greek.

Alleluia! Sing to Jesus (253)
What Child Is This? (207)

Dixon, Helen Cadbury Alexander

Dixon, Helen Cadbury Alexander (b. Birmingham, England, 1877; d. Birmingham, March 1, 1969) was the daughter of Richard Cadbury, a British industrialist and philanthropist, who was also a Quaker with interest in the cause of missions. She attended the University of Birmingham and studied music and languages in Germany. She married Charles M. Alexander, the singer for evangelist Rueben Archibald Torrey in 1904 and traveled with him in his ministry until his death in 1920. She married Amsji C. Dixon in 1924. With J. Kennedy Maclean she published *Charles M. Alexander: A Romance of Song and Soul-Winning* (1921).

Anywhere with Jesus (530)

Doane, George Washington

Doane, George Washington (b. Trenton, New Jersey, May 27, 1799; d. Burlington, New Jersey, April 27, 1859) was educated at Union College, Schenectady, New York, and at General Theological Seminary. He was ordained to the ministry of the Episcopal Church, served at Trinity Church, New York, at Trinity Church, Boston, and became bishop of New Jersey in 1832. He was also one-time professor of belle-lettres at Trinity College, Hartford, Connecticut. Doane was a promoter of missions and church schools, founding St. Mary's Hall, Burlington, New Jersey (1837), and Burlington College (1846). His interest in the Oxford Movement in England prompted him to publish an edition of John Keble's *The Christian Year* (1834). His hymns appeared in *Songs by the Way* (1824).

Softly Now the Light of Day (35)
Thou Art the Way (270)

Doane, William Howard

Doane, William Howard (b. Preston, Connecticut, February 3, 1832; d. South Orange, New Jersey, December 24, 1915) was educated at Woodstock Academy and directed the choir while a student there. He joined the Baptist Church at Norwich, Connecticut, worked in his father's cotton manufacturing business for three years, and then joined the firm of J. A. Fay and Company, which made woodworking machinery. He later moved with this firm to Cincinnati, Ohio, and became its president. Outside his business interests, his most important life work was in composing and editing hymn collections. He frequently collaborated with Fanny Crosby in producing hymns. Doane's most popular hymnal was *Silver Spray* (1867).

Blessed Hour (560)
BRACHIONI (647)
I Am Thine (599)
More Love to Thee (613)
Near The Cross (627)
Precious Name (524)
To God Be The Glory (79)

Doddridge, Philip

Doddridge, Philip (b. London, England, June 26, 1702; d. Lisbon, Portugal, October 26, 1751) was the son of a merchant and the youngest of twenty children. His paternal grandfather was a priest who had been ejected from his church by the Act of Uniformity (1662). His maternal grandfather was a Lutheran minister who was expelled from his native Prague, Bohemia, because of his faith. His parents died in 1715, and although offered an education for the Anglican ministry, he enrolled in the Nonconformist academy at Kibworth. He became minister at Northampton in 1729 and conducted an academy there until failing health forced him to give it up in 1751. Having contracted tuberculosis, he sailed for Portugal for rest in a warmer climate and died there. His friend Job Orton published Doddrige's hymns posthumously in 1755. Doddridge was a man of great learning. Alexander Campbell made use of Doddridge's translations in his edition of the New Testament (1826).

Awake, My Soul, Stretch Every Nerve (543)
Great God, We Sing That Mighty Hand (141)
O God of Bethel, by Whose Hand (140)

Doving, Carl

Doving, Carl (b. Norddalen, Norway, March 31, 1867; d. Chicago,

Illinois, October 2, 1937) came to the United States in 1890. He was educated at Luther College and Luther Seminary. He served churches in Minnesota and New York and was city missionary to Chicago. He also served on the committee which produced the *Lutheran Hymnary* (1913), for which he did extensive research.

Built on a Rock (362)

Draper, William Henry

Draper, William Henry (b. Kenilsworth, Warwickshire, England, December 19, 1885; d. Clifton, Bristol, England, August 9, 1933) was educated at Cheltenham College and at Keble College, Oxford. He became a minister in the Church of England (1880) and served as curate at St. Mary's Shrewsbury; vicar of Alfreton; vicar of the Abbey Church, Shrewsbury; rector of Adel, Leeds; master of the Temple, London (1919-1930); and from 1930 until his death, he was vicar of Axbridge, Somerset. He wrote more than 650 hymns and made several excellent translations from Greek and Latin. His publications include *Hymns for Holy Week* (1899), *The Victoria Book of Hymns* (1897), *Hymns for the Tunes of Orlando Gibbons* (1925), and *Seven Spiritual Songs by Thomas Campion* (1919).

All Creatures of Our God and King (66)

Dubois, Theodore

Dubois, Theodore (b. 1837; d. 1924). At an early age he studied at the Conservatoire in Paris, and later in Rome under Ambroise Thomas (1861). He afterwards returned to Paris and was appointed *maitre de chapelle* at Sainte-Clothilde. Dubois wrote "Les Sept Paroles du Christ" on Good Friday, 1867. In 1877 he became *maitre de chapelle* at the Madeleine and was organist there. Dubois became professor of harmony at the Conservatoire in 1871, and was its head from 1896 to 1905.

ADOREMUS TE CHRISTE (155)

Duffield, George Jr.

Duffield, George Jr. (b. Carlisle, Pennsylvania, September 12, 1818; d. Bloomfield, New Jersey, July 6, 1888) was the descendant of Presbyterian ministers. His grandfather was chaplain to the Continental Congress during the Revolutionary War. Educated at Yale University and Union Theological Seminary, he was ordained to the Presbyterian ministry in 1840 and served churches in Brooklyn, New York; Bloomfield, New Jersey; Philadelphia; Adrian, Michigan; Galesburg, Illinois; and Saginaw, Ann Arbor, and Lansing, Michigan. He retired to Bloomfield, New Jersey, in 1884 and lived with his son, Samuel W. Duffield, the author of *English Hymns, Their Authors and History* (1886).

Stand Up, Stand Up for Jesus (403)

Durham, Miss M.

No information has been found on this composer. The tune below was attributed to her by William Walker in his *Southern Harmony* (1835).

Promised Land (666)

Dwight, Timothy

Dwight, Timothy (b. Northampton, Massachusetts, May 14, 1752; d. New Haven, Connecticut, January 22, 1817). His mother was the daughter of Jonathan Edwards, the great Puritan scholar and preacher. He was educated at Yale University, beginning at age thirteen. Intense study injured his eyes, but he too became a great scholar. He was a chaplain in the Continental army and a close friend of George Washington. He became minister for the Congregational Church, Greenfield, Connecticut (1783), and president of Yale University (1795). He taught in the university in addition to his duties as president. In 1801 Dwight published a revision of Isaac Watts's *Psalms*, to which he added thirty-three of his own hymns.

I Love Thy Kingdom, Lord (408, 410)

Dykes, John Bacchus

Dykes, John Bacchus (b. Hull, England, March 10, 1823; d. Ticehurst, Sussex, England, January 22, 1876) was the son of a banker. At age ten he played the organ in the church at Hull, where his grandfather was minister. He was educated at Wakefield and at St. Catherine's College, Cambridge. He became a deacon and then a priest in the Church of England. Beginning in 1847, he served as minor deacon and precentor at Durham, and in 1862 became vicar of St. Oswalds, Durham where he remained for the rest of his life. Dykes is recognized as the greatest of the Victorian hymn tune composers. Most of his tunes originally appeared in *Hymns Ancient and Modern* (beginning in 1861) and in Chope's *Congregational Hymn and Tune Book*.

LUX BENIGNA (583)

MELITA (137)

NICAEA (69)

ST. AGNES (265, 438)

ST. SYLVESTER (564)

Earnshaw, Robert Henry

Earnshaw, Robert Henry (b. Todmordsen, England, 1856; d. Blackpool, England, 1929) served as organist at Morecambe parish church for three years and at St. Philip, Southport, for one year. Then for a number of years he was organist at Christ Church, Preston. Later he returned to Southport and was a member of the town council. During his later years in Southport, he was greatly interested in the cinema industry. He was living in retirement in Blackpool at the time of his death.

ARIZONA (113)

Edmeston, James

Edmeston, James (b. Wapping, London, England, September 10, 1791; d. Homerton, England, January 7, 1867) was educated to be an architect and surveyor, which vocation he followed from 1816 until his death. His grandfather, Samuel Brewer, was a minister of the Independents in England, but Edmeston joined the Church of England fairly early in life and continued in that church. He wrote nearly 2,000 hymns, many for children. His works include *The Search, and Other Poems* (1817), *Sacred Lyrics* (1820) *One Hundred Hymns for Sunday Schools, and for Particular Occasions* (1821), *Missionary Hymns* (1822), *The Woman of Shunam, and Other Poems* (1829), *Infant Breathings, being Hymns for the Young* (1846), and *Sacred Poetry* (1847).

Savior, Breathe an Evening Blessing (40)

Ellerton, John

Ellerton, John (b. London, England, December 16, 1826; d. Torquay, England, June 15, 1893) was educated at King William's College, Isle of Man, and at Trinity College, Cambridge. He was ordained to the ministry of the Church of England and served in various parishes for the rest of his life. While serving at Brighton, he first wrote hymns for children. He was also interested in social welfare work and was vice-president of the Mechanic's Institution, where he taught courses. Ellerton compiled *Hymns for Schools and Bible Classes* (1859) and gained the reputation of being an expert in hymnology. He wrote some fifty original hymns and also made translations from the Latin. He assisted in the compilation of *Hymns Ancient and Modern* (1875, 1889), *Church Hymns* (1871), and the *London Mission Hymn Book* (1884). His collected hymns were published as *Hymns, Original and Translated* (1888).

God the Almighty One (586)
Our Day of Praise Is Done (167)

Savior, Again to Thy Dear Name (11)
The Day Thou Gavest, Lord, Is Ended (39)
This Is the Day of Light (23)

Elliott, Charlotte

Elliott, Charlotte (b. Clapham, England, March 18, 1789; d. Brighton, England, September 22, 1871) because of a serious illness in 1821, became a complete invalid. In 1822 she met César Malan, the Genevan evangelist who encouraged her to devote her life to religious and altruistic projects. They were friends and correspondents for forty years. She compiled and published *The Invalid's Hymn Book* (1st ed., 1834). Henry Elliott, her brother, published other of her 150 hymns were published in his *Psalms and Hymns for Public, Private and Social Worship* (1835-1848), and in *Hours of Sorrow* (1836), *Hymns for a Week* (1839) and *Thoughts in Verse on Sacred* Subjects (1869).

Just as I Am (346)
My God, My Father, Though I Stray (611)

Ellor, James

Ellor, James (b. Droylsden, Lancashire, England, 1819; d. Newburgh, New York, September 27, 1899) was a hat maker by trade in his hometown. He had native musical talent and led the choir in his local Wesleyan chapel. He later worked for the railroad in England and came to the United States in 1843. Here he returned to his trade of hat making. Ellor was nearly blind for many years before his death and was living with his son in Newburgh at the time of his death.

DIADEM (251)

Elvey, George Job

Elvey, George Job (b. Canterbury, England, March 27, 1816; d. Windlesham, Surrey, England, December 9, 1893) was born of a musical family and was a chorister at Canterbury Cathedral while a boy. He was an accomplished organist during his late teens and served as organist at St. George's Chapel from 1835 to 1882. Elvey received the bachelor of music degree from New College (1838) and was knighted in 1871 after writing the *Festival March* for the marriage of Queen Victoria's daughter Princess Louise Alberta to John Douglas Sutherland Campbell. He also played for the wedding of the Prince of Wales, who became King Edward VII (1901).

DIADEMATA (255, 617)
ST. GEORGE'S WINDSOR (590)

Entwisle, J. Howard

Entwisle, J. Howard (b. 1863; d. 1901. No information is available on this composer.

Sweeter Then All (650)

Est, Thomas

Est, Thomas (b. London, England, c. 1540; d. London, January, 1608). His surname is variously spelled as Este, East, or Easte, as well as Est. A printer licensed to print in 1565 he specialized in music printing and published William Byrd's *Psalms, Sonnets, and Songs of Sadness and Piety* (c. 1587) and the works of other Tudor composers. In 1592 he published his own *Whole Book of Psalms*, which was the first hymnal to have all the musical scores in a single volume. Est printed the *Triumphs of Oriana* (1603), a book of madrigals honoring Queen Elizabeth's memory. He was recognized as the most famous publisher of his day.

WINCHESTER, OLD (131, 375)

Everest, Charles William

Everest, Charles William (b. East Windsor, Connecticut, May 27, 1814; d. Waterbury, Connecticut, January 22, 1877) graduated from Trinity College, Hartford (1838) and was ordained to the ministry of the Episcopal Church (1842). He was rector of the congregation at Hampden, Connecticut, for thirty-one years and was in charge of a school there. At the age of nineteen, he published *Visions of Death and Other Poems*, from which volume the hymn text included in *GSR* is taken.

Take Up Your Cross (503)

Everett, Asa Brooks

Everett, Asa Brooks (b. Virginia, 1828; d. near Nashville, Tennessee, September, 1875) studied to be a physician but abandoned this profession for a career in music. He and his brother L. C. studied in Boston, and Asa studied four more years in Leipzig, Germany. He was associated with his brother and with Rigdon M. McIntosh in the L. C. Everett Company. Asa edited a number of hymnals, the most popular of which was *The Sceptre,* which he compiled with his brother Benjamin (1871) for the Bigelow and Main Company.

FOOTSTEPS (426)

THURA (341)

Ewing, George Wilmeth

Ewing, George Wilmeth (b. Robstown, Texas, January 12, 1923) is the son of Patelford Poindexter and Eugenia Geneva Wilmeth Ewing. He was educated at Abilene Christian University (B.A. in Bible, 1948), and holds the M.A. (1952) and the Ph.D. (1962) degrees from the University of Texas at Austin. He and his wife Mellisse Miller Ewing have six children. He is a master carpenter and taught radar technology in the army during World War II. Ewing has preached among Churches of Christ for 48 years. He was a member of the English faculty at Abilene Christian University from 1955 to 1992, and served as chairman from 1967 to 1981. He is the author of *The Well-Tempered Lyre: Songs and Poems of the Temperance Movement* (SMU Press, 1977) and *In Sundry Times and Divers Manners* (Abilene: Quality Press, 1985).

*Sin Sorrow of Six Thousand Years*æTHE LAMB OF GOD (382)

Excell, Edwin Othello

Excell, Edwin Othello (b. Stark Co., Ohio, December 13, 1851; d. Louisville, Kentucky, June 10, 1921) was the son of a minister of the German Reformed Church. In his early years he was a plasterer and bricklayer, but his native gifts turned him to music. He became a popular singing teacher and was converted while leading the singing in a Methodist revival. He studied under George F. and Frederick Root (1877-1883), then moved to Chicago during in 1883. Here he began his publication of gospel song books. Excell was co-founder with John H. Vincent of the International Sunday School Lessons and was singer for the evangelists Sam Jones and Gypsy Smith. He composed more than 2,000 songs and compiled more than eighty hymnals. Excell was the original printer-publisher for *GS* (1921), which appeared about three weeks before his death.

Amazing Grace (122)
BLESSINGS (545)

Faber, Frederick William

Faber, Frederick William (b. Calverley, Yorkshire, England, June 18, 1814; d. London, England, September 26, 1863) was educated at Shrewsbury and Harrow Schools and at Balliol and University College, Oxford. He was ordained in the Anglican Church in 1849 and, although reared a strict Calvinistic Protestant, under the influence of the Oxford Movement and of John Henry Newman, became a Roman Catholic in 1846. From 1849 until his death, he served as superior in the Brompton Oratory in London. Faber admired the hymns of Newton and Cowper (the *Olney*

Hymns) and wished to produce similar compositions for the use of Roman Catholics. All of his hymns were published after he became a Catholic. These were collected in *Hymns* (1849), *Jesus and Mary—Catholic Hymns for Singing and Reading* (1849), *Oratory Hymns* (1854), and *Hymns* (1862).

Faith of Our Fathers (494)
Father of Mercies (125)
O Savior, Bless Us Ere We Go (13)
There's a Wideness in God's Mercy (308)

Fallersleben, August Heinrich Hoffman von

Fallersleben, August Heinrich Hoffman von (b. 1798; d. 1874) was a noted poet and scholar. With Ernst Friedrich Richter (1808-1879), he collected a number of Silesian sacred and secular folksongs. He assisted in the publication of *Schlesische Volkslieder* (1842), which contained these songs.

SCHÖNSTER HERR JESU (156)

Farjeon, Eleanor

Farjeon, Eleanor (b. Westminster, London, England, February 13, 1881; d. Hampstead, London, England, June 5, 1965) had among her family members the famous English novelist B. L. Farjeon and the actor, Joseph Jefferson. She received a private education. Her first book, *Nursery Rhymes of London Town*, was published in 1916. She published numerous works and received several medals for her publications. He works include *A Nursery in the Nineties* (1935), *The Glass Slipper* (1944), *Silversand and Snow* (1951), and *The Last Four Years* (1951). She became a Roman Catholic when she was seventy years old.

Morning Has Broken (470)

Fawcett, John

Fawcett, John (b. Lidget Green, near Bradford, Yorkshire, England, January 6, 1740; d. Hebden Bridge, England, July 15, 1817) at a young age came under the influence of George Whitefield, associated with the Methodists, and attended the Church of England. He later joined the Baptists, was ordained in 1763, and served churches at Wainsgate, Yorkshire, and Hebden Bridge. He founded the Northern Education Society (now Rawdon College) and published a number of religious writings. Fawcett had a very modest estimate of the value of his poems, most of which were written to be sung at the conclusion of the services which he was conducting. He published *Hymns Adapted to the Circumstances of*

Public Worship and Private Devotion (1782). Brown University conferred upon him the honorary D.D. degree (1811).

> *Lord, Dismiss Us with Thy Blessing* (10)
> *Blest Be the Tie* (394)

Featherstone, William Ralph

Featherstone, William Ralph (b. Montreal, Quebec, Canada, July 23, 1846; d. Montreal, May 20, 1873) was the son of John and Mary Stephenson Featherstone. He was a member of the Wesleyan Methodist Church in Montreal (now St. James United Church). Nothing further is known of this author.

> *My Jesus, I Love Thee* (453)

Fillmore, Frederick Augustus

Fillmore, Frederick Augustus (b. 1856; d. 1925) was a son of Augustus Damon Fillmore and a founder of the Fillmore Brothers Music House of Cincinnati. A farmer and a member of the Christian Church, he edited hymnals for both instrumental and non-instrumental segments of the Stone-Campbell Movement, including *Wonderful Story in Song* (Cincinnati: F. L. Rowe, 1917).

> *I Know That My Redeemer Lives* (507)

Fillmore, James Henry

Fillmore, James Henry (b. Cincinnati, Ohio, June 1, 1849; d. Cincinnati, February 8, 1936) was the oldest son of Augustus Damon and Hannah Lockwood Fillmore. The elder Fillmore was a widely known composer and singing school teacher among the Disciples of Christ. When James's father died in 1865, James assumed his singing school engagements in order to support the family. With his brothers he founded the Fillmore Brothers Music House in Cincinnati. They published Sunday School hymnals and church hymnals for many years, beginning with *Songs of Glory* (1874). Today the business publishes music for band and orchestra. J. H. Fillmore was active among Christian Churches and served as secretary for the American Christian Missionary Society for some years. He edited numerous hymnals, including *New Christian Hymn and Tune Book* (1882-1887). His son, Henry Fillmore, was a noted band director and composer of marches. Henry (1881-1956) often wrote under the pseudonym "Harold Bennett."

> *BATEMAN* (479)
> *Purer in Heart* (484)
> *RESOLUTION* (361)

Fischer, William Gustavus

Fischer, William Gustavus (b. Baltimore, Maryland, October 14, 1935; d. Philadelphia, Pennsylvania, August 12, 1912) attended singing schools and studied music at night while he worked as a bookbinder for J. B. Lippincott and Company in Philadelphia. He became a well-known teacher of music and a choral conductor. Fischer directed the chorus of the Welsh Societies at the bicentennial celebration of the landing of William Penn. He taught music at Girard College (1858-1868) and then went into the piano business with J. E. Gould. He published several Sunday School leaflets containing gospel songs.

HANKEY (309)
FISCHER (631)

Fisher, Albert Christopher

Fisher, Albert Christopher (b. New Bern, North Carolina, March 10, 1886; d. Dallas, Texas, February 6, 1946) was educated at Polytechnic College, Forth Worth, Texas; Vanderbilt University; and Southern Methodist University. He was a general evangelist for the Methodist Church, South, in Texas (1908-1918). He served as a chaplain in World War I and preached in Oklahoma as well as in Texas. Fisher edited *Best Revival Hymns* (Cokesbury Press, 1923).

There's a Glad New Song - REDEEMING LOVE (469)

Flemming, Friedrich Ferdinand

Flemming, Friedrich Ferdinand (b. Neuhausen, Saxony, Germany, February 28, 1778; d. Berlin, Prussia (Germany), May 27, 1813) was educated as a physician at Wittenberg, Jena, Vienna, and Trieste, and went to Berlin to practice, where he remained for the rest of his life. Music was his greatest hobby, and he composed a number of part songs for men's choral groups.

FLEMMING (568)

Flowerdew, Alice

Flowerdew, Alice (b. 1759; d. Ipswich, England, September 23, 1830) was the wife of Daniel Flowerdew, an official for the British government in Jamaica. Mr. Flowerdew died in 1801, and Alice returned to England where she kept a ladies' boarding school at Islington. While there she was a member of the Baptist church meeting in Worship Street. She later resided in Bury St. Edmunds and, for some years afterwards, in

Ipswich until her death. Mrs. Flowerdew published *Poems on Moral and Religious Subjects* (1st ed., 1803). In the 3rd edition (1811), the hymn included in *GSR* appeared, beginning "Fountain of Mercy, God of Love."

Father of Mercies, Day by Day (125)

Fosdick, Harry Emerson

Fosdick, Harry Emerson (b. Buffalo, New York, May 24, 1878; d. New York, New York City, October 5, 1969) was educated at Colgate University, Union Theological Seminary, and Columbia University. He began his ministry at the First Baptist Church, Montclair, New Jersey (1904-1915). He was also professor of practical theology at Union Seminary in Montclair. From 1919 to 1926 he was minister for the First Presbyterian Church in New York City and then of the Park Avenue Baptist Church, which became the Riverside Church in New York (1926-1946). He was one of the best-known and most influential preachers of his day. His published works include *The Meaning of Prayer* (1915), *A Guide to Understanding the Bible* (1938), *Living Under Tension* (1941), *On Being a Real Person* (1943), and his autobiography, *The Living of These Days* (1956).

God of Grace and God of Glory (581)

Foster, Frederick William

Foster, Frederick William (b. Bradford, England, August 1, 1760; d. Ockbrook, near Derby, England, April 12, 1835) was educated at Fulneck, Yorkshire, England, and at the Moravian College at Barby, Prussian Saxony. He was ordained a minister in the Moravian Church and in 1818 became a bishop. Foster edited the *Moravian Hymn Book* (1801) and the *Supplement* to that hymnal (1808). He was a good translator of German hymns.

God Himself Is with Us (7)

Foulkes, William Hiram

Foulkes, William Hiram (b. Quincy, Michigan, June 26, 1877; d. Smithtown, Long Island, New York, January 1962) had many ancestors who were Presbyterian ministers, as was he. Educated at Emporia College (Kansas), Kansas Wesleyan University, and McCormick Theological Seminary (Chicago), he also did graduate study at New College, Edinburgh, Scotland. He served Presbyterian churches in several states and was moderator of the General Assembly of the Presbyterian Church, USA (1937). Foulkes retired in 1941. He published many volumes of poetry, including *Living Bread from the Fourth Gospel* (1914), *Sunset by the*

Wayside (1917), and *Homespun, Along Friendly Roads* (1936). He also helped to compile the *Handbook* to the *Presbyterian Hymnal* (1935).
Take Thou Our Minds, Dear Lord (605)

Francis of Assisi

Francis of Assisi (b. Assisi, Italy, c. 1182; d. Assisi, October 4, 1226) was the son of Pietro Bernardoni, a wealthy cloth merchant. After a youth spent in self-indulgence, he fell ill in 1202, which caused a great reformation in his life. He gave the remainder of his life to prayer, poverty, and the caring for society's rejects. He founded the order of the Franciscans. Francis loved nature supremely, loved music, and had a great familiarity with the music of the troubadours.
All Creatures of Our God and King (66)

Franck, Johann

Franck, Johann (b. Guben, Brandenburg, Germany, June 1, 1618; d. Guben, June 18, 1677) was the son of Johann Franck, a lawyer and councilor at Guben. His father died in 1620, but his uncle, Adam Tielckau, adopted him and sent him to the University of Königsberg (1638) to study law. This was the only German university which was still intact during the Thirty Years War. He began the practice of law in 1645 in Guben. During the next several years he served on the town council (1648), was mayor (1661), and was a representative to the Diet of Lower Lusatia (1671). Franck ranks second only to Paul Gerhardt as a writer of hymns in German. He moved German hymnody to a more subjective and mystical sort of poetry. His hymns were published in the collections of his friends, Weichmann, Crüger, and Peter. Many of these were collected in his *Geistliches Sion* (1674).
Jesus, Priceless Treasure (350)

Franz, Ignaz

Franz, Ignaz (b. Protzau, Silesia, October 12 1719; d. Breslau, Germany, 1790) was educated at Glaz and Breslau, and ordained as a Roman Catholic priest at Olmutz in 1742. He was chaplain at Gross-Glogau (1753), and afterwards assessor to the office of the apostolic vicar in Breslau until the day of his death. He exerted a great influence on eighteenth-century Roman Catholic hymnody. His work includes the *Katholisches Gesangbuch* (1774) and a tunebook (1778).
Holy God, We Praise Thy Name (48)

Gabriel, Charles Hutchinson

Gabriel, Charles Hutchinson (b. Wilton, Iowa, August 18, 1856; d. Los Angeles, California, September 15, 1932) grew up on a farm in Iowa and early showed an interest in music. He taught himself to play the organ and became quickly and widely known as a singing-school teacher. He served as music director for Grace Methodist Episcopal Church in San Francisco (1890-1892) and then moved to Chicago. He published a number of song books between 1895 and 1912, and in the latter year became associated with the Homer Rodeheaver Company. He continued this relationship composing, writing, and editing until his death, . Gabriel's work touches the Stone-Campbell hymnody in that he helped to edit *The New Christian Hymn Book* with T. B. Larimore (Nashville: McQuiddy Printing Company, 1907). Gabriel often used the pseudonym "Charlotte G. Homer."

Hear the Sweet Voice - ONLY A STEP (319)
Higher Ground (630)
I Stand Amazed - MY SAVIOR'S LOVE (230)
In Loving-Kindness Jesus Came - HE LIFTED ME (264)
McDANIEL (471)
SHARON (486)
There's a Call Comes Ringing - McCABE (439)
When All My Labors and Trials Are O'er - GLORY SONG (658)

Gaither, Gloria

Gaither, Gloria (b. Battle Creek, Michigan, March 4, 1942) was educated at Anderson College, Anderson, Indiana, receiving a degree in English, French, and Sociology. During her college years she met William J. Gaither, who became her husband, . She taught school in Alexandria, Indiana, for three years and now sings as part of the Gaither Trio.

God Sent His Son (653)

Gaither, William J.

Gaither, William J. (b. Alexandria, Indiana, March 28, 1936) was educated at Anderson College, Anderson, Indiana, majoring in English. He taught at Alexandria High School for six years and is now president of the Gaither Music Company. Gaither has won numerous awards and has written over 200 songs. He was the Gospel Music Association's "Songwriter of the Year" for six consecutive years. He sings as part of the Gaither Trio, made up of himself, his wife Gloria, and his brother Dan.

God Sent His Son - RESURRECTION (653)

Gardiner, William

Gardiner, William (b. Leicester, England, March 15, 1770; d. Leicester, November 16, 1853) was the son of a hosiery manufacturer and followed in his father's footsteps. In addition, he was particularly a lover of music and devoted his life to introducing the works of Beethoven, Haydn, and Mozart into England. Gardiner's extensive travels in his business on the continent brought him knowledge of the best melodies being produced there. He published his *Sacred Melodies from Haydn, Mozart, and Beethoven, Adapted to the Best English Poets and Appropriated to the Use of the British Church* (London: 1812; Vol. II, 1815). Gardiner's two collections became a standard source book and model for other composers in the nineteenth century. The American Lowell Mason was particularly influenced by Gardiner. Other works by Gardiner include his *Music and Friends* (3 vols., 1838-1853); a translation of Beyle's *Lives of Haydn and Mozart*, from the French, and a work on the science of acoustics, *The Music of Nature* (1832).

BELMONT (388)
GERMANY (503)

Gauntlett, Henry John

Gauntlett, Henry John (b. Wellington, Shropshire, England, July 9, 1805; d. Kensington, London, England, February 21, 1876) was educated both in law and in music, was an organist, and composed more than 10,000 hymn tunes. He was an important figure in English Victorian church music. Gauntlett was organist in his father's church at Olney when he was nine years old. He was admitted to the bar but gave up his practice in 1844 to devote his life to music. The Archbishop of Canterbury conferred on him the honorary Mus.D. degree in 1843 for his contributions to church music. Gauntlett's publications include *Hymnal for Matins and Evensong* (1844), *The Church Hymnal and Tune-book* (1844-1851), *Cantus Melodici* (1845), *The Congregational Psalmist* (1851), and *Tunes, New and Old* (1868).

ST. ALPHEGE (673)
STUTTGART (17, 119, 123)

Gellert, Christian Furchtegott

Gellert, Christian Furchtegott (b. Hainichen, Saxony, July 4, 1715; d. Leipzig, Germany, December 13, 1769) was the son of a Lutheran minister and was educated at the University of Leipzig. He entered the ministry, but physical problems forced him to abandon it. He was a private tutor for a time and then taught at his university, ultimately becoming professor of philosophy. Goethe and Lessing were among his pupils. He published *Tales and Fables* (1746-1748) and *Spiritual Odes and Songs* (1757), which contained many of his own hymns.

Jesus Lives, and So Shall I (550)

Gerhardt, Paul

Gerhardt, Paul (b. Gräfenhainichen, near Wittenberg, Germany, March 12,1607; d. Lübben, Germany, May 27, 1676) was the son of a burgermeister of his native city and was educated in the Elector's school at Grimma and at the University of Wittenberg. He became tutor to the family of Andreas Barthold, an attorney in Berlin, in 1642. In 1655 he married Barthold's daughter Anna. Gerhardt began to write hymns during his stay in Berlin, and many of them were published in Johann Crüger's *Praxis Pietatis Melica*. He was ordained to the Lutheran ministry at the age of forty-four and preached in churches in Berlin and elsewhere. He served at St. Nicholas Church in Berlin where Crüger was located, but was removed from his post because of his siding against the Elector Friedrich Wilhelm in a dispute over Lutheran as opposed to Reformed Church doctrine. In 1668 his wife died, a disastrous blow to him. He became minister at Lübben and remained there until his death. William Reynolds says that Gerhard's hymns "mark the transition in Lutheran hymnody from the confession and ecclesiastical hymns of an earlier era to the hymns of subjective, devotional piety" (*Hymns of Our Faith*, 298).

Come, Give Now to Christ All Honor (184)
Give to the Winds Thy Fears (548)
Jesus, Thy Boundless Love to Me (621)
Now Rest Beneath Night's Shadow l(82)
O How Shall I Receive Thee (189)

Giardini, Felice de

Giardini, Felice de (b. Turin, Italy, April 12, 1716; d. Moscow, Russia, June 8, 1796) was a chorister in the Cathedral in Milan, Italy, and studied with Paladini. He also studied the violin with Somis. He played in various orchestras in Italy, toured Germany, and came to London in 1750. Giardini lived in England from 1751 to 1784 and had the applause of the aristocracy, including the Countess of Huntingdon. He wrote a few hymn tunes as a favor to Lady Huntingdon, which were included in Martin Madan's *A Collection of Psalms and Hymn Tunes* (1769). After going through several seasons in England, during which his operas were not accepted, he went to Russia in 1796 and died there a few months later.

ITALIAN HYMN (88, 400)

Gibbons, Orlando

Gibbons, Orlando (b. Oxford, England, c. December 25, 1583; d. Canterbury, England, June 5, 1625) was a chorister at King's College, Cambridge (1596), and was appointed organist of the Chapel Royal (1601), where he remained until his death. He was recognized as the outstanding organist of his day. In 1623 he became organist of Westminster Abbey and conducted the music for the funeral of King James I in 1625. Gibbons provided sixteen tunes for George Wither's *The Hymns and Songs of the Church* (1623).

SONG 13 (80)

SONG 34 (501)

Gibbs, Ada Rose

Gibbs, Ada Rose (b. 1865; d. 1905) was an English woman who was active in the Keswick Convention movement. She was the wife of William James Gibbs, superintendent of the Methodist Central Hall, Bromley, Kent. She published *Twenty-four Gems of Sacred Song* (c. 1900). No further information is available.

CHANNELS (596)

Gilmore, Joseph Henry

Gilmore, Joseph Henry (b. Boston, Massachusetts, April 29, 1834; d. Rochester, New York, July 23, 1918) was educated at Phillips Academy (Andover, Mass.), Brown University, and Newton Theological Seminary. He graduated in 1861 and was ordained to the Baptist ministry in 1862. During 1863-1864 he served as private secretary to his father, Joseph A. Gilmore, who was governor of New Hampshire. He taught Hebrew at the Rochester Theological Seminary (1867) and, beginning in 1868, was professor of logic, rhetoric, and English literature at the University of Rochester, remaining there until his retirement in 1911. His publications include *The Art of Expression* (1876), *Familiar Chats on Books and Reading* (1905), and *Outlines of English and American Literature* (1905).

He Leadeth Me! O Blessed Thought (133)

Gladden, Washington

Gladden, Washington (b. Pottsgrove, Pennsylvania, February 22, 1836; d. Columbus, Ohio, July 2, 1918) was educated at Williams College (1859) and ordained a Congregational minister in 1860. He served churches in New York and Massachusetts and then became minister for the First

Congregational Church, Columbus, Ohio (1882). He remained there until his retirement in 1914. Gladden was an early and strenuous proponent of the "social gospel" and of the theories of higher criticism.

O Master, Let Me Walk with Thee (441)

Gläser, Carl Gotthelf

Gläser, Carl Gotthelf (b. Weissenfels, Germany, May 4, 1784; d. Barmen, Germany, April 16, 1829) received his early training in music from his father and later studied under Johann Hiller and August Miller at St. Thomas's School, Leipzig. In Leipzig he also was trained in the violin under the Italian Campagnoli. Gläser moved to Barmen several years later and taught voice, piano, and violin. He also composed and conducted choral music.

AZMON (2, 504, 505)

Golden, William M.

No accurate information is available on this author/composer. George Pullen Jackson said that he lived in Mississippi.

To Canaan's Land I'm on My Way - GOLDEN (665)

Gordon, Adoniram Judson

Gordon, Adoniram Judson (b. New Hampton, New Hampshire, April 19,1836; d. Boston, Massachusetts, February 2, 1895) was named for the pioneer Baptist missionary to Burma, who was greatly admired by Alexander Campbell. He was educated at Brown University and Newton Theological Seminary and ordained to the Baptist ministry (1863). He served Baptist churches in Jamaica Plains, Massachusetts, and was in Boston, beginning in 1869. Gordon edited *The Service of Song for Baptist Churches* (1871) and *The Vestry Hymn and Tune Book* (1872). He was also editor of the monthly magazine *The Watchword*. Gordon was a great friend of Dwight L. Moody and assisted greatly in Moody's campaign in Boston. He also wrote a series of devotional books entitled *Quiet Talks*. Gordon College and Seminary near Boston are named for him.

GORDON (453)

Gottschalk, Louis Moreau

Gottschalk, Louis Moreau (b. New Orleans, Louisiana, May 8, 1829; d. Rio de Janeiro, Brazil, December 18, 1869), born of an English father and a French mother, he was a child musical prodigy. He studied in

Paris under Halle and Stamaty and toured France, Switzerland, and Spain in 1852. He returned to the United States and toured with great applause, being recognized as America's first piano virtuoso. Gottschalk incorporated into his compositions not only the prevailing eighteenth-century European style but also Creole and Caribbean folk music. He died of yellow fever while on a tour of South America. Gottschalk is remembered for such compositions as *The Dying Poet*, *La Mort*, *The Last Hope*, and a symphony, *La Nuit des Tropiques*.

MERCY (293, 637)

Goudimel, Claude

Goudimel, Claude (b. Besançon, France, c. 1505; d. Lyons, France, August 27, 1572). Little is known of Goudimel's life. He was a composer of both secular and sacred pieces and was providing polyphonic settings of the Geneva psalms for both Roman Catholic and Protestant choirs by 1551. Some sources declare that he was in Rome in 1540, where he conducted a school of music that included among its pupils Giovanni Pierluigi da Palestrina, the great Roman Catholic composer. This assertion, however, is very uncertain. About 1560 he became a Protestant and joined the Huguenots. His harmonizations of the psalm tunes used in the *Geneva Psalter* became the basis for future harmonizations by various composers. His works include *Les Pseaumes de David* (1564) and *Les Pseaumes mis en rime* (1565). When the St. Bartholomew's Day massacre, which had begun in Paris, spread to Lyons, Goudimel was murdered by Roman Catholics in that city.

TOULON (370)

Gould, John Edgar

Gould, John Edgar (b. Bangor, Maine, 1822; d. Algiers, Africa, March 4, 1875) showed musical talent very early in life and throughout his life was involved in the music business. With Edward L. White he compiled *The Modern Harp* (1846), *The Wreath of School Songs* (1847), *The Tyrolian Lyre* (1847) and *The Sunday School Lute* (1848). He owned music stores in New York City and in Philadelphia. Gould compiled *Harmonia Sacra* (1861) and *Songs of Gladness for the Sabbath School* (1869). He opened a music store and piano business with William Gustavus Fischer in Philadelphia (1868). When his health failed, he traveled to England, Europe, and Africa in a vain attempt to regain it.

PILOT (534)

Gower, John Henry

Gower, John Henry (b. Rugby, Warwickshire, England, May 25, 1855; d. Denver, Colorado, July 30, 1922) was musically inclined from childhood. At age twelve he was assistant organist at Windsor Castle. He was educated at Oxford (1876, 1883) and became master of music at Trent College, Nottingham (1876-1887). In 1887 he migrated to the United States and ultimately settled in Denver, Colorado, where he had mining interests. In Denver he served as organist at St. John's Cathedral and at the Central Presbyterian Church. In 1893 he moved to Chicago to be organist at the Church of the Epiphany. Gower's compositions include various songs and a cantata, *The Good Shepherd.* He published *Original Tunes* (1890), with a revision in 1919.

GOWER'S LITANY (5832)
MEDITATION (226)

Graeff, Frank E.

Graeff, Frank E. (b. Tamaqua, Pennsylvania, December 19, 1860; d. Ocean Grove, New Jersey, July 29, 1919) was reared in the so-called "Pennsylvania Dutch" country. Early in life he decided to be a minister and was ordained in 1890, serving in the Philadelphia Conference of the Methodist Church. He preached in various places until his retirement to Ocean Grove, New Jersey. Graeff loved little children and wrote many stories for them. He was the author of more than 200 hymns and a novel, *The Minister's Twins.*

Does Jesus Care? (642)

Grant, Robert

Grant, Robert (b. Bengal, India, 1779; d. Dalpoorie, India, July 9, 1838) was the son of Charles Grant, a director of the East India Company. He was educated for the law at Magdalene College, Cambridge, and was admitted to the bar in 1807. Afterwards he served as a member of Parliament and became Judge Advocate General in 1832. In 1833 he sponsored a bill in Parliament to give the Jews in England their civil liberties. In 1834 he was knighted by King William IV and sent to India as governor of Bombay. Grant is known to have written twelve hymns, which appeared in the *Christian Observer* and in H. V. Elliott's *Psalms and Hymns* (1835). These were published by his brother after his death and entitled *Sacred Poems* (1839).

O Worship the King (87)

Greatorex, Henry Wellington

Greatorex, Henry Wellington (b. Burton-on-Trent, Derbyshire, England, December 24, 1813; d. Charleston, South Carolina, September 10, 1858) was the grandson of Anthony Greatorex and the son of Thomas Greatorex, organist at Carlisle Cathedral and at Westminster Abbey during the reign of George IV. He received his musical training from his father. In 1839 he came to the United States and served as organist at Center Church in Hartford, Connecticut. In 1846 he moved to New York City and served as organist for St. Paul's Church and for Calvary Church. He moved to Charleston, South Carolina in 1853 as organist for an Episcopal church there, but died in a yellow fever epidemic. Greatorex compiled the *Collection of Psalm and Hymn Tunes, Chants, Anthems and Sentences for the Use of the Protestant Episcopal Church in America* (1851).

MANOAH (260, 625)

Green, Joseph Franklin

Green, Joseph Franklin (b. Waco, Texas, June 6, 1924) is the son of a Baptist minister. He graduated from Texas Wesleyan College and from Southwestern Baptist Theological Seminary. After serving in the army during World War II, he was ordained to the Baptist ministry, served churches in Texas and Colorado, and then went to work for the Broadman Press, Nashville, Tennessee. His works include *The Heart of the Gospel* and *Biblical Foundations for Church Music.* He has also published hymn interpretations in *The Church Musician* for the Sunday School Board of the Southern Baptist Convention.

Come, Come, Ye Saints (128)
Thy Supper, Lord, Before Us Spread (384)

Gregory the Great

Gregory the Great (b. Rome, Italy, 540; d. Rome, 604) was born of wealthy and pious parents. His father, Gordianus, was of senatorial rank in Rome; his mother's name was Silvia. He received a good education and was a member of the Roman senate. Upon his father's death, he used his immense fortune for religious purposes and became himself a Benedictine monk. He succeeded Pelagius as bishop of Rome, becoming Gregory I (590). It was Gregory who sent the monk Augustine to Britain in A.D. 597, thus bringing Christianity to the island. It was the work of Gregory to complete and authorize the liturgy of the Western Church. Edward Dickinson calls the chant named for Gregory "the true ideal of music." He says:

This ideal is found in the distinction of the church style from the secular style, the expression of the universal mood of prayer, rather than the expression of individual, fluctuating, passionate emotion with which secular music deals—that rapt, pervasive, exalted tone which makes no attempts at detailed painting of events or superficial mental states, but seems rather to symbolize the fundamental sentiments of humility, awe, hope, and love which mingle all particular experiences in the common offering that surges upward from the heart of the Church to its Lord and Master. (*Music in the Western Church,* 69).

Father, We Praise Thee (26)

Grindal, Gracia

Grindal, Gracia (b. Powers Lake, North Dakota, May 4, 1943) lived in North Dakota until the age of twelve, when her family moved to Salem, Oregon. She was educated at Augsburg College (1965) and the University of Arkansas (1969). She now teaches poetry and writing at Luther College. Her articles have appeared in various church journals and secular publications. She was a member of the hymn text committee of the Inter-Lutheran Commission on Worship (1973-1978) and is now a member of the editorial advisory board of *The Hymn,* which is the official organ of the Hymn Society in the United States and Canada.

Out of the Depths I Cry to You (549)

Grinfield, Thomas

Grinfield, Thomas (b. England, 1788; d. England, 1870) was educated at Paul's Cray, Kent, and at Trinity College, Cambridge. He became a priest in the Church of England (1813) and was rector of Shirland, Derbyshire, beginning in 1827. His published works include *Epistles and Miscellaneous Poems* (1815), *The Omnipresence of God, with Other Sacred Poems* (1824), and a *Century of Original Sacred Songs composed for Favourite Airs* (1836).

O How Kindly Hast Thou Led Me (142)

Grüber, Franz Xavier

Grüber, Franz Xavier (b. Unterweizberg, near Hochburg, Austria, November 25, 1787; d. Hallein, near Salzburg, Austria, June 7, 1863) was the son of a linen weaver who wished his son to follow his trade. Despite his father's objections, he learned to play the violin and later studied organ with Georg Hartdobler. He taught in the Catholic school at Arnsdorf (1807-

1829) and for a time was organist at St. Nikolaus Church at Oberndorf (1816). From 1828 to 1832, he was headmaster of a school in Berndorf and organist at Hallein from 1833 until his death. Although he wrote many compositions, his fame rests on his tune which is wedded to Joseph Mohr's "Silent Night."

STILLE NACHT (202)

Gruntvig, Nikolai Frederik Severin

Gruntvig, Nikolai Frederik Severin (b. Udby, Seeland, September 8, 1873; d. Vartov, Denmark, September 2, 1872) was the son of an Evangelical Lutheran minister and was educated at the University of Copenhagen. He went through a period of doubt during his years at the university, but the spiritual state of the people drove him back to his faith. In 1811 he was ordained to the Lutheran ministry and became one of Denmark's greatest preachers, educators, and hymnists. He led the way in bringing reforms to Denmark's educational system and was honored with the title of bishop by King Frederik VII (1863). Gruntvig published *Sang-Vark til den Danske Kirke* (1837) and *Nyeste Skilderie af Kjobenhagen* (1817). After his death, his works were published under the title *Hymns and Spiritual Songs*.

Built on a Rock (362)

Guirey, Ida

No information is available on this author.
Jesus, Rose of Sharon (486)

Gurney, John Hampden

Gurney, John Hampden (b. Serjeants' Inn, London, August 15, 1802; d. London, March 8, 1862) was the son of Sir John Gurney, a baron of the exchequer. He was educated at Trinity College, Cambridge (1824), and became a minister in the Church of England. From 1827 to 1844, he was curate of Lutterworth and was later prebendary of St. Paul's Cathedral. He supported various religious societies of his day, including the SPCK. His works include *Church Psalmody* (1853), the Lutterworth collection, entitled *A Collection of Hymns for Public Worship* (1838), and the Marylebone collection, entitled *Psalms and Hymns for Public Worship* (1851).

We Saw Thee Not (495)

Hall, J. Lincoln

Hall, J. Lincoln (b. Philadelphia, Pennsylvania, November 4, 1866; d. Philadelphia, November 29, 1930) was educated at the University of Pennsylvania and in later years was awarded the honorary Mus.D. degree by Harriman University. He helped to found the Hall-Mack Publishing Company of Philadelphia and edited, with others, a number of hymnals. He was a prominent song leader.

My Savior Cares (642)

Hammond, William

Hammond, William (b. Battle, Sussex, England, January 6, 1719; d. London, England, August 19, 1783) was educated at St. John's College, Cambridge. In 1743 he became a member of the Calvinistic Methodists and in 1745 joined the Moravian Brethren. Hammond was among the earliest of Englishmen to translate Latin hymns into English for congregational use. He wrote his autobiography in Greek. Among his published works is the hymnal *Psalms, Hymns, and Spiritual Songs* (1745).

Awake, and Sing the Song (153)
Lord, We Come Before Thee Now (4)

Handel, George Frederick

Handel, George Frederick (b. Halle, Germany, February 23, 1685; d. London, England, April 14, 1759) was a musical prodigy who gave his life to music even though his father wished him to become a lawyer. He studied under F. W. Zachaw in Halle, played in the Hamburg opera orchestra, and then performed in Italy. In 1713 he came to England and made his home there for the rest of his life. Handel was a great favorite of King George II. His most famous composition is the *Messiah* (1741), which was first performed in Dublin, Ireland. Handel became totally blind in 1752.

ANTIOCH (256)
BRADFORD (557)
CHRISTMAS (543)
JUDAS MACCABEUS (240)
SEMELE (563)

Hankey, Arabella Catherine

Hankey, Arabella Catherine (b. Clapham, England, 1834; d. London, England, 1911), usually known as "Kate," was the daughter of

Thomas Hankey, who belonged to William Wilberforece's "Clapham Sect." In her youth she began to teach Sunday School classes and organized a large class for shop girls and another for girls of her own social circle in London. A trip to South Africa to accompany her invalid brother home again stirred her interest in foreign missions, which never thereafter waned. She also spent much time in her later life visiting the London hospitals. Miss Hankey published *The Old, Old Story and Other Verses* (1879).

I Love to Tell the Story (309)

Hansen, Fred C. M.

Hansen, Fred C. M. (b. Vejle, Denmark, June 25, 1888; d. Blair, Nebraska April 4, 1965) migrated with his family to the United States in 1890. He was educated at Dana College and at Trinity Seminary in Blair, Nebraska, and became an ordained minister in the Danish Evangelical Lutheran Church. He served churches in Iowa, Wisconsin, and Chicago, Illinois. From 1939 to 1943 he was president of the Iowa district of the United Evangelical Lutheran Church. Hansen helped to found the Lutheran Bible Camp at Lake Okoboji, Iowa, and was editor of several religious papers. He was a member of the editorial committees for the *Hymnal for Church and Home* (1927), *The Junior Hymnal* (1928), and the *Service Book and Hymnal* (1958). He retired in 1958 and lived the remaining years of his life in Blair, Nebraska.

Built on a Rock (362)

Harding, James Proctor

Harding, James Proctor (b. London, England, May 19, 1850; d. London, February 21, 1911) was a clerk in the Inland Revenue Department in London (1867-1909). He was an amateur musician and organist for St. Andrew's Church, Islington, London, for thirty-five years. He composed a great deal of music for the children's choir festivals at the Giffords Hall Mission, London.

Morning Star (211)

Harrison, Ralph

Harrison, Ralph (b. Chinley, Derbyshire, England, September 10, 1748; d. Manchester, Lancashire, England, November 4. 1810) was the son of a dissenting minister, William Harrison. He was educated at Warrington Academy, a school under the auspices of the Unitarians. He became an Independent minister and preached at Shrewsbury beginning in 1769 and at Cross Street Chapel, Manchester, from 1771 until his death.

Harrison was co-founder of the Manchester Academy (1786) and was classical tutor there. He published *The Rudiments of English Grammar* (1777) and *Sacred Harmony* (1784, 1791). He seems to have exerted considerable influence over various independent hymn collections of his day.

CAMBRIDGE (11, 145)

Hart, Joseph

Hart, Joseph (b. London, England, 1712; d. London, May 24, 1768). His early life is quite obscure. His brother-in-law, John Hughes, declared him to have been "a teacher of the learned languages." He seems to have led a dissolute yet searching life in his early years. Hart was converted in the Moravian Chapel, Fetter Lane, London (1757), and in 1759 he became minister to the Jewin Street Independent Chapel, London, where he remained until his death. He was a powerful preacher and an ardent Calvinist. Twenty thousand people attended his funeral at Bunhill Fields. His works include *Hymns Composed on Various Subjects, with the Author's Experience* (1759) and a *Supplement* (1762).

Come, Ye Sinners, Poor and Needy (329)
That Dreadful Night (372)

Hartsough, Palmer

Hartsough, Palmer (b. Redford, Michigan, May 7, 1844; d. Plymouth, Michigan, October 24, 1932) was the son of Wells and Thankful Palmer Hartsough. His father was active in the Baptist Church and helped to organize the Michigan Baptist Convention (1836). He attended Kalamazoo College and Michigan State Normal College and became interested in music. Hartsough taught singing schools for several years and then opened a music studio in Rock Island, Illinois. He was also associated with the Fillmore Music House in Cincinnati, Ohio (1893-1903), writing many texts for James H. Fillmore. He became an ordained Baptist minister in 1906 and served a church in Ontario, Michigan for thirteen years (1914-1927). He retired in 1927 and lived his remaining years in Plymouth, Michigan.

I Am Resolved No Longer to Linger (361)

Hassler, Hans Leo

Hassler, Hans Leo (b. Nuremberg, Germany, October 15, 1564; d. Frankfurt, Germany, June 8, 1612) was the son of Isaak Hassler, an organist at Nuremberg. He studied in Italy with Andrea Gabrielli (1584). From 1585 to 1600, he was organist to Octavian II in Augsburg, and then became organist to Emperor Rudolph II in Prague. In this city he manufactured musical clocks. In 1601 Hassler returned to Nuremberg to be organist at the Frauenkirche and was also kappellmeister of the city (1601-1609). He married in 1604, and he and his wife resided in Ulm. Afterwards he was organist to the Elector of Saxony at Dresden. Hassler died of tuberculosis. His works include *Cantiones Sacrae* (1591), *Neue Deutsche Gesang* (1596), *Psalmen und christliche Gesang* (1607), and *Kirchengesänge, Psalmen und geistliche Lieder* (1608).

PASSION CHORALE (221)

Hastings, Thomas

Hastings, Thomas (b. Washington, Litchfield County, Connecticut, October 15, 1784; d. New York, New York, May 15, 1872) was the son of a physician. In 1786 the family moved to the then frontier of Clinton, New York. Hastings, an albino and nearsighted, taught himself music and at eighteen was directing the village choir. He compiled the *Utica Collection* (later entitled *Musica Sacra*) in 1816 and edited the *Western Recorder,* a religious paper, in Utica in 1828. In 1832 he moved to New York City and assisted Lowell Mason in editing *Spiritual Songs for Social Worship.* He also directed the choir of the Bleecker Street Presbyterian Church for many years. Hastings was ever an advocate for musical progress and excellence: he opposed shape-note music and notation; founded the *Musical Magazine* (1836); harmonized some American melodies in his *Indian Melodies* (1845); and, as a member of the Presbyterian Church, edited *The Presbyterian Psalmodist* (1855). He edited in all about fifty collections, and wrote over six hundred hymns and one thousand tunes. The University of the City of New York conferred the Mus.D. degree on him in 1858.

CONSOLATOR (338)
Hail to the Brightness of Zion's Glad Morning (425)
RETREAT (561)
TOPLADY (356)

Hatch, Edwin

Hatch, Edwin (b. Derby, England, September 4, 1835; d. Oxford, England, November 10, 1889) was born to nonconformist parents and was educated at King Edward's School, Birmingham, and at Pembroke College, Oxford (1857). He became an Anglican in 1853 and a priest in 1859. Hatch migrated to Canada shortly thereafter and taught at Trinity College, Toronto, and was rector of a high school in Quebec. He returned to England in 1867 and, subsequently, was vice-principal of St. Mary's Hall, Oxford, rector of

Purleigh, Essex (1883), and university reader in ecclesiastical history (1885-1889). He delivered the Bampton Lectures (1880) and the Hibbert Lectures (1888).

Breathe on Me, Breath of God (295)

Hatton, John

Hatton, John (b. Warrington, England, c. 1710; d. St. Helen's, England,

December, 1793) is a very obscure composer who wrote one of the world's most widely used tunes. He is believed to have resided in St. Helen's, in Windle township, on Duke Street. Apparently he was a member of the Presbyterian chapel in St. Helen's, where his funeral was preached.

DUKE STREET (67, 261, 359)

Hausman, Julie Katherina von

Hausman, Julie Katherina von (b. Riga, Latvia, 1825-26; d. Wosso, Estonia, August 15, 1901) was one of seven sisters, the children of a teacher. When she was quite young, her family moved to Mitau, where her father taught in the gymnasium, yet she was educated under private tutors. She suffered severely from migraine headaches. Her father was a town councilor, but moved to Riga shortly before his death in 1864. She afterwards lived with one of her sisters at Biarritz, France (1866-1870), and then with another sister, Elizabeth, in St. Petersburg, Russia. She was an intellectually active woman, served as governess in private homes from time to tome, and worked together with three of her sisters for several years. After the death of two of her sisters, she and another sister moved to Wosso, Estonia, where she lived until her death. Her works include *Hausbrot*, a devotional study, and *Maiblumen, Lieder einer Stillen im Lande*, which was published by Gustav Knak in Berlin.

Take Thou My Hands and Lead Me (527)

Havergal, William Henry

Havergal, William Henry, b. High Wycombe, Buckinghamshire, England, January 8, 1793; d. Leamington, Warwickshire, England, April 19, 1870), the son of William Havergal, was educated at St. Edmund's Hall, Oxford. He became a deacon in the Church of England (1816) and a priest (1817). A carriage accident forced him into retirement from his clerical duties for a number of years. During this interim, he pursued the study of church music. When he returned to active church work in 1842, he held, among other offices, that of honorary canon of Worcester Cathedral

(1845). Havergal reprinted Thomas Ravenscroft's *Whole Book of Psalms* with his own introduction (1845), and compiled *Old Church Psalmody* (1847), *A History of the Old Hundredth Psalm Tune* (1854), and *A Hundred Psalm and Hymn Tunes* (1859).

SWABIA (23)
FRANCONIA (379, 499)

Havergal, Frances Ridley

Havergal, Frances Ridley (b. Astley, England, December 14, 1836; d. Oystermouth, Glamorganshire, Wales, June 3, 1879) was the daughter of William Henry Havergal, who, at her birth, was rector of Astley. She was educated at Mrs. Teed's school while her father was rector at St. Nicholas, Worcester, but because of frail health received little formal education. She, however, made herself master of several modern languages, as well as Greek and Hebrew. She began writing verse at age seven, and at age fifteen she gave her heart completely to Christ. Miss Havergal lived with her father during his lifetime and wrote hundreds of poems. After his death, she resided at Caswall Bay, Swansea. Her poems are filled with the joy of salvation in Jesus Christ.

I Bring My Sins to Thee (347)
I Gave My Life for Thee (315)
Is It for Me, Dear Savior (171)
Lord, Speak to Me (622)
Take My Life and Let It Be (608)

Hawks, Annie Sherwood

Hawks, Annie Sherwood (b. Hoosick, New York, May 28, 1836; d. Bennington, Vermont, January 3, 1918) was the daughter of Marvin and Carolyn Bradt Sherwood. She lived most of her life in Brooklyn, New York, and attended the Hanson Place Baptist Church, where Robert Lowry, minister, greatly encouraged her in the writing of hymns. She is known to have written some four hundred. She married Charles H. Hawks in 1859. After his death in 1888, she lived with a son and his family in Bennington, Vermont.

I Need Thee Every Hour (574)

Haydn, Franz Joseph

Haydn, Franz Joseph (b. Rohrau, Austria, March 31, 1732; d. Vienna, Austria, May 31, 1809), the son of a wheelwright, received his initial musical training in the choir school of St. Stephen's in Vienna. His musical genius was soon recognized, and he ultimately became kapellmeister in the court of Prince Paul Esterhazy (1761-1791). Here he was afforded rich opportunities for composition and musical experimentation. He and Mozart were the two great musical masters of Europe in the late eighteenth century. Haydn visited England in 1797 and received a Mus.D. degree from Oxford. He wrote his famous work *The Creation* for an English text by Lidley. It was first performed in Vienna in 1798. Haydn was a deeply religious man and began all his manuscripts with the words "In nomine Domini" (in the name of the Lord), closing them with the words "Laus Deo" (Praise God), or "Soli Deo Gloria" (only to the glory of God).

AUSTRIAN HYMN (99, 436, 447)
CREATION (91)
HALLE (383)

Haydn, Johann Michael

Haydn, Johann Michael (b. Rohrau, Austria, September 14, 1737; d. Salzburg, Austria, August 10, 1806) was the younger brother of Franz Joseph Haydn. He served as kapellmeister at Grosswardein in 1757 and in 1762 became musical director for Archbishop Sigismund of Salzburg, where he remained until his death. His works number more than four hundred, most of which have never been published. He often adapted popular or traditional tunes for use as sacred music. His brother Franz considered Johann's work in this sort superior to his own.

LYONS (87)

Heath, George

Heath, George (b. c. 1750; d. 1822) was educated at Exeter in the Dissenter's academy there. He was for a time minister to the Presbyterian church at Honiton, Devonshire, but was dismissed from his office for proving "unworthy." Later he became a Unitarian minister. His works include *A History of Bristol* (1797) and *Hymns and Poetic Essays Sacred to the Public and Private Worship of the Deity* (1781).

My Soul, Be on Thy Guard (531)

Heber, Reginald

Heber, Reginald (b. Malpas, Cheshire, England, April 21, 1783; d. Trichinopoly, India, April 3, 1826) was educated at Brasenose College, Oxford, and became Fellow of All Soul's College in 1805. He went on the "grand tour" following his graduation and then became vicar of Hodnet

(1807-1823). Here he not only ministered to his church but also continued his literary work. He was a staff writer for the *Quarterly Review* and delivered the Bampton Lectures (1815). He was a friend of Sir Walter Scott, Robert Southey, and Henry Milman. Heber desired to produce a hymnal for used among Anglican churches so that the great vehicle of congregational song in use among the Dissenters might bear fruit in the established church. His bishop refused to authorize such a collection. In 1823, Heber was appointed Bishop of Calcutta, a longtime dream. Unfortunately his health proved too fragile, and he died while on a pastoral visit to Trichinopoly.

> *Bread of the World* l(373)
> *Brightest and Best* (211)
> *Holy, Holy, Holy* (69)

Hedge, Frederich Henry

Hedge, Frederich Henry (b. Cambridge, Massachusetts, December 12, 1805; d. Cambridge, August 21, 1890) was educated in Germany, beginning at age thirteen, and then at Harvard University (1825). He was ordained a Unitarian minister in 1829 and served churches in Massachusetts, Maine, and Rhode Island. He was professor of ecclesiastical history at Harvard (1857-1876) during most of which time he served as minister of the Brookline Unitarian Church. He was also professor of German at Harvard (1872-1881) and was recognized as an authority on German literature, evidenced in his great work *Prose Writers of Germany*. Hedge was co-compiler with F. D. Huntingdon of *Hymns for the Church of Christ* (1853).

> *A Mighty Fortress Is Our God* (104)

Heerman, Johann

Heerman, Johann (b. Raudten, near Wohlau, Silesia, October 11, 1585; d. Lissa, Posen, Germany, February 17, 1647) was the only survivor of five children born to his parents. His father was a poor furrier. His mother vowed that should God spare her only child she would dedicate him to the Christian ministry. He was educated at Fraustadt, Breslau, and Brieg, and spent part of 1609 at the University of Strassburg. An eye ailment forced him to leave his studies. From 1611 to 1634, Heerman was minister at Koben, and many of these years were marked by suffering. A great fire destroyed the city in 1616; in 1617 his wife died; and in 1618 the Thirty Years War began. During this conflict the city of Koben was plundered many times, and Heerman lost all his possessions. In 1631 the plague struck Koben, and in 1634 Heerman was forced to cease preaching because of a

chronic throat problem. Nevertheless, during these long periods of distress, Heerman wrote many of his great hymns. He ranks second only to Paul Gerhardt in German hymnody. Marilyn Stulken says: "Heerman marks the transition from the objective hymns of the Reformation to the more subjective hymns of the following period" (*Hymnal Companion*, 222).
Ah, Holy Jesus (222)

Helmore, Thomas

Helmore, Thomas (b. Kidderminster, Worcestershire, England, May 7, 1811; d. Westminster, England, July 6, 1890) was educated at Magdalen Hall, Oxford, and was ordained to the ministry of the Church of England. He was vicar of Lichfield Cathedral and then vice-principal and precentor at St. Mark's College, Chelsea (1842-1877). In 1846 he became master of the choristers at the Chapel Royal at St. James. Helmore was a pioneer in the restoration of the use of plainsong in the Church of England and was musical editor for John Mason Neale's translations of Latin hymns. His publications include *The Hymnal Noted* (1851-1854) and the article on plainsong in the *Dictionary of Musical Terms* (1881).
VENI EMMANUEL (182)

Hemy, Henri Frederick

Hemy, Henri Frederick (b. Newcastle upon Tyne, England, November 12,1818; d. Hartlepool, Durham, England, June 19, 1888) was born of German parents. He served for a time as organist at St. Andrew's Roman Catholic Church at Newcastle and later was professor of music at St. Cuthbert's College, Upshaw, Durham. He published *Royal Modern Tutor for the Pianoforte* (1858), which was widely used, and *Crown of Jesus Music* (1864), a collection very popular with Roman Catholics.
STELLA (13)
ST. CATHERINE (494, 621)

Henderson, Odie Colin

Henderson, Odie Colin (b. September 7, 1797, near Bells, Haywood Co., Tennessee; d. Uvalde, Texas, January 1971) left Tennessee after graduation from high school in order to improve his health. He came to South Texas and settled near Uvalde, where he at first grew vegetables for a living and later owned two ranches, raising sheep and hogs and keeping pecan orchards. He married Lucille Lanman (1930), and they had five children, one of whom was Colleen Blondeau, the wife of Rollie Blondeau, an associate editor of *GSR*. Henderson was a member of the Baptist Church, loved to sing and published a volume of poetry.

HENDERSON (428)

Herbert, George

Herbert, George (b. Montgomery Castle, England, April 3, 1593; d. Bemerton, near Salisbury, England, March 1, 1633) was educated at Westminster School and at Trinity College, Cambridge. He was a favorite courtier of King James I and became rector at Bemerton in 1630. Herbert had been orator for Cambridge University in 1619. His great poetic work, *The Temple*, was published posthumously in 1633, and his friend Isaak Walton published a notable biography of Herbert. As hymn material his poetry was neglected for many years until John Wesley made extensive use of it in his *Charleston Collection* (1737).

Let All the World in Every Corner Sing (81)

Hermann, Nicolaus

Hermann, Nicolaus (b. Altdorf, near Nuremberg, Germany, c. 1480; d. St. Joachimsthal in Bergstadt, Bohemia, c. May 3, 1561) was a teacher in the Latin school in Joachimsthal as early as 1518. He also served as organist and choirmaster for the Lutheran church there during the ministry of Johann Mathesius, whose sermons often inspired his poems and musical compositions. Hermann also wrote many hymns for children and youth. He published *Eyn gestreng vrteyl Gottes* (c. 1526), *Cantica Sacra* in two volumes (1554, 1558), and the hymnal *Die Historien von der Sintflut* (1562).

Let All Together Praise Our God (192)

Hérold, Louis Joseph Ferdinand

Hérold, Louis Joseph Ferdinand (b. Paris, France, January 28, 1791; d. Thernes, France, January 19, 1833) studied at the Paris Conservatory beginning in 1806 and won the first prize in the piano competition in 1810. He continued his studies in Italy. His first opera, *La giovento di Enrico Quinto*, was produced in Naples in 1815. He composed a great deal of music for the piano and is recognized as holding an important rank among French operatic composers. Hérold was chorusmaster of the Italian Opera in Paris (1824) and of the Grand Opera (1827).

MESSIAH (608)

Hewitt, Eliza Edmunds

Hewitt, Eliza Edmunds (b. Philadelphia, Pennsylvania, June 18, 1851; d. April 24, 1920) was the daughter of Captain James S. and Zeruiah Edmunds Stites. She was educated at the girl's Normal School in Philadelphia, graduating as the class valedictorian. She was a member of the Olivet Presbyterian Church, a public school teacher for several years, and the superintendent of the Sunday School at the Northern Home for Friendless Children in Philadelphia. She was also superintendent of the primary department of the Calvin Presbyterian Church for several years before her death. Eliza, the cousin of Edgar Page Stites, wrote hymn texts for several well-known song writers, including John R. Sweney, William J. Kirkpatrick, B. D. Ackley, Charles H. Gabriel, E. S. Lorenz, and Homer Rodeheaver.

More About Jesus (626)
Sing the Wondrous Love of Jesus (669)
There Is Sunshine in My Soul (463)

Hews, George

Hews, George (b. Weston, Massachusetts, January 6, 1806; d. Boston, Massachusetts, July 16, 1873) was a music teacher in Boston as early as 1830. He was a well-known tenor soloist and sang in the Handel and Haydn Society. He served as vice-president of the society from 1854 to 1858. Hews began to manufacture pianos in 1840 and made several improvements in the instrument, for which he obtained patents. He was organist of the Brattle Street Church in Boston for several years. The Harvard Medical Association made him an honorary member and held its meetings in his residence in Boston (1848-1851). He published several compositions both secular and sacred.

HOLLEY (340, 622)

Hey, Johann Wilhelm

Hey, Johann Wilhelm (b. Leina, Germany, March 26, 1789; d. Ichtershausen, Germany, May 19, 1854) was educated at the University of Jena and the University of Göttingen. He became licentiate in theology (1811) and in 1818 became minister to the church at Tottelstadt near Gotha. In 1827 he was court preacher at Gotha and for a time attracted large audiences. Because of his association with the Pietists, he became superintendent of Ichtershausen in 1832. His poems were written mostly for children and include the collection *Fabeln für Kinder* (1st series, 1833;

2d series, 1837). His works have been translated into English.
Can You Count the Stars of Evening (126)

Hill, Will

No information has been discovered on this composer.
HILL (46)

Hine, Stuart Wesley Keene

Hine, Stuart Wesley Keene (b. London, England, July 25, 1899) was educated at Cooper's Company School, London, and planned to attend Oxford University. This plan did not materialize, and he served in the British Army in France during World War I. He became a Methodist minister and served as a missionary in the Western Ukraine, in Romania, Poland, and Czechoslavakia from 1923 to 1939. After the outbreak of World War II, he returned to England (1939) and worked among the thousands of displaced persons from Eastern Europe who were in London. This work included the publication of literature in their languages. He now resides in Somerset, England.
O Lord, My God (60)

Hintze, Jacob

Hintze, Jacob (b. Bernau, near Berlin, Germany, September 4, 1622; d. Berlin, May 5, 1702) was court musician to the elector of Brandenburg at Berlin (1666-1695). He continued the work of Johann Crüger in editing the *Praxis Pietatis Melica,* adding sixty-five new melodies.
SALZBURG (58)

Hodges, John Sebastian Bach

Hodges, John Sebastian Bach (b. Bristol, Gloucestershire, England, 1830; d. Baltimore, Maryland, May 1, 1915) was the son of Edward Hodges, an organist in Bristol. The family moved to Canada in 1838, where the elder Hodges was organist at Toronto Cathedral. John came to the United States in 1845 and was educated at Columbia University. He became a deacon in the Episcopal Church (1854) and a priest (1855). After serving Episcopal churches in Pittsburgh, Chicago, and Newark (N. J.), he taught at Nashotah House, Wisconsin. For thirty-five years Hodges was rector of St. Paul's Church in Baltimore and there established the men and boys' choir and the parish school choir. He wrote some 100 tunes and anthems. His published works include the *Book of Common Praise* (1869) and *Hymn*

Tunes (1903). He also assisted in the publication of the Episcopal *Hymnal* (editions of 1874 and 1892).

EUCHARISTIC HYMN (373)

Hoffman, Elisha Albright

Hoffman, Elisha Albright (b. Orwigsburg, Pennsylvania, May 7, 1839; d. 1929) was educated in the public schools of Philadelphia and at Union Seminary of the Evangelical Association. He became a minister in the Evangelical Church and served eleven years with the Evangelical Association Publishing House in Cleveland, Ohio. He served various Evangelical churches and was minister of the First Presbyterian Church in Benton Harbor, Michigan. He wrote the words and music for many gospel songs and edited several collections.

Have You Been to Jesus (330)
What a Fellowship (108)

Holbrook, Joseph Perry

Holbrook, Joseph Perry (b. near Boston, Massachusetts, 1822; d. 1888) was music editor of Charles S. Robinson's *Songs of the Church* (1862) and of his *Songs for the Sanctuary* (1865). He was also music editor for the *Baptist Praise Book* (1872) and co-editor with Eben Tourjee of the *Hymnal of the Methodist Episcopal Church with Tunes* (1878). Holbrook also compiled and edited several books of music.

LYTE (656)

Holden, Oliver

Holden, Oliver (b. Shirley, Massachusetts, September 18, 1765; d. Charlestown, Massachusetts, September 4, 1844) moved with his family from Shirley to Holden in 1786. There he worked as a carpenter, helping to rebuild the city, which had been burned by the British at the time of the Battle of Bunker Hill. He also operated a general store and was in the real estate business. When a Baptist church was established in Charlestown, he gave the land for the building. Holden belonged to the Puritan Church in Holden, helped to build it a building, and served as its preacher for fifteen years. He was active in community affairs and served in the Massachusetts House of Representatives (1818-1843). In addition to all of these activities, Holden was a singing-school teacher and a hymnal compiler and editor. His works include *American Harmony* (Boston, 1792), *Union Harmony* (Boston, 1793), *The Massachusetts Compiler,* with Hans Gram and Samuel Holyoke (1795), *The Worcester Collection* (6th edition, 1797), *Sacred*

Dirges, Hymns and Anthems, Commemorative of the Death of George Washington (1800), *The Modern Collection of Sacred Music* (1800), *The Charlestown Collection of Sacred Songs* (1803), *Plain Psalmody* (1800), *The Young Convert's Companion: A Collection for the Use of Conference Meetings* (Boston, 1806), and, perhaps, the *Suffolk Collection of Church Music*. Holden's hymn tune CORONATION is the earliest American hymn tune still in use in modern times.

CORONATION (250)

Holland, Henry Scott

Holland, Henry Scott (b. Ledbury, Hertfordshire, England, January 27, 1847; d. Oxford, England, March 17, 1918) was educated at Balliol College, Oxford. He was ordained deacon in the Church of England (1872) and priest (1874). Holland was select preacher at Oxford 1879-1880, and again 1894-1896. He served at St. Paul's Cathedral from 1884 to 1910. In 1911 he returned to Oxford as lecturer and regius professor of divinity. He was a leader in the Christian Social Union and served as editor of its official organ, *The Commonwealth* (1896-1912). His works include *Jenny Lind, the Artist* (1891); *A Bundle of Memories* (1915); and *So as by fire; notes on the war* (1916). Holland was also an editor of the *Christian Psalter* and of the *English Hymnal* (1906).

Judge Eternal, Throned in Splendor (433)

Holmes, Oliver Wendell

Holmes, Oliver Wendell (b. Cambridge, Massachusetts, August 29, 1809; d. Boston, Massachusetts, October 7, 1894) was educated at Phillips Academy and Harvard University and became one of the leading literary men of the United States. After his graduation from Harvard in 1829, he studied medicine in Boston and in Paris and returned to teach anatomy at Dartmouth (1839-1847). He then became the long-time professor of anatomy and physiology at Harvard (1847-1882). Holmes wrote the anniversary poems at Harvard from 1851 to 1889. He belonged to the New England group of literati which included Bryant, Longfellow, Lowell, and Whittier. He was cofounder of the *Atlantic Monthly* (1857), to which he contributed articles headed "The Autocrat of the Breakfast Table," "The Professor at the Breakfast Table," and "Over the Teacups." His famous poem "Old Ironsides" is reputed to have helped save the famous *USS Constitution* from destruction.

Lord of All Being, Throned Afar (113)

Hopkins, Edward John

Hopkins, Edward John (b. Westminster, London, England, June 30, 1818; d. London, February 4, 1901) was a chorister at the Chapel Royal and studied music under T. F. Walmsley. He served as organist for various parish churches beginning in 1834 and was for 55 years organist at Temple Church, London, beginning in 1843. Hopkins was awarded the honorary Mus.D. degree by the Archbishop of Canterbury (1882) and by Trinity College, Toronto (1886). He retired in 1898. He published, with Edward F. Rimbault, *The Organ: Its History and Construction* (1855); completed the editorial work on the *Wesleyan Hymn Book* (1876), which had been begun by H. J. Gauntlett and George Cooper; and was music editor of the *Congregational Church Hymnal* (1887).

Savior, Again to Thy Dear Name (11)

Hopper, Edward

Hopper, Edward (b. New York, New York, February 17, 1816; d. New York, April 23, 1888) was educated at New York University and Union Theological Seminary (1842). As a Presbyterian minister, he served churches in Greenville, New York, Sag Harbor, Long Island, and, for many years, was minister for the Church of the Sea and Land, New York City. This church had a special ministry for seamen from all over the world. Lafayette College awarded Hopper the honorary D.D. degree in 1871. All of Hopper's hymns were originally published anonymously.

Jesus, Savior, Pilot Me (534)

Hopps, John Page

Hopps, John Page (b. London, England, November 6, 1834; d. 1912) was educated at the General Baptist College, Leicester, England. He began his ministerial labors in 1856, serving at Hugglescote, then at Ibstock, and afterwards with George Dawson at the Church of the Savior, Birmingham. From 1869 to 1876, he served various Unitarian congregations, and after 1876 he preached in Leicester. Hopps edited a religious paper *The Truthseeker* (beginning 1863) and edited various hymnals, including *Hymns for Public Worship and the Home* (1858), *Hymns of Faith and Progress* (1865), *Hymns for Public Worship* (1877), *The Children's Hymn Book* (1879), and *The Young People's Book of Hymns* (1881).

Father, Lead Me Day by Day (132)

Houghton, Will Henry

Houghton, Will Henry (b. South Boston, Massachusetts, June 28, 1887; d. Los Angeles, California, June 14, 1947) was the son of John William and Carrie Maude Grant Houghton. He was educated in the Boston public schools and briefly went on the stage. Deciding to give his life to Christ, he attended Eastern Nazarene College in Rhode Island and was ordained to the Baptist ministry (1915). He served churches in Canton, Pennsylvania (1915-1917), New Bethlehem, Pennsylvania (1918-1920), Norristown, Pennsylvania (1920-1923), Atlanta, Georgia (1925-1928), and New York City (1930-1934). Houghton was successful in his ministry and a strong fundamentalist in his preaching. He was active in various religious works and was an ardent evangelist. He held a religious campaign in Ireland (1924). In 1934 Houghton became president of Moody Bible Institute, Chicago, a post he held until his death. His first wife died in 1916, and he married Elizabeth Andrews (1918). His works include *The Living Christ* (1936); *Lessons in Soul-Winning*, which sold over 50,000 copies (1936); *Let's Go Back to the Bible* (1939); and *Back to the Bible* (1940). He wrote also many songs and choruses. Houghton served as a chaplain with the YMCA during World War I. He was awarded the D.D. degree by Wheaton College (1931) and the LL.D. by Bob Jones University (1942).

Lead Me to Some Soul Today (421)

How, William Walsham

How, William Walsham (b. Shrewsbury, Shropshire, England, December 13, 1823; d. Leenane, County Mayo, Ireland, August 10, 1897) was educated at Wadham College, Oxford. He entered the ministry of the Church of England in 1845, becoming priest in 1847. He served at Kidderminster, at Whittington, and at Oswestry. In 1879 he became Suffragan Bishop of East London, where he did great humanitarian work in the slums. He was called the "poor man's bishop." In 1888 How became the first Bishop of Wakefield. His published works include *Daily Prayers for Churchmen* (1852); *Psalms and Hymns*, with T. B. Morrell (1854); and *Church Hymns*, with John Elleton as co-editor (1871). He wrote more than 50 hymns. How died while on a vacation to Ireland.

For All the Saints (450)
O Word of God Incarnate (298)
We Give Thee but Thine Own (610)

Howard, Samuel

Howard, Samuel (b. London, England, c. 1710; d. London, July

13, 1782) was a chorister at the Chapel Royal under William Croft and studied under Johann Christoph Pepusch, a rival of Handel. He was concurrently organist at St. Clement Danes, the Strand, and at St. Bride's, Fleet Street. Howard assisted William Boyce in the compilation of *Cathedral Music* (1760-1778). He received the honorary Mus.D. degree from Cambridge (1769).

ST. BRIDE (548)

Hoyle, Richard Birch

Hoyle, Richard Birch (b. Cloughfold, Lancashire, England, March 8, 1875; d. London, England, December 14, 1939) was a Baptist minister and scholar. He came to the United States in 1934 and taught at Eastern Theological Seminary. He wrote the article on "The Holy Spirit" in the *Encyclopedia of Religion and Ethics* and was a close friend of Suzanne Bidgrain, the collector of the hymns for *Cantate Domino,* the hymnbook of the World Student Christian Federation.

Thine Is the Glory (240)

Hoyt, May Pierpont

No information is available on this author. The text attributed to her was published about 1889.

Here at Thy Table, Lord (376)

Hudson, Clarence

Little information is available on this composer. He served as choirmaster at the Wesleyan chapel in Delph, England, and edited and compiled the *Oldham Psalmody* (London, 1891). Dowston Castle was the name of his estate.

DOWSTON CASTLE (572)

Hudson, Ralph Erskine

Hudson, Ralph Erskine (b. Napoleon, Ohio, July 9, 1843; d. Cleveland, Ohio, June 1, 1901) served as a nurse in the Union Army at the General Hospital, Annapolis, Maryland, during the Civil War. After the war he taught music at Mount Vernon College, Alliance, Ohio (1864-1869). He was an ordained minister in the Methodist Episcopal Church and was active in evangelistic work as a singer. Hudson established his own publishing company at Alliance, Ohio. His works include *Salvation Echoes* (1882), *Gems of Gospel Song* (1884), *Songs of Peace, Love, and Joy* (1885), and *Songs of the Ransomed* (1887). These were later combined into a single volume, *Quartette*.

HUDSON (215)

Hughes, John

Hughes, John (b. Dowlais, Wales, November 22, 1873; d. Llantwit Fardre, Ponty pridd, Wales, May 14, 1932) moved with his family shortly after his birth to Llantwit, where he resided for the remainder of his life. He worked as a door boy at Glyn Colliery, a local mine, at age twelve, and later worked for the Great Western Railway in the traffic department. He was a member of the Salem Baptist Church, where he succeeded his father as deacon and precentor. Hughes compiled a number of marches, anthems, and hymn tunes for church use.

CWM RHONDDA (581, 587)

Hull, Eleanor Henrietta

Hull, Eleanor Henrietta (b. Manchester, England, January 15, 1860; d. London, England, January 13, 1935) was the founder and secretary of the Irish Text Society (1899) and was for a time president of the Irish Literary Society of London. She wrote several books on Irish history and literature and helped to renew interest in ancient Gaelic culture.

Be Thou My Vision (578)

Hunter, John

Hunter, John (b. Aberdeen, Scotland, July 12, 1848; d. Hampstead, London, England, September 15, 1917) was educated in the public schools of Aberdeen, but his family was too poor to send him to college. Consequently he became a draper's apprentice at age thirteen. A great revival in his city (1859-1861) moved him to become a minister, and he was able to attend Mansfield College, Oxford. Thereafter he preached for Congregational churches at York, Hull, Glasgow, and London. From 1904 to 1913, he again preached in Glasgow. Upon returning to London, he continued to preach each week in Aeolian Hall. Hunter published *Services for Public Worship* (1886), a most influential book; and also *Hymns of Faith and Life* (1889).

Dear Master, in Whose Life I See (571)

Hunter, William

Hunter, William (b. Ballymena, County Antrim, Ireland, May 26,

1811; d. Cleveland, Ohio, October 18, 1877) came at the age of six with his family to America and settled in York, Pennsylvania. He was educated at Madison College, Uniontown, Pennsylvania (1833), and became a Methodist minister. In 1836 he became editor of *The Pittsburgh Conference Journal* (1836-1840) and of its successor, the *Christian Advocate* (1844-1852; and 1872-1876). He also served as professor of Hebrew at Allegheny College (1855-1870). Hunter wrote over 100 hymns and edited the collections *Select Melodies* (1838-1851), *The Minstrel of Zion* (1845), and *Songs of Devotion* (1859). In 1876 he was appointed to a committee to revise the Methodist hymnal, which appeared after his death as the *Hymnal of the Methodist Episcopal Church with Tunes* (1878).

The Great Physician (173)

Hussey, Jennie Evelyn

Hussey, Jennie Evelyn (b. Henniker, New Hampshire, February 8, 1874; d. Concord, New Hampshire, 1958) began writing poetry at a very early age. Her family for four generations had been Quakers. She lived on her family's farm in New Hampshire until her final years, when she lived in the Home for the Aged, Concord, New Hampshire.

King of My Life, I Crown Thee Now (231)

Huston, Frank Claude

Huston, Frank Claude (b. Orange, Indiana, 1871; d. 1959) was a singing evangelist in the Christian Church. He studied music under D. B. Towner. In 1894 he married Bertha Martin and was converted to Christ that year. He became an evangelist in 1904 and served as a chaplain in World War I. He lived in Indianapolis, Indiana, for many years, and his closing years were spent in Jacksonville, Florida.

Here Before Thee, Savior (377)

Hutchins, Charles Lewis

Hutchins, Charles Lewis (b. 1838; d. 1920) was an editor and compiler of Episcopal hymnals. His works include *The Sunday School Hymnal and Service Book* (various editions 1871-1881), *Annotations of the Hymnal* (1872), *A Church Hymnal* (1870), *The Church Hymnal* (1872; later editions in 1892 and 1984), *The Chant and Service Book* (1884), and *The Church Psalter* (1897).

Lift Up, Lift Up Your Voices Now (448)

Ingalls, Jeremiah

Ingalls, Jeremiah (b. Andover, Massachusetts, March 1, 1764; d. Hancock, Vermont, April, 6, 1828) was the son of Abijah Ingalls, who died from the hardships of the Revolutionary War. Jeremiah married Mary Bigelow and settled in Newbury, Vermont. He made his living farming, carpentering, keeping a tavern, and teaching singing schools. All his children were musical, and the family often played together. Ingalls was a deacon in the Congregational Church at Newbury and led the choir there. In 1819 he moved his family first to Rochester, Vermont, and then to Hancock. He published his *Christian Harmony, or Songster's Companion* (1805). H. W. Foote suggests that Ingalls may have had help from his brother, who was organist for the Bromfield Street Methodist Church in Boston. At any rate, this book was a typical and popular collection of the times.

I Love Thee (446)

Irons, William Josiah

Irons, William Josiah (b. Hoddesdon, Hertfordshire, England, September 12, 1812; d. London, England, June 18, 1883) was the son of a non-conformist preacher and hymnwriter who was a friend of John Newton. He was educated at Queen's College, Oxford, and took orders in the Church of England (1835). He first served at St. Mary's Church, Newington (1835-1837), and here began to write and to translate hymns. He served several churches subsequently and delivered the Bampton Lectures in 1870. Irons was prebendary of St. Paul's Cathedral (1860-1883). His published works include *Christianity as Taught by St. Paul* (Bampton Lectures, 1870), *Metrical Psalter* (1857), *Appendix to the Brompton Metrical Psalter* (1861), *Hymns for Use in the Church* (1866) and *Psalms and Hymns for the Church* (1873, 1875).

Sing with All the Sons of Glory (249)

Irvine, Jessie Seymour

Irvine, Jessie Seymour (b. Dunottar, Scotland, July 26, 1836; d. Aberdeen, Scotland, September 2, 1887) was the daughter of a Scottish minister at Dunottar. She often accompanied her father in his preaching appointments. The tune name CRIMOND is for the town located in northeastern Aberdeenshire, Scotland.

CRIMOND (143)

Isaac, Heinrich

Isaac, Heinrich (b. Netherlands, c. 1450; d. Florence, Italy, 1517) was one of the greatest composers of the period just preceding the Reformation in Europe. Martin Luther greatly admired the work of Isaac, which reflected the musical styles prevalent in Italy, France, Germany, and the Netherlands. He wrote both sacred and secular works. Isaac entered the service of Lorenzo de Medici as court organist and music director (c. 1481) and was musical tutor to Lorenzo's sons, one of whom became Pope Leo X. He was also court composer for the Emperor Maximilian I beginning in 1497 in Vienna and Innsbruck. His declining years were spent in Florence, Italy.

INNSBRUCK (82)

Jackson, Robert

Jackson, Robert (b. Oldham, Lancashire, England, 1840; d. Oldham, July 12, 1914) was the son of the organist of St. Peter's Church, Oldham. He studied at the Royal Academy of Music and served at St. Mark's Church, Grosvenor Square, London, as organist. He was also a member of the Halle Symphony Orchestra in Birmingham. Jackson succeeded his father as organist for St. Peter's Church in 1868. Altogether this father and son were the organists for this church for 94 years (the father for 48, and the son for 46).

TRENTHAM (295)

Jackson, Thomas Albert

Jackson, Thomas Albert (b. Baltimore, Maryland, May 2, 1931) is a Baptist minister who was educated at the University of Richmond (1953), the Southeastern Baptist Theological Seminary (1957), and Johns Hopkins University (1970). He has served Baptist churches in Virginia and Maryland and has been active in Baptist associations and conventions. At present he ministers to the McLean Baptist Church, McLean, Virginia.

We Are Called to Be God's People (436)

Jameson, Love H.

Jameson, Love H. (b. Indiana, May 17, 1811; d. Indianapolis, Indiana, May 1, 1892) was the son of Thomas Jameson of Virginia. The family moved to Kentucky (c. 1800) and to Jefferson county in the then Indiana Territory (1810). The family became Christians in 1816. Love Jameson was baptized in 1829 and preached his first sermon that same year on Christmas Day. One of his great mentors was Walter Scott. He went to Ohio (1834), but returned to Indiana in 1840 and located in Madison, Indiana the following year. His wife died soon afterwards, and in 1842 he married Elizabeth R. Robinson. They moved to Indianapolis, which became his headquarters for the rest of his life.

> *Night with Ebon Pinion* (212)
> *There Is a Habitation* (664)

Jeffrey, John Albert

Jeffrey, John Albert (b. Plymouth, England, October 26, 1855; d. Brookline, Massachusetts, June 4, 1929) was the son of the organist of St. Andrew's Cathedral, Plymouth, England. He studied under his father and then in Germany under Franz Liszt and Reinecke. The musical conservatory at Leipzig later conferred on him the honorary Mus.D. degree. Jeffrey came to America in 1876 and became head of the Music department at St. Agnes's School in Albany, New York (1878). He moved to Yonkers (1893) and was organist there for the First Presbyterian Church. In 1900 he went to Boston, where subsequently he was a member of the faculty of the New England Conservatory of Music and where he served as organist for the North Cambridge Universalist Church.

> ANCIENT OF DAYS (56)

John of Damascus

John of Damascus (b. Damascus, c. 675; d. Jerusalem, December 4, 749?) was one of the fathers of the Greek Church and the greatest of the Greek Christian poets. He came from a good family in Damascus. The Italian hymnwriter Cosmas was his tutor. He served in a civil capacity under the Moslem caliph in Damascus and later entered the monastery at St. Sabas, near Jerusalem, along with his brother, Cosmas the Melodist. His greatest work was as a hymnodist and musician. John is given credit for the arrangement of the *Octoechus* (the Eight Tones), which were used to accompany the Sunday services of the churches. He seems to have done for the music of the Eastern churches what Gregory the Great did for the Western.

> *The Day of Resurrection* (242)

Johnson, Julia Harriette

Johnson, Julia Harriette (b. Salineville, Ohio, January 21, 1849; d. Peoria, Illinois, March 6, 1919) moved at the age of six with her family to Peoria, where she lived for the rest of her life. Her father, Robert Johnson, was minister of the First Presbyterian Church in Peoria (1855-1864). She taught the infant class and was superintendent of the younger children's department in the Sunday School of the church for forty-one years. She also wrote Primary Sunday School lessons for the David C. Cook Publishing Company for several years. Her publications include *School of the Master* (1880), *Indian and Spanish Neighbors* (1905), and *Fifty Missionary Heroes* (1913). She wrote some 500 hymn poems.

   Marvelous Grace of Our Loving Lord (124)

Jones, Lewis Edgar

   Jones, Lewis Edgar (b. Yates City, Illinois, February 8, 1865; d. Santa Barbara, California, September 1, 1936) was a graduate of Moody Bible Institute in the same class with the evangelist Billy Sunday. He became active in the work of the Young Men's Christian Association after graduation and stayed with this work for the rest of his life. Jones served as physical director at the YMCA in Davenport, Iowa, and was general secretary in Fort Worth, Texas. He served as general secretary in Santa Barbara, California, from 1915 until his retirement in 1925. Hymn writing was his hobby.

   Would You Be Free from the Power of Sin - POWER IN THE BLOOD (339)

Jones, Joseph David

   Jones, Joseph David (b. Brynerygog, Montgomery, Wales, 1827; d. Ruthin, Wales, September 17, 1870) was a singing teacher at Ruthin and in charge of the British school there. He published his collection of psalm tunes, *Y Perganiedydd,* in 1847.

   GWALCHMAI (72)

Jones, William

   Jones, William (b. Lowick, Northamptonshire, England, July 30, 1726; d. Nayland, England, January 6, 1800) was educated at the Charter house and at University College, Oxford (1749). He became a minister in the Church of England and was vicar of Betherscen, Kent (1764), rector at Pluckley and Paston, and then was appointed perpetual curate of Nayland, Suffolk (1777). He was a Fellow of the Royal Society and influential in church affairs. Jones founded the *British Critic* (1784). His publications include *Treatise of the Art of Music* (1784), *Ten Church Tunes for the Organ with Four Anthems in Score* (1789), *The Catholic Doctrine of the Trinity*

(1756), and *Physiological Disquisitions* (1781). He nicknamed himself "Oudeis" (a Greek work for "nobody"), and a dining club called "Nobody's Friends' is still in existence.

ST. STEPHEN (282)

Jorgenson, Elmer Leon

Jorgenson, Elmer Leon (b. Albion, Nebraska, 1886; d. Los Angeles, California, December 1968) was the son of Christopher Jorgenson, a Danish immigrant who had been a soldier in the personal guard of the King of Denmark. His mother had been seamstress to the Queen. The family migrated to the United States in 1884 and settled near the little town of Albion, Nebraska. Here Leon Jorgenson was born, and here the entire family became members of the Roselma Church of Christ. He was the youngest son in a family of six children. After his father's death in 1901, much of the responsibility of caring for the family fell on him. Despite this care, he took every advantage to receive an education, and early in his life he showed an interest in and love for music. He led singing in many evangelistic meetings in Nebraska and nearby Missouri. In 1907 he became head of the Music department of Western Bible and Literary College in Odessa, Missouri, under the presidency of J. N. Armstrong. Here he met and married Irene Doty in 1909, and shortly after their wedding the young couple moved to Louisville, Kentucky, where they made their home for the rest of their lives. Their only child, Martha Jane, was born in 1919, but the little girl died in her eighth year. In Louisville, Jorgenson studied under Robert Henry Boll and took courses at the Southern Baptist Theological Seminary and the University of Louisville. He was first a member and later president of the Louisville Chorus. Jorgenson began planning the compilation of his hymnal, *GS*, about 1910 and ultimately overcame all obstacles to publish it in 1921. For his contribution to Christian hymnody, he was elected to the Eugene Field Society and named to *Who's Who in America* in 1937. For many years E. L. Jorgenson was the publisher of *Word and Work*, a religious magazine edited by R. H. Boll, and conducted song tours across the United States promoting his hymnal and better church music. After Boll's death in 1956, he became editor of *Word and Work*. In 1958 he suffered a severe coronary, from which he never fully recovered. No man made a greater contribution toward improving congregational song among the Churches of Christ than Elmer Leon Jorgenson.

Thou Art Merciful, O Father (106)
Can You Count the Stars of Evening (126)

Jude, William Herbert

Jude, William Herbert (b. Westleton, Suffolk, England, September 1851; d. London, England, August 8, 1922) was the organist at Blue Coat Hospital, Liverpool, for a number of years and after 1889 was organist at the Stetford Town Hall near Manchester. He traveled extensively in England, and even to Australia, lecturing and giving recitals. He served as editor of *Monthly Hymnal,* a musical periodical, and compiled *Mission Hymns* (1911) and *Festival Hymns* (1916). He also wrote an operetta entitled *Innocents Abroad.*

GALILEE (615)

Judson, Adoniram

Judson, Adoniram (b. Malden, Massachusetts, August 19, 1788; d. at sea, Bay of Bengal, April 12, 1850) was one of the first American foreign missionaries. The son of a Congregational minister, he was educated at Rhode Island College (now Brown University) and at Andover Theological Seminary. Judson was married to Ann Hasseltine. In 1812 they sailed together to India under the auspices of the Congregationalists' American Board of Commissioners for Foreign Missions. Concluding that immersion only was baptism in the New Testament, he was baptized by the American Baptist missionary William Ward in Calcutta. He was afterwards forced out of India (1813) and became the pioneer missionary to Burma, suffering many hardships and imprisonments, but holding out faithfully. He translated the Bible into Burmese (1834). In 1845 he returned to the United States for a furlough, spent many years working on a Burmese-English dictionary, and died while on a sea voyage for his health. He was buried at sea in the Bay of Bengal. Adoniram Judson was greatly admired by Alexander Campbell, especially for his work in translating the Bible.

Come, Holy Spirit, Guest Divine (359)

Kaiser, Kurt Frederic

Kaiser, Kurt Frederic (b. Chicago, Illinois, December 17, 1934) is the son of Otto Kaiser. The elder Kaiser once served as chairman of a committee to compile a hymnal for the Plymouth Brethren. Kurt Kaiser was educated at Northwestern University and in 1973, was awarded the honorary Mus.D. degree by Trinity College, Deerfield, Illinois. He served as a deacon in the Seventh and James Baptist Church, Waco, Texas, and, since 1959, has been vice-president and director of music for Word, Inc. He collaborated with Ralph Carmichael in producing several religious musicals.

It Only Takes a Spark - PASS IT ON (459)
O How He Loves You and Me - KAISER (232)

Keble, John

Keble, John (b. Fairford, Gloucestershire, England, April 25, 1792; d. Bournemouth, England, March 29, 1866), the son of the vicar of Coln St. Aldwin's, was educated under private tutors and at Corpus Christi College, Oxford. There he made a more than enviable record. In 1811 he was elected a Fellow of Oriel College. Keble was ordained deacon (1815) and priest in the Church of England (1816), after which he served as a tutor and examiner at Oxford. Upon the death of his mother in 1823, he went to live with and assist his father in his ministerial duties. In 1825 he became curate of Hursley, but upon the death of his sister, Mary Ann, again returned to help and to be near his father. From 1831 to 1841, Keble was professor of poetry at Oxford. In 1833 he preached his famous *Assize Sermon* on the topic of "Our National Apostasy," which John Henry Newman believed was the commencement of the Oxford Movement. In 1835 Keble's father died, and he married a Miss Clarke. He accepted the vicarage of Hursley in 1836 and remained there for the rest of his life. Keble's published works include *The Christian Year: Thoughts in Verse for the Sundays and Holidays throughout the Year* (1827), *Psalter or Psalms of David in English Verse* (1839) *Lyra Innocentium* (1846) and the *Life of Bishop Wilson* (1863).

Hail Gladdening Light (32)
Sun of My Soul (42)

Kelly, Thomas

Kelly, Thomas (b. Kellyville, Stradbelly, County Queens, Ireland, July 13, 1769; d. Dublin, Ireland, May 14, 1854) was the son of Thomas Kelly, a judge of the Irish Court of Common Appeals. He was educated for a law career at Trinity College, Dublin, but a spiritual experience changed his mind, and he was ordained in the Irish Episcopal Church (1792). He began to engage in fervent evangelism, but was prohibited by his archbishop. Consequently, he left the Irish Church and formed an independent congregation. Kelly was a powerful preacher and generous with his means, which were considerable. He built church buildings and founded congregations at Athy, Portarling, and Wexford. He was also a fine classical scholar and wrote over 700 hymns. His published works include *A Collection of Psalms extracted from Various Authors* (1802), *Hymns on Various Passages of Scripture* (1804), and *Hymns by Thomas Kelly Not Before Published* (1815).

Look, Ye Saints! the Sight Is Glorious (252)
Praise the Savior, Ye Who Know Him (162)
The Head That Once Was Crowned with Thorns (257)

Ken, Thomas

Ken, Thomas (b. Berkhampstead, Hertfordshire, England, July 1637; d. Longleat, Wiltshire, England, March 19, 1711) was an orphan brought up in the home of his sister Ann, the wife of Isaak Walton, the author of the *Life of John Donne*, the *Life of George Herbert,* and *The Compleat Angler.* Ken was educated at Winchester College, Hart Hall, and New College, Oxford. He was ordained to the Anglican ministry in 1662, served various churches until 1666, and then returned to Winchester College The following year he became curate at Brightstone on the Isle of Wight, and then came again to Winchester as prebendary (1669). He served at the cathedral there and as chaplain to the bishop. Ken was a staunch moralist and a man of high principle. He spoke out against the immorality of the royal court and was sent to the Tower in 1688 upon his refusal to subscribe to James II's Declaration of Indulgence. Later he served as Bishop of Bath and Wells, but was deprived of his office for again refusing to subscribe under the reign of William and Mary. He lived the remainder of his life with his friend Lord Leymouth at Longleat. His most famous devotional work is the *Manual of Prayers for the Use of the Scholars of Winchester College* (1674).

All Praise to Thee, My God, This Night (30)
Praise God from Whom All Blessings Flow (73)

Kennedy, Benjamin Hall

Kennedy, Benjamin Hall (b. Summer Hill, Warwickshire, England, November 6, 1804; d. Torquay, Devonshire, England, April 6, 1889) was the son of Rann Kennedy, an Anglican priest at St. Paul's Birmingham. His father was the editor of *A Church of England Psalm-Book* (1821). Benjamin was educated at King Edward's School, Birmingham, at Shrewsbury School, and at St. John's College, Cambridge. He was fellow of St. John's (1828-1836), headmaster of Shrewsbury School (1836-1866), and, from 1867, was professor of Greek at Cambridge and Canon of Ely. His works include *Psalter, or the Psalms of David English Verse* (1860) and *Hymnologia Christiana, or Psalms and Hymns Selected and Arranged in the Order of the Christian Seasons* (1863). He also published Latin grammars and editions of the classics. Kennedy was elected honorary fellow of St. John's College in 1880.

Ask Ye What Great Thing I Know (304)

Kent, John

Kent, John (b. Bideford, Devonshire, England, December 1776; d. November 15, 1843) was a shipwright by trade and acquired only a limited education. Julian says: "His hymns are strongly worded, very earnest and simple, and intensely Calvinistic." Several of his hymns appeared in Samuel Reece's *Collection* (1799). In 1861 his *Collection of Original Gospel Hymns* (published in 1803) was in its 10th edition and contained "The Author's Experience" and a life of Kent by his son. The English evangelist Spurgeon made use of Kent's hymns in his collections employed in his tabernacle in London.

On Zion's Glorious Summit (177)

Kerr, Hugh Thompson

Kerr, Hugh Thompson (b. Elora, Canada, February 11, 1872; d. Pittsburgh, Pennsylvania, June 27, 1950) was educated at the University of Toronto and Western Theological Seminary. He became a Presbyterian minister upon his graduation from the seminary (1897) and first preached in Kansas and Illinois. He was minister of Shadyside Presbyterian Church, Pittsburgh (1913-1946). Kerr was a pioneer in religious broadcasting, conducting a weekly radio program from 1922 to 1944. In 1930 he served as moderator of the General Assembly of the Presbyterian Church, USA. Kerr published twenty-two books and was a long-time contributor to the Sunday School materials in use among the Presbyterians. He was chair of the committees for *The Presbyterian Hymnal* (1927).

God of Our Life (114)

Kethe, William

Kethe, William (b. Scotland; d. Dorsetshire, England, June 6, 1594). Few facts are known about this writer. He was an exile during the persecutions instigated by Queen Mary (1553-1558), first in Frankfurt, Germany, and then in Geneva, Switzerland. He took messages to and from the exiles in Basel and in Strassburg in 1558. The learned opinion inclines to his being one of the exiles left in Geneva to complete the *Geneva Bible* (1560) after Elizabeth I came to the throne. Kethe was chaplain to Elizabeth's forces under the Earl of Warwick at Havre (1563) and in the north country (1569). It is probable that he was rector to the church of Childe Okeford, Dorsetshire, beginning 1561. His metrical psalm paraphrases appeared in the *Anglo-Genevan Psalter* (1561) and in the *Scottish Psalter* (1564).

All People That on Earth Do Dwell (74)

Kingsley, George

Kingsley, George (b. Northampton, Massachusetts, 1811; d. Northampton, March 13, 1884) was a self-taught musician who was organist for the Old South Church, Boston, and for the Hollis St. Church, Boston. He taught music at Girard College, Philadelphia, and was supervisor of music for the Philadelphia Public Schools. Many of his hymn tunes were published in Charles Everest's *Sabbath* (1873).

FERGUSON (575)

MESSIAH (608)

Kinkel, Johanna

Kinkel, Johanna (b. 1810; d. 1858). No information is available on this composer. The quartet arrangement of KINKEL, which appeared in *GS* in 1937, was first published by Hope Publishing Company in 1912.

Kirkpatrick, William James

Kirkpatrick, William James (b. Duncannon, Pennsylvania, February 27, 1838; d. Philadelphia, Pennsylvania, September 20, 1921) was the son of Thompson and Elizabeth Kirkpatrick. He first studied music under his father and later under Pasqaule Rondinella, Leopold Meignen, and T. Bishop. He became a member of the Wharton St. Methodist Episcopal Church in Philadelphia, in 1855. He edited his first hymnal, *Devotional Melodies,* a collection of camp meeting songs in 1859. In 1861 Kirkpatrick married Miss. S. J. Doak and that same year began to serve as fife-major to the 91st Regiment of the Pennsylvania Volunteers in the Civil War. After the war he engaged in the furniture business, but upon the death of his wife (1878), he devoted his full time to musical work. He was music director at Grace Methodist Episcopal Church, Philadelphia from 1886 to 1897. In the latter year he married Mrs. Sara Kellogg Bourne. She died about 1910, and in 1917 he married the widow of John R. Sweney. Kirkpatrick published numerous collections from 1880 until his death and was president of the Praise Publishing Company, Philadelphia. His work touched the Stone-Campbell Movement in that he helped to edit three hymnals for the Gospel Advocate Company of Nashville, Tennessee: *Seventy-Seven Sweet Songs,* with T. B. Larimore (1906); *The New Christian Hymn Book*, with Larimore (1907); and *Praise Him,* with A. B. Lipscomb (1914).

AINOS (50)

COMFORTER (290)

DUNCANNON (231)

HIERON (8)

I've Wandered Far Away from God - COMING HOME (351)
JESUS SAVES (307)
KIRKPATRICK (467)
O for a Soul Aglow with Love - AGAPE (457)
PROIOS (174)
RONDINELLA (624)
REDEEMED (357)
TRUST IN JESUS (487)

Kitchin, George William

Kitchin, George William (b. Suffolk, England, December 17, 1827; d. Durham, England, October 13, 1912) was the son of Isaac Kitchin, who was rector of St. Stephen's, Ipswich. He was educated at Ipswich Grammar School, King's College School and College, and at Christ Church, Oxford. After graduation and ordination, he was subsequently Dean of Winchester (1883-1894), dean of Durham (1894), and chancellor of Durham University (1909). He published several works in the areas of archeology, biography, and history.

Lift High the Cross (224)

Knapp, Phoebe Palmer

Knapp, Phoebe Palmer (b. New York, New York, March 9, 1838; d. Poland Springs, Maine, July 10, 1908) was the daughter of Walter C. Palmer, a Methodist evangelist. At sixteen she married Joseph Fairfield Knapp, a Christian businessman who founded the Metropolitan Life Insurance Company. They were members with Fanny Crosby of the John Street Methodist Church in New York City. Upon her husband's death, she was left with a more than adequate income, much of which she gave away to charitable and religious causes. Her son, Joseph Palmer Knapp, was head of the Crowell-Collier Publishing Company. She wrote more than 500 gospel songs.

ALBERTSON (219, 324)
ASSURANCE (345)

Knapp, William

Knapp, William (b. Wareham, Dorsetshire, England, c. 1698; d. Poole, Dorsetshire, England, September 26, 1768) seems to have been of German descent. He was an organist and was parish clerk of St. James's Church, Poole, for thirty-nine years. His published works include *A Set of*

New Psalm Tunes and Anthems (1738) and *New Church Melody* (1753).
WAREHAM (141)

Kocher, Conrad

Kocher, Conrad (b. Dietzingen, Württemberg, Germany, December 16, 1786; d. Stuttgart, Germany, March 12, 1872) studied piano and composition in St. Petersburg, Russia. In 1819 he studied a capella singing in Italy and was greatly influenced by the work of Palestrina. He founded the School of Sacred Song in Stuttgart (1820) and later became director of music in the collegiate church in Stuttgart (1827). Kocher helped to reform German church music and to popularize four-part singing. The University of Tübingen conferred an honorary doctorate on him in 1852. He published *Die Tonkunst in der Kirche* (1823), which was a work on the chorale.
DIX (64, 94)

König, Johann Balthasar

König, Johann Balthasar (b. near Gotha, Germany, c. January 20, 1691; d. Frankfurt Germany, March 31, 1758) was a chorister at the age of twelve in Frankfurt. He studied and trained under Georg Philipp Telemann at St. Catherine's Church, Frankfurt (1711-1721), and succeeded Telemann as director of municipal music. König compiled the influential tunebook *Harmonischer Lieder-Schatz* (1738), which contained 1,784 tunes.
FRANCONIA (379, 499)

Kremser, Edward

Kremser, Edward (b. Vienna, Austria, April 10, 1838; d. Vienna, November 27, 1914) was a composer of operettas and works for the piano, voice, and orchestra. His work for male chorus, *Sechs altniederlandische Volkslieder* (1877) is well known. Beginning in 1869, he was chorusmaster of the Vienna Männergesangverein and of other choral groups. He edited *Wiener Lieder und Tänze* (2 vols., 1912, 1913).
KREMSER (1, 44)

La Feillée, François de

La Feillée, François de (fl. 1750) was a priest who was associated with the choir at Chartres Cathedral. Little information is available on this composer. He published *Nouvelle Methode de plain-chant* (1st ed., 1745; rev. ed. 1782). This book marks the change from the earlier modal music to tonal harmony and from free to isometric rhythms. The 1777 edition was dedicated to the bishop of Poitiers, and a revision was done in 1808 by F. D. Aynes.

CHRISTE SANCTORUM (26)
O QUANTA QUALIA (174)

Lampe, John Frederick

Lampe, John Frederick (b. Saxony, Germany, 1703; d. Edinburgh, Scotland, 1751) was a bassoon player who went to England in 1726 and played at Covent Garden Theatre and in Handel's orchestra. He collaborated with Henry Carey in producing several musical dramas. In 1745 Lampe, a close friend of Charles Wesley, began to be influenced by the work of John Wesley. He set twenty of Charles's hymns to music in *Hymns on the Great Festivals, and Other Occasions* (1746). He accompanied John Wesley on his preaching tour in Ireland (1748-1749) and there published *A Collection of Hymns and Sacred Poems* (1749).

IRISH (52)

Lane, Spencer

Lane, Spencer (b. Tilton, New Hampshire, April 7, 1843; d. Readville, Virginia, August 10, 1903), a soldier in the Union Army during the Civil War, afterwards studied at the New England Conservatory of Music and became a teacher of music in New York City. He later moved to Woonsocket, Rhode Island, where he established a music store. Lane was organist there and choirmaster at St. James's Protestant Episcopal Church for thirteen years. After serving churches in Massachusetts and Virginia, he moved to Baltimore, Maryland, where he was an associate in the Sanders and Stayman music business and where he also served as organist and choirmaster for the All Saints' Protestant Episcopal Church.

PENITENCE (538)

Lang, J. D.

No certain information is available on this translator. He seems to have lived in Australia at one time and there published his *Aurora Australis* (Sydney, 1826).

Jesus Lives, and So Shall I (550)

Lange, Martha D.

No information is currently available on this translator.

Take Thou My Hands and Lead Me (527)

Langran, James

Langran, James (b. London, England, November 10, 1835; d. Tottenham, England, June 8, 1909) studied organ under Jean Baptiste Calkin and J. F. Bridge. He was organist at St. Michael's, Wood Green (1856), Holy Trinity, Tottenham (1859), and St. Paul's, Tottenham (1870-1909). In 1878 he served as an instructor in St. Catherine's Training College, Tottenham. Late in life he received his B.Mus. degree from Oxford (1884). Several of his tunes were included in *Hymns Ancient and Modern*, and he served as music editor of the *New Mitre Hymnal* (1875).

LANGRAN (540)

Lathbury, Mary Artemisia

Lathbury, Mary Artemisia (b. Manchester, Ontario County, New York, August 10, 1841; d. East Orange, New Jersey, October 20, 1913) was the daughter of a Methodist minister and at first a professional artist. She served under John H. Vincent as general editor for the children's and young people's Sunday School publications of the Methodist Sunday School Union. She was founder of the "Look-Up Legion," a youth movement in the Methodist Sunday Schools (1878), and was closely associated with the summer conferences at Lake Chautauqua, New York.

Break Thou the Bread of Life (312)
Day Is Dying in the West (37)

Laufer, Calvin Weiss

Laufer, Calvin Weiss (b. Brodheadsville, Pennsylvania, April 6, 1874; d. Philadelphia, Pennsylvania, September 20, 1938) was educated at Franklin and Marshall College and at Union Theological Seminary. Following his graduation, he was ordained to the Presbyterian ministry and served both Dutch Reformed and Presbyterian churches in New York and New Jersey. He was field representative for the Presbyterian Board of Publication (1914-1924) and for the Presbyterian Board of Education (1924-1938). He was also assistant editor of music publication beginning in 1925. His published works include *Junior Church School Hymnal* (1928), *Songs for Men* (1928), *The Church School Hymnal for Youth* (1928), *Primary Worship and Music* (1930), *Hymn Lore* (1932) and *When the Little Child Wants to Sing* (1935). He was also an editor of the *Presbyterian Hymnal* (1933) and of the *Handbook to the Hymnal* (1935).

HALL (605)

LeFevre, Mylon Raymond

LeFevre, Mylon Raymond (b. Atlanta, Georgia, October 6, 1944) is the son of Urias and Eva Mae LeFevre, well-known gospel singers. He was educated at Bob Jones University and West Coast Bible College. He is a writer, producer, and singer, and has sung with the LeFevre Trio and the Stamps Quartet.

Without Him I Could Do Nothing - WITHOUT HIM (515)

Leavitt, Joshua

Leavitt, Joshua (fl. 19th Century). Little information is available on Leavitt. He was a Congregational minister who was active in the revivals led by Charles G. Finney on what was then the American frontier. He was the editor of *The Christian Lyre* (1831), a popular compilation which had run to twenty-six editions by 1846.

PLEADING SAVIOR (386)

Lee, Frederick George

Lee, Frederick George (b. 1832; d. ?) was educated at St. Edmunds Hall, Oxford. He entered the ministry of the Church of England, becoming deacon (1854) and priest (1856). In 1869 he was vicar of All Saints Church, Lambeth. His published works include *Lays of the Church, and Other Verses* (1851); *Poems* (2d ed., 1854); *The Beauty of Holiness: Ten Lectures on External Religious Observances* (1860); *The King's High way, and Other Poems* (1866); and *Essays on the Reunion of Christendom* (1867). Lee was also editor of the *Directorium Anglicanum* (2d ed., 1865) and was intensely interested in the emphasis on ritualism which grew out of the Oxford Movement.

When Day's Shadows Lengthen (544)

Leech, Bryan Jeffrey

Leech, Bryan Jeffrey (b. Buckhurst Hills, Essex, England, May 14, 1931) was educated at London Bible College, Barrington College in Massachusetts, and North Park Seminary, Chicago, Illinois. He served as a minister in Surrey, England, and then emigrated to the United States in 1955, where he became affiliated with the Evangelical Covenant Church. He has served churches in Boston, Massachusetts; Montclair, New Jersey; and San Francisco, California. He is the current minister of the Montecito Covenant Church in Santa Barbara, California. His publications include a musical play, *Ebenezer*; a novel, *It Must Have Been McNutt*; and *The*

Covenant Hymnal (1973), for which he was a member of the Hymnal Commission of the Evangelical Covenant Church. He was also an assistant editor of *Hymns for the Family of God* (1976).

Happy the Home When God Is There (438)

Leeson, Jane Eliza

Leeson, Jane Eliza (b. London, England, 1809; d. Leamington, Warwickshire, England, November 18, 1881) was a member of the Catholic Apostolic Church and a contributor to its hymnal, but later became a Roman Catholic. Her hymns were also included in Henry Formby's *Catholic Hymns arranged in order for the principal Festivals, Feasts of Saints, and other occasions of Devotion throughout the Year* (1851). Other of her publications are *Infant Hymnings: Hymns and Scenes of Childhood* (1842), *The Christian Child's Book* (1848), *The Child's Book of Ballads* (1849), and *Songs of Christian Chivalry* (1850).

Savior, Teach Me Day by Day (413)

Lemmel, Helen Howarth

Lemmel, Helen Howarth (b. Wardle, England, November 14, 1863; d. Seattle, Washington, November 1, 1961) came to the United States with her family at the age of nine. Her father had been a Wesleyan Methodist minister in England. The family lived for a short time in Mississippi and then settled in Wisconsin. Mrs. Lemmel possessed a fine voice and studied both in the United States and in Germany. She traveled with a woman's quartet on the Chautauqua Circuit for several years and also taught voice at Moody Bible Institute and at the Bible Institute of Los Angeles. After 1904 she made her home in Seattle. Mrs. Lemmel wrote over 500 hymns.

O Soul Are You Weary and Troubled - LEMMEL (311)

Lindeman, Ludvig Mathias

Lindeman, Ludvig Mathias (b. Trondheim, Norway, November 28, 1812; d. Christiana, Norway, May 23, 1887), the son of Ole Andreas Lindeman, was a concert pianist and organist at Vor Frue Kirke, Trondheim, for fifty-seven years. The grandfather, a physician, had changed the family name from Madsen. Ludvig studied under his father and at times was taking his father's place by the age of twelve. He chose music as his profession and succeeded his brother at Vor Frelsers Kirke in 1839, a position he held for the rest of his life. In 1848 he married Aminda Magnhilde Brynie, and later, with their son, Peter, established the Musikkonservatoriet in Oslo (1883). He published his hymnal, *Koralbog for den norske kirke* (1871).

Lindeman was also a great collector of Norwegian and Swedish folk tunes, a number of which he published in his *Aeldre og Nyere Norske Fjeldmelodier* (1853).

KIRKEN (362)

Lloyd, William Freeman

Lloyd, William Freeman (b. Uley, Gloucestershire, England, December 22, 1791; d. Stanley Hall, Gloucestershire, April 22, 1863) was engaged in Sunday School work from his youth, teaching both at Oxford and at London. He was secretary of the Sunday School Union (1810) and was associated with the Religious Tract Society (1816). He founded and edited the *Sunday School Teacher's Magazine*, the *Child's Companion*, and the *Weekly Visitor.* Lloyd also published many books for the use of Sunday School teachers.

My Times Are in Thy Hand (508)

Logan, John

Logan, John (b. Fala, Midlothian, Scotland, 1748; d. London, England, December 28, 1788) was the son of a farmer. Educated at the University of Edinburgh, he was ordained to the ministry of the Church of Scotland and served at South Leith (1777). He was also a member of the committee which prepared the *Translations and Paraphrases* of the Church of Scotland. Because of doctrinal difficulties, Logan was forced either to resign his church at Leith or to be deposed. He chose the former course, moved to London (1782), and for the rest of his life gained a living by his pen. Logan generated some controversy when he claimed several poems as his own which were known to have been written by Michael Bruce.

O God of Bethel, by Whose Hand (140)

Longfellow, Samuel

Longfellow, Samuel (b. Portland, Maine, June 18, 1819; d. Portland, October 3, 1892) was the brother of Henry Wadsworth Longfellow. He was educated at Portland Academy, at Harvard, and at Harvard Divinity School (1846). He was ordained a Unitarian minister and served churches at Fall River, Massachusetts; Brooklyn, New York; and Germantown, Pennsylvania. Longfellow was also involved in literary and hymnic projects. He published a *Life* of his brother (1886) and edited with Samuel Johnson *A Book of Hymns for Public and Private Use* (1846) and *Hymns of the Spirit* (1864). His works also include a book of hymns for evening worship, entitled *Vespers* (1859) and *A Book of Hymns and Tunes* (1860). He and

Johnson often altered the hymns which they included in their hymnals to fit their Unitarian sentiments.

God of the Earth, the Sky, the Sea (97)
Love for All (353)

Longstaff, William Dunn

Longstaff, William Dunn (b. Sunderland, England, January 28, 1822; d. Sunderland, April 2, 1894) was the son of a wealthy ship owner who used his money to assist charitable works. When his friend, Arthur A. Rees, left the Church of England to establish Bethesda Free Chapel, Longstaff went with him and served as treasurer for the chapel and supervisor of the building. He was also a close friend of William Booth, who founded the Salvation Army, and of Dwight L. Moody and Ira D. Sankey. Moody preached at Bethesda Chapel when on his campaign in England.

Take Time to Be Holy (487)

Lorenz, Edmund Simon

Lorenz, Edmund Simon (b. near Canal Fulton, Ohio, July 13, 1854; d. Dayton, Ohio, July 11, 1942) was the son of a missionary to German immigrants in Ohio. He was educated at Otterbein University, Union Biblical Seminary, and Yale Theological Seminary. He also studied music at the University of Leipzig. At the age of twenty, Lorenz was music editor of *Hymns of the Sanctuary and Social Worship* (1874)—the first United Brethren hymnal with tunes. An ordained minister among the United Brethren, he ministered to the High Street church, Dayton (1884-1886), and was president of Lebanon Valley College, Annville, Pennsylvania (1886-1888). He left local and collegiate work because of failing health, and in 1890 founded the music publishing firm of Lorenz and Company. His company published periodicals, including *The Choir Leader* (1894), *The Choir Herald* (1897), and *Kirchenchor* (1897). He edited *Notes of Triumph: for the Sunday School* (1886) with Isaiah Baltzell and was editor of *The Church Hymnal: the Official Hymnal of the United Brethren in Christ* (1935). His published works also include *Practical Church Music* (1909), *Church Music* (1923), *Music in Work and Worship* (1925), and *The Singing Church* (1937).

GRAMMATA (299)
In Vain in High and Holy Lays - WONDERFUL LOVE (273)

Loveless, Wendell Phillips

Loveless, Wendell Phillips (b. Wheaton, Illinois, February 2, 1892; d. October 3, 1987) grew up in Wheaton and went into business in Chicago. Beginning in 1914, he was a member of a touring musical group. He was a Marine Corps officer in World War I, was converted to Christ by reading the Bible for himself, and served as director of the radio department of Moody Bible Institute, Chicago (1926-1947). He was later minister to churches in Wheaton, in Boca Raton, Florida, and in Honolulu, Hawaii, where after his retirement he taught a class at the First Chinese Christian Church. His gospel songs and choruses appeared in his five-volume series, *Radio Songs and Choruses of the Gospel.*

LOVELESS (421)

Lowry, Robert

Lowry, Robert (b. Philadelphia, Pennsylvania, March 12, 1826; d. Plainfield, New Jersey, November 25, 1899) was educated at Bucknell University (1854) and was ordained to the Baptist ministry. He served churches in West Chester, Pennsylvania (1854-1858), and New York City (1859-1869), and the Hanson Place Baptist Church in Brooklyn, New York (1861-1869). While minister to a church at Lewisburg, Pennsylvania, he was also professor of belles-lettres at Bucknell University. In 1875 he became minister of the Park Avenue church in Plainfield, New Jersey, where he remained until his death. Lowry succeeded William B. Bradbury as editor for the Sunday School collections of Bigelow and Main, New York (1868), and collaborated with W. H. Doane in editing many of these volumes, including *Happy Voices* (1865), *Gospel Melodies* (1868), *Bright Jewels* (1869), *Pure Gold* (1871), *Royal Diadem* (1873); *Temple Anthems* (1873), *Brightest and Best* (1875), *Fountain of Song* (1877), *Good and Gold* (1880), and *Glad Refrain* (1886).

All The Way (651)
HANSON PLACE (551)
Low in the Grave He Lay - CHRIST AROSE (245)
Marching to Zion (68)
NEED (574)
Shall We Gather at the River (551)
Something for Jesus (609)
What Can Wash Away My Sin - NOTHING BUT THE BLOOD (344)

Lowry, Somerset Thomas Corry

Lowry, Somerset Thomas Corry (b. Dublin, Ireland, March 21, 1855; d. Torquay, England, January 29, 1932), the son of a lawyer, was educated at Trinity Hall, Cambridge. He was ordained to the ministry of the Church of England, becoming deacon (1879) and priest (1880). He served churches at Doncaster, Yorkshire, and at North Holmwood, and then became vicar of St. Augustine's, Bournemouth (1900-1911). He was rector at Wonston (1914-1919) and thereafter vicar of St. Bartholomew's, Southsea. His works include *The Work of the Holy Spirit* (1894), *Convalescence* (1897), *Lessons from the Passion* (1899), *The Days of Our Pilgrimage* (1900), and *Hymns and Spiritual Songs* (1910).

Son of God, Eternal Savior (161)

Luther, Martin

Luther, Martin (b. Eisleben, Saxony, November 10, 1483; d. Eisleben, February 18, 1546) was the son of a miner, Hans Luther, and his wife Margarete. He was educated at Magdeburg and Eisenach and was granted the M.A. degree from the University of Erfurt. He became an Augustinian monk in 1505 and a priest in the Roman Catholic Church (1507). In 1508 Luther became lecturer at Wittenberg University and was given the doctor of divinity degree (1512). As a result of his visit to Rome (1511) and his views of the work of John Tetzel in selling indulgences, he posted his Ninety-five Theses on the door of the Wittenberg Castle Church (October 31, 1517). During the furor that followed, Frederick, the elector of Saxony, kept Luther safe. Luther denied the supremacy of the pope in *The Babylonian Captivity of the Church* (1519) and was excommunicated (1520). He was summoned to the Diet at Worms (1521), where he refused to recant his beliefs, but was again preserved from death by Frederick. From 1521 to 1534, he worked on his translation of the Bible into the German language, one of his greatest literary achievements. In 1522 he returned to Wittenberg and prepared a revised service of the Mass and a hymnal, *Etlich Cristlich lider Lobegesang und Psalm* (1523-1524).

A Mighty Fortress Is Our God - EIN' FESTE BURG (104)
Christ Jesus Lay in Death's Strong Bonds (237)
Come, Holy Spirit, God and Lord (292)
From Heaven Above (199)
Out of the Depths - AUS TIEFER NOT (549)

Lutkin, Peter

Lutkin, Peter (b. Thompsonville, Wisconsin, March 27, 1858; d.

Evanston, Illinois, December 27, 1931) was educated in the public schools of Chicago and in the choir school of St. James's Cathedral (Episcopal). He served as organist at the latter school at age fourteen. He studied in Europe (1881-1891) and upon his return was organist at St. Clement's Church (1884-1891) and then at St. James's Church (1891-1896). By his teaching and lecturing, he exerted a great influence upon the teaching of music in American schools and colleges. He helped found the American Guild of Organists and was president of the Music Teachers' National Association (1911-1920). He was an editor of the *Methodist Hymnal* (1905) and of the Episcopal *Hymnal* (1918).

LUTKIN (632)

Lvov, Alexis Feodorovich

Lvov, Alexis Feodorovich (b. Reval, now Tallinn, Estonia, June 6, 1799; d. Romanovo, Lithuania, December 29, 1870) was educated under his father, who was director of the Russian Imperial Chapel Choir. He was trained also at the Institute of Road Engineering (1818) and served in the Russian army, rising to the rank of major general. Lvov succeeded his father at the imperial chapel (1837) and remained there for twenty-four years. His works include operas, chamber music, and compositions for the violin. He also edited a volume of chants for the ecclesiastical year as celebrated by the Greek Church. He retired because of deafness in 1867.

RUSSIAN HYMN (586)

Lynch, Thomas Toke

Lynch, Thomas Toke (b. Donmow, Essex, England, July 5, 1818; d. London, England, May 9, 1871) was educated at Islington and, briefly, at Highbury Independent College. He served as a Congregational minister at Highgate (1847-1849) and in Mortimer Street church (1849-1852). His hymn collection *The Rivulet: Hymns for Heart and Voice* (1855) caused a controversy among the Congregationalists because of the "personal" quality of its contents. Subsequent editions were published in 1856 and 1868. Julian says: "Lynch's hymns are marked by intense individuality, gracefulness and felicity of diction, picturesqueness, spiritual freshness, and the sadness of a powerful soul struggling with a weak and emaciated body." Lynch's hymnal was designed as a supplement to the *Hymns* of Isaac Watts. In 1856 he retired from preaching because of ill health, but returned to his pulpit in 1860, and, after it moved to new quarters on Hempstead Road, London (1862), remained there until his death.

Gracious Spirit, Dwell with Me (297)

Lyon, Meyer

Lyon, Meyer (b. 1751; d. Kingston, Jamaica, 1797), called also "Meier Leoni," was cantor to various Jewish synagogues in London, England. From 1768 to 1772 he was cantor to the Great Synagogue there. He tried to sing opera but was unsuccessful because of his unwillingness to sing on Jewish festivals and the Sabbath and also because of his lack of acting ability. In 1787 he became cantor to the Ashkenazic congregation, Kingston, Jamaica, and remained there for the rest of his life.

LEONI (43)

Lyte, Henry Francis

Lyte, Henry Francis (b. Ednam, Kelso, Scotland, June 1, 1793; d. Nice, France, November 20, 1847) was educated at Portora Royal School, Enniskillen, Ireland, and at Trinity College, Dublin. He was awarded the prize for the best poem in English three times during his college career. Although at first intending a career in medicine, he abandoned this idea and was ordained to the ministry of the Church of England (1815). He served churches at Wexford, Marazion, and Lymington. At Marazion in Cornwall he underwent a great spiritual change because of the death of a fellow minister. He began to study his Bible and to preach with a different emphasis. He became perpetual curate of Lower Brixham, Devonshire (1823), where he remained until his death. Lyte's works include *Tales on the Lord's Prayer* (1826), *Poems chiefly Religious* (1833), *The Spirit of the Psalms* (1834), *Poems of Henry Vaughan with a Memoir* (1846), and, posthumously, *Remains* (1850).

> *Abide with Me* (33)
> *Jesus, I My Cross Have Taken* (536)
> *Praise, My Soul, the King of Heaven* (53)

Mackay, William Paton

Mackay, William Paton (b. Montrose, Scotland, May 13, 1839; d. Portree, Scotland, August 22, 1885), educated at the University of Edinburgh, was a physician for a number of years. Feeling that he was called to the ministry, he gave up his medical practice and was ordained in the Presbyterian Church. He served the Prospect Street Presbyterian Church, Hull, beginning 1868. Several of his hymns were published in W. Reid's *Praise Book* (1872).

> *We Praise Thee, O God* (61)

Mackay, Margaret

Mackay, Margaret (b. Hedgefield, Inverness, Scotland, 1802; d. Cheltenham, England, January 5, 1887) was the daughter of Captain Robert Mackay. In 1820 she married Major William Mackay, a distinguished military officer, who died in 1845. Her works include a novel, *The Family at Heatherdale* and a volume of poetry, *Thoughts Redeemed; or Lays of Leisure Hours* (1854).

Asleep in Jesus (671)

Macmillan, Ernest Campbell

Macmillan, Ernest Campbell (b. Mimico, Ontario, August 18, 1893; d. Toronto, Canada, May 6, 1973) was the son of Dr. Alexander MacMillan, a Presbyterian minister who edited *The Hymnary of the United Church of Canada* (1930). Ernest played the organ by the age of ten and studied at the University of Toronto, the University of Edinburgh, and Oxford University (1910). While he was attending the Wagner Festival at Bayreuth, Germany in 1914, World War I began, and he was imprisoned at Ruhleben for the duration of the war. Here he composed his musical work *England*, based on the poet Swinburne's ode, for which Oxford University bestowed on him the honorary Mus.D. degree. He returned to Canada following the war and served subsequently as conductor of the Toronto Symphony Orchestra (1931-1965), principal of the Music Conservatory (1926-1942), and dean of the music faculty, Toronto University (1927-1952). For his musical services to Canada, he was knighted by King George V in 1935. MacMillan also published several books about native Indian and French-Canadian music.

TEMPUS ADEST FLORIDUM (196)

Madan, Martin

Madan, Martin (b. Hertingfordbury, England, 1726; d. Epsom, Surrey, England, May 2, 1790) was brother to the bishop of Peterborough and cousin to William Cowper, the poet. He was educated at Westminster School and at Christ Church, Oxford (1746). He was trained for the law and admitted to the bar. His life was changed, however, when, having been sent by a group of friends to gain material for ridiculing John Wesley, he was converted by Wesley's preaching. He was ordained to the ministry and served for a time as chaplain at Lock Hospital, a women's institution. His publication of *Thelyphthora* (1780), a work advocating polygamy as a solution for the problems of the women in Lock Hospital, raised such a furor that he retired from public ministry and moved to Epsom. In 1760 he published *A Collection of Psalms and Hymns,* which became one of the most popular hymnals of the day. He himself did not write hymns, but he did enduring revision work on the poems of others.

Lo! He Comes with Clouds Descending (289)

Main, Hubert Platt

Main, Hubert Platt (b. Ridgefield, Connecticut, August 17, 1839; d. Newark, New Jersey, October 7, 1925) was the son of the well-known singing teacher Sylvester Main. Although scarcely educated, he learned the music business and music through his association with music publishers. Main was co-editor with Philip Phillips of the *Methodist Episcopal Hymn and Tune Book* (1866). He joined the firm of William Bradbury (1867), and upon Bradbury's death the following year, when the firm of Bigelow and Main was formed, with his father as junior partner, he continued his work and stayed with the firm for the rest of his life. He was an authority on music copyrights, compiled numerous gospel songbooks, and wrote over one thousand compositions. He left his personal collection of hymnals and music books to the Newberry Library, Chicago.

MAIN (520)

Mainzer, Joseph

Mainzer, Joseph (b. Treves, Germany, March 7, 1801; d. Salford, Manchester, England, November 10, 1851) was a singing teacher and journalist. He served as a chorister at Treves Cathedral and studied at Darmstadt, Munich, and Vienna. He was ordained a priest in Germany (1826) and taught in a seminary there. Mainzer later lived in Brussels (1833-1839) and moved to England in 1839. He became an avid promoter of the teaching of sight-singing during the time he lived in Edinburgh (1842-1847). He published *Mainzer's Musical Times and Singing Circular,* which became the *Musical Times* (1847).

MAINZER (384)

Maker, Frederick Charles

Maker, Frederick Charles (b. Bristol, Gloucestershire, England, 1844; d. Bristol, 1927) was an influential figure in independent or "free" church music. He was a chorister in Bristol cathedral, studied the organ under Alfred Stone, and contributed tunes to Stone's *Bristol Tune Book* (1881). He was organist of the Milk Street Free Methodist Church (1882-1910) and during the same years played also at Clifton Downs and Redland Park Congregational churches. He was visiting professor for twenty years

at Clifton College and conducted the Bristol Free Church Choir Association.
ELTON (569)
INVITATION (334)
ST. CHRISTOPHER (229)
WENTWORTH (38)

Malan, Henri Abraham César

Malan, Henri Abraham César (b. Geneva, Switzerland, July 7, 1787 d. Vandoeuvres, Switzerland, May 18, 1864) was a man of many talents, being not only a preacher and musician, but also a printer, carpenter, mechanic, and artist. He was educated at the College of Geneva and, upon his ordination in 1810, became a popular preacher for the National Church of Geneva. In 1821 he withdrew from the Established Church in Geneva because of its Unitarian and formalist leanings and established a chapel in his garden. He preached there for the next forty-three years. Malan placed great emphasis on the viewpoints of John Calvin. The University of Glasgow gave him the honorary D.D. degree in 1826. He is said to have written one thousand hymns and is sometimes called "the greatest name in the history of French hymns." He published *Chants de Sion* (1841).
HENDON (94, 304)

Mann, Arthur Henry

Mann, Arthur Henry (b. Norwich, Norfolk, England, May 16, 1850; d. Cambridge, England, November 19, 1929) was educated at Norwich Cathedral and at New College, Oxford. While a chorister at Norwich at age eight, he could play the cathedral service. He served as organist at St. Pewer's Wolverhampton (1870), at Tettenhall Parish Church (1871-1875), at Beverly Minster (1875), and then at King's Chapel, Cambridge (1875-1928). Mann was a skillful trainer of boys' choirs, an authority on Handel, and music editor for Charles D. Bell's *Church of England Hymnal* (1895).
ANGEL'S STORY (620)

March, Daniel

March, Daniel (b. Millbury, Massachusetts, July 21, 1816; d. Woburn, Massachusetts, March 1, 1909), the son of Samuel and Zoa Park March, grew up on his father's farm and was educated at Millbury Academy and Amherst College. He traveled as a book agent and was principal of Chester Academy, Vermont. After graduation from Yale University (1840), he served as principal of Fairfield Academy, Connecticut (1840-1843). March was ordained to the Congregational ministry in 1845 and served churches in Connecticut, New York, Pennsylvania, and Massachusetts. He was a world traveler and often lectured on his experiences in various parts of the world. Jane P. Gilson became his wife in 1841, and upon her death in 1857, he married Anna B. Laconte (1859). She died in 1878. His son, Frederick William March, was a long-time missionary to Syria. March's works include *Our Father's Home, or, The Unwritten Word; From Dark to Dawn, or, Night Scenes of the Bible; The First Khedive, or, Lessons from the Life of Joseph; Days of the Son of Man; Home Life in the Bible;* and *Walks and Homes of Jesus.*

Hark, the Voice of Jesus Calling (416)

Marlatt, Earl Bowman

Marlatt, Earl Bowman (b. Columbus, Indiana, May 24, 1892; d. Winchester, Indiana, June 13, 1976) was educated at DePauw University and Boston University and did further graduate work at Oxford University and the University of Berlin. He was associate editor of the *Kenosha* (Wisconsin) *News* (1917-1918) and then served in World War I as a lieutenant in the field artillery. He joined the faculty at Boston University in 1923, becoming professor of the philosophy of literature and religious education (1925) and serving as dean of the School of Theology (1938-1945). From 1946 to 1957, Marlatt was professor of philosophy of religion at Southern Methodist University. He was an editor of *The American Student Hymnal* (1928) and a member of the Executive Committee of the Hymn Society of America.

Are Ye Able? (602)

Marriott, John

Marriott, John (b. Cottesbach, near Lutterworth, England, September 11, 1780; d. Broadclyst, near Exeter, England, March 31, 1825) was the son of R. Marriott, rector of Cottesbach. Educated at Rugby and at Christ Church, Oxford, he was ordained in the Church of England (1804) and for four years was tutor at Dalkeith Palace to George Henry, Lord Scott. Here he became a close friend of Sir Walter Scott. The Duke of Buccleugh appointed him to the rectory of Church Lawford, Warwickshire, which post he held the remainder of his life. The health of Marriott's wife prevented his living in Warwickshire, and he resided in Devonshire, where he served several churches. Although he wrote a number of hymns, none of these were published during his lifetime, except without his permission.

Thou, Whose Almighty Word (101)

Marsh, Charles Howard

Marsh, Charles Howard (b. Magnolia, Iowa, April 8, 1886; d. La Jolla, California, April 12, 1956) was the son of a Congregational minister, George Marsh. His parents arrived in the United States from England a few months before his birth. After Charles graduated from high school, J. Wilbur Chapman, the evangelist, invited him to play at the Winona Lake Chautauqua and Bible Conference, Indiana. He acquired additional musical training and taught at the Bible Institute of Los Angeles (1915-1919) and at the University of Redlands (1919-1926). He then went to France where he studied under Charles-Marie Widor and Henri Libert (1924), and under Philipp and Camille Decreaus, Marcel Dupre, and Nadia Boulanger (1926-1928). After returning to the United States, he was president of the European School of Music and Art, Fort Wayne, Indiana, and served as organist for the First Presbyterian Church there (1928-1932). In 1932 he became a professor at Orlando College of Music, Orlando, Florida, and later was organist at the University of Florida and organist-choirmaster at the First Baptist Church, Gainesville, Florida. He served as district supervisor of the Federal Music Project, San Diego, California (1935-1939), and was organist-choirmaster at St. James-by-the-Sea Episcopal Church, La Jolla, California.

CHAPMAN (283)

Marsh, Simeon Butler

Marsh, Simeon Butler (b. Sherburne, New York, June 1, 1798; d. Albany, New York, July 14, 1875) was reared on a farm. He attended his first singing at age sixteen in 1814. His enthusiasm for this work turned him into a singing-school teacher at age nineteen. He studied in a school taught by Thomas Hastings at Geneva, New York (1818), from whom he received great encouragement. Marsh was a member of the Presbyterian Church and served as Sunday School superintendent, choir director, and traveling singing-school teacher among the churches of the Albany Presbytery. He founded a newspaper, *The Intelligencer* (later *The Recorder*) at Amsterdam, New York (1837), and later *The Sherburne News* in Sherburne, New York. After his wife died in 1873, he resided with his son, John Butler Marsh, in Albany, New York. Marsh published three children's books for which he set the type himself.

MARTYN (278)

Martin, Civilla Durfee

Martin, Civilla Durfee (b. Jordan, Nova Scotia, August 21, 1866;

d. Atlanta, Georgia, March 9, 1948) was the daughter of James N. and Irene Harding Holden. She was a village school teacher for a number of years and studied music briefly. She married Walter Stillman Martin and helped him in his evangelistic work, joining him in writing gospel songs.
Be Not Dismayed (127)

Martin, Walter Stillman

Martin, Walter Stillman (b. Rowley, Essex County, Massachusetts, 1862; d. Atlanta, Georgia, December 16, 1935) was educated at Harvard University. He was ordained to the Baptist ministry, but later became a member and minister in the Christian Church (Disciples of Christ). He was professor of Bible at Atlantic Christian College in North Carolina (1916-1919) and then moved to Atlanta, where he resided the remainder of his life. He was married to Civilla Durfee Holden, a native of Nova Scotia. Together they conducted Bible conferences and evangelistic meetings across the United States.
God Will Take Care of You (127)

Mason, Henry Silvernale

Mason, Henry Silvernale (b. Gloversville, New York, October 17, 1881; d. Torrington, Connecticut, November 15, 1964) was educated at Syracuse University (1911) and Boston University School of Theology. He was a member of the faculty of Auburn Theological Seminary, Auburn, New York, where he was organist (1916-1939), instructor of music (1917-1935), and assistant professor of fine arts and religion (1935-1939). Although an Episcopalian, he was organist for the First Presbyterian Church and later for the Second Presbyterian Church in Auburn, the latter of which he served for 17 years.
BEACON HILL (602)

Mason, Lowell

Mason, Lowell (b. Medfield, Massachusetts, January 8, 1792; d. Orange, New Jersey, August 11, 1872) was descended from a family that had been in America since 1653. He learned music both vocal and instrumental from local citizens and was leading the choir in the village church and teaching singing schools at age sixteen. When he was twenty, he went to Savannah, Georgia, and worked as a bank clerk (1812-1827). There he studied music under Frederick L. Abel, a German musician, and also served as organist for the Independent Presbyterian Church. He returned to Boston (1827) and began his lifelong effort to improve church music in the United States. He was president of the Handel and Haydn Society (1827-1832) and directed the well-known Bowdoin Street Church choir in Lyman Beecher's church. In 1829 he began the publication of *The Juvenile Psalmist, or The Child's Introduction to Sacred Music*, and in 1833 established the Boston Academy of Music. He gained approval for the teaching of music in the public schools of Boston (1838). Mason traveled to Europe and studied with Johann Georg Nägeli. While there he collected material from Nägeli and others which served as bases for his tunes and harmonizations which he later published. He is credited with compiling or assisting in the compilation of over eighty hymnals and with composing 1,126 original tunes. He married Abigail Adams of Westboro, Massachusetts, in 1818. His music library was given to Yale University at his death.

> AZMON (2, 504, 505)
> BETHANY (636)
> BOYLSTON (600)
> GERAR (129)
> HAMBURG (233)
> LABAN (531)
> OLIVET (584)
> PEREZ (100)
> ROCKINGHAM (MASON) (510)
> UXBRIDGE (112)
> WESLEY (425)
> WORK SONG (418)

Massie, Richard

Massie, Richard (b. Chester, Cheshire, England, June 18, 1800; d. Pulford Hall, Coddington, England, March 11, 1887) was the son of R. Massie, rector of Coddington, Cheshire, England. He taught himself German and joined others such as Frances E. Cox, Henry J. Buckoll, Arthur T. Russel and Catherine Winkworth in translating German hymns. He published *Martin Luther's Spiritual Songs* (1854) and a translation of Carl J. Spitta's *Psalter und Harpfe*, which he entitled *Lyra Domestica* (1864; 2d series, 1868).

> *Christ Jesus Lay in Death's Strong Bands* (237)

Matheson, George

Matheson, George (b. Glasgow, Scotland, March 17, 1842; d. North Berwick, Scotland, August 28, 1906) was the son of a merchant in Glasgow. Although severely afflicted with approaching blindness from his childhood, and becoming completely blind at eighteen, he was an excellent student at Glasgow Academy (1852) and Glasgow University (1861-1862). He also attended the Divinity School of Glasgow University and was ordained to the Presbyterian ministry (1866). He was minister of St. Bernard's, Edinburgh, from 1866 until his retirement due to ill health in 1899. Matheson was an able preacher and published several theological works. He also published one volume of poetry, *Sacred Songs* (1890).

> *Make Me a Captive, Lord* (617)
> *O Love That Wilt Not Let Me Go* (619)

Maxwell, Mary E.

Maxwell, Mary E. (b. October 4, 1837; d. Richmond, Surrey, England, February 4, 1915). These dates are based on information found in Donald Hustad's *Dictionary-Handbook to Hymns of the Living Church* (1978). While the information is uncertain, it is probably correct. Her maiden name was Mary Elizabeth Braddon. She was educated by private tutors, married John Maxwell in 1874, and was associated with the Keswick Convention in northern England.

> *How I Praise Thee, Precious Savior* (596)

McAfee, Cleland Boyd

McAfee, Cleland Boyd (b. Ashley, Missouri, September 25, 1866; d. Jaffrey, New Hampshire, February 4, 1944) was educated at Park College, Parkville, Missouri, and Union Theological Seminary. He returned to Park College as a teacher and there preached for and directed the choir of the college church (1881-1901). He ministered to the Forty-first Street Presbyterian Church, Chicago (1901-1904) and to the Lafayette Avenue Presbyterian Church, Brooklyn (1904-1912). McAfee was professor of systematic theology at McCormick Theological Seminary, Chicago (1912-1930), and secretary of the Presbyterian Board of Foreign Missions (1930-1936). He made his home at Jaffrey, New Hampshire, following his retirement.

> *There Is a Place of Quiet Rest* - McAFEE (482)

McCann, Forrest Mason

McCann, Forrest Mason (b. Lometa, Texas, October 12, 1931) is the son of Dewey Forrest and Jean Olive Salyer McCann. He is a descendant, on his mother's side, of Francis Redford, who settled on land that is now part of Richmond, Virginia, in 1635. He was educated in the public schools of Texas, at Florida Christian College, Temple Terrace,

Florida (A.A., 1950); at the University of Florida (B.A., 1952; M.A., 1966); and at Texas Tech University (Ph.D., 1980). He married Clara Lugenia Moore of Gainesville, Florida (1952). They have three children: Forrest David, John Sterling, and Carol Jeananne. He has preached among the Churches of Christ since 1947 and taught three years in the public schools of Florida (1965-1968). From 1968 to 1996 he was Professor of English Literature and Language at Abilene Christian University, Abilene, Texas. McCann has served as both a deacon and elder in the Church of Christ. His Ph.D. dissertation at Texas Tech University was entitled "The Development of the Hymn in Old and Middle English Literature." He is co-editor of *Great Songs of the Church, Number Two, with Supplement* (1975) and chairman of the Revision Committee and general editor of *GSR* (1986). He is also the author of this *Handbook to Great Songs of the Church.*

    Come, Now O Lord of Victory (1790)

    Jesus, Wonderful Thou Art (562)

McCheyne, Robert Murray

McCheyne, Robert Murray (b. Edinburgh, Scotland, May 21, 1813; d. Dundee, Scotland, March 25,1843), the son of Adam McCheyne, was educated at Edinburgh University. McCheyne was licensed to preach in the Presbyterian Church (July 1835) and became the minister of St. Peter's Established Church, Dundee (1836). He was recognized as one of the most spiritually minded of the ministers of the Church of Scotland. In 1839 McCheyne was one of a deputation from the General Assembly of the Presbyterian Churches to Palestine on a "Mission of Inquiry to the Jews." He died of unknown causes which baffled all the physicians. His poems were published immediately after his death as *Songs of Zion to Cheer and guide Pilgrims on their way to the New Jerusalem* (1843).

    When This Passing World Is Done (652)

McCutchan, Robert Guy

McCutchan, Robert Guy (b. Mt. Ayr, Iowa, September 13, 1877; d. Claremont, California, May 15, 1958) was the son of Erastus Gilmore and Margaret Edie McCutchan. He was educated at Park College, Parkville, Missouri, and Simpson College, Indianola, Iowa. He taught at Baker University, Baldwin, Kansas (1904), and served as the head of its new Music department (1906). In 1911 he became dean of the School of Music, De Pauw University, Greencastle, Indiana, which post he held until his retirement (1937). McCutchan was one of the foremost hymnologists among American Methodists and was recognized as an authority on Christian song around the world. His handbook to *The Methodist Hymnal* (1935), entitled

Our Hymnody (1937), was the first significant handbook to a hymnal published in the United States. He married Carrie Burns Sharp (1904), and after her death (1941), he married Helen Laura Cowles (1944). He was honored with degrees from several universities. McCutchan served on the Commission of Church Music of the Methodist Episcopal Church (1924-1928), the Joint Commission for the Revision of the Methodist Hymnal (1928-1935), and, after 1937, on the General Conference Committee on Music of the Methodist Church. His published works, besides those mentioned above, include *American Junior Church and Church School Hymnal* (1928), *Standard Hymns and Gospel Songs* (1929), *Hymns in the Lives of Men* (1945), and *Hymn Tune Names* (1957).

All The World (91)

McDaniel, Rufus Henry

McDaniel, Rufus Henry (b. near Ripley, Brown County, Ohio, January 29, 1850; d. Dayton, Ohio, February 13, 1940) was educated in the public schools of Bentonville, Ohio, and at Parker's Academy, Claremont County, Ohio. He was ordained as a minister in the Christian Church (Disciples of Christ) in 1873. He married Margaret Dragoo and preached for various churches in the Southern Ohio Conference of the Christian Church. His last church was in Cincinnati, after which ministry he retired to Dayton, where he lived the remainder of his life. He wrote over one hundred hymns, many of which were published by the Rodeheaver Company.

What a Wonderful Change in My Life (471)

McFarland, John Thomas

McFarland, John Thomas (b. 1851; d. 1913). No information is available on this author. He is said to have written the stanza sometimes attributed to him between the years 1904 and 1908, at the request of Methodist Bishop William Anderson.

Away in a Manger (204)

McFayden, Henry Richard

McFayden, Henry Richard (b. Bladen County, North Carolina, February 1, 1877; d. ?) was the son of a Presbyterian minister and was himself the minister of the Presbyterian Church at Pinetops, North Carolina. He was also a traveling minister for the Nashville, Tennessee Presbytery. Nothing further is known.

The Lone Wild Bird (589)

McGranahan, James

McGranahan, James (b. near Adamville, Pennsylvania, July 4, 1840; d. Kinsman, Ohio, July 7, 1907) was a member of a family with roots in the Christian Church (Disciples of Christ). He received scant education but possessed native musical ability. He was teaching singing schools by age nineteen and was a student in William Bradbury's Normal Music School at Geneseo, New York (1861-1862). McGranahan was an associate of J. G. Towner in holding music conventions and singing schools in Pennsylvania and New York (1862-1864). By 1875 he had studied under George F. Root and was on the faculty of Root's Normal Musical Institute, Somerset, Pennsylvania. After Philip Bliss's death, McGranahan became song leader for Major Daniel W. Whittle, the American evangelist, and traveled throughout the United States and England. He possessed a fine tenor voice and was a pioneer in developing men's choirs. His health broke in 1887, and he lived thereafter in retirement at Kinsman, Ohio. McGranahan published *The Gospel Male Choir* (1878; vol. 2, 1883). He also collaborated with C. C. Case on *Harvest of Song* and with Ira. D. Sankey on *Gospel Hymns Nos. 3, 4, 5 and 6.*

> *Christ Returneth* (281)
> EL NATHAN (537)
> *My Redeemer* (407)
> *O How Love I Thy Law* (301)

McIntosh, Rigdon McCoy

McIntosh, Rigdon McCoy (b. Maury County, Tennessee, April 3, 1836; d. Atlanta, Georgia, July 2, 1899) was educated at Jackson College, Columbia, Tennessee, and studied music under L. C. and Asa B. Everett. He was an associate of the Everetts for several years, teaching in singing schools and helping to edit their publications. He was married to Sallie McClasson of Farmville, Virginia, and through her influence joined the Methodist Episcopal Church, South. He served as head of the music department of Vanderbilt University, Nashville, Tennessee (1875-1877), and was head of the music department of Emory College, Oxford, Georgia (1877-1895). During the 1860s he became music editor for the publishing house of the Methodist Episcopal Church, South, which post he continued into the 1880s. In 1895 he established the R. M. McIntosh Publishing Company and gave the remainder of his life to this work. McIntosh was widely known as a composer, editor, choral director, and teacher. He was employed by the Gospel Advocate Company, Nashville, Tennessee, to serve as music editor of its first hymnal, *Christian Hymns* (1889). His publications include *Tabor* (1866), *Hermon* (1873), the *Methodist Hymn and Tune Book*

(1880), *Prayer and Praise,* with Atticus G. Haygood (1883), *Gospel Grace, McIntosh's Anthems, Glad Tidings, and Amaranth.*

    The Kingdom is Coming (424)

    Promised Land (666)

McKinney, Baylus Benjamin

McKinney, Baylus Benjamin (b. Heflin, Louisiana, July 22, 1886; d. Bryson City, North Carolina, September 7, 1952) was the son of James Calvin and Martha (Heflin) McKinney. He was educated at Mt. Lebanon Academy, Louisiana; the Southwestern Baptist Theological Seminary, Fort Worth, Texas; Siegel-Myers Correspondence School of Music (1922); and Bush Conservatory, Chicago. He has been called the most outstanding Southern Baptist hymnwriter of the first half of the twentieth century. He served on the music faculty of Southwestern Baptist Theological Seminary (1919-1932) and was music editor for the publications of Robert H. Coleman (1918-1935). He married Leila Routh in 1918. During the great depression, he served on the staff of Travis Avenue Baptist Church, Fort Worth (1931-1935). In 1935 he became music editor for the Baptist Sunday School Board, Nashville, Tennessee, and in 1941 was secretary of the Church Music Department of the Sunday School Board. He was the first editor of *The Church Musician* (1950). McKinney was killed in a car wreck as he and his wife were returning to Nashville from the Ridgecrest Baptist Assembly in North Carolina. His publications include *Songs of Victory* (1937), *Broadman Hymnal* (1940), and *Voice of Praise* (1948).

    Blessed Savior, We Adore Thee - GLORIOUS NAME (154)

    Jesus Saves Forever - I SHALL NOT BE MOVED (657)

Medley, Samuel

Medley, Samuel (b. Cheshunt, Hertfordshire, England, June 23, 1738; d. Liverpool, Lancashire, England, July 17, 1799) was the son of a school teacher who was a friend of Isaac Newton. He joined the Royal Navy and was wounded off Port Lagos (1759). After leaving the navy, he read a sermon by Isaac Watts which led him to become a Christian. He joined the Baptist Church in Eagle Street, London, and was himself a school teacher for several years. Believing himself called to preach, he served as minister for the Baptist Church, Watvord, Hertfordshire (1767-1772), and the Byron Street Baptist Church, Liverpool (1772-1799). Most of Medley's hymns were first circulated as leaflets. His publications include *Hymns* (1785; 2d ed. 1785; enlarged, 1787); and *Hymns: the Public Worship and Private Devotion of True Christians Assisted in some Thoughts in Verse*

(1800). His daughter Sarah published his *Memoir* (1833), which contained forty-four additional hymns.

I Know That My Redeemer Lives (552)

Meinecke, Charles Christoph

Meinecke, Charles Christoph (b. Oldenburg, Germany, May 1, 1782; d. Baltimore, Maryland, November 5, 1850) was the son of Karl Meinecke, who was organist to the Duke of Oldenburg. He went to England in 1810 and came to the United States in 1820. Thereafter he was organist at St. Paul's Episcopal Church, Baltimore, serving for the remainder of his life. He published *Music for the Church. . . Composed for St. Paul's Church, Baltimore* (1844).

GLORIA PATRI (Meinecke) (76)

Mendelssohn, Felix

Mendelssohn, Felix (b. Hamburg, Germany, February 3, 1809; d. Leipzig, Germany, November 4, 1847) was the grandson of the great Jewish philosopher Moses Mendelssohn and the son of Abraham Mendelssohn, a banker. His mother, an artist, pianist, and singer, gave young Felix his first instruction. The family moved to Berlin (1811) because the French had occupied Hamburg. At this time the family joined the Lutheran Church, and the Father added Bartholdy to his name to indicate that he was now a Christian. Mendelssohn was a musical genius who at age nine gave his first public musical performance. By the age of twelve he had composed five symphonies. Greatly influenced by the music of Johann S. Bach, at the age of twenty he conducted Bach's *St. Matthew Passion,* its first performance since Bach's death. Mendelssohn wrote the oratorios *St. Paul* (1836) and *Elijah* (1846). He was town music director at Dusseldorf (1833), became director of the Gewandhaus Orchestra in Leipzig (1835), and founded the Leipzig Conservatory (1843).

CONSOLATION (496)
MENDELSSOHN (203)
MUNICH (298)
REYNOLDS (381)
SEASONS (6549)

Merrick, G. P.

No information is available on this composer.
ALDERSGATE (508)

Merrill, William Pierson

Merrill, William Pierson (b. Orange, New Jersey, January 10, 1867; d. New York, June 19, 1854) at age eleven became a member of the Belleville Congregational Church in Newburyport, Massachusetts, but transferred to the Second Dutch Reformed Church, New Brunswick, New Jersey, at age thirteen. Merrill was educated at Rutgers College (1887) and Union Theological Seminary (1890). In 1890 he became a Presbyterian minister and served churches in Pennsylvania; Chicago, Illinois; and New York City. In New York City he was minister to the Brick Presbyterian Church from 1911 until his retirement (1938). In 1917 Merrill was offered the presidency of Union Theological Seminary, but declined. He had a great interest in the theme of world brotherhood. His publications include *Faith Building* (1885), *Faith and Sight* (1900), *Footings and Faith* (1915), *Christian Internationalism* (1919), *The Common Creed of Christians* (1920), *The Freedom of the Preacher* (1922), *Liberal Christianity* (1925), *Prophets of the Dawn* (1928), *The Way* (1933), and *We See Jesus* (1934). Merrill was a successful minister and a widely heralded preacher. He was awarded honorary degrees by Rutgers, New York University, Columbia, and Rollins College in Deland, Florida. He married Clara Dwymour Helmer in 1896.

Rise Up, O Men of God (405)

Messiter, Arthur Henry

Messiter, Arthur Henry (b. Frome, Somersetshire, England, April 12, 1834; d. New York, New York, July 2, 1916) was educated under private tutors and studied music for four years at Northampton. He emigrated to the United States (1863) and at first sang in the choir at Trinity Church, New York City. He then served briefly as organist in Pultney, Vermont, and in Philadelphia, and then returned to Trinity Church as organist (1866), where for the next thirty-one years he was organist, maintaining the high standards of English church music. He also directed men's and boys' choirs. Messiter was music editor for the Episcopal *Hymnal* (1893); edited the *Psalter* (1889), *Choir Office Book* (1891), *Hymnal with Music as Used in Trinity Church* (1893); and wrote a *History of the Choir and Music of Trinity Church* (1906).

MARION (466)

Meyer, Johann David

Meyer, Johann David (17th century) was "Ratsheer" at Ulm in 1691 and published *Geistliche Seelenfreud* (1692). Nothing further is known

of this author/composer.
MEYER (149)

Miles, C. Austin

Miles, C. Austin (b. Lakehurst, New Jersey, January 7, 1868; d. Pitman, New Jersey, March 10, 1946) was educated at the Philadelphia College of Pharmacy and the University of Pennsylvania. He practiced his profession of pharmacist for several years, but upon the publication of his first song, "List, 'Tis Jesus' Voice," he abandoned pharmacy and went to work for the Hall-Mack Company, his publisher. He was their editor and manager for thirty-seven years (1898-1935). When Hall-Mack merged with the Rodeheaver Company (1935), Miles remained as an editor. He was a well-known director in churches, camp meetings, and conventions.

I Come to the Garden Alone - GARDEN (588)

Miller, John, or Johannes Müller

Miller, John, or Johannes Müller (b. Groshennersdorf near Herrnhut, Saxony, Germany, 1756; d. Pudsey, England, 1790), the son of Lutheran parents, was educated at the Moravian grammar school and the Moravian Theological College at Barby, near Magdeburg, Saxony. He went to Fulneck, England as assistant preacher and chaplain (1781). In 1788 he married and settled at Pudsey, where he died of tuberculosis in 1790. Miller made numerous contributions to *The Moravian Hymn Book* (1789).

God Himself Is with Us (7)

Milman, Henry Hart

Milman, Henry Hart (b. London, England, February 10, 1791; d. London, September 24, 1868) was the son of Sir Francis Milman, court physician. He was educated at Dr. Burney's school at Greenwich, at Eton, and at Bransenose College, Oxford, where he had a brilliant student career. He was ordained in the Church of England (1816) and entered upon a literary career as well as serving St. Mary's Church, Reading. In 1821 he was appointed professor of poetry at Oxford. His mind seems to have turned more and more to theological matters. He delivered the Bampton Lectures (1827) and published his *History of the Jews* (1829), a work which opened the door for German higher criticism in England. He became rector of St. Margaret's Church and Canon of Westminster (1835) and published his edition of Gibbon's *Decline and Fall of the Roman Empire* (1839). His greatest work, *Latin Christianity*, was published in 1854. He became dean of St. Paul's Cathedral (1849), a post he held for the remainder of his life.

Milman was a good friend of Reginald Heber, and thirteen of Milman's hymns were published in Heber's *Hymns Written and Adapted to the Weekly Service of the Church Year* (1827). His *Annals of St. Paul* was published posthumously.

Ride On! Ride On in Majesty (216)

Milton, John

Milton, John (b. London, England, December 9, 1608; d, Artillery Walk, St. Giles, England, November 8, 1674) was the son of John Milton, an English scrivener and amateur musician. He was educated at St. Paul's School and at Christ's College, Cambridge. After receiving his degrees, he lived with his parents for six years at Horton (1632-1638) and then traveled on the continent, meeting and conversing with eminent men of letters in France and Italy (1638-1639). He returned to England when he learned of the revolutionary rumblings there, settled in Aldersgate, and opened a school for a few years. He married Mary Powell in 1643, who bore him his children. She died in 1653, the year he became totally blind. He subsequently married Katherine Woodcock and, after her death, Elizabeth Minshull. He was Secretary to the Council of State during the years of the Commonwealth under Oliver Cromwell (1649-1659). Milton's fame rests upon his public writings in prose during the days of the Commonwealth, and more especially upon the poetry of the latter part of his life: *Paradise Lost* (1667), *Paradise Regained* (1671), and *Samson Agonistes*. At various times during his life, he published paraphrases of the Psalms.

Let Us with a Gladsome Mind (84)
The Lord Will Come and Not Be Slow (282)

Minor, George A.

Minor, George A. (b. Richmond, Virginia, December 7, 1845; d. Richmond, January 29, 1904) was educated at a military academy in Richmond. He served in the Confederate Army during the Civil War. After the war he taught in singing schools in Virginia and about 1875 founded the Hume-Minor Company of Richmond and Norfolk, manufacturers of pianos and organs. He married Jennie B. Pope, daughter of Captain J. H. Prince, of Green Plain, Virginia, in 1886. Minor was a member of the First Baptist Church of Richmond and led the music for the Sunday School. His publications include *Golden Light, No. 1* (1879); *Golden Light, No. 2; Golden Light, No. 3* (1884); *Standard Songs* (1896); and a children's collection entitled *The Rosebud*.

Bringing in the Sheaves (443)

Mohr, Joseph

Mohr, Joseph (b. Salzburg, Austria, December 11, 1792; d. Wagrein, Austria, December 4, 1848) was a chorister in the choir of the cathedral at Salzburg. He was ordained a priest in the Roman Catholic Church (1815) and served briefly as an assistant priest at St. Nicholas Church, Obendorf (August 1817-October 1819). J. Vincent Higginson says: "This was an accident in time as Mohr was assigned to another parish shortly thereafter." It was here at St. Nicholas Church that he wrote his world-famous carol. He was vicar at Hintersee (1828) and finally at Wagrein, near St. Johann, from 1837 until his death.

Silent Night, Holy Night (202)

Moment, John James

Moment, John James (b. Orono, Ontario, Canada, February 1, 1875; d. Plainfield, New Jersey, May 11, 1959) was educated at Princeton University (1896) and at Hartford Theological Seminary (1906). He taught at Lawrenceville School (1898-1904). Moment was ordained to the Presbyterian ministry and served churches in East Orange, New Jersey (1906-1908); Jersey City, New Jersey (1908-1911); and, in 1919, became minister to the Crescent Avenue Presbyterian Church, Plainfield, New Jersey, where he served until he retired. While at his last post, he often collaborated with his organist, Charlotte Lockwood Garden, in writing texts for anthems and oratorios. Moment served on the hymnal committee for *The Hymnal* (1933), which was published by the General Assembly of the Presbyterian Church in the United States of America.

Men and Children Everywhere (93)

Monk, William Henry

Monk, William Henry (b. Brompton, London, England, March 16, 1823; d. London, March 1, 1889) received his musical training under Thomas Adams, J. A. Hamilton, and G. A. Griesbach. By age eighteen he was organist for various churches in London. He then joined the faculty of King's College, London, becoming choir director (1847), organist (1849), and professor of vocal music (1874). He was organist at St. Matthias's Church, Stoke Newington, from 1852 until his death. He was also professor of music at the School for the Indigent Blind, the National Training School for Music, and Bedford College, London. Monk made important contributions to Victorian church music as editor of the *Parish Choir* (1840-1851) and as music editor for the early editions of *Hymns Ancient and Modern* (1861 and following). He also assisted in editing *The Book of*

Common Prayer, with Plain Song and Appropriate Music.
    Eventide (33)
    Victory (238)

Monsell, John Samuel Bewley

Monsell, John Samuel Bewley (b. St. Columb's, Londonderry, Ireland, March 2, 1811; d. Guildford, England, April 9, 1875) was the son of Thomas Bewley Monsell, archdeacon of Londonderry. He was educated at Trinity College, Dublin (1832), and entered the ministry of the Church of England (1834). During his career Monsell was chaplain to Bishop Mant, chancellor of the diocese of Connor, rector of Ramoan, vicar of Egham, and rector of St. Nicholas, Guildford. He died as the result of a fall when the stonework gave way during the rebuilding of St. Nicholas Church. Monsell is said to have written about 300 hymns. His published works include *Our New Vicar* (1867), *Hymns and Miscellaneous Poems* (1837), *Parish Musings, or Devotional Poems* (1850), *Spiritual Songs for the Sundays and Holy Days throughout the Year* (1857), *His Presence, Not His Memory* (1855), *Hymns of Love and Praise for the Church's Year* (1863) *Litany Hymns* (1869), *The Parish Hymnal after the Order of the Book of Common Prayer* (1873), and *Nursery Carols.*
    Fight the Good Fight (442)

Montani, Nicola Aloysius

Montani, Nicola Aloysius (b. Utica, New York, November 8, 1880; d. Philadelphia, Pennsylvania, January 11, 1948) studied music in the United States and then went to Rome, where he studied under Lorenzo Perosi and Filippo Capocci. He also studied Gregorian Chant under Dom Mocqueriau and Dom Endine (1905-1906). Upon his return to the United States, he served as organist and choirmaster at St. John the Evangelist Church in Philadelphia (1923-1924) and St. Paul's Church, New York City (1925). Because he had a deep interest in promoting and improving the performance of Gregorian Chant, he organized the Society of St. Gregory (1914) and the Palestrina Choir. He was honored as Knight Commander of the Order of St. Sylvester and served as a member of the Pontifical Institute of Sacred Music. Montani was the editor of the *St. Gregory Hymnal* (1920).
    MONTANI (544)

Montgomery, James

Montgomery, James (b. Irvine, Ayrshire, Scotland, November 4, 1771; d. Sheffield, Yorkshire, England, April 30, 1854) was the son of

John Montgomery, a Moravian minister. His parents, desiring to enter the mission field, left James at Bracehill, near Ballymena, County Antrim, Ireland, in 1783, and sailed for Barbados and Tobago, West Indies, where they both died (1790 and 1791). James then attended a school at Fulneck, near Leeds, but showed more interest in writing poetry than in his studies. He worked in a chandler's shop and finally found his way to London, hoping to find a publisher for his poems. Mr. Joseph Gales, the liberal and inflammatory editor of the *Sheffield Register,* took the young man into his business; and when Gales had to flee the country to avoid political persecution, Montgomery inherited the paper (1794). He changed the name to *The Sheffield Iris* and edited it for thirty-one years. As an editor he championed many liberal causes, including foreign missions and the abolition of slavery. He was also a lecturer on poetry. In 1833, the year slavery was abolished in the British dominions, Montgomery was granted a Royal pension of 200 pounds a year. Beginning about 1814, he developed close ties with the Methodists, and upon his death a Wesleyan chapel in Sheffield was named in his honor. Montgomery's publications include *Prison Amusements* (1797); *The West Indies* (1807); *Songs of Zion* (1822); *The Christian Psalmist* (1825); *Original Hymns for Public, Private, and Social Devotion* (1853); and *Poetical Works* (1st ed., 1828; 4th ed., 1854). Montgomery was a friend of Thomas Cotterill, who tried to introduce hymn singing into the Anglican churches, and of hymn writer William Mercer, vicar of St. George.

> *Angels, from the Realms of Glory* (194)
> *Go to Dark Gethsemane* (218)
> *In the Hour of Trial* (538)
> *Stand Up and Bless the Lord* (85)

Moody, May Whittle

Moody, May Whittle (b. Chicago, Illinois, March 20, 1870; d. Northfield, Massachusetts, August 20, 1963) was the daughter of Daniel Webster Whittle, the American evangelist and an associate of Dwight L. Moody. Her original given name was Mary. She was educated at the Girls' School, established by Moody in Northfield, Massachusetts, and at Oberlin College and the Royal Academy of Music in London, England. She had a fine singing voice and assisted Whittle and Moody in their evangelistic campaigns. May married the son of Dwight Moody, William R. Moody, in 1894. She was co-editor with Charles M. Alexander of the *Northfield Hymnal, No. 3.*

> WHITTLE (528)

Moore, Thomas

Moore, Thomas (b. Dublin, Ireland, May 28, 1779; d. Sloperton, Devizes, Wiltshire, England, February 25, 1852) was the son of John Moore, a small businessman in Dublin. He was educated at Trinity College, Dublin, and studied law in London. Moore served briefly as admiralty registrar in Bermuda (1803) and toured America and Canada. He is the author of some of the most popular songs written in English: "Believe Me If All Those Endearing Young Charms," "The Last Rose of Summer," and "Oft in the Stilly Night." He published a translation of the *Odes of Anacreon* (1800), *Fables for the Holy Alliance* (1823), *Odes on Cash, Corn, Catholics and Other Matters* (1828), *Sacred Songs* (1816-1824), *Lalla Rookh* (1817), *The Epicurean* (1827), and *History of Ireland* (1835). Lord John Russell published his *Memoirs, Journal, and Correspondence* (1855).

Come, Ye Disconsolate (338)

Moore, William

Moore, William (19th century) was the compiler of *The Columbian Harmony* (1825), published in Cincinnati, Ohio. At the time of publication, Moore seems to have resided in Lebanon, Wilson County, West Tennessee.

HOLY MANNA (419)

Moore, William Thomas

Moore, William Thomas (b. Henry County, Kentucky, August 27, 1832; d. 1926) was the son of Richard and Nancy M. Jones Moore. He was educated at Bethany College, West Virginia (1858; 1861). He married Mary A. Bishop, a daughter of the governor of Ohio (1864). Moore began his preaching career in 1853 and served churches in Frankfort, Kentucky (1858-1864), Detroit, Michigan (1865-1866), and Cincinnati, Ohio (1866-1878). In 1875 he helped organize the Foreign Christian Missionary Society, and that year he went to England as its missionary. For the next twenty-one years (1875-1896), he served there, first in Southport, then in Lancashire, and finally at the West London Tabernacle. He also founded the Christian Commonwealth, a religious paper of which he was the editor. In 1896 he returned to the United States to become dean of the Bible College at Columbia, Missouri. Moore's works include the *Christian Quarterly*, of which he was the editor (1869-1875, 1897); *The Living Pulpit of the Christian Church; Lectures on the Pentateuch by Alexander Campbell; The Plea of the Disciples of Christ* (1906); and *A Comprehensive History of the Disciples of Christ* (1909). Moore was one of the best-known promoters of the practice of open membership among the Christian

Churches (Disciples of Christ).
Praise God, Ye Heavenly Host Above (62)

Morris, Leila Naylor

Morris, Leila Naylor (b. Pennsville, Morgan County, Ohio, April 15, 1862; d. Auburn, Ohio, July 23, 1929) was the daughter of a Civil War veteran. When she was four years old, the family moved to Malt, Ohio. After her father's death, she opened, with her sister and mother, a millinery shop in McConnelsville, Ohio. Until her marriage to Charles H. Morris (1881), she was a member of the Methodist Protestant Church, but afterwards joined the Methodist Episcopal Church. About 1890 she began to write religious songs, in which effort she was assisted and encouraged by H. L. Gilmour. She often attended summer camp meetings in various parts of the United States. Her sight failed (1913-1914), but she continued to write hymns with the help of friends. In 1928 she moved to Auburn, Ohio, to live with her daughter, Mrs. W. R. Lunk, and remained there the rest of her life.

If You Are Tired of the Load of Your Sin - McCONNELSVILLE (317)
My Stubborn Will at Last Hath Yielded - SWEET WILL OF GOD (349)
Nearer, Still Nearer - MORRIS (483)

Morison, John

Morison, John (b. Cairnie, Aberdeenshire, Scotland, 1749; d. Canisbay, Caithness, Scotland, June 12, 1798) was educated at the University of Aberdeen (1771). He published poetry in the *Edinburgh Weekly Magazine* in his early life. In 1780 he began serving as minister of Canisbay in Caithness, remaining there for the rest of his life. He was a member of the committee appointed by the General Assembly of the Presbyterian Church (1781) to revise the *Translations and Paraphrases of Sacred Scripture* of 1745.

'Twas on That Night (367)

Mote, Edward

Mote, Edward (b. London, England, January 21, 1797; d. Horsham, Sussex, England, November 13, 1874) was the son of a keeper of a public house. He was apprenticed to a cabinetmaker and came under the influence of the preaching of John Hyatt, who was preacher for one of Lady Huntingdon's chapels on Tottenham Court Road in London. He settled in

Southwark (made famous by Chaucer in *The Canterbury Tales*) and worked as a cabinetmaker and a reporter for the press. He became a Baptist preacher (1852) and served at Horsham, Sussex for twenty-one years. Mote edited *Hymns of Praise, a New Selection of Gospel Hymns* (1836). His title may contain the earliest use of the term "gospel hymns."

My Hope Is Built on Nothing Less (558)

Moultrie, Gerard

Moultrie, Gerard (b. Rugby, England, September 16, 1829; d. Southleigh, England, April 25, 1885) was the son of John Moultrie, an Anglican minister. He was educated at Rugby School and Exeter College, Oxford (1851, 1856). His great-grandfather, who had immigrated to America, returned to England at the outbreak of the Revolutionary War, but his great-granduncle was General William Moultrie, who became governor of South Carolina (1785). He became a priest in the Church of England and served in various posts for the remainder of his life. Moultrie wrote a great number of hymns and was influenced by the Oxford Movement. His published works include *The Primer set forth at large for the use of the Faithful* (1864), *Hymns and Lyrics for the Seasons and Saints' Days of the Church* (1867), *The Espousals of Saint Dorothea and Other Verse* (1870), *The Devout Communicant* (1868), *Six Years' Work in Southleigh* (where he was vicar beginning in 1869), and *Cantica Sanctorum, or Hymns for the Black Letter Saints Days in the English and Scottish Calendars, to which are added a few Hymns for Special Occasions* (1880). He was also an excellent translator of Greek, Latin, and German hymns.

Let All Mortal Flesh Keep Silence (386)

Mozart, Wolfgang Amadeus

Mozart, Wolfgang Amadeus (b. Salzburg, Austria, January 27, 1756; d. Vienna, Austria, December 5, 1791) was the son of Leopold Mozart, kappellmeister to the prince-archbishop of Salzburg. He was perhaps the greatest musical genius in the history of the Western world. At age six he toured with his father and sister and amazed audiences everywhere by his virtuosity on the piano. He became famous throughout all Europe, but was never able to keep nor to handle money. He married Constanze Weber, the cousin of Carl Maria von Weber (1782). Mozart died at age thirty-six. He wrote over six hundred musical works.

ELLESDIE (536)

JORGENSON (106)

Mund, E. D.

This is a pseudonym for Edmund Simon Lorenz (q.v.)
In Vain, in High and Holy Lays (273)

Murray, James Ramsey

Murray, James Ramsey (b. Andover, Massachusetts, March 17, 1841; d. Cincinnati, Ohio, March 10, 1905) was the son of Walter and Christian Morrison Murray, who came to the United States in 1840. He studied under Lowell Mason, William B. Bradbury, George F. Root, and George Webb. Murray also studied at the Musical Institute, North Reading, Massachusetts (1856-1859). He served in the Union Army as a musician during the Civil War (1862) and after the war worked for the firm of Root and Cady, for whom he edited the monthly *The Song Messenger*. When the firm's offices were destroyed by the great Chicago fire (1871), he went to Andover, Massachusetts, to teach music (1871-1881). He joined the John C. Church Company, Cincinnati (1881), and remained with them for the rest of his life. He edited *The Musical Visitor* for the Church Company, and composed many songs. His publications include *The Prize, Royal Gems, Pure Diamonds, Murray's Sacred Songs,* and *Dainty Songs for Little Lads and Lasses.*

Away in a Manger (204)

Nägeli, Hans Georg

Nägeli, Hans Georg (b. Wetziken, near Zurich, Switzerland, May 26, 1774; d. Wetziken, December 26, 1836). At the age of eighteen, Nägeli established a music publishing firm which published the first printing of Beethoven's sonatas, Opus 31. He also founded the Zürcherische Singinstitut and was a pioneer in music education, to which he applied the educational methods of Pestalozzi. His works include *Gesangsbildungslehre nach Pestalozziaschen Grundsätzen* (1810) and *Christliches Gesangbuch* (1828).

DENNIS (394)
NAOMI (591)

Neale, John Mason

Neale, John Mason (b. London, England, January 23, 1818; d. East Grimstead, Sussex, England, August 6, 1866) was the son of Cornelius and Susanna Good Neale. He was educated at Sherbourne Grammar School, under private tutors, and at Trinity College, Cambridge. He was fellow and tutor in Downing College, Cambridge. Although both his parents were Evangelicals, and although he married Sarah Norman Webster, the daughter of an Evangelical minister, Neale was identified with the Oxford Movement and helped found the Ecclesiological, or Cambridge, Camden Society. He married and was ordained a priest in the Church of England (1842), but his high church opinions prevented his receiving a significant pastoral charge. In 1843 he discovered he had advanced tuberculosis and went to Madeira, where he stayed until 1844. In 1846 Neale was made Warden of Sackville College, East Grimstead, a home for elderly men. He remained in this post for the remainder of his brief life, spending his days in literary endeavors, in advancing the Oxford Movement, and in assisting the nursing sisterhood he had formed to help orphans and young women. Neale's great contribution to Christian song was in making known to the Western world the riches of the literature of the Greek Church. He was the greatest of the Greek and Latin translators. His publications include *Hymns for Children* (1842), *Medieval Hymns and Sequences* (1851, 1854), *Commentary on the Psalms* (1860), *Hymns of the Eastern Church* (1862), and *Hymns Chiefly Medieval, on the Joys and Glories of Paradise* (1865). Of the 105 hymns in the *Hymnal Noted*, 94 are by Neale. He also made a significant contribution to *Hymns Ancient and Modern*, as may be seen by the number of his hymns included.

> *All Glory, Laud, and Honor* (167)
> *Art Thou Weary?* (332)
> *Brief Life Is Here Our Portion* (673)
> *Christ Is Made the Sure Foundation* (364)
> *Creator of the Stars of Night* (160)
> *Good Christian Men, Rejoice* (206)
> *O Come, O Come, Emmanuel* (182)
> *O Sons and Daughters, Let Us Sing* (246)
> *The Day of Resurrection* (242)

Neander, Joachim

Neander, Joachim (b. Bremen, Germany, 1650; d. Bremen, May 31, 1680) was educated under his father at the Pedagogium in Bremen, and afterwards in the Gymnasium Illustre there. He led a rather carefree and non religious life, but was converted through the preaching of Theodore Under-Eyck of St. Martin's Church in Bremen. He acted as tutor to young men at Frankfurt-am-Main and later at the University of Heidelberg. He was appointed Rector of the Latin School at Dusseldorf (1874), but his association with the Pietists caused him to be suspended from his post. He returned to Bremen (1679) as assistant to Under-Eyck at St. Martin's Church, but died of tuberculosis the following year. He wrote about 60 hymns which have been widely used and has been called "the Paul Gerhardt of Calvinism" because he is the leading hymnist of the German Reformed Church.

ARNSBERG (7)
NEANDER (83)
Praise to the Lord, the Almighty (45)

Needham, John

Needham, John (b. ca. 1787) was the son of John Needham, a Baptist minister at Hitchin, Hertfordshire, England. He was probably educated by his father, whom John Julian calls "a tutor and in repute . . . a learned man." The younger Needham's life is a blank. In 1750 he was associate minister with John Beddome at the Baptist Church in Bristol. After Beddome retired, a controversy arose regarding the plan of having two men as ministers, and Needham was forced to withdraw. He and those who followed him met for a time with the Baptist Church in Callowhill Street, where a Mr. Foote was preacher, but they met as a separate congregation, merely using the Callowhill meeting house. The two churches united in 1758, with Foote and Needham as co-pastors. This arrangement continued until 1784. Needham published *Hymns, Devotional and Moral, on Various Subjects, collected chiefly from the Holy Scriptures* (1768).

Awake, My Tongue, Thy Tribute Bring (67)

Neumeister, Erdmann

Neumeister, Erdmann (b. Uchteritz near Weissenfels, Germany, May 12, 1671; d. Hamburg, Germany, August 18, 1756) was the son of Johann Neumeister, a schoolmaster and organist. He was educated at the University of Leipzig (1695) and was lecturer there for two years. In 1704 he became tutor to the daughter of Duke Johann George at Weissenfels and assistant court preacher. Following the death of the duke's daughter, Neumeister went to Sorau as senior court preacher (1706). Highly regarded as a preacher in his day, he was a strenuous opponent of Pietism and the Moravians and a defender of High Lutheranism. He is regarded as the originator of the church cantata. His works include *Der Zugang zum Gnaden-stuhle Jesu Christo* (1705), *Fünffache Kirchen-Andachten* (1716), and *Evangelischer Nachklang* (1718).

Sinners, Jesus Will Receive (324)

Newbolt, Michael Robert

Newbolt, Michael Robert (b. Lambourn, Berkshire, England, 1874;

d. Bierton, Buckinghamshire, England, February 7, 1956) was educated at St. John's College, Oxford. He became a deacon in the Church of England (1899) and a priest (1900). Newbolt then served as assistant curate of Wantage (1899-1905); vicar of St. Mary's, Iffley (1905-1910); principal of the Missionary College, Dorchester (1910-1916); perpetual curate of St. Michael and All Angels, Brighton (1916-1927); and canon of Chester Cathedral (1927-1946). In 1946 and following, he was licensed to officiate in the diocese of Oxford.

Lift High the Cross (224)

Newell, William Reed

Newell, William Reed (b. Savannah, Ohio, May 22, 1868; d. Deland, Florida, April 1, 1956) was educated at Wooster College (1891) and at Princeton and Oberlin Theological Seminaries. He was a Congregational minister and served the Bethesda Congregational Church in Chicago (1895). That same year he became assistant superintendent of the Moody Bible Institute, Chicago. D. L. Moody suggested that he conduct Bible classes not only in Chicago but in the other great cities in the United States and Canada. These classes were eminently successful and led to the publication of various study guides on Old and New Testament books.

Years I Spent in Vanity and Pride (268)

Newman, John Henry

Newman, John Henry (b. London, England, February 21, 1801; d. Edgbastgon, England, August 11, 1890) was the son of John Newman, a banker. He was educated at Ealing and at Trinity College, Oxford (1820). He became a Fellow of Oriel College, Oxford (1822) and was ordained in the Church of England (1824). Newman served as tutor at Oriel and was rector of St. Mary's, Oxford (1828). He was one of the most popular professors at Oxford during his tenure there. In association with John Keble and William Pusey, he wrote many of the "Tracts for the Times," which set forth the tenets of the Oxford Movement. "Tract 90" (1841) caused his retirement from Oxford and led to his recantation of all he had written against Roman Catholicism (1843) and his reception into the Roman Catholic Church (1845). After 1858 Newman lived at Edgbaston Oratory, Birmingham. He became a cardinal in the Roman Church in 1879. His published works, which are numerous, include *Lyra Apostolica* (1836), *The Development of Christian Doctrine* (1845), *Apologia pro Vita Sua (1864); Verses on Various Occasions* (1868), and *Essay in Aid of a Grammar of Assent* (1870). His series of lectures which have been entitled *The Idea of a University* (1852) is one of the classic statements of the value of a liberal education.

Lead, Kindly Light (483)

Newton, John

Newton, John (b. London, England, July 24, 1725; d. London, December 21, 1807) had a believing mother but an unbelieving father. His mother died when he was seven, and he went to sea with his father, where he grew more and more into a confirmed infidel. He experienced marvelous and horrible adventures at sea, undergoing floggings, slave trading, and the prospect of imminent death. He was led back to his mother's faith by the reading of Thomas à Kempis's *Imitation of Christ* and by the memory of his childhood sweetheart and future wife, Mary Catlett. From 1748 to 1754, he was the captain of a slave ship, but was growing closer to Christ. He left the sea in 1754 and served as tide surveyor in Liverpool, where he came under the influence of George Whitefield and the Wesleys. In 1764, though nearly forty years old, he became a minister in the Church of England, serving as curate of Olney. Here he collaborated with William Cowper to produce the *Olney Hymns* (1779). Later he was rector of St. Mary's Woolnoth, London (1779-1807), where he spent the remainder of his life. He wrote the following epitaph for his tombstone:

John Newton, Clerk
Once an infidel and libertine,
    A servant of slaves in Africa:
Was by the rich mercy of our Lord and Saviour, Jesus Christ
Preserved, restored, pardoned
    And appointed to preach the faith
    He had laboured long to destroy.
Near sixteen years at Olney in Bucks;
    And twenty-seven years in this church.

Amazing Grace (121,122)
Glorious Things of Thee Are Spoken (447)
How Sweet the Name of Jesus Sounds (279)
May the Grace of Christ Our Savior (17)

Nicetas of Remesiana

Nicetas of Remesiana (b. c. 335; d. c. 416) was bishop of Remesiana, who went as a missionary to Dacia (modern Romania) from 392 to 414. He was a contemporary of Jerome, the translator of the Latin

Vulgate, and a friend of Aurelius Clemens Prudentius, the hymnwriter.
We Praise Thee, God (63)

Nicholson, James

Nicholson, James (b. Ireland, c. 1828; d. Washington, D. C., November 6, 1876) came to the United States about 1850. For the next twenty years, he lived in Philadelphia, where he was a member of the Wharton Street Methodist Episcopal Church. He then moved to Washington, D. C. (1871) and worked as a clerk in the Post Office Department. His avocation was teaching Sunday School classes, leading singing, and helping with evangelism. Nicholson was buried in Philadelphia.
Lord Jesus, I Long to Be Perfectly Whole (631)

Nicholson, Sidney Hugo

Nicholson, Sidney Hugo (b. London, England, February 9, 1875; d. Ashvord, Kent, England, May 30, 1947) was the son of Sir Charles Nicholson, a founder and first chancellor of the University of Sydney. He was educated at Rugby and New College, Oxford, and the Royal College of Music. While a student at the latter institution, he served as organist at Barnet Parish Church (1897). He also served as organist at Eton College and at Carlisle Cathedral (1904). From 1908 to 1918, he was organist at Manchester Cathedral and then went to Westminster Abbey (1918-1927). He founded the School of English Church Music (1927) and served as its director until his death. He was knighted by King George VI (1938). Nicholson served as music editor of *Hymns Ancient and Modern* beginning in 1913 and was later chairman of the hymnal committee (1938-1947). His publications include *Boys Choirs* (1922), *A Manual of English Church Music* (1923), *Quires and Places Where They Sing* (1932), and *Peter—the Adventures of a Chorister* (1944).
CRUCIFER (224)

Nicholai, Philip

Nicholai, Philip (b. Mengeringhausen in Waldeck, August 10, 1556; d. Hamburg, Germany, October 22, 1608) was the son of a Lutheran minister. He was educated at the University of Erfurt and at Wittenberg (1579). For a time he assisted his father at Mengeringhausen and then served as minister at Herdecke. He was forced to leave this town when the Spanish invaded the city in 1568 because the town council was controlled by Roman Catholics. His life then entered a period of controversy. In 1588 he was chief pastor to Countess Margaretha of Waldeck and tutor to her son, Wilhelm Ernst. After disagreeing with the Calvinists, he moved to the city of Unna (1596). At Unna he again had a controversy with the Calvinists. In 1597-1598 a terrible plague struck this city, and here Nicolai published his *Frewden-Spiegel dess ewigen Lebens* (1599) as a devotional help to himself and others. When the Spaniards invaded Unna, Nicolai had to flee (1598). In 1601 he became minister to St. Catherine's Church, Hamburg, where he served the remainder of his life. Because of his powerful preaching he has been called a "second Chrysostom." He died of a fever in Hamburg.

> *How Brightly Beams the Morning Star* (186)
> *Wake, Awake, for Night Is Flying* (286)

North, Frank Mason

North, Frank Mason (b. New York, New York, December 3, 1850; d. Madison, New Jersey, December 17, 1935) was educated at Wesleyan University (1872; 1875) and ordained to the Methodist ministry (1872). He served churches in Florida, New York, and Connecticut (1872-1892). In 1892 he became editor of the *Christian City* and corresponding secretary of the New York Church Extension and Missionary Society of the Methodist Episcopal Church. He held these posts until 1912. In 1919 he became secretary of the Methodist Board of Foreign Missions. North was president of the Federal (now the National) Council of Churches of Christ in America (1916-1920).

> *Where Cross the Crowded Ways of Life* (415)

Nusbaum, Cyrus Silvester

Nusbaum, Cyrus Silvester (b. Middlebury, Indiana, July 27, 1861; d. Wichita, Kansas, December 27, 1937) was educated in the public schools of Indiana and began teaching school in Marion County, Kansas (1886). He became a Methodist minister (1886) and served various churches in Kansas. He was educational secretary of Southwestern College, Winfield, Kansas (1895-1897); minister at Ottawa, Kansas (1897-1903); presiding elder of the Independent District (1903-1907); and minister at Parsons, Kansas (1908-1914). In 1914 he became conference evangelist. President Woodrow Wilson appointed Nusbaum as an inspector of the Red Cross in France during World War I, with the rank of captain. Following the war he served as a lecturer and evangelist, holding meetings in Kansas, Nebraska, Oklahoma, and Texas. He married Harriett E. Erwin in 1886. Nusbaum spent his declining years ministering to small churches in Kansas. He is buried at Kingman, Kansas.

> *Would You Live for Jesus* (628)

O'Kane, Tullius Clinton

O'Kane, Tullius Clinton (b. Fairfield County, Ohio, March 10, 1830; d. Delaware, Ohio, February 10, 1912) was educated at Ohio Wesleyan University (1852- 1855). He tutored in mathematics at his university and was a school superintendent in Cincinnati (1857). He worked for the piano firm of Philip Phillips and Company (1864-1867) and then moved to Delaware, Ohio, where he worked as a traveling representative of the Smith American Organ Company of Boston. His music business interests led to his compiling collections of Sunday School songs, including *Fresh Leaves* (1868); *Dew Drops of Sacred Song, Songs of Worship* (1873); *Jasper and Gold* (1877); and with C. C. McCabe and John R. Sweney, *Joy to the World* (1878). He also published, with McCabe, Sweney, and W. J. Kirkpatrick, *Songs of Redeeming Love, No. 1* (1882) and *No. 2* (1887).

SOTER (171)

O'KANE (667)

Oakeley, Frederick

Oakeley, Frederick (b. Shrewsbury, Worcester, England, September 5, 1802; d. Islington, London, England, January 29, 1880) was the son of Sir Charles Oakeley, who served as governor of Madras, India. He was educated at Christ Church, Oxford (1824), and became a fellow of Balliol College (1827). Oakeley then entered the ministry of the Church of England and was appointed prebendary of Litchfield Cathedral (1832), preacher at Whitehall (1837), and minister of Margaret Chapel, Margaret Street, London (1839). While at the latter place, he translated hymns from the Latin and drew ever closer to those associated with the Oxford Movement. Through the influence of John Henry Newman, he left the Church of England and entered the Roman Catholic Church (1845). Subsequently, he became canon of the Catholic Pro-cathedral in Westminster, where he spent many years helping the poor. His published works include *Devotions Commemorative of the Most Adorable Passion of our Lord and Saviour Jesus Christ* (1842); *The Youthful Martyrs of Rome, a Christian Drama* (1856); and *Lyra Liturgica: Reflections in Verse for Holy Days and Seasons* (1865).

O Come, All Ye Faithful (210)

Oakeley, Herbert

Oakeley, Herbert (b. Ealing, Middlesex, England, July 22, 1830; d. Eastbourne, East Sussex, England, October 26, 1903) was the son of Herbert Oakeley, vicar of Ealing. He was educated at Rugby and at Christ

Church, Oxford (1853, 1856). He studied music at Leipzig, Dresden, and Bonn, Germany. Oakeley served as Reid Professor of Music at Edinburgh (1865-1891) and became influential in Scottish musical circles. He received several honorary degrees from British and Canadian universities and was knighted by Queen Victoria (1876) for having composed the music used at the inauguration of the Scottish monument to the Prince Consort Albert. He was named composer to the Queen in 1881. Oakeley was a skilled improviser on the organ.

ABENDS (36)

Oatman, Johnson, Jr.

Oatman, Johnson, Jr. (b. Franklin County, Ohio, October 10, 1841; d. Toledo, Ohio, October 14, 1897) was the son of Johnson and Rachel Ann Cline Oatman. He was educated at Herbert's Academy, Vincentown, New Jersey, and at the New Jersey Collegiate Institute, Bordentown. He entered the ministry of the Methodist Episcopal Church (1865), but never served in any permanent assignment. He was associated with his father in the mercantile business and later owned his own insurance business in Mount Holly, New Jersey. When he was about fifty, he began to write gospel song texts which were set to music by such notables as John R. Sweney, William J. Kirkpatrick, Charles H. Gabriel, and E. O. Excell.

Christ Will Me His Aid Afford (650)
I'm Pressing On (630)
When Upon Life's Billows (545)

Olearius, Johannes

Olearius, Johannes (b. Halle, Saxony, Germany, September 17, 1611; d. Weissenfels, Germany, April 24, 1684) was the son of the minister of St. Mary's Church and the superintendent at Halle. Johannes was educated at the University of Wittenberg, earning an M.A. (1632) and D.D. (1643). He was a member of the philosophy faculty at Wittenberg (1635) and superintendent of Querfurt (1637-1643). Later he was court preacher to Duke August of Sachsen-Weissenfels, private chaplain at Halle, and later its superintendent (1664). He later held the same post under Duke Johann Adolf at Weissenfels (1680-1684). Olearius wrote a commentary on the entire Bible and published *Geistliche Singe-Kunst* (1671), one of the most important German hymnals of the seventeenth century. He wrote over 300 hymns.

Comfort, Comfort Now My People (183)

Oliver, Henry Kemble

Oliver, Henry Kemble (b. Beverly, Massachusetts, November 24, 1800; d. Salem, Massachusetts, August 12, 1885) was educated at the Boston Latin School, at Philips Andover Academy and then at Harvard and Dartmouth (1818). He was a church organist at St. Peter's Church and at North Church in Salem, Massachusetts, and at the Unitarian church in Lawrence for thirty-six years. He also taught school in Salem for twenty-four years (1818-1842). During this time he served on the committee which helped to organize the forerunner of the National Education Association. His career included his being adjutant-general of the Massachusetts militia (1844-1858), Massachusetts state treasurer (1860-1865), director of the Massachusetts Bureau of Statistics of Labor (1869-1873), and mayor of Salem (1877-1880). He also founded the Salem Oratorio Society, the Salem Glee Club, and the Mozart Association. He edited with S. P. Tuckerman and A. Bancroft *The National Lyre* (1848), *Oliver's Collection* (1860), and *Original, Hymn Tunes* (1875). When he was seventy-two years old he conducted his tune FEDERAL STREET at the great Peace Jubilee in Boston (1872).

FEDERAL STREET (316)

Olivers, Thomas

Olivers, Thomas (b. Tregynon, near Newtown, Montgomeryshire, Wales, 1725; d. London, England, March 1799) was left an orphan at the age of four, and, passed from relative to relative, led an uneducated and careless life. By age eighteen, thoroughly steeped in ungodliness, he heard George Whitefield preach on the text "Is not this a brand plucked out of the fire?" This led to his conversion in Bristol, and he joined the Methodist church at Bradford-on-Avon, carrying on his trade of shoemaker. Here he also met John Wesley, who appointed him an itinerant preacher (1752). For the next twenty-five years he traveled more the 100,000 miles on horseback and preached throughout Cornwall. For a time he edited the *Methodist Magazine* but was dismissed from the post because of his lack of education (1789). He then retired to London for the remaining years of his life.

The God of Abraham Praise (43)

Olson, Ernst William

Olson, Ernst William (b. Skane, Sweden, March 15, 1870; d. Chicago, Illinois, October 6, 1958) emigrated with his parents to the United States (1875) and settled first near Wahoo, Nebraska, and then in Texas.

He was educated at Augustana College, Rock Island, Illinois (1891). He then served as editor for several Swedish publications and was office editor, first for the Engberg-Holmberg Publishing Company, Chicago (1906-1911), and then for the Augustana Book Concern (1912-1949). He was honored for his abilities in both Swedish and English. Olson published *A History of the Swedes in Illinois* (1908), served on the committee which published *The Hymnal* (1925) and the *Service Book and Hymnal* (1958). He contributed many translations and a few original English poems to *The Hymnal* (1925).

Children of the Heavenly Father (644)

Owen, William

Owen, William (b. Bangor, Caernarvonshire, Wales, December 12, 1813; d. Caernarvon, July 20, 1893) worked in the Penrhyn slate quarries at Bangor. He spent most of his life in the village of Caeathraw in his home county. From his youth he was well known for his singing ability, and he published a collection of anthems and hymn tunes in his old age entitled *Y Perl Cerddorol* (The Pearl of Music).

BRYN CALFARIA (252)

Owens, Priscilla Jane

Owens, Priscilla Jane (b. Baltimore, Maryland, July 21, 1829; Baltimore, December 5, 1907) was the daughter of Isaac and Jane Stewart Owens. She lived all her life in Baltimore, where she taught in the public schools for forty-nine years. She was a member of the Union Square Methodist Episcopal Church and did much work for the Sunday School there. Her writings appeared in the *Methodist Protestant* and in the *Christian Standard*.

We Have Heard the Joyful Sound (307)

Oxenham, John

Oxenham, John (b. Manchester, England, November 12, 1852; d. London, England, January 23, 1941) was the pseudonym of William Arthur Dunkerly, which he took in 1913, when he gave himself to a writing career. The name came from one of the sailor-heroes of Charles Kingsley's novel *Westward Ho!* He was educated at Old Trafford School and at Victoria University, Manchester. He engaged in business with his father and, after graduation from college, managed the French branch of the business. He married Margery Anderson, a Scottish woman, about 1876, and the couple came to the United States to open a branch of their business. Dunkerly returned to England (1881) and, having become interested in the *Detroit Free Press* in the U. S., published a London edition for several years. His first literary efforts, published in one of his newspapers, was so successful that he turned completely to a literary career. Dunkerly left London in 1913 and settled at Hanger Hill Farm at Ealing. Here he began to use his famous pseudonym. He published over forty novels and twenty volumes of verse and other prose. He was a member of the Congregational Church.

In Christ There Is No East or West (392)

Palestrina, Giovanni Pierluigi Sante da

Palestrina, Giovanni Pierluigi Sante da (b. Palestrina, Italy, 1525; d. Rome, Italy, February 2, 1594) was the son of wealthy parents in Palestrina and took the name "da Palestrina" to indicate his birthplace. He served as a chorister and was educated at the basilica of Santa Maria Maggiore (1534). In 1544 he returned to Palestrina, where he served as organist and choirmaster in the cathedral. When the bishop of Palestrina became Pope Julius II (1551), Palestrina was appointed choirmaster of the Cappella Guilia at St. Peter's, Rome. He served as a singer in the Papal chapel, but was dismissed because he was married (1555). He was choirmaster at St. John Lateran and then at Santa Maria Maggiore beginning in 1561. From 1565 to 1571, he taught at the Jesuit Seminary in Rome and, from 1572 until his death, was choirmaster of the Cappella Guilia at St. Peter's. After his wife died in 1580, he briefly considered entering the Roman priesthood, but instead he married the wealthy widow of a furrier and leather merchant. His complete works, as published by Breitkopf and Hartel, comprise thirty-three volumes.

Victory (238)

Palmer, Ray

Palmer, Ray (b. Little Compton, Rhode Island, November 12, 1808; d. Newark, New Jersey, March 29, 1887) was the son of Judge Thomas Palmer. He was educated at Phillips Academy and Yale University. Palmer was ordained to the ministry of the Congregational Church (1835) and served churches at Bath, Maine (1835-1850), and Albany, New York (1850-1865). He was corresponding secretary for the American Congregational Union, New York City (1866-1878). During these years he wrote and published various prose and poetic works, including *Spiritual Improvement* (1839), *Hymns of My Holy Hours and Other Pieces* (1868), and Complete *Poetical Works* (1876). He contributed several original and translated hymns to Park and Phelps's *Sabbath Hymn-Book* (1858). Palmer never allowed his hymn texts to be revised and never took any compensation for their use by others. He retired in 1878.

>*Jesus, Thou Joy of Loving Hearts* (263)
>*My Faith Looks Up to Thee* (584)

Palmer, Horatio Richmond

Palmer, Horatio Richmond (b. 1834; d. 1907) was an American music teacher. He was director of the Church Choral Union in New York City and in Brooklyn, New York. His works were often published by the Bigelow and Main Company of New York. These included *The Song Queen, The Song King, The Sovereign, Palmer's Theory of Music, Palmer's Piano Primer, The Common Sense Music Reader* (with A. T. Schauffler), and the *Choral Union* (1884).

>HAMARTOLOI (331)
>PALMER (54)

Parker, Edwin Pond

Parker, Edwin Pond (b. Castine, Maine, January 13, 1836; d. Hartford, Connecticut, May 28 1925) was educated at Bowdoin College and at Bangor Theological Seminary. He was an ordained Congregational minister and served the Center Church, Hartford, Connecticut, for fifty years. He had a great interest in church music, wrote over 200 hymns, and assisted in the compilation of several hymnals, including *Song Flowers* (1866) and *Book of Praise* (1868). He contributed hymns to the *Christian Hymnal* (1877).

>MERCY (293)

Parry, Joseph

Parry, Joseph (b. Merthyr Tydfile, Wales, May 21, 1841; d. Cartref, Penarth, Wales, February 17, 1903) was the son of a poor family and at age ten was already working the iron furnaces of his native village. His family emigrated to the United States in 1854, settling in Danville, Pennsylvania, where he was an ironworker. He studied his first music under his fellow ironworkers at Danville and attended the Normal Music School at Geneseo, New York (1861). In a few years he returned to Wales and won prizes in several singing competitions (Eisteddfod contests) between 1863 and 1866. He was afterwards able to study at the Royal Academy of Music (1868-1871) and was awarded degrees from Cambridge University (1871, 1878). Parry came again to the United States to conduct a private music school (1871-1873), but then returned to Wales to teach in the Welsh University

College, Aberystwyth (1873-1879). He then taught privately at Aberystwyth and Swansea (1870-1888) and finally at University College, Cardiff from 1888 until his death. His musical work was quite prolific in many forms, including over four hundred hymn tunes. He was honored in 1896 for his great contribution to Welsh music.

    ABERYSTWYTH (181, 276)

Peace, Albert Lister

    Peace, Albert Lister (b. Huddersfield, England, January 26, 1844; d. Liverpool, England, March 14, 1912) was a musical prodigy, gifted with perfect pitch, who at the age of nine became organist at the church in Holmfirth, Yorkshire. He was educated at Oxford University (1870-1875) and served as organist at Glasgow Cathedral (1879-1896) and St. George's Hall, Liverpool (1897-1912). Peace was one of Scotland's greatest organists, and when the Church of Scotland removed the ban on organs in the churches (1865), he gained popularity for his organ recitals. He was editor of *The Scottish Hymnal* (1884), *Psalms and Paraphrases with Tunes* (1886), *The Psalter with Chants* (1888), and *The Scottish Anthem Book* (1891).

    ST. MARGARET (619)

Peek, Joseph Yates

    Peek, Joseph Yates (b. Schenectady, New York, February 17, 1843; d. Brooklyn, New York, March 17, 1911) was a carpenter, farmer, and druggist's clerk who served in the Union Army during the Civil War. Peek had no formal musical training but played the violin, banjo, and piano. Music seems to have been his avocation. He worked as a florist (1881-1904) and in 1904 became a lay preacher in the Methodist Church. He preached in the states of Maine, Florida, and California, and received his full ministerial credentials about two months before his death. He was a member of the Nostrand-DeKalb Methodist Episcopal Church in Brooklyn at the time of his death.

    PEEK (427)

Perkins, William Oscar

    Perkins, William Oscar (b. Stockbridge, Vermont, May 23, 1831; d. Boston, Massachusetts, January 13, 1902) had two younger brothers: Julius Edson and Henry Southwick Perkins. He studied music in London with Wetherbee and in Milan, Italy under G. Perini. Upon returning to the United States, he settled in Boston. He established an academy (1871) in which he was also a teacher. Perkins was a conductor and a composer. He received the honorary Mus.D. degree from Hamilton College (1879). His publications include *The Church Bell* (1867), which he published with his brother H. S., and *The Choral Choir* (1882).

PERKINS (555)

Perronet, Edward

Perronet, Edward (b. Sundridge, Kent, England, 1726; d. Canterbury, England, January 2, 1792) was of Huguenot ancestry. The great grandfather, Pasteur Perronet, fled France to Switzerland, where he served a Protestant church at Chateau D'Oex. His son, David Perronet, came to England about 1680. Edward's father, Vincent Perronet, was a graduate of Queen's College, Oxford, and vicar of Shoreham, Kent (1728). He was sympathetic to the movement begun by the Wesleys and Whitefield. Edward, though brought up in the Church of England, was drawn to the Wesleys and became a preacher in their movement. He seems to have been always an independent thinker, however, even as a Methodist. He opposed John Wesley on the question of whether the Methodist preachers could administer the Lord's Supper. Wesley wanted all to continue to receive communion in the Anglican churches. Perronet began to administer it himself in 1755. He further offended Wesley and the Countess of Huntingdon, for one of whose chapels he was ministering at the time in Watling Street, Canterbury, by publishing a satire on the Church of England entitled *The Mitre*. He was forced out of the Countess's church and toward the end of his life became the minister of a Congregational Church in Canterbury. He was buried in the cloisters of Canterbury Cathedral. His works include small volumes of hymns: *Select Passages of the Old and New Testament versified* (1756); *A Small Collection of Hymns* (1782); *Occasional Verses, moral and sacred. Published for the instruction and amusement of the Candidly Serious and Religious* (1785).

All Hail the Power of Jesus' Name (250,251)

Peters, Mary Bowly

Peters, Mary Bowly (b. Cirencester, England, 1813; d. Clifton, England, July 29, 1856) was the daughter of Richard Bowly. She was married to John McWilliam Peters, rector of Quennington, Gloucestershire. Her hymns were included in *Psalms, Hymns and Spiritual Songs* (1842), published by the Plymouth Brethren and thereafter passed into several Church of England collections. She also published the *World's History from the Creation to the Accession of Queen Victoria,* in seven volumes.

Through the Love of God, Our Savior (117)

Petrus, Theodoricus

Petrus, Theodoricus. Also called Theodoric Petri Rutha, he flourished in the sixteenth century, but his dates of birth and death are unknown. He was a student of Jacob Finno, the Finnish reformer (c. 1598), who is called the "father of the Finnish literary language." Finno had collected and revised a volume of Latin hymns and school songs which were published by Petrus as the famous *Piae Cantiones* in Greifswald, Germany in 1582.

TEMPUS ADEST FLORIDUM (196)

Phelps, Sylvanus Dryden

Phelps, Sylvanus Dryden (b. Suffield, Connecticut, May 15, 1816; d. New Haven, Connecticut, November 23, 1895) was educated at the Connecticut Literary Institute, Brown University (1844), and Yale Divinity School. He was ordained to the Baptist ministry and served churches in New Haven, Connecticut (1846-1874), and in Providence, Rhode Island (1874-1876). In 1876 he became editor of the *Christian Secretary.* Brown University conferred the honorary D.D. degree on him in 1854. His writings include the *Holy Land, with Glimpses of Europe and Egypt, a Year's Tour* (1862). He was the father of the famous author and professor of English at Yale, William Lyon Phelps.

Savior, Thy Dying Love (609)

Pickup, F. H.

No information is available on this author.

To Love Someone More Dearly (460)

Pierpoint, Folliot Sandford

Pierpoint, Folliot Sandford (b. Bath, Somersetshire, England, October 17, 1835; d. Newport, England, March 10, 1917) was the son of William Horne Pierpoint. He was educated at Queen's College, Cambridge (1871), and served as classical master at Somersetshire College. Later he was a contributor to *Lyra Eucharistica* (2d ed., 1864) and wrote some of the hymns for the canonical hours in *The Hymnal Noted.*

For the Beauty of the Earth (94)

Pleyel, Ignaz Joseph

Pleyel, Ignaz Joseph (b. Ruppersthal, near Vienna, Austria, June 1, 1757; d. near Paris, France, November 14, 1831) was the twenty-fourth child of a village schoolmaster. He was a gifted musician and studied for five years under Franz Joseph Haydn and for some years thereafter in Italy. He was assistant director of music at Strasbourg Cathedral for some time and became director in 1789. Because of the French Revolution, he went to England in 1791 as conductor of Professional Concerts. Afterwards he went to Paris and engaged in a music publishing business known as Pleyel et Cie. In 1807 he began the piano factory of Pleyel, Wolff and Company. He is known primarily as a composer of instrumental works.

PLEYEL'S HYMN (468)

Plumptre, Edward Hayes

Plumptre, Edward Hayes (b. London, England, August 6, 1821; d. Wells, Somersetshire, England, February 1, 1891) was educated at King's College, London, and at University College, Oxford (1844). He was thereafter fellow of Bransenose College, but entered the ministry of the Church of England in 1846 and rose rapidly to fame as a preacher, scholar, and theologian. He held a number of posts in the Church of England, becoming dean of Wells in 1881. His published works are many, including *Lazarus, and Other Poems* (1864); the *Life of Bishop Ken* (1888); and a translation of Dante. Plumptre also served as a member of the Old Testament Company which helped to produce the English Revised Version of the Bible (1885).

Rejoice, Ye Pure in Heart (466)

Pollard, Adelaide Addison

Pollard, Adelaide Addison (b. Bloomfield, Iowa, November 27, 1862; d. New York, New York, December 20, 1934) was the daughter of James and Rebecca Smith Pollard. Her original name was Sarah Addison Pollard, but disliking the name Sarah, she took Adelaide. She received her education at the Denmark Academy, Denmark, Iowa, and in Valparaiso, Indiana, and at the Boston School of Oratory. In the 1880s, she lived in Chicago and taught in girls' schools for a number of years. She was attracted to the evangelistic and healing work of Alexander Dowie, became his assistant, and claimed to have received healing from diabetes. After her association with Dowie, she went to New England and worked with the evangelist Sanford, who predicted the near return of Christ. She desired to become a missionary, but when her plans did not materialize, she taught during the 1890s at the Missionary Training School at Nyack-on-the-Hudson. Shortly before World War I, she went to Africa, but because of the war she was taken to Scotland. She returned to New York after the war. Miss Pollard was reared in a Presbyterian family, but was attracted to extremist religious sects for most of her life. She seems always to have been in frail health.

Have Thine Own Way, Lord (597)

Pollock, Thomas

Pollock, Thomas (b. Stathallan, Isle of Man, May 28, 1836; d. Birmingham, England, December 15, 1896) was educated at Trinity College, Dublin (1859-1863). He entered the ministry of the Church of England (1861) and served as curate of St. Luke's Leek, Staffordshire; St. Thomas's, Stamford Hill, London; and St. Alban's, Birmingham. At the latter church, he was assistant to his brother, J. S. Pollock, for thirty years and succeeded him as vicar. Pollock's life was spent mainly in working among the poor in Birmingham. He was one of the compilers of *Hymns Ancient and Modern* and was chairman of the committee of compilation (1895-1896). In 1870 he published his *Metrical Litanies for Special Services and General Use*.

Father, Hear Thy Children's Call (582)

Pond, Sylvanus Billings

Pond, Sylvanus Billings (b. Milford, Vermont, April 5, 1792; d. Brooklyn, New York, March 12, 1871) composed Sunday School songs and conducted the New York Sacred Music Society and the New York Academy of Sacred Music. He was a partner in the firm of Firth, Pond, and Company, the publishers of the music of Stephen Foster. His publications include *Union Melodies* (1838), *United States Psalmody* (1841), and *The Book of Praise* (1866), a hymnal for the Dutch Reformed Church in America.

ARMENIA (391, 491)

Porter, W. T.

No information is available on this composer.

HATFIELD (478)

Pott, Francis

Pott, Francis (b. Southward, London, England, December 29, 1832; d. Speldhurst, England, October 26, 1909) was educated at Brasenose College, Oxford (1854, 1857). He entered the ministry of the Church of England (1856) and served as curate of Bishopsworth, Gloucestershire (1856-1858) and, subsequently, at Ardingly, Berkshire (1858-1861), and

Ticehurst, Sussex (1861-1866), and finally at Norhill, Ely (1866-1901). He gave up his parish ministry because of deafness and turned to study and the work of translation. Pott served on the committee for the original edition of *Hymns Ancient and Modern* (1861). That same year he published *Hymns Fitted to the Order of Common Prayer, and Administration of the Sacraments and Other Rites and Ceremonies of the Church, According to the Use of the Church of England, to Which are Added Hymns for Certain Local Festivals.* Interested in the revival of chanting in the churches, he published the *Free Rhythm Psalter* (1898).

The Strife is O'er, the Battle Done (238)

Pounds, Jessie H. Brown

Pounds, Jessie H. Brown (b. Hiram, Ohio, August 31, 1861; d. 1921) was educated at home because of frail health. At age fifteen, in 1876, she began to write articles for newspapers in Cleveland, Ohio, and for various religious publications of the Christian Church. Many of her early efforts in song are found under her maiden name, Jessie H. Brown, and were published by James H. Fillmore in Cincinnati. She married John E. Pounds, the minister of the Central Christian Church in Cincinnati (1897). They later moved to Hiram, Ohio, where he ministered to the college congregation. She was a staff writer for the *Christian Standard* and wrote over four hundred hymn texts.

Anywhere with Jesus (530)

Powell, Ada

No information is available on this hymn writer.
Sing to Me of Heaven (672)

Powell, Joseph P.

Powell, Joseph P. (b. in the 1830s in Oregon) was a member of a well-known Oregon family. He taught vocal music in the Christian Church from 1855 and worked with the Fillmore Brothers Music House in Cincinnati, Ohio. He was described as "a very useful man to the brotherhood, humble, sweet-spirited, and true" (*Christian-Evangelist,* August 1891). While living in Dundee, Oregon, in October 1880, he was appointed to the Committee of Revisers selected by the General Christian Missionary Convention to revise *The Christian Hymnal* (which was the final successor to the hymnals of Alexander Campbell). It was published under the title *The Christian Hymnal Revised: A Collection of Hymns and Tunes for Congregational and Social Worship; in Two Parts* (1882). In the

"Compilers' Preface" of *The Christian Sunday School Hymnal* (1883) under the signatures of J. H. Garrison, J H. Hardin, and George D. Smitherwood, stands this affirmation:

> The committee takes pleasure in acknowledging the very valuable services of J. P. Powell, whose labors on our Church Hymnal have been recognized and appreciated by the brotherhood. Having been appointed as musical editor of the Sunday School Hymnal, he meet with us in our several meetings, and gave us the benefit of his large experience and musical taste. To him we are largely indebted for the special features of the book above mentioned.

Ebon Pinion (212)

Prentiss, Elizabeth Payson

Prentiss, Elizabeth Payson (b. Portland, Maine, October 26, 1818; d. Dorset, Vermont, August 13, 1878) was educated in the schools of Portland, Maine. She had a love for writing from an early age and published articles in the *Youth's Companion,* beginning in 1834. She taught school for a number of years and married George Lewis Prentiss in 1845. A few years later, he became professor of homiletics and polity at Union Theological Seminary, New York, and they began residing there in 1851. Her published works include *Stepping Heavenward* (1869), *Religious Poems* (1873), and *Golden Hours, or Hymns and Songs of the Christian Life* (1874). Her *Life and Letters* were published after her death in 1878.

More Love to Thee, O Christ (613)

Prichard, Rowland Hugh

Prichard, Rowland Hugh (b. Graienyn, near Bala, North Wales, January 14, 1811; d. Holywell, Flintshire, Wales, January 25, 1887) was a man of humble means who was the grandson of the famous Welsh bard, Rowland Huw. He led the singing in his village church and was well known among Welsh musical circles. He published his *Cyfaill y Cantorion,* a collection for children, in 1844. In 1880 at the age of 69, he became a loomtender at the Welsh Flannel Manufacturing Company at Holywell.

HYFRYDOL (188, 253, 404)

Prynne, George Rundell

Prynne, George Rundell (b. West Looe, Cornwall, England, August 23, 1818; d. Plymouth, England, March, 1903) was the son of John Allen Prynne. He was educated at St. Catherine's College, Cambridge (1839), and ordained to the ministry of the Church of England (1841). He became vicar of St. Peter's, Plymouth, England, where he remained for the rest of his life. His works include *Hymnal suited for the Services of the Church* (1858) and *The Soldier's Dying Visions, and Other Poems* (1881).

Jesus, Meek and Gentle (572)

Pullen, Milton Aubrey

Pullen, Milton Aubrey (b. Houston, Texas, July 19, 1943) is the son of Milton Andrew and Alice LaNell Hill Pullen. He was educated at Texas A. & I. University (B.M.Ed. in voice) and at the University of Houston (M.Mus. in conducting). He has taught music and directed band and choral activities in Texas high schools for many years: Freer, Texas (1965-1968); League City, Texas (1968-1972); and Clear Lake City, Texas (1972-1979). In 1972 he established the Bay Area Chamber Singers in Clear Lake City. From 1979 to 1985 he was director of Abilene Christian University choral activities and associate professor in the department of Music. Since 1985 Pullen has been choral director at Clear Lake High School, League City, Texas. He a member of the Texas Music Educators Association, the American Choral Directors Association, and the Texas State Teachers Association, and has served as an officer in various musical associations in Texas. Milton Pullen was an associate editor for *GSR* (1980-1985) and rendered invaluable service in helping the general editor and the music editor produce a balanced and superior collection.

Purday, Charles Henry

Purday, Charles Henry (b. Folkestone, Kent, England, January 11, 1799; d. Kensington, London, England, April 23, 1885) was the son of a bookseller. He was engaged as a music teacher and publisher and was a popular lecturer on musical subjects. He was also precentor for the Scottish Church, Crown Court, Drury Lane, in London for many years and sang at the coronation of Queen Victoria (1837). Purday pioneered in the use of program notes for musical performances and worked hard for the reform of copyright laws. His publications include *The Sacred Musical Offering* (1822), *Crown Court Psalmody* (1854), *A few directions for Chanting* (1855), *Songs of Peace and Joy* (1879) with Frances Havergal, and *Copyright, a Sketch of Its Rise and Progress* (1877). He was also a contributor to *Groves's Dictionary of Music and Musicians.*

SANDON (114, 148)

Ramsey, Benjamin Mansell

Ramsey, Benjamin Mansell (b. Richmond, Surrey, England, 1849; d. West Wittering, Chichester, Sussex, England, August 31, 1923) "was for many years a well-known teacher in the Bournemouth area; a prolific composer of part-songs and pianoforte pieces and a writer of hymns and carols and on musical theory; retired from active professional life in 1916; during the last year of his life was in poor health, but organized and conducted a choral society in the village of Chichester" (From an obituary notice in the *Musical Times*, October 1, 1923).

Teach Me Your Way, O Lord - CAMACHA (523)

Rankin, Jeremiah Eames

Rankin, Jeremiah Eames (b. Thornton, New Hampshire, January 2, 1828; d. Cleveland, Ohio, November 28, 1904) was educated at Middlebury College, Vermont, and at Andover Theological Seminary. He was ordained to the Congregational ministry (1855) and served churches in New York, Vermont, Massachusetts, Washington, D.C., and New Jersey. He was appointed president of Howard University in Washington, D.C. (1889), which post he held until his death. He published many gospel song collections, including the *Gospel Temperance Hymnal* (1878), *Gospel Bells* (1883), and *German-English Lyrics, Sacred and Secular* (1897).

God Be with You Till We Meet Again (14)

Rawson, George

Rawson, George (b. Leeds, England, June 5, 1807; d. Clifton, Bristol, England, March 25, 1889) was educated at Manchester and for many years practiced law in Leeds. He assisted in the compilation of *Psalms, Hymns, and Passages of Scripture for Christian Worship* (1853), commonly called the *Leeds Hymn-book*, a hymnal for use in the Congregational Church of which Rawson was a member. He also assisted in compiling *Psalms and Hymns for the Use of the Baptist Denomination* (1858). The Religious Tract Society published many of his best poetic efforts in their *Songs of Spiritual Thought* (1885).

By Christ Redeemed, in Christ Restored (374)

Ray, Maude Louise

No information is available on this author.

To Love Someone More Dearly (460)

Read, Daniel

Read, Daniel (b. Rehoboth, now Attleboro, Massachusetts, November 16, 1757; d. New Haven, Connecticut, December 4, 1836) served under John Sullivan in the expeditions into Rhode Island during the Revolutionary War. He moved to New Haven near the end of the war and was associated with Amos Doolittle in engraving and in book publishing and selling. He married Jerusha Serman in 1785. Read was active in public affairs and was a worker in ivory and a comb maker. He was also a stockbroker in the bank in New Haven and a director of the library there. In addition, he was a singing teacher and published *The American Singing Book* (1785), which contained forty-seven of his own compositions. He also published *An Introduction to Psalmody* (1790), *The Columbian Harmonist* (1793), and *The New Haven Collection of Sacred Music* (1817). He compiled a collection which was never published entitled *Musica Ecclesia*. Read edited the first musical journal in America, the *American Musical Monthly* (1786).

WINDHAM (367)

Rebenlein, Georg

He is said to be the compiler of *Musicalische Handbuch* (1690). He was a member of an old family of printers in Hamburg, Germany. The volume attributed to him was published by his widow in 1690.

WINCHESTER, NEW (216)

Redhead, Richard

Redhead, Richard (b. Harrow, England, March 1, 1820; d. Hellingly, England, April 27, 1901) was trained as a chorister of Magdalen College, Oxford. He also studied organ under Walter Vicary. Frederick Oakeley brought Redhead from Magdalen to be organist at Margaret Street Chapel (1839-1864). He was also organist at St. Mary Magdalene, Paddington (1864-1894). With Oakeley he edited the first Gregorian psalter, *Laudes Diurnae* (1843). He also published *Church Hymn Tunes, Ancient and Modern, for the Several Seasons of the Church Year* (1853). These two books were significant in the Oxford Movement.

REDHEAD, NO. 76 (297)

Redner, Lewis Henry

Redner, Lewis Henry (b. Philadelphia, Pennsylvania, December 15, 1830; d. Atlantic City, New Jersey, August 29, 1908) was educated in the public schools of Philadelphia. In that city he became a wealthy real estate broker, was devoted to church work, and served as organist for churches, including Holy Trinity Episcopal, where Phillips Brooks was minister. He was also a very successful Sunday School superintendent. Redner never married but lived with his sister, Mrs. Sarah H. Sagers. He died on a visit to Atlantic City.

ST. LOUIS (193)

Reed, Andrew

Reed, Andrew (b. London, England, November 27, 1787; d. Cambridge Heath, Hackney, England, February 25, 1862) was the son of a watchmaker who was also a lay preacher among the Congregationalists. He followed his father's trade, but decided to enter the ministry and to that end attended Hackney College (1807). He was ordained in 1811 and served as minister of New Road Chapel, St. George's-in-the-East, London for fifty years (1811-1861). His great interest, besides preaching and music, was to help the poor and outcast. He helped found the London Orphan Asylum at Clapton, the Reedham Orphanage at Coulsdon, Surrey, an asylum for the insane at Earlswood, Surrey, the Royal Hospital for Incurables, Putney, Surrey, and the Eastern Counties Asylum at Colchester, Essex. He was awarded the honorary D.D. degree by Yale University on a trip to the United States in 1834. Reed published a supplement to Isaac Watts's *Psalms and Hymns* entitled *Hymn Book* (1817). His hymns, with those of his wife Eliza, were published in *Wycliffe Supplement* (1872).

Holy Spirit, Light Divine (293)

Reed, Edith Margaret Cellibrand

Reed, Edith Margaret Cellibrand (b. Islington, Middlesex, London, March 31, 1885; d. Barnet, Hertfordshire, England, June 4, 1933) was educated at St. Leonard's School, St. Andrew's, and at the Guildhall School of Music, London. She was an associate of the Royal College of Organists and assisted Percy Scholes as editor of *The Music Student* and *Music and Youth*. She was editor of the children's music magazine *Panpipes* (1923-1926). She also wrote *Story Lives of the Great Composers* and published two mystery plays for Christmas.

Infant Holy, Infant Lowly (209)

Rees, Bryn Austin

Rees, Bryn Austin (b. Chelsea, London, England, September 21, 1911) was educated at Neath Grammar School and at Hackney and New

College, London, where he was a candidate for the Congregational ministry. After being ordained, he served churches at Sawbridgeworth, Hertfordshire (1935-1940); Ipswich, Suffolk (1940-1945); Felixstowe, Suffolk (1945-1950); and Muswell Hill Congregational Church, London (1950-1962). In 1962 he became minister of Woodford Green United Free Church in Redbridge, London. He wrote the texts for Lloyd Webber's cantatas: *The Savior, The Meeting Race,* and *The Good Samaritan.*

    Have Faith in God, My Heart (499)

Reinagle, Alexander Robert

Reinagle, Alexander Robert (b. Brighton, East Sussex, England, August 21, 1799; d. Kidlington, England, April 6, 1877) was the grandson of Joseph Reinagle, Sr., who was trumpeter to the king, and the son of Joseph, Jr., an accomplished cellist. One of his uncles came to the United States in 1786 and served for more than two decades as a conductor, composer, teacher, and theatrical manager in Baltimore and Philadelphia. A. R. Reinagle was organist for the Church of St. Peter-in-the-East, Oxford (1822-1853). His published works include *Psalm Tunes for the Voice and Pianoforte* (1830).

    ST. PETER (279, 392)

Richter, Anne

Richter, Anne (d. 1857) was the daughter of Robert Rigby, vicar of St. Mary's Beverly, Yorkshire, England (1791-1823). She was married to W. H. Richter, who was chaplain of the county jail at Kirton Lindsey, Lincolnshire, and later rector of St. Paul's London. She was a descendant of John Bradshaw, whose name is the first in the list of the signatures on the death warrant of Charles I. She was also a great friend of the poet, Mrs. Felicia Hemans. Richter wrote for various magazines and published *The Nun and Other Poems* (1841).

    We Saw Thee Not (495)

Rimbault, Edward Francis

Rimbault, Edward Francis (b. London, England, June 13, 1816; d. London, September 26, 1876) was the son of Stephen Francis Rimbault, organist of St. Giles-in-the-Fields, London, and a noted composer. He studied with his father and later with Samuel Sebastian Wesley and William Crotch. He was a well-known musicologist, editor for the Motet Society, and also served as organist for St. Peter's, Verek Street, and St. John's Presbyterian Church in London. He was honored with degrees by Harvard

University and the Universities of Stockholm and Göttingen. Ribault's works include publication of an edition of Thomas Tallis's *Cathedral Service and Order of Daily Service*; Thomas Est's *The Whole Book of Psalms*; and Merbecke's *Book of Common Prayer Noted.*
RUTHERFORD (668)

Rinkart, Martin

Rinkart, Martin (b. Eilenburg, Saxony, Germany, April 23, 1586; d. Eilenburg, December 8, 1649) was educated at the Latin school at Eilenburg and at St. Thomas's School in Leipzig, where he was a foundation scholar and also served as a chorister. He studied theology at the University of Leipzig and served as cantor and then deacon at Eisleben, as minister at Ardeborn, and as archdeacon at Eilenburg (1617). Though frail physically, he was a man of great faith and courage. During the Thirty Years War (1618-1648), he was in Eilenburg, a walled city to which many refugees had fled for safety. A great plague struck the city in 1647, during which time Rinkart is said to have buried 5,000 persons, including his own wife.
Now Thank We All Our God (59)

Rippon, John

Rippon, John (b. Tiverton, Devonshire, England, April 29, 1751; d. London, England, December 17, 1836) became a member of the Baptist Church in 1767 and the following year studied for the Baptist ministry at the Baptist College, Bristol. He succeeded John Gill as preacher for the Baptist Church at Carter Lane, London, in 1772 at age twenty-one. Gill had preached for this church for fifty-four years, and Rippon remained there for sixty-three. A popular and influential minister, Rippon edited the revised edition of John Gill's *Exposition of the Old and New Testaments,* a great compendium of Baptist views; edited the *Baptist Annual Register* (1790-1802); and published his seminal hymn collection, the *Selection of Hymns from the Best Authors, Intended as an Appendix to Dr. Watts's Psalms and Hymns* (1787). He also published *A Selection of Psalms and Hymn Tunes* (1791).
How Firm a Foundation (493)

Rist, Johann

Rist, Johann (b. Ottensen, Holstein, March 8, 1607; d. Wedel, near Hamburg, August 31, 1667), the son of a minister, was educated at Hamburg, Bremen, and the University of Rinteln (1616). He then served as tutor for a family in Hamburg and studied Hebrew, mathematics, and medicine at the University of Rostock. While a student at Rinteln, Rist was encouraged by Josua Stemann to write hymns. Rist also studied at the Universities of Leyden, Utrecht, and Leipzig. He afterwards served as tutor to the family of Heinrich Sagen at Heide in Holstein (1633). Here he met and became engaged to Elisabeth Stapfel, whom he married in 1635. He settled at Wedel for the remainder of his life, ministering to both the spiritual and physical needs of his parishioners. Although Rist's life was relatively calm, during the Thirty Years War while at Rostock, he suffered greatly, falling prey to the plague, from which he ultimately recovered, and also losing all his musical instruments and his church organ. His published works include *Himmlische Lieder* (1641-1643); *Frommer und Gottseliger Christen alltägliche Haussmusik* (1654); *Neue musicalische Fest-Andachten* (1655); and *Neue musicalische Katechismus Andachten* (1656). He also wrote two plays which depicted the horrors of the Thirty Years War.

Break Forth, O Beauteous Heavenly Light (200)

Roberts, Daniel Crane

Roberts, Daniel Crane (b. Bridgehampton, Long Island, New York, November 5, 1841; d. Concord, New Hampshire, October 31, 1907) was educated at Kenyon College, Gambier, Ohio. He was soldier in the 85th Ohio Volunteers during the Civil War. Following the war, he entered the ministry of the Protestant Episcopal Church, becoming deacon (1865) and priest (1866). He ministered to churches in Vermont and Massachusetts and then went to St. Paul's Church in Concord, New Hampshire, where he remained for the final 29 years of his life. Roberts was president of the New Hampshire State Historical Society, chaplain of the New Hampshire Department of the Grand Army of the Republic, and active in the Knights Templar. Norwich University conferred upon him the honorary D.D. degree in 1885.

God of Our Fathers (566)

Roberts, John

Roberts, John (b. Tanrhiwfelen, Penllwyn, near Aberystwyth, Wales, December 22, 1822, d. Vron, Caernarvon, Wales, May 6, 1877) studied music under the singing-school teacher Richard Mills. He began to preach among the Calvinistic Methodists (1856) and was ordained in 1859. He served churches in Aberdare and Capel Cock, founded the singing festival Cymanfau Ganu in 1859, and edited the hymnal of the Calvinistic Methodists, *Llyfr Tonau Cynulleidfaol* (1859). He is recognized as one of the greatest of the Welsh hymnists of the nineteenth century.

LLANFAIR (236)

ST. DENIO (75)

Robinson, Robert

Robinson, Robert (b. Swaffhim, Norfolk, England, September 27, 1735; d. Showell Green, Warwickshire, England, June 9, 1790) was born in humble circumstances, and his father died when he was still a child. In 1749 he went to London and was apprenticed to a barber, but his inclinations were more to reading and to study than to his prospective trade. In 1752 his chance hearing of George Whitefield's preaching caused him much spiritual turmoil. In 1755 he finally professed faith in Christ and shortly thereafter began to preach, becoming minister of the Calvinistic Methodist chapel in Mildenhall, Norfolk. A few months later he was minister to an Independent Church in Norwich; and in 1759 he became a Baptist and ministered to the Baptist church at Cambridge, remaining there until 1790. Although without formal education, he was widely read and prominent as a preacher, scholar, and theologian. He published a *History of the Baptists* (1790). Late in his life, he became a friend of the Unitarian philosopher Joseph Priestly, who seems to have greatly influenced him to more liberal theological views.

Come, Thou Fount of Every Blessing (595)

Röntgen, Julius

Röntgen, Julius (b. Leipzig, Germany, May 9, 1855; d. Utrecht, Holland, September 13, 1932) was a noted composer, conductor, editor, musicologist, pianist, and professor. He studied music in Leipzig under Franz Lachner, Moritz Hauptmann, E. F. E. Richter, and Carl Reinecke. In 1877 he went to Amsterdam, where he was professor in the Amsterdam Conservatory. He succeeded Verhulst as the conductor of the Society for the Advancement of Musical Art in 1886. From 1918 to 1924 Röntgen was director of the Amsterdam Conservatory. He devoted his retirement years to composition. Röntgen was a friend of Liszt, Brahms, and Grieg.

IN BABILONE (308)

Root, George Frederick

Root, George Frederick (b. Sheffield, Massachusetts, August 30, 1820; d. Bailey's Island, Maine, August 6, 1895) was one of the most popular musicians in America. He studied first in his home town and then under A. N. Johnson and Lowell Mason in Boston. He was assistant organist to Johnson at the Winter and Park Street churches in Boston (1839) and assisted Lowell Mason in teaching in the Boston public schools (1841). In 1844 he went to New York, where he taught in Abbott's School for Young Ladies and in the New York Institution for the Blind, where Fanny Crosby was one of his students. In 1850 he went to Paris, France, for a year of study. Upon returning to the United States, he helped found the New York Musical Institute (1853) and then moved to Chicago where he associated with his brother, who was partner in the firm of Root and Cady. The business was destroyed in the Chicago fire (1871), and Root became associated with the John C. Church Company. He wrote many popular songs, especially during the Civil War, including "Tramp, Tramp, Tramp, the Boys Are Marching" and "Just Before the Battle, Mother." He helped edit approximately seventy-five collections, including *The Shawm* with William B. Bradbury and the *Diapason* (1860).

> *Come to the Savior* (336)
> JOYFUL (336)

Rosecrans, James Holmes

Rosecrans, James Holmes (b. New York, c. 1845; d. Breakabeen, New York, February 18, 1926) was a member of a musical family. His father died when he was eight, and the boy went to work to help to support the family. At age twenty he attended his first music school at Friendship, New York, and spent the next four years studying music, working for support during vacation times. He became a school teacher for two years and then joined the Fillmore Brothers Music House and contributed to their Sunday School collections, beginning with *Songs of Glory* (1874). Rosecrans was a member of the Christian Church and became a traveling singer, teacher, and preacher among these churches. He was State Sunday School Evangelist for California (1884). Later he was associated with Sunday School, evangelistic, and educational enterprises in Texas. He published more than twenty collections, including *The Voice of Joy; The Children's Hallelujahs; Gems and Jewels* with J. H. Fillmore (1890); and *Crown of Beauty* with Leonard Daugherty (Cincinnati, 1902). During his declining years, he lived in retirement with relatives in Breakabeen, New York.

> JAMESON (664)
> ROSECRANS (541)

Rowley, Francis Harold

Rowley, Francis Harold (b. Hilton, New York, July 25, 1854; d. Boston, Massachusetts, February 14, 1952) was the son of John R. and Mary Jane Smith Rowley. He was educated at the University of Rochester (1875), and Rochester Theological Seminary (1878). From 1879 until 1910, he served Baptist churches in Titusville, Pennsylvania; North Adams, Massachusetts; Oak Park, Illinois; Fall Riber, Massachusetts; and finally the First Baptist Church, Boston. In 1910 he became president of the

Massachusetts Society for the Prevention of Cruelty to Animals, serving in this capacity until 1945, when he became chairman of the board at age ninety-one. The Rowley School of Humanities at Oglethorpe University, Atlanta, Georgia, was named in his honor.

> *I Will Sing the Wondrous Story* (165)

Runyan, William Marion

Runyan, William Marion (b. Marion, New York, January 21, 1870; d. Pittsburgh, Kansas, July 29, 1957) was the son of William White, a Methodist preacher, and Hannah Orcutt Runyan. The family moved to Marion, Kansas, in 1884. He studied music as a youth and was ordained to the Methodist ministry at age twenty-one (1891). He preached at various places in Kansas, and in 1903 he became the evangelist for the Central Kansas Methodist Conference, in which capacity he served for some twenty years. He was afflicted with increasing deafness, resigned his evangelistic duties, and became associated with John Brown University, Sulphur Springs, Arkansas (1924). There he preached for the Federated Church and edited the *Christian Workers' Magazine.* In 1925 he moved to Chicago, became associated with Moody Bible Institute, and served as editor for Hope Publishing Company until he retired in 1948.

> FAITHFULNESS (147)

Russell, Arthur Tozer

Russell, Arthur Tozer (b. Northampton, England, March 10, 1806; d. Southwick, Brighton, England, November 18, 1874) was the son of Thomas Clout (who changed his name to Russell) a Congregational minister and scholar who edited the works of Tyndale, Frith, Barnes, and John Owen. A. T. Russell was educated at St. Saviour's School, Southwark; the Merchant Taylors' School, London; Manchester College, York; and St. John's College, Cambridge. He entered the ministry of the Church of England (1829) and became curate of Great Gransden, Huntingdonshire (1829-1852). In 1851 he was appointed vicar of Whaddon, Cambridgeshire, and in 1866 became vicar of St. Thomas, Toxtett Park, Liverpool. The next year he was curate at Wronckwardine Wood, Shropshire, and finally curate of Southwick, near Brighton (1874). Russell was at first a high churchman, but during the struggles of the Oxford Movement became an effective opponent of those who favored the Anglo-Catholic position. He published a number of works, including *Hymn Tunes, Original and Selected, from Ravenscroft and other old Musicians* (1840) and *Psalms and Hymns, partly original, partly selected, for the use of the Church of England* (1851).

> *Let All Together Praise Our God* (192)
> *O How Shall I Receive Thee* (189)

Sammis, John H.

Sammis, John H. (b. Brooklyn, New York, July 6, 1846; d. Los Angeles, California, June 12, 1919). No information is available on the early years of his life. At age twenty-three (1869), he moved to Logansport, Indiana, and became a successful businessman and an active member of his church. He was an active worker in the YMCA and made his decision to enter the ministry. He attended McCormick Theological Seminary and graduated from Lane Theological Seminary (1881). After being ordained to the Presbyterian ministry, he served churches in Glidden, Iowa; Indianapolis, Indiana; Grandhaven, Michigan; Red Wing, Minnesota; and Sullivan, Indiana. In 1901 he moved to California and served on the faculty of the Bible Institute of Los Angeles until his death.

When We Walk with the Lord (513)

Sandell-Berg, Caroline Vilhelmina

Sandell-Berg, Caroline Vilhelmina (b. Froderyd, Sweden, October 3, 1832; d. Stockholm, Sweden, July 27, 1903) was the daughter of a Swedish minister. She became paralyzed at age twelve but later recovered. In 1858 her father was drowned in her presence when he fell from a boat. In 1860 her mother died. The next year she took residence in a home maintained by the Evangelical National Foundation and joined their editorial staff. She thus became acquainted with Carl Rosenius and Oscar Ahnfelt, leaders in the spiritual revival which was sweeping northern Europe. Ahnfelt set many of her poems to music. She wrote more than 650 hymns and has been called "the Fanny Crosby of Sweden." In 1867 she married Carl Oscar Berg, a wealthy merchant and leader in the temperance movement in Sweden.

Children of the Heavenly Father (644)
Day by Day (134)

Sanderson, Lloyd Otis

Sanderson, Lloyd Otis (b. near Jonesboro, Arkansas, May 18, 1901; d. Memphis, Tennessee, January 19, 1992). His Christian mother was responsible for his giving his life to Christ. He was baptized by James E. Laird and began preaching among the Churches of Christ in 1923. He was educated at Harper Junior College (Harper, Kansas), Southwest Missouri State College, the University of Oklahoma, Little Rock Conservatory of Music, Friends University, and the University of Arkansas. His works include *Theory of Music, First Lessons in Singing, Song Leader's Manual*, and *Harmony and Theory of Music*. He served as editor of the *Christian*

Counselor and as music editor of Gospel Advocate publications. He was associate editor of *Christian Hymns* (1935) and editor of *Christians Hymns No 2* (1948) and *No.Three* (1966).

> *Broken Life* (326)
> *Buried with Christ* (355)
> SANDERSON (579)
> *The Solemn Feast* (372)

Sankey, Ira David

Sankey, Ira David (b. Edinburgh, Pennsylvania, August 28, 1840; d. Brooklyn, New York, August 13, 1908) was reared on his family's farm in western Pennsylvania and educated in the public schools of Edinburgh and Newcastle, Pennsylvania, to which latter town the family moved in 1857. He joined the Methodist Episcopal Church in Newcastle and served as choir director and Sunday School superintendent. Sankey served in the Union Army during the Civil War and, following the war, assisted his father, who was a collector of internal revenue. The great work of Sankey's life began in 1870 when he met Dwight Lyman Moody at a YMCA convention in Indianapolis, Indiana. Six months after their meeting, he became Moody's song leader, and for the next thirty years he traveled with Moody in both the United States and England in evangelistic meetings. In 1873, during a meeting in England, Sankey published the first edition of his *Sacred Songs and Solos,* which became one of the most popular hymnals ever published and has sold more than eighty million copies. The final edition in 1903 contained 1200 songs. Sankey was also responsible for the *Gospel Hymns* series. He published *Gospel Hymns and Sacred Songs* (1875), *Gospel Hymns No. 2* (1876), *No. 3* (1878), *No. 4* (1883), *No. 5* (1887), And *No. 6* (1891). These were combined into a single volume, *Gospel Hymns Nos. 1-6 Complete* (1894).

> HINGHAM (643)
> INTERCESSION (328)
> METASOU (641)
> SANKEY (4980
> *Trusting Jesus* (514)

Schlegel, Katharina Amalia Dorothea von

Schlegel, Katharina Amalia Dorothea von (b. October 22, 1697, in Germany). Little is certain except that she wrote the hymn attributed to her. James Mearns in Julian's *Dictionary* says that she was probably "a lady attached to the little ducal court at Cothen." Others have conjectured that she was the head of a Protestant nunnery at Cothen. Her hymns were published in *Einige gantz neue Lieder zum Lobe des Dreyeinigen Gottes und zur gewünschten reichen Erbauung vieler Menschen* (c. 1733), known also at the *Cothenische Lieder.*

Be Still, My Soul (547)

Schmolck, Benjamin

Schmolck, Benjamin (b. Brauchitzchdorf, Silesia, December 21, 1672; d. Schweidnitz, Silesia, February 12, 1737) was the son of Martin Schmolck, a Lutheran minister at Brauchitzchdorf. He was educated at the gymnasium at Laubau and at the University of Leipzig, where he studied theology. He returned to his home town as his father's assistant in 1701. On February 12, 1702, he married Anna Rosina, the daughter of a merchant in Laubau. That same year he was appointed deacon of the Friedenskirche at Schweidnitz, where he remained for the rest of his life. Schmolck was a tireless and effective preacher, even though he was hampered by the Peace of Westphalia (1648), which had put great restraints on Lutherans in the district where he worked. His greatest fame came through his hymns, which earned him the name of the "second Gerhardt." He wrote over 900 hymns. In 1730 he began to suffer strokes of paralysis, probably due to his strenuous labors, and from which he died on the anniversary of his wedding in 1737.

My Jesus, As Thou Wilt (533)
Open Now Thy Gates of Beauty (83)

Schneider, Friedrich

Schneider, Friedrich (b. Alt-Waltersdorf, Saxony, January 3, 1786; d. Dessau, Germany, November 23, 1853) was educated at the University of Leipzig. He served as organist at St. Paul's Church in Leipzig (1807), conducted the Seconda Opera Company (1810), was organist at St. Thomas' Church (1812), and director of the Municipal Theatre (1817). Some time after 1821, he moved to Dessau, where he established a music school and served as a musical conductor. His works include oratorios, operas, symphonies, cantatas, masses, and overtures.

LISCHER (20)

Schnyder, Xavier von Wartensee

Schnyder, Xavier von Wartensee (b. Lucerne, Switzerland, April 16, 1786; d. Frankfurt, Germany, August 27, 1868) descended from a noble family, was trained in music at an early age. He taught in the Pestalozzian

Institute, Yverdun, and then settled in Frankfurt (1817), where he taught and composed music. Schnyder won many high honors at Swiss music festivals.

HORTON (353)

Scholtes, Peter

No information is available on this author/composer.

ST. BRENDAN'S (456)

We Are One in the Spirit (456)

Schop, Johann

Schop, Johann (b. probably at Hamburg, c. 1590; d. Hamburg, c. 1664) was a performer on the violin, lute, trumpet, and zinke. He was a member of the Court Orchestra at Wolfenbüttel (1615) and at Copenhagen (1618). In 1621, according to Zahn, he was director of the town council music and kapellmeister of Hamburg. He was a good friend of Johann Rist and contributed a number of tunes to Rist's *Himmlische Lieder* (16741).

ERMUNTRE DICH (200)

Schumann, Robert Alexander

Schumann, Robert Alexander (b. Zwickau, Saxony, June 8, 1810; d. Endenich, near Bonn, July 29, 1856) was the son of a bookseller and editor, who died in 1826. His mother wished him to become a lawyer and accordingly sent him to Leipzig, but there he gave himself more to the study of music than of law, studying under Friedrich Wieck, his future father-in-law. Subsequently, his mother sent him to Heidelberg and then to Italy, but he again studied music rather than law. In 1840 he married Clara Wieck, one of the leading pianists of the day. Because of a finger injury, Schumann turned from a career as a pianist to that of a composer. He was the embodiment of the Romantic Movement in European music and edited the influential journal *Neue Zeitschrift für Musik* (1834-1844). In his later years Schumann became mentally unstable and attempted to drown himself in 1854. He voluntarily entered the asylum at Enderich, where he died two years later.

CANONBURY (21)

SCHUMANN (610)

Schumann, Valentin

Schumann, Valentin (fl. 16th century). Other than that he published

his *Geistliche Lieder aufs new gebessert und gemehrt* (Leipzig, 1539), nothing is known of this editor.
VOM HIMMEL HOCH (199)

Schütz, Johann Jakob

Schütz, Johann Jakob (b. Frankfurt-am-Main, Germany, September 7, 1640; d. Frankfurt-am-Main, May 22, 1690) studied law at Tübingen and was a practicing attorney in Frankfurt. He was a brilliant lawyer and also an ardent Pietist. He is said to have influenced his friend Philipp Jacob Spener to begin his famous prayer meetings (Collegia pietatis). In 1686 Schütz came under the influence of J. W. Petersen and separated himself from the Lutheran Church. Schütz was interested in the Frankfurt Company, which purchased land from William Penn in Germantown, Pennsylvania (1683). His works include *Christliche Lebensregeln* (1677) and a little collection of hymns, *Christliches Gedenckbüchlein zur Beforderung eines anfangenden neuen Lebens* (1675).
Sing Praise to God Who Reigns Above (109)

Schwedler, Johann Christoph

Schwedler, Johann Christoph (b. Krobsdorf, Silesia, December 21, 1672; d. Niederwiese, Silesia, January 12, 1730) was educated at the gymnasium at Zittau and at the University of Leipzig (1696). He was ordained to the Lutheran ministry and became famous as a preacher in the church at Niederwiese (1701-1730). Great crowds attended his meetings. He was a friend of Count Zinzendorf and of Johann Mertzer, and wrote more than 500 hymns. He also assisted in founding an orphanage.
Ask Ye What Great Thing I Know (304)

Scott, Clara H. Jones

Scott, Clara H. Jones (b. Elk Grove, Cook County, Illinois, December 3, 1841; d. Dubuque, Iowa, June 21, 1897) was the daughter of Abel Fiske and Sarah Rockwell Jones. She attended the first musical institute conducted in Chicago by C. M. Cady (1856) and taught music at the Ladies' Seminary in Lyons, Iowa (1859). She married Henry Clay Scott (1861). Mrs. Scott was a friend of Horatio R. Palmer, who greatly encouraged her in writing hymn texts and tunes. She contributed many songs to his collections. Her works include *The Royal Anthem Book* (1882), *Happy Songs: Truth in Song for Lovers of Truth* (1896), and *Short Anthems* (1897). She was killed while on a visit to Dubuque, Iowa, where she was

thrown from a buggy by a runaway horse.
  Open My Eyes, That I May See (607)
  SCOTT (607)

Scott, Robert Balgarnie Young

   Scott, Robert Balgarnie Young (b. Toronto, Canada, July 16, 1899) was educated at Knox College and the University of Toronto. He went to Europe for a year of study and was subsequently ordained to the ministry of the United Church of Canada (1926). He was minister in Long Branch, Ontario, taught at Union College in Vancouver, and then at United Theological College, McGill University, Montreal (1921 -1955). Dr. Scott served as honorary flight lieutenant and chaplain in the Royal Canadian Air Force during World War ll. For four years he served as president of the Fellowship for a Christian Order and wrote several hymns during this time. In 1955 Scott became professor of religion at Princeton University and served as chairman of the department in 1963. He is now living in retirement. His works include *The Relevance of the Prophets* (1944); *Treasures from Judean Caves* (1955); *The Psalms as Christian Praise* (1958); and, with Gregory Vlastos, *Towards the Christian Revolution* (1936).
  O Day of God Draw Nigh (440)

Scriven, Joseph Medlicott

   Scriven, Joseph Medlicott (b. Seapatrick, County Down, Ireland, September 10, 1819; d. Bewdley, Rice Lake, Ontario, Canada, August 10, 1886) was the son of Captain John Scriven of the Royal Marines. His mother was sister to Joseph Medlicott, an Anglican minister at Pottern, Wiltshire. He entered Trinity College, Dublin (1835), but deciding on a military career, entered Addiscombe Military College, Surrey. His health cut short these plans, and he returned to Trinity, from which he graduated in 1842. He planned to be married, but his fiancé was accidentally drowned on the eve of their wedding. Scriven then moved to Canada (1844) and taught school at Woodstock and Brantford and served as tutor to the family of Lieutenant Pengelley, a retired naval officer, near Bewdley. He planned a second time to marry, but again his fiancé, Eliza Roche, died shortly before the wedding. Scriven was a member of the Plymouth Brethren and devoted himself to work among the poor and handicapped. In his later years, he himself suffered from poor health and scant income. He died by drowning, whether accidental or intentional has never been determined. He published *Hymns and Other Verses* (1869).
  What a Friend We Have in Jesus (567)

Sears, Edmund Hamilton

Sears, Edmund Hamilton (b. Sandisfield, Massachusetts, April 6, 1810; d. Weston, Massachusetts, January 16, 1876) was the son of Joseph Sears. He was educated at Union College, Schenectady, New York (1834), and Harvard Divinity School (1837). Sears was ordained to the Unitarian ministry (1839) and served churches at Wayland and Lancaster, Massachusetts. Although a Unitarian, he once wrote to Bishop E. H. Bickersteth: "Though I was educated in the Unitarian denomination, I believe and preach the divinity of Christ." Sears's works include *Regeneration* (1854); *Pictures of the Olden Time* (1857): *Athanasia, or Foregleams of Immortality* (1858); *The Fourth Gospel. the Heart of Christ* (1872); and *Sermons and Songs of the Christian Life* (1872). He was also for a time co-editor of *Monthly Religious Magazine.*

It Came Upon the Midnight Clear (195)

Shaw, Knowles

Shaw, Knowles (b. Butler County, Ohio, October 13, 1834; d. near McKinney, Texas, June 7, 1878) was the son of Albin and Huldah Griffin Shaw. He moved in infancy with his family to Rush County, Indiana, where his father died when Knowles was twelve. For the next six years, he strove to help his widowed mother by working wherever he could, teaching school, and playing the violin at dances and other public gatherings. He seems to have been a natural musical genius. After hearing the gospel preached with power, he was overpowered by his conscience and his meager knowledge of God's word. He was immersed into Christ September 13, 1852. Although many expected Shaw to return shortly to the ways of the world, he remained faithful. He married Martha Finley on January 11, 1855, and in October 1858 Shaw was called upon to make a talk at church. He did so acceptably that all encouraged him to preach. Consequently, he gave himself to public preaching and joined with it his musical ability. He was soon known as the "Singing Evangelist." Over the next twenty years Shaw preached north, south, east, and west. In some meetings over 200 would be added to the church, and over 12,000 were led to Christ through his ministry. Knowles Shaw was killed in a train wreck on his way from Dallas to McKinney, Texas. His last words were: "Oh, it is a grand thing to rally people to the Cross of Christ." Shaw published a number of Sunday School and revival collections. Among them were *Shining Pearls* (1868), *Sparkling Jewels* (1871), and *The Gospel Trumpet* (1875).

AMPELOS (262)
I Am the Vine (262)
SHAW (495)

Sowing in the Morning (443)
Tarry With Me (635)

Shelton, Thomas J.

Shelton, Thomas J. (b. Kentucky, June 1849; d. Denver, Colorado, March 6, 1929) was a minister of the Stone-Campbell Movement beginning in the late 1860s. He dealt much in sensationalism in his preaching, desiring to rival Moody and Sankey. For a time in the 1870s, James Holmes Rosecrans was singer for Shelton. In the early 1880s his speculative preaching and sensationalism alienated him from the church. In 1881 he claimed membership in the Milton Church, Pike County, Illinois. His complete separation from the Disciples occurred in March 1891. He had migrated to Little Rock, Arkansas, where he preached and published a paper called *The Christian*. The brethren there dismissed him. In his final sermon he said: "I am Jesus Christ...I leave here next Tuesday morning for Kansas City, and Lucy goes with me [Lucy Brack was the wife of one of the members of the church in Little Rock]. . . .We will await orders in Kansas City from God. We may go to Denver or San Francisco" (Reported by George C. Christian in *The Christian-Evangelist,* March 9, 1891: 182). Apparently Shelton did go to Denver. Harold Holland reported to me that in Denver Shelton preached and published a book entitled *The Law of Vibrations*, which got him in trouble with the postal authorities. He also published *I Am Sermons* (1900), a volume of unusual sermons which commended Mrs. Mary Baker Eddy and Christian Science.

One Step at a Time (541)

Shepherd, Thomas

Shepherd, Thomas (b. England, 1665; d. Bocking, Essex, England, January 29, 1739) was the son of William Shepherd. He was at first a minister in the Church of England, but left it and in 1694 became a minister of the independent Castle Hill Meeting House, Nottingham, where Philip Doddridge would later minister. In 1700 he moved to Bocking, near Braintree, Essex, and preached in a barn for seven years. At the end of these years, a chapel was built in which he preached for the remainder of his life.

Must Jesus Bear the Cross Alone (629)

Shepherd, Franklin Lawrence

Shepherd, Franklin Lawrence (b. Philadelphia, Pennsylvania, August 7, 1852; d. Philadelphia, February 15, 1930), the son of Isaac A.

Sheppard, was educated at the University of Pennsylvania. Following his graduation with highest honors (1872), he joined his father's business of manufacturing stoves and heaters, as manager of the foundry. Sheppard was organist and vestryman of the Zion Protestant Episcopal Church in Baltimore, Maryland, where he was a member. He later joined the Second Presbyterian Church in Baltimore, where he served as music director and taught in the Sunday School. He was a delegate to the Presbyterian General Assembly, president of the Presbyterian Board of Publication, and served on the editorial committee of the Presbyterian *Hymnal* (1911). He also edited the Sunday School compilation *Alleluia* (1915).

TERRA BEATA (629)

Sherwin, William Fiske

Sherwin, William Fiske (b. Buckland, Massachusetts, March 14, 1826; d. Boston, Massachusetts, April 14, 1888) received his musical training under Lowell Mason. He taught in the New England Conservatory of Music, Boston, Massachusetts. Although Sherwin was a Baptist, his ability to organize and direct amateur choruses led John H. Vincent to employ him as musical director of the Methodist Chautauqua Institution, in western New York.

Bread of Life (312, 376)
CHAUTAUQUA (37)

Showalter, Anthony Johnson

Showalter, Anthony Johnson (b. Rockingham County, Virginia, May 1, 1858; d. Chattanooga, Tennessee, September 16, 1924) was the son of John A. and Susanna Miller Showalter. He studied music under his father and under B. C. Unseld, H. R. Palmer, and George F. Root. Showalter also studied music in Europe in 1895. In 1880 he began to teach music and that year published his first book, *Harmony and Composition*. He became associated with the Reubush-Kieffer Company of Dayton, Virginia, and in 1884 moved to Dalton, Georgia, to establish a branch office. Soon afterwards he founded his own publishing company, through which he edited over sixty song books. He also edited and published *The Music Teacher* for over twenty years. He was widely known and honored as a music teacher, particularly throughout the South. Showalter served as an elder and music director for the First Presbyterian Church, Dalton, Georgia.

SHOWALTER (108)

Shurtleff, Ernest Warburton

Shurtleff, Ernest Warburton (b. Boston, Massachusetts, April 4, 1862; d. Paris, France, August 24, 1917) was educated at Boston Latin School, at Harvard University, and at New Church Theological Seminary and Andover Theological Seminary. He entered the Congregational ministry and served churches at Ventura, California; Old Plymouth and Palmer, Massachusetts; and at Minneapolis, Minnesota (1898-1905). In 1906 he became director of student activities for American students at the Academy Vitti in Paris. Shurtleff married Helen S. Cramer of Cameron, Texas, and they were relief workers during World War 1. His works include *Poems* (1883), *New Year's Peace* (1885), *Song of Hope* (1886), and *Shadow of the Angel* (1886).

Lead On, O King Eternal (259)

Sibelius, Jean

Sibelius, Jean (b. Tavastehus, Finland, December 8, 1865; d. Jarvenpaa, Finland, September 20, 1957) studied under Martin Wegelius, who conducted the Finnish Opera, and also in Berlin and Vienna. He taught at the Helsingfors Music Institute and at Philharmonic Orchestra School. He is recognized as the greatest of Finnish composers. His work in providing music for Finnish myths has been compared to that of Wagner's in helping to preserve ancient Germanic legends. His works include *Five Christmas Songs* (1895) and *Musique Religieuse* (1927).

FINLANDIA (547)

Silcher, Friedrich

Silcher, Friedrich (b. near Schorndorf, Württemberg, Germany, June 27, 1789; d. Tübingen, Germany, August 28, 1860) conducted and taught music in Ludwigsburg and Stuttgart. He founded the university Choral Society and was director of music at the University of Tübingen (1817-1860). His works include *Sammlung deutscher Volkslieder*, a 12-volume collection of folk songs; the *Württemberg Choralbuch. Geschichte der evangelischen Kirchengesänge* (1844), and also three volumes of hymns.

SO NIMM DENN MEINE HÄNDE (527)

Simpson, Larry Leonard

Simpson, Larry Leonard (b. Miami, Florida, February 22, 1954) is the son of Wells Leonard and Betty Lee Bryant Simpson. He was educated at Abilene Christian University (B.S., 1975) and the University of Florida College of Medicine in Miami (M.D., 1978). He married Gene Randy Bishop (1983), and they have one daughter. Dr. Simpson is a diplomat of the American Board of Emergency Medicine and a fellow of the American College of Emergency Physicians. He resides in Riverview, Florida.

    Jesus Is Lord (159)

Skene, Robert

No certain information is available on this composer. He edited *The Concordia* (Louisville, 1861) and, with Augustus Damon Fillmore, *The Christian Psaltery* (1867). It is more than probable that Robert Skene is the grandson of Benjamin Skene, whose obituary is given ample space in the *Millennial Harbinger* (April 1859: 237-38). Benjamin Skene had a son Robert, who resided in Louisville, Kentucky.

    SKENE (177)

Skoog, Andrew L.

Skoog, Andrew L. (b. Varmland, Sweden, December 17, 1856; d. Minneapolis, Minnesota, October 30, 1934) was the son of a tailor and his father's apprentice at age ten. He came with his family to the United States at age three and settled in Minneapolis. Although possessing scant formal education, he had great natural talents and became proficient in photography, printing, publishing, teaching, selling, and writing. He edited and published a popular Swedish language journal. Skoog served as organist and choir director for churches in Chicago and Minneapolis, wrote many texts, and edited several hymnals. His works include *Evangelii Basun I* (1881) and *Jubelklangen* (1886). He also assisted in the publication of three hymnals of the Mission Covenant Church.

    Day by Day and with Each Passing Moment (134)

Slade, Mary Bridges Canedy

Slade, Mary Bridges Canedy (b. Fall River, Massachusetts, 1826; d. Fall River, 1882) was the wife of a minister in Fall River and spent her entire life there. She was a school teacher and served as assistant editor of *The New England Journal of Education*. She wrote a number of hymn texts.

    From All the Dark Places (424)
    Hark! the Gentle Voice (320)
    Sweetly, Lord, Have We Heard Thee Calling (426)
    Who at the Door Is Standing? (341)

Slater, William Washington

Slater, William Washington (b. Logan County, Arkansas, February 2, 1885; d. Fort Worth, Texas, August 22, 1959) was a minister of the Church of Christ and a well-known singer and singing-school teacher. He received his music education under E. T. Hildebrand and Will M. Ramsey at the Eureka Normal School, Eureka, Oklahoma. He led the singing for many prominent evangelists among Churches of Christ. His son is J. Nelson Slater, and his grandson is William Slater Banowsky, who has served as president of Pepperdine University (Malibu, California) and the University of Oklahoma. Slater published several hymnals including *Spiritual Melodies* (1926), *Church and Revival Songs* (1930), *Song Evangel* (1934), *Gospel Chimes* (1934), *Songs of Praise and Devotion* (1936), *Victory Songs* (1939), *Gospel Songs and Hymns* (1944), and *Sunbeam Songs* (1947).

SLATER (41)

Sleeper, William True

Sleeper, William True (b. Danbury, New Hampshire, February 9, 1819; d. Wellesley, Massachusetts, September 24, 1904) was the son of Jonathan and Mary Parker Sleeper. He was educated at Phillips-Exeter Academy, the University of Vermont, and Andover Theological Seminary. He entered the ministry of the Congregational Church and served mission churches in Worcester, Massachusetts, and in Maine. In 1876 he returned to Worcester as minister for the Summer Street Congregational Church and remained for more than thirty years. His works include a book of poems, *The Rejected King and Hymns of Jesus* (1883).

Out of My Bondage (352)

Smart, Henry Thomas

Smart, Henry Thomas (b. London, England, October 26, 1813; d. London, July 6, 1879) was educated at Highgate for the law but later abandoned this profession for music. He studied under his father and W. H. Kearns, but was largely self-taught. He served as organist at Blackburn, Lancashire (1831-1836); St. Philip's Church, Regent Street, London (18381839); St. Luke's Church, Old Street (1844-1864); and St. Pancras Church, London (1865-1879). He helped to design and install organs in both England and Scotland. Although he became blind in 1865, his memory and skill allowed him to continue to play until his death. His works include *Choral Book* (1865), *Psalms and Hymns for Divine Worship* (1867), and the *Presbyterian Hymnal* (1875).

LANCASHIRE (242, 259)

REGENT SQUARE (194, 289, 364)

Smith, Alfred Morton

Smith, Alfred Morton (b. Jenkintown, Pennsylvania, May 20, 1879; d. Brigantine, New Jersey, February 26, 1971) was educated at the University of Pennsylvania (1901) and received two degrees from Philadelphia Divinity School (1905, 1911). He entered the ministry of the Episcopal Church as deacon (1905) and priest (1906). He served churches briefly in Philadelphia and Long Beach, California, and then became minister of St. Matthias' Church, Los Angeles (1906-1916). He served as a chaplain in the United States Army during the First World War. Returning to the United States in 1919, he served as part of the staff of the Episcopal City Mission, Philadelphia, and was chaplain at Eastern State Penitentiary and at city hospitals. He then served St. Clement's Church (1920-1928) and afterwards ministered to St. Elizabeth's Church (1930-1933). He retired in 1955 and lived for a time in Druim Moir, a retirement home for Episcopal clergy. He went to live in Brigantine, New Jersey, in 1968.

SURSUM CORDA (378)

Smith, Carolyn Sprague

Smith, Carolyn Sprague (b. Salem, Massachusetts, 1827; d. 1886) was the wife of Charles Smith, minister to the South Church, Andover, Massachusetts. Nothing further is known of her life.

Tarry with Me, O My Savior (635)

Smith, Henry Percy

Smith, Henry Percy (b. England, 1825; d. Bournemouth, Hampshire, England, January 28, 1898) was educated at Balliol College, Oxford. He entered the ministry of the Church of England as deacon (1849) and priest (1850). He served as curate to Charles Kingsley, the well-known English writer (1849-1851). Thereafter he served St. Michael's Church, Yorktown, Camberley, Surrey (1851 -1868); Great Barton, Suffolk (1868-1882); was chaplain of Christ Church, Cannes, France (1882-1895); and canon of the cathedral at Gibraltar in Spain beginning in 1892.

MARYTON (263, 441)

Smith, Oswald Jeffray

Smith, Oswald Jeffray (b. Odessa, Ontario, Canada, November 8, 1889) was educated at Canadian Bible College, McCormick Theological Seminary in Chicago, Illinois, and at Manitoba College. He entered the ministry of the Presbyterian Church and served the Dale Presbyterian

Church, Toronto (1915-1919). He was later minister of the Alliance Tabernacle, Toronto, and then founded the People's Church in that city. He served as minister of this church until 1959 and then became its missionary pastor. Smith was known as one of the greatest evangelists and missionary promoters of the twentieth century. He served as editor of *The People's Magazine,* published many books, and wrote over 1200 hymn poems.

DEEPER AND DEEPER (618)

Into the Heart of Jesus (618)

Smith, Walter Chalmers

Smith, Walter Chalmers (b. Aberdeen, Scotland, December 5, 1824; d. Kinbuch, Perthshire, Scotland, September 20, 1908) was educated at the University of Aberdeen and at New College, Edinburgh. He entered the ministry of the Free Church of Scotland and served at Chadwell Street, Islington, London (1850-1857); Roxburgh Free Church, Edinburgh (1857-1876); and the Free High Church, Edinburgh (1876-1894). He also served as moderator of the Free Church of Scotland (1893). His works include *The Bishop's Walk* (1860), *Olrig Grange* (1872), *Hilda Among the Broken Gods* (1878), *North Country Folk* (1883), *Kildrostan* (1884), and *Hymns of Christ and the Christian Life* (1876).

Immortal, Invisible, God Only Wise (75)

Spafford, Horatio Gates

Spafford, Horatio Gates (b. North Troy, New York, October 20, 1828; d. Jerusalem, Israel, October 16, 1888) spent his early life in New York and moved to Chicago (1856) to practice law. In Chicago he not only had a highly successful practice but also served as professor of medical jurisprudence at Lind University, later called Chicago Medical College. Spafford was a member of the Presbyterian Church, and a Sunday School teacher, was active in YMCA work, and served as director and trustee for Presbyterian Theological Seminary of the Northwest (now McCormick Theological Seminary). He lost the greater portion of his fortune in the Chicago fire (1871). Two years later his four daughters were drowned on a voyage across the Atlantic, and his son died in 1880. Disappointed at the unsympathetic attitude of Chicago friends, the Spaffords left the United States (1881) and settled in Jerusalem, establishing the American colony there. The Spafford's story is told in the book *Our Jerusalem,* by their daughter, Bertha Spafford Vester.

When Peace Like a River, Attendeth My Way (646)

Speiss, Johann Martin

Speiss, Johann Martin (b. Switzerland, 1696; d. Bern, Switzerland, June 4, 1772) was organist at Bergazbern and also a professor music at Heidelberg Gymnasium. He served as organist at St. Peter's Church, Heidelberg (1745), and was organist at Bern Cathedral from 1746 until his death. His works include *David's Harpffen-Spiel* (1751), *Geistliche Arien* (1761), and *Musikalische Bibel-Andachten* (1762).

SWABIA (23)

Spohr, Ludwig

Spohr, Ludwig (b. Brunswick, Germany, April 5, 1784; d. Cassel, France, October 22, 1859) belonged to a musical family, and he himself early showed musical talent. He was a famous violinist and composed in various musical forms. Spohr was critical of the works of Beethoven and von Weber but championed those of Wagner.

SPOHR (343)

Stainer, John

Stainer, John (b. London, England, June 6, 1840; d. Verona, Italy, March 31, 1901), the son of a schoolmaster, was a chorister at St. Paul's Cathedral. He was educated at Christ Church, Oxford, and at St. Edmund's Hall. He served as organist at Magdalen College (1860) and at University College (1861). Stainer succeeded Sir John Goss as organist at St. Paul's Cathedral (1872) and continued there until his eyesight failed (1888). At that point he retired and returned to Oxford, where he taught until his death. He was knighted by Queen Victoria (1888). Stainer published a popular textbook on organ playing and wrote over 150 hymn tunes. His works include *The Dictionary of Musical Terms* (1879), of which he was coeditor; *The Music of the Bible* (1879); and *Church Hymnary* (1898).

The First Noel (208)

Stead, Louisa M. R.

Stead, Louisa M. R. (b. c. 1850, Dover, England; d. Penkridge, near Umtali, Southern Rhodesia (now Zimbabwe), January 18, 1917) was born of Christian parents and converted at age nine. In her teens she felt she was called to be a missionary. In 1871 she came to America and lived with friends in Cincinnati, Ohio. She offered herself for missionary service at a meeting at Urbana, Illinois, but her health did not permit service at that time. She married Mr. Stead in 1875, and they had one daughter, Lily.

Mr. Stead drowned a few years later, and Mrs. Stead went to South Africa as a missionary to the Cape Colony (1880-1895). There she married Robert Wodehouse, a South African. When her health again became fragile, they returned to the United States, and Wodehouse served Methodist churches as a local minister. After she regained her health, the Wodehouses were delegates to the Ecumenical Missionary Conference in New York (1900) and again entered missionary service for the Methodist Church. She served at Umtali from 1901 until her retirement in 1911 and lived there until her death. She was buried near her home on the side of Black Mountain in a grave hewn from solid rock.

'Tis So Sweet to Trust in Jesus (497)

Stebbins, George Coles

Stebbins, George Coles (b. Orleans County, New York, February 26, 1846; d. Catskill, New York, October 6, 1945) grew up on a farm in New York. He studied music in Buffalo and Rochester, New York. In 1869 he moved to Chicago, where he worked with the Lyon and Healy Music Company and served as music director for the First Baptist Church. In Chicago he met most of the leading religious musicians of the day, including Root, Bliss, Palmer, and Sankey. Stebbins went back East, where he served as music director for the Clarendon Street Baptist Church, Boston (1874-1875), and, for about six months, at the Tremont Temple, Boston (1876). In the summer of 1876, he joined the team of Dwight L. Moody and Ira D. Sankey, and worked with Moody and others for twenty-five years. He helped compile many gospel songbooks and was coeditor with Sankey and McGranahan of *Gospel Hymns*, Nos. 3, 4, 5, and 6. He published his *Memoirs and Reminiscences* (1924). Stebbins died just a few months short of his 100th birthday.

ADELAIDE (597)
Calling Today (321)
Evening Prayer (40)
Holiness (487)
Jesus, I Come (352)

Steele, Anne

Steele, Anne (b. Broughton, Hampshire, England, 1716; d. Hampshire, November 11, 1778) was the daughter of William Steele, a timber merchant and minister of the Baptist Church at Broughton. She seems to have had a taste for literature while quite young. She began to write poetry but never published any verse until 1760. Miss Steele was a semi-invalid all of her life, and her health was further diminished by the death by drowning of her fiancé a few hours before their marriage. She has been recognized as one of the first English women hymn writers. Often she wrote under the pseudonym "Theodosia" and had a number of her poems published in Richard Steele's *Spectator*.

Father, Whate'er of Earthly Bliss (591)

Stennett, Samuel

Stennett, Samuel (b. Exeter, England, 1717; d. London, England, August 25, 1795) was the son of Joseph Stennett, a Baptist minister at Exeter. In 1737 the family moved to London, where the father served as minister of the Little Wild Street Baptist Church, Lincoln's Inn Fields. Stennett was educated under the tutelage of John Hubbard of Stepney and John Walker of the Academy at Mile End because as a dissenter he could not attend the universities. He became his father's assistant at Little Wild Street (1747) and minister of the church upon his father's death (1758). He also preached for the Sabbatarian Baptist Church in London each Saturday (1736-1756). His grandfather, Joseph Stennett, had been the minister of this sabbatarian church for twenty-three years. Samuel Stennett was one of the most influential dissenting ministers of his day, was a personal friend of King George lll, and was a hard worker for religious freedom. The English philanthropist and prison reformer John Howard was a member of the church at Little Wild Street. King's College, Aberdeen, awarded Stennett the honorary D.D. degree In 1763. Several of his hymns were published in John Rippon's *Selection*.

Majestic Sweetness Sits Enthroned (260)
On Jordan's Stormy Banks (666, 667)

Stephen the Sabaite

Stephen the Sabaite (b. c. 725; d. 794). According to Samuel Duffield in his *English Hymns. Their Authors and History* (1886), Stephen was a monk at the monastery of Mar Saba, near Jerusalem. This monastery was supposedly founded in the sixth century and is located on a cliff overlooking the Kedron Valley. Stephen was placed in the monastery at the age of ten by his uncle, John of Damascus, who was himself an inmate. Cosmas the Melodist was also a member of the Mar Saba community. Stephen remained in the monastery until his death. Whether the words of the hymns attributed to him are really his cannot be determined.

Art Thou Weary (332)

Stites, Edgar Page

Stites, Edgar Page (b. Cape May, New Jersey, March 22, 1836; d. Cape May, January 7, 1921) was a descendant of the *Mayflower* pilgrim, John Howland. He was also a cousin of Eliza Edmunds Hewitt. He served in the Union Army during the Civil War and was in charge of feeding the troops passing through Philadelphia. After the war he was a pilot on the Delaware River, became a Methodist preacher for a time in the Dakotas, and then lived in Cape May for the remainder of his life. He was a member of the First Methodist Episcopal Church there, and each year attended the Ocean Grove Assembly. He sometimes used "Edgar Page" as his pseudonym.

Simply Trusting Every Day (514)

Stockton, John Hart

Stockton, John Hart (b. New Hope, Pennsylvania, April 19, 1813; d. Philadelphia, Pennsylvania, March 25, 1877). His parents were Presbyterians, but he was converted in a Methodist meeting in Paulsboro, New Jersey (1832). He entered the Methodist ministry, becoming a member of the New Jersey Conference (1857). Stockton retired from full-time ministry because of poor health (1874) but continued an interest in evangelism and assisted in the Moody-Sankey meetings in Philadelphia. His published works include *Salvation Melodies* (1874) and *Precious Songs* (1875).

Come, Every Soul (327)
Great Physician (173)
STOCKTON (327)

Stone, Samuel John

Stone, Samuel John (b. Whitmore, Staffordshire, England, April 25, 1839; d. Charterhouse, England, November 19, 1900) was the son of William Stone, an Anglican minister. He was educated at the Charterhouse and at Pembroke, College, Oxford (1862, 1872). He entered the ministry of the Church of England and served as curate at Windsor (1862) and at St. Paul's, Haggerston (1874). Subsequently he was rector of All-Hallows-on-the-Wall, London, from 1890 until his death. His works include *Lyra Fidelium* (1866), *The Knight of Intercession and Other Poems* (1st ed., 1872), *Sonnets of the Christian Year* (1875), *Hymns* (1866), and *Order of the Consecutive Church for Children. with Original Hymns* (1883). His collected *Poems and Hymns* were edited by F. G. Ellerton posthumously. Stone served on the committee which published *Hymns Ancient and Modern*

(ed. 1909). Julian says: "Usually the key-note of his song is Hope."
    The Church's One Foundation (365)

Stowe, Harriet Beecher

Stowe, Harriet Beecher (b. Litchfield, Connecticut, June 14, 1812; d. Hartford, Connecticut, July 1, 1896) was the daughter of Lyman Beecher. She moved with her family, which included her brother, Henry Ward Beecher, to Cincinnati, Ohio (1832), where her father served as president of Lane Seminary. She married Calvin E. Stowe, a professor of languages and biblical literature in the seminary (1836). Mrs. Stowe wrote the well-known anti-slavery novel *Uncle Tom's Cabin* in 1852. Her husband was later a professor at Bowdoin College and at Andover Theological Seminary. She published over forty volumes of prose and one volume of poems. Several of her hymns were included in Henry Ward Beecher's *Plymouth Collection* (1855).
    Still, Still with Thee (641)

Stowell, Hugh

Stowell, Hugh (b. Douglas, Isle of Man, England, December 3, 1799; d. Salford, England, October 8, 1865) was the son of Hugh Stowell, rector of Ballaugh, near Ramsey. He was educated at St. Edmund Hall, Oxford (1822, 1826). He entered the ministry of the Church of England (1823) and was curate of churches in Gloucestershire, Huddersfield, and Salford. He became rector of Christ Church, Salford (1831), and canon of Chester Cathedral (1845). In 1851 he was appointed chaplain to the Bishop of Manchester. Stowell was an effective preacher and a popular writer of hymns for children. His works include *The Peaceful Valley* (1826), *A Selection of Hymns Suited to the Services of the Church of England* (1831), *Pleasures of Religion and Other Poems* (1832), *Tractarianism Tested* (1845), and *A Model for Men of Business* (1854). J. B. Marsden published his *Memoir* (1868).
    From Every Stormy Wind That Blows (561)

Su Yin-Lan

Su Yin-Lan (b. Tientsin, China, 1915; d. Tientsin, 1937) graduated from the music department of Yenching University, Peking (Beijing) in 1935. She married after her graduation and returned to Tientsin. In the summer of 1937, she gave birth to a son. That same summer the Japanese bombed Tientsin, and she was frightened to death by the noise of the exploding bombs.
    SHENG EN (39)

Sullivan, Arthur Seymour

Sullivan, Arthur Seymour (b. Bolwell Terrace, Lambeth, England, May 13, 1842; d. Westminster, England, November 22, 1900) was a chorister of the Chapel Royal under Thomas Helmore at the age of twelve. He was educated at the Royal Academy of Music and the Leipzig Conservatory, where he studied under the notable music teachers of his day. Sullivan is known for his music which he prepared for the texts of W. S. Gilbert. The best known of their operettas are *H.M.S. Pinafore* (1878) and *The Mikado* (1885). Sullivan was organist in several churches and professor of composition at the Royal Academy of Music (1866). He did not believe that popular tunes ought to be used for hymns. He was musical editor of *The Hymnary* (1872) and *Church Hymns with Tunes* (1874). He was knighted by Queen Victoria (1883).

HANFORD (611)

ST. GERTRUDE (412)

Swain, Joseph

Swain, Joseph (b. Birmingham, England, 1761; d. London, England, April 14, 1796) became an orphan in childhood. He was apprenticed to an engraver and subsequently came to London. He was converted through the reading of the Scriptures and was baptized by John Rippon (1783). From the time of his conversion, he began to express his warm religious emotions in hymns. In 1791 Swain became the minister of the Baptist congregation in East Street, Walworth, London, after having been a member of Rippon's Carter Lane Baptist Church in Southwark for some years. His ministry was extremely successful, but he died after a short illness and was buried in Bunhill Fields, in London. His works include *A Collection of Poems on Several Occasions* (1781); *Redemption. A Poem in Five Books* (1789); *Experimental Essays on Divine Subjects* (1791); *Walworth Hymns* (1792); its *Supplement* (1794); and *A Pocket Companion and Directory* (1794).

How Sweet, How Heavenly Is the Sight (390)

O Thou, in Whose Presence (634)

Sweatmon, Thomas R.

Sweatmon, Thomas R. Not much certain information is available on this poet. Joseph Nelson Slater, the son of Will W. Slater, who provided the music for the poem listed below, believes that Sweatmon was a student with his father in the Eureka Normal Music School in Stigler, Oklahoma, in 1915. Slater probably bought the text from Sweatmon at that time. The following advertisement appeared in the *Musical Visitor*, published by the Fillmore Music House: "Song Poems and Harmony Fittings from 50 cents and up by Thomas. R. Sweatmon. Newnan, Ga. Coweta Co." (Jan. 1915). "Versification and Composition. Something New. Each phrase of the subject is well discussed and explained. Price 25 cents. Thos. R. Sweatmon. Sargent, Ga. Coweta Co." (Nov. 1915). "Song Poems Revised. Rev. Thomas R. Sweatmon. Louisville, Ky." (Nov. 1917). I am indebted to Harold Holland of Pepperdine University for this information from the *Musical Visitor.*

 Walking Alone at Eve (41)

Sweney, John Robson

 Sweney, John Robson (b. West Chester, Pennsylvania, December 31, 1837; d. Chester, Pennsylvania, April 10, 1899), the son of John H. Sweney, seems to have evidenced musical talent when quite young, for at age twenty-two he was teaching music at Dover, Delaware. He served as band director of the Third Delaware Regiment during the Civil War. After the War he became a professor of music at the Pennsylvania Military Academy and remained there for twenty-five years. During this time he also served as music director for Bethany Presbyterian Church. The millionaire John Wanamaker was superintendent of the Sunday School of this church, and he and Sweney compiled two hymnals together: *Living Hymns for Use in the Sabbath School. Young People's Meeting. and Church Home* (1890) and *The New Living Hymns* (1902), the latter which Wanamaker compiled from materials left him by Sweney. He married Lizzie A. Gould, who died in 1871. They had two children, Frank G. and B. Hilyard. His second wife was also named Lizzie. They had one daughter, Josephina, who married William J. Kirkpatrick in 1917. Sweney was a popular song leader and worked in summer assemblies in many places in the United States. He composed more that one thousand gospel songs and helped to compile more than sixty hymnals.

 Jesus Leads (272)
 Sing On (473)
 Story of Jesus (305)
 Sunshine (463)
 SWENEY (626)

Swertner, John

 Swertner, John (b. Haarle, Netherlands, September 12, 1746; d. Bristol, England, March 11, 1813), an artist, was the son-in-law of John Annich. He served as a Moravian missionary at various churches in England

and also at Fairfield, Dublin, Ireland. Swertner edited hymnals for the Moravian Church from 1798 to 1801.

Sing Hallelujah, Praise the Lord (179)

Synesius of Cyrene

Synesius of Cyrene (b. Cyrene, c. 375; d., 430) was descended from a wealthy and illustrious family, which, according to the historian Gibbon, could trace its descent back seventeen centuries. He was educated under the Neo-Platonist Hypatia and became known an eloquent man, a philosopher, and a statesman. When the Gothic invasions were threatening his country, he tried to persuade the Emperor Arcadius of the imminent danger, but without success. How thoroughly converted Synesius really was is open to some doubt. He married a Christian lady in A.D. 403 and in 410 was made Bishop of Ptolemais against his will.

Lord Jesus, Think on Me (529)

Tallis, Thomas

Tallis, Thomas (b. Leicestershire, England, c. 1505; d. Greenwich, England, 23, 1585) is called "the Father of English cathedral music." He is clearly the greatest English musician of the sixteenth century. Still more marvelous is that he was able to survive the various political and social changes of all the Tudor rulers—Henry Vll, Henry Vlll, Edward Vl, Mary, and Elizabeth 1. He was a very adaptable man. Tallis arranged the music for the second prayer book prepared under Edward Vl and wrote motets and masses during the reign of the Catholic Queen Mary. Elizabeth granted to Tallis and to William Byrd, who were joint organists at the Chapel Royal, the exclusive right to print music and music paper (1575-1596). Several of Tallis's tunes were included in Archbishop Matthew Parker's *Whole Psalter Translated into English Metre* (1561 -1567).

TALLIS' CANON (30)
TALLIS' ORDINAL (70)

Tappan, William Bingham

Tappan, William Bingham (b. Beverly, Massachusetts, October 24, 1794; d. West Needham, Massachusetts, June 18, 1849) was a Boston clockmaker's apprentice at age twelve. He moved to Philadelphia in 1815 and practiced his profession there. In 1822 Tappan became interested in and began to work for the American Sunday School Union, a connection he maintained for the remainder of his life. In 1840 he entered the ministry of the Congregational Church and became a successful evangelist. He published ten volumes of poems, including *New England and Other Poems* (1819) and *Poems* (1822, 1860).

'Tis Midnight and on Olive's Brow (213)

Tate, Nahum

Tate, Nahum (b. Dublin, Ireland, 1652; d. Southwark, London, England, August 12, 1715) was the son of Faithful Tate (originally Teate), a minister of the Church of Ireland. He was educated at Trinity College, Dublin. Tate went to London in 1668 to seek his fortune as a writer, but lacked the talent to become great. He was appointed poet laureate (1692) and royal historiographer (1702). He is remembered principally for his work with Nicolaus Brady to produce a new version of the psalter. This work, entitled *The New Version of the Psalms of David,* appeared in 1696 and a *Supplement to the New Version* in 1698. Tate was a man of spendthrift habits and died in the Mint at Southwark, a debtors' refuge.

Through All the Changing Scenes (52)
While Shepherds Watched Their Flocks (197)

Taylor, Austin

Taylor, Austin (b. Morgantown, Kentucky, October 14, 1881; d. Uvalde, Texas, 1973) was the son of Garrard B. and Susan Holloway Taylor. His parents were baptized at Cane Ridge, Kentucky in 1868, and the family moved to Sherman, Texas, in 1890. He studied music under Horatio R. Palmer and Dr. H. N. Lincoln, well-known music teachers of the day. Taylor married Augusta Barbara Jerger in 1908. He published his first song book, *The Gospel Messenger*, in 1905 and spent a lifetime teaching singing schools and leading singing for evangelistic meetings. He was used widely as a singer among the Churches of Christ in the South and Southwest. For many years he assisted in editing hymnals for the Firm Foundation Company of Austin, Texas, including *New Songs of Victory* (1911), *New Songs of Praise* (1916), *Rudimental Nugget* (1912) included in *Gospel Songs Number Two* (1919), and *The New Ideal Gospel Hymn Book* (1930). His hymnal collection was given to Abilene Christian University after his death.

Closer to Thee (573)

Teddlie, Tillit Sidney

Teddlie, Tillit Sidney (b. Swan, Texas, June 3, 1885; d. Greenville, Texas, 1987) was educated at North Texas State Teachers College (now the University of North Texas) in Denton. He was baptized in 1903, attended his first singing school under his brother, V. O. Teddlie, in 1904, and that year published his first song. He married Edna Webb and began preaching among Churches of Christ in 1923. He served as superintendent of Boles Home in Quinlan, Texas (1927-1928). Teddlie's preaching was mainly in Texas and Tennessee, and he was well known as a singer, song writer, and compiler of hymnals. His published works include *Whispers of Love* (1936), *Songs of Salvation* (1937), *Spiritual Melodies* (1938), *Eternal Praise* (1939), *Select Revival Songs* (1939), *Standard Gospel Songs* (1943), *Songs of Praise* (1952), *Songs of Faith and Love* (1958), *Songs of Redemption* (1959), *The Great Christian Hymnal* (1965), and *Golden Harvest Hymns* (1974). Teddlie's manuscripts are now in the library of Abilene Christian University, Abilene, Texas. He died at the age of one hundred two.

THE LORD'S SUPPER (366)
When We Meet in Sweet Communion (366)
Worthy Art Thou (168)
Worthy of Praise Is Christ Our Redeemer (168)

Tersteegen, Gerhardt

Tersteegen, Gerhardt (b. Mors, Westphalia, Germany, November 25, 1697; d. Mülheim, Germany, April 13, 1769) was intended by his parents to be a minister in the Reformed Church. His father died in 1703, and the family finances could not afford to educate Gerhardt beyond the local Latin school, Mors Gymnasium. He was apprenticed to a merchant, underwent a religious experience, and eked out a meager living by weaving and selling silk ribbons. He adopted an overly strict regimen of eating only one small meal a day so that he could give his money to the poor. This diet caused a severe depression which lasted for five years. At the end of that period, he wrote his new covenant with God in his own blood and gave himself to Christian service outside the Reformed Church. He spent his time in prayer, in visiting the poor, and in writing. He gathered to himself a number of followers who supported him in his preaching and work. Tersteegen went to Holland to preach for many years (1732-1755), since no one outside the state church could preach in his district of Germany. His home, which he called "The Pilgrim's Cottage," was a refuge for those who sought a new way of life. Tersteegen is considered one of the most important hymn writers to come out of the Reformed Church in Germany. His hymns have both a tenderness and an urgency in all matters spiritual.

God Calling Yet! Shall I Not Hear (316)
God Himself Is with Us (7)

Teschner, Melchior

Teschner, Melchior (b. Fraustadt, Silesia, 1584; d. Oberpritschen,

Posen, Germany, December 1, 1635) was the son of a chief steward. He studied while a child under Johann Klee in the gymnasium at Zittau. He was later educated at the University of Frankfurt-an-der-Oder (1602), studying philosophy and theology, and music under Bartholomaus Gesius. He then served as cantor and teacher at Schieger (1605-1608) and, having saved his money, studied also at Wittenberg. In 1609 he became cantor of the Church of the Kripplein Christi, in his home town of Fraustadt. In 1614 he became pastor of the church at Oberpritschen and married Elisabeth Klee, the daughter of his old teacher, in 1616. Teschner died as the result of an attack by the Cossacks in 1635. One of his sons and a grandson succeeded to his ministry at Oberpritschen.

ST. THEODULPH (167,189)

Thalben-Ball, George Thomas

Thalben-Ball, George Thomas (b. Sydney, New South Wales, Australia, 1896) is the son of George Thomas Thalben-Ball of Newquay, Cornwall, England. He was educated at the Royal College of Music, London. He served as organist at Whitefield's Tabernacle (1911-1914); Holy Trinity, Castelnau (1914-1916); and Paddington Parish Church (1916-1919); and as assistant at Temple Church (1919-1923). Since 1923 he has been organist in succession to Walford Davies. Thalben-Ball received the honorary D.Mus. degree from Lambeth College (1938), and was president of the Royal College of Organists (1948). He also helped to edit the *B.B.C. Hymn Book* (1951).

LLANHERNE (95)

Theodulph of Orleans

Theodulph of Orleans (b. probably Spain, ca. 750; d. Langers, France, September 18, 821) was the son of a noble Gothic family. He was a monk in a monastery at Florence but was brought by Charlemagne to France (c. 781). Here he became abbot of Fleury and then bishop of Orleans. Upon the death of the Englishman Alcuin, Theodulph became Charlemagne's chief theologian. He was accused of conspiracy against Charlemagne's successor, Louis I (818), and died three years later, probably still in prison and probably of poison.

All Glory, Laud, and Honor (167)

Thompson, John O.

No information is available on this author. The song attributed to him was published in John H. Vincent's *The Epworth Hymnal containing*

standard hymns (New York: Phillips and Hunt, 1885).
  Far and Near the Fields Are Teeming (399)

Thompson, Will Lamartine

Thompson, Will Lamartine (b. East Liverpool, Ohio, November 7, 1847; d. New York, New York, September 20, 1909) was educated at Mt. Union College, Alliance, Ohio, and at the Boston conservatory of Music. He also studied music in Leipzig, Germany. Thompson established the publishing firm of Will L. Thompson and Company, in East Liverpool and in Chicago, Illinois, through which he published numerous songs, both sacred and secular, and also several collections. The story is told that Thompson visited Dwight L. Moody on his death bed. Although no visitors were allowed, when Moody learned that Thompson had come, he asked to see him. During their conversation, Moody said, "Will, I would rather have written 'Softly and tenderly Jesus is calling' than anything I have been able to do in my whole life." According to Kenneth Hanson, Thompson's religious roots were in the Stone-Campbell Movement.
  ELIZABETH (500)
  Jesus Is All the World to Me (500)
  Softly and Tenderly Jesus Is Calling (323)
  THOMPSON (323)

Thomson, Mary Ann

Thomson, Mary Ann (b. London, England, December 5, 1834; d. Philadelphia, Pennsylvania, March 11, 1923) grew up in England but later came to the United States. Here she married John Thomson (or Thompson). She was a member of the Episcopal Church of the Annunciation, Philadelphia, in which church her husband was accounting warden. He was also the first librarian of the Free Library in Philadelphia. Her poems were often published in *The Churchman,* New York, and in *The Living Church*, Chicago.
  O Zion, Haste, Thy Mission High Fulfilling (414)

Threlfall, Jeannette

Threlfall, Jeannette (b. Blackburn, Lancashire, England, March 24, 1821; d. Westminster, England, November 30, 1880) was the daughter of a Blackburn wine merchant, Henry Threlfall, and his wife Catherine Eccles Threlfall, a member of a prominent family of the region. The Eccles family disapproved of the union. Both father and mother died while their daughter was quite young, and she lived with relatives. A sad accident left

Miss Threlfall lame, mutilated, and an invalid for life. Julian says: "She bore her long, slow sufferings brightly, and to the end retained a gentle, loving sympathetic heart, and always a pleasant word and smile, forgetful of herself." Her poems were published in various periodicals, and collected in *Woodsorrel. or Leaves from a Retired Home* (1856) and in *Sunshine and Shadow* (1873), for which later publication Christopher Wordsworth, the bishop of London, wrote the introduction.

Hosanna, Loud Hosanna (163)

Thring, Godfrey

Thring, Godfrey (b. Alford, Somersetshire, England, March 25, 1823; d. Shamley Green, Guildford, England, September 13, 1903) was the son of J. G. D. Thring, a minister in the Church of England. He was educated at Shrewsbury School and at Balliol College, Oxford (1845). He entered the ministry of the Church of England (1846) and served churches at Stratfield-Turgis (1846-1850) and at Strathfieldsaye (1850-1853). In 1858 he succeeded his father at Alford, and in 1878 became prebendary of East Harptree in Wells Cathedral. His works included *Hymns Congregational and Others* (186), *Hymns and Verses* (1866), *Hymns and Sacred Lyrics* (1874), and *The Church of England Hymn Book* (1880; rev. ed. 1882).

Crown Him with Many Crowns (255)

Thrupp, Dorothy Ann

Thrupp, Dorothy Ann (b. London, England, June 20, 1779; d. London, December 14, 1847) was the daughter of Joseph Thrupp of Paddington Green. Little is known of her life. She wrote hymns, mostly for children, which were published in W. Carus Wilson's *Friendly Visitor* and in his *Children's Friend,* under the pseudonym of Iota. She also published several hymns in Mrs. Herbert Mayo's *Selection of Hymns and Poetry for the Use of Infant Schools and Nurseries* (1838; rev. ed. 1846) under her initials D. A. T. Miss Thrupp had earlier edited *Hymns for the Young* (c. 1830). In this 1830 collection appeared "Savior, Like a Shepherd Lead Us," but since all the hymns are unsigned, there is no way to know certainly that it was written by Miss Thrupp.

Savior, Like a Shepherd Lead Us (606)

Tickle, Gilbert Young

Tickle, Gilbert Young (b. 1819; d. 1888) was a resident of Liverpool, England (1847) and assisted Alexander Campbell in going through customs when he arrived there for his tour through England,

Scotland, and Ireland. He was an associate of David King, one of the leaders among the Churches of Christ in England, and assisted in editing some of the editions of *Hymns for Churches of Christ*. In my copies of this hymnal (2d rev. ed., 1910; 3d ed. 1913), over twenty of Tickle's compositions are included. In the *Church of Christ Hymn Book* (1957), published at Wigan, Lancashire, England, are ten of his hymns, and in *Favourite Hymns of the Church* (Aylesbury, England,1995), at least a half dozen are still in use.

> *Another Week with All Its Cares Hath Flown* (370)
> *Lord of Our Highest Love* (379)

Tisserand, Jean

Tisserand, Jean (b. date and place unknown; d. Paris, France, 1494) was a preaching friar of the Franciscans in Paris. He was also an early writer of cantiques. Tisserand founded an order for penitent women and may be the author of an office (a formal worship service order) honoring members of his order who were martyred in Morocco (1220). His hymn, *O filii et filiae,* was published after his death.

> *O Sons and Daughters, Let Us Sing* (246)

Tomer, William Gould

Tomer, William Gould (b. October 5, 1833; d. New Jersey, September 26, 1897) received his musical education through singing schools and also sang in the choir at Finesville, New Jersey. He served in the Union Army in the Civil War as a member of 153rd Pennsylvania Infantry and was on the staff of General Oliver O. Howard, for whom Howard University (Washington, D.C.) was later named. Tomer became a government employee following the war, which job he filled for twenty years. His final years were spent in New Jersey teaching school.

> *God Be With You Till We Meet Again* (14)

Toplady, Augustus Montague

Toplady, Augustus Montague (b. Farnham, Surrey, England, November 5, 1740; d. London, England, August 11, 1778) was the son of Major Richard Toplady, who died in the siege of Carthagena (1741). He was educated at Westminster School, London and, after his mother's move to Ireland, at Trinity College, Dublin. He traced his conversion to a sermon by James Morris, a Methodist preacher, which he heard in a barn in Ireland. Toplady entered the ministry of the Church of England (1762) and became vicar of Broadhembury, Devonshire (1766). He moved to London (1775) and was preacher for the French Calvinist church in Leicester Fields the following year. He was an ardent and very partisan Calvinist and an avowed opponent of John Wesley. His works include *Psalms and Hymns* (1775), *Poems on Sacred Subjects* (1769), and *Historic Proof of the Doctrinal Calvinism of the Church of England* (1774). He died of tuberculosis at thirty-eight.

Rock of Ages, Cleft for Me (356)

Towner, Daniel Brink

Towner, Daniel Brink (b. Rome, Pennsylvania, March 5, 1850; d. Longwood, Missouri, October 3, 1919) was the son of J. G. Towner, a widely-known singer and music teacher. He studied music under his father and also under John Howard, George F. Root, and George G. Webb. He was music director of Centenary Methodist Episcopal Church, Binghamton, New York (1870-1882); York Street Methodist Episcopal Church, Cincinnati, Ohio (1882-1884); and Union Methodist Episcopal Church, Covington, Kentucky (1884-1885). In 1885 he became one of the singers for Dwight L. Moody in his evangelistic campaigns. Towner was appointed head of the music department of Moody Bible Institute, Chicago, Illinois (1893), and did an influential work in training singers and musicians. He is said to have written over 2,000 songs and to have assisted in the compilation of fourteen collections. He died while leading singing in a meeting at Longwood, Missouri .

Calvary (268)
MOODY (124)
SECURITY (530)
TOWNER (342)
Trust and Obey (513)

Troutbeck, John

Troutbeck, John (b. Dacre, Cumberland, England, November 12, 1832; d. London, England, October 11, 1899) was the son of George Troutbeck. He was educated at Rugby and at University College, Oxford (1856, 1858), and was ordained to the ministry of the Church of England (1859). Troutbeck was precentor of Manchester Cathedral (1865-1869) and in 1869 became chaplain and priest in ordinary to Queen Victoria. From 1870 to 1881 he served as secretary to the New Testament Revision Company, which produced the English Revised Version of the New Testament. He did translation work for Novello and Company, London. His published works include the *Manchester Psalter and Chant Book* (1867), the *Westminister Abbey Hymn Book* (1883), and the *Cathedral*

Paragraph Psalter (1894). The archbishop of Canterbury conferred the
D.D. degree upon him in 1883.

Break Forth, O Beauteous Heavenly Light (200)

Troyte, Arthur Henry Dyke

Troyte, Arthur Henry Dyke (b. Killerton, near Exeter, England,
May 3, 1811; d. Bridehead, England, June 19, 1857) was the son of Sir
Thomas Dyke Acland. He was educated at Harrow and at Christ Church,
Oxford. He studied to be a lawyer and had a great interest in science. In
1852 he legally changed his surname to Troyte. His hymn tunes and chants
were published in the *Salisbury Hymn Book* (1857).

TROYTE'S CHANT No.1 (62, 374)

Tucker, John Ireland

Tucker, John Ireland (b. Brooklyn, New York, 1819; d. New York
City, 1895) was educated at Columbia College (1837). He organized boys
choirs in the Church of the Holy Cross, Troy, New York (1844), and led
the singing at the first Choral Eucharist in New York City (1852). His
works include the *Old Parish Hymnal* (1870); *Tunes. Old and New: Adapted
to The Hymnal as set forth by the General Convention of 1871 and Revised
and Enlarged by that of 1874* (New York, 1875); *The Service Book* (1873);
and *The Children's Hymnal* (1874).

CANONBURY (21)

Tucker, Francis Bland

Tucker, Francis Bland (b. Norfolk, Virginia, January 6, 1895; d.
Savannah, Georgia, 1984) was educated in the public schools of Lynchburg,
Virginia, the University of Virginia (1914), and Virginia Theological
Seminary (1920, 1944). He entered the ministry of the Episcopal Church
following service in France during World War 1, becoming deacon in 1918
and priest in 1920. Tucker served churches in Lawrenceville, Virginia (1920-
1925); Georgetown, Washington, D.C. (1925-1945); and Christ Church,
Savannah, Georgia, from 1945 until his retirement. He was a member of
the joint commission which compiled *The Hymnal. 1940* (19361946); the
joint commission on church music (1946-1958); and served until his death
as a member of the theological committee which was helping to prepare
The Hymnal 1982 (1985).

Father, We Thank Thee (387)

Tullar, Grant Colfax

Tullar, Grant Colfax (b. Bolton, Connecticut, August 5, 1869; d. Ocean Grove, New Jersey, May 20, 1950) was the son of Austin M. and Rhoda Maine Tullar. He received his given names from General U. S. Grant and Schuyler Colfax, who were president and vice-president of the United States when he was born. His mother having died when he was two years old, he was reared by unloving relatives. In his early years he worked in a woolen mill and clerked in a shoe store. He was converted at a Methodist meeting near Waterbury, Connecticut (1888), and attended Hackettstown Academy, New Jersey (1889-1891), where he received his only formal education. Tullar entered the Methodist ministry and served at Dover, Delaware, for one year. At that time he entered evangelistic work and was song leader for Major George A. Hilton for ten years. In 1893 he and Isaac H. Meredith founded the Tullar-Meredith Publishing Company in New York. He remained with this firm, publishing many hymn tunes and editing many hymnals until his death.

> *Face to Face* (660)
> TULLAR (269)

Turle, James

Turle, James (b. Somerton, Somersetshire, England, March 5, 1802; d. the Cloisters, Westminster Abbey, June 28, 1882) was the son of James Turle. He was a chorister at Wells Cathedral (1881-18113). Later, having studied under J. J. Goss, he was organist at Christ Church, Blackfriars (1819-1829); at St. James's, Bermondsey (1829-1831); and then became assistant at Westminster Abbey, where he served as organist and master of the choristers (1831 -1875). After retirement he resided in the precincts of the Abbey until his death.

> TE DEUM LAUDAMUS (63)

Turner, H. L.

Turner, H. L. (fl. 19th century). No certain information is available on this author. His hymn "It May Be at Morn" was published in J. E. White's *Supplement to the Song Anchor* (Battle Creek, Michigan: Review and Herald Publishing Association, 1880). James McGranahan's tune CHRIST RETURNETH was published in F. E. Belden's *Christ in Song* with the indication that the piece was copyrighted in 1877 and renewed in 1905.

> *It May Be at Morn* (281)

Tweedy, Henry Hallam

Tweedy, Henry Hallam (b. Binghamton, New York, August 5, 1868; d. Brattlebury, Vermont, April 11, 1953) was a descendant of the colonial governor William Bradford through his mother. He was educated at Phillips Andover Academy; Yale University (1901, 1909); Union Theological Seminary, New York; and the University of Berlin. He was ordained to the ministry of the Congregational Church (1898) and served churches in Utica, New York (1898-1902), and Bridgeport, Connecticut (1902-1909). Tweedy was professor of practical theology at Yale Divinity School (1909-1937). While at Yale, he was a popular preacher in boys' schools, seemingly having a great appeal to young men. He edited *Christian Worship and Praise* (New York: A. S. Barnes and Company, 1939). His missionary hymn, which we have included in *GSR*, is believed by many to be the greatest missionary hymn written in the twentieth century. In his later years, Tweedy became an invalid.

Eternal God, Whose Power Upholds (396)

Twells, Henry

Twells, Henry (b. Ashted, near Birmingham, England, March 23, 1823; d. Bournemouth, England, January 19, 1900) was educated at St. Peter's College, Cambridge (1848, 1851), and entered the ministry of the Church of England (1849). He was curate of Great Berkhamsted (1849-1851); subvicar at Stratford-upon-Avon (1851-1854); master of St. Andrew's House Schools at Mells, Somersetshire (1854-1856); and head master of Godolphin School, Hammersmith (1871-1890). In 1890 he moved to Bournemouth, where he built and partially endowed the Church of St. Augustine, remaining there until his death.

At Even, When the Sun Was Set (36)

Vadney, Victor Jonathon

Vadney, Victor Jonathon (b. San Diego, California, March 26, 1950) is the son of John William Vadney and Imogene E. Vadney Noel. He was educated at Abilene Christian University (1972) and Baylor College of Medicine (1972-1975). He did his residency at the University of Oregon Health Sciences Center (1975-1978). After a private practice in Abilene, Texas, Dr. Vadney went for a time on a medical mission to Africa. He is presently staff physician at Abilene State School, Abilene, Texas. He is married to Janet Lynn Black Vadney, and they have two children, Joanna and Jonathan.

My Brethren, Let Us Be as One (395)

Vail, Silas Jones

Vail, Silas Jones (b. Brooklyn, New York, October 6, 1818; d. Brooklyn, May 10, 1884) was by trade a hatter and a clerk. He later became a successful businessman. Vail was an amateur composer and compiled *The Athenaeum Collection,* a notable songbook which contained several previously unpublished songs by Stephen Collins Foster. He also compiled, with William F. Sherwin, *Songs of Grace and Glory* (1874).

LYNDHURST (489)

Van De Venter, Judson W.

Van De Venter, Judson W. (b. near Dundee, Michigan, December 5, 1855; d. Tampa, Florida, July 17, 1939) was the son of John W. and Eliza Wheeler Van De Venter. He was educated in the Dundee public schools and at Hillsdale College in Michigan. He studied music in local singing schools. Van De Venter also studied and taught art in various public schools for several years, toured Europe in 1885, visiting the famous galleries while there, and was supervisor of art in the high school at Sharon, Pennsylvania. He was an active member of the Methodist Episcopal Church and, believing he had received a call to public ministry, became first a local preacher among the Methodists and then entered evangelistic work. His song leader was Winfield Scott Weeden. He spent his last years in Temple Terrace, a suburb of Tampa, Florida, where he influenced Billy Graham. It was my privilege, while attending Florida Christian College in Temple Terrace (1946-1950), to know the widow of J. W. Van De Venter, his second wife. She often came over to the college and played the piano for us in the parlor of the girls' dormitory and would sometimes share the fruit from her orange and grapefruit groves in Temple Terrace .

All to Jesus I Surrender (604)

Van Dyke, Henry

Van Dyke, Henry (b. Germantown, Pennsylvania, November 10, 1851; d. Princeton, New Jersey, April 10, 1933) was educated at Brooklyn Polytechnic Institute, Princeton University, and Princeton Theological Seminary. After graduation he entered the ministry of the Presbyterian Church. He served the United Congregational Church, Newport, Rhode Island (18791883), and the Brick Presbyterian Church, New York City (1883-1899). In 1899 he became professor of English literature at Princeton, where he taught until 1923. Woodrow Wilson was president of Princeton while Van Dyke taught there; and when he became President of the United States, he appointed Van Dyke as minister to the Netherlands and

Luxembourg (1913-1916). Van Dyke also served in the United States Navy Chaplains Corps and was moderator of the General Assembly of the Presbyterian Church. He served as chairman of the committee to prepare the *Book of Common Worship* (1905; rev. 1932). His works include *The Reality of Religion* (1884), *The Story of the Psalms* (1887), *The Poetry of Tennyson* (1889), *Sermons to Young Men* (1893), *The Story of the Other Wise Man* (1896), and *The Gospel for an Age of Doubt* (1896). After his retirement from Princeton (1923), he gave his efforts entirely to literary work.

> *Joyful, Joyful, We Adore Thee* (55)

Vaughan Williams, Ralph

Vaughan Williams, Ralph (d. Down Ampney, Gloucestershire, England, October 12, 1872; d. St. Marylebone, England, August 26, 1958) was the son of A. Vaughan Williams, a minister of the Church of England. He was educated at Charterhouse School, the Royal College of Music, and Trinity College, Cambridge (1894, 1895, 1901). He served as organist at South Lambeth Parish Church (1896-1899). Afterwards he studied with Max Bruch at the Akademie der Künste, Berlin, and with Maurice Ravel in Paris. He was a lecturer at Oxford University and professor of composition at the Royal College of Music. Vaughan Williams spent much time collecting English folk songs in East Anglia and Hertfordshire, which work influenced all of his later efforts. He served as music editor of *The English Hymnal* (1906) and, with Martin Shaw, of *Songs of Praise* (1925, 1931). He is recognized as the greatest English composer since Henry Purcell.

> FOREST GREEN (396)

Vulpius, Melchior

Vulpius, Melchior (b. Wasungen, Thuringia, c. 1560; buried at Weimar, Germany, August 7, 1615) was cantor at the gymnasium at Weimar from 1602 to 1615. He was noted as an arranger of harmonies for multiple voices and also for his original chorale melodies. His works were published in *Cantiones Sacrae* (1602-1604), *Kirchengesänge und geistliche Lieder* (1604), and in *Ein schönes geistliches Gesangbuch* (1609). Vulpius also published a translation of Heinrich Faber's *Musicae Compendium* (1610).

> DAS NEUBEBORNE KINDELEIN (292)

Wade, John Francis

Wade, John Francis (b. c. 1710; d. Douay, France, August 16, 1786) was one of the English exiles living among the Catholic community at Douay. There he made his living as a music teacher and bookseller, acting as copyist of plainchant and hymn collections for use in the chapels of the English Roman Catholic families. Nothing further is known of his life.

ADESTE FIDELIS (210)

Walch, James

Walch, James (b. Edgerton, near Bolton, England, June 21, 1837; d. Llandudno, Caernarvonshire, Wales, August 30, 1901) received his musical education from his father and, afterwards, from Henry Smart. He served as organist at Duke's Alley Congregational Church in Bolton (1851), then simultaneously at Walmsley Church (1857) and Bridge Street Wesleyan Chapel (1858). He served also as organist at St. George's Parish Church, Bolton (1863). Walch conducted the Bolton Philharmonic Society (1874-1877) and was engaged in the music business in Barrow-in-Furness, where he was honorary organist (1877-1901).

TIDINGS (414)

Walford, William

Walford, William (b. Bath, Somersetshire, England, 1772; d. Uxbridge, England, June 22, 1850) was educated at Homerton Academy and became a Congregational minister. He served churches at Sowmarket, Suffolk (1798-1800); Great Yarmough, Norfolk (1800-1813); and at Uxbridge twice (1824-1831 and 1833-1848). During his second tenure at Uxbridge, he seemed to suffer from some kind of mental illness but during this time served as classical tutor at Homerton. He published *The Manner of Prayer* (1836). From a comparison of this book with the hymn text "Sweet Hour of Prayer," many have concluded that Walford really is the author of this famous hymn.

Sweet Hour of Prayer (559)

Walker, Annie Louise

Walker, Annie Louise (b. Kiddermore, Staffordshire, England, 1836; d. Bath, England, 1907) was the daughter of Robert Walker, a civil engineer. The family moved to Canada in 1857, where the father was employed in helping to construct the Canadian Grand Trunk Railway. While in Canada for six years, she conducted a school for girls with her sisters. She returned to England (1863) and served as a governess. During her stay in Canada, she published several of her poetic pieces in a collected volume, *Leaves from the Backwoods* (1861). Her hymn "Work for the Night Is

Coming" was published in Canada (1854) while she was there visiting her brothers prior to the family's moving there in 1857. In 1883 she married Harry Coghill, a merchant, and they lived near Hastings. Mrs. Coghill's works include, *Oak and Maple* (1890), a volume of verse, and *Autobiography and Letters* of her cousin Mrs. Oliphant (1898). She also wrote six novels and a volume of children's plays.

Work, for the Night Is Coming (418)

Wallace, William Vincent

Wallace, William Vincent (b. Waterford, Ireland, June 1, 1812; d. Chateau de Bages, France, October 12, 1865) was of Scottish ancestry. He studied music with his father, who was a bandmaster and bassoon player. William was master of the violin at quite an early age and presented his first concert in 1827. His first marriage ended in divorce, and he afterwards wandered over Australia, New Zealand, India, and South America. He returned to England and presented his first opera, *Maritana,* at Drury Lane (1845), and a second, *Matilda of Hungary* (1847). He then resumed his wanderings, traversing the United States, Mexico, and South America, giving concerts in exchange for anything he could turn into money. In 1850 he married the pianist Helen Stoepel and ultimately composed seven operas and one cantata, besides several shorter piano works. After another successful tour of the United States, he lost his eyesight. Upon the advice of his physician, he retired to the Pyrenees.

SERENITY (444)

Walmsley, Robert

Walmsley, Robert (b. Manchester, England, March 18, 1831; d. Sale, October 30, 1905) was a jeweler. He was a member of the Congregational Church, and was a worker in the Manchester Sunday School Union for twenty-eight years. He wrote many of his hymns for the annual Pentecost (Whitsunday) Festival. In 1870 he went to Sale, where he conducted his business until his death. Forty-four of his hymns were published in his *Sacred Songs for Children of All Ages* (Dec.1900). James Mearns, who wrote the information on Walmsley in Julian's *Dictionary*, says concerning Walmsley's poems: "They are simple, musical, full of a deep love of God, of the works of God in nature, and of little children, and deserve to be more extensively used."

The Sun Declines O'er Land and Sea (38)

Walter, Howard Arnold

Walter, Howard Arnold (b. New Britain, Connecticut, August 19, 1883; d. Lahore, India, November 1, 1918) was educated at Princeton University and Hartford Theological Seminary and later studied in the Universities of Edinburgh, Glasgow, and Göttingen. He afterwards taught English at Waseda University in Tokyo, Japan. Walter served as assistant minister at Asylum Hill Congregational Church, Hartford, Connecticut (1910-1913), and in 1913 joined the executive staff of the YMCA. With the encouragement of John R. Mott, he went to India to work with Moslem students in Foreman Christian College, Lahore, India. He died there during an influenza epidemic in 1918.

I Would Be True (427)

Walter, William Henry

Walter, William Henry (b. Newark, New Jersey, July 1, 1825; d. New York, New York, 1893) made himself master of the organ and as a boy played in the Presbyterian and Episcopal churches in Newark. He studied under Edward Hodges and became organist of the Church of the Epiphany in New York City (1842). He afterwards served as organist for St. John's Chapel, St. Paul's Chapel, and Trinity Chapel in New York until 1869. He was awarded the Mus.D. degree from Columbia University (1864), and became the university organist beginning in 1865. His publications include *Chorals and Hymns* (1857), *Manual of Church Music* (1860), and *The Common Prayer, with Ritual Song* (1868).

FESTAL SONG (85, 405)

Walther, Johann

Walther, Johann (fl. 16th century). Nothing is known of this composer other than that he published the *Geistliche Gesangbuchlein* (Wittenberg, 1524). This collection contained many of Martin Luther's compositions.

CHRIST LAG IN TODESBANDEN (237)

Walton, George William

Walton, George William (b. Brownfield, Texas, October 15, 1941) is the son of Oscar Lewis and Bessie Faye Chisholm Walton. He was educated at Abilene Christian University (B.A., 1963), the University of Arkansas (M.A., 1964), and Texas Tech University (Ph.D., 1976). Since 1964 he has been a member of the English faculty at ACU and currently serves as chairman of the department. Walton is the author of "Bunyan's Proverbial Language" in *Bunyan in Our Time* (ed. Robert G. Collmer). He is a member of the Minter Lane Church of Christ in Abilene, Texas.

Father of Mercy (563)

Walworth, Clarence Augustus

Walworth, Clarence Augustus (b. Plattsburg, New York, May 30, 1820; d. Albany, New York, September 19, 1900) was educated at Union College, Schenectady, New York, where he studied law. He was admitted to the bar in 1841. Although brought up a Presbyterian, he studied for the Episcopal ministry at General Theological Seminary, New York. While there he came under the influence of the Oxford Movement and became a Roman Catholic priest. He was one of the founders of the Paulist Fathers in the United States. In 1866 he became rector of St. Mary's Church in Albany, New York, where he remained for the rest of his life. His published works include *The Oxford Movement in America* (1895) and *Andiatorocte. . . and Other Poems* (1888).

Holy God, We Praise Thy Name (48)

Ward, Samuel Augustus

Ward, Samuel Augustus (b. Newark, New Jersey, December 28, 1847; d. Newark, September 28, 1903) received his musical education under Jan Pychowske in New York City. He later opened a music store business in Newark. Ward was the successor to Henry S. Cutler as organist of Grace Episcopal Church, Newark (1880). He also founded the Orpheus Club of Newark (1889) and was its director until 1900.

MATERNA (435)

Wardlaw, Ralph

Wardlaw, Ralph (b. Dalkeith, Scotland, December 22, 1779; d. Glasgow, Scotland, December 17, 1853) was educated in the local schools at Dalkeith and at Glasgow University. Wardlaw became an influential and eminent theological and biblical expositor and controversialist. He assisted in publishing with Charles Stewart a *Selection of Hymns* (1803) and a *Supplement* (1817). He died at Easterhouse near Glasgow, where his funeral was attended by a vast multitude from all walks of life. Julian says: "Critically and regarded as literature, his hymns have little of poetry in them; no 'winged words' to lift the soul heavenward. They reflect simply and plainly the lights and shadows of every-day experience of the spiritual life, rather than its etherialities and subtleties."

Hail, Morning, Known Among the Blest (21)

Ware, Henry Jr.

Ware, Henry Jr. (b. Hingham, Massachusetts, April 21, 1794; d. Framingham, Massachusetts, September 25, 1843) was the son of Henry Ware, who was minister of the Unitarian congregation at Hingham and later Hollis Professor of Divinity at Harvard University. The younger Ware graduated from Harvard with high honors (1812) and became a Unitarian minister (1815). He served as minister for the Second Unitarian Church in Boston (1817-1829). When his health began to fail, Ralph Waldo Emerson became his associate minister. Ware served as professor of pulpit eloquence and pastoral care at Harvard Divinity School (1829-1842). He retired to Framingham in 1842 and died there a year later. Ware founded and edited *The Christian Disciple,* later called *The Christian Examiner,* in 1813. Harvard awarded him the D.D. degree (1834).

Happy the Home When God Is There (438)

Waring, Anna Laetitia

Waring, Anna Laetitia (b. Plas-y-Velin, Neath, Glamorganshire, Wales, April 19, 1823; d. Clifton, Bristol, England, May 10, 1910) was reared in the Society of Friends (Quakers) but was baptized in the Church of England (1842). She published a small collection of nineteen of her hymns under the title *Hymns and Meditations. by A. L. W.* (1850). Successive editions were published, culminating with the tenth edition (1863), which contained thirty-eight hymns. She also published *Additional Hymns* (1858) and contributed hymns to the *Sunday Magazine* (1871). Miss Waring was active in prison visitation and supported the Discharged Prisoners' Aid Society.

In Heavenly Love Abiding (649)

Warner, Anna Bartlett

Warner, Anna Bartlett (b. Long Island, New York, 1820; d. Constitution Island, near West Point, New York, 1915) was the daughter of Henry W. Warner, a lawyer in New York City. After 1837 she lived with her father and her sister Susan on Constitution Island, near the United States Military Academy at West Point. Their home, "Good Crag," now a national shrine, was willed to the academy. She and her sister conducted Bible classes for the cadets at West Point for many years. Her love was returned; and when she died at age 95, she was buried with full military honors. Her published works include *Hymns of the Church Militant* (1858) and *Wayfaring Hymns. Original and Translated* (1869). She also published novels under the pseudonym "Amy Lothrop."

We Would See Jesus (496)

Warren, George William

Warren, George William (b. Albany, New York, August 17, 1828; d. New York, New York, March 17, 1902) was a self-taught musician. He was educated at Racine College, Wisconsin. Warren served as organist at St. Peter's Church, Albany (1846-1858) and then at St. Paul's Albany (18581860). Afterwards he moved to Brooklyn, where he was organist for Holy Trinity Church (1860-1870). Finally, he served as organist for St. Thomas' Church in New York City (1870-1890). Warren published *Warren's Hymns and Tunes as Sung at St. Thomas' Church* (1889). He received the honorary Mus.D. degree from Racine College.

NATIONAL HYMN (566)

Washburne, Henry S.

Washburne, Henry S. (b. Providence, Rhode Island, June 10, 1813; d. 1903) spent his early years in Kingston, Massachusetts. After finishing the local grammar school, he worked in a bookstore in Boston. Later he attended Worcester Academy and entered Brown University (1836), but because of health problems he received no degree. Washburne became the director of publications for the New England Sabbath School Union for a time and then entered business in Worcester and Boston. Ultimately, he was employed at the Union Mutual Life Insurance Company and rose to be president of the company. In 1876 he surveyed the condition of the insurance business in Europe for his company. Washburne also served on the Boston School Board for nine years, was state representative (1871-1872), and state senator (1873).

Let Every Heart Rejoice and Sing (49)

Watts, Isaac

Watts, Isaac (b. Southampton, England, July 17, 1674; d. Stoke Newington, England, November 25, 1748) has been called "the father of English hymnody." We are indebted to Watts for rescuing the churches from the dull Psalm paraphrases and for introducing the reverent and passionate hymn singing of modern times. Watts's parents were dissenters, and his father was twice imprisoned for his dissent. The father later conducted a boarding school at Southampton. There Isaac, the first of nine children, was born. He was educated at the grammar school at Southampton, learning Greek, Latin, and Hebrew. His fine abilities induced a local physician to offer to send him either to Oxford or Cambridge if he would become a minister in the Church of England. Isaac refused and was educated under Mr. Thomas Rowe at the Nonconformist Academy at Stoke

Newington (1690). He left the academy in 1694 and spent two years at home, where he wrote the bulk of his *Hymns and Spiritual Songs* (1707-1709). For six years he served as tutor to the son of the Puritan leader Sir John Hartopp. His extensive study during these years filled him with materials for the numerous works that he published but also permanently injured his health. In 1702 Watts became minister of the Independent congregation in Mark Lane. Since his health was fragile, an assistant minister, Mr. Samuel Price, was also appointed. Price became co-minister (1812) when Watts's health further declined. At about this time Watts became a guest in the home of Sir Thomas Abney and continued there for the next thirty-six years, even after Sir Thomas's death (1722). In addition to his influential hymn collections, Watts published many other works, including *Logic*, which was used at Oxford for many years; *Catechisms. Scripture History* (1732); and *The Improvement of the Mind* (1741). His hymn compilations included *Horae Lyricae* (1706, 1709); *Hymns and Spiritual Songs* (1707-1709); *The Psalms of David. Imitated in the Language of the New Testament* (1719); *Sermons with Hymns* (1721-1727); *Reliquiae Juveniles* (1734); and *Remnants of Time* (1736).

> *Alas! and Did My Savior Bleed* (215)
> *Am I a Soldier of the Cross* (546)
> *Before Jehovah's Awful Throne* (110)
> *Come, Let Us Join Our Cheerful Songs* (5)
> *Come, Sound His Praise Abroad (111)*
> *Come, Ye That Love the Lord* (68)
> *From All That Dwell Below the Skies* (78)
> *How Shall the Young Secure Their Hearts* (302)
> *I'm Not Ashamed to Own My Lord* (504)
> *Jesus Shall Reign Where'er the Sun* (261)
> *Joy to the World* (256)
> *My Shepherd Will Supply My Need* (645)
> *O God Our Help in Ages Past* (136)
> *The Heavens Declare Thy Glory, Lord* (112)
> *This Is the Day the Lord Hath Made* (18)
> *When I Survey the Wondrous Cross* (233)

Webb, George James

Webb, George James (b. Rushmore Lodge, Salisbury, England, June 24, 1803; d. Orange, New Jersey, October 17, 1887) was the son of a prosperous farmer who wished his son to enter the ministry. George chose instead to be a musician and studied under Alexander Lucas at Salisbury. For a brief time he served as organist at Falmouth and then migrated to

Boston, Massachusetts (1830). He was soon appointed organist for the Old South Church, which post he held for forty years. At this church he became friends with Lowell Mason and served with Mason as a professor in the Boston Academy of Music (1833). Many years later (1870) he joined him in musical ventures in New York. Webb also served as president of the Boston Handel and Haydn Society (1840). He was one of the most influential of American music teachers. His works include *The Massachusetts Collection of Psalmody* (1840), *The American Glee Book* (1841), and, with Lowell Mason, *The Psaltery* (1845), *The National Psalmist* (1848), *Cantica Laudis* (1850), and *Cantica Ecclesiastica* (1859). For a short time he also edited the periodicals *Music Library* and *Musical Cabinet*.

> WASHBURNE (49)
> WEBB (403)

Webbe, Samuel Sr.

Webbe, Samuel Sr. (b. London, England, 1740; d. London, May 25, 1816) was the son of a government official newly appointed to Minorca. The father died, however, before his wife and son could join him at his new post. In 1751 Samuel was apprenticed to a cabinetmaker, with whom he remained until about 1760. Having saved his money, he took a job as a music copyist with the London publisher Weleker and then studied under the organist Carl Barbandt. Webbe also studied languages, including Latin, Greek, Hebrew, French, Italian, and German. He was a Roman Catholic and was employed as organist for the Spanish, Portuguese, and Sardinian embassies in London beginning in 1776. He won many prizes in the competitions held by the Catch Club, for which he was secretary (1784-1816). His published works include *A Collection of Masses for Small Choirs* (1792); *A Collection of Sacred Music as Used in the Chapel of the King of Sardinia in London* (1793); *Antiphons in Six Books of Anthems* (1818); and, with his son Samuel Jr., *A Collection of Motets and Antiphons* (1792).

> CONSOLATOR (338)

Weber, Carl Maria Friedrich Ernst von

Weber, Carl Maria Friedrich Ernst von (b. Eutin, Germany, November 18, 1786; d. London, England, June 5, 1826) was the son of a theatrical empressario and traveled with his father throughout Europe, where he gained knowledge of the stage. He studied under Michael Haydn and Abbe Georg Joseph Vogler (concerning whom Robert Brown wrote his famous poem "Abt Vogler") and was conductor of the Breslau Municipal Theater and, later, of theaters in Stuttgart, Prague, and Dresden. He gained

fame for his operas *Der Freischütz, Preciosa, Euryanthe,* and *Oberon.* His works also include symphonies, masses, cantatas, and chamber music.
JEWETT (533)
SEYMOUR (35,413)

Webster, Joseph Philbrick

Webster, Joseph Philbrick (b. Manchester, New York, March 22, 1819; d. Elkhorn, Wisconsin, January 18, 1875) received his education at an academy at Pembroke, New Hampshire. He later studied music under Lowell Mason in Boston and spent several years teaching music and performing both in New York and Connecticut. Webster played several musical instruments. He held anti-slavery views and settled sometime before the Civil War, in Elkhorn, Wisconsin. He was a prolific composer and compiled *The Signet Ring* (Chicago, 1868).
Sweet By and By (659)

Weeden, Winfield Scott

Weeden, Winfield Scott (b. Middleport, Ohio, March 29, 1847; d. Bisby Lake, New York, July 31, 1908) was the son of Isaac and Sarah Faar Weeden. He was educated in his home town and for several years taught singing schools. Having a good voice, he entered evangelistic work and often led the singing at YMCA, Christian Endeavor, and Epworth League conventions. He was singer with the evangelistic campaigns of Judson W. Van de Venter for several years. He is best known for his tune SURRENDER, composed for Van de Venter's "I Surrender All." These words are inscribed on his tombstone. He lived his last years in New York City and is buried there in Woodlawn Cemetery. Weeden was named for the famous American general of the Mexican War, Winfield Scott. He composed many gospel songs, and his published works include *The Peacemaker* (1894), *Songs of Sovereign Grace* (1897), and *Songs of the Peacemaker* (1895).
SURRENDER (604)

Weisse, Michael

Weisse, Michael (b. Neisse, Silesia, ca. 1480; d. Landskron, Bohemia,1534) was educated for the Roman Catholic priesthood and for a time was a monk at Breslau. The writings of Martin Luther having fallen into his hands, he, with a brother priest, left the Roman Church and entered the Bohemian Brethren's House at Leutomischl in Bohemia. He became a minister among the Brethren (1531) and was sent as emissary to Luther regarding points of difference in doctrine. Weisse edited the first German-language hymnal in use among the Bohemian Brethren, *Ein Neu Gesangbuchlen* (1531). This compilation contained 155 songs, most of which were either translated or composed by Weisse.

Christ the Lord Is Risen Again (247)

Weissel, Georg

Weissel, Georg (b. Domnau, Prussia, 1590; d. Königsberg, Prussia, August 1,1635) was the son of Johann Weissel, a judge who was later mayor of Domnau. He was educated at Königsberg (1608-1811) and also studied at Wittenberg, Leipzig, Jena, Strasbourg, Basel, and Marburg. He served briefly as rector of a school at Friedland (1614), but returned to Königsberg to continue the study of theology. He served as minister of the Altrossgart church at Königsberg (1623-1635). Weissel is recognized as an important Prussian hymn writer, and some twenty of his hymns, most written for festivals of the ecclesiastical year, have survived.

Lift Up Your Heads, Ye Mighty Gates (191)

Wesley, Charles

Wesley, Charles (b. Epworth, Lincolnshire, England, December 18, 1707; d. Marylebone, London, England, March 29, 1788) was the eighteenth and youngest son of Samuel and Susanna Wesley and the brother of John Wesley. Charles was educated at home by his parents, at Westminster (beginning 1716), and at Christ College, Oxford (1726). At Oxford he formed the Oxford Holy Club with John and with George Whitefield, thus beginning the Methodist movement. In 1735 Charles was ordained deacon and then elder in the Church of England. This same year he accompanied John to the colony of Georgia, where he served as secretary to General Oglethorpe on St. Simon's Island. He returned to England the following year. His life was greatly influenced by the noted religious leader William Law, as well as by the equally famous Count Nicholas von Zinzendorf. He traced his conversion experience to May 21, 1738. In that year he and John set out to spread their views throughout England, Ireland, and Wales. He sang the ideas that John preached and did much to spread Methodism. Charles disagreed with his brother's inclination to separate from the Church of England and remained a member of that communion all of his life. He married Sarah Gwynne (1749), and to their union eight children were born. Their sons Samuel and Charles both made names for themselves in music. Next to Isaac Watts, Charles Wesley has had the greatest influence on modern Christian song.

A Charge to Keep I Have (600)

All Praise to Our Redeeming Lord (391)
Arise, My Soul, Arise (342)
Christ, the Lord, Is Risen Today (235)
Come, Thou Long-Expected Jesus (188)
Forth in Thy Name (501)
Hark! The Herald Angels Sing (203)
I Know That My Redeemer Lives (557)
Jesus, Lover of My Soul (276, 278)
Love Divine, All Loves Excelling (267)
My Lord, My Truth, My Way (575)
O for a Heart to Praise My God (491)
O for a Thousand Tongues to Sing (2)
Rejoice, the Lord Is King (474)
Soldiers of Christ, Arise (401)
Ye Servants of God (175)

Wesley, John Benjamin

Wesley, John Benjamin (b. Epworth, Lincolnshire, England, June 17, 1703; d. London, England, March 2, 1791) was the son of the Anglican minister Samuel Wesley and his wife Susanna. He was educated at Charterhouse School and at Christ Church, Oxford (1724, 1726-27). John was ordained to the ministry of the Church of England (1728) and served as curate under his father at Epworth. In 1729 he became a tutor at Oxford and was active in the Holy Club with his brother Charles. In 1735 the Society for the Propagation of the Gospel sent John and several others to Georgia as missionaries. John served as a parish priest in Savannah. He was deeply moved by the religious demeanor of a group of Moravians on the voyage to America. In Georgia he published his first hymnal, *A Collection of Psalms and Hymns* (Charleston, 1737), which included psalm paraphrases, standard English hymns, and translations of German poetry. Upon his return to England (1738), John had a deep religious experience while attending a Moravian meeting. He never joined them, however, and later openly dissented from their position. In 1739, accompanied by his brother Charles, John began to preach over all England, Ireland, and Wales a fervent evangelical message which urged a return to holiness of life. His own hymns, and especially those of his brother Charles, sang his message into the hearts of thousands. In 1780 he published *A Collection of Hymns for the People Called Methodists*, which was the ancestor of all subsequent Methodist hymnals both in England and in the United States.

Give to the Winds Thy Fears (548)
Jesus, Thy Boundless Love to Me (621)
O Thou to Whose All-Searching Sight (510)

Wesley, Samuel Sebastian

Wesley, Samuel Sebastian (b. London, England, August 14, 1810; d. London, April 19, 1786) was the son of Samuel Wesley, and grandson of Charles Wesley. He studied music under his father and was a chorister at the Chapel Royal (1820-1826). His ability as an organist was widely recognized. He served churches in London (1826-1832) and at Hereford Cathedral (1832-1835), Exeter Cathedral (1835-1842), Leeds Parish Church (1842-1849), Winchester Cathedral (1849-1865), and Gloucester Cathedral (1865-1876). Oxford conferred the Mus.D. degree upon him (1849), and in 1850 he became professor of organ at the Royal Academy of Music. Wesley wrote over one hundred hymn tunes and also various anthems, glees, and church service music. He published *A Few Words on Cathedral Music and the Musical System of the Church. with a Plan of Reform* (1849).
> AURELIA (365)
> CAMBRIDGE (111, 145)
> SERUG (525)

Westendorf, Omer

Westendorf, Omer (b. Cincinnati, Ohio, February 24, 1916) was educated at the University of Cincinnati (M.M., 1950) and has been organist at St. Bonaventure Church in that city since 1936. His text mentioned below is a translation of a ninth-century Latin text and arose out of the revisions of the Roman Catholic liturgy which emerged from Vatican Council ll. Westendorf, in cooperation with other Catholic seminarians, compiled *The People's Hymnal* (1955), which first introduced Catholics to the riches of Protestant hymnody. He is founder and president of the World Library of Sacred Music and of World Library Publications. Westendorf also compiled *The People's Mass Book* (1964), which volume, in that and in succeeding editions, has been the most popular Catholic hymnal in America.
> *Where Charity and Love Prevail* (452)

White, J. T.

White, J. T. (fl. 19th century). No certain information is available on this composer. His name is attached to the tune ALL IS WELL in William Walker's *Southern Harmony* and in B. F. White's *Sacred Harp* (1844). David W. Music has found the tune printed two years earlier in *Revival Melodies, or Songs of Zion* (Boston, 1842), where it is credited to C. Dingley, a music teacher in New York City, but the "Dingley" tune is in a different meter. Doubtless White's connection with the tune was that of arranger. The tune is probably of English or American folk origin. It was included in A. D. Fillmore's *New Harp of Zion* (Cincinnati, 1872; p. 292), with the words referred to the *Christian Hymn Book* (Cincinnati, 1865; No. 1084). The tune was usually attached to the text "What's this that steals, that steals upon my frame? Is it death, is it death?"

All Is Well (423)

Whitfield, Frederick

Whitfield, Frederick (b. Threapwood, Shropshire, England, January 7, 1829; d. Croyden, England, September 13, 1904) was the son of H. Whitfield. He was educated at Trinity College, Dublin (1859). Whitfield entered the ministry of the Church of England and served as curate of Otley, vicar of Kirby-Ravensworth, senior curate of Greenwich, and vicar of St. John's, Bexley. In 1875 he began to serve at St. Mary's, Hastings. Whitfield published more than thirty volumes of prose and verse, including *Spiritual Unfolding from the Word of Life, Voices from the Valley Testifying of Jesus, The Word Unveiled,* and *Gleanings from the Scripture.* His *Sacred Poems and Prose* appeared in 1861, with a second series in 1864. His verse is also found in *The Casket* and *Quiet Hours in the Sanctuary.*

There Is a Name I Love to Hear (455)

Whiting, William

Whiting, William (b. Kensington, England, November 1, 1825; d. Winchester, England, May 3, 1878) was educated at Clapham School and Winchester College. He served as Master of the Winchester College Choristers' School for some thirty years. Whiting published his poems as *Rural Thoughts and Other Poems* (1851), but he included none of his hymns in this compilation. Although other of his hymns appear in well-known English hymnals, his fame rests chiefly on the one hymn listed below.

Eternal Father, Strong to Save (137)

Whittier, John Greenleaf

Whittier, John Greenleaf (b. Haverhill, Massachusetts, December 17, 1807; d. Hampton Falls, New Hampshire, September 7, 1892) was born of Quaker parents. He was of English descent on his father's side and of French Protestant on his mother's. He grew up in relative poverty, working on the family's farm and later as a shoemaker and teacher. Other than the education he received at the local village school, he was able to attend for a short time the Haverhill Academy. A volume of poems by Robert Burns whetted the young man's appetite, and by age fourteen he was himself writing verse. William Lloyd Garrison published Whittier's early poems, and Garrison assisted Whittier in obtaining a position with a Boston paper (1829). Afterwards he served as editor of *The American Manufacturer* (1828), *The New England Review* (1830), *The Pennsylvania Freeman* (1836), and the *National Era* (1847). Whittier was an ardent abolitionist and considered himself one of the founders of the Republican Party. He did not, however, consider himself a hymn writer. He once said: "I am really not a hymn-writer, for the good reason that I know nothing of music. Only a very few of my pieces were written for singing. A good hymn is the best use to which poetry can be devoted, but I do not claim that I have succeeded in composing one." Most of his hymns in use today are centos from longer poems and were first made popular through the collections of Samuel Longfellow and Samuel Johnson. For an excellent evaluation of Whittier as hymnist, see *The Hymn* 8 (October 1957) 105-10.

> *Dear Lord and Father of Mankind* (569)
> *Immortal Love, Forever Full* (444)
> *O Brother Man, Fold to Thy Heart* (428)

Whittle, Daniel Webster

Whittle, Daniel Webster (b. Chicopee Falls, Massachusetts, November 22, 1840; d. Northfield, Massachusetts, March 4, 1901) as a youth moved to Chicago from his home town and worked as a cashier in a Wells Fargo bank. He served as a lieutenant in the 72nd Illinois Infantry beginning in 1861 during the Civil War. Whittle also served as provost marshall on the staff of Gen. O. O. Howard, was wounded in the battle of Vicksburg, and accompanied General Sherman on his march through Georgia to the sea. He attained the rank of major at the end of the war and was always thereafter called by this title. After the war, Whittle returned to Chicago, where he was treasurer for the Elgin Watch Company until 1873. Encouraged by Dwight L. Moody, Whittle became an evangelist and conducted campaigns all over the United States. P. P. Bliss, James McGranahan, and George C. Stebbins served with Whittle as his singers. Many of his hymns, most of which he wrote late in life, were published under the pseudonym "El Nathan."

> *Dying with Jesus* (528)
> *I Know Not Why* (537)

Wigner, John Murch

Wigner, John Murch (b. King's Lynn, Norfolk, England, June 19, 1844, d. London, England, March 31, 1911) was the son of John Thomas Wigner, who was minister of the church at King's Lynn. He was educated

at London University and entered government service, serving in the India Home Office, London. He retired in 1909. Wigner was active in the Baptist Church and became a well-known children's evangelist. He served on the Council of the Children's Special Service Mission.
Come to the Savior Now (334)

Wilkes, John Bernard

Wilkes, John Bernard (b. 1785; d. 1869) was educated at the Royal Academy of Music in London (1842-1846). He served as organist at St. David's Church, Merthyr Tydfil, Wales, and later at Llandaff Cathedral (1861-1865). Wilkes also served as organist at Monkland Church, near Leominster, where Henry W. Baker was vicar. In this service and association with Baker, Wilkes also contributed to the first edition of *Hymns Ancient and Modern* (1861).
MONKLAND (84)

Williams, Aaron

Williams, Aaron (b. London, England, 1731; d. London, 1776) was a music teacher in West Smithfield, London. He also served as clerk of the London Wall Scots Church. Williams published several compilations for church use, including *The Universal Psalmodist* (1763), *The Royal Harmony* (1766), *The New Universal Psalmodist* (1770), and *Psalmody in Miniature* (pub. posthumously, 1778). Daniel Bailey brought out an American edition of Williams's *Universal Psalmodist* under the title *The American Harmony of Universal Psalmodist* (1769).
ST. THOMAS (16, 153, 408)

Williams, Peter

Williams, Peter (b. Llansadurnin, Carmarthenshire, Wales, January 7, 1722; d. Llandyfeilog, Wales, August 8, 1796) was educated at the Carmarthen Grammar School and, while there, was converted by the preaching of George Whitefield. He was ordained in the Church of England (1744) and ministered in the parish of Eglwys Cymmyn. His fervent preaching was the cause of his dismissal. In 1746 he joined the Calvinistic Methodists and became an important itinerant evangelist throughout Wales. The Methodists expelled him for heresy, and he established his own chapel in Cater Street, Carmarthen. His publications include a Welsh hymnbook (1759), the Bible in Welsh with annotations (1767-1770), a concordance (1773), and *Hymns on Various Subjects* (1771).
Guide Me, O Thou Great Jehovah (587)

Williams, Robert

Williams, Robert (b. Mynydd Ithel, Anglesey County, North Wales, c. 1781; d. Mynydd Ithel, 1821) was born blind but became a skilled basketmaker, by which trade he earned his living. Tradition says he had an unusual musical gift, sang well, and could copy down a tune perfectly after hearing it but once. He never married.

LLANFAIR (236)

Williams, Thomas

Williams, Thomas (fl. 18th century). No certain information is available on this composer other than that he published *Psalmodia Evangelica: A Collection of Psalms and Hymns in Three Parts for Public Worship* (2 vols., 1789). Truro was an ancient town in Cornwall, England.

TRURO (191, 552)

Williams, William

Williams, William (b. Cefn-y-coed, near Llandovery, Wales, February 11, 1717; d. Pantcelyn, Wales, January 11, 1791), known as the "Sweet Singer of Wales," has been compared in influence and productivity to Paul Gerhardt of Germany and Isaac Watts of England. His father was a well-to-do farmer, and William received his education at Llwynllwyd Academy at Carmarthen, intending to become a physician. While there he was so moved by the preaching of Howell Harris in 1738 that he resolved to enter the ministry. He was ordained deacon in the Church of England and served as curate at Llanwrtyd and Llanddewi-Abergwesyn, but refused to enter the priesthood because of his views on evangelism. In 1746 he left the Established Church and joined the Calvinistic Methodists, assisting David Rowlands and Harris in their revival campaigns. He was an itinerant evangelist in Wales for fifty years. During these years his wife accompanied him as his singer. Williams wrote over 800 hymns in Welsh and more than 100 in English. He is buried in the churchyard of Llanfair. His son John published a collected edition of his father's hymns (1811). Williams himself published *Halleluiah* (1744); *Y Mor o Wydr* (The Sea of Glass, 1752); and *Gloria in Excelsis, or, Hymns of Praise to God and the Lamb* (1771).

Guide Me, O Thou Great Jehovah (587)

Willis, Love Maria

Willis, Love Maria (b. Hancock, New Hampshire, June 9, 1824; d. Elmira, New York, November 26, 1908). Her maiden name was Whitcomb. She married Frederick L. H. Willis, a Boston physician (1858). Mrs. Willis

served as editor of *The Banner of Light* in Boston and later of *Tiffany's Monthly Magazine*. She was a member of the Unitarian Church.
Father, Hear the Prayer We Offer (564)

Willis, Richard Storrs

Willis, Richard Storrs (b. Boston, Massachusetts, February 10, 1819; d. Detroit, Michigan, May 7, 1900) was the son of Nathaniel Willis. He was educated at Chauncey Hall, Boston, and Yale University (1841). At Yale he composed and arranged music for student performances and was president of the Beethoven Society. He went to Germany after graduation to study with Xavier Schnyder von Wartensee at Frankfurt and with Moritz Hauptmann in Leipzig. While in Leipzig, he became a good friend of Felix Mendelssohn, who helped revise several of Willis's compositions. Willis returned to the United States (1847) and taught German at Yale. In 1848 he became music critic for the *New York Tribune*, the *Albion* and *The Musical Times*. From 1852 to 1864 he edited *The Musical Times*, *The Musical World*, and *Once a Month*. His published works include *Church Chorals and Choir Studies* (1850), *Our Church Music* (1856), *Waif of Song* (1876), and *Pen and Lute* (1883).
CAROL (185)
SCHONSTER HERR JESU (156)

Wilson, Carrie M.

This is one of the many pen names used by Fanny J. Crosby.
Sing On, Ye Joyful Pilgrims (473)

Wilson, Emily Divine

Wilson, Emily Divine (b. Philadelphia, Pennsylvania, May 24, 1865; d. Philadelphia, June 23, 1942) was the daughter of John and Sarah Lees Divine. Her father had immigrated from Ireland and her mother from England. She married John G. Wilson, a Methodist minister (1887), and they worked together in church labors until his death (1933). Her ability in music and drama was a great inspiration to him in his work. Both she and her husband attended the annual summer assemblies at Ocean Grove, New Jersey, as long as they lived.
HEAVEN (669)

Winkworth, Catherine

Winkworth, Catherine (b. London, England, September 13, 1827;

d. Monetier, Savoy, France, July 1, 1878) was the daughter of Henry Winkworth. She spent most of her early life near Manchester. In 1862 she moved to Clifton, where she lived with her father and sisters. Miss Winkworth devoted her life to spiritual and moral causes. She was especially active in the Clifton Association for the Higher Education of Women. She is recognized as the foremost English translator of German hymns. Her poems and translations appeared in her *Lyra Germanica* (1855; 2d series, 1858) and in her *Chorale Book for England* (1863). This latter publication had for its music editors William Sterndale Bennett, the founder of the Bach Society (1849), and Otto Goldschmidt, the husband of the singer Jenny Lind and founder of the Bach Chair (1875). She brought out her biographical work, the *Christian Singers of Germany,* in 1869. Miss Winkworth died of a heart ailment in 1878.

Blessed Jesus, at Thy Word (25)
Christ the Lord Is Risen Again (247)
Come, Holy Spirit, God and Lord (292)
Comfort, Comfort Now My People (183)
Jesus, Priceless Treasure (350)
Lift Up Your Heads, Ye Mighty Gates (191)
Lord Jesus Christ, Be Present Now (3)
Now Rest Beneath Night's Shadow (82)
Now Thank We All Our God (59)
Praise to the Lord, the Almighty (45)
Wake, Awake, for Night Is Flying (286)

Winter, Gloria Frances

Winter, Gloria Frances (b. Passaic, New Jersey, June 14, 1938) is a member of the Medical Mission Sisters of the Roman Catholic Church, in which order she is known as Sister Miriam Therese. She was educated in Bayley-Ellard Regional High School, Madison, New Jersey, and at Trinity College and Catholic University, Washington, D.C. She received her master's degree from McMaster Divinity College, Hamilton, Ontario. In 1955 she entered the Society of Catholic Medical Missionaries. She served this sisterhood as Director of Public Relations for the Northeast District and Coordinator of Public Relations for the USA (1963-1972). She has been a leader in liturgy and music among the Medical Mission Sisters and has written several mass settings and 138 songs.

Come Down, Lord, My Son Is Ill (522)
COME DOWN, LORD (522)

Witter, William E.

Witter, William E. (b. 1854; d. ?). Little information is available on this author. He was a school teacher in Wyoming Valley, New York (1877) and was deeply touched by the tragic death of Philip Bliss (1876). He asked God to help him write hymns similar to those of Bliss with which to touch hearts.

While Jesus Whispers to You (331)

Wolcott, Samuel

Wolcott, Samuel (b. South Windsor, Connecticut, July 2, 1813; d. Long Meadow, Massachusetts, February 24, 1880) was educated at Yale University (1833) and Andover Theological Seminary (1837). In 1840 he went to Syria as a missionary, but returned in 1842 because of ill health. Thereafter he was minister for Congregational churches in Rhode Island, Massachusetts, Illinois, and in Cleveland, Ohio. He also served as secretary for the Ohio Home Missionary Society. Wolcott began writing hymns late in his life and wrote over two hundred.

Christ for the World We Sing (400)

Wordsworth, Christopher

Wordsworth, Christopher (b. Lambeth, England, October 30, 1807; d. Harewood, England, March 20, 1885) was the youngest son of the elder Christopher Wordsworth and a nephew of the poet William Wordsworth. His mother was Priscilla Lloyd Wordsworth. He was educated at Winchester School, where he was both a scholar and an athlete, and then at Cambridge University (1830). He was a classical lecturer at Cambridge for some time and orator for the University (1836). That same year he was appointed headmaster of Harrow School, where he instituted many moral reforms. In 1838 he married Susan Hatley Freere. Wordsworth was canon of Westminster Cathedral (1844), Hulsean lecturer at Cambridge (1848-1849), and from 1850 to 1869 served as parish priest at Stanford-in-the-Vale cum Goosey. Wordsworth became Bishop of Lincoln in 1869, which post he held until just before his death. He visited his uncle William every year at Rydal Mount until the poet died in 1850. His published work related to hymnology is his *Holy Year, or Hymns for Sundays and Holydays* (1862).

Alleluia! Alleluia! Hearts to Heaven (244)
O Lord of Heaven and Earth and Sea (149)

Wreford, John Reynell

Wreford, John Reynell (b. Barnstaple, England, December 12, 1800; d. St. Marylebone, England, 1881) was educated for the Unitarian ministry at Manchester College, York, England. In 1826 he began to serve as co-minister with John Kentish at the New Meeting, Birmingham. Five years later his voice failed, and he left the ministry and opened a school at Edgbaston with Hugh Hutton, the minister of the Old Meeting. In later years he retired to Bristol. Wreford's published works include *A Sketch of the History of Presbyterian Nonconformity in Birmingham* (1832) and *Lays of Loyalty* (1837). This latter work celebrated the accession of Victoria as queen. He also contributed fifty-five hymns to J. R. Beard's *Collection of Hymns for Public and Private Worship* (1837).

When My Love to Christ Grows Weak (219)

Xavier, Francis

Xavier, Francis (b. Castle Xavier, near Pampeluna, Spain, April 7, 1506; d. Sancian, near Canton, China, December 11, 1642) was the son of Don Juan Giasso and Doña María d'Azpilqueta y Xavier. He was educated at the University of Paris and at first devoted himself to teaching. He came under the influence of Ignatius Loyola, the founder of the Jesuits, and became one of the first seven men to form the Order of the Jesuits at Montmartre near Paris, August 15, 1534. He was ordained in 1537 and went with Loyola first to Venice in that year and later to Rome. King John III of Portugal recognized the zeal of the Jesuits, and Xavier was selected to go to the Portuguese colony of Goa. He sailed for that place in 1541 and began his work the following year. From then until his death he traversed not only India but also China, Japan, and many of the islands of the East Indies. He is buried in the Cathedral of Goa.

My God, I Love Thee (451)

Yates, John Henry

Yates, John Henry (b. Batavia, New York, November 21, 1837; d. Batavia, September 5, 1900) was the son of John H. and Elizabeth Taylor Yates. His parents had come to the United States from England. He was educated at Batavia Union School and after his graduation engaged in selling shoes. He was a department manager for the E. L. and G. D. Kenyon Hardware Store (1871-1886). In 1886 he became editor of the local paper, which he edited until 1896. In 1858, Yates became an ordained Methodist minister, but later became a Baptist and served as minister of the West Bethany Free Will Baptist Church. Ira Sankey took notice of Yates and persuaded him to write the hymn text included in *GSR*. Yates also published Poems and Ballads (1897).

Encamped Along the Hills of Light (498)

Young, John Freeman

Young, John Freeman (b. Pittston, Maine, October 30, 1820; d. New York, New York, November 15, 1885) was educated at Wesleyan University, Middletown, Connecticut, but later joined the Episcopal Church and attended Virginia Theological Seminary, Alexandria, Virginia. He was ordained in 1845 and served churches in Florida, Texas, Mississippi, Louisiana, and New York. From 1867 to 1885 he served as the second Episcopal Bishop of Florida. He was interested in education and opened a school for boys in Jacksonville, Florida, and a girls' school in Fernandina, Florida. He was also active in reopening the University of the South in Sewanee, Tennessee, following the Civil War (1869) and often lectured in the school. Young published *Hymns and Music for the Young* (1860-1861), and J. H. Hopkins, Jr., published posthumously Young's *Great Hymns of the Church* (1887). Bishop Young also had an interest in architecture and assisted in erecting many church buildings.

Silent Night, Holy Night (202)

Zelley, Henry J.

Zelley, Henry J. (b. Mount Holly, New Jersey, March 15, 1859; d. Trenton, New Jersey, March 16, 1942) was educated in the Mount Holly public schools, at Pennington Seminary, and at Taylor University. He was an ordained Methodist minister and first served in the New Jersey Conference (1882) as statistical secretary, treasurer, and trustee. Dr. Zelley was noted for his evangelistic fervor. He wrote over 1500 poems, hymns, and gospel songs. He retired in 1929.

Walking in Sunlight (462)

Zinzendorf, Nicolaus Ludwig von

Zinzendorf, Nicolaus Ludwig von (b. Dresden, Germany, May 26, 1700; d. Herrnhut, May 9, 1760) was the son of noble parents, but was reared by his aunt and grandmother. He was educated at the Adelspädagogium in Halle and at Wittenberg University. Although educated for the law, he was early interested in religion, being moved by a picture of Christ crowned with thorns, underneath which picture were the words "This have I done for thee, What hast thou done for Me?" In 1722 he purchased an estate in Saxony, which he called Herrnhut. It served as a refuge for persecuted Moravians. In 1737 Count Zinzendorf was appointed bishop among the Moravians; and although banished from Saxony, he helped establish Moravian colonies in other parts of Germany and England, Holland, and North America. He wrote more that 2,000 hymns and had a strong influence on John Wesley in the early years of his movement.

O Thou, to Whose All-Searching Sight (510)

Zundel, John

Zundel, John (b. Hochdorf, Germany, December 10, 1815; d. Cannstadt, Germany, July 1882) was educated in Germany, but for seven years served as organist of St. Anne's Lutheran Church in St. Petersburg, Russia. While there he was also bandmaster of the Imperial Horse Guards. He came to America in 1847, where he successively served as organist at the First Unitarian Church, Brooklyn, New York; St. George's, New York; and Plymouth Congregational Church, New York, to which church Henry Ward Beecher ministered. Just before his retirement, he served briefly at Central Methodist Church in Detroit, Michigan. With Henry and Charles Beecher, he edited the *Plymouth Collection of Hymns* (1855). He also published *The Choral Friend* (1822), *Psalmody* (1855), and *Christian Heart Songs* (1870). Zundel founded the *Monthly Choir and Organ Journal* (1863), but only issued one volume. In 1873 he edited the musical journal *Zundel and Brandt's Quarterly*. Upon retirement he returned to his native Germany.

BEECHER (267)

INDEX OF FIRST LINES

(All Editions)

	1921	1922	1925	1937	1975	1986
A Charge to Keep I have	1	1	1	—	601	600
A Joyful Song	—	—	—	1	1	—

Ambrose Nichols Blatchford (1842-1924). Written for S. S. Anniv. of Lewin's Mead Meeting (1876), Bristol, England. Pub. W. R. Stevenson's *School Hymnal* (1880).

	1921	1922	1925	1937	1975	1986
A Mighty Fortress	—	—	—	326	326	104
A Sunbeam, a Sunbeam	—	—	—	577	577	—

Nellie Talbot. Text pub. 1900 and owned by Hope Pub. Co.

	1921	1922	1925	1937	1975	1986
A Wonderful Savior	2	2	2	2	2	467
Abide with Me	3	3	3	327	327	33
After the Life-paths	—	—	376	3	3	—
Again the Lord of Light	—	—	4	328	328	28
Ah, Holy Jesus	—	—	—	—	—	222
Alas! and Did my Savior	4	4	5	4,5,6	4,5,6	215
All Creatures of Our God	—	—	—	—	602	66
All for Jesus	—	—	6	329	329	—

Mary Dagworthy Yard James (1810-1883). No further information is available.

	1921	1922	1925	1937	1975	1986
All Glory, Laud and Honor	—	—	—	—	—	167—
All Hail the Power	5	5	7	330/331	330/331	250/251
All My Heart This Night	—	—	—	578	578	—

Paul Gerhardt (1607-1669), q.v. Pub. in Crüger's *Praxis Pietatis Melica* (1653). Tr. Catherine Winkworth (1829-1878). Pub. in *Lyra Germanica*, 2d Series (1858)

	1921	1922	1925	1937	1975	1986
All People That on Earth	—	—	—	332	332	74
All Praise to Our Redeeming	—	—	—	—	—	391
All Praise to Thee, My God	—	—	—	333	333	30
All the way my Savior leads	—	—	—	334	334	651
All Things are Ready	6	6	8	7	7	—

Charlotte G. Homer, a pseudonym for Charles Hutchinson Gabriel, q.v. Pub. 1895; owned by W. E. M. Hackleman.

	1921	1922	1925	1937	1975	1986
All Things Come of Thee	—	—	—	8	8	—

Anonymous paraphrase of 1 Chronicles 29:14.

	1921	1922	1925	1937	1975	1986
All Things Praise Thee	—	401	9	335	335	64

	1921	1922	1925	1937	1975	1986
Awake, My Soul, in Joyful	—	—	22	346	346	—

Samuel Medley, q.v. Orig. pub. in J. H. *Meyer's Collection of Hymns for Lady Huntingdon's Chapel* (1782). Text alt. in John Rippon's *Selection* (1787).

	1921	1922	1925	1937	1975	1986
Awake, My Soul, Stretch	18	18	23	347	347	543
Awake, My Tongue, Thy	19	19	24	348	348	67
Away from Earth My Spirit	20	20	—	—	—	—

Ray Palmer, q.v. Pub. in Lowell Mason's *Union Hymns* (1833). Based on John 6:51.

	1921	1922	1925	1937	1975	1986
Away in a Manger	388	388	437	579	579	204
Be Like Jesus, This My Song	—	—	—	580	580	—

James Rowe (1865-1933). Pub. 1912. Owned Hope Pub. Co. See below, "Earthly Pleasures."

	1921	1922	1925	1937	1975	1986
Be Not Dismayed	24	24	29	18	18	127
Be Still, My Soul	—	—	—	—	603	547
Be Thou My Vision	—	—	—	—	604	578
Be with Me, Lord	—	—	—	—	605	579
Beautiful Valley of Eden	—	—	—	19	19	—

William Orcutt Cushing, q.v. Hymn written 1875, while he prayed for blessing from God. Pub. 1877.

	1921	1922	1925	1937	1975	1986
Beautiful Zion, Built Above	21	21	25	—	—	—

George Gill (1820-1880), missionary to South Sea Islands. Written on island of Mangaia, April 1850. Pub. in *Juvenile Missionary Magazine* (1852)

	1921	1922	1925	1937	1975	1986
Before Jehovah's Awful	22	22	26	349	349	110
Behold a Stranger at the Door	—	405	27	350	350	340
Beneath the Cross of Jesus	23	23	28	351	351	229
Beneath the Forms of	—	—	—	—	—	388
Beyond the Smiling and the	25	25	30	—	—	—

Horatius Bonar, q.v. Text written April, 1849. Pub in his *Hymns of Faith and Hope*, 1st Series (1057).

	1921	1922	1925	1937	1975	1986
Bless Me Now	—	—	—	20	20	—

Alexander Clarke (1834-1879). Text written 1872. The chorus of a hymn beginning "Heavenly Father, Bless Me Now..." Pub. in Bliss and Sankey's *Gospel Hymns* No. 1 (1875) under motto of 2 Cor. 6:2.

	1921	1922	1925	1937	1975	1986
Beyond the Sunset	—	—	—	1950 cvr	606	662
Blessed Assurance	27	27	31	21	21	345
Blessed Be the Fountain of	—	—	—	22	22	—

Eden Reeder Latta (b. 1839). Pub. in Sankey's Sacred Songs and Solos and in his *Gospel Hymns*, No. 5 (1887).

	1921	1922	1925	1937	1975	1986
Blessed Jesus at Thy Word	—	—	—	—	—	25
Blessed Savior, We Adore	—	—	—	—	—	154
Blessing and Honor	—	—	—	—	—	174
Blest Be the Tie	26	26	32	352	352	394
Bread of the World	28	28	33	353	353	373
Break Forth, O Beauteous	—	—	—	—	—	200
Break Thou the Bread of Life	29	29	34	354	354	312
Breathe on Me, Breath of God	—	—	—	—	607	295
Brethren, We Have Met to	—	—	—	—	608	419
Brief Life Is Here Our Portion	—	—	—	355	355	673

	1921	1922	1925	1937	1975	1986
Come, Thou Long-Expected	—	—	—	—	615	188
Come to Jesus Just Now	37	37	—	—	—	—

Anonymous folk poem. No further information available.

	1921	1922	1925	1937	1975	1986
Come to the Savior	—	—	—	—	—	336
Come to the Savior Now	—	—	—	—	—	334
Come, Ye Disconsolate	39	39	44	362	362	338
Come, Ye Faithful, Raise the	—	—	—	363	363	—

Job Hupton (1762-1849). Pub. in *Gospel Magazine* (Sept. 1805) Orig. first line read "Come Ye saints, and raise…" Alt. J. M. Neale (q.v.) in *Christian Remembrance* (1863).

	1921	1922	1925	1937	1975	1986
Come, Ye Sinners, Poor and	—	—	—	28	629	329
Come, Ye Thankful People	—	—	—	364	364	590
Come, Ye that Love the Lord	38	38	43	29	29	68
Comfort, Comfort Now My	—	—	—	—	—	183
Coming, Coming, Yes They	40	40	45	—	—	—

Wakefield MacGill. Text pub. ca. 1909 in J. H. Allan's *Redemption Songs,* No. 360.

	1921	1922	1925	1937	1975	1986
Consider the Lilies of the	41	41	46	542	542	—

Anonymous paraphrase of Matt. 6:28, 29. Pub. by E. O. Excell (1890).

	1921	1922	1925	1937	1975	1986
Creator of the Stars of Night	—	—	—	—	—	160
Crown Him with Many	42	42	47	365	365	255
Day by Day and with Each	—	—	—	—	—	134
Day Is Gone, Gone the Sun	—	—	—	31	31	—

Anonymous but familiar version for the Army bugle call "Taps."

	1921	1922	1925	1937	1975	1986
Day Is Dying in the West	43	43	48	30	30	37
Dear Lord and Father of	—	408	49	366	366	569
Dear Master, in Whose Life	—	—	—	—	—	571
Did Christ O'er Sinners Weep	44	44	—	—	—	—

Benjamin Beddome, q.v., wrote, text for use before the sermon. Pub. in John Rippon's *Selection.*

	1921	1922	1925	1937	1975	1986
Does Jesus Care	—	—	—	32	32	642
Down in the Valley with My	45	45	50	33	33	—

William Orcutt Cushing, q.v., pub. text in 1908 under title "Follow On."

	1921	1922	1925	1937	1975	1986
Dying with Jesus by Death	46	46	51	34	34	528
Each Cooing Dove	—	—	—	35	35	—

Robert Morris (1818-1888) wrote text while seated amid ruins of Capernaum (1868). Pub. in H. R. Palmer's *Songs of Love for the Bible School* (1874). Orig. first line read "Each gentle dove…"

	1921	1922	1925	1937	1975	1986
Early, My God, Without Delay	—	—	52	367	367	—
Earth Holds No Treasures	—	—	—	36	36	—

Tillit Sidney Teddlie, q.v., wrote text under a hickory tree near Golden, Texas (1912), where he had obeyed the gospel in 1903.

	1921	1922	1925	1937	1975	1986
Earthly Pleasures Vainly	47	47	—	—	—	—

James Rowe (1865-1933). Text pub. 1912. Owned by Hope Pub. Co. The 1937 and 1975 editions of *GS* pub. chorus only: "Be like Jesus, this my song…"

	1921	1922	1925	1937	1975	1986
Encamped along the Hills	48	48	54	37	37	498
Encamped about the Saints	—	—	53	—	—	—

Elmer Leon Jorgenson, q.v., pub. text in *GS* (1925). No other information is available.

	1921	1922	1925	1937	1975	1986
Enter into His Gates with	390	390	390	582	582	—

Anonymous paraphrase of Psalm 100:4, 5. Pub. 1907 by Leyde & Burgener.

	1921	1922	1925	1937	1975	1986
From Heaven Above to Earth	—	—	—	—	—	199
From the Cross the Blood Is	61	61	—	—	—	—

Horatius Bonar, q.v., wrote this text for Good Friday. Pub. in his *Hymns of Faith and Hope*, 3d Series (1866).

From the Table Now Retiring	62	62	—	—	—	—
Gentle Mary Laid Her Child	—	—	—	—	—	196
Give Me the Bible	63	63	73	46	46	299
Give Me the Wings of Faith	64	64	—	—	—	—

Isaac Watts, q.v., pub. in his *Hymns and Spiritual Songs*, (2d ed., 1709), entitled "The Examples of Christ and the Saints."

Give to the Winds Thy Fears	—	—	—	—	—	548
Glorious Things of Thee Are	—	—	74	545	545	447
Glory Be to God on High	—	—	—	47	47	—

A paraphrase of Luke 2:14, probably by Charles Heinrich Christoph Zeuner (1795-1857), organist for the Park Street Church, Boston, and for the Handel and Haydn Society.

Glory Be to the Father	—	—	—	380	380	76
Glory to His Name	—	—	—	48	48	—

Chorus to "Down at the Cross" by Elisha Albright Hoffman, q.v., and first pub. in T. C. O'Kane, C. C. McCabe, and John R. Sweney's *Joy to the World* (Cincinnati, 1878).

Go Home and Tell	—	—	—	49	49	—

Chorus to "Go Home and Tell to Those You Love" by Ada Ruth Habershon (1861-1918) and first pub. in Charles M. Alexander's *Gospel Songs* (1908).

Go, Labor On: Spend and Be	—	—	—	381	381	—

Horatius Bonar, q.v., wrote text in 1836. Pub. in his *Hymns for the Wilderness* (1843).

Go to Dark Gethsemane	—	—	—	—	—	218
God Be in My Head	—	—	—	—	618	—

Text derives from French poem beginning "Jesus soit en ma tête..." (ca. 1497), celebrating the Hours of Mary. Pub. in *"Horae beatae marie virginis ad usum insignis ac praeclare ecclesiae Sarum"* (England, 1514). English text from *Sarum Primer* (1558).

God Be with You Till We Meet	65	65	75	50	50	14
God Calling Yet! Shall I Not	—	—	—	—	—	316
God Give Us Christian Homes	—	—	—	—	619	—

Baylus Benjamin McKinney, q.v., wrote text 1949 especially for "Christian Home Week." Pub in *Baptist Home Life* (May 1950). Introduced that year at the Southern Baptist Convention.

God Himself Is with Us	—	—	—	—	620	7
God Is Calling the Prodigal	66	66	76	51	51	322

Charles Hutchinson Gabriel, q.v. Pub. by Rodeheaver Co. 1889. The following entry is a rewrite of this text with different tune.

God Is Calling the Prodigal	—	—	—	—	—	322
God Is Love; His Mercy	—	—	—	382	382	119
God Is the Fountain Whence	67	67	77	383	383	129
God Moves in a Mysterious	—	—	78	384	384	139
God of Grace and God of Glory	—	—	—	—	621	581
God of Our Fathers, Whose	—	—	—	546	546	566
God of Our Life, through All	—	—	—	—	—	114
God of the Earth, the Sky, the	—	—	—	—	—	97

	1921	1922	1925	1937	1975	1986
God Sent His Son	—	—	—	—	—	653
God the Almighty One	—	—	—	—	622	586
God's Tomorrow Is a Day of	—	—	—	52	52	—

Alfred Henry Ackley (1887-1960). An accomplished cellist and Presbyterian minister. Text written 1928 and pub. in Homer A. Rodeheaver and Ackley 's *New Songs for Service* (1929).

Good Christian Men, Rejoice	—	—	—	—	—	206
Grace! 'Tis a Charming Sound	—	—	—	547	547	—

Philip Doddridge, q.v., wrote this text shortly before his death in 1751. Pub. posthumously in Job Orton's collection of Doddridge's works, *Hymns founded on Various Texts in the Holy Scriptures* (1755).

Gracious Spirit Dwell with Me	—	—	—	—	—	297
Great God, We Sing That	—	—	—	—	—	141
Great Is Thy Faithfulness	—	—	—	—	—	147
Guide Me, O Thou Great	68	68	79	385	385	587
Hail, Gladdening Light of His	—	—	—	—	623	32
Hail, Morning Known Among	—	412	80	386	386	21
Hail the Day That Sees Him	—	—	—	—	—	236
Hail, Thou Long-Expected	71	71	—	—	—	—
Hail, Thou Once Despised	70	70	81	—	—	—

John Bakewell (1721-1819) is credited with text in its original form. First pub. in *A Collection of Hymns to the Holy, Holy, Holy, Triune God, in the Person of Christ Jesus, Our Mediator and Advocate* (London, 1757). Martin Madan (1760) and Augustus Toplady (1776) gave hymn its modern form.

Hail to the Brightness of	—	—	82	387	387	425
Hail to the Lord's Anointed	72	72	—	388	388	—

James Montgomery, q.v., wrote text, which was sung at a Moravian convocation, Dec. 25, 1821. Adam Clarke heard it and included it in his commentary on Psalm 72. Afterwards revised and pub. in Montgomery's *Songs of Zion* (1822).

Hallelujah Chorus	—	—	—	548	548	—

George Frederick Handel, q.v., is author and composer. Best-known section of his oratorio, *The Messiah*. First performed in Dublin, Ireland (1741).

Hallelujah, Praise Jehovah	73	73	83	53	53	50
Happy the Home When God Is	—	—	—	—	—	438
Hark! Ten Thousand Harps	74	74	85	—	—	—

Thomas Kelly, q.v. Pub. in his *Hymns on Various Passages of Scripture*, 2d ed. (1806).

Hark, the Glad Sound	76	76	—	390	390	—

Philip Doddridge, q.v., wrote text to accompany a Christmas sermon, Dec. 25, 1735. Pub. in *Translations and Paraphrases for the Scottish Church* (1745).

Hark! the Gentle Voice	75	75	86	54	54	320
Hark! the Herald Angels Sing	77	77	87	391	391	203
Hark! the Vesper Hymn	—	—	—	549	549	—

Thomas Moore, q.v. It appears as early as 1818 in Sir John Steven- son's *Collection of Popular National Airs*.

Hark! The Voice of Jesus	78	78	88	392	392	416
Hark! 'Tis the Shepherd's	—	—	—	584	584	—

Alexcenah Thomas. No information available. Pub. in William A. Ogden and Edmund S. Lorenz's *Notes of Victory for the Sunday Schools* (Chicago, 1885).

	1921	1922	1925	1937	1975	1986
Harvest Fields with Gold	—	—	—	585	585	—

Anonymous text, pub. in Eleanor Smith, Charles H. Farnsworth, and C. A. *Fullerton's The Children's Hymnal* (New York, 1918).

	1921	1922	1925	1937	1975	1986
Have Faith in God, My Heart	—	—	—	—	—	499
Have Thine Affections Been	79	79	—	116	116	—
Have Thine Own Way, Lord	80	80	89	55	55	597
Have You Any Room for Jesus	—	—	91	56	56	—

Daniel Webster Whittle, q.v., wrote poem under initials W. W. D. His song leader James McGranahan pub. it in 1878. Present text arr. by L. W. M. (identity unknown) and pub. by Charles M. Alexander (1914).

	1921	1922	1925	1937	1975	1986
Have You Been to Jesus	—	—	90	57	57	330
Have You Heard the Glorious	81	81	92	550	550	—

Catherine Booth-Clibborn (1865-1950). Hymn pub. 1918. No further information available.

	1921	1922	1925	1937	1975	1986
He Is Able to Deliver Thee	—	—	—	58	58	—

William Augustus Ogden (1841-1897). Chorus to song beginning "'Tis the grandest theme through the ages sung..." Pub. in E. O. Excell's *Triumphant Songs for Sunday School and Gospel Meetings* (1887). Ogden studied under Lowell Mason and Thomas Hastings, pub. many Sunday School hymnals, and the last 20 yrs. of his life was supervisor of music for Toledo, Ohio, schools.

	1921	1922	1925	1937	1975	1986
He Leadeth Me, O Blessed	85	85	96	59	59	133
He Is Able—This My Peace	84	84	95	—	—	—

Elmer Leon Jorgenson, q.v., pub. this text in the first edition of *GS* (1921).

	1921	1922	1925	1937	1975	1986
He Took Me out of the Pit	—	—	—	60	60	—

Text assigned to James Fitch. James Fitch (1672-1722) is known to have pub. hymn, but whether he is the author is unknown. Text was pub. in Harry D. Clarke's (1888-1957*) Gospel Truth in Song*, No. 2 (1923).

	1921	1922	1925	1937	1975	1986
He Will Hold Me Fast	—	—	—	61	61	—

Ada Ruth Habershon, q.v., wrote text in 1906. Chorus of hymn beginning "When I Fear My Faith Will Fail..." pub. in Charles M. Alexander's *Alexander's Gospel Songs*, No. 2 (1908).

	1921	1922	1925	1937	1975	1986
Hear the Sweet Voice of Jesus	82	82	93	62	62	319
Hear Us, Heavenly Father	—	—	—	63	63	—

The identity of the author of this chorus is unknown.

	1921	1922	1925	1937	1975	1986
Hear What God, the Lord	83	83	—	—	—	—

William Cowper, q.v., pub. this text in *Olney Hymns*, Book I (1779). Poem was entitled "The future peace and glory of the Church."

	1921	1922	1925	1937	1975	1986
Heavenly Father, God over	—	—	—	—	—	593
Heirs of Victory Are We	—	—	94	—	—	—

Henry Ostrom (d. Dec. 1941). A Methodist minister, member of the extension staff of Moody Bible Institute, who put great emphasis on the second coming of Christ in all his hymn poems.

	1921	1922	1925	1937	1975	1986
Here at Thy Table, Lord	—	—	—	—	—	376
Here before Thee, Savior	—	—	—	393	393	377
Here, O My Lord, I See Thee	86	86	97	394	394	381
Here We Are But Straying	—	—	—	64	64	555
His Yoke Is Easy, His Burden	—	—	—	65	65	—
Hold Thou My Hand	—	—	98	395	395	520
Holy God, We Praise Thy	—	—	—	—	624	48

	1921	1922	1925	1937	1975	1986
Holy, Holy, Holy	87	87	99	396	396	69
Holy Spirit, Light Divine	—	—	—	—	—	293
Hosanna, Loud Hosanna	—	—	—	—	—	164
How Blest and How Joyous	—	—	flyleaf	flyleaf	—	—

Marshall Clement Kurfees (d. 1931), minister in Church of Christ and staff writer for the *Gospel Advocate*. First pub. in J. H. Fillmore's *New Christian Hymn and Tune Book*, Part III (1887).

How Brightly Beams the	—	—	—	—	—	186
How Calm and Beautiful the	88	88	—	—	—	—

Thomas Hastings, q.v. Pub. in his *Presbyterian Psalmist* (1855, p. 21).

How Firm a Foundation	89	89	100	398/399	398/399	493
How Happy Are They Who	90	90	101	—	—	—

Charles Wesley, q.v. Text pub. in his *Hymns and Sacred Poems* (1749), entitled, "For one Fallen from Grace."

How I Praise Thee, Precious	—	—	—	—	—	596
How Precious Is the Book	91	91	102	—	—	—

John Fawcett, q.v. Text pub. in his *Hymns adapted to the circumstances of Public Worship and Private Devotion* (1782).

How Shall I My Savior Set	92	92	103	—	—	—

Maxwell is the author of text. No other information available. Pub. in John Rippon's *Selection* (1791).

How Shall the Young Secure	93	93	104	399	399	302
How Sweet, How Heavenly	94	94	105	400	400	390
How Sweet the Name of Jesus	95	95	106	401	401	279
Hungry and Faint and Poor	96	96	107	402	402	—

John Newton, q.v. Text pub. in *Olney Hymns* (1779). Intended as a hymn to be sung "before Sermon."

I Am a Poor, Wayfaring	—	—	—	—	625	—

Anonymous American folk hymn.

I Am a Stranger Here	97	97	108	66	66	—

Elijah Taylor Cassel (1849-1930), a physician and Baptist minister, wrote text in 1902. Pub. in E. O. Excell's *International Praise* (1902).

I Am Coming to the Cross	—	—	—	67	67	—

William McDonald (1820-1901) an evangelist in the National Holiness Conference. He saw Fischer's tune, to which song is now always sung, and wrote words, which were used first at the national camp meeting, Hamilton, Mass., June 22, 1870.

I Am Dwelling on the Mount	142	142	156	68	68	—

Harriet W. ReQua. No information is available on this author. All editions of *GS* before 1937 began text, "Is not this the land of Beulah..."

I Am Feasting on the Living	—	—	—	69	69	—

Anonymous text.

I Am Redeemed but not with	—	—	—	70	70	—

James M. Gray (1851-1935). No other information available.

I Am Resolved No Longer to	—	—	—	—	626	361
I Am So Glad That Our Father	—	—	—	71	71	—

Philip P. Bliss, q.v., wrote text in the home of D. W. Whittle (June 1870). Pub. in Bliss's *The Charm for Sunday Schools* (1871).

I Am the Vine and Ye Are	98	98	109	72	72	262
I Am Thine, O Lord	99	99	110	73	73	599

	1921	1922	1925	1937	1975	1986
I Am Thinking Today of That	100	100	111	73	73	—

Eliza Edmunds Hewitt, q.v. Text pub. in John R. Sweney, H. L. Gilmore, and J. H. Entwisle's *Songs of Love and Praise,* No. 4 (1897).

I Ask Not, Lord for Less to	101	101	112	—	—	—

M. Hopkins pub. text in J. H. Fillmore's *New Christian Hymn and Tune Book,* Part III (1887, No. 730). Poem entitled "My Prayer."

I Bring My Sins to Thee	102	102	113	75	75	347
I Can Hear My Savior Calling	103	103	114	76	76	—

W. Blandy (erroneously spelled "Blandly") wrote text. No other information available. J. S. Norris, who wrote the music, copyrighted the song (1890).

I Come to the Garden Alone	104	104	115	77	77	588
I Do Believe, I Now Believe	—	—	—	78	78	—

Charles Wesley, q.v., wrote the words to chorus. I have been unable to find original full poem.

I Gave My Life for Thee	344	344	389	79	79	315

In all editions of *GS* before 1937, opening line read "Thy life was given for me..."

I Have a Savior	105	105	116	80	80	328
I Have Heard of a Land	106	106	117	81	81	—

Mrs. F. A. F. White. No other information available. Song with music copyrighted by Mark M. Jones (1889). Owned by the Evangelical Pub. Co., Chicago, Ill.

I Hear the Savior Say	108	108	118	82	82	—

Elvina Mabel Hall (1820-1899), wrote text one Sunday morning in 1865 on the flyleaf of her *New Lute of Zion* as her minister led a long prayer at Monument St. Methodist Church, Baltimore, Md. Later gave minister a copy.

I Hear Thy Welcome Voice	109	109	119	83	83	—

Lewis Hartsough (1828-1919) wrote poem while engaged in a revival in Epworth, Iowa (1872). Pub. that year in *The Revivalist,* a collection edited by Joseph Hillman, and also in Sankey's *Gospel Hymns and Sacred Songs* (1875).

I Heard an Old, Old Story	—	—	—	—	—	517
I Heard the Voice of Jesus Say	107	107	120	403	403	343
I Know I Love Thee Better	110	110	121	84	85	—

Frances Ridley Havergal, q.v., is credited with this text. No other information available.

I Know My Heavenly Father	111	111	122	85	85	—

S. M. I. Henry, of whom nothing further is known, is credited with this text. First pub. in 1897 and owned by E. O. Excell and Hope Pub. Co., who controlled copyright until 1925.

I Know Not Why God's	112	112	123	86	86	537
I Know That My Redeemer Lives (Wesley)	—	—	124	404	404	557
I Know That My Redeemer Lives (Fillmore)	—	—	—	—	627	507
I Know That My Redeemer Lives...	—	—	—	87	87	—

Elmer Leon Jorgenson, q.v., recast hymn by Jessie Brown Pounds. Pub. and copyrighted in *GS* (1937).

I Know That My Redeemer Lives...	113	113	126	—	—	—

Jessie Brown Pounds, q.v. wrote text and pub. it in 1893. It appeared in J. H. Fillmore and Gilbert Ellis's *The Praise Hymnal* (1896).

I Know That My Redeemer Lives... (COMFORT)	—	414	125	405	405	552

	1921	1922	1925	1937	1975	1986
I Lay My Sins on Jesus	—	415	—	—	—	—

Horatius Bonar, q.v. Text pub. in his *Songs in the Wilderness,* 1st Series (1843), entitled "The Fullness of Jesus."

I Love Thee, I Love Thee	—	—	—	—	628	446

In the present revision of *GS* this opening stanza is omitted. The hymn now begins: "O Jesus, My Savior..." (q.v.).

	1921	1922	1925	1937	1975	1986
I Love Thy Kingdom, Lord	114	114	127	406/407	406/407	408/410
I Love to Tell the Story	115	115	128	88	88	309
I Must Needs Go Home	116	116	129	89	89	—

Jessie Brown Pounds, q.v., wrote text in 1906. Pub. that year in Charles H. Gabriel and W. W. Dowling's *Living Praises,* No. 2.

I Must Tell Jesus	—	—	—	90	90	—

Elisha Albright Hoffman, q.v., wrote text of this chorus. Opening line read: "I must tell Jesus all of my trials..." Pub. in Henry Date's *Pentecostal Hymns* (1894).

I Need Thee Every Hour	117	117	130	91	91	574
I Saw One Hanging on a Tree	118	118	131	—	—	—

John Newton, q.v., pub. text in the *Olney Hymns* (1779).

I Shall See Them Again	119	119	—	—	—	—

Husband is credited with this text. No further information is available.

I Sing the Mighty Power	—	—	—	—	—	92
I Stand Amazed	120	120	132	92	92	230
I Think When I Read	—	—	—	586	586	—

Jemima Thompson Luke (1813-1906) wrote text in 1841 after a visit to the Normal Infant School in Gray's Inn Road. There she heard the Greek Air SALAMIS, which prompted her to find a text to fit tune. Unable to do so, she wrote this text while riding a stagecoach to Wellington, England. *GS* text is st. 1 and half of st. 2. A third stanza, making this a missionary hymn, added later.

I Want to Be a Worker	—	—	—	93	93	—

Isaiah Baltzell (1832-1893). Text pub. 1880. No other information.

I Was Sinking Deep in Sin	—	—	133	94	94	—

James Rowe (1865-1933) wrote text in 1912. Howard E. Smith (1863-1918) provided music. Rowe would hum a bar or two, and Smith, badly crippled with arthritis, would play it and write it. Song written in Saugatuck, Conn. Rowe born in England, migrated to the U.S. in 1890. Associated at one time with the Trio Music Co. Waco, Texas. Text pub. by Robert H. Coleman in his *Select Gospel Songs* (1916).

I Washed My Hands This	391	391	441	587	587	—

Lucinda M. Beal Bateman, q.v., wrote text for children. Pub. by Fillmore Brothers Music House, Cincinnati, Ohio (1886).

I Will Arise and Go to Jesus	—	—	—	—	629	329

In *GSR* (1986) text begins with orig. reading "Come, ye sinners, poor and needy..."

I Will Sing of My Redeemer	—	—	134	95	95	404/407
I Will Sing the Wondrous	—	—	—	96	96	165
I Will Sing You a Song	—	—	—	97	97	—

Ellen Huntington Gates (b. 1835) was wife to Isaac E. Gates. Born Torrington, Conn. Text seems to have been pub. ca. 1865, and later pub. in Sankey's *Sacred Songs and Solos.*

I Would Be True	—	—	—	—	—	427
If Human Kindness Meets	—	416	135	—	—	—

Gerard Thomas Noel (1782-1851) was an Anglican minister educated at Cambridge Univ. Pub. text in his *Psalms and Hymns* (1810).

	1921	1922	1925	1937	1975	1986
If I Have Wounded Any Soul	—	—	—	551	551	—

M. Battersby wrote text about 1913. Pub. by Homer Rodeheaver.

If Jesus Goes with Me, I'll Go	—	—	—	105	105	—

Austin Miles, q.v., wrote this chorus and tune. Pub. in 1908 by the Rodeheaver Co. First line of song, "It may be in the valley..."

If on a Quiet Sea	121	121	136	—	—	—

Augustus Montague Toplady, q.v., wrote a poem of eight double stanzas for the *Gospel Magazine* (Feb. 1772). Text taken from this. Revised text radically altered. Present first stanza may be an original introduction to the poem.

If Our First Fathers	122	122	—	—	—	—

Herbert E. Tickle is the author. He was related to Gilbert Young Tickle, q.v., the hymn writer well known among British Churches of Christ. Poem originally began "If earthly fathers ..." and was in seven stanzas. Our text stanzas 1, 2 ,3, and 5.

If the Name of the Savior	123	123	137	106	106	—

Jessie Brown Pounds, q.v., pub. text in J. H. Fillmore's *New Christian Hymn and Tune Book,* Part III (1887).

If You Are Tired of the Load	—	—	—	132	132	317

In previous editions of *GS* only the chorus of this song appeared, beginning "Just now your doubtings give o'er..."

If You Could See Christ	124	124	138	—	—	—

Carolyn Sawyer wrote this text. No other information available. Pub. 1899, appears in Daniel B. Towner and Charles M. Alexander's *Revival Hymns* (Chicago, 1905, No. 130).

I'll Be Present When My Name	—	—	—	98	98	—

Judson W. Van de Venter, q.v., wrote this chorus. An evangelist among Methodists. Influenced Billy Graham when Graham was student at Florida Bible Institute, then located in Temple Terrace, Fla., on what is now the campus of Florida College, formerly Florida Christian College.

I'm a Pilgrim and I'm a	125	125	139	99	99	—

Mary Stanley Bunce Dana Shindler, q.v. Text pub. in her *Southern Harp* (1842).

I'm Not Ashamed to Own My	126	126	—	408	408	504
I'm Pressing on the Upward	127	127	141	100	100	630
I've a Home Prepared	—	—	—	—	—	670
I've Found a Friend in Jesus	—	—	—	101	101	—

Charles William Fry (1837-1880) wrote text in the home of Mr. Wilkinson in Lincoln, England. Poem found after Fry's death and pub. in *The War Cry* (Dec. 29, 1881).

I've Found a Friend Who Is	146	146	160	—	—	—

Jack P. Scholfield (1882-1972) wrote text in 1911, while leading singing for evangelist M. F. Ham. Pub. in Robert H. Coleman's *New Evangel* (1911). Scholfield, born in Beulah, Kan., was also a teacher and realtor. He died in Poplar Bluff, Mo.

I've Reached the Land of Corn	—	—	—	103	103	—

Edgar Page Stites, q.v., wrote text ca. 1875, while attending camp meeting at Ocean Grove, N.J. John R. Sweney, who was leading the singing at the meeting, set it to music. Pub. in *Goodly Pearls* by John J. Hood Co.

I've Wandered Far Away from	—	—	—	104	104	351
Immortal, Invisible, God Only	—	—	—	—	—	75
In Christ there Is No East	—	—	—	—	630	392
In Heavenly Love Abiding	128	128	143	410	410	649
In His Rude Manger-Bed	392	392	442	—	—	—

Palmer Hartsough, q.v., wrote text which was pub. by Fillmore Brothers Music House, Cincinnati, Ohio. No other information.

	1921	1922	1925	1937	1975	1986
In Loving-Kindness Jesus	129	129	143	107	107	264
In Memory of the Savior's	—	—	144	411	411	375
In Sorrow I Wandered	—	—	—	108	108	—

James Rowe (1865-1933). Pub. in H. A. Rodeheaver, B. D. Ackley, and Charles H. Gabriel's *Great Revival Hymns No. 2* (1915).

In the Christian's Home in	131	131	145	109	109	—

Samuel Y. Harmer (b. 1809). No other information available.

In the Dark and Cloudy Day	132	132	—	—	—	—

George Rawson, q.v., wrote text. Pub. in *Leed's Hymn Book* (1853).

In the Cross of Christ I Glory	130	130	146	412	412	480
In the Desert of Sorrow and	133	133	147	110	110	—

H. R. Trickett (d. 1909). Member of the Christian Church. Pub. in J. H. Fillmore's *New Christian Hymn and Tune Book, Part III* (Cincinnati, 1887, No. 723, entitled "The Water of Life.")

In the Hour of Trial	134	134	148	413	413	538
In the House of Ancient Story	135	135	149	414	414	—

Miss H. M. Bolman is credited with text. No other information known.

In the Hush of Early Morning	136	136	150	415	415	274
In the Land of Fadeless Day	137	137	151	111	111	661
In the Shadow of His Wings	138	11138	152	112	112	—

B. Atchinson. No information known. Text pub. by E. O. Excell (1872).

In the Time of Roses	—	—	—	552	552	—

Louise Reichardt (1779-1826) wrote music for this anonymous text. Tune is HOFFNUNG. Erroneously credited to her father, Johann Friedrich Reichardt in *GS* editions before 1975.

In the Trees the Birds Are	393	393	443	—	—	—

Charles I. Junkin is credited with text. Written about 1906 and owned by Congregational Sunday School and Publication Society. No other information available.

In Vain in High and Holy Lays	139	139	153	113	113	273
In Weakness, Lord, Thou Art	140	140	154	—	—	—

Anonymous text. May be found in William Urwick's *Collection of Hymns Adapted to Congrega-tional Worship* (Dublin, 1829).

Infant Holy, Infant Lowly	—	—	—	—	—	209
Into My Heart	—	—	—	114	114	—

Harry D. Clarke (1888-1957). Pub. in his *Gospel Truth in Song* (1924). Born in Wales, he migrated to Canada and then to the U.S., and was a singer for Billy Sunday during the evangelist's declining years.

Into the Heart of Jesus	—	—	—	553	553	618
Is It for Me, Dear Savior	141	141	155	115	115	171
Is Not This the Land of Beulah	142	142	156	68	68	—

For information, see under "I am dwelling on the mountain."

Is Thy Heart Right with God	—	—	—	116	116	—

For information, see under "Have thine affections been nailed."

Is Your Life a Channel of	143	143	157	117	117	—

Harper G. Smith (1873-1945). Pub. in James McGranahan's *Hymns, Psalms, and Gospel Songs* (Pittsburgh, 1904).

It Came Upon the Midnight	144	144	158	416	416	195
It May Be at Morn	—	—	—	118	118	281

	1921	1922	1925	1937	1975	1986
It May Not Be on the Mount	145	145	159	119	119	—

Charles Hutchinson Gabriel, q.v., wrote first st. ca. 1894. Sts. 2, 3 by Charles Edwin Prior (1856-1927), a banker and organist from Connecticut. Text pub. 1894.

It Only Takes A Spark	—	—	—	—	—	459
Jerusalem, My Happy Home	—	—	—	417	417	—

Original probably based on a passage in Augustine of Hippo's *Liber Meditationes* and a Latin hymn by Cardinal Damian (1553). Modern trans. by a priest who signed himself "F. B. P." From Williams and Boden's *Collection* (1801).

Jerusalem the Golden	147	147	181	418	418	—

Bernard of Cluny, q.v. From his *Contemptu Mundi* (ca. 1145) Modern translation by John Mason Neale (1839) of the portion beginning *"Urbs Sion aurea..."* as found in Richard Chenevix Trench's *Sacred Latin Poetry*. Pub. in Neale's *Medieval Hymns and Sequences* (1851).

Jesus, All-Atoning Lamb	148	148	—	—	—	—

Charles Wesley, q.v. The date of publication of this poem unknown.

Jesus, and Didst Thou Leave	—	—	162	—	—	—

Anne Steele, q.v. This text, part of a nine-stanza poem, begins with st. 4. See below under "Jesus, in Thy transporting name."

Jesus, and Shall It Ever Be	149	149	163	419	419	—

Joseph Grigg, q.v., pub. original version in his *Four Hymns on Divine Subjects* (1765). Modern text said to be by Benjamin Francis (1734-1799), a Baptist minister at Horsley, England. Pub. in John Rippon's *Selection* (1787).

Jesus Bids Us Shine	394	394	444	588	588	—

Anna Bartlett Warner, q.v., pub. text in E. O. Excell's *The Gospel in Song* (1884). Text erroneously attributed to Anna's more famous sister Susan in *GS* (1921, 1922).

Jesus Calls Us	150	140	164	420	420/631	614/615
Jesus, I My Cross Have Taken	151	151	165	421	421	536
Jesus, in Thy Transporting	152	152	—	—	—	—

Anne Steele, q.v., pub. these stanzas in her *Centos and Altered Texts* (1760). See above under "Jesus, and didst Thou leave the sky."

Jesus Is All the World to Me	—	—	—	120	120	500
Jesus Is Calling, Calling	153	153	166	121	121	—

Palmer Hartsough, q.v. Text pub. by Fillmore Music House in 1909.

Jesus Is Coming to Earth	154	154	167	—	—	—

Leila Naylor Morris, q.v. Pub. in H. L. Gilmour, George W. Sanville, Wm. J. Kirkpatrick, and Melvin J. Hill's *The King's Praises,* No. 3 (Philadelphia, 1912).

Jesus Is Lord, My Redeemer	—	—	—	—	632	159
Jesus Is Mighty to Save	—	—	—	122	122	—

Anonymous chorus. No information available.

Jesus Is Our Loving Shepherd	155	155	168	123	123	—

Mrs. W. S. Stroud of Atlanta, Ga. She assisted in the editing of hymnals produced by S. H. Hall and Flavil Hall. No other information.

Jesus Is Passing This Way	—	—	—	24	124	—

Elisha Albright Hoffman, q.v., wrote this chorus in 1887. Pub. that year in Sankey's *Sacred Songs and Solos*. Full text begins "Is there a sinner awaiting ..."

Jesus Is Tenderly Calling	156	156	169	125	125	321
Jesus, Keep Me Near the	157	157	170	126	126	627
Jesus Lives, and So Shall I	—	—	—	—	—	550
Jesus, Lover of My Soul	158	158	171	127/422	127/422	276/278

	1921	1922	1925	1937	1975	1986
Jesus Loves Me	395	395	445	589	589	—

Anna Bartlett Warner, q.v. Poem first appeared in the novel *Say and Seal* (1859). Written in collaboration with sister Susan.

Jesus Loves the Little	—	—	—	590	590	—

H. Woolston. No other information.

Jesus Meek and Gentle	159	159	172	423	423	572
Jesus Master, Whose I Am	—	418	—	—	—	—

Frances Ridley Havergal, q.v. Text written for nephew, J. H. Shaw, Dec. 1865. First printed as leaflet and then pub. in her *Ministry of Song* (1869).

Jesus, Merciful and Mild	160	160	173	—	—	—

Thomas Hastings, q.v., pub. this text in his *Church Melodies* (1858). No other information known.

Jesus My Lord Will Love Me	—	—	—	—	—	461
Jesus, My Savior, to	161	161	174	128	128	—

This text, of unknown date, appears under the initials "A. N." in some of the early books of Charles M. Alexander. No other information available.

Jesus Only When the Morning	162	162	175	—	—	—

Elias Nason (1811-1887). Text written ca. 1856 and pub. in the Boston *Wellspring*. Later pub. in Edward Kirk's *Songs for Social and Public Worship* (1863). Nason was born at Wretham, Mass. educated at Brown Univ., and became a Congregational minister.

Jesus, Priceless Treasure	—	—	—	—	633	350
Jesus, Rose of Sharon	—	—	—	129	129	486
Jesus Said of Little Children	—	—	—	590	590	—

Clifford R. Lanman pub. text in 1937. No other information available.

Jesus, Savior, Pilot Me	163	163	1176	424	424	486
Jesus Saves Forever	—	—	—	—	—	657
Jesus, Savior, Pilot Me	—	—	—	—	—	534
Jesus Shall Reign Where'er	—	—	177	425	425	261
Jesus, the Loving Shepherd	164	164	178	—	—	—

William Augustine Ogden (1841-1897). No other information available.

Jesus, the Very Thought of	165	165	179	46	426	265
Jesus, Thou Joy of Loving	—	420	180	427	427	263
Jesus, Thy Boundless Love	—	421	182	—	—	621
Jesus, Thy Name I Love	166	166	182	428	428	656
Jesus Walked This Lonesome	—	—	—	—	634	—

American folk hymn. No other information available.

Jesus Wept: Those Tears	167	167	—	—	—	—

John Ross MacDuff (1818-1895). Text pub. in his *Altar Stones* (1853). The *GS* editions which contained the hymn erroneously attributed it to Edward Denny. MacDuff was educated at Edinburgh Univ. and became a minister in the Church of Scotland in 1842.

Jesus, Wonderful Thou Art	—	—	—	—	635	562
Joy to the World	168	168	183	429	429	256
Joy-Bells Ringing	—	—	—	592	592	—

Josephine Pollard wrote this text for children. No other information.

Joyful, Joyful, We Adore Thee	—	—	—	—	636	55
Judge Eternal, Throned in	—	—	—	—	—	433
Just a Few More Days	—	—	184	130	130	556

	1921	1922	1925	1937	1975	1986
Just As I Am	169	169	185	131	131	346
Just Now Your Doubtings	—	—	—	132	132	317

Leila Naylor Morris, q.v., wrote this chorus. See "If you are tired of the load of your sin."

King Jesus, Reign Forever	170	170	186	—	—	—

Ralph Wardlaw, q.v., was an eminent Scottish minister. No further information available.

King of My Life I Crown Thee	—	—	—	—	—	231
Know, My Soul, Thy Full	171	171	—	430	430	536

Henry Francis Lyte, q.v. In previous editions of *GS* this portion of the complete text of "Jesus, I My Cross Have Taken" (q.v.), was printed separately. It is now incorporated.

Lamp of Our Feet	172	172	—	—	—	—

Bernard Barton, q.v., pub. this text in 11 sts. in *The Reliquary* (1836, p. 116). *GS* text included stanzas 1, 2, 9, and 11.

Lay Hold on the Hope	173	173	186	—	—	—

Fanny Jane Crosby, q.v. Text pub. in E. O. Excell's *Coronation Hymns* (1910).

Lead, Holy Shepherd	—	—	188	—	—	—

Titus Flavius Clemens (Clement of Alexandria), q.v. Text a translation of Clement's *Paidagogos (The Tutor)*, A.D. 200, by Hamilton Montgomerie Macgill (1807-1880), pub. in the Scottish *Presbyterian Hymnal* (1876).

Lead, Kindly Light	174	174	189	431	431	583
Lead Me Gently Home	—	—	190	133	133	—

Will Lamartine Thompson, q.v., pub. text in 1879. Copyright later owned by Hope Pub. Co.

Lead Me to Some Soul	—	—	—	134	134	421
Lead on, O King Eternal	—	—	—	432	432	259
Lead Us, O Father	—	—	—	—	—	540
Let All Mortal Flesh Keep	—	—	—	—	—	386
Let All the World in Every	—	—	—	—	—	81
Let All Together Praise Our	—	—	—	—	—	192
Let Every Heart Rejoice and	178	178	191	554	554	49
Let the Beauty of Jesus Be	—	—	—	135	135	—

Albert Orsbon wrote text. No other information available. Edwin E. Young made arr. in 1930.

Let the Whole Creation Cry	—	—	—	—	—	58
Let the Words of My Mouth	175	175	192	136	136	—

Text a quotation from Psalm 1914 set to Anglican chant. No other information available.

Let Us Walk in the Light	176	176	—	—	—	—

Anonymous text, probably of folk or camp meeting origin.

Let Us with a Gladsome Mind	—	—	—	433	433	84
Lifetime is Working Time	179	179	—	—	—	—

Carrie E. Breck, q.v. Text pub. by Edmund S. Lorenz in 1905.

Lift High the Cross	—	—	—	—	—	224
Lift Up, Lift Up Your Voices	—	—	—	—	—	448
Lift Up Your Heads, Ye	—	—	—	—	—	191
Like a Shepherd, Tender	—	—	—	138	138	272

	1921	1922	1925	1937	1975	1986
Like a Star of the Morning	—	—	—	139	139	—

B. Hartzler wrote text. Pub. by Edmund S. Lorenz, q.v., who wrote music. No other information.

Light of the World	—	—	193	137	137	—

Laura Ormiston Dibdin Chant (1848-1923). Text written at the request of S. Collier of Central Wesleyan Mission of Manchester, England (June, 1901). She wished it to be as tender as, but gladder than, Newman's "Lead, Kindly Light."

Lo, He Comes with Clouds	180	180	194	434	434	289
Lo, How a Rose E'er Blooming	—	—	—	—	—	180
Lo, What a Glorious Sight	—	—	195	555	555	—

Isaac Watts, q.v., pub. text in his *Hymns and Spiritual Songs* (1707), in 6 sts. *GS* text omitted Watts's st. 3.

Look, Ye Saints, the Sight	—	422	196	140	140	252
Lord and Savior, True and	—	—	—	—	637	

Handley Carr Glyn Moule (b. 1841) was Anglican bishop of Durham. Text pub. in *The Council School Hymn Book* (Novello & Co., 1905).

Lord, Christ, When First	—	—	—	—	—	288
Lord, Dismiss Us with Thy	181	181	197	141/435	141/435	10
Lord, Have Mercy, Have	11182	182	198	—	—	—

A paraphrase of ancient Christian prayers based on the Psalms. The chant arr. is by S. P. Tuckerman. No other information.

Lord, I Care Not for Riches	—	—	—	142	142	—

Mary Ann Kidder (1820-1905) was a Methodist who resided for nearly half a century in New York City. No other information known.

Lord, I Hear of Showers	183	183	199	143	143	—

Elizabeth Codner (1824-1919). Wife of Daniel, curate of Peter- borough, England, edited *Woman's Work*, a missionary magazine. No other information known.

Lord Jesus Christ, Be Present	—	—	—	—	—	3
Lord Jesus, I Long to Be	184	184	200	144	144	631
Lord Jesus, Think on Me	—	—	—	—	—	529
Lord of All Being, Throned	—	423	201	436	436	113
Lord of Our Highest Love	—	424	202	437	437	379
Lord, Speak to Me That I May	185	185	203	438	438	622
Lord, We Come before Thee	186	186	204	439	439	4
Love Divine, All Loves	187	187	205	440	440	267
Love For All, and Can It Be	188	188	206	441	441	353
Love Him, Love Him, All Ye	—	—	—	593	593	—

Carey Bonner is probably the author of this text. It was pub. in his *Child Songs* (London, 1908) and attributed to E. Rawdon Bailey, one of Bonner's pseudonyms.

Low in the Grave He Lay	190	190	20-8	145	145	245
Lullaby and Goodnight	—	—	—	556	556	—

Karl Simrock is the reputed author of the German original. The translator of stanza 1 is unknown. E. L. Jorgenson, q.v., translated stanza 2 and pub. it in *GS* (1937).

Majestic Sweetness Sits	191	191	208	4421	442	260
Make Me a Captive, Lord	—	—	—	—	—	617
Marvelous Grace of Our	—	—	—	—	—	124

	1921	1922	1925	1937	1975	1986
Master, the Tempest Is Raging	—	—	—	146	146	—

Mary A. Baker wrote this text at the request of H. R. Palmer, q.v., for songs to go with current Sunday School lessons. It is based on Mark 4:35-41 and pub. in 1874. This song was sung during the days when Pres. James Abram Garfield lay dying after, having being shot by Charles J. Guiteau, and was sung at his funeral.

May the Grace of Christ Our	—	425	209	—	—	17
Men and Children Everywhere	—	—	—	—	—	93
Mid Pleasures and Palaces	—	—	—	557	557	—

John Howard Payne (1792-1852) wrote this text. His mother died when he was 13, and at 17 he became an actor. He lived abroad after age 21. In England he wrote the drama *Clari, the Maid of Milan,* and when it was presented as an opera, he introduced into it this beloved poem of home. He returned to America in 1832 and was later appointed consul to Tunis, where he died.

Mighty God, While Angels	—	—	210	—	—	—

Robert Robinson, q.v., wrote this text. The probable date is 1774, although both date and circumstances are uncertain.

Mighty Rock, Whose Towering	192	192	211	—	—	—

Fanny Jane Crosby, q.v., is the author of this text. The circumstances and date are unknown.

More About Jesus	193	193	212	147	147	626
More Holiness Give Me	194	194	213	443	443	488
More Love to Thee, O Christ	195	195	214	148	148	613
Morning Has Broken	—	—	—	—	—	470
Must Jesus Bear the Cross	196	196	215	444	444	629
My Brethren, Let Us Be as	—	—	—	—	—	395
My Country, 'Tis of Thee	—	—	—	558	558	—

Samuel F. Smith (1808-1895), a Baptist minister from Boston, Mass., wrote this text. He came across the tune "God Save the King" one gloomy February day in 1832 while thumbing through some German music books and was inspired to write these noble words.

My Days Are Gliding Swiftly	—	—	—	149	149	—

David Nelson (1793-1844) wrote this text in 1837 while fleeing from slave-holding neighbors in Missouri and going to Quincy, Illinois. The words came to him while he was hiding on the river bank on the Missouri side and were written on a letter he had with him.

My Faith Looks Up to Thee	197	197	216	445	445	584
My Father Is Rich in Houses	198	198	217	—	—	—

Harriet Eugenia Pech Buell (1834-1910) composed this text while walking home from a Sun- day service at Thousand Island Park, New York, in 1878. It was pub. in the *Northern Christian Advocate,* Syracuse, N.Y. and set to music that same year.

My God, I Love Thee	—	—	—	—	—	451
My God, My Father, Though I	—	—	—	—	—	611
My Gracious Redeemer, I	199	199	218	—	—	—

Benjamin Francis (1734-1799), a Welshman who did not learn English until age 20, wrote this text. He was a Baptist preacher. The hymn was pub. in John Rippon's *Selection* (1787).

My Heavenly Home Is Bright	—	—	—	150	150	—

William Hunter (1811-1877) was an Irish immigrant to the U.S. who settled in Pennsylvania and became a Methodist preacher and editor of the *Christian Advocate.* He edited several hymnals, and this text is from his *Select Melodies* (Pittsburgh, 1838).

	1921	1922	1925	1937	1975	1986
O Could I Speak the	213	213	234	453	453	—

Samuel Medley, q.v., pub. text in his *Hymns: The Public Worship and Private Devotions of True Christians* (3d ed., 1789).

O Day of God, Draw Nigh	—	—	—	—	—	440
O Day of Rest and Gladness	—	426	236	—	—	—

Christopher Wordsworth (1807-1885), Anglican bishop of Lincoln, pub. text in his *Holy Year* (1862).

O Do Not Let the Word Depart	214	214	237	161	161	—

Eliza Holmes Reed (1794-1867), wife of a minister, Andrew Reed, who was greatly given to works of charity. Text pub. in her husband's *Wycliffe Chapel Supplement* (1872).

O for a Closer Walk with God	—	—	—	454	454	576
O for a Faith That Will Not	215	215	238	455	455	505
O for a Heart to Praise My	216	216	239	456	456	491
O for a Soul Aglow with Love	—	—	—	—	—	457
O for a Thousand Tongues	—	—	—	457	457	2
O for the Peace	217	217	240	—	—	—

Jane Fox Crewdson (1809-1863) was daughter of George Fox of Perraw, Cornwall, Eng. Married Thomas Crewdson (1836), was in ill health most of her life, and composed her poems under difficult conditions. Text pub. in her posthumous work *A Little While, and Other Poems* (1864).

O God of Bethel, by Whose	—	427	241	458	458	140
O God of Earth and Altar	—	—	—	—	—	434
O God, Our Help in Ages Past	218	218	242	459/460	459/460	136
O God, We Praise Thee and	—	—	—	—	—	70
O Happy Day That Fixed My	219	219	243	162	162	—

Philip Doddridge, q.v. Text based on 1 Chron. 15:15. Pub. in Job Orton's edition of Doddridge's *Hymns* (1755) without refrain.

O Heart Bowed Down with	220	220	244	163	163	337
O Holy City, Seen of John	—	—	—	—	—	431
O How He Loves You and Me	—	—	—	—	—	232
O How Kindly Hast Thou Led	221	221	245	461	461	142
O How Shall I Receive Thee	—	—	—	—	—	189
O If My House Is Built Upon	—	—	—	164	164	—

William Augustine Ogden, q.v., wrote text. No other information available.

O Jesus, I Have Promised	—	—	246	462	462	620
O Jesus, King Most Wonderful	—	428	247	463	463	—

Bernard of Clairvaux, q.v., wrote text as part of his *"Jesu dulcis memoria."* These lines begin *"Jesu, rex admirabilis ..."* Trans. Edward Caswall, q.v., pub. in *Lyra Catholica* (1849).

O Jesus Is Coming Again	—	—	—	165	165	—

J. H. Painter. Chorus is part of full text beginning "O I wonder when Jesus is coming again..." pub. in J. H. Fillmore's *Grateful Praise* (1884).

O Jesus, My Savior	—	—	—	—	628	446

Anonymous text orig. beginning "I love Thee, I love Thee..." in Jeremia Ingall's *Christian Harmony* (1805).

O Jesus, Thou Art Standing	—	429	248	—	—	—

	1921	1922	1925	1937	1975	1986
O Sons and Daughters, Let	—	—	—	—	—	246
O Soul, Are You Weary and	—	—	—	—	—	311
O Splendor of God's Glory	—	—	—	—	—	158
O Spread the Tidings Round	—	—	—	—	645	290
O the Bitter Pain and Sorrow	231	231	263	—	646	—

Theodore Monod (b. 1836) wrote text during a series of "consecration" meetings at Broadlands, England (July 1874). First printed by Lord Mount-Temple on back of a program card in Oct. 1874. Monod was educated at Western Theological Seminary, Allegheny, Pa., and served as a minister in Paris, France, for many years.

O the Crowning Day is	—	—	—	171	171	—

Daniel Webster Whittle, q.v., wrote this text. It is found in *Sankey's Sacred Songs and Solos* (complete ed. No. 176). First line of text begins "The Lord is now rejected..." Pub. 1881.

O the Precious Love of Jesus	232	232	264	172	172	—

Eliza Sherman wrote text. It appeared as early as 1882 in J. H. Fillmore's *New Christian Hymn and Tune Book* (No. 643). No other information available.

O They Tell Me of a Home	—	—	—	173	173	—

J. K. Alwood (1828-1909) composed text one cloudless, moonlit night as he rode his horse home from preaching. Wrote text and melody down the next day. It was harmonized by J. F. Kinsey, who pub. it in his *Living Gems* (Chicago, 1890).

O Think of the Home Over	233	233	—	174	174	—

Dewitt Clinton Huntingdon (1830-1912) wrote text. He was a Methodist presiding elder and later professor of Bible at Nebraska Wesleyan Univ. It was pub. at T. C. O'Kane's *Additional Fresh Leaves, a Supplement to Fresh Leaves* (New York, 1868).

O Thou in Whose Presence	—	—	—	—	—	634
O Thou to Whose All-Searching	—	—	—	—	—	510
O to Be like Thee	235	235	266	175	175	624
O Weary Pilgrim, Lift Your	—	—	—	176	176	—

M. M. Wienland wrote text, for which Edmund S. Lorenz, q.v., supplied music. Pub. in 1897.

O Weary Soul, the Gate Is	—	—	—	177	177	—

James Rowe (1865-1933) wrote text. Pub. by Rodeheaver Co. (1912). No other information known.

O What Will You Do With	236	236	267	—	—	—

Nathaniel Norton wrote text. Pub. in 1886. No other information.

O Word of God Incarnate	—	—	—	—	647	298
O Worship the King	237	237	268	473	473	87
O Worship the Lord in the	397	397	447	594	594	—

A paraphrase of Psalm 110:3, pub. by Ida F. Leyda (1911). No other information available.

O Wounded Feet of Jesus	—	—	—	178	178	—

Anonymous text. No information available.

O Zion, Haste, Thy Mission	238	238	269	474	474	414
Of One the Lord Has Made	239	239	270	179	179	—

John Moody McCaleb (1861-1953) wrote this stirring missionary hymn. McCaleb was a pioneer missionary to Japan, going there in 1895. I have not found this text in any hymnal earlier than *GS* (1921).

On a Hill Far Away	—	—	271	180	180	655
On Jordan's Stormy Banks	242	242	272	181/2/3	181/2/3	666/7
On Zion's Glorious Summit	246	246	273	475	475	177

	1921	1922	1925	1937	1975	1986
Renew Thy Church, Her	—	—	—	—	—	423
Rescue the Perishing	—	—	294	193	193	411
Ride On! Ride On in Majesty	—	—	—	—	—	216
Rise Up, O Men of God	—	—	—	—	649	405
Rock of Ages, Cleft For Me	256	256	295	484	484	356
Safe in the Arms of Jesus	—	—	296	194	194	647
Safely Through Another Week	257	257	297	485	485	—

John Newton, q.v., wrote and published this hymn in Richard Conyers's *A Collection of Psalms and Hymns* (1774). Also pub. in the *Olney Hymns* (1779).

Saved to the Uttermost	258	258	—	—	—	—

William James Kirkpatrick, q.v., pub. text in 1903, with revisions in 1917. No other information.

Saints of God, Rejoice and	—	—	—	486	486	—

Austin Taylor (1881-1973) pub. text in 1928. He was a singer and hymnal compiler among Churches of Christ for many years. No other information.

Savior, Again to Thy Dear	259	259	298	487	487	11
Savior, As in Dust to Thee	260	260	—	—	—	—

Robert Grant, q.v., wrote text. Printed in the *Christian Observer* (1815) and pub. first in a hymnal in Elliott's *Psalms & Hymns* (1835). Usual opening line is, "Savior, when in dust..."

Savior, Blessed Savior	—	—	299	—	—	—

Godfrey Thring, q.v., wrote text in 1862. Pub. in his *Hymns, Congregational and Others* (1866).

Savior, Breathe an Evening	261	261	399	488	488	40
Savior, Grant Me Rest and	262	262	301	489	489	479
Savior, Hear Me While Before	263	263	—	195	195	—

H. H. Booth, the Salvation Army singer, wrote this text. First pub. in *Salvation Army Songs*. No other information available.

Savior, Lead Me Lest I Stray	264	264	302	196	196	—

Frank M. Davis (1839-1896). Pub. in *Carols of Joy*. No other information.

Savior, Like a Shepherd Lead	398	398	448	490	490	606
Savior, More Than Life to Me	—	—	—	197	197	—

Fanny Jane Crosby, q.v., wrote text after receiving tune from W. H. Doane with request for a hymn entitled "Every day and hour." Pub. in Robert Lowry and Doane's *Brightest and Best* (1875).

Savior, Teach Me Day by Day	265	265	303	491	491	413
Savior, Thy Dying Love	266	266	304	492	492	609
Seek Ye First, Not Earthly	269	269	—	—	—	—

Georgiana M. Taylor is the author of this text. No other information.

Seek Ye First the Kingdom	268	268	306	198	198	—

Eliza Edmunds Hewitt (1851-1920). No other information available.

Seeking the Lost	267	267	305	199	199	—

William Augustine Ogden (1851-1897). No other information available.

Shall I Crucify My Savior	—	—	—	200	200	269
Shall Songs of Grateful Love	—	—	—	201	201	—

James John Cummins (1795-1867) wrote text. It was altered from an earlier form in 1839. No other information available.

Shall We Gather at the River	270	270	307	202	202	551

	1921	1922	1925	1937	1975	1986
Something Beautiful	—	—	—	—	—	511
Sometime the Burden Will Be	283	283	319	—	—	—

E. E. Richardson authored the text. Music by E. O. Excell. This was Excell's last song. Pub. 1920.

Somewhere the Sun Is Shining	—	—	—	—	651	—

Jessie Brown Pounds, q.v. A popular hymnist and writer for Fillmore Bros. and the Christian Standard. Wife of John Pounds, a minister in the Christian Church. Text pub. 1897.

Somebody Did a Golden Deed	—	—	—	596	596	—

John Ralston Clements (1868-1946) Pub. 1901. No other information.

Son of God, Eternal Savior	—	—	—	—	—	161
Songs of Praise Awoke the	285	285	321	—	—	—

James Montgomery, q.v. pub. text in T. Cotterill's *Selection* (1819) and his own *Christian Psalmist* (1825). *GS* text has sts. 2, 3, 5, 6. Stanza 1 begins, "Songs of praise the angels sang..."

Soon Will Our Savior from	284	284	—	—	—	—

Ada Ruth Habershon (1861-1918) wrote text in 1906. Pub. that year by Charles M. Alexander.

Soul, A Savior Thou Art	287	287	323	—	—	—

Jessie Brown Pounds, q.v. Pub. by Fillmore Bros. Music House, 1897.

Sound, Sound the Truth	288	288	324	—	—	—

Thomas Kelly, q.v., pub. text in his *Hymns on Various Passages of Scripture* (1820).

Sowing in the Morning	289	289	325	215	215	443
Sowing the Seed by the Day	—	—	—	216	216	—

Emily Sullivan Oakeley (1829-1883) was from Albany, N.Y. Text pub. in the *Family Treasury* (Edinburgh, 1861).

Speak to My Soul, Dear Jesus	290	290	326	—	—	—

Leander Lycurgus Pickett (b. 1859). American evangelist and temperance advocate. Text pub. 1897.

Speed Away! Speed Away!	291	291	327	496	496	—

Fanny Jane Crosby, q.v. Text pub. in Sankey's *Gospel Hymns, No. 6* (1980). Based on a secular lyric taken from a Seneca Indian myth of the white dove sent out by the mother of a dead maiden to find her soul. Orig. text may be seen in *The Franklin Square Song Collection* (New York: Harper, 1884, p. 10).

Stand Up, and Bless the Lord	—	—	—	—	—	85
Stand Up, Stand Up for Jesus	293	293	328	497	497	403
Standing by a Purpose True	—	—	—	217	217	—

Philip P. Bliss, q.v. Text pub. by John C. Church Co. and also appears in Sankey's *Gospel Hymns,* Nos. 1-6 Complete (1894).

Standing on the Promises	292	292	329	218	218	554
Still, Still with Thee	—	—	—	flyleaf	652	641
Still with Thee, O My God	—	—	—	—	—	612
Sun of My Soul	294	294	339	498	498	42
Sunset and Evening Star	—	—	—	219	219	—

Text by the English poet-laureate Alfred, Lord Tennyson (1809-1892). Written near the end of his life (Oct. 1889). He asked his son Hallam always to place it last in his collected poems.

Sweet Are the Promises	—	—	—	220	220	—
Sweet Hour of Prayer	295	295	331	499	499	559

	1921	1922	1925	1937	1975	1986
Sweet Is the Promise	297	297	332	221	221	—

Charles Hutchinson Gabriel, q.v. Text pub. in E. O. Excell's *Triumphant Songs,* No. 2 (1889).

Sweet Is the Solemn Voice	—	438	333	500	500	—

Henry Francis Lyte, q.v. The text possesses a sad tenderness and was first pub. in his *Spirit of the Psalms* (1889).

Sweet Is the Task, My	—	—	—	222	222	—

Henry Francis Lyte, q.v., wrote this text. No other information known.

Sweet Is the Work, My God	—	439	334	—	—	—

Isaac Watts, q.v. A portion of his paraphrase of Psalm 92 and pub. in his *Psalms of David* (1719).

Sweetly, Lord, Have We Heard	296	296	335	223	223	426
Take My Life, and Let It Be	298	298	336	501	501	608
Take My Life, O Father, Mold	—	—	—	502	502	603
Take the Name of Jesus with	299	299	337	224	224	524
Take the World but Give Me	—	—	338	225	225	—

Fanny Jane Crosby, q.v. Pub. in T. C. O'Kane, C. C. McCabe, and John R. Sweney's *Joy to the World, or Sacred Songs for Gospel Meetings* (New York: Phillips & Hunt, 1878).

Take Thou My Hands and	301	301	339	—	—	527
Take Thou Our Minds, Dear	—	—	—	—	—	605
Take Time to Be Holy	300	300	340	503	503	487
Take Up Thy Cross	—	—	—	—	—	503
Tarry With Me, O My Savior	302	302	342	226	226	635
Teach Me Your Way, O Lord	—	—	—	—	—	523
Tell Me the Old, Old Story	—	—	342	227	227	—

Katherine Hankey, q.v. Text is taken from her life of Christ in verse: *The Old, Old Story.* Part One was entitled "The Story Wanted." Pub. Jan. 29, 1866.

Tell Me the Story of Jesus	—	—	343	228	228	305
Tempted and Tried	—	—	—	—	653	—

W. B. Stevens. Pub. in *Starlit Crown* (Dallas: Stamps-Baxter Music Co., 1937. No. 138).

That Dreadful Night before	—	—	—	—	654	372
The Church's One Foundation	303	303	344	504	504	365
The Day of Resurrection	304	304	345	—	—	242
The Day Thou Gavest, Lord	—	440	346	505	505	39
The Father Kind Above Sent	—	—	—	229	229	—

Palmer Hartsough, q.v. Pub. in Gilbert J. Ellis and J. H. Fillmore's *The Praise Hymnal* (1895).

The Fight Is On, the Trumpet	—	—	—	230	230	—

Leila Naylor Morris, q.v., wrote text. Pub. by Haldor Lillenas.

The First Noel	—	—	—	231	231	208
The God of Abraham Praise	306	306	347	506	506	43
The God of Harvest Praise	307	307	—	—	—	—

Text attributed to James Montgomery, q.v. No other information.

The Gospel Bells Are Ringing	—	—	—	232	232	—

Samuel Wesley Martin (b. 1839) in Plainfield, Ill. Orig. titled "The Gospel Message." No other information.

	1921	1922	1925	1937	1975	1986
The Grace of the Lord	—	—	—	237	237	—

A paraphrase of 2 Cor. 13:14 by Van Denman Thompson. No other information available.

The Grace of the Lord Jesus	—	—	—	568	568	—

Richard E. Maxwell, a member of the Church of Christ, is author of this text. Paraphrase of 2 Cor. 13:14, pub. in *GS* 1937.

The Great Physician	305	305	348	234	234	173
The Greatness of God	—	—	—	—	—	190
The Hand That Was Nailed	308	308	349	235	235	—

Hattie Pierson and Fred Morris collaborated on text. Pub. by Hope Pub. Co. (1905).

The Head That Once Was	—	441	350	507	507	257
The Heavens Declare Thy	—	—	351	—	—	112
The King of Love My	—	—	—	—	—	118
The King Shall Come When	—	—	—	—	—	284
The Kingdoms of Earth Pass	309	309	352	—	—	—

H. R. Trickett (d. l909). Minister in Christian Church. Pub. in Fillmore's *New Christian Hymn and Tune Book* (Part III, 1887). Text written in 1884.

The Lion of Judah Goes	3410	310	353	—	—	—

W. C. Martin wrote text. Pub. by A. J. Showalter (1899). No other information available.

The Lone, Wild Bird	—	—	—	—	—	589
The Lord Bless You and Keep	—	—	flyleaf	508	508	—

This paraphrase of Numbers 6: 24-26 by E. L. Jorgenson, orig. compiler of *GS*. Pub. 1934.

The Lord Bless You and Keep	—	—	—	—	655	632
The Lord Is in His Holy	399	399	449	597	597	8
The Lord Is My Shepherd, I	—	—	—	236	236	—

A paraphrase of Ps. 23:1, 2, set to chant by Lowell Mason, q.v.

The Lord Is Nigh	312	312	354	—	—	—

Arr. of Psalm 145:18 by E. L. Jorgenson, q.v. First pub. in *GS* (1921).

The Lord Jehovah Reigns	—	—	—	—	—	105
The Lord My Pasture Shall	313	313	355	569	569	—

Joseph Addison, q.v., pub text in an essay in the *Spectator* (July 26, 1712).

The Lord My Shepherd Is	314	314	356	509	509	145
The Lord Will Come and Not	—	—	—	—	—	282
The Lord's My Shepherd, I'll	—	442	357	510	510	143
The Name of Jesus Is So	315	315	358	237	237	—

W. C. Martin, of whom no information is available, wrote text. Pub. by E. S. Lorenz (1901).

The Night Is Fast Passing	316	316	359	238	238	—

Adoniram Judson Gordon, q.v. No other information available.

The Peace of God Now Guard	—	—	—	239	239	—

Paraphrase of Phil. 4:7, set to chant by George MacFarfren. No other information available.

The Radiant Morn Has Passed	—	443	360	—	—	—

Godfrey Thring, q.v. Wrote text in 1864. Pub. in his *Hymns, Congregational and Others* (1866). Second stanza rev. 1899.

Anonymous text, set to music by Charlie D. Tillman (1861-1943). A popular song with older folk.

Reginald Heber, q.v., wrote text while he was Anglican bishop of Calcutta, India. It is a song for St. Stephen's Day (Dec. 26) and pub. in his *Hymns Written and Adapted to the Weekly Church Service of the Year* (1827).

Robert Grant, q.v., authored text. No other information available.

H. B. Hartzler is author of text. Pub. before 1912. No other information.

Edward C. Avis. pub. text in 1901. No other information available.

Jessie Brown Pounds, q.v. Pub. in 1889.

James Deforest Murch (1892-1973) pub. text under title "I'll Put Jesus First in My Life." Song came out of his experience with liberalism and worldliness in the church. Almost despairing, he awoke one night with Rom. 12:1, 2 in his mind. He resolved on a plan of consecration, restudy of Scripture, and experimental action. Out of this arose the personal commitment of putting Jesus first in everything. This text came to him at 3:00, one morning in 1933.

Jessie Brown Pounds, q.v., pub. text in 1913. No other information.

Josephine Pollard (b. ca. 1840).

George Cooper (1840-1907) wrote text. No other information available.

Ada Ruth Habershon (1841-1917) wrote text. This poem ("Will the Circle Be Unbroken") has been one of the most popular of sentimental texts.

Gerard Moultrie (1829-1885) was an Anglican priest, educated at Rugby and Oxford. He pub. various hymns and translations.

Peter Philip Bilhorn (1861-1936), whose orig. family name was Pulhorn, pub. text in his *Crowning Glory* (1888). He was converted to Christ by George Pentecost after singing in beer halls for a time, traveled with George C. Stebbins, invented a portable organ, and was Billy Sunday's first song leader.

Lydia Baxter (1809-1874) was born in Petersburg, New York, and was a Baptist. She was an invalid for many years. Her poems were pub. in *Gems by the Wayside* (1855).

	1921	1922	1925	1937	1975	1986
There Is a Habitation	326	326	—	252	252	664
There Is a Land of Pure	—	—	—	515	515	—

Isaac Watts, q.v., pub. text in his *Hymns and Spiritual Songs* (1707).

There Is a Name I Love to	—	—	—	—	—	455
There Is a Peace That Cometh	—	—	371	—	—	—

Jessie Rose Gates authored the text. It was pub. with a tune by E. L. Jorgenson, q.v., in *GS* (1925).

There Is a Place of Quiet Rest	—	—	—	—	657	482
There Is a Sea Which Day by	327	327	372	572	572	—

This text contains two anonymous stanzas and a third by Lula Klingman Zahn (d. 1948), the wife of R. A .Zahn, preacher in the Church of Christ and sister to George A. Klingman. In a letter to me, dated July 27, 1970, Irene Jorgenson attributed the first two stanzas to E. L. Jorgenson. Perhaps he revised them, for he never claimed them in any printing of *GS*.

There Is a Place of Quiet Rest	—	—	—	—	657	482
There Is a Spot to Me More	—	—	—	254	254	—

William Hunter (1811-1877) was born in County Antrim, Ireland, came to the U.S. as a child, attended Madison College, Uniontown, Pa., and became a Methodist preacher. He edited several hymnals and was one of a committee of twelve who edited the *Methodist Hymnal* (1878).

There Is, Beyond the Azure	—	—	—	—	—	107
There Is Rest for the Weary	—	—	—	255	255	—

Jessie Brown Pounds, q.v., pub. text in J. H. Fillmore's *New Christian Hymn and Tune Book* (Part III, 1887).

There Is Rest, Sweet Rest	—	—	—	256	256	—

Eliza Edmunds Hewitt, q.v., pub. text in John R. Sweney and Wm. J. Kirkpatrick's *Glad Hallelujahs* (1887).

There Is Sunshine in My	—	—	—	257	257	463
There Shall Be Showers of	328	328	374	258	258	—

Daniel Webster Whittle, q.v., wrote text under his pen name "El Nathan." Pub. in Sankey's *Gospel Hymns*, No. 4 (1883).

There Stands a Rock on	329	329	374	259	259	—

S. S. Journal authored text. No other information available.

There Was One Who Was	330	330	375	260	260	—

Carrie (Mrs. Frank A.) Breck, q.v., wrote text. Pub. by Grant Colfax Tullar in 1899.

There Will Be Light at the	—	—	376	3	3	—

Jennie Wilson, as an invalid, wrote this text. See "After the Life-Paths," which is the first stanza of poem. She is included in A. J. Showalter's *The Best Gospel Songs and Their Composers* (Dalton, Georgia, 1904).

There's a Book That Surpasses	331	331	377	—	—	—

An anonymous poem. No information is available.

There's a Call Comes Ringing	332	332	378	261	261	439
There's a Church in the	—	—	—	262	262	—

William S. Pitts, an American singing teacher. While traveling through Cedar Valley, Iowa, in 1857, he saw a beautiful spot filled with wild flowers and large trees. That fall, in his native Wisconsin, he wrote this text. A few years later an actual church was built on the site in Iowa.

There's a Garden Where	—	—	—	263	263	—

Eleanor Allen Schroll authored the text. It was pub. by Fillmore Bros. Co. of Cincinnati (1920) and later owned by the Lillenas Pub. Co.

	1921	1922	1925	1937	1975	1986
Through the Night of Doubt	—	—	388	—	—	—

Bernhardt Severin Ingeman (1789-1862), Danish poet and professor, wrote original *"Igjennem nat og traengsel."* Pub. in the *Nyt Tillaeg til Evangelist-christelig. Psalmebog* (Copenhagen, 1859). The trans. is by Sabine Baring-Gould, q.v., in the *People's Hymnal* (1867). Current text modified by editors of *Hymns Ancient and Modern* (1875).

Through the Love of God Our	—	—	—	—	—	117
Throw Out the Life-Line	—	—	—	271	271	—

Edward Smith Ufford (1851-1929), a Baptist who had been viewing wrecks on Nantucket beach when he wrote the text and tune. Harmony by George C. Stebbins, q.v., and pub. in Ira David Sankey's *Male Chorus* (1888).

Thy Life Was Given for Me	344	344	389	(79)	(79)	(315)

See " I Gave My Life for Thee."

Thy Supper, Lord, before Us	—	—	—	—	—	384
"Till He Come": O Let the Words	—	446	390	518	518	383
Time Is Filled with Swift	—	—	—	—	660	—

Jennie Wilson, a blind poet, wrote text. Tune written by Franklin Lycurgus Eiland one evening in 1905, as he sat in the backyard of the log cabin home of J. W. Gaines in Palo Pinto Co., Texas. No other information.

'Tis Midnight, and on Olive's	346	346	391	519	519	213
'Tis My Happiness Below	345	345	392	520	520	—

William Cowper, q.v., pub. text in Lady Huntingdon's *Collection* (1774). Also pub. in the *Olney Hymns* (1779).

'Tis Religion That Can Give	—	—	—	272	272	—

Mary Masters is credited with text. Pub. in her *Familiar Letters and Poems* (1775). She was an English woman of scant education, but a great friend of Thomas Scott, the Anglican minister at Norwich.

'Tis So Sweet to Trust in	357	347	393	274	274	497
'Tis the Blessed Hour of	348	348	394	275	275	560
'Tis the Old Time Religion	—	—	—	275	275	—

An anonymous American folk hymn. The tune may go back to English folk origins.

'Tis the Promise of God	—	—	—	276	276	—

Philip P. Bliss, q.v., wrote text. Pub. in his *Gospel Songs* (1874). Written to replace a copyright text which the owners would not allow to be published in his collection.

'Tis the Savior Pleading	349	349	395	—	—	—

Palmer Hartsough, q.v., wrote text. Pub. in Gilbert J. Ellis and J. H. Fillmore's *The Praise Hymnal* (1896).

To Canaan's Land I'm on My	—	—	—	—	661	665
To God Be the Glory	—	—	—	—	663	79
To Christ Be Loyal and Be	—	—	—	—	—	—

Elisha Albright Hoffman (1839-1929). Music by Dr. D. M. Wilson. Apparently first pub. in A. J. Showalter and E. G. Sewell's *Gospel Praise* (1900) and claimed as a *Gospel Advocate* copyright. The copyright, however, is not claimed in the *Advocate's Christian Hymns* (1935).

To Him Who Spread the Skies	—	—	396	—	—	—

Horatius Bonar, q.v. Included in a posthumous collection of his poems by his son entitled *Until the Day Break and Other Hymns and Poems Left Behind* (1890). Poem originally written in 1866.

To Love Someone More	—	—	—	574	574	460
To Our Redeemer's Glorious	—	447	397	521	521	—

Harriet Binney Steele (b. 1826) is author of text. No other information.

	1921	1922	1925	1937	1975	1986
To the Work, to the Work	—	—	—	277	277	—

Fanny J. Crosby, q.v., wrote text. Pub. in 1869.

To Us a Child of Hope Is Born	350	350	398	522	522	—

John Morrison (1749-1798) is credited with text, which was apparently pub. about 1781. Sankey, in *Sacred Songs and Solos,* attributes it to Michael Bruce (1746-1867).

True-Hearted, Whole-Hearted	351	351	399	278	278	—

Frances Ridley Havergal, q.v., wrote text at Ormont Dessous, Switzerland, Sept. 1874. Pub. in her *Loyal Responses, or Daily Melodies for the King's Minstrels* (1878).

Trying to Walk in the Steps	—	—	—	—	—	518
'Twas on That Night	—	—	400	523	523	367
Two Little Hands to Work	—	—	—	598	598	—

William Augustine Ogden, q.v., wrote text. Orig. pub. date is unavailable. It was re-printed by permission of David C. Cook in E. O. Excell's *Triumphant Songs* No. 3 (1894). There the opening line reads, "I've two..."

Under His Wings	—	—	—	279	279	643
Unto the Hills Around Do I	—	448	401	524	524	148
Wake, Awake, for Night Is	—	—	—	—	—	286
Walk in the Light	—	—	—	—	—	625
Walking Alone at Eve	—	—	—	—	—	41
Walking in Sunlight All of	—	—	—	280	280	462
Walking with Jesus, by His	—	—	—	281	281	—

This is a chorus to a hymn by L. C. Voke. Pub. 1919. No other information available.

Watchman, Tell Us of the	—	—	—	525	525	181
We Are Called to be God's	—	—	—	—	—	436
We Are Going Down the	—	—	—	282	282	—

Jessie Brown Pounds, q.v. Pub. by Fillmore Bros. Music Co. (1890) in three stanzas. E. L. Jorgenson, q.v., added the hopeful 4th st. in *GS* (1937).

We Are One in the Spirit	—	—	—	—	—	456
We Bless the Name of Christ	—	—	—	—	—	358
We Gather Together to Ask	—	—	—	flyleaf	664	1

This text entered *GS* in 1940, printed inside the front cover.

We Give Thee but Thine Own	352	352	402	526	526	610
We Have Heard the Joyful	—	—	—	283	283	307
We Praise Thee, God	—	—	—	284	284	63
We Praise Thee, O God	353	353	403	285	285	61
We Praise Thee, O God, Our	—	—	—	—	—	44
We Saw Thee Not, When Thou	354	354	404	286	286	495
We Would See Jesus, for the	355	355	405	527	527	496
We'll Walk in the Light	—	—	—	599	599	—

Anonymous chorus, probably of American frontier origin. It appears as a chorus to "Hark! the herald angels sing" as arr. by George D. Elderkin in James M. Black's *The Chorus of Praise* (New York: Eaton & Main, 1898).

Welcome, Delightful Morn	356	356	406	528	528	20
Were You There When They	—	—	—	—	665	228
What a Fellowship	—	—	—	287	287	108
What a Friend We Have in	357	357	407	529	529	567
What a Wonderful Change	—	—	—	—	—	471

	1921	1922	1925	1937	1975	1986
What a Wonderful Savior	—	—	—	288	288	—

Elisha Albright Hoffman, q.v., from a song beginning "Christ has for sin atonement made..." Pub. by Bigelow and Main Co. (1891) and also appeared in Sankey's *Gospel Hymns 1-6 Complete* (1894).

	1921	1922	1925	1937	1975	1986
What Can Wash Away My Sin	358	358	408	289	289	344
What Child Is This	—	—	—	—	—	207
What Wondrous Love Is This	—	—	—	—	667	225
When All My Labors and	359	359	409	291	291	658
When All Thy Mercies, O My	360	360	410	530	530	131
When at Thy Footstool, Lord	361	361	411	—	—	—

Henry Francis Lyte, q.v . Pub. in his *Poems Chiefly Lyrical* (1833).

When Comes to the Weary	—	—	—	292	292	—

Lizzie DeArmond lived in Swarthmore, Pa. Wrote this text after the death of her daughter, ca. 1922. Homer Rodeheaver sang the song at her funeral and at that of the evangelist Billy Sunday. Ironically, it was also sung at the funeral of the gangster, John Dillinger.

When Days of Toil Have All	362	362	412	293	293	—

Civilla Durfee (Mrs. Walter Stillman Martin). Pub. 1906. No other information available.

When Day's Shadows	—	—	—	531	531	544
When He Calls Me I Will	—	—	—	294	294	—

Anonymous American gospel song text. In *GS* (1937) copyright was credited to C. B. Clark as of 1935. In *GS*, 1940 printing, arr. credited to E. L. Jorgenson.

When He Cometh	400	400	450	600	600	—

William Orcutt Cushing, q.v. Text appeared in Sankey's *Sacred Songs and Solos* (ed. 1903, No. 140). Text written much earlier.

When I See the Blood	—	—	—	295	295	—

John Foote. Chorus from a non- copyrighted song beginning, "Christ our Redeemer died on the cross..."

When I Shall Come to the End	—	—	—	296	296	—

William Charles Poole (1875-1949) was educated at Washington College, Chestertown, Md., and became a Methodist preacher. Charles H. Gabriel encouraged him to write gospel song texts. This text, entitled "Sunrise," pub. in *Songs of Faith and Triumph* (Hall-Mack Co., 1924).

When I Shall Reach the More	363	363	413	297	297	—

W. A. Spencer wrote text. First pub. in 1897. No other information.

When I Shall Wake in That	363	363	413	297	297	—

Horatius Bonar, q.v., is credited with text. Set to music by E. L. Jorgenson in *GS* (1921).x

When I Survey the Wondrous	365	365	414	532	532	233
When Jesus Comes to Reward	366	366	415	298	298	—

Fanny Jane Crosby, q.v., pub. text in *Gospel Music* (1876). It was entitled "Watching."

When Morning Gilds the Skies	—	—	—	533	533	152
When Morning Lights the	367	367	416	—	—	—

A metrical version of Psalm 143:8-10. It appears as part of a full version of that psalm in my copy of *The Psalter of the United Presbyterian Church of North America* (Pittsburgh: 1889, No. 444) A revised version of the text appears in *The Hymnbook* (Presbyterian), 1955, where it is attributed to *The Psalter,* 1912.

When My Love to Christ	—	449	417	534	534	219
When Peace Like a River	368	368	418	299	299	646

	1921	1922	1925	1937	1975	1986
Who Is on the Lord's Side	376	376	427	—	—	—

Frances Ridley Havergal, q.v., wrote text Oct. 1877. Pub. in her *Loyal Responses* (1878) in five 12-line stanzas. *GS* text contains Sts. 1, 2, 3, and 4.

	1921	1922	1925	1937	1975	1986
Who Will Follow Jesus	379	379	—	—	—	—

Eliza Edmunds Hewitt, q.v. Pub. by John C. Church Co. (1912). No other information available.

	1921	1922	1925	1937	1975	1986
Whosoever Heareth, Shout	—	—	428	322	322	335
Why Did My Savior Come to	380	380	429	312	312	369
Why Do You Wait, Dear	381	381	430	313	313	—

George F. Root, q.v. No other information available.

	1921	1922	1925	1937	1975	1986
Why Should He Love Me So	—	—	—	314	314	—

Robert Harkness (1880-1961). On whom see above under "When we cross the valley." Pub. by Robert H. Coleman (1925).

	1921	1922	1925	1937	1975	1986
Will You Come, Will You	—	—	—	315	315	—

Fanny Jane Crosby, q.v. No other information available.

	1921	1922	1925	1937	1975	1986
Will You Take Jesus Today	—	—	—	316	316	—

William W. Rock. Pub. in Charles M. Alexander's *Gospel Songs,* No. 2 (New York, 1910). The chorus of a poem beginning "Will you take Jesus to be your Guide?" No other information.

	1921	1922	1925	1937	1975	1986
___	—	—	—	317	317	—

Priscilla Jane Owens, q.v. Pub. in 1882. No other information.

	1921	1922	1925	1937	1975	1986
Without Him I Could Do	—	—	—	—	—	515
Wonderful, Wonderful Jesus	—	—	—	318	318	—

Haldor Lillenas (1885-1959) wrote text. He emigrated to U.S. from his native Norway as an infant. At first a Lutheran and then a member of the Church of the Nazarene. Wrote songs for Charles M. Alexander and founded the Lillenas Pub. Co.

	1921	1922	1925	1937	1975	1986
Wonderful, Wonderful Savior	—	—	—	319	319	—

D. C. Carson. (No information available.) Carson altered this chorus from an original poem by George Starke Schuler (1882-1973). Pub. 1927.

	1921	1922	1925	1937	1975	1986
Work for the Night Is Coming	382	302	431	538	538	418
Worthy of Praise Is Christ	—	—	—	—	670	168
Would You Be Free from Your	383	383	432	320	3230	339
Would You Live for Jesus	384	384	433	321	321	628
Ye Christian Heralds, Gov	—	—	—	539	539	—

Bourne Hall Draper (1775-1843), an English Baptist and student at Bristol, England, where the poem was written. Pub. in Elias Smith and Abner Jones's *Hymns for the Use of Christians* (1805). Original of the hymn appeared in a newspaper (probably Elias Smith's) and then in the hymnal mentioned, divided into two hymns: "Ruler of Worlds, display Thy power"; and "Ye Christian Heroes! Go, proclaim." In *Hymns and Songs of Praise* (1874), "heroes" is changed to "heralds."

	1921	1922	1925	1937	1975	1986
Ye Servants of God, Your	—	—	—	—	—	175
Years I Spent in Vanity	—	—	—	322	322	268
Yes, for Me, for Me He Careth	385	385	434	323/540	323/540	639
Yesterday, Today, Forever	—	—	—	324	3243	—

Albert B. Simpson (1843-1919), founder of the Christian and Missionary Alliance. Only a portion of the original chorus is included in *GS*. The original poem begins "O how sweet the glorious message / Simply faith may claim: / Yesterday, today, forever / Jesus is the same..."

	1921	1922	1925	1937	1975	1986
Yield Not to Temptation	386	386	435	325	325	—

Horatio Richmond Palmer, q.v. Text and tune came to him one day in a flash as he was working on the "dry" subject of music theory. Pub. in his *Sabbath School Songs* (Chicago, 1868).

	1921	1922	1925	1937	1975	1986
Zion Stands with Hills	387	387	436	—	—	—

Thomas Kelly, q.v., pub. his *Hymns on Various Passages of Scripture* (Dublin, 1804). This text pub. in 2d ed. (1806).